Introduction

Advanced Biology for You is designed to support your studies in AS and A2 biology modules. It is suitable for any of the specifications offered by AQA, Edexcel, OCR, WJEC and NICCEA, as you will find all the essential concepts and components written *specifically* for the new AS and A2 examinations.

Advanced Biology for You aims to be both interesting and helpful to you. As you will see, the book is based on the same formula and approach as the highly successful GCSE *Biology for You*. The text is designed to be lively, informative and understandable, whether you will be using it to cover AS or to take it further to A2.

Building on your earlier work in biology, new ideas are introduced in a clear, straightforward way. The book is carefully planned so that each new concept is developed on a single page or, more usually, on two facing pages.

The chapters are designed to be either AS or A2, as you can see on the Contents page. Pages marked with a red corner are *usually* only needed for your A2 core modules and those without are the AS level pages.

However there are exceptions, for instance all of chapters 13, 14 and 15 are required for the OCR AS Biology syllabus.

Also Edexcel, OCR, WJEC and NICCEA require some of chapters 22, 23 and 24 for AS.

If you look at page 459 you will see a specification grid which matches the chapters with the particular requirements of the syllabus that you are following.

In any case, I advise you to obtain an up-to-date copy of the syllabus that you are following, either from your teacher or from the Examination Board.

You need to be sure that you don't miss out on work that you should have covered, but equally you don't want to be learning things that are not relevant to your syllabus!

Most of the A2 chapters link up and develop the work already covered in the AS chapters.

This makes it easier to review your previous work before tackling the more demanding A2 units.

Each new biological term is printed in **bold** and key ideas are presented in a highlighted box.

At the end of each chapter you will find a useful summary, which is ideal for revision.

This is followed by questions to reinforce your understanding of the chapter.

At the end of the six main sections of the book, there are recent past examination questions.

You can use these to test your application of the work that you have covered and also to improve your exam technique.

You can't miss these pages as they are coloured to match the chapters that they refer to.

In the last section of the book you will find guidance on practical skills, revision, examination techniques and Key Skills in biology.

Throughout the book there are Biology at Work pages. These focus on showing how the concepts that you learn about are relevant to all our lives … or will be, because we have included some of the most exciting breakthroughs taken from the 'cutting edge' of current biological research.

I would like to thank my family, Diana, Jill and Gail, for all the help and encouragement that they have given me over the two years that it has taken to complete this book.

If you enjoyed using GCSE *Biology for You*, then I am sure that *Advanced Biology for You* will make biology easier to understand at this level and help you to achieve success in your examinations. Good luck!

Gareth Williams

Contents

Advanced
Biology
for You

Gareth WILLIAMS

First published in 2000 by:
Stanley Thornes (Publishers) Ltd
Delta Place
27 Bath Road
Cheltenham GL53 7TH
England

00 01 02 03 04 / 10 9 8 7 6 5 4 3 2 1

A catalogue record of this book is available from the British Library.

ISBN 07487–5298–6

Typeset by Tech-Set Ltd, Tyne & Wear
Printed and bound in Spain by Graficas Estella S.A.
Artwork by Oxford Designers and Illustrators, Harry Venning

Also available: **Advanced Chemistry for You**   ISBN 0 7487 52978
                Advanced Physics for You   ISBN 0 7487 5296X

I would like to record my special thanks for the excellent work of Damian Allen and Nick Paul who were responsible for writing the Biology at Work sections of this book.

Everest

The first question which you will ask and which I must try to answer is this, 'What is the use of climbing Mount Everest?' and my answer must at once be, 'It is no use.' There is not the slightest prospect of any gain whatsoever. Oh, we may learn a little about the behaviour of the human body at high altitudes, and possibly medical men may turn our observation to some account for the purposes of aviation. But otherwise nothing will come of it. We shall not bring back a single bit of gold or silver, not a gem, nor any coal or iron. We shall not find a single foot of earth that can be planted with crops to raise food. It's no use. So, if you cannot understand that there is something in man which responds to the challenge of this mountain and goes out to meet it, that the struggle is the struggle of life itself upward and forever upward, then you won't see why we go. What we get from this adventure is just sheer joy. And joy is, after all, the end of life. We do not live to eat and make money. We eat and make money to be able to enjoy life. That is what life means and what life is for.

George Leigh-Mallory, 1922

Chapters marked * are usually not in AS level, only in A2.
Chapters marked † check the specification you are following.
For further details see: www.nelsonthornes.com/ab4u.htm

1 Biological molecules

Recent explorations in space have led to the discovery of large amounts of biological molecules in outer space.
They are mainly small molecules made up of carbon, hydrogen, nitrogen, oxygen and sometimes sulphur or silicon.
It has been speculated that if these molecules were to become concentrated on dust grains, they could well combine into more complex molecules, even polymers.

Meteorites landing from outer space have been found to contain organic material.
The Murchison meteorite fell in Murchison, Australia in 1969.
On examination, it was found to contain a variety of different amino acids – the molecules that build proteins.

Could it be that the origin of some of the biological molecules that make up living organisms was not in our atmosphere but in outer space?

Comet Hale-Bopp

▷ Atoms

All matter is made up of **atoms**.
But what do you think atoms are made up of?
There are *three* different particles that make up an atom:

- **protons**, which have a positive charge,
- **neutrons**, which have no charge,
- **electrons**, which have a negative charge.

The protons and neutrons are found in the nucleus, at the centre of the atom.
The electrons are found circling the nucleus in 'orbitals' or 'shells'.

If the overall charge of an atom is neutral, what do you think this tells us about the number of protons and the number of electrons?

If an atom is neutral, then the number of protons must **equal** the number of electrons.

Atoms of a particular element always contain the **same** number of protons.
For example, carbon atoms always contain six protons, and oxygen atoms always contain eight protons.

The **atomic number** of an element is the number of protons contained in the nucleus.

The **mass number** of an element is the number of protons **plus** the number of neutrons contained in the nucleus.

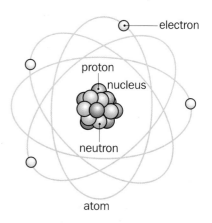

atom

▷ Molecules

Do you remember what a molecule is?

A **molecule** consists of two or more atoms joined together chemically.

Molecules can be made from atoms of the **same** element joined together. For example, a molecule of oxygen (O_2) contains two atoms of oxygen. Usually, molecules contain atoms of **different** elements joined together. For example, a molecule of carbon dioxide (CO_2) contains an atom of carbon and two atoms of oxygen.

A molecule that is made up of different atoms is called a **compound**. So carbon dioxide is a compound.

▷ Ions

Ions are charged particles. They are formed when atoms or groups of atoms gain or lose electrons.

What charge will atoms have if they **gain** electrons?
What charge will atoms have if they **lose** electrons?

Since electrons have a negative charge:

- Atoms that gain electrons will be negative (**anions**).
- Atoms that lose electrons will be positive (**cations**).

We write ions with the chemical symbol of their elements and a negative or positive sign to show the charge.
A sodium atom that loses an electron becomes the ion Na^+.
A chlorine atom that gains an electron becomes the ion Cl^-.
Groups of atoms can also form ions.
For example, NO_3^- is a nitrate ion and PO_4^{3-} is a phosphate ion.

Cat-ions are 'pussytive'!
Cations go to the cathode
When they get there they receive electrons

▷ Isotopes

Atoms of the same element always contain the same number of protons. For example, a carbon atom always contains six protons in its nucleus.

But the number of neutrons in its nucleus can change.
Usually carbon atoms have six neutrons.
So the **mass number** = 6 protons + 6 neutrons = 12.
But some carbon atoms have eight neutrons.

What do you think their mass number will be?
The mass number of this form of carbon will be 14.

> **Atoms of the same element with different mass numbers are called isotopes.**

Many isotopes are radioactive so biologists have been able to use them as tracers.
For instance, the isotope carbon-14 (^{14}C) is radioactive.
So if ^{14}C-labelled carbon dioxide is fed to plants, we can look at the formation of compounds made in photosynthesis by tracing what happens to the ^{14}C.

Nitrogen-15 is a 'heavy', non-radioactive isotope (the normal form of nitrogen is ^{14}N).
This isotope has been used to label the nitrogen in DNA to find out how new DNA is made.

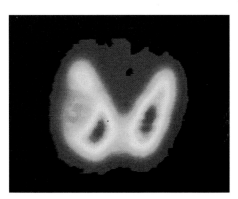

Gamma camera scintigram of a human thyroid gland, using radioactive isotope Iodine 131 to show cancerous cells

▷ Acids and bases

Hydrogen has an atomic number of 1 and a mass number of 1. This means that it has one proton and one electron but no neutrons. A hydrogen ion (H^+), which is an atom that has lost an electron, is simply one proton by itself.

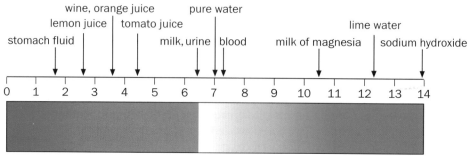

The pH scale

The **pH** of a solution is a measure of the concentration of hydrogen ions present. The **higher** the concentration of hydrogen ions present, the **more** acidic the solution.

On the pH scale, a value of 1 indicates a strong acid, 7 is neutral and 14 is a strong alkali.
The pH scale is logarithmic, so a solution with a pH of 1 is ten times more acidic than a solution with a pH of 2, which is ten times more acidic than pH 3, and so on.

Can you work out how much more acidic a solution with a pH of 1 is than a solution with a pH of 7?

An acid is a substance that splits up, or **dissociates,** into ions when in solution, releasing hydrogen ions. For example:

$$HCl \longrightarrow H^+ + Cl^-$$
$$\text{acid} \qquad \text{hydrogen} \qquad \text{base}$$
$$\text{ion}$$

Hydrochloric acid is a strong acid since it releases a lot of hydrogen ions into solution.

Carboxylic acids such as ethanoic acid are weak acids. Relatively few of their molecules dissociate and release hydrogen ions into solution.

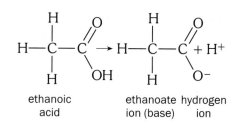

ethanoic acid → ethanoate ion (base) + hydrogen ion

Can you see that when an acid dissociates it loses an H^+, leaving a base? A base is a compound that can combine with hydrogen ions.

What do you think happens when a base accepts a hydrogen ion?

$$-NH_2 + H^+ \longrightarrow -NH_3^+$$
$$\text{base} \quad \text{hydrogen} \qquad \text{acid}$$
$$\text{ion}$$

It forms an acid.

Buffers

Living organisms have to maintain their cell contents at a fairly stable pH because their enzymes only work effectively over a relatively narrow pH range. Some chemicals in the cytoplasm are able to:

● act as bases by mopping up hydrogen ions to help neutralise an acidic solution,
● act as acids by donating hydrogen ions to help neutralise an alkali solution.

Some substances are able to carry out both roles. Chemicals that can act as bases and as acids are called **buffers**. Plasma proteins act as buffers to keep the blood pH constant and prevent it from becoming too acidic or too alkaline.

When acids and bases react together they form salts. For example:

$$HCl + NaOH \longrightarrow NaCl + H_2O$$
$$\text{acid} \qquad \text{base} \qquad \text{salt}$$

Using an electronic pH meter

▷ Chemical bonds

Atoms are held together inside molecules by chemical bonds.
The making and breaking of these chemical bonds involves energy.

Ionic bonds

Electrons that circle the nucleus are found in orbitals or shells.
The first shell around the nucleus can hold two electrons,
the second and third shells can each hold eight electrons.
Subsequent shells can hold an increasing number of electrons.

Atoms are stable when their outer electron shell is full.
For example, a sodium atom has one electron in its outer shell.
It becomes more stable if it *loses* this electron.
It then forms the positive ion Na^+.

A chloride atom has seven electrons in its outer shell.
It becomes stable if it *gains* an electron to fill the outer shell.
It then forms the negative ion Cl^-.

What do you think will happen to the positive sodium ions and
the negative chloride ions?

The oppositely charged ions will attract each other.
Electrostatic forces draw these ions together forming an **ionic bond**.
Ionic bonds often occur in inorganic compounds such as sodium chloride.

Covalent bonds

Covalent bonds also involve atoms becoming more stable when their
outer electron shells become full.
For instance, a hydrogen atom has a single electron in its outer shell.
It would become more stable if it gained an electron.

Two hydrogen atoms are able to *share* their electrons.
This forms a **covalent bond,** which holds the two hydrogen atoms
together in a hydrogen molecule.

A carbon atom has four electrons in its outer shell.
It would become more stable if it gained another four electrons.
Methane (CH_4) consists of a carbon atom and four hydrogen atoms.

It has four covalent bonds, where each of the hydrogen atoms shares its
electron with the carbon atom to make a stable methane molecule.

Hydrogen bonds

A molecule of water consists of two hydrogen atoms and one oxygen atom.
Each oxygen atom has six electrons in its outer shell and
each hydrogen atom has one electron, so each of the two hydrogen atoms
shares an electron with the oxygen atom.
Each hydrogen atom forms a single covalent bond with the oxygen atom,
so forming a stable molecule of water.

But the oxygen atom has more protons in its nucleus than each of the
hydrogen atoms. These positively charged particles tend to pull the shared
electrons in the bond.
So the oxygen end of the molecule has a slight negative charge ($2\delta^-$)
and the hydrogen ends of the molecule have a slight positive charge (δ^+).
The molecule is said to be **polar**.

When two water molecules are in close contact, their opposing charges
attract each other. This forms a **hydrogen bond**. (See top of page 10.)

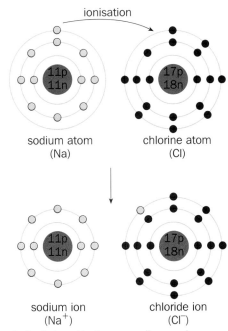

An ionic bond between sodium and
chloride ions

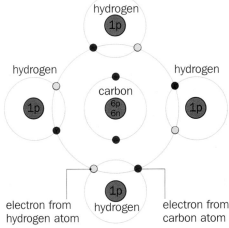

Covalent bonds between a carbon atom and
four hydrogen atoms

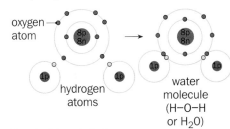

Covalent bonds between an oxygen atom
and two hydrogen atoms

▷ Water

Water is perhaps the most important biochemical molecule.

- Three-quarters of the Earth's surface is covered by water.
- Water provides the environment for many living organisms that live in freshwater or seawater.
- Water makes up 70% of a human cell and anything up to 95% of the mass of a plant cell.

Let's stick together

The most important property of water molecules is that they can 'stick together' by forming hydrogen bonds with other water molecules.

A water molecule has no overall charge. It is electrically neutral.
Overall there are 10 protons and 10 electrons.
But, as you have seen, the nucleus of the oxygen atom tends to pull electrons away from the nucleus of each hydrogen atom, creating polar molecules.
Polar molecules allow the formation of hydrogen bonds.
Although these hydrogen bonds are weak, there are lots of them, so they stick together in a strong lattice framework.
This sticking together is called **cohesion**.
It gives water many of its special properties.

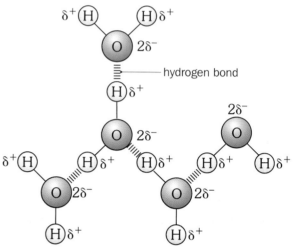

Water molecules are held together by hydrogen bonds

Water as a solvent

Many biochemical reactions take place in the watery cytoplasm of cells.
When a chemical dissolves in water it is free to move about and to react with other chemicals.
Because water has slightly positive and slightly negative parts, it will attract other charged particles, such as ions, and other polar molecules, such as glucose.
For example, in a solution cations such as sodium and potassium become surrounded by water molecules.
The slightly negative charge on the oxygen atom is attracted to the positive cation.
The same thing happens with anions such as chloride; they attract the slightly positive hydrogen ions.

In contrast, non-polar molecules such as lipids will not dissolve in water.
In this case, the water molecules tend to be attracted **to each other**, to the exclusion of the non-polar molecules.

This **hydrophobic** (water-hating) property of lipids is important in giving stability to the cell membrane.

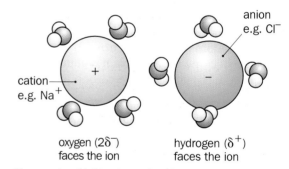

The way in which water molecules arrange themselves around ions in solution

Water as a metabolite and transport medium

In many reactions in cells, water is either used up or produced.
For example, it is used up in photosynthesis and produced in respiration.
Water is a transport medium both inside and outside the cell.
In animals, blood and lymph transport many dissolved substances.
In plants, water is vital to the ways in which xylem and phloem function.
The properties of water as a solvent are important here.

Thermal properties

Most cells can only tolerate a narrow range of temperature.
This is mainly because the enzymes within the cell can only funtion effectively over this temperature range.

A large amount of energy is needed to raise the temperature of water.
This is because the movement of water molecules is restricted by the hydrogen bonds that form between them.
We say that water has a high **specific heat capacity**.
This means that it takes a lot of energy to warm water up.
Equally, water has to lose a lot of heat energy to cool down.

As a result, aquatic habitats have relatively stable temperatures.
Aquatic organisms do not have to endure rapid and extreme temperature changes.

It also means that it is easier for mammals to maintain a stable internal body temperature. Sweating involves the conversion of water to a gas.
This requires the transfer of a great deal of energy and is an effective method of cooling the body.

Density changes

Water is unique because its solid form, ice, is less dense than its liquid form.
This is why ice floats on the surface of a lake or pond.
It forms an insulating layer, which prevents the water underneath from freezing.
If ice were denser than water, then a pond would freeze from the bottom up, killing all the living organisms within it.

Water is usually most dense at 4 °C.
So even when a pond is frozen over, there is a layer of water below the ice at 4 °C where organisms can survive.

Cohesion and surface tension

The hydrogen bonds that hold water molecules together give water its cohesive properties.
This cohesion means that long columns of water molecules don't break.
They can be drawn up xylem vessels to the tops of the tallest trees, a bit like sucking water up a straw.

At the air/water interface of a pond, the cohesion between water molecules produces surface tension.
This acts almost like a skin that covers the water.
Insects such as the pond skater exploit this property.
The insect's body is supported by the high surface tension at the water surface

Freshwater invertebrates

Evaporation of sweat cools the skin of this boxer

Ice floats on the surface of this frozen pond

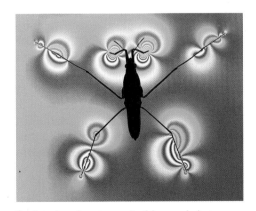

Surface tension supports this pond skater (Gervis lacustris) on the water surface

11

▷ Carbohydrates

Carbohydrates are compounds of carbon, hydrogen and oxygen.
In a carbohydrate, there is usually the same number of carbon atoms and oxygen atoms but twice as many hydrogen atoms.
One molecule of water (H_2O) combines with one atom of carbon to form the sub-unit (CH_2O). These sub-units can be repeated, $(CH_2O)_n$, to form many different molecules.

Carbohydrates are the source of energy in all living organisms. Carbohydrate polymers add strength and support to cell membranes, plant cell walls and insect skeletons.

Pasta is rich in carbohydrates

There are **three** main types of carbohydrates:

- **monosaccharides** or simple sugars,
- **disaccharides** or double sugars (formed from two monosaccharides),
- **polysaccharides**, polymer chains of many hundreds of monosaccharides.

Monosaccharides

Monosaccharides are the simplest forms of carbohydrate.
They provide the building blocks for larger carbohydrate molecules.
They also act as a respiratory substrate, providing cells with an energy source.

The names of monosaccharides depend upon the number of carbon atoms in the molecule:

- **Trioses** have three carbon atoms ($n = 3$).

For example, glyceraldehyde is an important intermediate in respiration.

- **Pentoses** have five carbon atoms ($n = 5$).

For example:
Ribose is an important part of the **RNA** molecule involved in passing on the genetic code.
Deoxyribose is an important part of the **DNA** molecule.
Ribulose helps to fix carbon atoms from carbon dioxide into carbohydrate molecules in the first stages of photosynthesis.

- **Hexoses** have six carbon atoms ($n = 6$) with the formula $C_6H_{12}O_6$.

Glucose is the main energy source for most living cells.
It is one of the first carbohydrates produced in photosynthesis and forms the building blocks of many other carbohydrates.
Fructose is a very sweet sugar. It combines with glucose to form the disaccharide molecule sucrose, the sugar you put in your tea.
Galactose is found in milk. It combines with glucose to form the disaccharide milk sugar molecule lactose. You put this in your tea too!

Monosaccharides usually exist as ring structures when they dissolve in water.
Can you see any differences between the α-glucose and β-glucose molecules?
These two molecules have the same chemical formula ($C_6H_{12}O_6$) but they have different structural formulas.
We say that they are **structural isomers**.

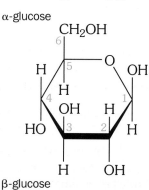

α-glucose

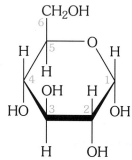

β-glucose

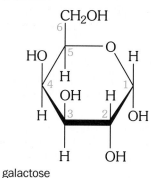

galactose

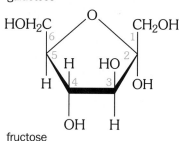

fructose

Disaccharides

Disaccharides are formed when **two** monosaccharides join together.
This reaction releases water so it is called a **condensation reaction**.
The link between the monosaccharide rings is called a **glycosidic bond**.

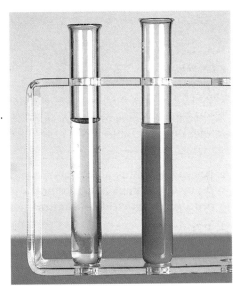

monosaccharide   monosaccharide   disaccharide (α-form of maltose)
(α-glucose)   (α-glucose)

−H_2O (condensation)
+H_2O (hydrolysis)

Look at the diagram.

Between which carbon atoms does the glycosidic bond form?

It forms between carbon atom number one (C_1) of one
α-glucose molecule and carbon atom number four (C_4)
of the other α-glucose molecule.
These two carbon atoms end up sharing an oxygen atom.

Disaccharides can be formed by joining together

- two **similar** monosaccharides, as in the case of maltose,
  which is made from two glucose molecules,

- two **different** monosaccharides, as with sucrose and lactose.

Disaccharide	Source	Monosaccharide units
sucrose	stored in plants such as sugar beet and sugar cane	glucose + fructose
lactose	milk sugar — the main carbohydrate found in milk	glucose + galactose
maltose	malt sugar — found in germinating seed such as barley	glucose + glucose

Look at the table to find out which monosaccharide units make
up sucrose (cane sugar) and which make up lactose (milk sugar).

Disaccharides can be broken back down into monosaccharides.
This type of reaction is called **hydrolysis** (a molecule of water is **added**).

Disaccharides are still relatively small molecules.
They are water-soluble and taste sweet.
Disaccharides are more suitable for transport and storage than monosaccharides.
Sucrose is stored in sugar beet and sugar cane. It is the main form in which
carbohydrates are transported in the phloem sieve tubes of plants.

Reducing sugars

Monosaccharides, such as glucose, fructose and galactose, and
disaccharides, such as maltose and lactose, are known as reducing sugars.
They have **carbonyl groups** (C=O) which can be **oxidised**
to **carboxylic acids** (—COOH).
(Remember, in an oxidation reaction oxygen is added.)
Thus they reduce other compounds, such as **Benedict's reagent**,
producing a precipitate.
The colour of the precipitate depends upon the **concentration** of the
reducing sugar.

A positive Benedict's test

Benedict's test is used to estimate the amount of reducing sugar present
in a solution. Sucrose is a non-reducing sugar but it will give a positive
result with Benedict's if it is first boiled with dilute acid to hydrolyse (split)
it into its monosaccharides.

Look at the table to estimate the amount of reducing sugar
in the test-tube in the photograph.

Amount of reducing sugar	Colour of solution and precipitate
no reducing sugar increasing quantity of reducing sugar	blue green yellow brown red

13

Polysaccharides

Polysaccharides are polymers made up of hundreds of monosaccharide units.
A condensation reaction occurs between each monosaccharide unit.
Long chains of monosaccharides are held together by glycosidic bonds.
These long molecules can be branched or unbranched.

Polysaccharides are insoluble and not sweet to taste.
Storage polysaccharides tend to be folded to give a compact molecule like starch.
Structural polysaccharides tend to be coiled or straight chained (as with cellulose).

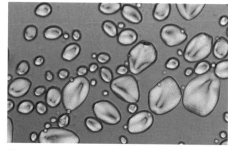

Starch grains from potato

Starch

Starch is the main carbohydrate food reserve in plants.
Many food crops, such as maize, wheat, millet and potatoes, contain a lot of starch.
So it is the major food energy resource for most of the world's population.

Can you name any foods that are rich in starch?

Starch is a polymer made up of many α-glucose molecules.
These α-glucose sub-units are held together by glycosidic bonds.
Starch is actually a mixture of two different compounds:

- **Amylose** is a linear, unbranched polymer, which makes up about 80% of starch.
- **Amylopectin** is a polymer with some 1,6 linkages that give it a branched structure.

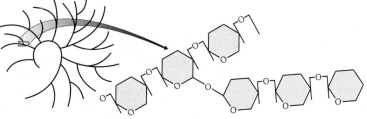

amylose polymer coils
into a helix held in place
by hydrogen bonds
which form between
hydroxyl groups

part of *amylose*
molecule with glucose
monomers joined by
glycosidic bonds

amylopectin has glycosidic bonds,
which form branches, giving a molecule
with a brush-like shape

What makes starch a good food store?
Try to explain how each of the following properties make starch
an ideal storage molecule.
Starch is:

- *compact* – think about the space available in cells,
- *insoluble* – think about osmosis,
- *readily converted to sugars* – when would the store be needed?

Starch grains are made up of successive layers of amylose and
amylopectin, which show up as growth rings in starch grains.

Starch gives a blue-black colour with iodine solution

Glycogen is a storage polysaccharide, sometimes called 'animal starch'.
It is the only carbohydrate store in animals.
Chemically it is very similar to amylopectin.
In humans, glycogen is stored in the liver and skeletal muscle.
During prolonged periods of exercise, blood glucose may fall below
the threshold level.
Liver glycogen is quickly converted to glucose to meet the body's energy needs.

Which hormone promotes the conversion of glucose to liver glycogen
when blood glucose is high?

'She must have been out jogging again!'

Cellulose

Cellulose is a structural polysaccharide made up of thousands of glucose units. In this case, β-glucose units are held together by 1,4 glycosidic bonds, forming long, unbranched chains.

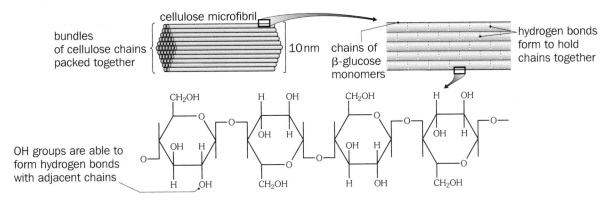

Can you see from the diagram how these chains are linked together to form long **microfibrils**?
The microfibrils are held together by hydrogen bonds to form strong cellulose fibres.
It is these fibres that give plant cell walls their strength and rigidity.

Humans cannot digest cellulose but animals such as cows, sheep and horses can.
These herbivores have bacteria in their guts that make **cellulases**.
These enzymes break down the bonds within the cellulose molecule to release units of glucose.
This is an example of **mutualism**: both the herbivore and the bacterium benefit.
The bacterium gets a food source and a sheltered environment.
The herbivore gets a rich source of energy – glucose.

We use a lot of cellulose.
It is found in all plant cells and is therefore a readily available raw material.
Probably the best known use is in the manufacture of paper.
The words that you are reading on this page are printed on cellulose.
Cellophane is a clear film used in food packaging.
Celluloid is used in the manufacture of photographic film.
Cellulose films are used in the production of dialysis membranes, Sellotape and sweet wrappers.
Even cotton clothes and tea towels are made from cellulose.
Tough, synthetic rayon is used in tyre cords owing to its high tensile strength.
Viscose is a synthetic fibre derived from cellulose and used in a range of textiles.

Some items manufactured from cellulose

Chitin

Chitin has many chemical and structural similarities to cellulose.
It is a polysaccharide with amino acids added to form a **mucopolysaccharide**.
Chitin forms the exoskeletons of insects and other arthropods.
It is also present in the cell walls of fungi.
Chitin is strong, lightweight and waterproof.

Why do you think chitin is so important to insect body structure?

Chitin makes this insect's exoskeleton strong and light

▷ Lipids

Lipids are a large and varied group of organic compounds.
They include **fats** and **oils**.
Like carbohydrates, they are made up of carbon, hydrogen and oxygen,
though they have a lot less oxygen.
They are non-polar compounds and so are insoluble in water.
They can be extracted using non-polar solvents, such as alcohol and ether.

Fats and oils are chemically very similar,
but at room temperature, fats are solid and oils are liquid.

Triglycerides are one of the most common types of lipids.
They are formed by joining two **different** kinds of organic molecules
together: **fatty acids** and **glycerol**.

The glycerol molecule in any lipid is always the same.
It is the fatty acids that vary.
Fatty acids are organic acids with a **carboxyl** (—COOH) group at one end.
Joined to the carboxyl group is a long hydrocarbon tail.
Different fatty acids have different hydrocarbon tails.
The properties of any particular lipid depend upon the fatty acids it contains.

There are hundreds of different fatty acids that might react with glycerol.
They vary in two ways:

- the length of the hydrocarbon tail,
- how **saturated** the molecule is.

Saturated fatty acids only have C—C bonds.
You can see from the diagram below that in stearic acid all the carbon atoms
are joined by a **single** C—C bond.

Unsaturated fatty acids have at least one C=C double bond.
Polyunsaturates have more than one double bond, as in linoleic acid below.

How many double bonds does linoleic acid have?

Triglycerides

Triglycerides consist of one molecule of glycerol and three fatty acid molecules.
They are formed as a result of three condensation reactions involving
the —OH groups of glycerol and the —COOH group of each fatty acid.
For each condensation reaction, an **ester bond** is formed.

When oxidised, triglycerides release more energy for use in respiration
than an equal mass of carbohydrate.
Triglycerides also produce a lot of metabolic water when oxidised.
This is important to desert animals – the camel's hump is made of fat.
Triglycerides are stored under the skin where they act as a heat-insulator.

Which properties of fats make them ideal as an energy store?

A field of oilseed rape

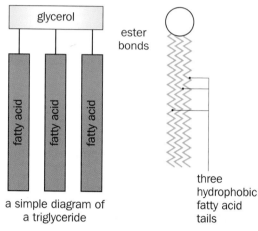

a simple diagram of a triglyceride

three hydrophobic fatty acid tails

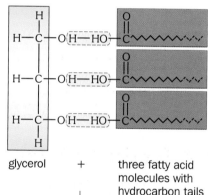

glycerol + three fatty acid molecules with hydrocarbon tails

→ 3H₂O

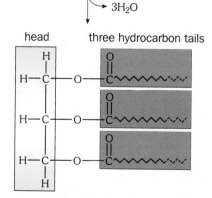

triglyceride molecule

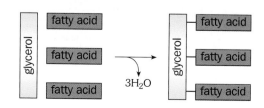

Phospholipids

Phospholipids are similar to triglycerides but one of the fatty acids molecules is replaced by a phosphate group (PO_4^{3-}).

The lipid and the phosphate parts of the molecule have very different properties.
The lipid part is non-polar and insoluble in water – we call it **hydrophobic** or 'water-hating'.
But the phosphate part is polar and dissolves in water – we say that it is **hydrophilic** or 'water-loving'.

When in contact with water, phospholipids spread out over the surface.
Their hydrophilic heads are attracted to the water and 'dip into' it.
The hydrophobic tails move away from the water.
The molecules can become tightly packed forming a **monolayer**.

What do you think would happen if this arrangement were shaken up?

The phospholipids would form tiny, spherical structures called **micelles**.
The hydrophobic tails turn inwards and become protected from the water by the hydrophilic heads.

As you will see in Chapter 3, these properties are very important in determining the structure and function of the cell surface membrane.

Waxes

Waxes are similar to fats and oils but their long-chained fatty acids are linked to a long-chained alcohol.

Waxes are very insoluble and form a waterproof layer over some cells.
This stops water getting in, but more importantly for land-living plants and animals, it prevents too much water getting out.

Can you think of examples of this property of waxes?

Insects have a waxy cuticle that helps them cut down water loss.
Similarly, many leaves have waxy cuticles to reduce transpiration.

Steroids

Structurally, steroids have little in common with other lipids, although they do share some properties.
For instance, they are insoluble in water and soluble in many organic solvents.
Chemically, they have a four-ring structure with various side-chains.
They are of great biological importance, especially as hormones.
Human steroids are synthesised from **cholesterol**.

Many people associate cholesterol with heart disease but in fact it is an important constituent of body cells, especially the cell membrane.
However, ***too much*** cholesterol and saturated fat can produce **atheroma** deposits.
These can reduce the blood flow in arteries and even block them.
High cholesterol diets increase the risk of heart attacks and strokes.
Steroid hormones include **oestrogen**, **progesterone** and **testosterone**.
You can find out more about cholesterol and anabolic steroids on page 24.

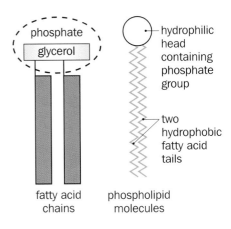

fatty acid chains   phospholipid molecules

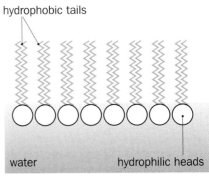

A monolayer

A micelle

cholesterol

testosterone

▷ Proteins

Apart from water, proteins make up most of the content of cells.
Proteins perform an enormous range of biological activities.

- As enzymes they catalyse chemical reactions.
- Carrier proteins transport materials across cell membranes.
- Antibodies defend the body against disease-causing microbes.
- Structural proteins support cells and tissues.
- Hormones transmit information.
- Transport proteins such as haemoglobin carry oxygen.
- Contractile proteins such as actin and myosin bring about contraction in muscle.

The structure of a protein is closely linked to its function.
For instance, haemoglobin has a different structure to that of an antibody.
Proteins are big compounds with large molecular masses.
The main chemical constituents are carbon, hydrogen and oxygen but, in addition, they **all** contain nitrogen and some also have sulphur and phosphorus.

Proteins are polymers composed of sub-units called **amino acids**.
There are only about 20 different types of amino acids but thousands of different proteins.
The specific function of a protein depends upon its shape.
This is determined by the specific sequence of amino acids in the chain.

Amino acids

All amino acids have the same basic structure.
They have an amino ($-NH_2$) group at one end of the molecule and a carboxyl ($-COOH$) group at the other end.
The R group differs from one amino acid to another.
For example, in glycine the side-chain is a single hydrogen atom, whilst in alanine it is a methyl ($-CH_3$) group.

In solution, the amino end of the molecule can act as a base by accepting hydrogen ions (H^+), so forming a positively charged amino acid ion.
Alternatively, the carboxyl end can act as an acid by giving up hydrogen ions, so producing a negative amino acid ion.

Molecules such as amino acids, which can act as acids or as bases, are said to be **amphoteric**.
When amino acids form protein chains there is still an amino group at one end and a carboxylic acid group at the other end.
So, like amino acids, proteins can accept or give up hydrogen ions.
This gives a protein the ability to resist pH changes and act as a **buffer** (see page 8).

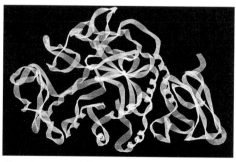

The structure of the enzyme taka amylase

amino group (base) *gains* a hydrogen ion (H^+) and becomes *positively* charged

carboxyl (acid) group *loses* a hydrogen ion (H^+) and becomes *negatively* charged

glycine

alanine

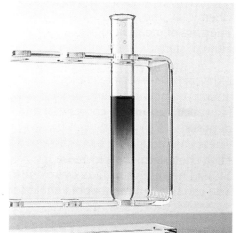

The biuret test gives a lilac colour if positive for proteins

The peptide bond

Amino acids are the sub-units that join together to form polypeptide chains.
Each amino acid is joined to the next one in the chain.
A reaction takes place between the amino group of one amino acid and
the carboxyl group of another.
This is a condensation reaction and a molecule of water is lost.
The chemical bond that is formed is called a **peptide bond**.

Can you remember other molecules formed by condensation reactions?

Disaccharides, polysaccharides and fats are all condensation products.

Can you see from the diagram how a peptide bond forms between two amino acids
to form a **dipeptide**?

A polypeptide contains many hundreds of amino acids.
When a polypeptide bonds with other polypeptides, it forms a protein
containing thousands of amino acids.

Protein structure

The **primary structure** of a protein is the sequence of amino acids in the chain.
It determines the eventual shape of the protein and hence its function.
As we have seen, amino acids in the chain are held together by peptide bonds.
For example:

NH_2— leucine—valine—cysteine—arginine—leucine—glutamine—serine—COOH

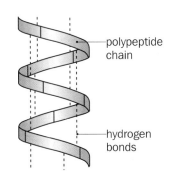

A polypeptide chain wound into an α-helix

There are 20 different amino acids, not far off the 26 letters in the alphabet.
Think about all the different words in a dictionary.
This gives you some idea of all the different combinations of amino acids
that can build the 100 000 known proteins.

But proteins are three-dimensional molecules.
The amino acid chains do not lie flat like a string of beads on a table.
The chains of amino acids form helices and pleated sheets
held together by **hydrogen bonds**.
This gives the protein its **secondary structure**.

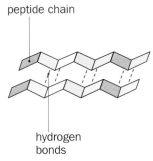

β-sheets of a fibrous protein

The **tertiary structure** of a protein is the complex
three-dimensional shape the molecule takes when the
polypeptide helix twists and folds around itself.

How do you think this tertiary structure is held together?

The **quaternary structure** of a protein involves the linking
together of a number of polypeptide chains.

Haemoglobin consists of four separate polypeptide chains.

Tertiary structure

Quaternary structure

19

Protein bonding

The structure of a protein is held together by three types of chemical bond.

- **Hydrogen bonds** occur between some hydrogen atoms and some oxygen and nitrogen atoms in the polypeptide chain.
  The hydrogen atoms have a small positive charge and the oxygen and nitrogen atoms have a small negative charge.
  The opposite charges attract to form hydrogen bonds.
  Although these bonds are weak, the large number of them maintains the molecule in a three-dimensional shape.

- **Ionic bonds** occur between any charged groups that are not joined together by a peptide bond.
  These ionic bonds are stronger than hydrogen bonds but they can be broken by changes in pH and temperature.

- Some amino acids such as cysteine and methionine contain sulphur atoms.
  Disulphide bonds can form between the sulphur atoms of amino acids that are close together.
  These disulphide bonds are very strong and contribute to the strength of structural proteins such as keratin and collagen.

- The **hydrophobic effect** helps some proteins to maintain their structure.
  When globular proteins are in solution, their hydrophobic 'water-hating' groups point inwards, away from the water.

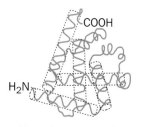

Types of chemical bonds found in a polypeptide

Stability

As you have seen, a protein is held in its three-dimensional shape by hydrogen bonds, ionic bonds and covalent bonds.
Under certain circumstances, such as increasing temperature, the three-dimensional shape can change.

An increase in temperature will cause the atoms in the protein molecule to vibrate.
Raising the temperature can cause the atoms to vibrate so violently that the bonds holding the protein together break.
The three-dimensional structure of the protein changes, altering the protein's shape.
These changes affect the tertiary and the quaternary structures.
The primary structure of the protein is unaffected.

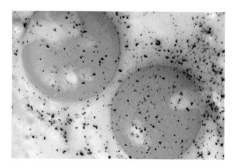

This polypeptide is held together by hydrogen bonds, ionic bonds and disulphide bonds.

If this loss of shape is permanent, it is called **denaturation**.
Altering the tertiary structure of a protein affects its biological function (as you will see in Chapter 4 on 'Enzymes').
A denatured enzyme is unable to bind with its substrate (the molecule on which it normally acts).

Can you think of anything else that could cause a protein to denature?

Denaturation can also be brought about by extreme changes of pH and by the presence of heavy metal ions and organic solvents.

Heating up an egg denatures the protein albumen so you can't 'un-fry' eggs!

Eddie's feeling the heat will he ever be the same?

Globular and fibrous proteins

Proteins can be divided into two groups depending on their final three-dimensional structure: **globular** or **fibrous**.

Globular proteins are compact molecules.
The highly twisted polypeptide chains roll up into a ball.

As the protein rolls up, the amino acids with hydrophobic (water-hating) R groups point to the centre of the molecule.
This leaves the amino acids with hydrophilic (water-loving) R groups on the outside.
As a result, globular proteins are water-soluble.

Globular proteins tend to be less stable and are involved in metabolic reactions.
All enzymes are globular proteins, as are antibodies and some hormones.

Haemoglobin is a globular protein involved in metabolism.
It picks up oxygen in the lungs to form oxyhaemoglobin.
Oxyhaemoglobin breaks down (dissociates) in the tissues, giving up its oxygen and reverting to haemoglobin.

Haemoglobin consists of **four** polypeptide chains.
Disulphide bridges hold the chains together.
At the centre of each polypeptide chain is an iron-containing group called **haem**.
This is an example of a non-protein **prosthetic group**.
The protein combines with the prosthetic group forming a **conjugated protein**.

Each haem group contains an iron ion (Fe^{2+}).
Since each iron ion can bind with one molecule of oxygen, each haemoglobin molecule can pick up **four** oxygen molecules.

Fibrous proteins consist of polypeptides laid down in parallel chains, linked together to form long fibres or sheets.

Fibrous proteins are very stable, insoluble and strong.
Collagen is a good example of a fibrous protein.
It provides the tough properties needed in tendons and bone.

A single collagen fibre consists of three polypeptide chains.
Each polypeptide chain is twisted in the form of a helix.
The three polypeptide helices wind around each other like a rope with three strands.
Hydrogen bonds hold the three strands in place.

You can find out more about the uses of collagen on page 25.

Comparison of fibrous proteins and globular proteins	
Fibrous proteins	**Globular proteins**
stable structure	relatively unstable structure
insoluble in water	soluble
strength gives structural functions	metabolic functions
polypeptide chains form long strands	polypeptide chains 'roll up' into spherical shape
e.g. collagen in bone and keratin in hair	e.g. all enzymes, antibodies, some hormones (e.g. insulin), haemoglobin

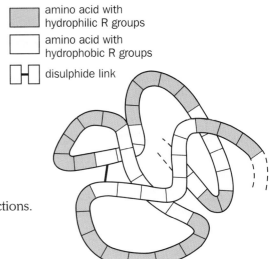

amino acid with hydrophilic R groups

amino acid with hydrophobic R groups

disulphide link

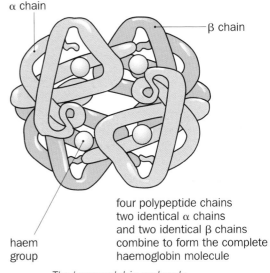

Part of a globular protein molecule

α chain

β chain

four polypeptide chains two identical α chains and two identical β chains combine to form the complete haemoglobin molecule

haem group

The haemoglobin molecule

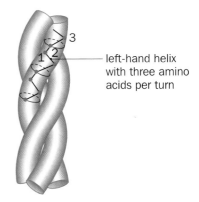

left-hand helix with three amino acids per turn

3 polypeptide helices wind together like a rope in this molecule of collagen

▷ Inorganic ions

Inorganic ions play many important roles in cell metabolism. They can be divided into two groups:

- **Macronutrients** are only needed in small amounts in living organisms.
- **Micronutrients** are needed in *minute* quantities (a few parts per thousand).

The absence of either of these can lead to deficiency diseases.

Calcium

- Important in plants because calcium pectate is a major component of the middle lamella. Deficiency can lead to stunted growth.
- The main component in bones and teeth. Calcium also has an important role in muscle contraction and blood clotting. Deficiency in animals causes rickets and affects blood clotting.

Milk provides a rich source of calcium

Sodium

- Important to the cell membrane in maintaining the electrical and osmotic balance. It is also important in active transport mechanisms.

Potassium

- As with sodium, potassium is important to the functioning of the cell membrane.
- Vital for nerve impulse transmission and other active transport systems.
- Needed for protein synthesis and is an important cofactor in respiration.
- Its absence in plants leads to yellowing of the leaf edges and dead spots.

Magnesium

- Important constituent of chlorophyll; its absence leads to **chlorosis** (yellow leaves).
- Present in bones and teeth.

Chloride

- Important to the electrical and osmotic properties of the cell membrane.
- Needed for carbon dioxide transport in the blood and is a component of stomach acid.

Chlorosis is a yellowing of the leaves due to magnesium deficiency

Nitrate

- Important constituent of many biological molecules including amino acids, proteins, nucleic acids, coenzymes, ATP and some hormones.
- Deficiency in plants causes stunted growth and chlorosis of the leaves.

Phosphate

- Again found in many important biological molecules such as ATP, nucleic acids, coenzymes and some proteins.
- Has a role in the phospholipid component of cell membranes.
- Major structural role in bones and teeth.
- Deficiency in plants results in poor root growth and purple younger leaves.

Spreading pellets of chemical fertiliser

▷ Biology at work: Electrophoresis

Electrophoresis is a technique that allows scientists to separate and identify the proteins present in body fluids such as blood plasma, and also to identify the individual amino acids that make up a protein.

It is similar to chromatography but whereas chromatography separates chemicals according to their solubility in a given solvent, electrophoresis separates them according to their overall electrical charge. Different proteins have different electrical charges because they are made up from different amino acids.

The basic structure of an amino acid

R-group

amino group   carboxyl group

The solution to be analysed is placed on a support medium, for example silica gel in buffer solution (to keep the pH constant). For most proteins the required pH is typically between 7 and 9.

An electrical current is then passed through the medium and the proteins move on the medium at different rates according to their overall electrical charge.
As a result of this differential movement, the proteins become separated from each other.

The next step is to reveal the positions of the proteins using a developing agent (essentially a stain).
The distance travelled by each protein can be measured and this data compared with standard samples of known proteins in order to identify the particular proteins in the sample.

In order to study the individual amino acids in a protein, the protein must be broken down into its constituent amino acids. This requires protease enzymes, which break the peptide bonds that join one amino acid to another.

This technique is useful in medicine as it allows doctors to identify abnormalities in blood chemistry, which may lead to the diagnosis of a patient's medical condition.
It is also a significant part of the procedure of genetic fingerprinting, where it is used in the separation of fragments of DNA.

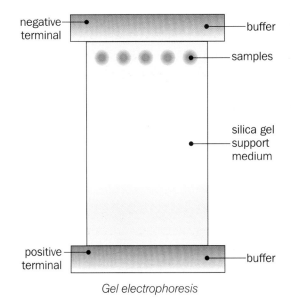

Gel electrophoresis

▷ Biology at work: Cholesterol

Cholesterol is a lipid and although most people associate it with heart disease, it is in fact a normal and important constituent of body cells. It is found in the cell membranes of animal cells, as well as being involved in the formation of hormones and bile salts.

Cholesterol is manufactured in the liver, particularly from saturated fats, although a small amount can be absorbed directly from cholesterol-rich foods such as eggs.

Some people have naturally high cholesterol levels irrespective of their diet; this is an inherited condition known as **hypercholesterolaemia**.

Cholesterol, like other lipids, does not dissolve in the blood. It is carried in the circulation attached to a protein. This combination of lipid and protein is called **lipoprotein**. Cholesterol is mainly carried by **low density lipoprotein (LDL)**, and it is in this form that cholesterol can be deposited in arteries.
This condition, known as **atherosclerosis**, can reduce the blood flow and therefore the oxygen supply to vital organs such as the heart.

High density lipoproteins (HDL) tend to pick up excess cholesterol and transport it to the liver for removal.

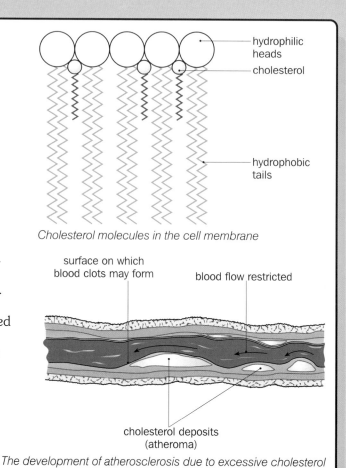

Cholesterol molecules in the cell membrane

hydrophilic heads
cholesterol
hydrophobic tails

surface on which blood clots may form
blood flow restricted
cholesterol deposits (atheroma)

The development of atherosclerosis due to excessive cholesterol

▷ Biology at work: Anabolic steroids

Anabolic steroids are substances similar to the male sex hormone testosterone. They work by mimicking the protein building (anabolic) effects of this hormone. Research has shown that steroids can pass into the nucleus and directly promote the production of the proteins actin and myosin that make up muscle fibres.

Anabolic steroids are used by athletes to build muscle and also because they speed up the recovery of muscles after strenuous exercise. This allows the athlete to undertake a more demanding training schedule.

The use of these drugs is banned in international sport mainly because of the unfair advantage one athlete may gain over another.
However, there are also a number of harmful side effects of excessive use of anabolic steroids.
These include impotence, sterility, liver damage and heart disease.
An additional risk for women is the condition known as **virilisation** – the development of male characteristics such as excessive body hair.

A number of sportsmen have benefited from the use of steroids

▷ Biology at work: Collagen replacement therapy

Collagen replacement therapy (CRT) is a quick, non-surgical technique, which involves injecting collagen implants to replace the skin's natural collagen.
CRT helps to smooth facial lines, scars and deformities on the surface of the skin by supplementing the collagen under the skin.
It can also be used to enhance lip shape and definition.

Collagen structure and function

Collagen is a **fibrous** protein found in bone, cartilage, tendons and connective tissue.

Outside the cell, many collagen molecules join to form collagen fibrils. Electron micrographs show that the collagen fibrils are striated, or striped, with alternate light and dark bands due to the displacement of each triple helix.
This adds to the strength of the fibril as well as generating the pattern.

Collagen is also found in connective tissue such as the dermis of the skin. The dermis also contains many elastic fibres within its matrix of collagen fibres. One consequence of ageing is that the collagen fibres become compressed whilst the elastic fibres reduce in number.
This reduces the skin's elasticity and causes wrinkles and lines to develop.

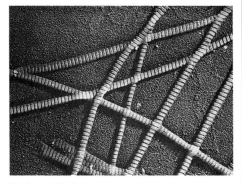

Collagen fibrils

The development of collagen replacement therapy

The medical use of collagen dates back to when animal collagen was used in surgical sutures.
Continued research led to the wide use of collagen in a number of applications, including heart valves and as an agent to help stop bleeding during surgery.
A group of American biochemists and medical scientists experimenting with alternative materials for skin grafts pioneered the use of purified bovine collagen to replace lost tissue.
Research by commercial companies has led to the development of various forms of collagen implants.
These are intended to provide an immediate, visible difference in facial appearance.

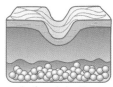

How collagen replacement therapy works

The collagen used in CRT is injected to just below the surface of the epidermis, using a fine gauge needle.
Here it is incorporated into the body's own network of collagen fibres.`

The natural appearance of the skin may be enhanced as the contour of the support structure is restored.

Like natural collagen, injectable collagen begins to lose its form and will eventually wear down depending on age, skin condition, and amount of sun damage.
Full correction is maintained only with a series of ongoing treatments.
There are some risks associated with CRT and all patients undergo a skin allergy test four weeks before treatment.
In 3% of cases patients prove to be allergic to bovine collagen.

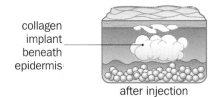

Young, ageing and treated skin

Summary

- Carbon atoms bond strongly to each other forming chains and rings.
- Carbohydrates include monosaccharides, disaccharides and polysaccharides. They can act as an energy source or provide structural support.
- Monosaccharides include glucose, fructose and galactose. They have the same chemical formula but different chemical structures – we call them isomers.
- Monosaccharides can become linked together by a glycosidic bond to form disaccharides such as maltose, sucrose and lactose, and polysaccharides, such as starch and cellulose.
- Polysaccharides can perform structural roles, for example cellulose in plant cells, and energy storage roles, for example starch in plants and glycogen in animals.
- Lipids are composed of carbon, hydrogen and a little oxygen. Most are non-polar and insoluble in water.
- Lipids are used as energy stores, for insulation and protection, and in cell membrane structure. They include fats, oils, phospholipids, waxes and steroids.
- Fats and oils are condensation products (esters) of fatty acids and glycerol.
- Fatty acids vary in the length of their side-chains and whether they are saturated or unsaturated.
- Phospholipids are similar to triglycerides but a phosphate replaces one fatty acid. They form monolayers in water and are vital to the structure of cell membranes.
- Proteins are condensation polymers of up to 20 different amino acids. Proteins have a vast variety of functions as enzymes, hormones, antibodies and as transport and structural proteins.
- All amino acids have an amino group and a carboxyl group but differ in their R groups. Amino acids are linked by peptide bonds as a result of condensation reactions.
- Every protein has a different amino acid sequence, giving it a primary structure. The secondary structure is the arrangement of the polypeptide chain into a helix or pleated sheet. The tertiary structure involves the folding of the secondary structure to give a three-dimensional shape. The quaternary structure involves the association of two or more polypeptide chains to give a protein.
- Fibrous proteins such as collagen form tough fibres that give support. Globular proteins such as enzymes, antibodies and some hormones are involved in cellular reactions.
- Water is a fundamental biological molecule. It is an important solvent and is involved in biochemical reactions and in temperature regulation.

▷ Questions

1 Simple carbohydrate molecules can be written as $(CH_2O)_n$.
   a) What name is given to the carbohydrate in which n is
      i) 6
      ii) 5
      iii) 3
   b) State two different functions of carbohydrates in living organisms.
   c) Simple carbohydrates can be combined to form disaccharides and polysaccharides. What else is produced in these reactions?
   d) i) Name the reagent used to test for reducing sugars.
      ii) Describe the result if this test were to be positive.
      iii) Name a sugar that would **not** give a positive result with this test.

2 The diagram shows part of a cellulose molecule.

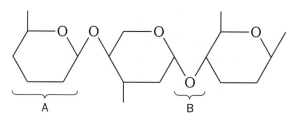

   a) Name the sub-unit labelled A on the diagram.
   b) Name the reaction that produced the bond labelled B.
   c) What is the name of bond B?
   d) Explain how the structure of the cellulose molecule is related to its role as a component of plant cell walls.
   e) Name two commercial uses of cellulose.

3 a) Copy and complete the table by ticking (✓) which
       property applies to each biological molecule.

Property	Biochemical compound				
	Monosaccharide	Starch	Cellulose	Lipid	Protein
is a polymer					
contains nitrogen					
is soluble in water					

   b) The diagram shows a small polypeptide with eight
       amino acids s to z.

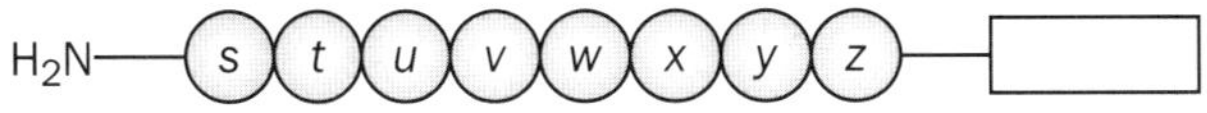

       i) Write down the formula of the chemical group
           that would appear in the box.
       ii) Name the type of reaction by which amino
           acids are joined together.
       iii) Name the reagent or reagents used to test for
           the presence of a protein.

4 Look at the diagram
   of the triglyceride.

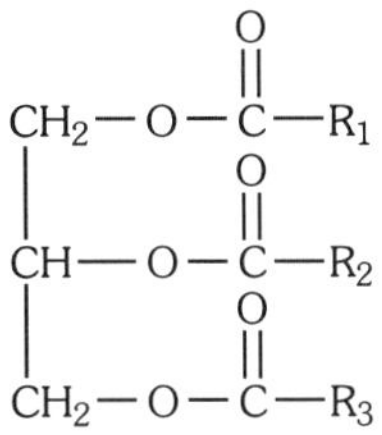

   a) Name the two different types of molecule that
       make up a triglyceride.
   b) What is the name of the bonds that form between
       them?
   c) What is the name of the process by which these
       bonds can be broken?
   d) Look at the data in the table. Use the data to suggest
       possible roles of fats in the metabolism of animals.

	Heat produced in calorimeter (kJ)	Water produced on oxidation (g)
1 g protein	23.4	0.41
1 g carbohydrate	17.6	0.55
1 g fat	38.9	1.07

5 The diagram
   shows a
   dipeptide.

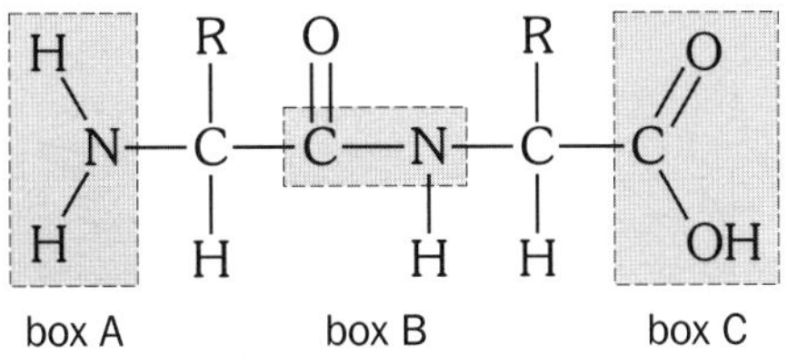

   box A   box B   box C

   a) Draw a diagram to show the two molecules
       produced if this dipeptide is hydrolysed.
   b) What is the name of the chemical group shown in
       box A?
   c) What is the name of the chemical group shown in
       box C?
   d) What is the name of the chemical bond shown in
       box B?
   e) Name two elements, other than carbon, hydrogen
       and oxygen, that may be present in the groups R.

6 Starch, cellulose, phospholipids and proteins are all
   macromolecules.
   a) Which of these molecules is
       i) *not* a polymer?
       ii) *not* found in a chloroplast?
   b) Give one chemical element present in all proteins
       but not present in starch, cellulose and
       phospholipids.
   c) Explain how two features of a starch molecule
       make it a good storage carbohydrate.

7 The table compares monosaccharides and amino
   acids. Copy and complete the table by ticking (✓)
   each statement that you think is correct and putting a
   cross (✗) where you think the statement is incorrect.

Statement	Monosaccharides	Amino acids
always contain nitrogen		
may be polymerised into macromolecules		
released by complete hydrolysis of nucleic acids		
insoluble in water		
may be linked by glycosidic bonds		
released by complete hydrolysis of cellulose		
always contain carbon, hydrogen and oxygen		

8 Match each level of protein structure with the correct
   description:
   a) primary structure
   b) secondary structure
   c) tertiary structure
   d) quaternary structure

   A) the twisting of the amino acid chain into a helix
       held together with hydrogen bonds,
   B) the association of a number of polypeptide chains,
   C) the sequence of amino acids in the polypeptide
       chain,
   D) the folding of the polypeptide into a complex
       three-dimensional shape.

9 a) Name two biological molecules that contain
       calcium and give the function of each.
   b) Name two biological molecules that contain iron
       and give the function of each.
   c) Name one biological molecule that contains
       magnesium and give its function.

2 Cells

Some cells are able to tolerate extreme conditions.
Unicellular microbes can be found in water heated to boiling point by volcanoes, and at temperatures below zero.
They can be found in pools saturated with salt or sodium carbonate.
These microbes are known as **extremophiles** and some are thought to be closely related to the earliest forms of life on Earth.

Extremophiles include **thermophiles**, bacteria that are able to thrive at 70 °C in hot volcanic springs.
Halophiles are able to tolerate the extreme salinity in salt lakes where evaporation concentrates and crystallises the seawater.
Alkalinophiles can survive at a pH of 10 and above.
They are found in soda lakes rich in sodium carbonate and sodium chloride.
Acidophiles, such as the bacterium *Thiobacillus ferro-oxidans*, are able to tolerate pHs below 1!

These conditions would be enough to kill most cells because their enzymes would denature, or water would be drawn out of the cells by osmosis.
These organisms may provide clues about how and where life originated.

Thermophilic bacteria can live in these hot springs in Yellowstone National Park, USA

▷ Beginnings

Robert Hooke was the first person to observe cells in 1665.
He looked at a thin slice of cork under a primitive microscope.
It had a honeycomb appearance made up of lots of 'little boxes' that he called cells.

Cork is in fact dead bark taken from the cork tree.
Hooke didn't realise that the small, dark holes that he was seeing were once filled with a living material – **protoplasm**.
Following his discovery, Hooke and other early microscopists found that different types of plant material were all composed of cells.

In 1883, botanist Matthias Schleiden and zoologist Theodor Schwann proposed that all plants and animals were composed of cells and that cells were the basic building blocks of life.
In 1855, Rudolf Virchow stated that new cells could only arise from the division of pre-existing cells and that the chemical reactions of life took place inside cells.

These observations led to the formulation of the modern **cell theory**.

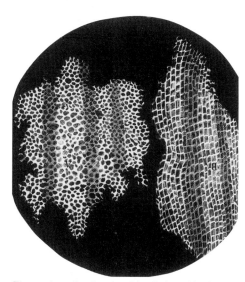

The cork cells observed by Robert Hooke

> **All living things are made up of cells.**
> **New cells are formed by the division of pre-existing cells.**
> **Cells contain genetic material, which is passed on from parent to daughter cells.**
> **All metabolic reactions take place inside cells.**

Some organisms are made up of just *one* cell.
We say that they are **unicellular**.
Other organisms are **multicellular** and are composed of millions of cells.
Each of us is made up of over 50 million million cells.

What are the four main principles of the cell theory?

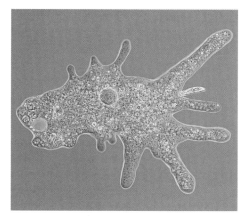

Amoeba is unicellular

▷ Prokaryotic cells

There are two distinct types of cell: **prokaryotic cells** and **eukaryotic cells**.
Prokaryotic cells are more primitive than eukaryotic cells and have
a simpler structure.
They have no nucleus nor do they have distinct cell organelles.

Organisms made of prokaryotic cells are called **prokaryotes**.
Organisms made up of eukaryotic cells are called **eukaryotes**.

Prokaryotes are relatively simple organisms, such as bacteria and blue-green bacteria.
Cells like these were probably the first living things to evolve on Earth –
a few billion years ago.
The word 'prokaryote' means 'before the nucleus' and if you look at
the diagram of the bacterium you can see why.
The single chromosome containing the bacterial DNA is not surrounded
by a nuclear membrane.

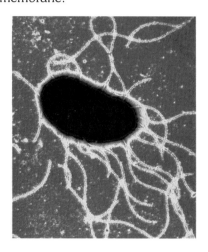
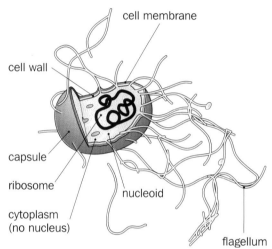

In addition to the main chromosome, bacteria may have other
small rings of DNA called **plasmids**.
Plasmids can replicate themselves independently of the main chromosome.
Bacteria have a rigid **cell wall** outside the cell surface membrane containing
a strengthening material called **murein** to protect the cell.
The cell surface membrane sometimes develops inner extensions called **mesosomes**.
This is where respiration takes place.

Bacteria feed by **extracellular digestion**.
They release enzymes onto their potential food and absorb the digested products.
These enzymes are made inside **ribosomes**.

Some bacteria have **flagella**, which beat to propel the cell along.

	Prokaryotes	Eukaryotes
organisms	bacteria and blue-green bacteria	plants, animals, fungi and protoctists
size	small, ranging from 1 to 10 μm	large, usually between 10 and 100 μm
nucleus	no distinct nucleus as the main chromosome is not surrounded by a nuclear membrane	distinct nucleus with linear chromosomes surrounded by a nuclear membrane
cell walls	rigid cell wall containing the polysaccharide murein	present in plants, fungi and some protoctists but not containing murein
organelles	few organelles except for small ribosomes	many membrane-bound organelles such as mitochondria and chloroplasts
flagella	flagella, if present, lack microtubules	flagella have microtubules

▷ Eukaryotic cells

Eukaryotic cells probably evolved from prokaryotic cells some 1000 million years ago.
'Eukaryote' means 'true nucleus'. The DNA in these cells is held within a nuclear membrane.
Eukaryotic cells have organelles such as mitochondria and chloroplasts.
These are surrounded by membranes, which allow metabolic processes such as respiration and photosynthesis to take place within the organelle.
The enzymes controlling these processes are often located **within** the membranes.
This greater degree of organisation led to an increase in cell size.

> **Eukaryotes have a proper nucleus: their DNA is enclosed
> by a nuclear membrane.**
> **Prokaryotes do not have a nucleus: their DNA is in direct contact with
> the cytoplasm.**

▷ Animal cells

What does a typical animal cell look like?

That's not an easy question, because there are many different types.
The structure of a cell is adapted to carry out a particular function.
For instance, a sperm cell has a tail to swim; a nerve cell has
a long cell process called an axon to transmit impulses.
However, animal cells have many things in common.

Animal cells are surrounded by a **cell membrane** or **plasma membrane**.
Inside the membrane is the jelly-like **cytoplasm**, which contains the **nucleus**
and other organelles.
These other cell components include the **endoplasmic reticulum,
mitochondria, Golgi bodies, centrioles, lysosomes, ribosomes**
and **cytoskeleton**.
This detailed organisation is known as the **ultrastructure** of the cell.

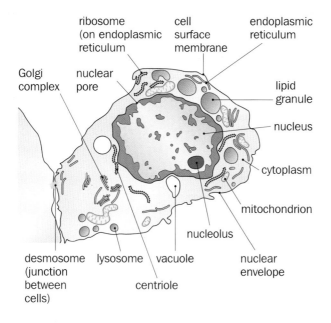

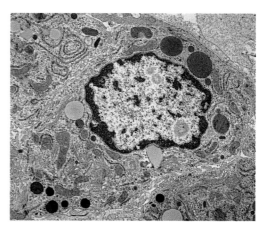

A liver cell as seen under the electron microscope

▷ Plant cells

Plant cells have all the structures found in animal cells.
Look at the diagram. Can you see any *additional* features?

All plant cells are enclosed by a **cellulose cell wall**, outside the cell surface membrane.
This supports the cell and gives it its regular geometric shape.
The cell wall may contain a number of small holes called **pits**.
The pits allow strands of cytoplasm, called **plasmodesmata**,
to link different cells together.
Most of the inside of the cell is taken up by a fluid-filled **vacuole**.
A large vacuole is a permanent feature of plant cells. It is surrounded
by a membrane called the **tonoplast**.
The presence of **chloroplasts** is one of the most important features of plant cells
as this is where **photosynthesis** takes place.

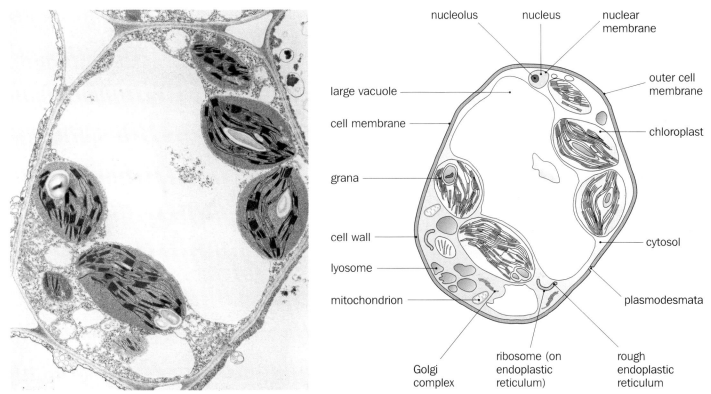

Note the typical plant cell features in this palisade cell: chloroplasts, starch grains,
cellulose cell wall and a large vacuole

Differences between plant and animal cells	
Plant cells	**Animal cells**
cellulose cell wall	no cell wall
plasmodesmata	no plasmodesmata
chloroplasts	no chloroplasts
large, permanent vacuole filled with cell sap	small, temporary vacuoles
tonoplast around vacuole	no tonoplast
no centrioles	centrioles present
starch grains for storage	glycogen granules for storage

▷ Cellulose cell wall

The plant cell wall consists of tiny cellulose fibres called **microfibrils**, glued together by a mixture of polysaccharides. Each microfibril is made up of thousands of cellulose molecules bound together by pectins and hemicelluloses (see page 15).

Cell walls have the following functions:

- They provide support for the cell by allowing it to become **turgid**. As water enters the vacuole by osmosis, the plant cell expands. The cell wall has to be strong enough to resist this expansion and so enable the cell to become turgid.

- They provide mechanical strength to support the cell. The cellulose microfibrils are very strong. The strength may be increased by the addition of **lignin** in tissues such as xylem. In cells such as **collenchyma**, extra cellulose is added to the cell wall to increase mechanical support.

- They are freely permeable to water and substances in solution.

- They have narrow pores (**pits**) through which fine strands of cytoplasm (**plasmodesmata**) are able to pass. These connections allow exchange of materials between the living cell contents.

- The cell walls of adjacent cells are glued together by the **middle lamella**. This is a jelly-like substance made up of calcium and magnesium pectate.

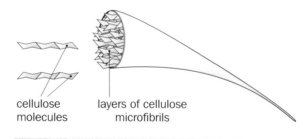

cellulose molecules

layers of cellulose microfibrils

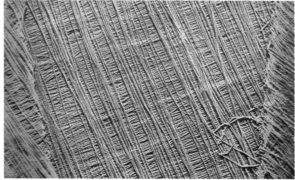

Microfibrils make up this cellulose cell wall

▷ Vacuole

Plant cells have a large, permanent vacuole bounded by a membrane called the **tonoplast**.
The vacuole contains cell sap, which is a solution of sugars, amino acids, mineral salts and waste chemicals dissolved in water. In some cells the sap contains pigments; for instance, beetroot cells contain anthocyanins, which give them their characteristic purple colour.

Plant cell vacuoles have a number of functions:

- Water tends to enter the vacuole by **osmosis**. The cell contents expand and push against the cell wall, which resists this stretching with an equal and opposite force. The cell can take in no more water and is said to be turgid (see page 55).

- Vacuoles act as stores of foods like sugars and amino acids.

- Vacuoles accumulate waste products such as tannins. If these wastes accumulate in the vacuoles of leaf cells, they are excreted when the leaves fall.

- The vacuoles of some cells contain pigments, which give colour to parts of the plant like petals.

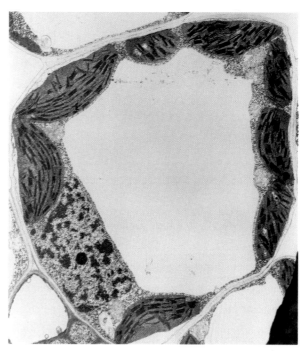

In this mature plant cell, the vacuole, bounded by the tonoplast takes up most of the cell volume

▷ Nucleus

The nucleus is the largest organelle in the cell and can be seen with a light microscope.
Nuclei are spherical and each is about 10 μm in diameter.

The nucleus is surrounded by a nuclear membrane.
The nuclear membrane is a double membrane with a space in between.

There are many large pores in the membrane, which allow materials to pass in and out of the nucleus.

As you can see in the diagram, the nuclear membrane is connected to a system of membranes called the endoplasmic reticulum.

Nucleoplasm is the name given to the material inside the nucleus. It contains **chromatin**, which is made up of DNA attached to proteins called **histones**.
In a non-dividing cell the chromatin is spread throughout the nucleus in the form of tiny granules.
At times of cell division, the chromatin condenses, pulling the DNA into thread-like **chromosomes**.
This is why chromosomes only become visible at times of cell division.

The nucleus also contains a spherical structure called a **nucleolus**.
The nucleolus is important as it makes ribonucleic acid (RNA), which is needed to make **ribosomes**. We will look at this in Chapter 6.

- The nucleus contains the genetic material DNA, together with histone proteins in the chromosomes.

- The DNA carries genetic information for the synthesis of proteins, including enzymes.

- The DNA in the nucleus codes for the production of enzymes. Enzymes control the chemical reactions taking place in the cell. So the genetic material of the nucleus controls the metabolism of the cell.

- The nucleus produces new chromosome material at cell division so that each daughter cell has the same amount of DNA and is genetically identical.

Can you think of any cells that **do not** have a nucleus?

Red blood cells lose their nuclei and this enables them to carry more **haemoglobin** and so pick up more oxygen.
Phloem sieve tubes provide the transport system for sucrose in plants.
They have lost most of the cell organelles including their nuclei.
This makes it easier for materials to flow through the cell.

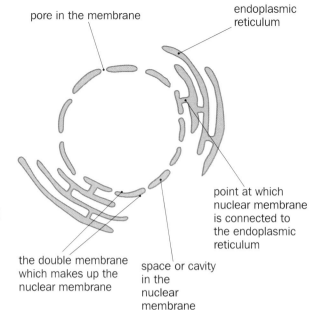

pore in the membrane

endoplasmic reticulum

point at which nuclear membrane is connected to the endoplasmic reticulum

the double membrane which makes up the nuclear membrane

space or cavity in the nuclear membrane

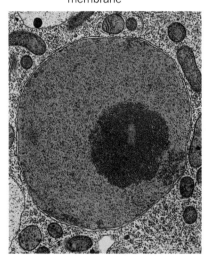

A false colour electron micrograph of a cell nucleus

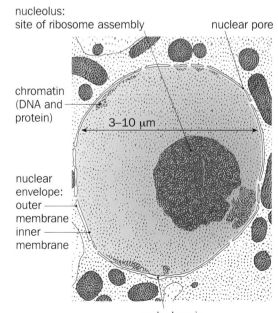

nucleolus: site of ribosome assembly

nuclear pore

chromatin (DNA and protein)

3–10 μm

nuclear envelope:
outer membrane
inner membrane

endoplasmic reticulum

33

▷ Endoplasmic reticulum

The **endoplasmic reticulum** (ER) is a complex system of double membranes.
The fluid-filled spaces between the membranes are called **cisternae**.
As the ER is connected with the nuclear membrane and the
cell surface membrane, the cisternae form a system of little passages,
which allow materials to be transported throughout the cell.

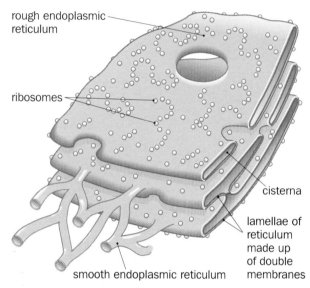

Where **ribosomes** are present on their outer surface, the membranes are
called rough endoplasmic reticulum.
The main function of rough ER is to package and transport proteins made
by the ribosomes. Cells that manufacture a lot of protein, for instance those
making digestive enzymes in the gut, have large amounts of rough ER.

Not all ER is covered in ribosomes.
ER with no ribosomes is called **smooth ER**.
Smooth ER is the site of lipid synthesis.
So large amounts of smooth ER are located in cells that make
lipids and steroids, for example cells of the liver and testis.

Endoplasmic reticulum has the following functions:

- to form an extensive transport system throughout the cell,
- production and packaging of proteins (rough ER),
- synthesis of lipids and steroids (smooth ER),
- collection, storage and distribution of these materials.

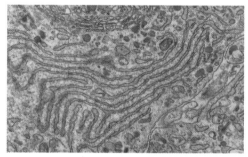

TEM of smooth endoplasmic reticulum (SER)
No attached ribosomes

▷ Ribosomes

Ribosomes are small, dense organelles that are found in huge numbers in
all cells.
They are about 20 nm in diameter in eukaryotic cells but slightly smaller
in prokaryotic cells.

Ribosomes can occur free in the cytoplasm where they synthesise enzymes
that are used in the cytoplasm, such as those enzymes involved in glycolysis
(the first stage of respiration).
Many of the cell's ribosomes are attached to ER (rough ER).

Ribosomes are manufactured in the nucleolus from ribosomal RNA and
protein.
Each ribosome is made up of one small sub-unit and one large sub-unit.
Ribosomes are the sites of protein synthesis in the cell.

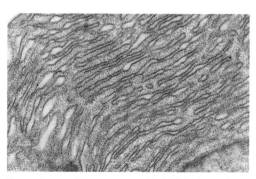

*Can you see ribosomes on this TEM of rough
endoplasmic reticulum (RER)?*

▷ Golgi body

These organelles were first observed by the Italian scientist Camillo Golgi at the end of the last century. They appear as stacks of flattened sacs.

Electron micrographs show how Golgi bodies are formed. Small pieces of rough ER are pinched off at the ends to form small vesicles. A number of these vesicles then join up and fuse together to make a Golgi body.

Proteins which were made and stored in the rough ER are transported in the small vesicles and collect in the Golgi bodies. Here the proteins are modified and combined with carbohydrates or fats to make new molecules such as glycoproteins.

Small vesicles can then become pinched off from the Golgi body, carrying the new chemical products away. These chemicals can be secreted when the vesicle moves to the cell surface membrane. Sometimes the vesicles that are pinched off from the Golgi body become **lysosomes**.

The main functions of the Golgi body are:

- assembling glycoproteins such as **mucin** by combining carbohydrate and protein,
- transporting and storing lipids,
- formation of lysosomes,
- production of digestive enzymes,
- secretion of carbohydrates for the formation of plant cell walls and insect cuticles.

TEM of a Golgi body in section

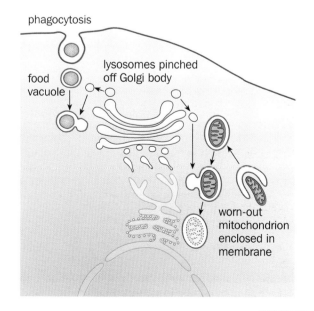

vesicles fuse with the cell surface membrane and release the secretions

vesicles containing secretions are pinched off the Golgi body

the Golgi body– stack of flattened sacs lined with smooth endoplasmic reticulum

vesicles pinch off the rough endoplasmic reticulum and fuse to form flattened sacs

rough endoplasmic reticulum

▷ Lysosomes

Lysosomes are small vacuoles formed when small pieces of the Golgi body are pinched off at the end.
They contain a variety of hydrolytic enzymes, which can digest material within the cell.
The membrane around the lysosome prevents these enzymes from digesting the cell itself.

The main functions of lysosomes are linked to the actions of these enzymes.

- Lysosomes release enzymes that destroy worn-out organelles in the cell.

- They digest material that has been taken into the cell.
  For instance, some white blood cells are able to engulf bacteria. The bacterium is taken into the cytoplasm inside a vesicle. Lysosomes discharge their contents into the vesicle and digest the bacterium.
  This process is known as **phagocytosis** (see page 58).

- Lysosomes release their enzymes to the outside of the cell to digest other cells.
  This process is called **exocytosis** (see page 58).

- They can cause the cell to self-destruct.
  The lysosome's membrane breaks down, releasing its enzymes and digesting the entire cell (**autolysis**).

phagocytosis

lysosomes pinched off Golgi body

food vacuole

worn-out mitochondrion enclosed in membrane

▷ Mitochondria

Mitochondria are relatively large organelles found in all eukaryotic cells.
They are barely visible under the light microscope but the electron microscope
reveals them as sausage-shaped structures about 1 μm wide and 5 μm long.

Each mitochondrion has a double membrane, the outer one of which controls
the entry and exit of materials.
The inner membrane forms many folds called **cristae**.
The surface of each crista is covered in stalked particles, where energy-rich **ATP**
(**adenosine triphosphate**) is made.
The mitochondrion is filled with a jelly-like **matrix**, where some of the enzymes
used in respiration are found.
The matrix contains ribosomes and loops of DNA,
which enables the mitochondria to replicate themselves when the cell divides,
so that both daughter cells produced will have enough mitochondria of their own.

Mitochondria are the sites of **aerobic respiration** in the cell.
They are often described as the 'power plants' of the cell.
Enzymes involved in different stages of cell respiration are located
on the cristae and in the matrix.
Details of aerobic respiration are covered in Chapter 16.

Not surprisingly, the numbers of mitochondria present reflect the
metabolic activity of a cell. For instance, insect flight muscle and liver cells
contain vast numbers of mitochondria.

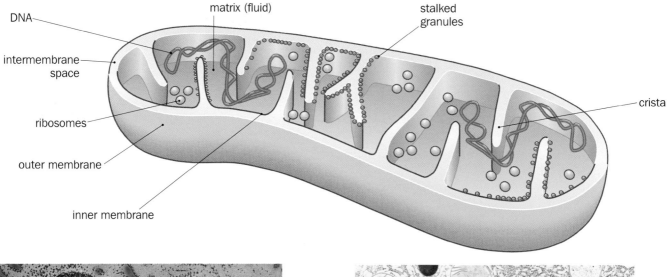

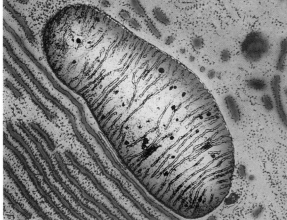

TEM of a mitochondrion in section

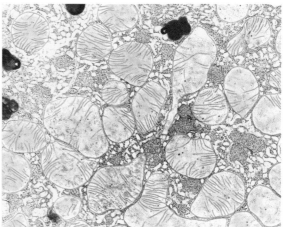

TEM of a mitochondria mainly cut in cross section, note the cristae

▷ Chloroplasts

Chloroplasts are found inside the photosynthetic tissues of plants and some protoctists.
They are particularly abundant in the palisade mesophyll cells of leaves.
They belong to a group of organelles called **plastids**, many of which
contain pigments.

Chloroplasts are similar in size to mitochondria and, like mitochondria, they have
a double membrane – the **chloroplast envelope**.
Inside this double membrane is the fluid **stroma**, which contains enzymes
involved in the reactions of photosynthesis.

Within the stroma is a network of flattened sacs called **thylakoids**.
Grana (singular **granum**) are formed when many of these thylakoids are stacked
together like piles of coins.
The chlorophyll molecules, which trap light energy, are located within
the thylakoids of each granum.
The grana combine the ability to present a large surface area for
light absorption with economy of space.
Also visible in the stroma are large starch grains, which form a temporary store
for the products of photosynthesis.
Details of the biochemistry of photosynthesis are covered in Chapter 17.

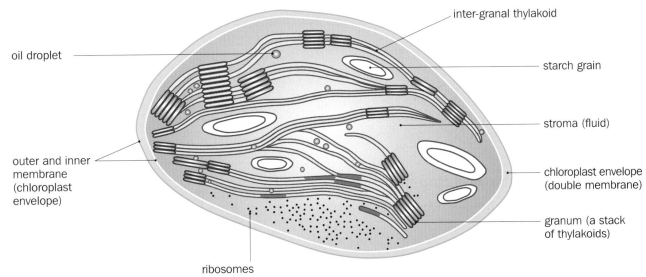

inter-granal thylakoid

oil droplet

starch grain

stroma (fluid)

outer and inner
membrane
(chloroplast
envelope)

chloroplast envelope
(double membrane)

granum (a stack
of thylakoids)

ribosomes

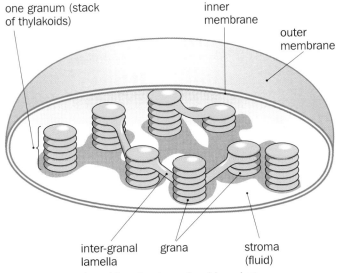

one granum (stack
of thylakoids)

inner
membrane

outer
membrane

inter-granal
lamella

grana

stroma
(fluid)

3-D representation of the structure of a chloroplast

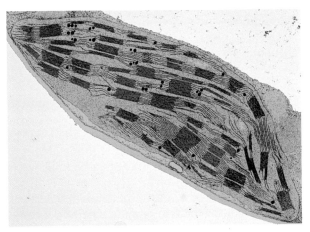

TEM of section of a chloroplast

▷ Cytoskeleton

Despite its appearance, the cytoplasm is not a clear, formless blob of jelly.

Throughout the cell there is a complex network of fibrous proteins that make up the **cytoskeleton**.

However, the cytoskeleton is not a rigid framework since the protein fibres can be built up and broken down in different parts of the cell at the same time.

This means the cytoskeleton will allow movement as well as giving the cell shape and support.

Microtubules are fine, tubular, unbranched structures.
They run through the cell providing the basis of the supporting scaffolding.
Microtubules are made up of the protein **tubulin**.

Microfilaments are much thinner strands, composed of the protein **actin**.
Because this protein is involved in muscle contraction, it is thought that microfilaments may be linked to cell movements and transport within the cell.
The single-celled *Amoeba* and some white blood cells are capable of this sort of independent movement.

Functions of the cytoskeleton as a whole are:

- to provide an internal framework which supports the cell,
- to organise and move organelles within the cell,
- to move the whole cell,
- to construct the spindle during cell division,
- to provide the components of cilia and flagella.

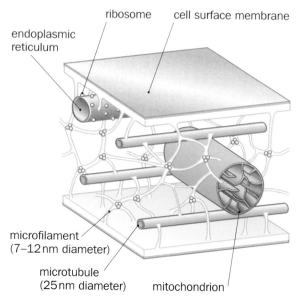

ribosome   cell surface membrane
endoplasmic reticulum
microfilament (7–12 nm diameter)
microtubule (25 nm diameter)   mitochondrion

The cytoskeleton has a complex 3-D framework

▷ Centrioles, cilia and flagella

Centrioles are two short bundles of microtubules positioned at right angles to each other.
They are located just outside the nucleus in a clear area of cytoplasm called the **centrosome**.
The wall of each centriole is made up of nine triplets of microtubules arranged at an angle.
At times of cell division, they migrate to opposite poles of the cell where they produce the **spindle**.
This arrangement of microtubules assists the movement of chromosomes.

Cilia and **flagella** are very similar in structure to each other.
Each has a ring of nine pairs of microtubules surrounding two central pairs.
Cilia are much shorter (5–10 μm) and are found in greater numbers.

Flagella often occur singly and can be anything up to 1000 μm long.
They are often used to help cells to move. Many unicellular organisms and the tails of sperm cells have flagella to allow them to move.

Cilia are often used to move materials about.
For instance, cilia beat to provide a conveyer belt carrying mucus from the respiratory passages up to the throat.

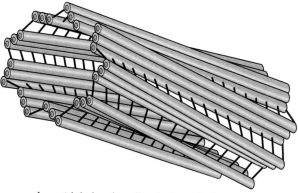

A centriole is a bundle of microtubules

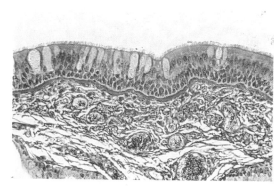

Light microscope of the ciliated epithelial cells of the respiratory passages

▷ Viruses

Viruses are much smaller than bacteria and are only visible with an electron microscope.
They range in size from 20 nm to 400 nm and do not have a proper cell structure.
As such they are exceptions to the cell theory.
These 'non-cells' have no cytoplasm, no organelles and no chromosomes.

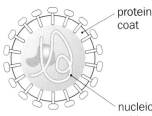

protein coat

nucleic acid strand

the human immunodeficiency virus (HIV)

Herpes simplex virus causes cold sores

Viruses can only become active inside a living host cell.
Outside the cell they exist as inert virus particles called **virons**.
When they invade a host cell they are able to take over the cell's metabolic machinery and make new virus particles.
So 'reproduction' is the only characteristic that viruses share with other living organisms.

Viruses consist of

- a core of nucleic acid,
- a protein coat or **capsid**.

The core of nucleic acid can be RNA or DNA.
The influenza virus and the human immuno-deficiency virus (HIV) contain RNA, as do most of the viruses that cause diseases in plants.
Herpes simplex, the virus that causes cold sores, and *Parvovirus*, which causes gastroenteritis, both contain DNA.

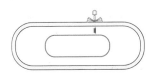

tobacco mosaic virus infects tobacco plants

As you can see from the diagrams, viruses have distinct structures and come in a variety of shapes and sizes.
Because of the absence of cytoplasm, viruses cannot carry out any chemical reactions on their own.
They are totally dependent on the cellular machinery of other cells.
As such viruses are regarded as **parasites**.

bacteriophages are viruses which infect bacteria

It's a take over

Many viruses cause disease.
Some are even named by the symptoms they produce in their hosts.
For example, tobacco mosaic virus (TMV) produces a distinctive mosaic pattern on tobacco leaves.

The sequence of events that occur when a virus takes over a cell and makes new viral particles is similar in most cases.
In the example here, we will look at the **bacteriophage** *lambda*.
Bacteriophages are viruses that replicate inside bacterial cells.

- The viral nucleic acid enters the host cell.
  This can occur by the viral membrane joining to the cell surface membrane of the host cell or, as in the case of bacteriophages, the DNA is injected into a bacterial cell (see page 99).

- The viral DNA is 'read' by the host cell.

- The host cell uses this information to make new viral DNA and new viral protein.

- The viral DNA is surrounded by protein coats and the host cell bursts, releasing the new viruses.

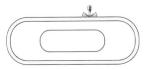

1. attachment of virus to host cell

2. insertion of viral nucleic acid

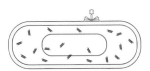

3. replication of viral nucleic acid

4. synthesis of viral protein

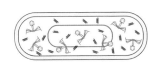

5. assembly of virus particles

6. lysis of host cell

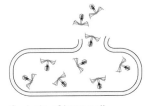

39

▷ Levels of organisation

Most organisms are multicellular and their bodies contain a variety of different cells.
During development, cells **differentiate**, developing different structures and shapes. This means that they can carry out different functions.

Cells that differentiate in the same way form a **tissue**, for example cardiac muscle.
So tissues are made up of cells of the same type.
Different tissues combine to form **organs**, such as the heart.
Organs then work together as **systems**, for instance the circulatory system.
All the systems in an individual make up the **organism**, for example you!

More and more complex

What makes up an organism?
We can identify different levels of organisation.
Starting at the lowest level and getting more complex:

- **Chemical level**: atoms make up important biological molecules, such as carbohydrates, proteins, lipids and nucleic acids.
  These are needed for the maintenance and metabolism of an organism.

- **Organelle level**: as you have seen, specialised structures within cells are called organelles.
  The Golgi body, for instance, is composed of membranes made up of phospholipids and proteins.

- **Cellular level**: cells are the basic structural unit of life.
  Different cells differentiate to carry out particular functions.
  These specialised cells show division of labour, since they carry out different jobs.
  For instance, red blood cells transport oxygen.

- **Tissue level**: a tissue is a collection of specialised cells of the same type, all working together to carry out a particular function.
  For example, muscle tissue is composed of individual muscle cells.
  When these cells contract, the muscle tissue contracts.

- **Organ level**: organs may be made up of several tissues.
  For instance, the heart is made up of cardiac muscle, nervous tissue and connective tissue.
  Organs are structures in the body with a definite form and function.

- **System level**: a system involves a number of organs working together to perform a common function.
  The organs of the digestive system include the stomach, intestines, liver and pancreas.
  These organs work together to digest and absorb your food.

- **The organism**: all the systems of the body together make up an organism.

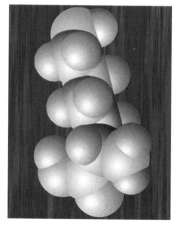

Model of an amino acid

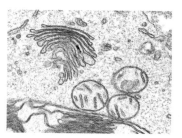

Mitochondria and a Golgi body in kidney tubule cells

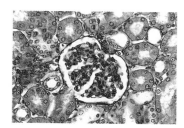

A Bowman's capsule in kidney tissue

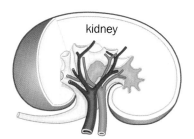

kidney

urinary system

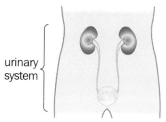

▷ Specialised cells

Look at the photographs of specialised animal and plant cells on this page.
What special features does each one have?
How do these features help the cell to carry out its particular role?

Copy and complete the table using your observations of these cells.

Type of cell	Specialised features	Function of the cell within the body
ciliated epithelial cells of bronchus		
spermatozoa		
striated muscle fibres		
neuro-muscular connections		
red blood cells		
phloem sieve tubes		
a stoma		
root hair cells		

▷ The light microscope

The diagram shows the basic structure of a **light microscope**.
It is also known as a **compound microscope** because it
has two lenses: the **eyepiece** lens and the **objective** lens.
These lenses combine to produce a much greater magnification
than could be obtained by a single lens.
The magnification of each lens is usually written on the
eyepiece and objective mountings.
So how do you know the total magnifying power of
a microscope?
You simply **_multiply_** the two magnifications together.
A ×10 eyepiece lens and a ×40 objective lens together produce
a total magnification of ×400.
Light microscopes have the ability to magnify up to ×2000.
This is sufficient to observe cells and some of the larger organelles.

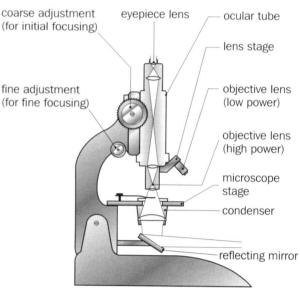

A light microscope

Resolving power

The ability to magnify is not the only quality needed of a microscope.
It also needs to produce a **_clear_** image showing all the fine detail
of the specimen.
This ability is known as **resolving power** and it can be expressed as:
'the minimum distance between two points at which they are still visible
as two separate points'.
Two objects close together may appear as a single image when viewed
under the light microscope.
Increasing the magnification will only show the objects as **_one_** larger image.
The microscope is unable to **resolve** the two objects into separate images.

The maximum resolution of a light microscope is 200 nm.
So two objects closer together than 200 nm cannot be distinguished
as being separate.
The reason for this is the nature of light itself.

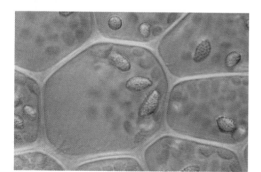

Poor resolution in this photomicrograph taken under the light microscope

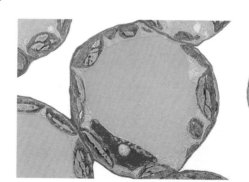

High resolution in this transmission electron micrograph

The wavelength of visible light is about 500–650 nm.
Organelles such as mitochondria (about 1000 nm in diameter) are large enough
to interfere with light rays.
But ribosomes (20 nm in diameter) are too small to interfere with light rays.
So ribosomes cannot be seen under a light microscope whereas
mitochondria can.
A general rule is that if two objects are each smaller than half the wavelength
of the radiation used to view them, then they cannot be seen as being separate
from each other.
So in the case of light microscopes, if each object is smaller than 200 nm,
then they will not be seen as separate from each other.

▷ The electron microscope

The **electron microscope** was developed in the 1950s.
It relies upon an electron beam instead of light rays.
The image is formed as the electrons are scattered by the biological specimen, rather like light rays are scattered in a light microscope.

The average wavelength of light is about 550 nm whilst the average wavelength of an electron beam is 0.005 nm.
The shorter the wavelength of the radiation used to produce the image, the greater the resolving power of the microscope.
A good light microscope can resolve two objects that are 200 nm apart.
But an electron microscope can resolve objects that are only 1 nm apart.

So how does an electron microscope work?

- At the top of the electron microscope column the filament of an electron gun is heated, causing it to emit electrons.

- These negatively charged electrons are attracted to a positively charged electrode called the anode.
  As they move, the electrons are concentrated into a beam by the negatively charged cathode.

- The condenser and objective are electromagnets.
  They straighten the electron beam, focusing it onto the specimen.

- The projector focuses an image of the specimen onto a screen.

- A vacuum has to be maintained inside the microscope otherwise the electron beam would be scattered when it hit air molecules.

- Any specimens to be viewed have to be dead if they are to be placed in a vacuum.
  Skilled preparation is needed to dehydrate and fix the material.

There are two types of electron microscopes:

Transmission electron microscopes (TEMs) pass the electron beam *through* the specimen.
The electrons are deflected as they pass through the thin slices of material, and the pattern produced is converted into an image.

Scanning electron microscopes (SEMs) record the electrons that are reflected off the surface of a specimen.
Consequently, thin sections of material are not required and three-dimensional images of intact specimens can be produced.

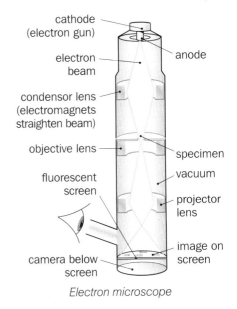

Electron microscope

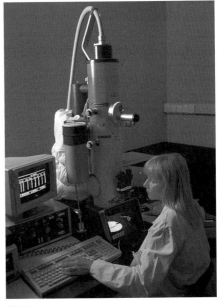

TEM in use

Comparison of light microscopes and electron microscopes		
	Light microscope	**Electron microscope**
radiation used	light rays	electron beams
magnification	×2000	×500 000
resolving power	200 nm	1 nm
focused by	glass lenses	electromagnets
biological material	living or dead	dead
size	small and portable	very large and static
preparation of material	quick and simple	time-consuming and complex
cost	relatively cheap	very expensive

SEM of human head louse (×25)

▷ Cell fractionation

Cell fractionation is a technique used to separate the different parts of cells. Each part can then be studied to determine its structure, using an electron microscope, and its function.

The following steps are involved:

- The tissue to be studied (for example, liver) is cut into small pieces and placed in cold isotonic buffer solution (that is, at the same concentration as the liver tissue).

- The pieces of tissue are ground into very small fragments in a type of liquidiser called an **homogeniser**, to break open the cells.

- The suspension of cell fragments is filtered to remove large pieces of tissue debris.

- The filtrate is then placed into a centrifuge.

A centrifuge is a machine that can spin tubes of liquid at very high speeds. The spinning exerts a force on the contents similar to, but much greater than, the force of gravity.
The faster the speed at which the tubes are spun, the greater is this force.

Cell organelles separate out in order according to their density and shape.
At slower speeds, larger organelles, such as nuclei, collect at the bottom of the tube and form a pellet.
Other less dense organelles remain in suspension in the liquid above the pellet, which is called the **supernatant**.
Increasing the speed of the centrifuge results in other organelles separating out from the supernatant.
Centrifuging at different speeds results in new pellets forming, each of which has relatively pure samples of one type of organelle.
You can see from the table that the length of time centrifuging is important, as well as the speed.

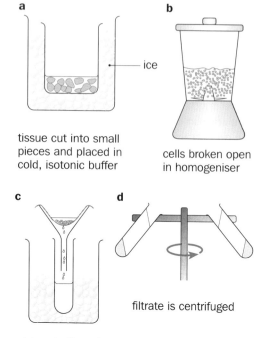

a

b

tissue cut into small pieces and placed in cold, isotonic buffer

cells broken open in homogeniser

ice

c

d

mixture is filtered to remove cell debris

filtrate is centrifuged

	Organelle	Centrifuge setting (g)	Time
first to separate out	nuclei	800–1000	5–10 min
	mitochondria lysosomes	10 000–20 000	15–20 min
	rough ER	50 000–80 000	30–50 min
	plasma membranes smooth ER	80 000–100 000	60 min
last to separate out	free ribosomes	150 000–300 000	>60 min

In what order would you expect the following organelles to separate out: ribosomes, nuclei and mitochondria?

The buffer solution used is 'isotonic' with the liver tissue (the same concentration). What might happen to the organelles if the buffer was
a) *less* concentrated   b) *more* concentrated?

Liver tissue contains many lysosomes. Why do you think this might make the study of liver mitochondria difficult?

Biochemical activity of isolated organelles is soon lost.
What *two* features of cell fractionation help to reduce this loss?

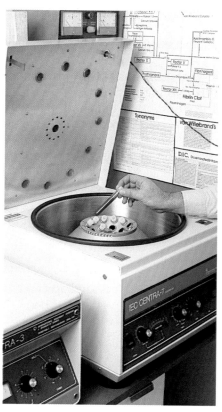

A high speed centrifuge in use

▷ Biology at work: Laser microscopes

The use of light microscopes and electron microscopes to look at biological specimens has been fundamental to the advancement of biological research.

Now there is a new type of microscope called a **laser confocal microscope.** This uses laser beams to excite chemical stains called **fluorochromes**, which emit fluorescent signals.

These stains can be attached to the DNA in the nucleus of a cell to reveal its structure.

Computer analysis

The fluorescent images that are produced are converted into a format which computers can analyse in depth.
This includes three dimensions but only after electronic colour enhancement.
Different signal strengths are given different computer colours, so a colour-coded image can be developed.
The whole process is known as **colour thresholding**.

A major advantage of laser imaging is that the images of specimens are extremely clear.
The same images under a light microscope would be blurred.
For thick samples, such as cervical smears, **optical sections** are taken at different depths through a cell nucleus.

A vertical profile of images is then built up so that all are clearly in focus. Obtaining an all round view of the fluorescent signals with this technique is difficult.
This can be overcome by using **3D-laser imaging.**
This involves taking a series of six images of the same nucleus, with each being rotated by 30°.

Lasers and cancer

Laser imaging techniques can be applied to a wide range of cytological studies, including cancer.
The natural fluorochrome known as Schiff's reagent binds to those elements of DNA that are released during the early stages of cancer.
The intensity of staining is proportional to the amount of cancerous growth, allowing quantitative assessment.

This application has revealed a number of novel features specific to cancerous cells, such as the occurrence of 'hot spots' of localised fluorescence in cell nuclei.
The use of laser microscopy enables much clearer viewing of previously known cancer cell abnormalities.
These include the bending and breakdown of the nuclear envelope and the appearance of 'holes' in the nucleoplasm.

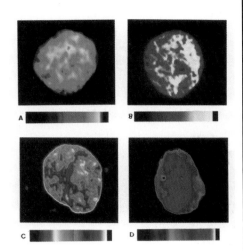

Laser images of nuclei from lung cancer cells. Colour bars indicate descending signal intensity from right to left.

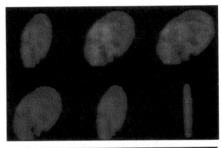

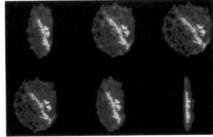

(Top) Serial 3-D images of a cervical nucleus from a normal smear turned stepwise through 30°
(Bottom) Similar images of a cervical smear nucleus with cancer, showing bands of high fluorescence

Summary

- All living organisms (except viruses) are made up of units called cells.
- Prokaryotes include bacteria and blue-green bacteria. Eukaryotes include plants, animals, fungi and protoctists.
- Eukaryotic cells have a true nucleus. They are relatively large with a high degree of internal organisation.
- Animal and plant cells contain many similar organelles, including a cell surface membrane, cytoplasm containing mitochondria, lysosomes, endoplasmic reticulum, Golgi apparatus and ribosomes, and a nucleus with a nucleolus and chromatin.
- In addition, plant cells have chloroplasts, a large permanent vacuole and a rigid cell wall.
- Animal cells have centrioles, which are not found in plant cells.
- The genetic material of plant and animal cells is found inside the nucleus.
- Mitochondria provide the sites where most ATP is produced. ATP provides the energy for the processes taking place inside the cell.
- Chloroplasts are able to trap light energy as chemical bond energy, which can later be released and used by cells.
- Most cell organelles cannot be seen with a light microscope because of the limit of resolution when using light rays.
- Electron microscopes can be used to see smaller structures in greater detail. They can resolve these small structures because electron beams have a shorter wavelength than light rays.

▷ Questions

1 Match the structures i)–x) with the descriptions of their functions a)–j).

   i) mitochondria
   ii) Golgi body
   iii) lysosome
   iv) ribosome
   v) centriole
   vi) cell wall
   vii) vacuole
   viii) chloroplast
   ix) cell surface membrane
   x) nucleus.

a) manufactures ribosomal RNA
b) site of protein synthesis
c) controls the substances that pass into and out of a cell
d) contains the genetic material of the cell
e) converts light energy into chemical energy
f) makes ATP from the oxidation of glucose
g) gives mechanical support to the cell
h) contains digestive enzymes involved in intracellular digestion
i) organises the fibres of the spindle in animal cells
j) modifies proteins after their production.

2 The diagram at the top of the next columnshows part of an electron micrograph of a cell.
a) Match the letters A—G with the following labels:
   i) cell surface membrane
   ii) vacuole
   iii) chromatin
   iv) Golgi body
   v) crista of mitochondrion

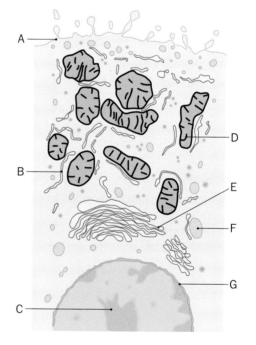

   vi) smooth endoplasmic reticulum
   vii) pore in nuclear envelope.
b) Give three features that suggest that this is a secretory cell.
c) Why do you think that this is an animal cell?

3 The table at the top of the next page refers to structures that may be contained within a bacterial cell, a liver cell and a palisade mesophyll from a leaf. Copy and complete the table, placing a tick (✔) in the appropriate box if the structure is present and a cross (✗) if the structure is absent.

Feature	Bacterial cell	Liver cell	Palisade cell
Nuclear envelope			
Cell wall			
Glycogen granules			
Microvilli			
Chloroplasts			

4 Draw a table to compare the advantages and disadvantages of the light microscope and the electron microscope.

5 Copy and complete the following sentences.
   a) Cell organelles that are likely to be abundant at sites of active transport are ___.
   b) A cell organelle that is particularly rich in hydrolytic enzymes is the ___.
   c) Parts of the endoplasmic reticulum that break off as vesicles are thought to form ___ ___.
   d) Microtubules are a component of ___.
   e) The organelle that converts light energy into chemical energy is the ___.

6 Liver cells were ground to produce an homogenate. The flow diagram shows how centifugation was used to separate organelles from liver cells.

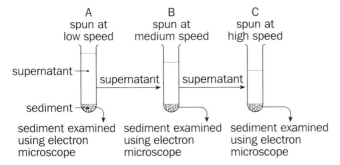

Drawing of electron micrographs of three organelles separated by the centrifugation are shown below. The drawings are **not** to the same scale.

a) Copy and complete the table below.

Electron micrograph	Name of organelle	Centrifuge tube in which the organelle would be the main constituent of the sediment
1		
2		
3		

b) Explain why it is possible to separate the organelles in this way.

7 The diagram (drawn from an electromicrograph) shows a secretory cell from a memmary gland and its relationship to a blood capilliary. The globules (A) consist only of triglycerides.

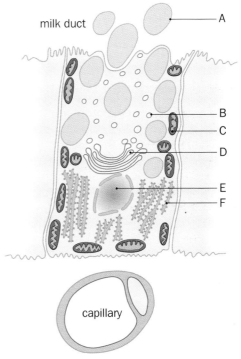

a) i) Identify the structures labelled C, D, E and F.
    ii) Radioactivity-labelled amino acids supplied to such cells grown in tissue culture were later found in milk protein (casein) produced by the cells. Give, in correct sequence, the letters of those structures which show the likely route taken through the cell by those amino acids after absorption.

3 The cell membrane and transport

Many of the organelles that we looked at in the last chapter are composed of or surrounded by membranes.

Can you name some of these cell organelles?

Mitochondria, chloroplasts, lysosomes, Golgi bodies, the nucleus and the endoplasmic reticulum are all enclosed by membranes.

In this chapter we will focus on the cell surface membrane. This acts as a boundary to the cytoplasm and defines the limits of the cell.
It also controls which substances are able to pass into and out of the cell.

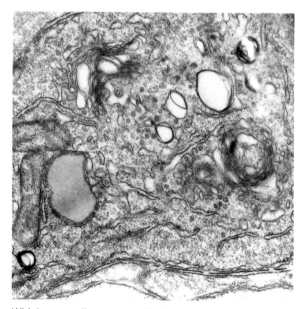

Which organelles can you find in this photomicrograph?

▷ The structure of the cell surface membrane

The cell surface membrane is about 7 nm thick.
Under the light microscope this merely appears as a single line.
However, the development of the electron microscope has made it possible to investigate the detailed structure of biological membranes.

Chemical analysis has shown the membrane to be 75% phospholipid.
In addition, the membrane contains proteins, cholesterol and polysaccharides.
However, it is the phospholipids that form the key elements in the structure.

As you saw in Chapter 1, simple lipids are made up of glycerol and three fatty acid molecules. Lipids are **non-polar** molecules.
In a phospholipid, one of the fatty acids is replaced by a phosphate group.

This phosphate end of the phospholipid molecule is a **polar** molecule.
It has an attraction for other polar molecules such as water.
The other end of the molecule (made up of two fatty acid tails) remains **non-polar** and will not mix with water.

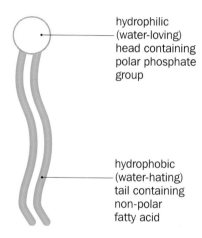

hydrophilic (water-loving) head containing polar phosphate group

hydrophobic (water-hating) tail containing non-polar fatty acid

The polar phosphate heads of the molecule, are water-loving (**hydrophilic**), whereas the non-polar tails are water-hating (**hydrophobic**).

As you saw in Chapter 1, phospholipids can form monolayers and micelles.
Perhaps more importantly though, phospholipids can form **bilayers**.

One sheet of phospholipids forms over another.
Can you see in the diagram that the hydrophilic heads point outwards, facing the water, and the hydrophobic tails face inwards?

This phospholipid bilayer is the basis of the structure of the cell surface membrane and all other membranes.

What is meant by the terms **hydrophilic** and **hydrophobic**?
How do the hydrophilic and hydrophobic properties of phospholipids help to explain the basic structure of the cell surface membrane?

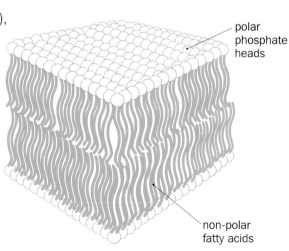

polar phosphate heads

non-polar fatty acids

A phospholipid bilayer

▷ The fluid mosaic theory

The **fluid mosaic theory** was first proposed by Singer and Nicholson in 1972.
With the increased magnification and resolution of the electron microscope, the cell surface membrane could be distinguished as two black lines, referred to as 'tram lines'.
Singer and Nicholson suggested that the cell surface membrane was made up of two layers of phospholipids.

Further chemical analysis showed that a large number of different proteins were located in the cell surface membrane.
It was thought that these proteins 'floated about' in the fluid phospholipid layer.

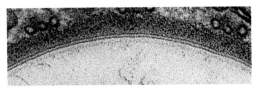
Electron micrograph of a cell surface membrane

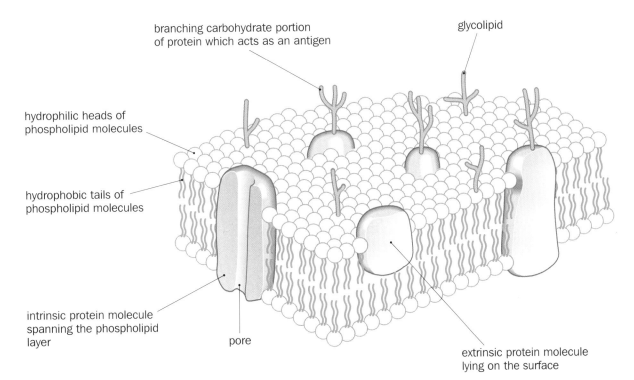

branching carbohydrate portion of protein which acts as an antigen

glycolipid

hydrophilic heads of phospholipid molecules

hydrophobic tails of phospholipid molecules

intrinsic protein molecule spanning the phospholipid layer

pore

extrinsic protein molecule lying on the surface

As you can see, some of the proteins completely span the membrane. These are called **intrinsic proteins**.
Other proteins are found only on the inner surface or on the outer surface of the membrane.
These are known as **extrinsic proteins**.
Just like the phospholipids that make up the bulk of the membrane, the proteins have polar and non-polar regions.
Weak hydrogen bonds between the polar regions of the proteins and the phospholipids keep the membrane stable.

The fluid mosaic model for the cell surface membrane has been described as 'a number of protein icebergs floating in a sea of lipids'.

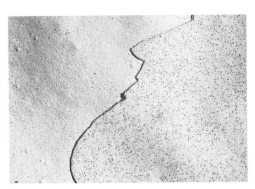
Freeze-fracture TEM of the surface of a plasma membrane showing the double membrane system

▷ How fluid is fluid?

As you saw in Chapter 1, fatty acids can be saturated or unsaturated.
Some phospholipids, then, will have saturated fatty acid tails.
Other phospholipids will have unsaturated fatty acid tails.

- The more unsaturated fatty acids present in the phospholipid bilayer, the more fluid the membrane.

- The shorter the fatty acid tails, the more fluid the membrane.

- The greater the steroid content of the membrane, the **less** fluid it is. **Cholesterol** is a steroid that makes up about 20% of the lipids found in animal cells but is rarely found in plant cells. Cholesterol can fit between the phospholipid molecules, increasing the rigidity and stability of the membrane as a whole.

- An increase in temperature increases the fluidity of the membrane.

Glycolipids make up about 5% of the lipids found in the membrane.
These are lipids that have combined with polysaccharides.
They are usually found in the outer layer of the membrane,
and are thought to play a role in cell-to-cell recognition.

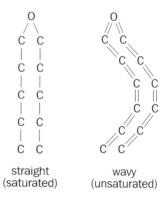

Fatty acids

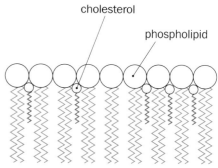

Cholesterol fits between the phospholipids giving the membrane more stability

▷ What about the proteins?

Thousands of different protein types appear in membranes.
It is the proteins that give each type of membrane its own important functions.

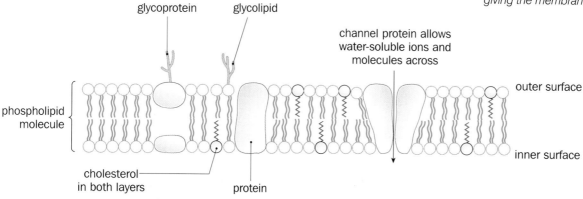

- **Carrier proteins** and **channel proteins** assist and control the movement of water-soluble ions and certain molecules across the membrane. They can maintain different concentrations of ions on either side of the membrane. This can maintain an electrochemical gradient between the inside and the outside.

- Other proteins are involved in **active transport**. This involves the use of energy from ATP to ferry certain ions and molecules across the membrane, against a concentration gradient. A good example is the sodium–potassium pump, where a specific protein uses energy from ATP in nerve impulse transmission.

- **Receptor proteins** recognise and bind with specific molecules outside the cell, such as hormones.

- Some **enzymes**, such as ATPase, are located within membranes.

- **Glycoproteins** are combinations of proteins and polysaccharides. As with glycolipids, they stick out from the surface of some membranes like antennae and are important in cells recognising each other. Some glycoproteins act as **antigens**.

▷ Diffusion

You soon notice if someone has put on too much after-shave or perfume. The molecules of after-shave spread out in all directions of the room.

Molecules and ions in a gas or in a liquid are always on the move. This tendency to spread out through the gas or liquid is called **diffusion**.

> **Diffusion is the movement of molecules (or ions) from a region of high concentration to a region of lower concentration until they are spread out evenly.**

What happens if you drop a crystal of dye into a beaker of water?

First the crystal starts to dissolve, forming a region of high concentration.
Then the molecules of dye diffuse out in all directions.
Eventually the molecules are spread evenly throughout the water.

Can you think of any examples of diffusion in living organisms?

Oxygen diffuses across the air sacs of the lungs into the blood.
Carbon dioxide diffuses out of the blood in the opposite direction.
Some digested food diffuses across the gut wall into the blood.
Mineral salts diffuse from water in the soil into root hairs.

'Oh no it's aftershave man'

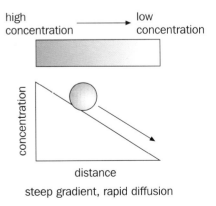

What affects the rate of diffusion?

- The greater the difference in the concentration of a substance in two areas, the faster the rate of diffusion.
  This difference in concentration is known as the **concentration gradient**.

  Can you see from the diagram that the rate of diffusion is directly proportional to the concentration gradient?

- Small particles tend to diffuse faster than larger particles.

- Diffusion takes place more quickly through thin membranes because there is only a short diffusion pathway.
  Think about the air sacs (alveoli) in the lungs.

- Diffusion is quicker if the membrane has a large surface area, as in the case of the spongy mesophyll cells of a leaf, for instance. They provide a huge surface area over which diffusion can take place.

- The shorter the distance between two regions, the faster the rate.

- An increase in temperature increases the rate of diffusion because the particles will have greater kinetic energy.
  In effect, this increase in particle movement is quite small.

shallow gradient, slow diffusion

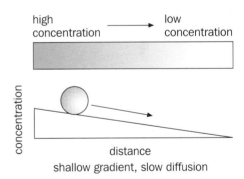

steep gradient, rapid diffusion

Facilitated diffusion

This special form of diffusion allows faster movement.
It involves the use of proteins to assist or **facilitate** diffusion.
There are two main types of protein involved:
channel proteins and **carrier proteins**.

Charged ions, such as Na^+, K^+, Ca^{2+} and Cl^-, cannot diffuse easily across the non-polar centre of the phospholipid bilayer.
Channel proteins open up spaces or pores across the membrane, and so allow entry or exit.
These pores are lined with polar groups allowing charged ions to pass through.

Usually each channel protein is **specific** for one type of ion.
That is, each protein will only let one particular ion through.
The channel proteins can also open or close their pores, acting like gates depending upon the cell's needs.

Carrier proteins are more sophisticated in the way they work.
They are able to allow the diffusion across the membrane of larger polar molecules such as sugars and amino acids.
A particular molecule attaches to the carrier protein at its particular binding site.
This causes the carrier protein to change its shape.
As it does so it 'delivers' the molecule through the membrane.

Carrier proteins and channel proteins both increase the rate of diffusion along a concentration gradient.
It is important to remember that neither requires ATP from respiration. Each is a **passive** process.

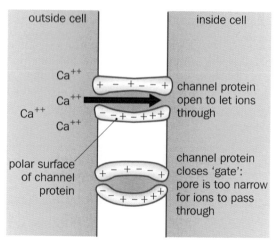

Channel proteins act like 'gates', which open to let ions through

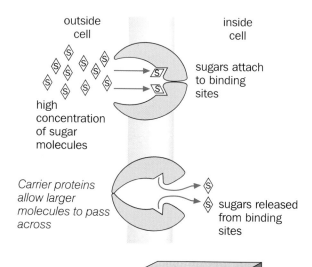

Carrier proteins allow larger molecules to pass across

Diffusion and surface area

As a cell increases in size, its surface area to volume ratio decreases.
You can prove this with a simple exercise.
Look at the drawings of the four 'cells'.
Copy and complete the table to work out the surface area/volume ratio.

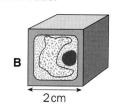
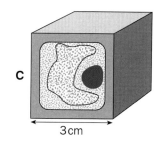
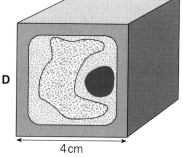

A   1 cm   B   2 cm   C   3 cm   D   4 cm

	Cube A	Cube B	Cube C	Cube D
surface area of one face	$1\ cm \times 1\ cm = 1\ cm^2$			
surface area of cube	$6 \times 1\ cm^2 = 6\ cm^2$			
volume of cube	$1\ cm \times 1\ cm \times 1\ cm = 1\ cm^3$			
ratio: surface area/volume	$6\ cm^2 / 1\ cm^3 = 6{:}1$			

As the cell increases in size there is less surface area in proportion to its volume.
This means that, **relatively**, there is less surface area of cell membrane over which diffusion can occur.
But some cells are able to increase their surface area, as is the case with microvilli in epithelial cells.

▷ Osmosis

The cell surface membrane separates the cell contents
from the surrounding environment.
As you have seen, the membrane allows some molecules
to pass through but not others.
We say that it is a **partially permeable membrane**.

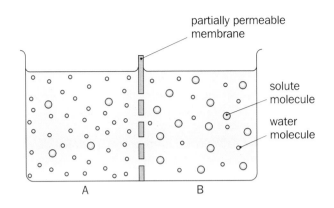

Look at the diagram.
It shows two solutions separated by a partially permeable
membrane.
(Remember that a solution consists of solute molecules dissolved
in a solvent, for example sugar molecules dissolved in water.)

Which solution, A or B, is the most concentrated?
Which solution contains the most water molecules?

The solute molecules are too large to pass through the pores
in the membrane.
But the water molecules are small enough to pass through.
Since A has a greater concentration of water molecules than B,
there will be *diffusion* of water molecules through the membrane,
from solution A into solution B.
This special type of diffusion is called **osmosis**.

> **Osmosis is the diffusion of water molecules from a
> region of high concentration to a region of lower
> concentration through a partially permeable
> membrane.**

A matter of potential

A 'weak' solution will have a high concentration of water molecules.
These 'free' water molecules will have a tendency to move about.
We say that the solution has a **high water potential**.

Pure water has the highest water potential at zero.
So all lower water potentials will have negative values.

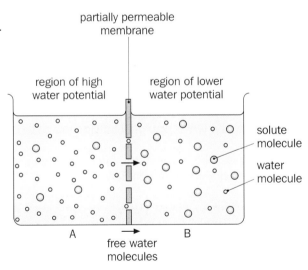

A 'concentrated' solution will have a lower concentration of
water molecules.
There will be fewer free water molecules moving about.
We say that this solution has a **low water potential**.
By low water potential we mean a potential that is more negative.

Water will diffuse out of cells with a high water potential
into cells with a lower water potential.
Perhaps we should give a more accurate definition of osmosis.

> **Osmosis is the diffusion of water molecules from a
> region of high water potential to a region of lower
> water potential through a partially permeable
> membrane.**

Water potential is expressed as Ψ, the Greek letter psi.

▷ Osmosis in plant cells

Can you make a simple but accurate drawing of a plant cell?

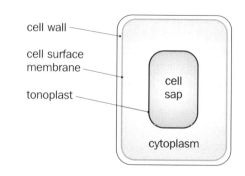

- Surrounding the cell is the cell wall.
  The cell wall is freely permeable, allowing all molecules in and out.

- Flush against the cell wall is the cell surface membrane.
  As you know, this is a partially permeable membrane.

- Inside the cell surface membrane is another membrane – the **tonoplast**.
  The tonoplast separates the contents of the vacuole from the cytoplasm.

▷ Solute potential (Ψ_s)

The concentration of dissolved substances inside the cell is called the **solute potential**.
This value is **always** negative because the forces of attraction between the solute molecules and the water molecules **reduce** the movement of the water molecules.

(Remember that the water potential of pure water is zero. So anything that reduces the ability of water molecules to move must **lower** the potential, that is, make it **more** negative.)

The **more** solute molecules present, the **lower** the water potential.
The **fewer** solute molecules present, the **higher** the water potential.

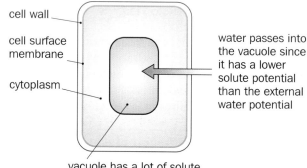

water passes into the vacuole since it has a lower solute potential than the external water potential

vacuole has a lot of solute molecules: a low solute potential

> The solute potential (Ψ_s) is a measure of the reduction in water potential due to the presence of solute molecules.

▷ Pressure potential (Ψ_p)

Water enters a plant cell if the solute potential inside the cell is lower than the water potential outside the cell.

As water passes into a plant cell, the cell contents start to swell.
But this does not go on indefinitely.

Soon the cellulose cell wall starts to become stretched.
It starts to physically resist the swelling caused by the influx of water.
The pressure that the cell wall develops is called the **pressure potential**.
The pressure potential is usually, though not always, positive.

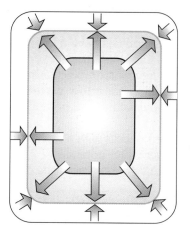

as water enters the cell, the cell wall resists stretching and develops an opposing pressure potential

> Pressure potential (Ψ_p) is the pressure exerted on the cell contents by the cell wall and cell membrane.

At any time, the water potential of a plant cell is the sum of the solute potential and the pressure potential:

Water potential = solute potential + pressure potential
$$\Psi \qquad\qquad \Psi_s \qquad\qquad \Psi_p$$

▷ Turgidity

What happens if you put a plant cell into distilled water or a weak solution (sometimes called a **hypotonic** solution)?

The water potential inside the cell will be **lower** than the water potential of the external solution.
So water enters the cell by osmosis.

This influx of water causes the cell to swell.
The contents press against the cell wall, producing a pressure potential.
As more water enters, the pressure potential rises until it is equal (and opposite) to the solute potential.
The water potential is now zero.
No more water can enter the cell.
A cell in this state is said to be **turgid**.

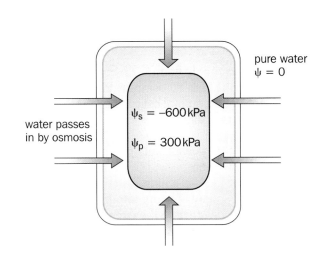

▷ Plasmolysis

What happens if you put a plant cell into a strong solution (sometimes called a **hypertonic** solution)?

In this case, the external solution has the lower water potential.
So water passes out of the cell by osmosis.

As water leaves the cell, the cell surface membrane starts to shrink away from the rigid cell wall.
The pressure potential is now zero, and the cell is **flaccid**.

As more water leaves the cell, the cell contents continue to shrink.
The cell membrane peels away from the cell wall.
A cell in this condition is **plasmolysed**.

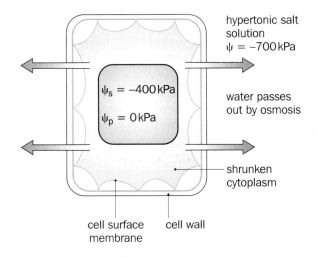

Turgid cells are firm because they are full of water.
They give mechanical support to many soft plant stems and keep them upright.
If these cells lose water, they become flaccid.
They are no longer firm and cannot give the same support.
As a result, the plant stems **wilt**.
But watering them will enable them to regain their turgidity!

What would happen if a plant were placed in **isotonic** solution, that is, a solution with the **same** water potential as that of the cells?
There would be no net movement of water in either direction.
The cells would be in equilibrium.

Try to predict the water movement in these cells:

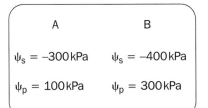

A	B
$\psi_s = -300\,\text{kPa}$	$\psi_s = -400\,\text{kPa}$
$\psi_p = 100\,\text{kPa}$	$\psi_p = 300\,\text{kPa}$

A	B
$\psi_s = -600\,\text{kPa}$	$\psi_s = -700\,\text{kPa}$
$\psi_p = 100\,\text{kPa}$	$\psi_p = 200\,\text{kPa}$

A	B
$\psi_s = -400\,\text{kPa}$	$\psi_s = -600\,\text{kPa}$
$\psi_p = 200\,\text{kPa}$	$\psi_p = 300\,\text{kPa}$

▷ Osmosis in animal cells

What do you think would happen if you put some animal cells (let's say red blood cells) into distilled water?

You can see in the diagram.
Water enters the cells by osmosis, the cells swell and burst.
The reason is that animal cells have no cell wall to limit the expansion of the cell.

The cells have negative solute potential and therefore have a low water potential.
The water outside has a high water potential of zero.
So there is an inflow of water into the cells by osmosis.
Without a cell wall to stop the expansion of the cell, water keeps entering the cell until it bursts.
When this happens to red blood cells it is called **haemolysis**.

What do you think would happen if the red blood cells were put into strong salt solution (a hypertonic solution)?

This time the solute potential of the external solution is more negative than that inside the cells.
This time water will diffuse out of the cells, so they will shrink.
Red blood cells look crinkled, or **crenated**, like those in the photograph.
This can happen in cases of severe dehydration.

We have blood plasma and tissue fluids that are isotonic with our cells (they have the same solute potential).
Our kidneys are able to maintain a constant water level in our bodies.
This example of homeostasis is called **osmoregulation**.

▷ *Amoeba* stays in shape

Amoeba is a single celled organism (one of the Protoctist group).
Some species of *Amoeba* live in freshwater and some are marine.

What problem could *Amoeba* have when living in freshwater?
Water is continuously entering *Amoeba*, because its cell has a negative solute potential.

So why doesn't *Amoeba* burst?

Inside its cell *Amoeba* has an organelle called a **contractile vacuole**.
Water accumulates inside the contractile vacuole.
When it is full the vacuole passes to the cell membrane and releases the water to the outside.
A new contractile vacuole then starts to fill up.

Why do you think that the species of *Amoeba* that live in the sea do not have contractile vacuoles?

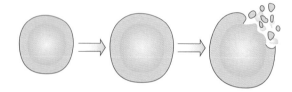

red blood cell   when placed in water the cell swells up ...   ... and bursts! (haemolysis)

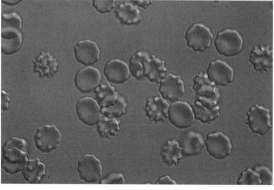

These red blood cells are crenated

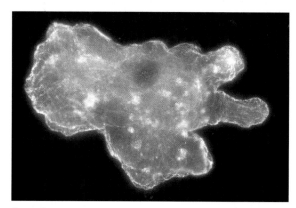

Amoeba

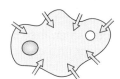

water enters Amoeba by osmosis

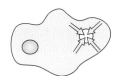

water taken into contractile vacuole

contractile vacuole bursts removing water from the cell

▷ Active transport

Look at the histogram showing the concentration of ions inside and outside the cells of a freshwater alga.
Can you detect any pattern?

The ions are present in far higher concentrations inside the cell than they are on the outside.
There must be some mechanism at work in the membrane. Otherwise the ions would diffuse out of the cell.

The cell is able to accumulate molecules and ions against a concentration gradient.
This involves the use of energy provided by ATP from respiration.
So the process at work is called **active transport**.

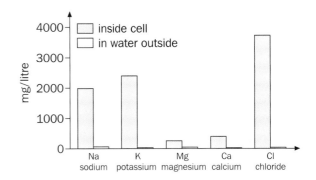

> **Active transport is the uptake of molecules or ions against a concentration gradient using energy from respiration.**

How does it work?

There are specific carrier proteins present in the cell membrane.
As in facilitated diffusion, each carrier protein can combine with a particular molecule or ion.
But unlike facilitated diffusion (which is a passive process), active transport needs an input of energy.
This energy is provided by ATP made in cellular respiration.

- The molecule or ion combines with a specific carrier protein.

- ATP transfers a phosphate group to the carrier protein on the inside of the membrane.

- As a result, the carrier protein undergoes a change of shape, which carries the molecule or ion to the inside of the membrane.

- The molecule or ion is released to the inside of the membrane and the carrier protein reverts to its original shape.

Due to the energy needed for active transport, cells involved in the process:

- tend to contain many mitochondria,
- have a high rate of respiration.

Their ability to take up molecules or ions against a concentration gradient is affected by temperature, oxygen concentration and the presence of poisons such as cyanide, all factors that affect the rate of respiration.

Can you name any processes that involve active transport?

Here are a few:

- nerve impulse transmission,
- muscle contraction,
- absorption of amino acids in the gut,
- absorption of mineral salts by plant roots,
- protein synthesis,
- excretion of urea by the kidney.

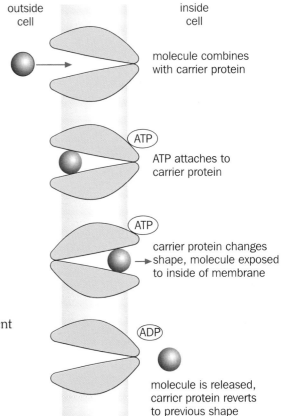

▷ Endocytosis and exocytosis

So far, we have looked at the ways in which the cell surface membrane is able to transport individual molecules and ions.
There are processes where the cell can transport large quantities of material (solids or liquids) *into* the cell (**endocytosis**) or *out* of the cell (**exocytosis**).

Endocytosis

During endocytosis, the cell wraps the cell surface membrane around the material and brings it into the cytoplasm inside a vesicle. There are two main types of endocytosis.

- **Phagocytosis** – solid material is taken into the cell in a vesicle. Lysosomes fuse with the vesicle, emptying their enzymes into it. The enzymes digest the material and the products are absorbed into the cytoplasm.

White blood cells, called **phagocytes**, remove bacteria and cell debris by phagocytosis.
Amoeba engulfs its food by phagocytosis. The food is taken into the cytoplasm inside a food vacuole. Lysosomes release digestive enzymes into the vacuole and the soluble products are absorbed.

- **Pinocytosis** – sometimes called 'cell drinking', is similar to phagocytosis but in this case liquid material is taken into the cell. The vesicles formed during pinocytosis can be extremely small. A human egg cell can take up nutrients from surrounding cells by pinocytosis.

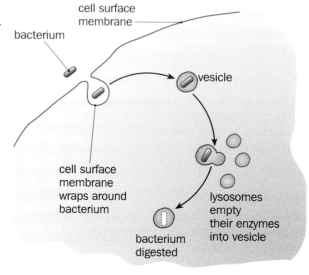

Exocytosis

Exocytosis is the reverse of endocytosis.
It is the passage of materials *out* of the cell.
Often this material is a useful **secretion**, as in the case of digestive enzymes, hormones or mucus.

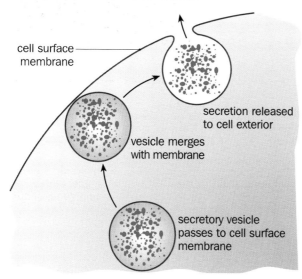

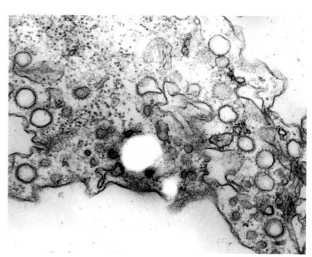

EM showing pinocytosis and vesticles (× 150,000)

Secretory vesicles carry their contents to the cell surface membrane.
The vesicle merges with the membrane and the secretion is released.

▷ Biology at work: Cryopreservation

The Antarctic Ocean is the coldest ocean in the world, with average temperatures as low as $-1.87\,^{\circ}C$.
The Antarctic Toothfish has evolved to survive temperatures as low as $-2.2\,^{\circ}C$.
It contains a natural antifreeze substance, a type of **glycoprotein** molecule.

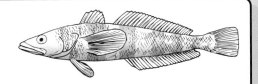

An Antarctic toothfish which lives, feeds and reproduces on the ocean floor

The freezing process

Water cooled to below its freezing point without the formation of ice is said to be **super-cooled**.
In the cells of most organisms, only a proportion of the water is converted to ice.
The removal of liquid water increases the concentration of solutes in the remaining solution.
Adding a **cryoprotectant** such as glycerol reduces this effect and also reduces the amount of ice formed during cooling.

Biological membranes act as efficient barriers to ice crystals.
External freezing of the cell causes its interior to have a lower concentration than the surrounding solution.
Water must therefore be lost from the cell to maintain equilibrium.
This loss can occur in two ways:

- Water can move osmotically from the cell to the hypertonic solution around it.

- Liquid water can be removed by the formation of intracellular ice.

The direct observation of cells during freezing and thawing is now possible using a specialised microscope called a **cryomicroscope**.

This can be used to show that cell survival following freezing and thawing is determined by two potentially damaging processes:

- the effect of concentrated solutions at slow rates of cooling,

- the formation of intracellular ice at faster rates.

Maximum survival varies for different cell types and is determined by the extent to which the two damaging processes overlap.

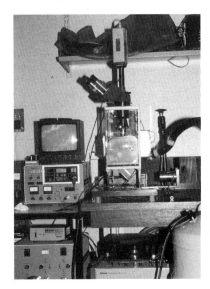

A cryomicroscope

Effects of low temperatures upon biological membranes

A cell's response to freezing and thawing is determined by the properties of its cell surface membrane.
The membrane is composed of both lipid and protein components.

The consistency of the lipid bilayer is affected by heat.

At low temperatures the fatty acids of the **phospholipids** are in a relatively rigid, crystalline state.

At higher temperatures the fatty acids assume a more random fluid structure.

The temperature at which these changes occur is largely determined by the composition of the fatty acid molecules.
The more double bonds a fatty acid molecule contains, the greater the degree of **unsaturation,** and the lower the temperature at which the lipid becomes **'fluid'**.

Once cooled, membrane lipids become solid and so the membrane proteins are no longer free to move.
The membrane becomes less **'dynamic'**.

At rapid rates of cooling, there is insufficient time for the proteins to migrate.
They become set in a configuration similar to that found at normal temperatures.

During slow cooling, a gradual change in state occurs, with proteins being pushed into areas of still-fluid membrane.
This results in an aggregated distribution of proteins.

Certain important membrane processes will occur only if the membrane is sufficiently fluid.
Examples include membrane synthesis, transport and the activity of membrane-bound enzymes.
Living organisms therefore maintain a semi-fluid lipid composition at normal temperatures.
This is achieved by regulating the amount of unsaturated fatty acids.

This knowledge has been used to develop artificial **cryoprotectant** substances and techniques for use in medical and veterinary applications.
These include the preservation of human bone marrow cells for transplantation to cancer patients, and the storage of sperm and ova for in-vitro fertilisation.

Differences between cells account for some of the difficulties experienced in the preservation of organs.
Each of the organ's cell types has a specific cooling rate required for optimum survival.
Exceptions are human skin grafts and heart valve grafts where there is no need to reconnect blood vessels.

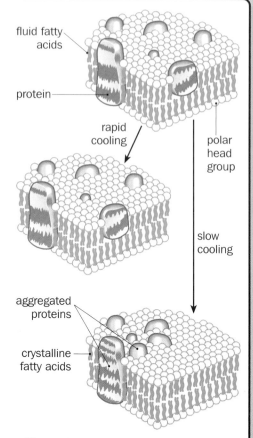

Effects of slow and rapid cooling on the Fluid Mosaic model of membrane structure

Human bone marrow being placed in a controlled rate freezer

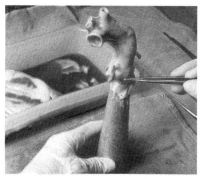

A human aortic valve being prepared for presentation

Summary

- The cell surface membrane around a cell is made up of phospholipids and proteins.
- The cell surface membrane regulates the movement of molecules and ions into and out of the cell.
- Diffusion is the movement of molecules or ions from a region of high concentration to a region of lower concentration until an equilibrium is reached.
- The cell surface membrane is thin and provides a large surface area over which diffusion can occur.
- Facilitated diffusion increases the rate of diffusion. It involves the use of transporter proteins present in the cell surface membrane.
- Osmosis is a specialised form of diffusion. It can be defined as the diffusion of water from a region of high water potential to a region of lower water potential across a partially permeable membrane.
- The ability of a cell to take in water is known as the water potential (Ψ_{cell}). This can be determined by solute potential (Ψ_s) and the pressure potential (Ψ_p).
- Active transport is the movement of molecules or ions across the cell surface membrane against a concentration gradient. This involves the use of energy in the form of ATP from respiration.
- Pinocytosis and phagocytosis are different forms of endocytosis. Pinocytosis involves droplets of fluid being taken into the cell. Phagocytosis involves solid particles being taken in.
- Exocytosis occurs when substances are passed out of the cell.

▷ Questions

1 a) Name the molecules labelled A and B.
   b) Why is this model described as being *fluid*?
   c) Give two functions in the membrane of the molecules labelled B.

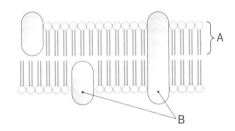

2 The graph shows how the rate of uptake of glucose by red blood cells depends upon the concentration of glucose outside the cells.

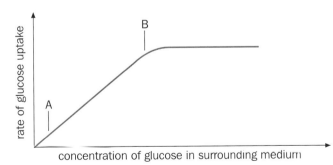

   a) i) What limits the rate of uptake of glucose from the surrounding medium between points A and B on the graph?
      ii) What evidence from the graph supports your answer?
   b) What do you think is limiting the rate of uptake of glucose after point B?

3 The effect of temperature on the permeability of cell membranes can be investigated using fresh carrot. When the carrot discs are placed in water there is a slow release of chloride ions from the vacuoles of the carrot cells.
A number of sets of equal-sized discs were cut and placed into water at different temperatures, from 35 °C to 70 °C. The graph shows the release of chloride ions over this temperature range.

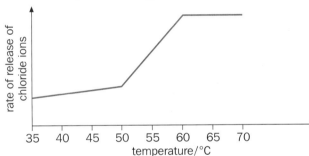

   a) Why is it necessary to wash the discs before placing them in water at different temperatures?
   b) Explain the increase in the rate of release of chloride ions between the temperatures
      i) 35 °C and 45 °C
      ii) 50 °C and 60 °C.
   c) What assumption is made about the cell wall of carrot cells in this investigation?

4 a) Give a definition of osmosis.

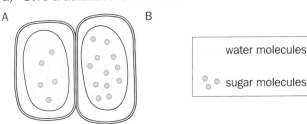

b) i) Which cell has the highest water potential?
    ii) Which cell has the highest solute potential?
    iii) In which direction will the water move?
c) i) In cell A the solute potential (Ψ_s) = −1400 kPa,
       the pressure potential (Ψ_p) = 600 kPa.
       What is the water potential (Ψ_{cell})?
    ii) In cell B the solute potential (Ψ_s) = 2000 kPa,
       the pressure potential (Ψ_p) = 800 kPa
       What is the water potential (Ψ_{cell})?
    iii) What will be the water potential (Ψ_{cell}) at
       equilibrium?

5 Some plant tissue was placed in distilled water until
   the cells became fully turgid.
   It was then placed into concentrated sucrose solution
   until the cells became plasmolysed.
   The table shows some of the values of the potentials
   of the cells.

Conditions of cell	Potential / kPa		
	ψ_{cell}	ψ_s	ψ_p
Fully turgid	0		+300
Plasmolysed		−500	

a) Copy the table and complete the missing values.
b) The diagram shows a turgid plant cell. Draw the
    same cell in a plasmolysed condition.

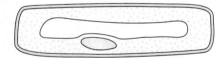

6 Measurements were made of the rate of uptake of
   substances P and Q across the cell surface membrane
   of some cells. The cells were placed in different
   concentrations of either P or Q and the results are
   shown in the table.

Concentration mM 1^{-1}			Rate of Uptake μM h^{-1}	
External (E)	Internal (I)	(E-I)	P	Q
25	50		0	20
50	50		0	40
75	50		12	60
100	50		24	68
125	50		36	70
150	50		48	71

a) Copy the table and complete the column E minus I
    (E − I).
b) From the data in the table, what is the condition
    that is essential for the transport of P to take place?
c) Describe the relationship between the
    concentration gradient and the rate of uptake of P.
d) What process is responsible for the type of
    transport shown by P?
e) i) What type of transport is shown by Q?
    ii) Give one piece of evidence to support your
       answer.
    iii) Apart from Q, name two other molecules
       associated with the membrane that are needed
       for this process to take place.
f) i) Compare the increase in the rate of uptake of
       Q between 25 and 50 mM litre^{-1} (external
       concentration) with the increase between
       125 and 150 mM litre^{-1}.
    ii) Explain the reason for this difference.

7 a) Draw a simple diagram to show the arrangement
       of phospholipid molecules in the cell surface
       membrane.
   b) The graph shows the results of an investigation
       into the movement of various molecules across the
       membrane.

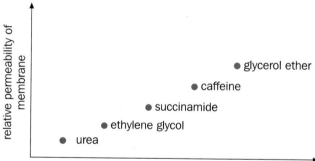

The graph shows an important property of cell
surface membranes.
   i) Describe this property.
   ii) Explain how the structure of the cell surface
      membrane determines this property.
c) Use only information in the graph to explain why:
   i) urea has to be actively excreted,
   ii) it would be a disadvantage for a cell to excrete
      a waste molecule having a higher relative oil to
      water solubility than urea.

Have you ever wondered how they make chocolates with a soft-centre?
How can you pour liquid chocolate over a liquid centre?
Enzymes provide the answer.
The liquid chocolate is poured over a solid centre of polysaccharide.
Then, after the chocolate has set, an enzyme starts to break down the
polysaccharide to a runny, sugary centre.

Enzymes are the molecules that control the reactions in your body.
They are the caretakers of your cells and tissues.
They make sure that your body chemistry is kept in good shape.

Each enzyme has a particular job to do. There is:

● an enzyme that clears the fat out of your bloodstream after dinner,
● an enzyme that can detect the level of glucose in your blood,
● an enzyme in your liver that breaks down the alcohol in beer or wine.

Thousands of chemical reactions take place in your body every second.
Together these reactions make up your **metabolism**.
Enzymes control your metabolism by determining when
and how reactions take place.

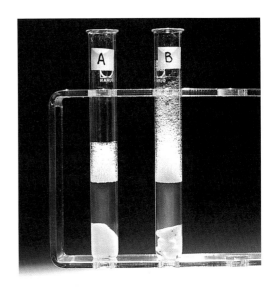

$$A \xrightarrow{\text{enzyme}} B \quad + \quad C$$

substrate · · · · · · · · · · · · · · products
(the substance that the · · · · · · · · · (the substances produced
enzyme works on) · · · · · · · · · · · · · by the reaction)

Enzymes are **catalysts** that speed up the rate of metabolic reactions.
These reactions would still take place without enzymes — but in
years rather than milliseconds!
There are two types of metabolic reaction:

● Reactions where larger molecules are broken down into smaller ones.
  One example is hydrogen peroxide being broken down
  to water and oxygen by the enzyme **catalase**.

$$2H_2O_2 \xrightarrow{\text{catalase}} 2H_2O \;+\; O_2$$
hydrogen peroxide · · · · · · water · · · oxygen

● Reactions where small molecules are built up into larger,
  more complex ones.
  For example, two amino acids can join together to form a dipeptide:

(chemical structure diagram)

amino acid · · · · · · · · amino acid · · · · · $\xrightarrow{\text{enzyme}}$ · · · · · dipeptide · · · · · $+H_2O$ · · · · water

Which of the following reactions do you think break molecules down
and which build molecules up?

● a glycogen molecule formed from glucose molecules,
● a protein formed from amino acids,
● the digestion of starch to maltose,
● urea formed from ammonia and carbon dioxide.

▷ The chemical structure of enzymes

All enzymes are **globular** proteins.
As you already know, proteins consist of long chains of amino acids.
In a globular protein, the amino acid chain is folded and wound into a spherical or globular shape.

Can you see how this protein is held in its globular shape?

Hydrogen bonds, ionic bonds and disulphide bridges hold the amino acid chain in its distinct three-dimensional shape.
This shape is the **tertiary structure** of the protein?

Do you remember what the primary and secondary structures of a protein are?

The **primary structure** of a protein is the actual sequence of amino acids in the chain.
There are 20 naturally occurring amino acids.
Since there are thousands of amino acids in one protein chain, the number of possible permutations is vast.
Each type of enzyme has its own sequence of amino acids, different from any other type of enzyme.

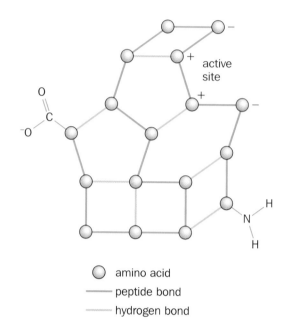

	amino acid
——	peptide bond
——	hydrogen bond

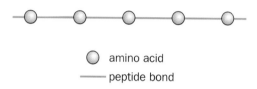

○ amino acid
—— peptide bond

Primary structure of a protein

The **secondary structure** of a protein is the way in which the amino acid chain is organised.
In the globular protein here, the secondary structure involves twisting the amino acid chain into a spiral or helix.

The **tertiary structure** of a globular protein involves the helix folding back on itself to give the molecule its own complex three-dimensional shape.
The enzyme's tertiary structure is very important, since it gives the enzyme many of its properties.
The exact three-dimensional shape enables an enzyme to form receptor sites for its substrates.
The enzyme molecule is held in its tertiary form by hydrogen bonds, ionic bonds and disulphide bridges.

The shape of the protein also depends upon its environment, that is, its immediate surroundings.
So changes in conditions, such as pH and temperature, can cause the three-dimensional shape of the protein to change.

Before going on to see how an enzyme's structure can be linked to its properties, see if you can answer these questions:

What is the primary structure of an enzyme?
What is the secondary structure of an enzyme?
Why is the tertiary structure so important to an enzyme?

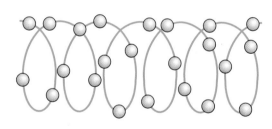

○ amino acid

Secondary structure of a protein

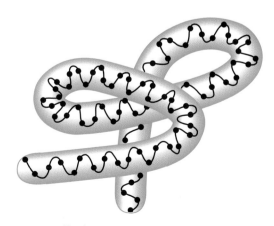

Tertiary structure of a protein

▷ Properties of enzymes

As you know, enzymes are catalysts. They speed up chemical reactions.
But they also have other properties that result from their complex globular shape.

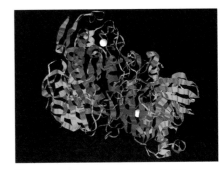

Computer simulation of an enzyme

- Enzymes are **specific**.
  This means that each enzyme will catalyse only **one** particular reaction.

- Enzymes are not used up in the reactions that they catalyse,
  so they can be used again and again.

- When enzymes react, they combine with their substrates to form
  enzyme/substrate complexes.
  When the reaction has taken place, the products are released, leaving
  the enzyme as it was at the start.

- Only a small amount of enzyme is needed to catalyse a lot of substrate.

- Enzymes are fast acting. We say that they have a high **turnover number**.
  This means that they can convert many molecules of substrate per unit time.

- Enzymes are affected by changes in temperature and pH.

- Many enzymes are only able to work if another chemical called a **cofactor**
  is present.

- Enzyme-catalysed reactions can be slowed down or stopped altogether
  by chemicals called **inhibitors**.

Specificity

Each enzyme can catalyse only one particular reaction,
because an enzyme can only react with a specific substrate molecule.
For instance, amylase can only catalyse the hydrolysis of starch
into smaller disaccharide maltose molecules.
This is because amylase can only react with starch molecules.

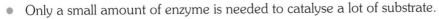

starch molecule   amylase   maltose molecules

The name of an enzyme comes from the particular substrate on
which it acts.
In fact, the name of the enzyme gives you a clue about the substrate
it reacts with.

- **Lact**ase acts upon the milk sugar **lact**ose.
- **Amyl**ase works on starch, or to give it its proper name **amyl**ose.
- **Cellul**ase, made by microbes in the herbivore gut, breaks down **cellul**ose.

Which substrate do you think each of these enzymes acts upon?

- sucrase,
- lipase,
- protease.

. . . You're the one that I want'

The explanation for the specificity of enzymes lies in the tertiary structure
of their protein molecules, that is, their three-dimensional shapes.
As you will see, the enzyme is thought to provide receptor sites where only
a certain substrate will fit so that the chemical reaction takes place.

The lock and key theory

This theory was put forward to try to explain why enzymes are specific
and will only work on particular substrates.
You know that enzymes have a specific three-dimensional shape.
They are large molecules, usually much bigger than their substrates.
But only a relatively small part of the enzyme actually comes into contact with the substrate.
This area of the enzyme is called its **active site**.
The active site has a shape into which part of the substrate fits because of its shape.
Only 3–12 amino acids make up the active site but its shape is an exact fit for the substrate.

The substrate molecule is like the key that fits the enzyme's lock.
The two molecules form a temporary structure called an **enzyme/substrate complex**.

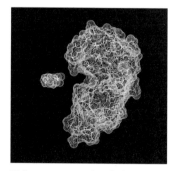

This computer simulation shows the substrate entering the active site

The reaction takes place at the active site and this is where the products are formed.
Since the products have a different shape from the substrate, they no longer fit
the active site and are repelled.
The active site is then free to react with more substrate.

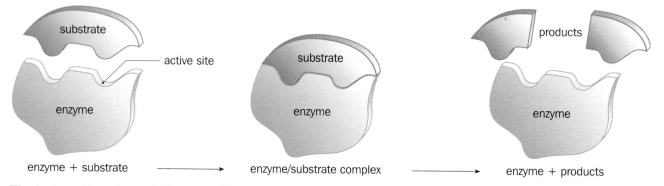

The lock and key theory helps to explain many of the properties of enzymes.
For instance, an enzyme is specific because only a particular shape of substrate
will fit its active site.

Induced fit theory

This is an updated version of the lock and key theory.
It suggests that the active site of the enzyme may not **exactly** correspond to
the shape of the substrate.
The active site has a more flexible shape and is able to mould itself around the substrate.
Only when it binds closely to the substrate does the active site catalyse the reaction.
As in the lock and key theory, the products no longer fit the active site and are repelled.
The enzyme reverts to its 'relaxed' state and is able to attach to more substrate.

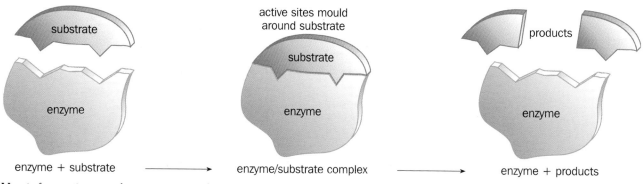

Use information on this page to explain:
- why enzymes are specific and will catalyse only one or a few chemically related compounds,
- why the shape of the active site is determined by the enzyme's tertiary structure,
- why altering the shape of the active site of an enzyme will affect its activity.

Activation energy

Do you remember about rates of reaction in GCSE Science?
Particles in gases and liquids are continually moving.
If the particles bump into each other, then a chemical reaction may occur.

How would you speed up a chemical reaction?

Heating the particles increases their kinetic energy and so they move about more quickly.
This means that there is a greater chance of collisions and the rate of reaction increases.

Reactions need energy to start them off.

> **The energy needed to start a chemical reaction is called the activation energy.**

Another way of thinking about it is as though there is an energy barrier to get over before the reaction can get underway.
It's a bit like pushing a boulder over the top of a hill.
First, you have to supply some energy to get it to the top and over before it can roll down the other side.

In the same way chemical reactions need activation energy to start them off.
This energy is needed to break the existing chemical bonds inside molecules.
Activation energy can be supplied in the form of heat.
But why would this be no good for the reactions that take place in your body cells?

Enzymes lower the activation energy needed to make chemical reactions start.
This means that we don't need extra heat for the reactions in our body cells.
The reactions can take place at lower temperatures.

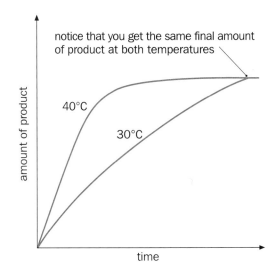

notice that you get the same final amount of product at both temperatures

40°C

30°C

amount of product

time

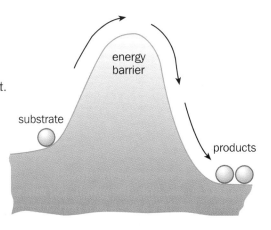

energy
barrier

substrate

products

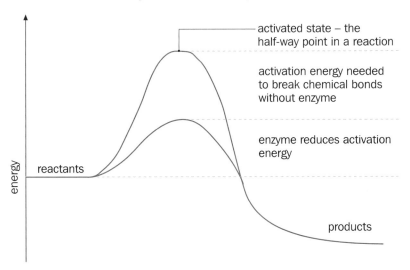

activated state – the half-way point in a reaction

activation energy needed to break chemical bonds without enzyme

enzyme reduces activation energy

reactants

products

energy

By *lowering* the activation energy of a reaction, the enzyme provides a different pathway for the reaction to follow.
By lowering the activation energy, enzymes reduce the input of energy needed and allow reactions to take place at the lower temperatures found in the cells of organisms.

Look back to page 65.
What other factors affect the rate of an enzyme-controlled reaction?
The main factors affecting enzyme activity are shown in the box to the right.

- **temperature**
- **pH**
- **enzyme concentration**
- **substrate concentration**
- **the presence of cofactors**
- **the presence of inhibitors**

67

Temperature

Heating increases the rate of most chemical reactions.
As you know, heating gives molecules greater kinetic energy and they move around more quickly.

This means there is a greater chance of the molecules colliding and the rate of reaction increases.
Also, since the particles are moving faster, their impact will be greater when they collide, making a reaction more likely.
So raising the temperature makes it more likely that the collisions will result in a reaction taking place.

Particles must collide before they can react!

Increasing the temperature of an enzyme-controlled reaction brings about an increase in rate of reaction, but only up to a point.
For some enzymes, increasing the temperature to about 40 °C brings about a corresponding increase in the rate of reaction.
This is due to the increased kinetic energy of both the substrate and the enzyme molecules.

> **Over this sort of range, the effect of temperature T on the rate of a reaction can be expressed by the temperature coefficient Q_{10}:**
>
> $$Q_{10} = \frac{\text{rate of reaction at T} + 10\,^{\circ}\text{C}}{\text{rate of reaction at T}}$$

If we choose T as 20 °C, and taking values from the graph:

$$Q_{10} = \frac{\text{rate of reaction at 30}\,^{\circ}\text{C}}{\text{rate of reaction at 20}\,^{\circ}\text{C}} = \frac{3.5}{1.75} = 2$$

The rate of reaction **doubles** for each 10 °C rise in temperature.

But this does not go on indefinitely.
As you can see from the graph, the rate of enzyme-catalysed reactions reaches a peak at a particular temperature.
This is the **optimum temperature** for the reaction.

What is the optimum temperature for the enzyme in the graph?

Any increase in temperature also causes the atoms making up the enzyme molecule to vibrate more.
Eventually this vibrating causes the breaking of hydrogen bonds and the other bonds that hold the enzyme molecule in its tertiary structure, with its specific shape.

This causes a change in the tertiary structure of the enzyme.
Its three-dimensional shape alters, including the active site, which will no longer fit the substrate molecule.
We say that the enzyme is **denatured**.
This is a **permanent** change that cannot be reversed by cooling.
The enzyme has lost its activity since it is no longer able to form enzyme/substrate complexes.

Cooling below the optimum temperature inactivates the enzyme but does not denature it.
The enzyme can work faster again when it is warmed up.

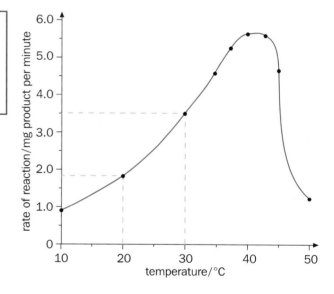

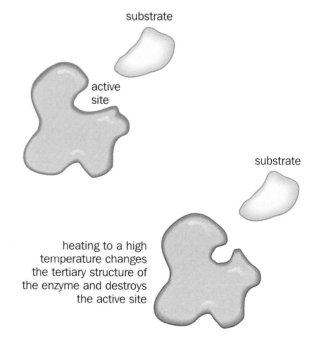

heating to a high temperature changes the tertiary structure of the enzyme and destroys the active site

pH (hydrogen ion concentration)

Most enzymes have an optimum pH at which the rate of reaction is fastest.

Look at the graphs.

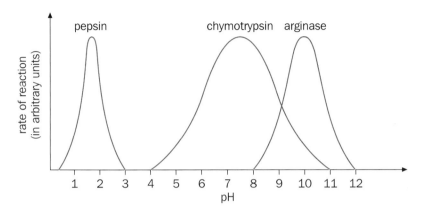

What do you think is the optimum pH for each enzyme?
Why do you think that pepsin and chymotrypsin are active in different regions of the gut?
Which enzyme is active over

   i)   the narrowest range of pH and
   ii) the widest range of pH?

As you have seen, the three-dimensional shape of an enzyme is vital
if it is to function properly.
Many of the chemical bonds holding this tertiary structure in place
are hydrogen bonds.
Small changes in pH can affect the rate of reaction without denaturing the enzyme.
However, at the **extremes** of its pH range an enzyme can become unstable and denature.

Acidity and alkalinity can affect the active site of an enzyme.
Free hydrogen ions (H^+) or hydroxyl ions (OH^-) can affect the
charges on the amino acid side-chains of the enzyme's active site.
This will affect the hydrogen bonding and so change the three-dimensional shape
of the enzyme and the shape of its active site.
The substrate will no longer fit the active site, the enzyme loses its activity
and the rate of reaction falls.

If the active site becomes flooded with hydrogen ions or hydroxyl ions,
it can prevent the enzyme and the substrate from fitting together.
Look at the diagrams below to see how this could happen.

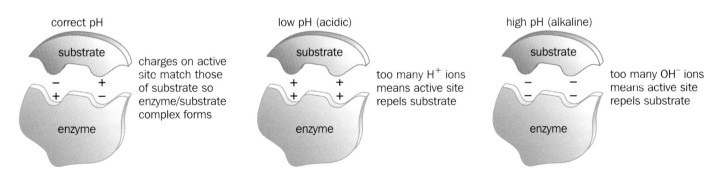

If the enzyme and the substrate both have the **same** charges, they
repel each other and an enzyme/substrate complex is not formed.

Enzyme concentration

As you know, the active site of an enzyme can be used again and again.

So only a small amount of enzyme is needed to catalyse a lot of substrate because after the reaction takes place at the enzyme's active site, the products are released and the active site is free to accept more substrate.

The number of substrate molecules that one molecule of enzyme can turn into products in 1 minute is called the **turnover number**. You can see from the table that turnover numbers can vary a lot.

Carbonic anhydrase is found in red blood cells.
It catalyses the reaction in which carbon dioxide dissolves in water.

$$CO_2 + H_2O \xrightarrow{\text{carbonic anhydrase}} H^+ + HCO_3^-$$

This reaction does happen naturally but it is ten million times faster if the enzyme is present.

Hydrogen peroxide is a common waste product of reactions in cells. The only problem is that hydrogen peroxide is poisonous.

How many molecules of hydrogen peroxide can one molecule of catalase split in 1 minute?
Why do you think that catalase has such a high turnover number?

Enzyme	Turnover number
carbonic anhydrase	36 000 000
catalase	5 600 000
β-galactosidase	12 000
chymotrypsin	6 000
lysozyme	60

(Source: Biochemical Society Guidance Notes 3, *Enzymes and their role in biotechnology*.)

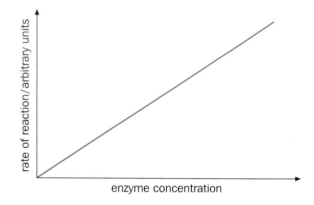

> Provided conditions such as temperature and pH are suitable and there is an excess of substrate, then the rate of reaction will be *directly proportional* to the enzyme concentration. So, increasing the enzyme concentration will increase the rate of reaction.

Substrate concentration

If the amount of enzyme stays the same, the rate of reaction will increase with an increase in substrate concentration, **up to a point**.

Look at the graph.

Are many enzyme active sites filled at low substrate concentration?
What happens to the active sites as the substrate concentration increases?
What happens to the rate of reaction when **all** the active sites are filled?

When the enzyme's active sites are all working as quickly as they can, adding more substrate brings about no further increase in the rate of reaction.
The enzyme is working flat out.

Scientists working in industry often need to know how much substrate to add to an enzyme-catalysed reaction.
Why do you think this is?

Well, if they add too little substrate, then less of the product is produced, and if they add more substrate than is needed, then the costs are higher.

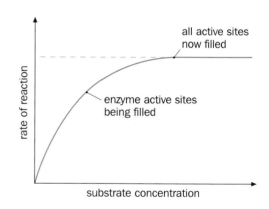

Cofactors

Some enzymes need the presence of another molecule if they are to work.
These molecules are called **cofactors**.
Cofactors are non-protein molecules.
They modify the chemical structure of the enzyme in some way so that it can function more effectively.

There are three types of cofactors:

- prosthetic groups,
- coenzymes,
- activators.

Prosthetic groups are organic molecules that form a *permanent* attachment to the enzyme.
Haemoglobin contains the prosthetic group **haem**, which contains iron and bonds permanently to the protein molecule.
Haem enables the haemoglobin molecule to carry oxygen.
It is also present as the prosthetic group in the enzyme **catalase**.

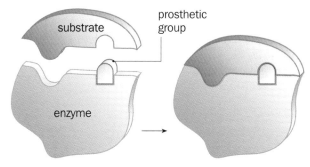

enzyme/substrate complex

Coenzymes are small, non-protein organic molecules.
Unlike prosthetic groups, they are not permanently attached to the enzyme.
Coenzymes help enzymes and substrates to bond with each other.
The enzyme can only function if the coenzyme is present.

Many coenzymes are derived from vitamins.
An example is the coenzyme **NAD**, formed from the vitamin **nicotinic acid**.
NAD is the coenzyme for a number of **dehydrogenase** enzymes.
It acts as a hydrogen acceptor.

Why do you think people develop deficiency diseases if some vitamins are lacking in their diet?

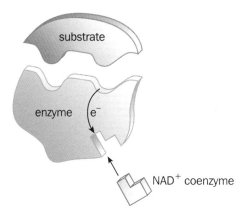

NAD^+ is a coenzyme that works by removing an electron from the active site. The substrate is then able to engage

Activators are inorganic metal ions.
Examples include magnesium (Mg^{2+}), iron (Fe^{2+}), calcium (Ca^{2+}) and zinc (Zn^{2+}).
Activators form a temporary attachment to the enzyme and change its active site so that the reaction is more likely to take place.
For example, the synthesis of any protein in your body cannot take place without magnesium as a cofactor.
The reaction does not take place without it.
Calcium is needed for muscle contraction and nerve impulse transmission.
Most metal activators are obtained from our diet.

Why do you think metal activators are often found in dietary supplements?

Fruit and vegetables are a rich source of vitamins and minerals

Inhibitors

An inhibitor is a substance that can slow down or stop a reaction. The inhibitor combines with the enzyme and stops it from attaching to the substrate.
Inhibitors are either **reversible** or **non-reversible**.

The effects of reversible inhibitors are temporary and when the inhibitor is removed, the enzyme regains its full activity.

There are two types of reversible inhibitors.

A **competitive inhibitor** has a structure similar to that of the substrate.
The competitive inhibitor competes with the substrate for the active site of an enzyme. This means that it has a shape that allows it to fit into the active site of the enzyme instead of the substrate. This prevents the formation of enzyme/substrate complexes and the rate of reaction decreases.

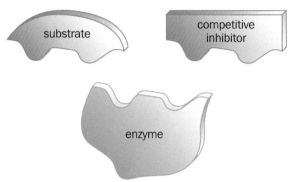

A competitive inhibitor can fit into the active site and exclude the substrate

In respiration, the enzyme **succinate dehydrogenase** removes hydrogen from its substrate **succinate**.
But the enzyme's activity can be inhibited if **malonate** is present.
Malonate *competes* with succinate for the active site on succinate dehydrogenase.

Increasing the concentration of the substrate can reduce the effects of a competitive inhibitor.
Since the inhibitor binds reversibly with the active site, as it leaves there is a chance of the substrate occupying the site.
The more substrate molecules there are present, the greater chance there is of them getting into the active site at the expense of the inhibitor.

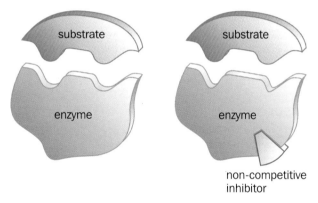

A **non-competitive inhibitor** does not bind to the active site of the enzyme. It attaches to some other part of the enzyme molecule.
This alters the overall shape of the enzyme molecule, including the active site, and the substrate can no longer bind to the active site.
Notice that, this time, the inhibitor and the substrate are not competing for the active site.
So increasing the amount of substrate will not reduce the inhibition.

non-competitive inhibitor

A non-competitive inhibitor does not attach to the active site but indirectly changes its shape

Look at the graph. Can you see that the non-competitive inhibitor affects the action of the enzyme at **all** concentrations of substrate? Why do you think this is?

Non-reversible inhibitors alter the enzyme permanently.
Heavy metal ions such as silver (Ag^+) and mercury (Hg^+) cause the disulphide bonds holding the enzyme together to break.
This alters the tertiary structure of the enzyme and it loses its catalytic activity.

Cyanide is a non-reversible inhibitor of **cytochrome oxidase**, an important enzyme in respiration.

Many pesticides are non-reversible inhibitors (see page 77).
Can you suggest an explanation for the way in which they act?

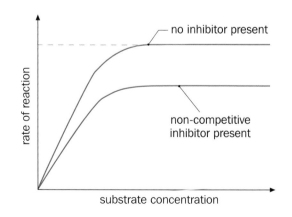

▷ Controlling metabolic pathways

A metabolic pathway consists of a series of enzyme-controlled reactions.
Look at this pathway:

$$A \xrightarrow{e_1} B \xrightarrow{e_2} C \xrightarrow{e_3} D \xrightarrow{e_4} E$$

Can you see that the product of one reaction becomes the substrate of the next?
For example, B is the product of the first reaction and then becomes the substrate
for the second reaction. Each reaction is catalysed by a different enzyme.
This is an example of a **multi-enzyme pathway**.

Enzymes in a pathway like this are often fixed to the inner membrane
of cell organelles such as mitochondria.
This keeps the enzymes close together and so increases the chance
of collisions occurring between enzyme and substrate molecules.

A multi-enzyme pathway is often controlled by the end product.
This is called **end product inhibition**.
This happens because the end product acts as an inhibitor of one
of the enzymes at the start of the pathway:

$$A \xrightarrow{e_1} B \xrightarrow{e_2} C \xrightarrow{e_3} D \xrightarrow{e_4} E \text{ (end product)}$$
$$\underset{\text{inhibition}}{\underline{\qquad\qquad\qquad\qquad\qquad\qquad}}$$

In this example, the end product E inhibits the enzyme e_1.
If too much of E is produced, it inhibits e_1 and the pathway
is slowed down. As a result, the level of product falls.

What do you think would happen if there was a shortage of product E?
There would be less of E to inhibit enzyme e_1, so more A
would be converted to B. The pathway would no longer be blocked
and the level of end product E would rise.

Time for some negative feedback!

This type of self-regulating mechanism is called **negative feedback**.
This is a concept that you will come across again in this book.
It means that the output from a system affects the input.
In this case, if the amount of product E rises then action is taken to reduce it.

This type of control of metabolic pathways must involve reversible inhibitors
since the enzymes are not permanently damaged.
The end product acts as a type of non-competitive inhibitor.
It attaches to a specific site on the surface of the enzyme away from the active site.

This affects the overall shape of the active site and slows down the rate of reaction.
Such inhibitors are called **allosteric inhibitors**, because the enzyme has
more than one shape.
One shape makes the enzyme *active*, the other shape makes it *inactive*.

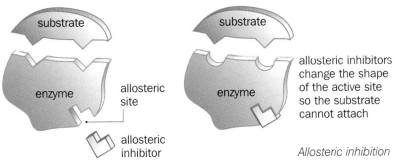

allosteric inhibitors
change the shape
of the active site
so the substrate
cannot attach

Allosteric inhibition

So the end product acts as a *molecular switch* that can turn the enzyme
on or off depending upon the concentration of the end product.

▷ Classifying enzymes

Usually, an enzyme is named by taking its substrate and adding the suffix '-ase'.
For example,

- prote**ase** catalyses the hydrolysis of proteins,
- amyl**ase** catalyses the hydrolysis of amylose (starch),
- lip**ase** catalyses the hydrolysis of lipids.

Some enzymes have older names that give no clue to the substrate they catalyse,
for example trypsin and pepsin.

Enzymes may be classified according to the *type* of reaction they catalyse.
For example, alcohol dehydrogenase removes hydrogen from alcohol,
and DNA polymerase catalyses the formation (and breakdown) of DNA by polymerisation.

Enzymes are classified into six main groups by the nature of their action.

- **Hydrolases** catalyse the hydrolysis of a substrate by the addition
  of a molecule of water:

$$\underset{\text{substrate}}{AB} \quad + \quad \underset{\text{water}}{H.OH} \quad \xrightarrow{\text{hydrolase}} \quad \underset{\text{products}}{A.H \quad + \quad B.OH}$$

  Hydrolases include the digestive enzymes that work in our gut
  and the enzyme in a germinating seed:

$$\text{maltose} \xrightarrow{\text{maltase}} \text{glucose} + \text{glucose}$$

$$\text{lipid} \xrightarrow{\text{lipase}} \text{fatty acids} + \text{glycerol}$$

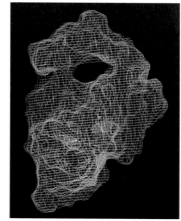

Computer graphic of the enzyme
taka amylase

- **Oxoreductases** are involved in oxidation and reduction, or **redox**, reactions.
  They include:
  dehydrogenases, which oxidise the substrate by catalysing the removal
  of hydrogen, passing it on to a hydrogen acceptor or coenzyme:

$$\underset{\text{substrate}}{AH_2} + \underset{\text{coenzyme}}{2NAD^+} \rightleftharpoons \underset{\text{oxidised substrate}}{A} + \underset{\text{reduced coenzyme}}{2NADH}$$

  oxidases, which catalyse the addition of oxygen to hydrogen, forming water:

$$\underset{\text{substrate}}{AH_2} + \underset{\text{oxygen}}{\tfrac{1}{2}O_2} \rightleftharpoons \underset{\text{oxidised substrate}}{A} + \underset{\text{water}}{H_2O}$$

- **Transferases** transfer a group of atoms from one molecule to another.
  They include:
  transaminases, which transfer amino groups (NH_2) from one molecule
  to another, so enabling organisms to make certain amino acids.
  phosphotransferases, which control the transfer of phosphate groups in respiration:

$$\text{glucose} + ATP \longrightarrow \text{glucose-6-phosphate} + ADP$$

- **Isomerases** control the conversion of one isomer to another by transferring
  a group of atoms from one molecule to another.

- **Lyases** are able to break chemical bonds *without* the addition of water (hydrolysis).
  decarboxylases remove carboxyl groups (COOH) from respiratory substrates to
  release carbon dioxide.

- **Ligases** catalyse reactions in which new chemical bonds are formed, using ATP
  as a source of energy. For example, DNA ligase is involved in the synthesis of DNA.

▷ Biology at work: Commercial use of enzymes

High-fructose corn syrups

Fructose is the sweetest natural sugar.
But naturally occurring sources of fructose, such as honey, are
not always available in sufficient amounts to meet commercial
demands.
These natural sources also tend to be expensive.
World wide, there is a huge demand for sweeteners in
soft drinks and confectionery.

Millions of tonnes of **high-fructose syrup** are now produced
every year from corn starch.
Corn starch is a cheap feedstock, *especially* in the USA.
Enzymes can break down the starch into glucose.
The glucose is then converted into fructose.

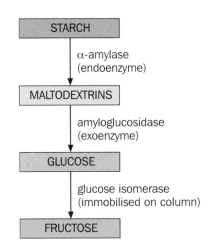

Three enzymes are involved.
Bacterial amylase first hydrolyses the starch.
As the name suggests, the enzyme is extracted from a bacterium.
Amylase is an **endoenzyme**, hydrolysing bonds *within* the starch.
So the large polysaccharide molecule is broken down into
small chains called **maltodextrins**.

The next step is to hydrolyse the maltodextrins to glucose.
The second enzyme, **amyloglucosidase**, is an **exoenzyme**,
which removes glucose units from the ends of the maltodextrin
molecules.
The enzyme is extracted from a fungus.

Why do you think it is useful to hydrolyse a large polymer
first with an endoenzyme and secondly with an exoenzyme?

The endoenzyme chops the large polymer into smaller strips.
Each strip has two ends that the exoenzyme can get to work on.
If the exoenzyme were used first, there would be only two ends
of the large molecule that it could attack!

The third enzyme is **glucose isomerase** and, like bacterial amylase,
it is also made by a bacterium.
Glucose isomerase converts glucose to fructose.
Fructose is much sweeter than glucose.
The enzyme is fixed onto beads of calcium alginate and
packed into glass columns.
The enzyme is **immobilised**, because it is fixed to the beads.

The glucose is run into the top of the column and reacts
with the isomerase enzyme as it trickles down the column.
Eventually high-fructose syrup runs out at the bottom of the column.

Can you think of any advantages of using immobilised enzymes in
industry?
Once a column has been set up, it can be used many times.
Also, it costs money separating the products of a reaction from the enzyme.
If the enzyme is 'fixed' then it does not get mixed up with the products,
so the cost of commercial production is lower.

▷ Biology at work: Immobilised enzymes

As you have already seen, when enzymes are used commercially it makes economic sense to use them in an immobilised form. However, immobilisation of enzymes did not develop purely for economic reasons.

In the mid-1960s, biological washing powders became widely available. These powders contained protease enzymes in a free powdered form. Very quickly there were reports of allergic reactions in both workers and users. This led to bad publicity and a big fall in protease production. The allergic reactions were thought to be caused by the powdered enzyme coming into contact with the skin. As a result of these problems, detergents now contain immobilised proteases, which do not react with the skin.

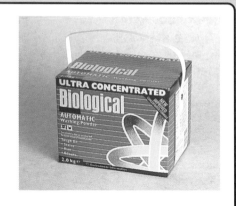

So, just how are enzymes put into an immobilised form?

Entrapment involves the enzyme being mixed with another chemical that forms a gel capsule around it. The substrate that the enzyme acts upon is able to diffuse through the gel, although this may be quite slow.

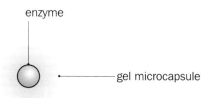

Adsorption is a more expensive process that involves the enzyme particles being held by weak forces on an adsorbing agent, for example glass beads or carbon particles. With this method there is no barrier slowing down the enzyme/substrate contact.

Biosensors

The third method is called cross-linkage. This method involves large numbers of enzyme particles being linked together. This is carried out by a so-called cross-linking agent such as glutaraldehyde. The drawback with this method is that it can damage the enzymes.

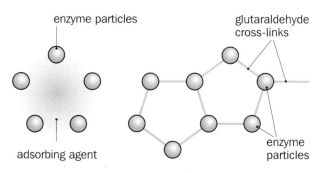

As you have already seen in this chapter, enzymes are highly specific chemicals and biotechnologists have combined this characteristic together with electronics to develop **biosensors**. These devices use immobilised enzymes to detect chemicals such as blood sugar, and the reaction between the enzyme and its substrate is measured electronically.

Biosensors have great potential in the areas of medical diagnosis and environmental monitoring, because they can detect minute amounts of chemicals.

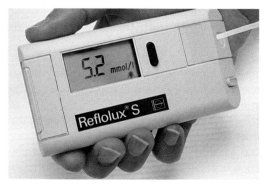

An electronic biosensor

▷ Biology at work: Insecticide resistance in pests

The increased use of pesticides is one of the factors that have led to an increase in the yield of crops.
A particular insecticide does not affect all members of a pest species equally.
Some individuals are genetically less susceptible and may survive to pass on their **resistance** to the next generation.
The more frequently an insecticide is used, the more likely resistance in the pest insect species is to evolve.

Mode of action of insecticides

The majority of insecticides in use today belong to the organophosphate group.
They work by blocking the activity of the enzyme **acetylcholinesterase.**
This enzyme is involved in the transmission of nerve impulses across the synapse.

- The chemical transmitter substance **acetylcholine** is released from the pre-synaptic membrane.
- It crosses the synaptic gap and binds with the surface receptors on the post-synaptic membrane.
- The enzyme then breaks down the acetylcholine.
- This prevents the continuous transmission of nerve impulses in the post-synaptic membrane.

Insecticides mimic the action of acetylcholine by binding with the acetylcholinesterase.
This prevents the enzyme from breaking down acetylcholine and is a form of **competitive inhibition.**
Nervous dysfunction follows and quickly leads to the death of the insect.

Biochemical basis of resistance

Resistant insects appear to have different forms of acetylcholinesterase to non-resistant insects.
They display a small number of mutations in the base sequence of the DNA in the acetylcholinesterase gene.
Once transcribed, these mutations cause changes in the amino acid sequence of the enzyme.
These amino acid changes occur close to the active site, as revealed by research into the three-dimensional structure of the enzyme.
Changes to the shape of the active site result in it becoming smaller.
Consequently, the larger insecticide molecules are prevented from entering the active site.
This then allows the smaller acetylcholine substrate molecules to enter the active site.

This knowledge is being used to investigate the identification and synthesis of new insecticides to reduce resistance.

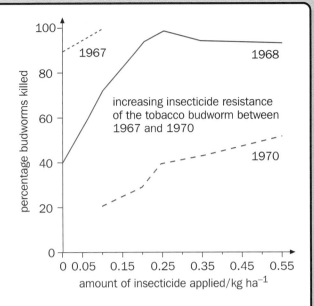

increasing insecticide resistance of the tobacco budworm between 1967 and 1970

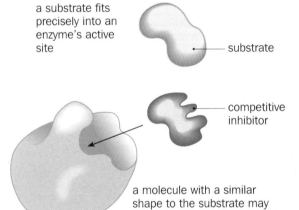

a substrate fits precisely into an enzyme's active site

substrate

competitive inhibitor

a molecule with a similar shape to the substrate may fit into the enzyme's active site

Competitive inhibitors can have a similar shape to that of the enzymes normal substrate.

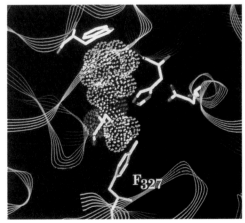

A 3-D computer model of acetylcholinesterase with its substrate acetylcholine (purple) in the active site

Summary

- Enzymes are globular proteins and their properties are related to their tertiary structure.
- Enzymes speed up the rate of reaction by lowering the activation energy required to start the reaction.
- An enzyme works by combining with a substrate to form an enzyme/substrate complex. The substrate molecule becomes temporarily attached to the enzyme's active site.
- Enzymes are specific because they act only on a particular substrate.
- Enzymes are unchanged after the reaction and can be used again and again.

- Temperature, pH and the concentration of the reactants affect the rate of an enzyme-catalysed reaction.
- Some enzymes only work in the presence of cofactors. These cofactors include prosthetic groups, coenzymes and activators.
- Enzymes can be prevented from working by reversible and non-reversible inhibitors. Reversible inhibitors can be competitive or non-competitive.
- The name of an enzyme can give a clue to the substrate upon which it works and the type of reaction that it catalyses.

▷ Questions

1 Copy and complete the following:

Enzymes are ___ proteins with an exact ___ ___ shape. The ___ structure of an enzyme is held together by ionic and ___ bonds. During a reaction the ___ fits into a region on the surface of the enzyme called the ── ──. Enzymes are ── because they will act only on a particular substrate.
Increasing the temperature of an enzyme-catalysed reaction by 10 °C usually ___ the rate. Increasing the temperature beyond 40 °C ___ many human enzymes. Chemicals that slow down or stop the action of an enzyme are called ___.

2 a) Explain what is meant by an enzyme.
   b) Explain how each of the following affects the rate of an enzyme-controlled reaction:
      i)   temperature
      ii) enzyme concentration
      iii) substrate concentration.

3 a) Define the following terms:
      i) enzyme
      ii) coenzyme
   b) Explain how the following properties of enzymes depend upon the structure of the enzyme molecule:
      i)   substrate specificity
      ii) temperature denaturation
      iii) inhibition.

4 a) Explain, with the use of diagrams, the lock and key theory of enzyme action.
   b) How does the induced fit theory modify the lock and key theory?

5 The graph shows the effect of increasing substrate concentration on the rate of an enzyme-catalysed reaction.

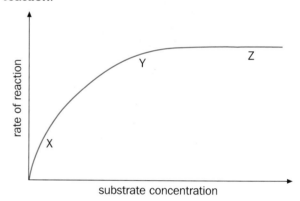

Explain **exactly** what is happening at the points X, Y and Z on the graph.

6 a) Enzyme-catalysed reactions normally have a temperature coefficient (Q_{10}) of 2 between 0 °C and 40 °C. Explain what this means.
   b) At higher temperatures the enzyme is rapidly denatured. Explain what happens and the effect that this has upon enzyme action.

7 a) What is meant by the activation energy of a chemical reaction?
   b) Explain how enzymes act to lower the activation energy.
   c) In many chemical reactions, heat supplies this activation energy. Why would this be inappropriate for reactions that take place in cells?

8 An experiment was carried out investigating the effects of temperature on the action of the enzyme sucrase on the substrate sucrose. The following data were obtained:

Temperature (°C)	Time taken to complete hydrolysis of sucrose (min)	Reaction rate (1/time)
0	50	
10	15	
20	8	
30	4	
40	6	
50	28	
60	110	

a) Using this information, plot a graph to show how the rate of reaction varies with temperature. Calculate the rate of reaction.

b) Describe and explain the results obtained between 10 °C and 30 °C.

c) Explain what is happening to the enzyme molecules between 40 °C and 60 °C.

d) Using information on your graph, calculate the Q_{10} value for this reaction between 15 °C and 25 °C.

9 The results of an investigation into the effect of increasing substrate concentration on the rate of an enzyme-catalysed reaction are shown in the graph.

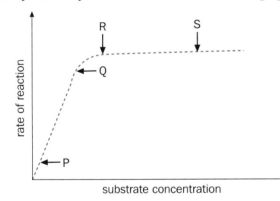

a) i) Name the factor that determines the rate of the reaction between points P and Q.

ii) What has happened to the rate of reaction between points R and S?

iii) Name two factors that could account for this occurrence.

b) i) State two conditions that should be kept constant in this investigation.

ii) What should be measured in order to determine the rate of an enzyme-catalysed reaction?

c) The investigation was repeated with the addition of a competitive inhibitor. The same amount of inhibitor was added to the substrate at each concentration.
Copy the graph below and add to it the curve you would expect if the inhibitor were present.

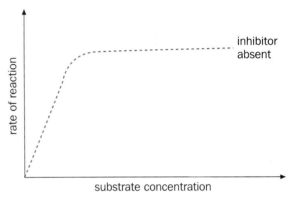

10 a) What is a cofactor?

b) What are the three main groups of cofactors?

c) Explain the differences between these three groups.

11 An investigation was carried out into the effects of pH on the action of the enzyme amylase on starch. Eight test tubes were set up at different pHs and incubated in a water bath at 30 °C for 1 hour. The amount of reducing sugar (product) was then estimated. The results are shown in the table.

pH	4.0	5.0	6.0	6.5	7.0	8.0	9.0	10.0
amount of reducing sugar produced	1	12	26	32	33	27	13	5

a) Plot a graph to show these results.

b) Explain the effects of pH on the action of amylase in this investigation.

5 Digestion

▷ The prehistoric supershark

Dozens of teeth marks on the fossil remains of a whale show that it was the victim of a massive predatory shark.
Scientists have used a formula relating tooth size of sharks to their body length.
They calculate that the shark, *Carcharodon megalodon*, could have grown to a length of 17 metres.
A scaled-up version of the great white shark of *Jaws* fame, megalodon preyed on whales up to 9 metres long.
Megalodon was probably the largest carnivorous fish that ever lived on the Earth.
Weighing an estimated 65 tonnes, it would have made the great white shark of today look like a kitten.

▷ Heterotrophic nutrition

Autotrophs such as green plants, algae and some bacteria are able to use light energy or energy from chemical reactions to make their own food.

Heterotrophs are unable to do this and have to feed on other organisms. Heterotrophs include all animals, fungi, some protoctists and some bacteria. There are a number of different types of heterotrophic nutrition:

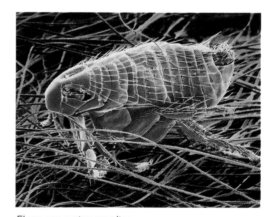

- **Saprophytes** (sometimes called saprobionts) feed on dead or decaying material using **extracellular digestion**.
  Saprophytes include fungi and bacteria.
  They feed by secreting digestive enzymes onto their food externally. The food is then digested and the soluble products are absorbed.
  Microscopic saprophytes are called **decomposers**.

- **Parasites** feed on other living organisms, their **hosts**.
  They digest the cells of the host and absorb the products.
  The relationship between the parasite and the host is beneficial to the parasite but harmful to the host.
  Parasites may be animals, plants, fungi, protoctists or bacteria.
  Examples of parasites are tapeworms, liver flukes and potato blight.
  Some parasites cause human disease, such as the malarial parasite.

Fleas are ectoparasites

- **Holozoic feeders** include virtually all animals.
  They take their food into their bodies and digest it.
  Many do this inside a specialised digestive system.
  Holozoic feeders include **herbivores** (plant eaters), **carnivores** that feed on other animals, and **detritivores**, animals that feed on dead and decaying material, digesting it internally.

- **Mutualism** is a form of nutrition where there is a close association between two species where both partners benefit.
  Lichens are made up of fungal cells and algal cells.
  The fungal hyphae store water for the algal cells and in return get sugars from the photosynthetic alga.

Brown bear feeding on salmon in Alaska

▷ The human digestive system

The components of the human diet are covered in Chapter 13. Here we will look at the human digestive system and its five main functions.

- **Ingestion**: taking food into the body.
  Other animals employ a variety of different feeding mechanisms depending upon the nature of their food.

- **Peristalsis**: propelling food along the alimentary canal by muscular contractions of the gut wall.

- **Digestion**: the breakdown of large, insoluble food molecules into simple, soluble molecules.
  Digestion can be **mechanical**, involving the physical breaking up of food by our teeth when biting or chewing.
  Digestion can also be **chemical**, involving the hydrolysis of complex food molecules by digestive enzymes (as we have seen in the previous chapter).

- **Absorption**: the passage of digested food through the gut wall into the bloodstream.

- **Egestion**: the elimination of undigestible food from the body, mainly plant cell wall material such as cellulose.

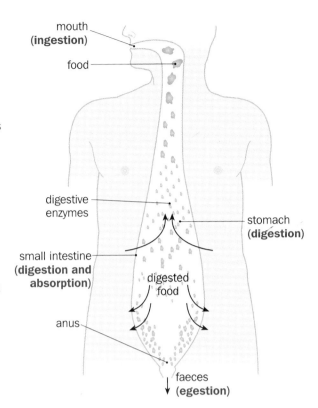

▷ The structure of the gut wall

The alimentary canal is a muscular tube that runs from mouth to anus. Throughout its length the gut wall consists of four different layers of tissue:

- The **inner mucosa** lines the gut wall.
  It secretes mucus, which lubricates the passage of food and helps to protect the gut from damage.
  The cells of the mucosa are layered (stratified) for protection.
  In some regions of the gut, the mucosa secretes digestive juices, whereas in others it absorbs digested food.

- The **sub-mucosa** contains blood and lymph vessels, which take away the absorbed food products.
  It also contains a rich network of nerve fibres that coordinate the muscular contractions involved in peristalsis.

- The **muscle layer** consists of two layers of muscle running in different directions.
  The inner circular muscle has fibres arranged in rings.
  The outer longitudinal muscle has fibres running lengthways.
  Both layers are made up of smooth involuntary muscle and are responsible for the waves of muscular contraction that move food along the gut. This is called **peristalsis**.

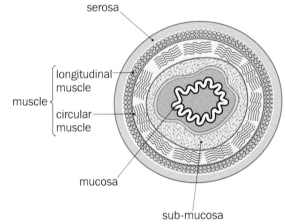

General structure of the gut wall in section

Behind the ball of food, the circular muscle contracts and the longitudinal muscle relaxes. This helps move the food along. In front of the ball of food, the longitudinal muscle contracts and the circular muscle relaxes. This causes the gut to widen and shorten, so that it can receive the food as it is pushed forward.

- The outer **serosa** is a layer of tough connective tissue which protects the gut wall from friction from other organs in the abdomen.

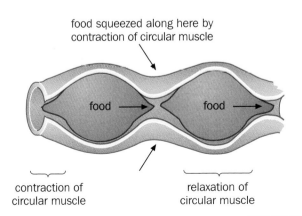

▷ The gut: an overview

The human digestive system consists of the alimentary canal and its associated organs, such as the **salivary glands**, **liver** and **pancreas**.

In adults, the alimentary canal is about 10 metres long. It is divided up into distinct parts, which have been adapted to carry out different functions.

Food passes from the mouth to the stomach down a tube called the **oesophagus**.
Food leaves the stomach and enters the **duodenum**, the first part of the **small intestine**.
The second and longer part of the small intestine is called the **ileum**.
The rest of the alimentary canal is made up of the **large intestine**, which can be sub-divided into the **caecum**, the **appendix**, the **colon** and the **rectum** ending at the **anus**.

▷ Mechanical digestion

Teeth are important in the mechanical digestion of food.
Mastication is the chewing of ingested food.
This makes the food easier to swallow and also increases the surface-area for enzyme action.

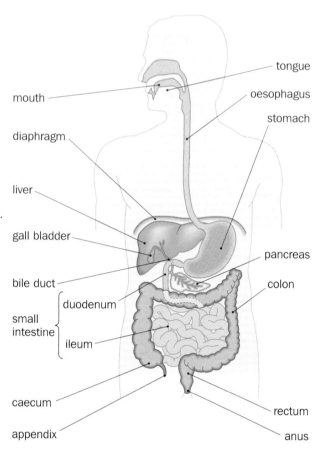

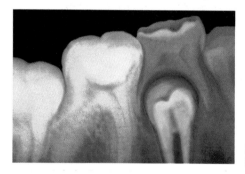

Permanent tooth (green) erupting under a child's milk teeth

Humans have two sets of teeth: the **milk teeth** and the **permanent teeth**.
We have different types of teeth, which perform different roles:

- **Incisors** are chisel-shaped for biting and cutting.

- **Canines** are pointed in many carnivores for piercing and tearing. In humans their role is more like that of incisors.

- **Premolars** have uneven 'cusps' for grinding and chewing.

- **Molars** are like premolars and are used for chewing. The lack of specialisation of our teeth reflects the mixed plant and animal nature of our diet: we are **omnivores**.

A tooth is made up of the **root**, which is embedded in the jaw, and the visible **crown**.
The hard outer layer of the crown is made up of **enamel**.
This covers the bone-like layer of **dentine**, which makes up the bulk of the tooth and surrounds the **pulp cavity**.
Inside the pulp cavity are nerves and blood vessels.
The dentine of the root is kept firmly in place in the jaw by a layer of **cement** and by **periodontal fibres**.

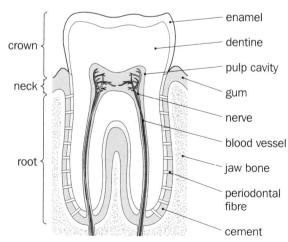

Section of a molar

▷ Chemical digestion

As you saw in Chapter 4, some enzymes are involved in the **hydrolysis** of complex food molecules to smaller ones. The digestive enzymes are classified as **hydrolases**.

Usually more than one enzyme is needed for the complete digestion of a particular food molecule.
For instance, **amylase** will hydrolyse starch to the disaccharide maltose but a second enzyme, **maltase**, is then needed to digest the maltose into the monosaccharide glucose.

Proteins, as you know, are large, complex molecules. They may require several different enzymes to digest them. **Peptidases** is the name given to protein-digesting enzymes.

Endopeptidases hydrolyse peptide bonds within the protein molecule. This essentially slices the protein up into shorter lengths of amino acids.
The peptide bonds at the ends of these short lengths are then hydrolysed by **exopeptidases**.

Why do you think that endopeptidases act on proteins before exopeptidases?

Well, if exopeptidases were to act first, they would only have two 'ends' of the molecule to work on.
By using endopeptidases first, the protein is split up and far more 'ends' become available for exopeptidases to work upon.

Compared with proteins, fats are much smaller molecules. They can be hydrolysed to fatty acids and glycerol by just one enzyme, **lipase**.

Different parts of the alimentary canal have different pHs. As you know, different enzymes have different optimum pHs. For instance, pepsin in the stomach has an optimum pH of 2.0, whereas lactase in the ileum has a pH optimum of 8.5.

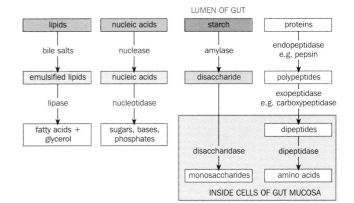

endopeptidases hydrolyse peptide bonds at specific points along the protein chain leaving smaller polypeptide sections

exopeptidases hydrolyse peptide bonds on terminal amino acids

carboxypeptidase liberates terminal amino acid with a free carboxyl (–COOH) group

aminopeptidase liberates terminal amino acid with a free amino (–NH$_2$) group

Summary of the digestive enzymes in the human gut

Region of gut	Secretion	Site of production	pH	Enzymes produced	Substrate	Products
mouth	saliva	salivary glands	6.5–7.5	amylase	starch	maltose
stomach	gastric juice	gastric glands	2.0	pepsin rennin	protein milk protein	polypeptides
duodenum	pancreatic juice	pancreas	7.0	amylase trypsin chymotrypsin carboxypeptidase lipase nuclease	starch protein protein polypeptides fats nucleic acids	maltose polypeptides polypeptides amino acids fatty acids + glycerol nucleotides
ileum	intestinal juice	ileum mucosa	8.5	maltase sucrase lactase peptidases lipase nucleotidase	maltose sucrose lactose polypeptides fats nucleotides	glucose glucose + fructose glucose + galactose amino acids fatty acids + glycerol sugar, base, phosphate

▷ Digestion in the mouth

In the mouth food is chewed by the teeth and mixed with saliva.
Saliva is secreted by three pairs of **salivary glands**.
Saliva is a solution containing the following dissolved substances:

- **Salivary amylase**, which hydrolyses starch to maltose.

- **Mineral salts**, mainly sodium hydrogen carbonate, which helps
  to keep the pH in the mouth at about 6.5–7.0 (the optimum for
  amylase). Chloride ions in saliva activate salivary amylase.

- **Mucin**, a slimy glycoprotein which helps to bind particles of food
  together and lubricates its passage down the oesophagus.

After chewing, the food is rolled into a ball or **bolus** by the tongue
and pushed to the back of the mouth to be swallowed.

Swallowing involves a number of reflexes.
Look at the diagram.

What prevents the food from going

a) into your nasal passage,
b) down your windpipe?

Once inside the oesophagus, the bolus is forced down to the stomach
by a wave of muscular contraction known as **peristalsis**.

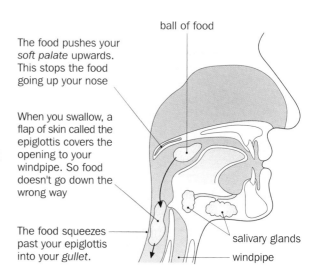

The food pushes your *soft palate* upwards. This stops the food going up your nose

When you swallow, a flap of skin called the epiglottis covers the opening to your windpipe. So food doesn't go down the wrong way

The food squeezes past your epiglottis into your *gullet*.

ball of food

salivary glands

windpipe

▷ Digestion in the stomach

The stomach is a large, muscular bag that can hold up to 2 dm³ of food.
Food is kept in the stomach by contraction of the **cardiac sphincter**
and **pyloric sphincter**, two rings of smooth muscle.
Food may stay in the stomach for up to 4 hours depending upon
what has been eaten.
During this time the contractions of the muscular stomach wall
churn up and mix the food with **gastric juice** secreted by
cells in **gastric pits** in the mucosa of the stomach lining.
Gastric juice is a solution containing the following dissolved substances:

- **Hydrochloric acid**, secreted by **oxyntic cells**, gives the stomach
  contents a pH of 2.0.
  This activates the stomach enzymes and provides the optimum pH
  for their action.
  It also kills most bacteria in the food and inactivates salivary amylase.

- **Pepsin** is secreted in inactive form by **zymogen** cells.
  It becomes activated by stomach acid.
  Pepsin is an endopeptidase, breaking specific peptide bonds within
  the protein molecule, so hydrolysing it to polypeptides.

- **Rennin** is also secreted by zymogen cells. This is activated
  by acid and converts soluble caseinogen in milk into insoluble **casein**.
  The milk curdles and so it stays in the stomach longer for digestion.
  Why do you think this is particularly important in young mammals?

- **Mucus** is secreted by **goblet cells** and is important in
  protecting the stomach wall from the digestive actions of pepsin
  and hydrochloric acid. A peptic ulcer can form if too much
  acid is secreted as a result of irregular eating, stress or smoking.

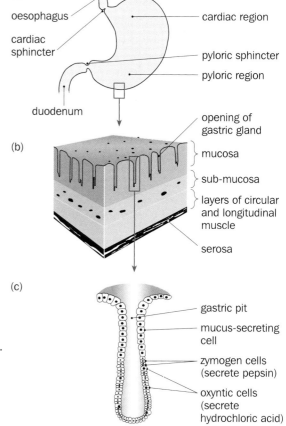

(a)

oesophagus

cardiac sphincter

duodenum

cardiac region

pyloric sphincter

pyloric region

(b)

opening of gastric gland

mucosa

sub-mucosa

layers of circular and longitudinal muscle

serosa

(c)

gastric pit

mucus-secreting cell

zymogen cells (secrete pepsin)

oxyntic cells (secrete hydrochloric acid)

*(a) section through stomach (b) part of stomach wall
(c) gastric gland*

84

▷ Digestion in the small intestine

After a few hours in the stomach, the food becomes a creamy fluid called **chyme**.
Periodic relaxation of the pyloric sphincter releases the chyme into the duodenum a little at a time.

Most of the digestive activities of the small intestine take place in the duodenum. The role of the ileum is mainly absorption.

There are three main secretions concerned with digestion that are released into the duodenum: **bile**, **pancreatic juice** and **intestinal juice**.

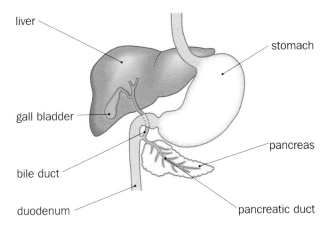

Bile

Bile is made in the liver and stored in the **gall bladder**.
It enters the duodenum along the **bile duct**.
Bile contains no digestive enzymes but it does contain substances that have an important role in digestion:

- **Sodium hydrogen carbonate** neutralises the acid chyme as it enters the duodenum from the stomach to produce a neutral pH (pH 7) at which the enzymes in the small intestine work best.

- **Bile salts** (sodium glycocholate and sodium taurocholate) **emulsify** fats (break them down into minute droplets) and give them a much larger surface area over which lipase can act.

Pancreatic juice

Pancreatic juice is made in the pancreas by secretory cells.
It is released into the pancreatic duct in response to the presence of acid food in the duodenum.
It is alkaline and performs a similar role to bile in neutralising stomach acid.
Pancreatic juice contains a lot of water, as is the case with other digestive juices.
This water must eventually be reabsorbed into the blood in the large intestine, otherwise we would dehydrate.

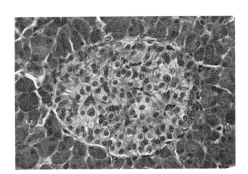

Secretory cells in the pancreas

Pancreatic juice contains the following enzymes:

- **trypsin**, an endopeptidase.
  Its role is to hydrolyse proteins to polypeptides.

- **chymotrypsin**, another endopeptidase.
  When activated in the presence of trypsin, it hydrolyses proteins to peptides.

- **carboxypeptidase**, also activated by trypsin.
  This enzyme is an exopeptidase that hydrolyses polypeptides to smaller peptides and some amino acids.

  Trypsin, chymotrypsin and carboxypeptidase together continue the digestion of proteins.

- **pancreatic amylase** completes the hydrolysis of starch to maltose, which was started by salivary amylase in the mouth.

- **lipase** hydrolyses fats to fatty acids and glycerol.

- **nuclease** breaks down nucleic acids into their constituent nucleotides.

Splitting starch the hard way!

Intestinal juice

There are deep folds in the wall of the duodenum called the **crypts of Lieberkühn**.

Here, **Brunner's glands** secrete intestinal juice, which contains water, mucus and sodium hydrogen carbonate. Intestinal juice does not contain any enzymes but it protects the mucosa of the duodenum from the effects of stomach acid.

Enzymes released by the secretory cells at the tips of the villi complete digestion.

Digestion enzymes are also present in the cell surface membrane and cytoplasm of these cells.

- **Aminopeptidase** is an exopeptidase that hydrolyses peptides to smaller peptides and amino acids.

- **Dipeptidase** breaks down dipeptides to amino acids.

- **Nucleotidase** hydrolyses nucleotides into their constituent sugars, phosphates and bases.

- **Maltase** breaks down maltose to glucose.

- **Lactase** converts lactose to glucose and galactose.

- **Sucrase** hydrolyses sucrose to glucose and fructose.

▷ Absorption in the small intestine

As a result of digestion, there is a high concentration of small, simple molecules inside the lumen of the ileum.
These have to be absorbed across the wall of the ileum so that they can be transported around the body in the bloodstream.

Although there is a concentration gradient established, simple diffusion would be too slow to supply the body's needs for some of these molecules.
So the following methods of transport occur:

- **Diffusion**
  Fatty acids, glycerol and most vitamins diffuse easily into the epithelial cells.
  The fatty acids and glycerol recombine inside the cells to form triglycerides.
  They leave the epithelial cells and enter a **lacteal**, to be circulated by the **lymph system** (see page 194).

- **Facilitated diffusion**
  As you saw in Chapter 3, some molecules, such as fructose, cross the cell surface membrane of the epithelial cell via carrier proteins.
  This form of transport does not involve energy from ATP.

- **Active transport**
  As you saw in Chapter 3, the epithelial cells of the small intestine use energy from ATP for the active uptake of glucose, galactose, amino acids, dipeptides and some salts.
  Dipeptides are then digested **intracellularly** (within the epithelial cells) into simple amino acids.

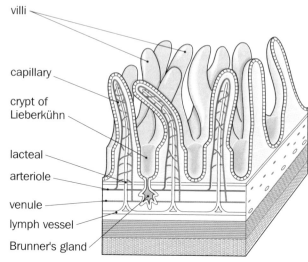

3-D diagram of a section of the duodenum

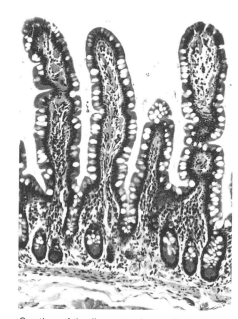

Section of the ileum to show villi

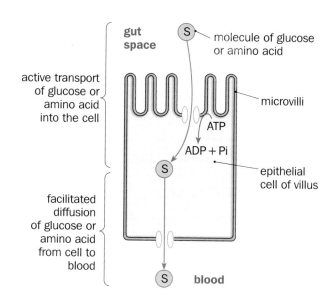

The structure of the small intestine

The ileum is well adapted for absorption.
It has a number of structural features that significantly increase the surface-area over which absorption can take place.

- The ileum is very long – about 6 metres in adult humans.

- The internal lining is thrown into folds, giving a much larger surface area than a simple, smooth tube would.

- On the folds are numerous finger-like projections called **villi**.

- The epithelial cells lining the villi have microscopic projections called **microvilli**. These vastly increase the absorptive surface of the cell surface membrane of the epithelial cells.

Simple sugars, amino acids, salts and vitamins that have been absorbed pass out of the epithelial cells into a blood capillary inside the villus.
From here, the blood travels along the **hepatic portal vein** to the liver, where the levels of absorbed food are monitored and regulated, before being delivered to all the cells of the body.

Any excess glucose is converted to the polysaccharide glycogen and stored in the liver.
Excess amino acids are broken down by a process called **deamination** to make **urea**, which is excreted by the kidneys.

As we shall see in Chapter 11, triglycerides are transported by the lymph system, which joins to the blood system near the heart.
In the blood, the triglycerides break down into fatty acids and glycerol and are transported to cells to be used to make lipids.

The large intestine

The large intestine is about 1.5 metres long and can be divided up into the **caecum**, the **appendix**, the **colon** and the **rectum**.

Any undigestible food not absorbed by the ileum enters the caecum.
In humans this is little more than a short connection between the ileum and the colon.
At the base of the caecum is a small tube called the appendix.
In humans neither of these two parts of the large intestine are important in digestion but, they have a major function in the alimentary canals of herbivores.

About 10 dm³ of digestive fluids may be secreted into the human gut every day. The vast majority of this is water, which has to be reabsorbed into the blood, otherwise we would dehydrate. This is one of the major roles of the colon.
As reabsorption takes place, the consistency of the undigestible food changes from liquid to semi-solid.
The semi-solid **faeces** consist of undigested food, particularly fibre, dead cells lost from the gut lining, bacteria and waste material from bile. These are stored and compacted in the rectum before **defaecation**.

Populations of microbes such as *Escherichia coli* (*E. coli*) present in the colon are responsible for the manufacture of vitamin K and folic acid.

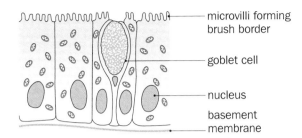

microvilli forming brush border
goblet cell
nucleus
basement membrane

Detailed structure of the epithelial cells lining the small intestine

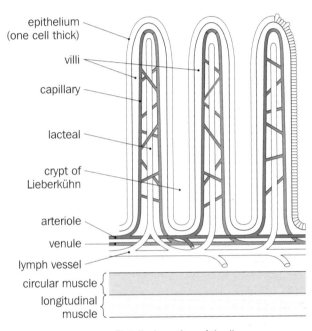

epithelium (one cell thick)
villi
capillary
lacteal
crypt of Lieberkühn
arteriole
venule
lymph vessel
circular muscle
longitudinal muscle

Detailed section of the ileum

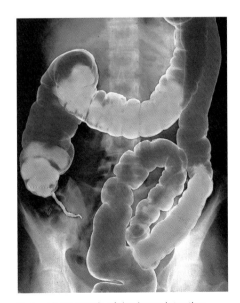

X-ray photograph of the large intestine after a barium meal

▷ Control of digestive secretions

Have you ever thought what causes you to produce saliva?
The sight, smell, taste and even the thought of food are
enough to cause you to salivate.

The release of digestive juices in the gut is under the sophisticated
control of both the **nervous system** and the **hormonal system**.

Hormones are chemical messengers that are carried around
the body in the bloodstream to affect **target organs**.
We will look more closely at the hormonal and nervous systems
in Chapters 18 and 19.

Control of saliva production

The release of saliva by the salivary glands is entirely under
nervous control.
The presence of food in your mouth triggers a **simple reflex**
to the brain, which sends out nervous impulses along
the **vagus nerve** instructing the glands to secrete saliva.

But the mere thought of food can cause you to salivate due to
a **conditioned reflex** action involving the brain.
In other words, your brain learns to associate the thought
of food with its presence in the mouth.

Control of gastric juice production

At the same time, the brain stimulates the stomach lining to
secrete gastric juice by nerve impulses passing along the
vagus nerve.

The presence of food in the stomach stimulates the release of
the hormone **gastrin** from **G cells** in the stomach wall.
This further stimulates the secretion of gastric juice for up to
4 hours.

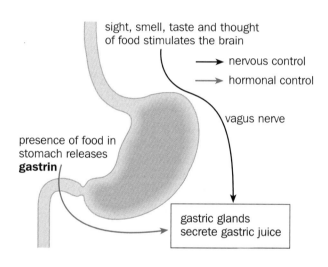

sight, smell, taste and thought
of food stimulates the brain

→ nervous control
→ hormonal control

vagus nerve

presence of food in
stomach releases
gastrin

gastric glands
secrete gastric juice

Control of bile and pancreatic juice production

When food leaves the stomach, it enters the duodenum.
The presence of acid food in the duodenum stimulates the
production of *two* hormones from the duodenal wall:

- **Secretin** travels to the liver in the bloodstream,
  where it stimulates the production of bile.
  Secretin also passes to the pancreas, where it stimulates
  the secretion of an alkaline fluid.

- **Cholecystokinin** (CCK) causes the gall bladder to contract,
  so releasing bile into the duodenum.
  CCK also stimulates the pancreas to secrete pancreatic juice.

The control of the release of digestive secretions in the gut
highlights the differences between nervous and hormonal control.
One relies upon the transmission of nerve impulses from the brain
along the vagus nerve.
The other involves the transport of chemical messengers to
target organs via the bloodstream.

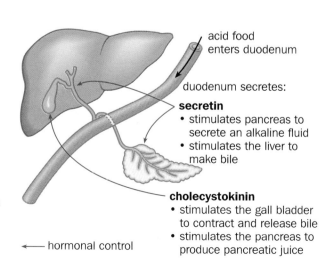

acid food
enters duodenum

duodenum secretes:

secretin
- stimulates pancreas to
  secrete an alkaline fluid
- stimulates the liver to
  make bile

cholecystokinin
- stimulates the gall bladder
  to contract and release bile
- stimulates the pancreas to
  produce pancreatic juice

← hormonal control

▷ Other types of heterotrophic nutrition

Saprophytism

Saprophytes (also called saprobionts) feed on dead organisms and waste organic matter.
Most saprophytes are fungi or bacteria.
They secrete powerful digestive enzymes to the outside of their cells. This is called **extracellular digestion**.
The digestive enzymes include proteases, amylases, lipases, cellulases and lignases.
Can you suggest which substrate each of these enzymes hydrolyses?

The digestive enzymes break down organic material into smaller, soluble molecules, which can then be absorbed across cell membranes.
The bread mould *Rhizopus* is a saprophytic fungus.

As we shall see in Chapter 9, many saprophytic fungi and bacteria are important in the large-scale production of chemicals such as antibiotics, as well as the commercial production of foods such as yoghurt, cheese and bread.

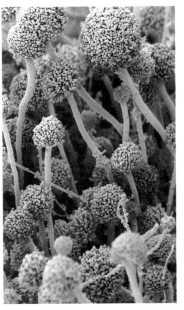
SEM of the bread mould Rhizopus

Parasitism

A parasite feeds on another living organism, its host.
It is a one-sided relationship because the parasite gains food and harms the host.

Ectoparasites, such as fleas, feed on the outside of their hosts.

Endoparasites, such as the tapeworm *Taenia*, live inside the host.
The tapeworm embeds its head, or **scolex**, into the lining of the human small intestine by means of a crown of hooks and four suckers.
A long chain of segments, or **proglottids**, grows from the scolex.

The tapeworm lies in the gut surrounded by predigested food.
It absorbs this predigested food across its body wall by a combination of diffusion and active transport.
(Tapeworms have no mouth and no gut.)
The tapeworm's body wall is resistant to digestive enzymes and to the immune response of the host.

The scolex of the tapeworm Taenia

Mutualism

Mutualism is an association between two organisms in which both benefit in some way, often nutritionally.

As you will see in Chapter 23, different types of bacteria are vital to the nitrogen cycle. **Nitrogen-fixing** bacteria are able to convert atmospheric nitrogen into an organic usable form.
Rhizobium is a nitrogen-fixing bacterium that lives in the roots of plants of the Papilionacae, the family to which peas, beans and clover belong. The bacteria cause swellings on the plant roots called **root nodules**.

The association is a good example of mutualism.
On the one hand, the bacterium provides the plant with a source of nitrogen to make amino acids and proteins.
In return, the plant provides the bacterium with sugars.
Nitrogen-fixing bacteria are very important in maintaining soil fertility.

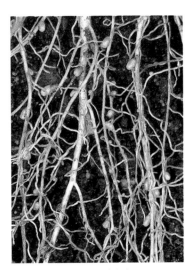
Root nodules contain nitrogen-fixing bacteria

▷ Biology at work: Protein producers

Most of the meat and milk consumed by humans comes from cows and sheep.
These animals have the ability to eat grass and forage, unlike pigs or poultry.
Cows and sheep provide about 70% of the total animal protein eaten by humans.

Like other herbivorous mammals, cows and sheep do not secrete **cellulase** enzymes.
Instead they have **mutualistic** bacteria that produce the enzymes for them.
In return, the bacteria gain other digestive products and suitable conditions for growth.
The bacteria live in a specific part of the specialised stomach of cows and sheep,
called the **rumen**. Such animals are called **ruminants**.
The 'stomach' has four chambers, with three chambers deriving from the lower
part of the oesophagus and one chamber which is the true stomach.

Cellulose digestion takes place in six stages:
1. *Mouth* – grass is cropped by teeth, ground with saliva into a 'cud' and swallowed.
2. *Rumen* – the cud is mixed with cellulose-digesting bacteria to produce glucose, which is then fermented to organic acids. These are absorbed into the blood and provide a major source of energy. Carbon dioxide and methane are belched out. Rumen bacteria also form protein from inorganic nitrogen.
3. *Reticulum* – the cud is formed into balls and regurgitated into the mouth for further chewing before being re-swallowed and passing into the omasum.
4. *Omasum* – here much water is reabsorbed from the cud. The firmed up remainder then passes into the abomasum.
5. *Abomasum* – here normal gastric secretions begin to digest proteins from the grass and bacteria.
6. *Duodenum* – chyme passes into here and then into the small intestine where the products of digestion are absorbed.

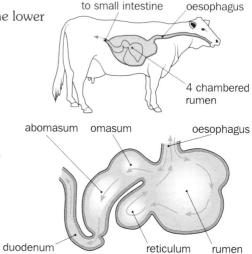

Protein sources

Data from the Food and Agricultural Organisation (FAO) shows that
ruminants provide 16.5% of all the protein in the human diet.
This is mainly in the form of milk and meat produced by ruminants
feeding on grass, forage and other fibrous vegetation that humans
cannot digest.
Poultry and pigs provide a further 12.2% of our total protein
consumption.
This is only achieved by feeding high levels of grain, grown on land
that could otherwise produce food for direct human consumption.

Other feed sources for ruminants include grain, which is fed in
large quantities to high producing cattle in developed countries.
However, 90% of the feed available to ruminants throughout
the world consists of forage, legumes, hay and straw.

Animals produce 35% of all the protein eaten by humans and of
this nearly half comes from ruminants eating mainly grass and forage.
Grass and forage are therefore a major resource that must be
maintained and carefully developed.
They play a vital part in helping to produce our dietary protein needs.
Without productive, sustainable pastures, the ability of the world to
feed itself would be considerably reduced.

	Consumption	
Commodity	Grams/ day	% of all protein
Milk and products	6.9	9.7
Meat – cattle	3.8	5.3
Meat – sheep and goats	0.6	0.8
Offal – ruminants*	0.5	0.7
Eggs	1.9	2.7
Meat – poultry	2.6	3.6
Meat – pig	3.7	5.2
Offal – pig*	0.5	0.7
Fish, etc.	4.1	5.8
Meat – other**	0.3	0.4
Vegetable protein***	46.4	65.1
Sub-totals		
Ruminant protein	11.8	16.5
Other animal proteins	13.1	18.4
Vegetable proteins	46.4	65.1
Total protein consumption	71.3	100.0

*Assumed that equal quantities of offal were produced from pigs and ruminants.
**Meat from horses, rabbits, reindeer, wild animals, etc.
***Protein in separated cereal grains, pulses, vegetables, root crops etc.

Mean daily consumption of different sources of protein by humans in the world during 1988–1990 (FAO data)

Summary

- The human digestive system has five basic functions: ingestion, peristalsis, digestion, absorption and egestion.
- The human alimentary canal is composed of four different layers of tissue: the inner mucosa, the sub-mucosa, the muscle layer and the outer serosa.
- Mechanical digestion involves mastication by the teeth and churning by the muscular stomach wall.
- Chemical digestion involves enzymes called hydrolases, which hydrolyse food substrates.
- Salivary amylase starts the digestion of starch in the mouth before the food is swallowed.
- The stomach secretes gastric juice containing hydrochloric acid, pepsin, rennin and mucus.
- Bile is released into the duodenum from the gall bladder. It emulsifies fats and neutralises the acid chyme entering the duodenum from the stomach.
- Pancreatic juice containing a number of enzymes enters the duodenum from the pancreas.
- Digested food molecules are absorbed in the ileum by diffusion, facilitated diffusion or by active transport.
- The ileum is well adapted for absorption because it has a large surface-area: it is very long, and it has a folded inner lining with villi and epithelial cells with microvilli.
- Saprophytes feed on dead organisms and waste organic matter.
- Parasites feed on other living organisms (the host).
- Mutualism is an association between two organisms in which both benefit, often nutritionally.

▷ Questions

1 a) Describe the digestion of carbohydrate in the human alimentary canal.
   b) How is the structure of the wall of the ileum (small intestine) adapted to its function in the absorption of the products of digestion?

2 Copy and complete the table showing some of the enzymes in the human gut.

Name of enzyme	Site of production	Substrate	Product(s)
	duodenal mucosa		trypsin
	pancreas	fat	fatty acids, glycerol
lactase		lactose	

3 a) Explain exactly what the following types of enzymes do:
      i)   endopeptidases
      ii) exopeptidases
      iii) nucleases
   b) Why are endopeptidases secreted into the gut **before** exopeptidases?

4 a) Describe one function of the muscle layers in the stomach wall.
   b) i) Name the type of protein-digesting enzyme secreted by the gastric glands.
      ii) Describe the function of this type of enzyme.
   c) Explain briefly why a different enzyme is required for the digestion of each type of food substance.

5 The drawing shows the human digestive system.

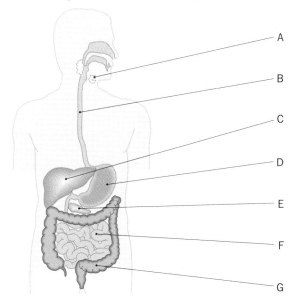

   a) Give the letter of the organ where each of the following is produced:
      i) endopeptidase
      ii) maltase
   b) Name the compounds produced when triglycerides are digested.
   c) Describe two roles of bile in the digestion of triglycerides.

6 The diagram on the following page shows some of the cells that form the lining of the small intestine of a mammal.

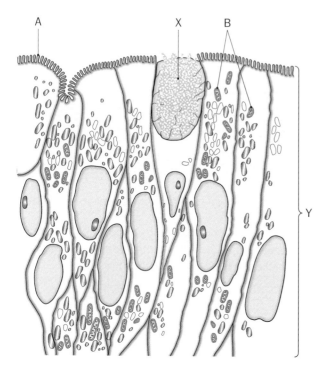

a) What is the general name given to tissue such as that labelled Y?
b) i) Name the features labelled A and B on the diagram.
   ii) Explain fully how A and B function in this tissue.
c) i) Name the secretion labelled X.
   ii) State two functions of this secretion.

7 The diagram shows the human digestive system.

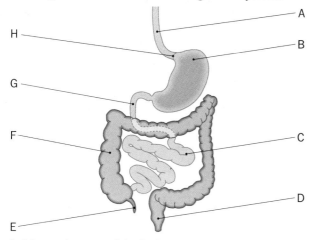

a) Name the parts labelled A to H.
b) Different regions of the gut have different pH values.
   i) Why is it important to have a particular pH in a particular region?
   ii) Name a region where the gut has a low pH and one where it has a high pH.
c) Use one of the letters A to H to indicate the main region where absorption of each of the following occurs:

i) digested proteins
ii) glucose
iii) water

8 a) What are the main features of
   i) autotrophic nutrition
   ii) heterotrophic nutrition?
The diagram shows part of a transverse section of the ileum.

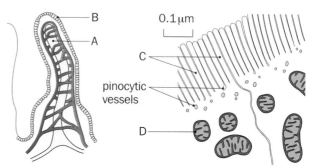

b) Name the parts labelled A to D.
c) Briefly describe how three features shown in the diagram enable the ileum to carry out its function of absorption.

9 A number of fungal spores were scattered on the surface of a sterile growth medium containing starch. All the spores germinated and each formed a typical fungal growth consisting of a mass of hyphal threads. At this time iodine solution was poured over the surface of the growth medium.
The result is shown in the diagram.

a) Explain the clear area around most of the fungal growths.
b) Despite the fact that all these spores were produced asexually from the same fungus, one of them did not have a clear area around it. Suggest an explanation for this.

10 a) Copy and complete the table about the method of feeding of each organism. Tick (✓) if the statement is true or cross (✗) if the statement is not true.

Statement	Saprophytic fungus	Tapeworm	Human
takes undigested food into its body			
carries out extracellular digestion			
carbohydrates absorbed as monomers, such as glucose			

▷ **Biological molecules**

1 The statements in the table below refer to three polysaccharide molecules. Copy and complete the table. If the statement is correct, place a tick (✔) in the appropriate box and if the statement is incorrect, place a cross (✗) in the appropriate box.

Statement	Starch	Glycogen	Cellulose
Polymer of α-glucose			
Glycosidic bonds present			
Unbranched chains only			
Energy store in animal cells			

(Edex) **[4]**

2 a) Explain what is meant by the term *reducing sugar*. [2]
b) The diagram below shows two molecules of glucose. Draw these molecules again to show how they are linked together when they form a molecule of maltose.

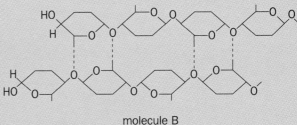

[2]

c) How does the molecular structure of sucrose and of lactose differ from that of maltose? [4]
d) i) Name *three* different polysaccharides found in organisms and for each polysaccharide state one of its roles. [3]
ii) Give *one* example of the commercial importance of each of two polysaccharides which occur in plants. [2]

(O&C) **[13]**

3 a) Cellulose is the most abundant naturally occurring carbon compound on Earth. Where is cellulose most likely to be found? [1]
b) The diagram below shows part of a molecule of cellulose.

i) Name the carbohydrate labelled Z. [1]
ii) Which of these terms correctly describes the molecule labelled Z?
hexose   pentose   tetrose   triose [1]

iii) 1. Describe how units in this diagram are arranged in a complete molecule of cellulose. [1]
2. Describe *one* property this molecular structure gives to cellulose. [1]

(WJEC) **[5]**

4 The diagrams of molecule A and molecule B show part of the molecular structure of two polysaccharides. The hexagonal shapes represent hexose sugars.

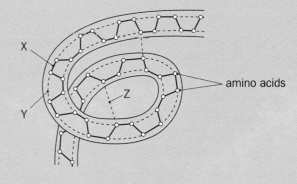

Key: ---- Hydrogen bonds

a) Give the name of molecule A. [1]
b) Give *one* difference between the hexose sugars in molecules A and B. [1]
c) Both polysaccharides contain hexose sugars joined by glycosidic bonds.
i) Explain, using an annotated diagram, how these bonds in molecule A are hydrolysed in the process of human digestion. [2]
ii) Using information in the diagram of molecule B, suggest *one* reason why it cannot be digested by humans. [1]

(AEB) **[5]**

5 The diagram below shows part of a protein molecule.

a) i) Name the bonds labelled X and Y. [2]
ii) Name *one* other type of bond which might form the bond labelled as Z. [1]
b) i) What level of protein structure is shown? [1]
ii) Suggest a function that such a structure might perform in the body. [1]
iii) Explain how a structural feature of this protein allows the performance of this function. [2]
(*WJEC*) **[7]**

6   Silk fibroin is a fibrous protein produced by certain insects. The β sheet secondary structure occurs in the silk fibroin molecule.
a) How could you show that silk is a protein? [2]
b) Explain what is meant by each of the following.
i) A fibrous protein [1]
ii) The secondary structure of a protein [2]
iii) A β sheet protein [3]
(*O&C*) **[8]**

7   The diagrams below show the molecular structure of a triglyceride, a phospholipid and a glycolipid.

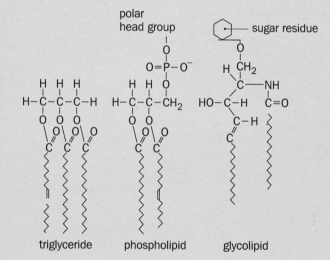

triglyceride   phospholipid   glycolipid

a) What is the main structural feature common to all three molecules? [1]
b) Copy and complete the table below to show how the different role in cells of each of these molecules is related to differences in their molecular structure.

Molecule	Molecular structure	Role in cells
Triglyceride		
Phospholipid		
Glycolipid		

[6]
(*O&C*) **[7]**

8   The diagram below shows the tertiary structure of a molecule of a protein called lactalbumin.

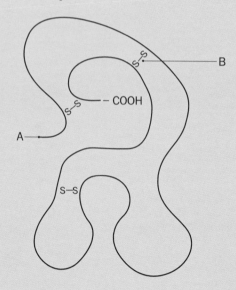

a) What is the name of the chemical group found at A? [1]
b) What is the name of the bond shown at B? [1]
c) What is meant by the *tertiary structure* of a protein? [1]
d) Lactalbumin lacks a quaternary structure. What does this mean? [1]
e) Lactalbumin is not a conjugated protein. What does this mean? [1]
(*NICCEA*) **[5]**

▷ **Cells**

9   Some structures found in cells are listed below.

cell surface membrane	cellulose cell wall
centriole	flagella
Golgi body	lysosome
microtubules	middle lamella
mitochondria	plasmodesmata
rough endoplasmic reticulum	starch granule
tonoplast	

From this list, select *five* structures which are found in plant cells but not in animal cells. [5]
(*O&C*) **[5]**

10 a) An electron microscope has a much greater resolving power than an optical microscope.
i) Explain the meaning of the term *resolving power*. [1]
ii) Explain why these microscopes have this difference in resolving power. [1]
b) The diagram opposite shows the structure of an animal cell as it would appear when seen with an electron microscope.

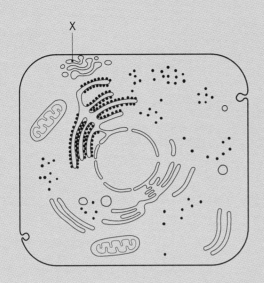

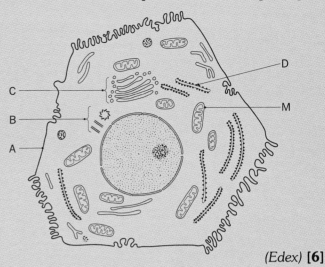

(Edex) **[6]**

i) Name *one* structure that is present in this cell but would *not* be in a bacterial cell [1]

ii) Name *one* structure that is *not* present in this cell but may be present in a bacterial cell [1]

c) Describe one function of the organelle labelled **X**. [1]

(AEB) **[5]**

11 The table below gives descriptions of organelles found in eukaryotic cells. Copy and complete the table by writing the name of each organelle in the spaces provided.

Description	Name of organelle
Usually rod-shaped, 1 μm wide and up to 7 μm long; have a double membrane; the inner membrane is folded to form cristae	
Rounded organelle approximately 25 nm in diameter; consists of RNA and protein	
Disc-shaped structure, about 1 μm wide and up to 5 μm long; contains a system of thylakoids	
Hollow, cylindrical structure; consists of nine triplets of microtubules	
Contains the genetic material of a cell; surrounded by a double membrane	

(Edex) **[5]**

12 The diagram at top of the next column shows the structure of a liver cell as seen using an electron microscope.
a) Name the parts labelled A, B, C and D. [4]
b) The magnification of this diagram is x 12 000. Calculate the actual length of the mitochondrion labelled M, giving your answer in μm. Show your working. [2]

13 The diagram below shows part of an animal cell and is based on a series of electron micrographs.

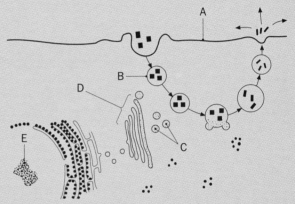

a) Name the structures labelled A, B, C, D and E. [5]
b) i) Name the structure where the protein contents of D are synthesised. [1]
ii) Describe *two* functions that D may have in cells. [2]

(WJEC) **[8]**

14 The diagram below shows part of a cell as seen under an electron microscope.

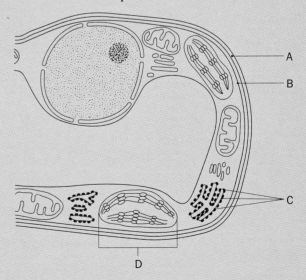

95

Further questions on core principles

a) Identify the structures labelled A, B, C and D. [2]
b) Explain why some of the detail shown in this diagram would not be seen using a light microscope. [4]
(NEAB) **[6]**

▷ Cell surface membrane

15 The diagram below shows the fluid mosaic structure of the cell surface membrane.

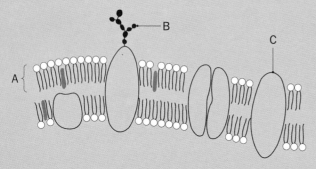

a) Copy and complete the table by naming the parts of the membrane labelled A, B and C in the diagram and state the function of each. [6]

Structure	Name	Function
A		
B		
C		

b) Using the diagram explain the path followed by water as it enters the cell. [1]
(WJEC) **[7]**

16 The diagram below shows a phospholipid molecule.

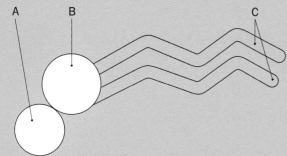

a) i) Name the parts of the molecule labelled A, B and C. [1]
   ii) Explain how the phospholipid molecules form a double layer in a cell membrane. [2]
b) Cell membranes also contain protein molecules. Give *two* functions of these protein molecules. [2]
(NEAB) **[5]**

17 The diagram below represents part of an animal cell which has been put in distilled water.

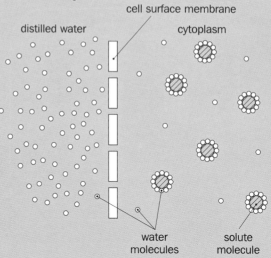

a) Use the diagram to:
   i) explain why the water potential of the distilled water is higher than the water potential of the cytoplasm of the cell; [2]
   ii) describe the property of the cell surface membrane which allows osmosis to take place. [1]
b) Osmosis has been described as a special case of diffusion. Describe *two* ways in which you would expect the movement of water into a cell by osmosis to be similar to the diffusion of oxygen into a cell. [2]
(AEB) **[5]**

18 a) Give *two* differences between osmosis and active transport. [2]
b) Samples of red blood cells were placed in a series of sodium chloride solutions of different concentrations. After 3 hours, the samples were examined to find the percentage of the cells which had burst. The results are given in the graph below.

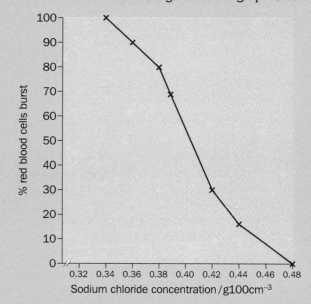

i) Explain why all the red blood cells burst when placed in a 0.34% sodium chloride solution. [3]

ii) The red blood cells burst over a range of sodium chloride concentrations. Suggest a reason for this. [1]

c) When cells from an onion were placed in the same range of sodium chloride solutions, none of the cells burst. Explain why. [1]

(NEAB) **[7]**

▷ Enzymes

19 The diagrams below illustrate one model of enzyme action.

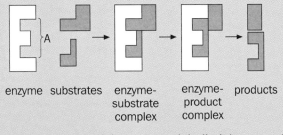

enzyme   substrates   enzyme-substrate complex   enzyme-product complex   products

a) Name the part of the enzyme labelled A. [1]
b) Explain how this model can account for enzyme specificity. [2]
c) With reference to this model, explain the effect of a competitive inhibitor on an enzyme-catalysed reaction. [2]

(Edex) **[5]**

20 a) Explain how the following are related to the protein structure of enzymes.
   i) The effect of high temperature on an enzyme catalysed reaction
   ii) Substrate specificity
   iii) The effect of inhibitors [10]
b) Suggest a simple method by which you could find out whether an enzyme catalysed reaction is being inhibited by a *competitive* or a *non-competitive* inhibitor. [2]

(NEAB) **[12]**

21 The diagram below illustrates the induced fit model of enzyme action.

enzyme   substrate   enzyme + substrate   enzyme   product

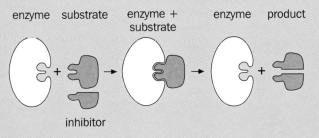

inhibitor

a) Use the diagram to explain the following.
   i) The induce fit model [2]
   ii) Competitive inhibition [2]

b) How would the diagram be different if it were used to illustrate the lock and key hypothesis? [1]

(AEB) **[5]**

22 Hexokinase is an enzyme. It catalyses the phosphorylation of glucose in cellular respiration.

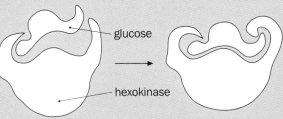

glucose + ATP $\xrightarrow{\text{hexokinase}}$ glucose-6-phosphate + ADP

The polypeptide chains of this enzyme are folded into the shape shown in the diagram below. There is a deep groove in the molecule. ATP binds at the surface of this groove. Glucose can also bind at this groove, but as it does this it causes a change in the shape of the enzyme molecule. The product cannot dissociate from the enzyme until the shape reverts to that of the free enzyme.

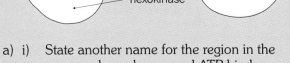

glucose

hexokinase

a) i) State another name for the region in the groove where glucose and ATP bind. [1]
   ii) Explain how the structure of the enzyme enables the reaction to take place. [4]
b) i) Sketch a curve to show how increasing the substrate concentration affects the rate of an enzyme-catalysed reaction. [3]
   ii) Explain the shape of the curve you have drawn. [3]
c) The optimum pH for hexokinase is pH 7. Suggest why only a little glucose-6-phosphate is produced when the enzyme is in a buffered solution of pH 6. [2]

(Camb) **[13]**

23 a) i) Copy the axes below. Sketch a graph to show the expected effects of temperature on the rate of an enzyme catalysed reaction. [3]

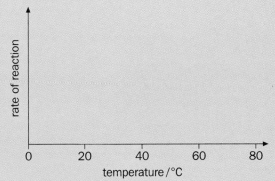

ii) Explain the effects of temperature on this reaction. [4]

b) The rates of enzyme catalysed reactions can also be affected by pH. Explain how change in pH affects enzyme structure. [4]
(O&C) **[11]**

24 Succinate dehydrogenase is an enzyme which catalyses the conversion of succinate to fumarate.
a) Use your knowledge of enzyme structure to explain why succinate dehydrogenase catalyses this reaction only. [2]
b) Malonate is an inhibitor of succinate dehydrogenase. The structural formulae of malonate and succinate are shown in the diagram below.

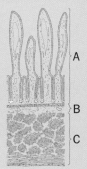

succinate   malonate

Use the information in the diagram to explain how malonate inhibits the enzyme. [2]
(NEAB) **[4]**

▷ **Digestion**

25 The diagram below shows a part of a transverse section through the ileum as seen using a low magnification with a light microscope.

a) Name the parts labelled A, B and C. [3]
b) Describe the function of part C. [2]
(London) **[5]**

26 The flow chart below represents the breakdown of starch in the human gut.

starch $\xrightarrow{amylase}$ maltose $\xrightarrow{maltase}$ glucose

a) Name *two* organs which produce amylase in humans. [1]
b) Describe how the release of amylase from each of these organs is controlled. [3]
c) Describe the precise location of maltase in the human gut. [2]
(AEB) **[6]**

27 The table below refers to some enzymes involved in the digestion of carbohydrates in the human digestive system. Copy and complete the table by writing the correct word or words in the empty boxes.

Name of enzyme	Site of production	Products of reaction
	Wall of intestine	Glucose 1 galactose
Sucrase		
	Pancrease	Maltose

[4]
(London) **[4]**

28 The diagram below shows the human digestive system.

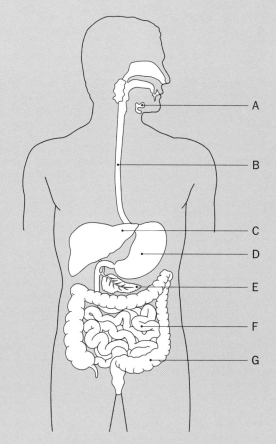

a) Give the letter of an organ where each of the following is produced.
i) endopeptidase
ii) maltase [2]
b) Name the compounds which are produced by the digestion of triglyceride. [1]
c) Describe *one* role of bile in digestion of triglycerides. [2]
d) i) Name the hormone which causes the gall bladder to contract. [1]
ii) What is the stimulus that initiates the release of this hormone? [1]
(NEAB) **[7]**

6 Nucleic acids and protein synthesis

The genome is 'all the DNA sequences contained in the chromosomes of an organism'.
The Human Genome Project aims to trace every single human gene
and map its particular position on the appropriate chromosome.
It is a truly international project, with contributions from many countries.
It is being coordinated by the Human Genome Organisation.
They intend to unravel the structure of each gene and the protein for which it codes.
The significance of this is that we will be able to understand
how people are affected by certain diseases and target early treatments.
The information will also be used to create new drugs to fight
cancers, heart diseases, immune disorders and other illnesses.

▷ Does DNA carry the genetic information?

For many years scientists were not sure whether it was DNA or protein
that carried the genetic information.
In 1952, Frank Hershey and Martha Chase set up an experiment that
proved that it is in fact DNA that codes for the production of proteins.

Bacteriophages are viruses that live inside bacterial cells.
The T_2 bacteriophage (phage for short) lives on the gut bacterium
Escherichia coli (*E. coli*).
The phage consists of a protein coat containing a core of DNA.
The phage is able to inject its DNA into the bacterial cell.
There it takes over the bacterium's biochemical machinery
to replicate itself and make lots of new phages.

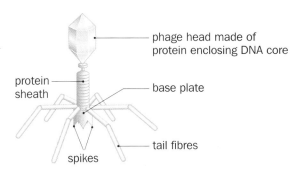

Hershey and Chase set up two cultures of bacteria and phage
to test whether the genetic material was DNA or protein.
DNA contains phosphorus but no sulphur.
Protein contains sulphur but hardly any phosphorus.

The growth medium in culture A contained the radioactive isotope
of phosphorus, ^{32}P.
The growth medium in culture B contained the radioactive isotope
of sulphur, ^{35}S.
The radioactively labelled phage was then allowed to infect the
separate cultures of *E. coli* bacteria.

Which molecules of the phage will be radioactive in

- culture A,
- culture B?

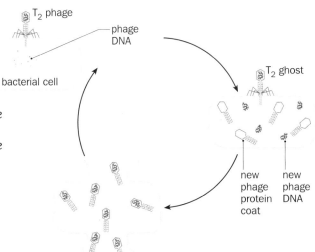

After an appropriate time, the empty phage heads (called ghosts)
were separated from the bacterial cells in a blender.
The two fractions were tested for radioactivity, giving the following results:

Why do you think that the offspring of phage type A
were radioactive?
Why do you think that the offspring of phage type B
were not radioactive?
How do the results support the view that DNA carries
the genetic information?

Phage type	E. *coli* bacteria fraction	Phage ghost fraction	Phage offspring
A (^{32}P)	radioactive	non-radioactive	radioactive
B (^{35}S)	non-radioactive	radioactive	non-radioactive

▷ The structure of nucleic acids

There are two types of nucleic acid: **deoxyribonucleic acid (DNA)** and **ribonucleic acid (RNA)**.
Both are polymers made up of sub-units called **nucleotides**.

> **Each nucleotide is made up of three parts:**
> - **a phosphate group,**
> - **a pentose sugar (either ribose or deoxyribose),**
> - **a base which contains nitrogen.**

The phosphate, sugar and base join together
as shown in the diagram.

Deoxyribonucleic acid (DNA) always contains the sugar **deoxyribose**.
Ribonucleic acid (RNA) always contains the sugar **ribose**.
The phosphate groups are the same in both DNA and RNA.

There are five different types of bases, which we put into two groups.

- **Pyrimidines** are bases with a single ring structure.
  There are three pyrimidine bases: **cytosine**, **thymine** and **uracil**.

- **Purines** are bases with a double ring structure.
  There are two purine bases: **adenine** and **guanine**.

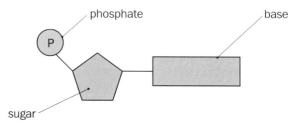

A single nucleotide

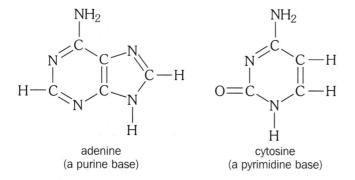

adenine
(a purine base)

cytosine
(a pyrimidine base)

One nucleotide can join to another by a condensation reaction.
This takes place between the sugar and phosphate groups.
Many nucleotides joining up in this way form a polynucleotide chain.

> **In DNA molecules, the nucleotides contain one of the four bases adenine, guanine, cytosine or thymine.**
> **In RNA molecules, the nucleotides contain one of the bases adenine, guanine, cytosine or uracil.**
> **So in RNA uracil replaces thymine.**

What are the **two** main differences between the structure of
DNA and the structure of RNA?

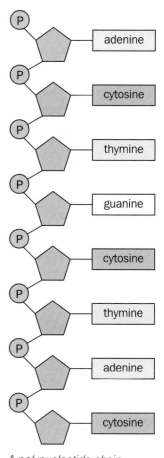

A polynucleotide chain

▷ The structure of DNA

In 1951, the American chemist Erwin Chargaff analysed DNA.
He used chromatography to separate the four bases in DNA from different species.
The amounts of each base were measured quantitatively.
Look at the table showing some of Chargaff's results.
Can you see any pattern in the amounts of the bases estimated?

Organism	Percentage of each base present			
	Adenine	Cytosine	Guanine	Thymine
yeast	32	18	18	32
tuberculosis bacterium	16	34	36	14
locust	29	21	21	29
human	31	19	19	31

Chargaff noted that the amounts of adenine and thymine were similar
and that the amounts of cytosine and guanine were similar.
This was to help later workers, who realised that the bases in
a DNA molecule always pair up.
They deduced that adenine must always pair up with thymine
because their amounts were always the same.
Similarly they deduced that cytosine must always pair up with guanine.
This is called the '**rule of base pairing**'.

> **The bases always pair in the same way:**
> **ADENINE with THYMINE**
> **CYTOSINE with GUANINE**

DNA is made up of *two* polynucleotide chains.
The structure is a bit like a ladder. The 'uprights' of the ladder
are made up of alternating sugar and phosphate groups.
The 'rungs' of the ladder are made up of the bases.

The bases are held together by weak hydrogen bonds.
Two hydrogen bonds hold adenine to thymine
and three hydrogen bonds hold cytosine to guanine.

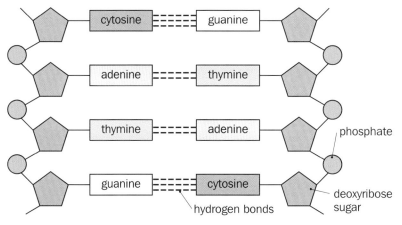

The ladder-like structure is twisted into a helix so that it really
resembles a spiral staircase with the bases as the steps.
This structure was given the nickname 'the double helix'.

If one half of a strand of DNA has the base sequence
TACCTGATGTCAAG, what do you think the
sequence of bases on the other strand will be?

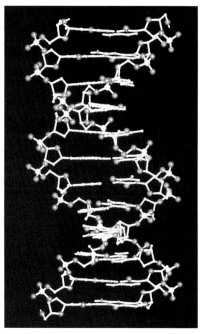

A 3-D model of DNA

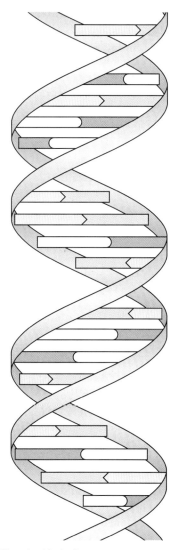

The double helix

101

▷ The discovery of the double helix

The working out of the structure of the DNA molecule remains one of the outstanding scientific events of the twentieth century. Scientists recognised the importance of DNA in the cells of living organisms and by the early 1950s the following facts were known about it:

- DNA is a very long, complex molecule made up of nucleotides.
- It contains four bases – adenine, cytosine, guanine and thymine.
- The amount of adenine is the same as the amount of thymine and the amount of cytosine is the same as the amount of guanine.
- The molecule is likely to be a helix held together by hydrogen bonds.

What scientists could not work out was how the molecular structure was put together.
How could the molecule store all the genetic information of an organism?
How could it copy itself exactly, time after time?

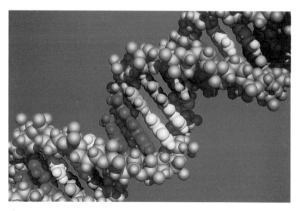
Computer simulation of DNA structure

Evidence from X-ray diffraction

A technique called X-ray diffraction has been used to work out the structures of many different molecules, including proteins. The technique involves firing a beam of X-rays at a protein crystal. As the X-rays hit the atoms in the protein, they are deflected and caught on a photographic plate.
The scattered X-rays produce a pattern that can be used by experts to deduce the arrangement of the atoms in the molecule.

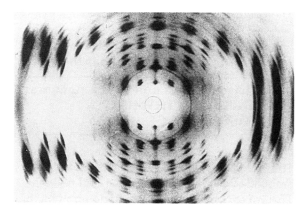
X-ray diffraction pattern of DNA

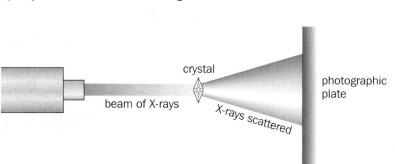

In 1953, Rosalind Franklin and Maurice Wilkins worked at King's College, London, on the X-ray crystallography of DNA. The work was difficult because DNA does not form crystals easily.

However, they succeeded in producing X-ray diffraction photographs like the one shown here.
From these they were able to deduce that the phosphate groups of DNA must be positioned on the outside of the molecule.

This work proved to be of vital importance to the later discovery of the double helix.
Tragically, Rosalind Franklin died of cancer in 1958 at the age of 37. Four years later, Maurice Wilkins was awarded the Nobel Prize. Unfortunately, Nobel Prizes are not awarded posthumously.

Rosalind Franklin

▷ The DNA detectives

The molecular structure of DNA was finally deduced by
James Watson and Francis Crick working at the Cavendish Laboratory
in Cambridge in 1953.
Watson was an American biologist visiting Europe and Crick was a
British physicist turned biologist.
They collected all the recent information on DNA, including Chargaff's data
on base composition and the X-ray diffraction work of Franklin and Wilkins,
and used this to put together a three-dimensional model of DNA.

Watson and Crick with their DNA model

Any model would have to satisfy all the available information
and explain how the molecule was able to reproduce itself.
It took hours of discussions and pain-staking manipulation of the
models before they hit on the correct solution.
Both Chargaff's results and the X-ray diffraction patterns could be
explained if the model consisted of **two** polynucleotide chains
twisted around each other in the form of a double helix.

X-ray diffraction had shown that *every* complete turn of the helix measured 3.4 nm.
Watson suggested that if cytosine paired with guanine (a pyrimidine with a purine)
and if thymine paired with adenine (again a pyrimidine with a purine)
then 10 bases could fit into one complete turn of the helix (3.4 nm).
The bases would be held together by hydrogen bonds.
Watson and Crick made accurate cut-out models of the four nucleotides
and were able to fit them together like a jig-saw puzzle.
They went on to make a three-dimensional DNA model,
like the one in the photograph.

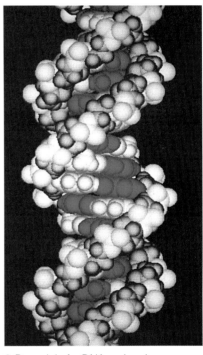

The amount of DNA in a cell is known to double before cell division.
So DNA must be able to make exact copies of itself.
Watson and Crick's model could do this if the hydrogen bonds
holding the bases together were to break.
The two strands could separate and each produce a new double helix.
Watson and Crick were awarded the Nobel Prize for their immense
contribution to molecular genetics.

Chromosomes are known to consist of DNA and histone protein.
The DNA is thought to be highly coiled so that a huge amount
of DNA is condensed into one chromosome containing up to
300 million nucleotides!

3-D model of a DNA molecule

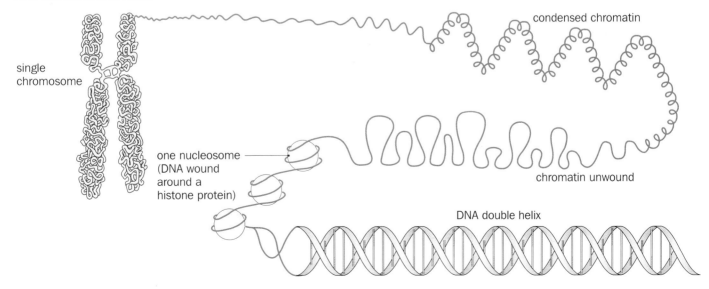

single
chromosome

one nucleosome
(DNA wound
around a
histone protein)

condensed chromatin

chromatin unwound

DNA double helix

▷ DNA replication

Chromosomes must make copies of themselves so that the new cells
formed at cell division have all the correct genetic information.
Similarly, chromosomes must make copies of themselves so that
the genetic information can be passed on to the offspring in
the sperm and the egg. This copying of DNA is known as **replication**
and it takes place in every cell before cell division occurs.

First, the hydrogen bonds holding the base pairs together break.
As the bonds break, the two halves of the molecule separate.
It's a bit like a zipper unzipping, and each half of the
molecule acts as a mould, or **template,** on which a new strand
of DNA can be built.

When the two halves of the molecule separate, the DNA bases are exposed.
Free nucleotides enter the nucleus from the cytoplasm and assemble
on the template DNA according to the law of base pairing.
Nucleotides containing adenine join up with those containing thymine
and nucleotides containing cytosine join up with guanine nucleotides.
This happens against each original polynucleotide chain.
The enzyme **DNA polymerase** joins the new nucleotides together,
forming a new sugar–phosphate backbone.

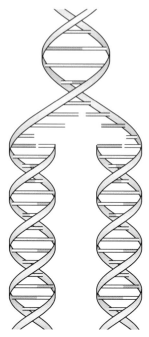

A DNA molecule replicating

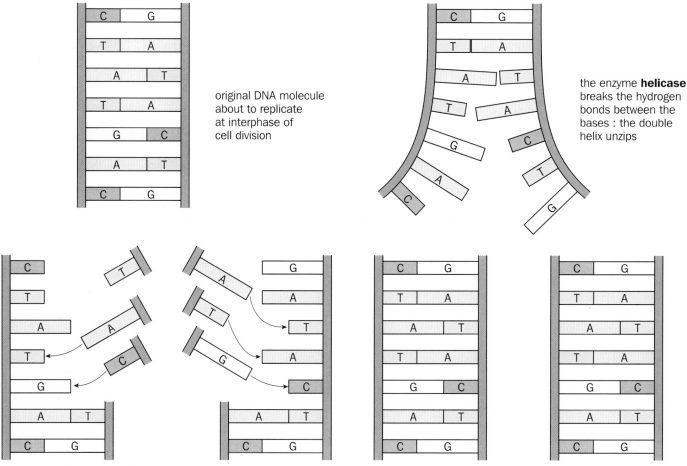

original DNA molecule
about to replicate
at interphase of
cell division

the enzyme **helicase**
breaks the hydrogen
bonds between the
bases : the double
helix unzips

free nucleotides attach to each template
DNA where bases are compatible

the nucleotides join up producing
two identical DNA molecules

▷ Evidence for DNA replication

This method of replication is known as '**semi-conservative**' because each new DNA double helix contains one complete polynucleotide strand from the original DNA molecule.

Shortly after Watson and Crick's discovery, Meselson and Stahl produced evidence to support this method of DNA replication. They grew the bacterium *E. coli* in a medium containing amino acids made with the isotope ^{15}N ('heavy nitrogen'). The bacterium took up the isotope and so all its DNA contained ^{15}N. Meselson and Stahl were able to extract the bacterial DNA and centrifuge it in caesium chloride solution. Depending on the mass of the molecule, the DNA would settle out at a particular point in the tube.

A high-speed centrifuge

The ^{15}N bacteria were then transferred to a growth medium containing the normal, lighter isotope of nitrogen, ^{14}N, where they reproduced by cell division. Extracts of DNA from the first generation offspring were shown to have a lower density, since half the DNA was made up of the original strand containing ^{15}N and the other half was made up of the new strand containing ^{14}N. At succeeding generation times, the DNA extracts were found to have a lower proportion of ^{15}N as more ^{14}N was incorporated into the bacterial DNA. This was conclusive evidence for the semi-conservative method of DNA replication.

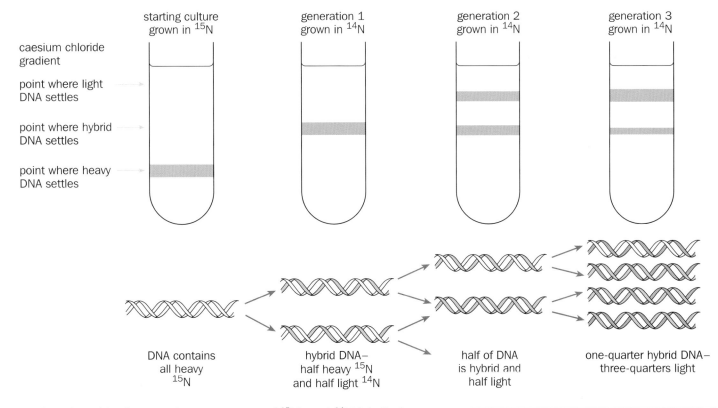

Look at the table showing the proportions of ^{15}N- and ^{14}N-labelled DNA at each generation time.
Predict the percentage of ^{15}N-labelled DNA that would occur in the third and fourth generations.

Generation	%DNA	
	^{15}N	^{14}N
1	50	50
2	25	75
3		
4		

▷ The genetic code

You now know how DNA is able to copy itself.
DNA also acts as a store of genetic information.

As you know, each chromosome is made up of a long,
super-coiled strand of DNA.
This strand can be divided up into thousands of shorter sections
called **genes**.
So a gene is a small part of a DNA strand.

The length of DNA making up a particular gene carries
the information needed to make a particular protein.
This information is known as the **genetic code**.

Remember that inside every cell there are thousands of
chemical reactions taking place.
Enzymes control all these chemical reactions.
You should remember that *all* enzymes are proteins.

So because DNA codes for proteins, it must determine
which enzymes are produced and therefore *which*
chemical reactions can take place in cells.

The information in the genetic code is found in the
sequence of bases along the length of DNA.
These determine the sequence of amino acids in the protein.

But how many bases do you think code for a single amino acid?

A triplet code?

As you know there are *four* different bases found in DNA:
adenine, thymine, guanine and cytosine.
There are *twenty* different amino acids that make up our protein.

So how many amino acids could be coded for if *one* base coded
for *one* amino acid?
The answer is only four as there are only four codes: A, T, G and C.

How about *two* bases coding for one amino acid?
No, still not enough, although this time we could have 16 different
codes for 16 different amino acids:
AA, AT, AC, AG, TT, TA, TC, TG, CC, CA, CT, CG, GG, GC, GA, GT

Let's try *three* bases for each amino acid.
That would give us 64 different codes – that's more than enough for
20 amino acids: ATA, ACG, TAC, etc.

In fact, most amino acids are coded by more than one DNA base triplet.
For instance, TTC and TTT both code for the amino acid lysine.
AGC, AGT, AGG and AGA all code for the amino acid serine.
What seems to be important is the first two bases in the sequence.
But there are two amino acids that are coded by just one base triplet.
TAC codes for methionine and ACC codes for tryptophan.

These DNA base triplets are called DNA **codons**.

A bit of light reading 'The secret of life'!

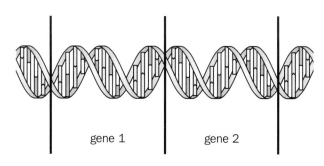

gene 1   gene 2

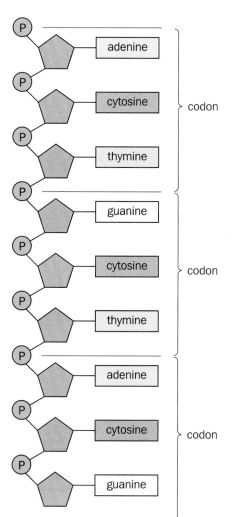

106

▷ Ribonucleic acid (RNA)

Do you remember how RNA differs from DNA?
RNA always has **ribose** sugar and the base **uracil** replaces thymine.

There are other differences between RNA and DNA.
RNA molecules tend to be short-lived.
RNA is found inside the nucleus and in the cytoplasm.
RNA molecules are involved in the synthesis of proteins.

There are *three* different types of RNA.

Messenger RNA (mRNA)

A messenger RNA molecule is a single strand (not a double strand) about a thousand nucleotides long.
Messenger RNA is involved in carrying the genetic code from the DNA in the nucleus to the ribosomes in the cytoplasm where protein is made.

Ribosomal RNA (rRNA)

Molecules of ribosomal RNA are large and complex, often forming a double helix. Ribosomes are made up of rRNA and protein.

Transfer RNA (tRNA)

These are small molecules, about 80 nucleotides long.
Transfer RNA molecules bring amino acids to the ribosomes so that the protein can be assembled.

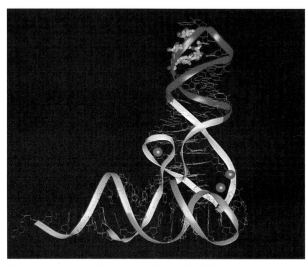

Computer simulation model of transfer RNA

▷ Making a protein

There are *two* main steps in converting the DNA code into a new protein.
These are **transcription** and **translation**.

As you know, DNA carries the information to build proteins from amino acids.
But DNA never leaves the nucleus.
So how does the information get from DNA to the site of protein synthesis in the ribosomes?
There must be some kind of 'messenger molecule'.
It must be able to carry the base sequence of DNA to the ribosomes.
Here the message can be *translated* into the correct amino acid sequence for the protein.

This 'messenger molecule' was eventually isolated and found to be RNA.
It was given the name **messenger RNA** (mRNA).
Can you see from the diagram that DNA is now involved in three processes?
Use the diagram to explain what we mean by replication, transcription and translation.

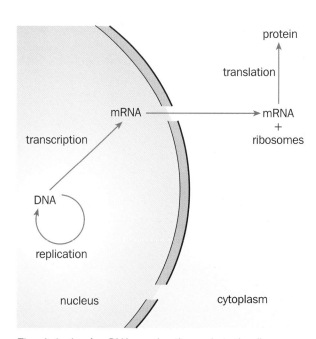

The vital role of m-RNA carrying the code to the ribosomes

▷ Transcription

So how do you think mRNA is made in the nucleus?
The mRNA is copied from a specific region of DNA
called the **cistron**.
The cistron is a length of DNA that forms a mRNA
molecule.
Often a cistron is equivalent to a gene and codes for
a specific polypeptide.

First, the DNA unwinds due to the breaking of the
hydrogen bonds between the base pairs.
One of the two DNA strands acts as a **template** against
which a matching mRNA strand can be formed.
The exposed bases on this template strand of DNA
attract RNA nucleotides with a ***complementary***
base, for example cytosine on DNA will attract a
guanine nucleotide.
But remember that ***adenine will attract a uracil
nucleotide, not one containing thymine.***

The enzyme **RNA polymerase** moves along the DNA,
forming bonds that add nucleotides one at a time to
the RNA .
Behind the RNA polymerase the DNA strands join
up to reform the double helix.

You should remember that each amino acid was coded
for by a DNA codon, or a sequence of three bases.
As you can see from the diagram, the RNA molecules
carry mirror images of these base triplets.
These mirror images are called **RNA codons**.
Each mRNA codon codes for a certain amino acid.
In this way, the mRNA carries the DNA code out of
the nucleus to the ribosome, where it is used to
assemble proteins.

(a)
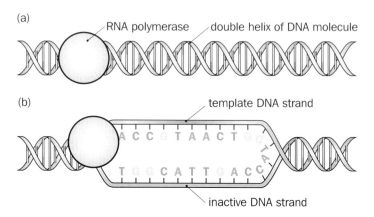
RNA polymerase   double helix of DNA molecule

(b)
template DNA strand

inactive DNA strand
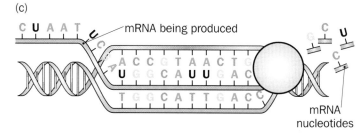

(c)
mRNA being produced

mRNA nucleotides
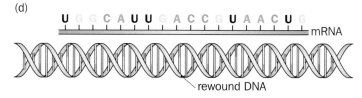

(d)
U G G C A U U G A C C G U A A C U G
mRNA

rewound DNA

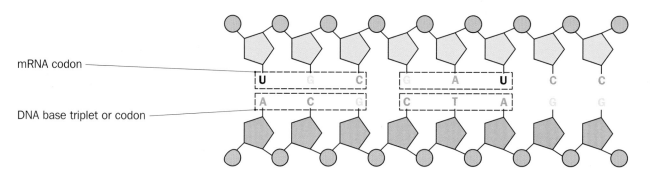

mRNA codon

DNA base triplet or codon

What do you think the base sequence of mRNA will be
if it is transcribed from the following DNA sequence?
TAC—CGC—CAT—TTA—ACG—ACT—AAA

▷ Translation

Translation is the process that converts the coded information of mRNA into the correct sequence of amino acids in a polypeptide.

First of all mRNA arrives from the nucleus with the genetic code.
The mRNA strand contains the codons for each particular amino acid in the protein.
This coded message is then read from the mRNA and **translated** into a polypeptide molecule.

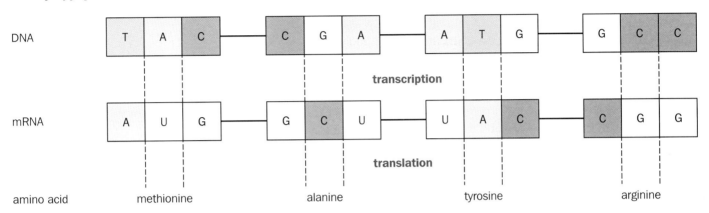

Amino acids are carried to the ribosomes by smaller RNA molecules called **transfer RNA** (tRNA).
Molecules of tRNA are single strands folded back on themselves.
They are often referred to as 'clover leaf' structures.
If you look at the diagram, you will see why.

Can you see that the bases are paired to each other?
How are these bases held together?

Hydrogen bonds give tRNA a stable structure.

The role of tRNA is to carry amino acids to the ribosomes.
To do this it has an amino acid attachment site at one end.

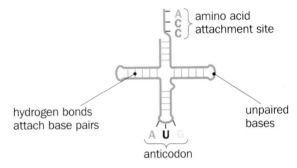

Structure of tRNA

Each amino acid has its own specific tRNA molecule.
So there are 20 different types of tRNA molecules for the 20 different amino acids.
The tRNA attaches itself to a specific amino acid in the presence of a specific enzyme and ATP.
This is sometimes called **amino acid activation**.

The tRNA/amino acid complex is then ferried to the ribosome where the amino acid becomes attached to the polypeptide chain.
At one end of the tRNA is a base triplet called an **anticodon**.
The anticodon is different for each amino acid: for instance, CGA for alanine, AGU for serine and UUC for lysine.
The anticodon attaches itself to the compatible mRNA codon.
For instance, anticodon CGA will attach itself to codon GCU.

A ribosome is made up of **ribosomal RNA** (rRNA) and protein.
Each ribosome consists of two sub-units.
The smaller sub-unit has two sites for attaching molecules of tRNA: the P site (peptide site) and the A site (amino acid site).
So two tRNA molecules are associated with a ribosome at any one time.

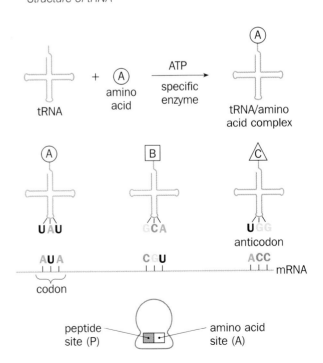

▷ Building a protein

The process of translation begins when the mRNA molecule with the **start codon** AUG attaches itself to the ribosome.
AUG codes for methionine, the amino acid that most polypeptide chains start with.
The tRNA molecule carrying the amino acid methionine attaches itself at the P site of the ribosome.

Can you see that the tRNA anticodon UAC attaches to a compatible mRNA codon, AUG?

Now a second tRNA molecule attaches to the ribosome's A site.
The two amino acids methionine and alanine are close enough for a **peptide bond** to form between them.
The bond between the first tRNA and methionine now breaks.
This provides the energy to form the peptide bond between methionine and alanine.

The first tRNA leaves the ribosome and the P site becomes vacant.
The whole ribosome now moves one codon along the mRNA strand.
So the second tRNA molecule now occupies the P site.
This leaves the A site free.
A third tRNA comes in to fill the A site.
Can you see its anticodon AGU matches the next codon on mRNA: UCA?
A peptide bond forms between alanine and serine.

The ribosome moves along the mRNA strand reading off the message a codon at a time.
As it does so, more tRNAs slot into the A site and bring with them their amino acids.
And so the polypeptide chain grows.
The process is repeated until a **stop codon** occurs in the mRNA, for example UAG, UGA or UAA.
These do not code for any amino acids.
The mRNA separates from the ribosome and the completed polypeptide chain is released to the cytoplasm.

Both the ribosome and the mRNA can be used again.
Each mRNA can code for the production of many molecules of a particular polypeptide before stopping.
Usually a number of ribosomes can be found on a single mRNA, each reading off the coded information at the same time.

Such structures are known as **polyribosomes** or **polysomes**.

Try to complete the table by putting in the correct tRNA anticodon, amino acid and DNA base sequence.
You can find the full table of mRNA codons on page 112.

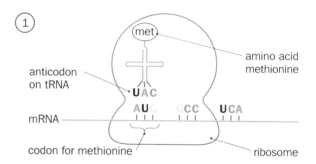

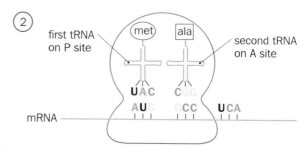

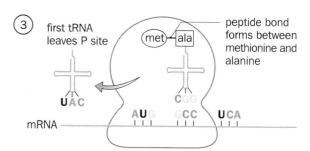

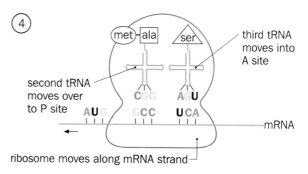

ribosome moves along mRNA strand

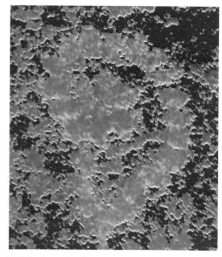

TEM of a polyribosome

mRNA codon	tRNA anticodon	Amino acid	DNA base sequence
GGA			
UAC			
CCA			
CUG			
UUU			
AAG			
UGC			

110

Summary

- A chromosome is made up of a long, super-coiled strand of DNA.
- A gene is a length of DNA that codes for the production of a particular protein.
- The DNA molecule consists of a double helix with pairs of bases bonded together.
- The sequence of bases on DNA is called the genetic code. It can be read off in base triplets called codons. Each codon codes for a particular amino acid.
- DNA is able to make new DNA identical to itself by semi-conservative replication.
- DNA can make messenger RNA by a process called transcription. Messenger RNA carries the coded information from DNA in the nucleus to the ribosomes where proteins are synthesised.
- Transfer RNA carries specific amino acids to the ribosomes to be assembled into protein.

▷ Questions

1 Copy and complete the following:
A molecule of DNA is made up of many sub-units called ___. Each nucleotide is made up of a ___ joined to a ___ sugar with a phosphate group. The DNA molecule consists of two strands running parallel to each other and coiled into a ___ ___. The bases in each strand are held together by ___ bonds. In RNA the base ___ is replaced by ___ and the pentose sugar present is ___. There are ___ different types of RNA and all are involved in the synthesis of ___. One type, called ___ RNA, forms the ribosomes in association with proteins. ___RNA is formed from a single strand of DNA by a process called ___. The third type of RNA is called ___RNA and its role is to pick up specific ___ ___ and carry them to the ribosomes.

2 Copy the table comparing DNA and RNA. If you think the feature is correct put a tick (✓) in the box. If you think the feature is incorrect put a cross (✗) in the box.

Feature	DNA	RNA
contains ribose		
is a single strand		
contains adenine, guanine and cytosine		
contains uracil		
contains equal proportions of purines and pyrimidines		

3 The diagram shows a nucleotide from a DNA molecule.

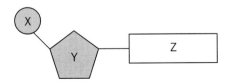

a) Name the parts labelled X, Y and Z.

b) Write down the base sequence of part of a strand of messenger RNA made from the following portion of a DNA molecule:
ATC GGA CTC TTC ATA GCG ACG GTA

c) The percentage of bases on one strand of DNA is thymine = 40% and cytosine = 22%.
What is the percentage of the bases adenine and guanine in this same strand of DNA?

4 Look at the diagram of part of a molecule of messenger RNA:
A U G A C G C A U G C A G U C C G A
a) How many codons are shown in this section of mRNA?
b) What is the role of each of these codons in protein synthesis?
c) Write down the transfer RNA anticodons specified by this mRNA strand.

5 Copy and complete the table showing three types of nucleic acid involved in protein synthesis.

Type of nucleic acid	Where formed	Function(s)	Where function(s) takes place
DNA			
mRNA			
tRNA			

6 Copy and complete the following table (the table of mRNA codons on page 112 will help you).

DNA double helix	non-coding strand		TGT			
	coding strand	AGC				
transcribed mRNA					GUA	
tRNA anticodon				GAG		UUU
amino acid incorporated into polypeptide			Tyr		Met	

111

Table of mRNA codons and the amino acids for which they code

First base	Second base				Third base
	G	A	C	U	
G	GGG glycine GGA glycine GGC glycine GGU glycine	GAG glutamic acid GAA glutamic acid GAC aspartic acid GAU aspartic acid	GCG alanine GCA alanine GCC alanine GCU alanine	GUG valine GUA valine GUC valine GUU valine	G A C U
A	AGG arginine AGA arginine AGC serine AGU serine	AAG lysine AAA lysine AAC asparagine AAU asparagine	ACG threonine ACA threonine ACC threonine ACU threonine	AUG start AUA isoleucine AUC isoleucine AUU isoleucine	G A C U
C	CGG arginine CGA arginine CGC arginine CGU arginine	CAG glutamine CAA glutamine CAC histidine CAU histdine	CCG proline CCA proline CCC proline CCU proline	CUG leucine CUA leucine CUC leucine CUU leucine	G A C U
U	UGG tryptophan UGA stop UGC cysteine UGU cysteine	UAG stop UAA stop UAC tyrosine UAU tyrosine	UCG serine UCA serine UCC serine UCU serine	UUG leucine UUA leucine UUC phenylalanine UUU phenylalanine	G A C U

7 a) What will be the sequence of amino acids in a protein coded by this section of DNA?
GTG ACG GTG CAC ATT

b) The removal or substitution of a base of a DNA strand results in a point mutation. Suppose a point mutation occurs on the DNA strand in part (a) producing:
   i) GTG ACG GTG CTC ATT
   ii) GTG ACG TGC ACA TTC
   What effect would each of these mutations have on the protein molecule to be made?

8 The table at the top of the page shows some of the RNA codons (triplets of bases) together with the amino acids for which they code.
a) What sequence of amino acids does the following code in the DNA (deoxyribonucleic acid) give rise to?
— GCAGGACCAGCAACATAC —
b) The following amino acid sequence is from the beginning of the protein molecule of insulin.
Lysine – glutamine – threonine – alanine – alanine – alanine – lysine
What is the DNA code in the chromosome for this fragment of the protein?
c) What are the t-RNA anti-codons that will 'plug in' to the code in a)?

9 Indicate whether you think the following statements are true or false.
a) DNA is a protein.
b) DNA is a double helix.
c) The molecular shape of DNA is maintained by hydrogen bonding between complementary base pairs.

d) DNA contains four bases, adenine, guanine, cytosine, and uracil.
e) Transcription, the transfer of information from DNA to RNA occurs only when DNA is replicating.
f) In messenger RNA (m-RNA) there are codons, each consisting of three bases.
g) Transfer RNA (t-RNA) carries specific amino acids to ribosomes where complementary anticodons on t-RNA match codons on m-RNA.

10 The table lists amino acids and the base sequences on a messenger RNA (mRNA) strand which code for them in protein synthesis.

Amino acid	mRNA triplet code
Tyrosine	UAU
Alanine	GCG
Phenylalanine	UUU
Leucine	UUA
Arginine	CGU
Glycine	GGG
Arginine	AGG

A DNA strand has the base sequence:
AATCGCAAATCCCGCATAATTTAG

a) Name the amino acid which would be placed **third** in the growing polypeptide chain.
b) Name the **fifth** amino acid in the chain if a single base deletion occurred after the sequence AAA.
c) Suggest a specific factor which could have caused this change.
d) A transfer RNA (tRNA) molecule carries the anticodon CCC. Name the specific amino acid carried by this tRNA molecule

7 Cell division

One of the main principles of the cell theory states:
'New cells are formed by the division of pre-existing cells.'
Since all living things are able to grow and reproduce,
then the cells of all living organisms must be able to
reproduce themselves.

As you have seen in Chapter 2, most of your body cells become
specialised in order to perform particular functions.
The cells in your pancreas secrete the hormone insulin whilst
those in your brain transmit electrical impulses.
Once you are fully grown, little cell division occurs in your body,
apart from your skin and gut cells, and the cells that form gametes.
In fact, any other incidences of cell division in a fully grown adult
may result in a cancer.
Tumours can develop if things go wrong in tissues where
cell division is normally very active.

Cells increase in number by **cell division**.
The parent cell divides and passes on genetic material
to the daughter cells.
As you already know, this genetic material (DNA) is found
inside the nucleus.
The most important part of cell division concerns events
inside the nucleus.

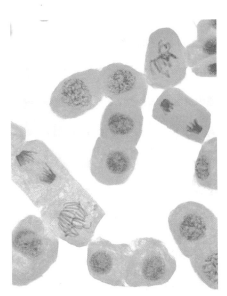

Cells at various stages of cell division

▷ Chromosomes

Each chromosome is a single thread-like structure made up
of a long molecule of DNA combined with histone protein.
The DNA molecule is made up of many small sections called **genes**.
When the cell is not dividing, the chromosomes are not visible and
are dispersed throughout the nucleus as **chromatin**.

When the cell is about to divide, each chromosome condenses and
becomes visible.
Each chromosome appears as *two* threads.
Each of the threads is called a **chromatid** and they are joined
together at a point called the **centromere**.

Where does the second thread come from?
Shortly before cell division occurs, each DNA molecule makes a
copy of itself.
So the one thread of DNA becomes two identical threads, the
chromatids.
As the two chromatids are identical, they will have identical genes.
These identical genes are known as **alleles**.

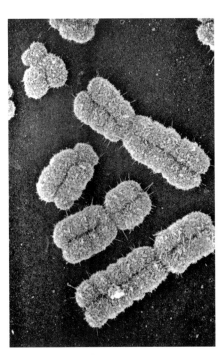

SEM of human chromosomes

113

▷ Numbers of chromosomes

Look at the table.
It shows the number of chromosomes found in different plant and animal species.

Different species have different chromosome numbers.
Can you see any other pattern?

Notice that they are all *even* numbers.
This is because chromosomes occur in pairs.

What about size? Do bigger organisms have more chromosomes?
No. There is no relationship between the size of an organism and the number of chromosomes that it possesses.

Species	Number of chromosomes
fruit fly	8
broad bean	12
onion	16
locust	24
lily	24
yeast	34
cat	38
mouse	40
human	46
potato	48
chimpanzee	48
horse	64
dog	78

▷ Pairs of chromosomes

Look at the chromosome preparation made from a human male.
This sort of photograph is called a **karyotype**.
It is made by cutting out the chromosomes from a photograph and putting them in their pairs.

Can you see that:

- They are not all the same size.
  They have been arranged in decreasing order, starting with the biggest.

- They have been put into matching pairs according to their size and shape.
  These are called **homologous pairs** of chromosomes.
  Each homologous pair is given a number.

- The last pair of chromosomes displayed are the **sex chromosomes**.
  All the other chromosomes are termed **autosomes**.
  We can quickly identify the sex of an individual by looking at the sex chromosomes.
  In females, the two sex chromosomes are alike and are termed X chromosomes.
  In males, there is one X chromosome but the other is much shorter and is called the Y chromosome.

Human cells have 46 chromosomes – that's 23 homologous pairs.
This total number of chromosomes is called the **diploid** number (**2n**).
Gametes (sex cells) have *half* the normal diploid number.
This is called the **haploid** number, shown as (**n**).
So human sperms will have 23 chromosomes and human eggs will have 23 chromosomes.

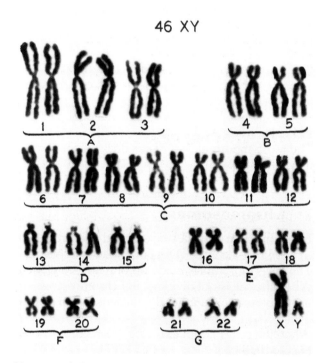

46 XY

Human male karyotype

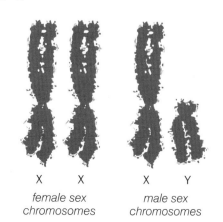

X   X   X   Y
female sex   *male sex*
chromosomes   *chromosomes*

114

▷ Halving and doubling

So why is it important that gametes are haploid?
What would happen if a diploid sperm fertilised a diploid egg?
That would be 46 sperm chromosomes and 46 egg chromosomes,
giving 92 chromosomes in the fertilised egg – double the normal number!

Normally cell division produces identical daughter cells,
each with a full complement of chromosomes.
There has to be a special type of cell division that produces gametes
with a haploid chromosome number.
So at fertilisation a diploid **zygote** (fertilised egg) is produced.

Half your chromosomes came from your father in the sperm.
These are called the **paternal** chromosomes.
The other half came from your mother in the egg.
These are called **maternal** chromosomes.
Each homologous pair is made up of one paternal and one
maternal chromosome.

The zygote divides by mitosis, producing diploid cells
with identical chromosomes.
These chromosomes must therefore carry the same genes (**alleles**)
as those found in the zygote.
This is why you have inherited characteristics from each of your parents.
Half your alleles came from your father and half came from your mother.

▷ The dividing cell

Cell division involves the division of the nucleus and then the
division of the cytoplasm.
There are **two** types of cell division:

- **Mitosis**, which produces two daughter cells that are genetically
  identical to the parent cell.

- **Meiosis**, which produces four genetically different haploid cells.
  Meiosis, unlike mitosis, involves two consecutive divisions.

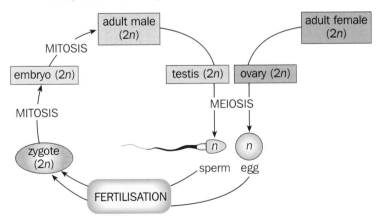

Mitosis occurs during growth and asexual reproduction when
it is important that each daughter cell has the same chromosomes
as the parent cell and the same genes.

Meiosis occurs during sexual reproduction, when it is important
that haploid gametes are produced.

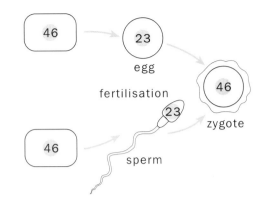

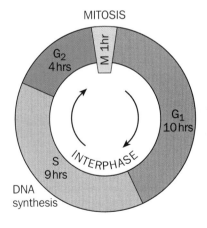

A fertilised human egg or zygote

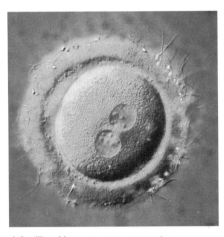

*The cell cycle consists of mitosis (the **M phase**) and
a period between divisions called **interphase**.
Interphase is divided into 3 **growth phases**:
G1 phase a period of rapid cell growth when new
organelles are synthesised. **S phase** when the
amount of DNA in the cell doubles.
G2 phase when the centrioles replicate and
microtubules start to construct the spindle.*

▷ Stages in mitosis

The function of mitosis is to increase the number of cells that are genetically identical to the parent cell.

Mitosis occurs during growth and asexual reproduction.
A fertilised egg divides many times by mitosis to form an embryo.
But so do the cells in your skin, bone marrow and in a healing wound.
In flowering plants, growth is greatest at the shoot and root tips.
Here mitosis occurs in particular areas called **meristems**.

The use of time lapse photography with a phase-contrast microscope enables us to observe mitosis as a continuous process. However, for convenience, mitosis can be divided into a number of stages when particular events take place.

If you look at a section of root tip under the microscope, most cells will not be dividing.
This stage between divisions is known as **interphase**.
It is sometimes called the 'resting stage' but in actual fact the cell is metabolically active.
During interphase:

● the amount of DNA in the nucleus doubles,

● new organelles, for example mitochondria, are made.

No chromosomes are visible at interphase because the chromosome material, **chromatin**, is dispersed throughout the nucleus in a diffuse form.

Prophase

Prophase is the longest stage in mitosis.

● The chromosomes become visible as long thin threads.

● The chromosomes start to coil up and become shorter and thicker.

● In animal cells, the centrioles divide and move to opposite ends (**poles**) of the nucleus.

● Protein microtubules develop from each centriole, forming **spindle fibres**. Some of these extend from pole to pole. In plant cells, there are no centrioles and the **spindle** forms independently.

● Towards the end of prophase, each chromosome can be seen to consist of two **chromatids** held together by a **centromere**.

● At the end of prophase, the nucleolus disappears and the nuclear envelope breaks down. The chromosomes now lie free in the cytoplasm.

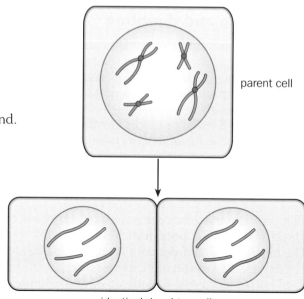

parent cell

identical daughter cells

At mitosis the parent cell divides to produce two daughter cells with identical chromosomes

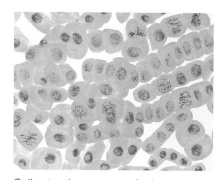

Cells at various stages of mitosis

Early prophase

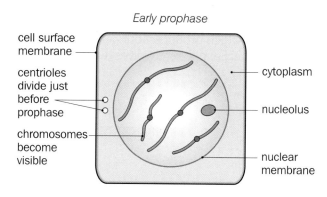

cell surface membrane

centrioles divide just before prophase

chromosomes become visible

cytoplasm

nucleolus

nuclear membrane

Late prophase

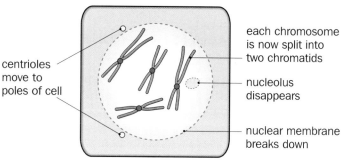

centrioles move to poles of cell

each chromosome is now split into two chromatids

nucleolus disappears

nuclear membrane breaks down

116

Metaphase

Metaphase is a relatively short stage in mitosis.
Consequently, it can be difficult to observe on a slide section.

- The chromosomes move towards the **equator** of the spindle.

- Here they attach themselves to a spindle fibre by means of a centromere.

Anaphase

Anaphase is also a short stage in mitosis.

- The centromeres holding each pair of chromatids together divide.

- The free chromatids move to the poles, centromere first. This movement results from the contraction of the spindle fibres.
  As they shorten, they pull the chromatids apart.

Telophase

- The chromatids have now reached the poles and can be regarded as distinct chromosomes.

- This final stage of mitosis can almost be regarded as the reverse of prophase.
  The nuclear envelope forms around each group of chromosomes and the nucleolus reappears.
  The chromosomes uncoil to form diffuse chromatin.

- The cytoplasm divides by a process called **cytokinesis**.

Cytokinesis

Division of the cytoplasm often starts during telophase.
In animal cells, the centre of the cell 'pinches in' to form a **division furrow**.
This forms in the same plane as the equator.
The furrow forms due to the contraction of a ring made up of two proteins, actin and myosin.
As the division furrow deepens, the cell surface membrane on each side joins up and two separate cells result.

Cytokinesis is different in plant cells.
First, vesicles produced by the Golgi body collect on the equator.
These vesicles contain carbohydrates, such as pectins and hemicelluloses.
The vesicles fuse together to form a **cell plate**.
The cell plate eventually stretches right across the cell, forming the **middle lamella**.
Cellulose builds up on each side of the middle lamella to form the cell walls of two new plant cells.

Metaphase

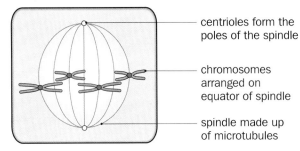

centrioles form the poles of the spindle

chromosomes arranged on equator of spindle

spindle made up of microtubules

Anaphase

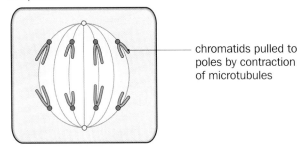

chromatids pulled to poles by contraction of microtubules

Telophase

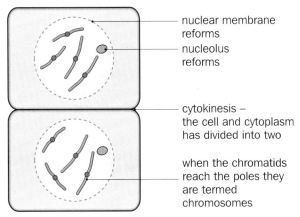

nuclear membrane reforms

nucleolus reforms

cytokinesis – the cell and cytoplasm has divided into two

when the chromatids reach the poles they are termed chromosomes

Cytokinesis in an animal cell

division furrow

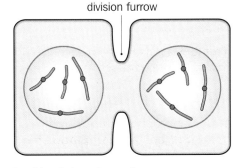

Cytokinesis in a plant cell

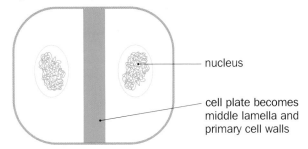

nucleus

cell plate becomes middle lamella and primary cell walls

▷ Photomicrographs of stages in mitosis

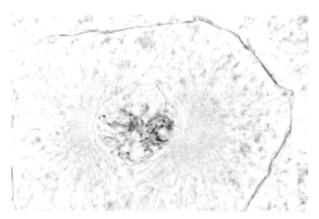

Prophase: chromosomes become visible as chromatin condenses

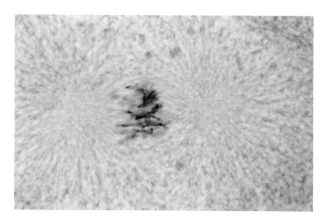

Late prophase: fully organised chromosomes, split into chromatids, move to the centre of the cell. The spindle fibres are well formed

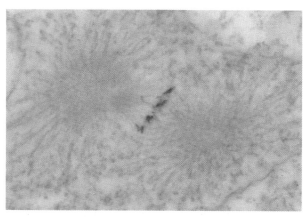

Metaphase: the spindle fibres are well formed from microtubules. The centrioles are located at the poles of the spindle and the chromosomes arrange themselves on the equator

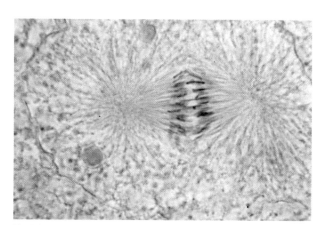

Early anaphase: the chromatids separate and start to move to their respective poles

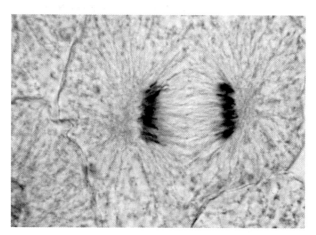

Late anaphase: the chromatids reach the poles drawn by the contractile microtubules in the spindle

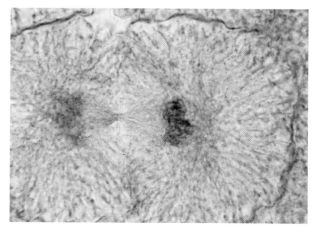

Telophase: the chromatids once they reach the poles are fully organised chromosomes. A cell membrane forms between the two cells (cytokinesis)

These stages of mitosis are shown from photomicrographs of whitefish

▷ Significance of mitosis

Mitosis produces cells that are an **exact** copy of the parent cell.
These daughter cells have the same number of chromosomes and
are genetically identical to the parent cell.

Mitosis is important for the following processes:

- **Growth**
  As multicellular organisms grow, the number of cells making up
  their tissues increases.
  The new cells must be identical to the existing ones.
  Growth by mitosis takes place over the whole body in animals.
  In plants, growth is confined to certain areas called meristems.

- **Repair of tissues**
  Damaged cells must be replaced by identical new cells.
  Your skin cells and the cells lining your gut are constantly dying
  and being replaced by identical cells.
  This is achieved by mitosis.

- **Asexual reproduction**
  Asexual reproduction results in offspring that are identical to the
  parent.
  Mitosis occurs when unicellular organisms, such as yeast and
  Amoeba, reproduce.

Mitosis can also produce new offspring in multicellular organisms.
Hydra is a primitive animal that lives in freshwater habitats.
It produces 'buds', which eventually break away and form
new individuals identical to the parent.

In flowering plants, organs such as bulbs, corms, tubers, rhizomes
and runners are produced by mitotic division.
When they separate from the parent they form a new individual.
Mitosis can result in the production of large numbers of offspring
in a relatively short period of time.
But there is little or no variation between each individual.
As you will see, mitosis of cells grown in tissue culture have
important applications in both genetic engineering and biotechnology.

▷ Meiosis

Meiosis is a type of cell division that is vital for sexual reproduction.
Meiosis takes place in the reproductive organs.
It results in the formation of gametes with half the normal
chromosome number.
So haploid sperms are made in the testes and haploid eggs are
made in the ovaries.

In flowering plants, haploid gametes are made in the anthers and
ovules.
In contrast to mitosis, meiosis produces cells that are not
genetically identical.
So meiosis has a key role in producing new genetic types,
that is, it results in **genetic variation**.

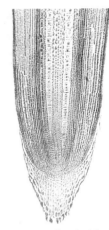

Mitosis takes place first behind the root tip

Budding in Hydra

Micropropagation: plants grown in tissue culture

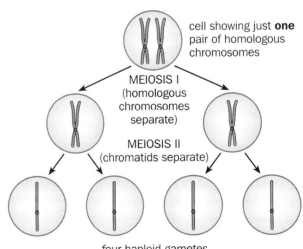

cell showing just **one** pair of homologous chromosomes

MEIOSIS I
(homologous chromosomes separate)

MEIOSIS II
(chromatids separate)

four haploid gametes

▷ Stages in meiosis

Meiosis involves *two* divisions of the cell.
These two divisions are termed meiosis I and meiosis II.
As with mitosis, the cell is said to be in interphase when it is not dividing.
During interphase the DNA content of the cell doubles and new cell organelles are formed.

▷ Meiosis I

Prophase I

- The chromosomes condense and are seen to have split into two chromatids.

- As in prophase of mitosis, the chromosomes shorten and thicken by coiling.

- One of the most important features of prophase I of meiosis is that the paternal and maternal chromosomes come together in **homologous pairs**.

- This pairing of the chromosomes is called **synapsis**. Each homologous pair of chromosomes is called a **bivalent**. So a bivalent consists of *four* strands: *two* chromosomes, each split into *two* chromatids.

- As the chromosomes pair up, they shorten and twist around each other. This causes a tension, and sections of chromatid may break off and exchange with corresponding sections of a different chromatid. The points where this exchange of chromatid material occurs are called **chiasmata** (singular **chiasma**). This swapping of chromatid material is called **crossing over**.

- Towards the end of prophase I, the nucleolus disappears and the nuclear envelope breaks down.

Prophase I is the longest and most complex stage in meiosis. The key events are:

- the pairing of homologous chromosomes (bivalents),

- the exchange of chromatid material at chiasmata (crossing over).

Prophase I

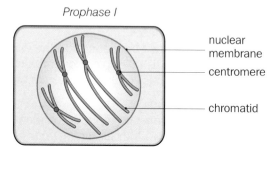
- nuclear membrane
- centromere
- chromatid

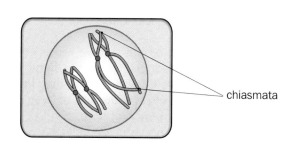
bivalent – two chromosomes split into two chromatids

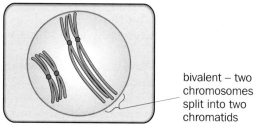
chiasmata

Metaphase I

- At the start of metaphase I, the spindle will have formed.

- As in mitosis, the chromosomes assemble on the equator of the spindle.

How does the arrangement of chromosomes differ from that at metaphase of mitosis? The key difference in meiosis metaphase I is that the chromosomes are joined in homologous pairs (bivalents).

Metaphase I

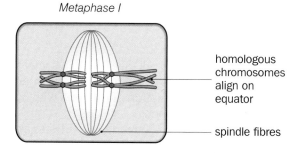
homologous chromosomes align on equator

spindle fibres

Anaphase I

- At anaphase I the ***chromosomes*** in each bivalent separate. Compare this with anaphase of mitosis, when the ***chromatids*** separate.

- As a result of anaphase I, each pole receives only ***one*** of each homologous pair of chromosomes.

- As in mitosis, the contraction of the spindle fibres pulls the homologous chromosomes apart. Each pole receives a ***haploid*** number of chromosomes.

Anaphase I

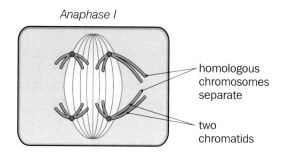
homologous chromosomes separate

two chromatids

Telophase I

- The chromosomes reach the opposite poles of the spindle.
- The nuclear envelope forms around each group of **haploid** chromosomes.
- Usually the chromosomes stay in their condensed form and meiosis II follows on straight away.
- Cytokinesis occurs to produce two haploid cells.

What has happened to the number of chromosomes in each cell at the end of meiosis I?

Telophase I

new nuclear membrane forms

▷ Meiosis II

Prophase II
- The new spindle fibres develop at right angles to the old spindle.

Metaphase II
- The separate chromosomes arrange themselves on the equator of the spindle.
- Each chromosome attaches to a spindle fibre by means of its centromere.

How is this different from the arrangement of chromosomes at metaphase I of meiosis?

Metaphase II

chromosomes align on spindle together

Anaphase II
- The centromeres divide.
- The spindle fibres contract to pull the two chromatids to the poles, centromere first.

How is this different from the events that take place at anaphase I of meiosis?

Anaphase II

chromatids separate and move to opposite poles of spindle

Telophase II
- On reaching the poles, the chromatids lengthen and become indistinct.
- The spindle disappears and the nuclear envelope reforms.
- Cytokinesis takes place, resulting in four haploid cells, each with a different genetic make up.

Can you identify the **two** main ways in which the genetic make up of these cells has been changed.

Try looking back over the events that take place during meiosis on these two pages.

Telophase II

4 haploid cells each with a different genetic make up

▷ Meiosis and genetic variation

There are two main ways in which genetic variation occurs at meiosis.

Random segregation of chromosomes

At metaphase I the pairs of homologous chromosomes arrive at the equator.
They arrange themselves in a random order on the equator.

Look at the diagram.
It shows two cells with just **two** homologous pairs of chromosomes (4n).

What do you think determines whether the blue chromosome or the red chromosome is uppermost?
The answer is that it is down to chance.

The diagram shows that there are **two** ways that a pair of chromosomes can arrange themselves on the equator.

As a result, it is possible to produce **four** different types of gamete.

Our example had just two pairs of chromosomes.
But a human cell contains 23 pairs of chromosomes.

Can you work out how many possible types of gamete could be produced?
The answer is 2^{23} – that's over 8 million different types of gamete!

And during fertilisation **any** male gamete can join with **any** female gamete.
So thousands of millions of new genetic combinations are possible!

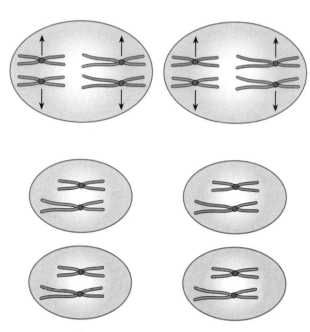

four different types of gamete

Random arrangement of homologous chromosomes at metaphase I of meiosis

Crossing over

During prophase I of meiosis the homologous chromosomes come together in pairs.
Each chromosome is divided into two chromatids.
The homologous chromosomes twist around each other.
This creates a tension, which may cause breaks to occur along the length of the chromatids.

During crossing over, corresponding fragments of chromatid may get swapped over.
This 'cutting and sticking' of chromatids means that genetic material is exchanged.
In this way, new genetic combinations are produced and variation in the gametes is increased.

So, together with random segregation of chromosomes, crossing over can produce an enormous amount of variation, both in the gametes and the resulting offspring.

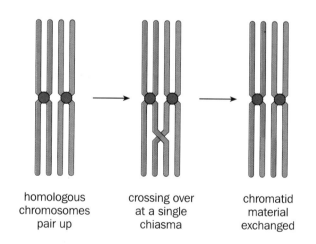

| homologous chromosomes pair up | crossing over at a single chiasma | chromatid material exchanged |

▷ Cell division and DNA

As you have seen, the number of chromosomes can change at different stages of cell division.

The chromosomes are made up of DNA and histone proteins. So it should not be a surprise to you that the DNA content of a cell changes at different stages of mitosis and meiosis.

Look at the diagram.
The normal amount of DNA in this diploid cell is $2x$.

What happens to the amount of DNA just before mitosis?
The amount of DNA doubles (to $4x$) due to replication.

At the end of mitosis I, the DNA content is back to $2x$.
This is because the $4x$ content has been distributed equally between the two daughter cells.

At interphase of meiosis, the DNA content again doubles (to $4x$).
What do you think happens to the DNA content after meiosis I?

The amount of DNA halves because each homologous chromosome separates into each daughter cell.

What do you think happens after meiosis II?

The DNA content of the cell is now down to $1x$.
This is because the chromatids have separated, effectively halving the DNA content.

After fertilisation the DNA content is back to $2x$,
because the haploid gametes (each $1x$) have joined together.

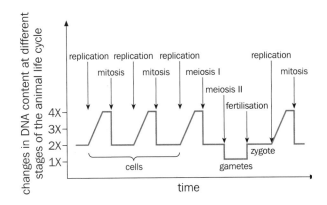

▷ Differences between mitosis and meiosis

The differences between mitosis and meiosis can be summarised in the form of a table.

Mitosis	Meiosis
one division	two divisions
the number of chromosomes remains the same	the number of chromosomes is halved
homologous chromosomes do not pair up	homologous chromosomes pair up to form bivalents
chiasmata do not form and crossing over never occurs	chiasmata form and crossing over occurs
daughter cells are genetically identical	daughter cells are genetically different from the parent cells
two daughter cells are formed	four daughter cells are formed

▷ Biology at work: The biology of cancer

Cancer is the second most common cause of death in the western world (after heart disease). It is, however, not one single disease but a group of diseases, all resulting from uncontrolled mitotic cell division.

There are over 100 different forms of cancer and it affects more than one in four of the UK population at some time in their lives. The likelihood of developing cancer increases with age, with the risk roughly doubling with each decade beyond the age of 30.

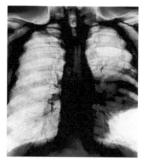

X-ray of human chest showing cancer of the lung

Cell division is controlled by genes, and normally stops when enough cells have been made to perform a particular task. If these genes undergo **mutation**, they form **oncogenes**. Cell division runs out of control and the cells simply continue to divide. This results in the development of a tumour, which is a group of abnormal cells that divide more rapidly than the normal surrounding cells.

Tumour cells usually lack differentiation. This means that they do not carry out the specialised function of the cells in their host tissue. They interfere with the normal activity of these cells, for example restricting the blood flow to them.

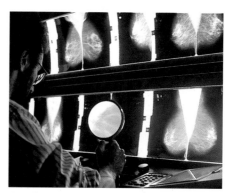

Human lung tissue (pink) invaded by a malignant tumour (blue)

At this point a small tumour may not be producing any noticeable symptoms, but cancerous cells may be breaking free and may be transported around the body in the bloodstream. If this happens then secondary tumours (called **metastases**) may develop in a variety of other body tissues.

Tumours that behave in this way are called **malignant**. Some tumours remain inactive and are relatively harmless. These inactive growths are called **benign** tumours.

A radiographer studying mammograms

What factors cause the mutation of genes to form oncogenes, and what treatment can be given to cancer patients?

Although mutations occur spontaneously, smoking and excessive exposure to strong sunlight are two activities known to increase the likelihood of mutation. There is also a range of **carcinogenic** (cancer causing) agents to which you could be exposed, for example asbestos, ionising radiation and benzene.

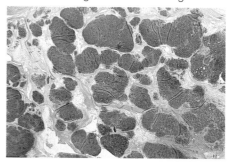

Primary tumours may be treatable by surgical removal, and this is often combined with radiotherapy and/or chemotherapy. These treatments use ionising radiation and drugs to inhibit the cell division of the tumour. However, they can have unpleasant side effects owing to their effect on other tissues.

▷ Biology at work: Cancer by infection

As you know the genes that cause cancer are called **oncogenes**.
These are the mutated forms of the genes that normally regulate cell division.
The rate of mutation can be increased by a number of factors,
for example a virus infection.
Viruses usually carry oncogenes or regulatory genes that can become oncogenes.
An example of one such virus is the **Human Papillomavirus (HPV)**,
a serious form of which is responsible for cervical cancer.

Cervical cancer

Cervical cancer is one of the most common forms of disease in women.
A successful screening programme in Britain has led to a decline in
the number of women dying from cervical cancer.
Originally, the disease was thought to be caused by a sexually transmitted infection.
A small sub-group of 'high risk' viruses known as HPV16 need to be present
before cervical cancer will develop.
The specific gene sequence is known for this virus, as are the identities of
the two oncogenes labelled E6 and E7. It seems likely that the development
of the cancer starts when these two oncogenes bind to the proteins known to
control cell division in cervical epithelial cells.

Screening

The early stages of cervical cancer occur in surface cells.
This has two useful implications, which have aided the development of
an effective screening programme.

- Cervical cells can be scraped off during a **smear test** and later
  identified under a microscope.

- As the cancer remains superficial, it is possible to remove it using
  a simple surgical technique.

Smear test cells are classified according to their appearance.
These can range from 'normal' to 'invasive cancer'.
If necessary, this diagnosis is later confirmed by taking
a small tissue sample or **biopsy**.

Regular repetition of the screening reduces the incidence of false negatives.
Up to 15% of pre-cancerous cells can be missed in the initial smear.

Treatment

In its early stages, cancerous tissue can be destroyed with heat, by using
laser treatment, or by the technique of cryosurgery, which uses extreme cold.
More advanced cases, where the cancer has spread to the organs of the pelvis,
usually require radiotherapy.

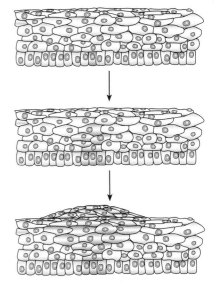

The establishment of an HPV requires the infection of a basal stem cell

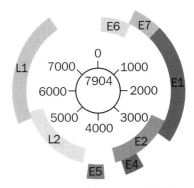

The genetic organisation of HPV16. Each segment represents a gene. The red genes E6 and E7 encode proteins with oncogenic potential

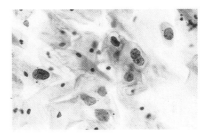

Cervical biopsy reveals pre-cancerous cells are present

Summary

- There are two types of cell division: mitosis and meiosis.
- Mitosis occurs during growth and repair of cells and during asexual reproduction.
- The daughter cells produced at mitosis are genetically identical to the parent cell.
- At interphase, the DNA content of the nucleus doubles.
- The main stages of mitosis are prophase, metaphase, anaphase and telophase.
- Meiosis occurs during the formation of gametes (and spores in plants like mosses and ferns).
- During meiosis, four haploid cells are produced, each being genetically different.
- It is important that gametes are haploid so that at fertilisation a diploid zygote is formed.
- During meiosis, chromosomes come together in homologous pairs.
- Meiosis has two divisions and exchange of chromosome material results in variation.
- Cancers can develop from the uncontrolled division of cells.

▷ Questions

1 a) Copy and complete the table to show which processes take place during mitosis and which take place during the first division of meiosis.
Use a tick (✓) if you think that the process does occur and a cross (✗) if you think that it does not.

Process	Mitosis	First division of meiosis
homologous		
chromosomes pair		
crossing-over		
chromatids separate		

b) Why do you think that mitosis is a suitable type of cell division for repairing tissues but meiosis is not?

2 a) Explain why root tips are suitable material to show stages in mitosis.
b) When preparing root tips to show stages in mitosis, why is it important to:
   i) stain the tissue,
   ii) pull the tissue apart with a needle and gently apply pressure to the cover slip?
c) Look at the drawing showing a cell undergoing mitosis.

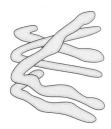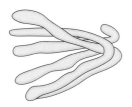

   i) Which stage of mitosis is shown in the drawing?
   ii) Using evidence visible in the drawing, give one reason why this cell is not in the first division of meiosis.

3 a) Make a table to show the differences between mitosis and meiosis.
b) Explain the advantages and disadvantages for organisms in which meiosis takes place during the life cycle, compared with those that only reproduce by mitosis.

4 a) Explain two ways in which meiosis contributes to genetic variation.
b) The bar chart shows the amount of DNA present in one cell of an organism at different stages of mitosis.

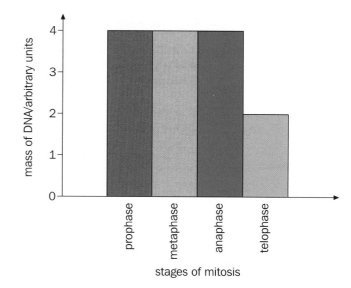

How many units of DNA would you expect to be present in one cell of this organism
   i) during the first division of meiosis,
   ii) in one of the gametes formed as a result of meiosis?

5 The diagrams show stages in cell division in an organism.

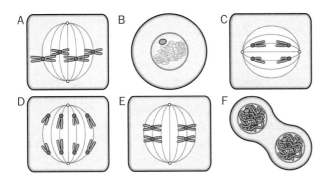

a) Match the letter of each diagram A to F with the correct description of each of the stages below. (You may use each letter once, more than once, or not at all.)
   i) metaphase of mitosis,
   ii) anaphase II of meiosis,
   iii) cell normally increases in size,
   iv) DNA replicates,
   v) bivalents become arranged at equator,
b) What is the main significance of mitosis in the growth of organisms?
c) Explain two ways in which meiosis contributes to genetic variation.

6 The diagram shows meiosis in an animal cell.

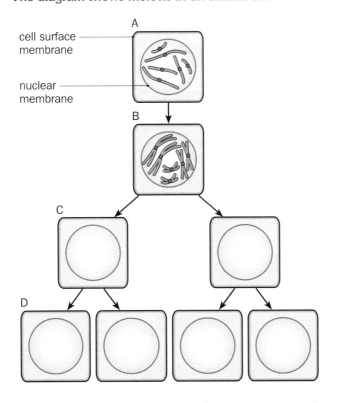

a) What is the diploid number of chromosomes in this cell?

b) Where do you think this cell could be found in an animal?
c) What is the stage of cell division shown at B? Give a reason for your choice.
d) Copy and complete the cells at C and D, drawing in the chromosomes that could be found in them.

7 The diagram shows the quantity of DNA, measured in arbitrary units, during several cell divisions in animal tissue.

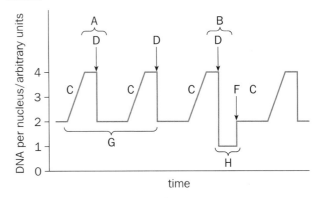

a) Name the type of cell division occurring at A and B. Give reasons for your answer.
b) What do you think is occurring at the points marked C, D, E and F?
c) What type of cell is produced at G and H?

8 The diagram shows four animal cells at different stages of mitosis.

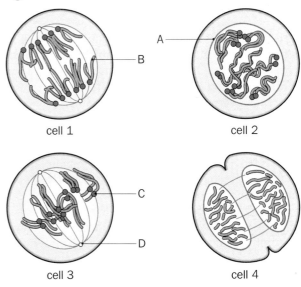

a) Name the structures labelled A, B, C and D.
b) i) Name the stages of division shown by cells 1 and 3.
   ii) Use the number of each cell to arrange the stages in the correct sequence in mitosis.
c) How does mitosis maintain genetic stability in an organism?

8 Reproduction

The human embryo starts its life sexually neutral.
As it grows it develops into either a male or a female.
Male embryos have an X and a Y chromosome.
A gene on the Y chromosome codes for the production of
factor SRY, which stimulates the development of the testes,
so the embryo develops into a boy.
Female embryos have two X chromosomes and so
do not have the gene that codes for SRY.

Until recently it was thought that this was the only genetic
factor that determined the sex of the embryo.
However, recent research has found another gene that is
thought to code for a protein that stimulates the
development of female characteristics.
This gene has been named *Wnt-4* and it is hoped that further
research may give more insight into the problems of infertility
that some women experience.

▷ Sexual reproduction

Animals have diploid body cells and haploid sex cells, or **gametes**.
Body cells with the full chromosome number are made by mitosis.
Haploid gametes with half the chromosome number are made by meiosis.
At fertilisation a haploid sperm fuses with a haploid egg to produce
a diploid fertilised egg. This then divides many times by mitosis to
eventually grow into a new individual.

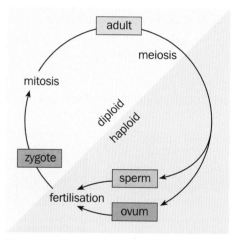

The life cycle of most animals

In flowering plants, there are two distinct phases of the life cycle:
the diploid **sporophyte** and the haploid **gametophyte**.
The diploid sporophyte produces haploid **spores** by *meiosis*
(the diploid chromosome number is halved).
The spores develop into the haploid gametophyte, which then
produces haploid gametes by *mitosis* (the chromosome number
stays the same).

In plants such as mosses and ferns, the main plant is the diploid sporophyte.
It produces haploid spores by meiosis, which are genetically different.
A spore grows into the gametophyte, which produces haploid gametes
by mitosis. These gametes will be genetically identical.
What has happened in flowering plants is that the water-dependent
gametophyte stage in the life cycle has become much reduced.
The dominant stage in the life cycle is the sporophyte.

Sexual reproduction in flowering plants and in animals results in
offspring that show **variation**. This is the result of:

- random segregation of chromosomes at metaphase I of meiosis,
- crossing over during prophase I of meiosis,
- random fertilisation of gametes,
- random mating between organisms of the same species.

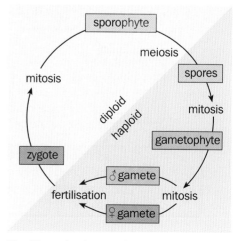

The life cycle of most plants

▷ Flower structure

Most adult flowering plants are diploid.
Meiosis occurs within their reproductive tissues to make haploid spores.
The male spores are the **pollen grains**, which are made in the anther.
A pollen grain has a tough wall around it that is resistant to desiccation.
So pollen grains can be transferred from one flower to another without drying out.
At pollination, each pollen grain produces two male gametes by mitosis.
The female spores are the **ovules**, which are made in the ovary.
The female gamete, or **egg nucleus**, develops inside an ovule.
Can you identify the sporophyte and gametophyte phases of development?

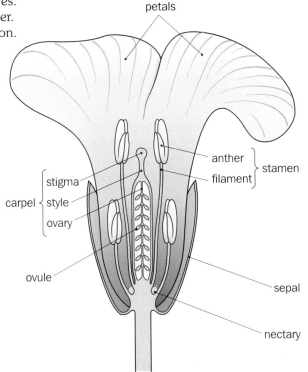

Flowers vary in structure depending on their method of pollination.
Basically though, each flower consists of fours sets of modified leaves.
The **sepals**, **petals**, **stamens** and **carpels** are attached to the swollen end of the stem, called the **receptacle**.

- The sepals are the outermost ring of structures.
  They are usually green and leaf-like and their main function is to protect the flower when it is in bud.
  Sometimes, the sepals are coloured and indistinguishable from the petals, as in tulips and lilies.

- Inside the sepals is a ring of colourful petals called the **corolla**.
  Petals of insect-pollinated flowers usually have scent and make **nectar** in order to attract insects.

- Immediately inside the petals are the male parts of the flower, called the stamens.
  Each stamen consists of an **anther** attached to the receptacle by a long stalk called a **filament**.
  The pollen is made inside the anther in four pollen sacs by a process involving meiosis.
  The pollen sacs eventually split to release the pollen.

- In the centre of the flower are one or more carpels.
  These are the female parts of the flower containing the ovules.
  Each carpel is made up of a **stigma** connected to the **ovary** by a long **style**.
  The ovules are made inside the ovary and contain an egg cell formed by a process involving meiosis.
  After fertilisation, the ovules eventually form the **seeds**.

Insect pollination in the foxglove

The design of any flower is related to its method of pollination.
Insect-pollinated flowers have colourful petals.
They are scented and they have nectar, to attract insects.
Flowers that are pollinated by the wind do not need any of these.
Thus, wind-pollinated flowers, such as grasses, tend to be dull and have no scent. They often dispense with petals altogether, so that the anthers and stigmas are exposed to the wind.

Insect-pollinated flowers have:	Wind-pollinated flowers have:
• colourful, scented petals and nectar to attract insects	• anthers hanging outside the flower to catch the wind
• anthers and stigmas inside the flower for insects to rub against	• large, feathery stigmas which catch pollen grains in the air
• small amounts of sticky pollen that can easily stick to insect's bodies	• lots of smooth, light pollen that can easily be blown by the wind

▷ Pollination

Pollination is the transfer of pollen grains from the anther to a stigma of a plant of the same species.
Self-pollination occurs when pollen is transferred from the anther to a stigma of the same flower or to a different flower but on the same plant.
Cross-pollination occurs when pollen is transferred to a stigma of *another* plant of the same species.
Cross-pollination may be carried out by insects or by the wind, and flowers can become highly adapted to either mechanism.

When an anther is ripe, it splits open along its length and opens out. This process is called **dehiscence** and it releases the pollen so that pollination can occur.

Pollination is needed in order to bring the two male gametes (inside a pollen grain) near to the female gamete so that fertilisation can occur.

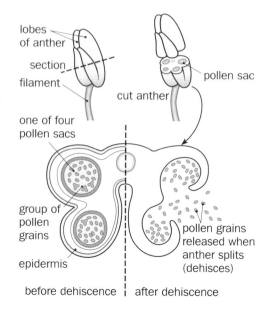

Insect pollination

Look at the diagram of the white deadnettle (*Lamium album*).
You can see a number of adaptations for insect pollination.
The deadnettle is pollinated by bees, which land on the lower lip of the corolla tube.
Bees have long tongues and are able to reach the nectaries at the base of the corolla tube.
The bees feed upon the sugary nectar made in the nectaries.
The anthers are positioned in such a way that sticky pollen from them will brush against the bee's back as it pushes its head down the corolla tube.
When the bee enters another flower, it brushes some of the pollen against the ripe stigma and cross-pollination is achieved.
In the white deadnettle, the anthers ripen before the stigma, a condition known as **protandry**.
The tip of the stigma opens to expose the receptive surface some time after the anthers have released their pollen.
This prevents the bee from accidentally self-pollinating the flower.
Lots of separate deadnettle flowers are clustered together to form a more conspicuous **inflorescence**, which is easier for bees to see.

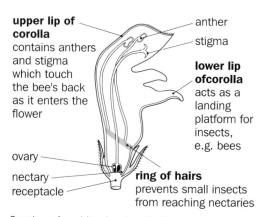

Section of a white dead nettle flower

Wind pollination

Grasses and cereals are all pollinated by the wind.
Rye grass (*Lolium perenne*) has many features typical of a wind-pollinated flower.
The flowers are small, green and inconspicuous compared with an insect-pollinated flower.
They have no scent and no nectar.
The anthers hang outside the flower so the wind can blow away the large quantities of small, smooth and light pollen that they produce.
The feathery stigmas are also positioned outside the flower.
They act like a net, providing a large surface-area for catching pollen grains that get blown into them.

Wind-pollination can waste a lot of pollen, which is why the anthers produce so much.
But the fact that plants such as grasses and cereals grow in close proximity to one another means that cross-pollination is more likely to occur.

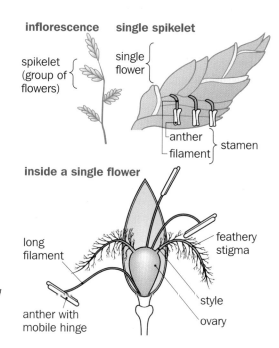

Mechanisms to ensure cross-pollination

Self-pollination can be an advantage to plants that are scattered over a wide area.
However, it is a form of inbreeding that can reduce the amount of variation in the population and its potential for evolutionary change.
Also, any undesirable recessive characteristics will tend to persist in the population.
Cross-pollination is less reliable than self-pollination but results in far greater genetic variation in a population (outbreeding).
It is not surprising that mechanisms have evolved that are designed to make cross-pollination more likely.

Self-pollination will not occur if the anthers and the stigma of a flower mature at different times.
As you saw in the white deadnettle, **protandry** is the condition where the anthers ripen before the stigma is able to receive pollen.
Protogyny is the condition where the stigma matures before the anthers, as in the bluebell.

A **dioecious** species is one in which individual plants either have all male flowers or all female flowers.
Clearly, self-pollination is impossible in these species.
Willow is an example of a dioecious plant but in general the number of completely dioecious species is few.

White dead nettle flowers are protandrous: the anthers ripen before the stigma

▷ **Fertilisation**

In flowering plants the female gamete is protected within the ovary.
The only way that the male gamete can reach it is by means of a **pollen tube**.

If a pollen grain lands on the stigma of a plant of the same species, it absorbs water, swells and splits open.
The germinating pollen grain grows a pollen tube down the style.
It is thought to grow in response to chemicals secreted by the ovary.
At the tip of the pollen tube are three nuclei.
The **tube nucleus** precedes the other two and controls the growth of the pollen tube.
Behind the tube nucleus are two haploid **male gametes,**
which have originated from the division of a generative nucleus.

SEM of pollen grains germinating on a stigma

The pollen tube secretes enzymes as it grows, digesting its way through the loosely packed cells of the style.
When it reaches the ovary, it enters an ovule through the **micropyle**.
The tube nucleus disintegrates and the tip of the pollen tube bursts.
The two male gametes are released into the **embryo sac**.
One male gamete fuses with the egg nucleus to form a diploid **zygote**.
The other male gamete fuses with the diploid nucleus at the centre of the embryo sac to form a triploid **endosperm nucleus**.
So a **double fertilisation** occurs, a process that only occurs in flowering plants.

The ovule forms the seed and the endosperm nucleus forms the food store inside the seed.
The zygote eventually develops into an embryo and grows into a new plant.
The ovary wall forms the fruit but the other floral structures wither.

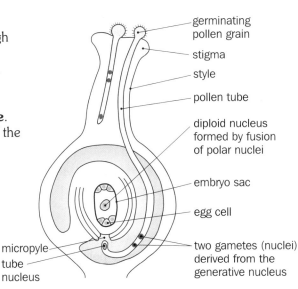

germinating pollen grain
stigma
style
pollen tube
diploid nucleus formed by fusion of polar nuclei
embryo sac
egg cell
micropyle
tube nucleus
two gametes (nuclei) derived from the generative nucleus

131

▷ Human male reproductive system

The organs that are responsible for producing gametes are called the **gonads**.
In male mammals, the gonads are the **testes** (singular **testis**).
The testes produce the male gametes, the **spermatozoa** (sperm).
The male hormone **testosterone** is also made in the testes.

The testes develop inside the abdomen and descend into a sac of skin called the **scrotum** just before birth.
The temperature in the scrotum is about 3 °C cooler than the temperature within the body, giving the optimum conditions for sperm production.

Each testis is an oval structure, about 5 cm long.
Each testis is divided up into many compartments called **lobules**.
Each lobule contains a number of tightly coiled tubes called **seminiferous tubules**.
The seminiferous tubules are lined by the **germinal epithelium**, which is made up of cells called **spermatogonia**.
The spermatogonia are the cells that divide to form the sperm.
The seminiferous tubules merge together to form a network of tiny tubes called the **vasa efferentia**, which in turn join up to form a 6 metre long coiled tube lying just outside each testis, called the **epididymis**.
The epididymis empties into the **vas deferens**, a tube which carries the sperm out of the testis to the **urethra**.
Sperm is stored in both the epididymis and the vas deferens.

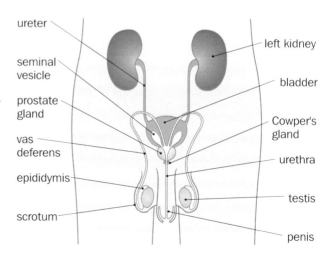

Male reproductive system

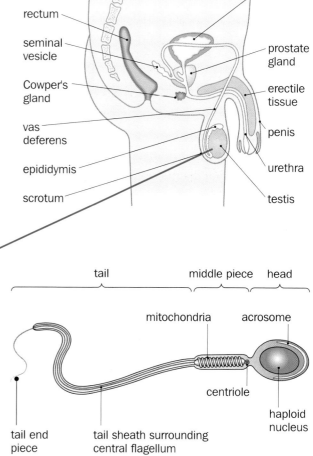

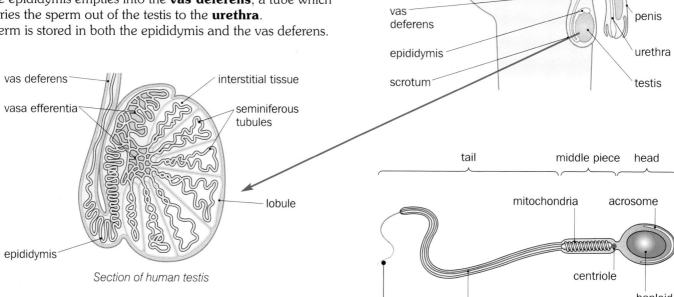

Section of human testis

A human sperm

A number of glands also have ducts joining the urethra.
The **seminal vesicles**, **Cowper's glands** and the **prostate gland** secrete fluids that nourish the sperm and make it alkaline.
This neutralises any acidic urine present in the urethra and combats the acid environment in the vagina, which is hostile to sperm.
The resulting mixture of sperm and these secretions is called **semen**.
The semen passes along the urethra and out of the penis during copulation.

The mature sperm is about 60 μm in length and well adapted to swimming to the egg. The mitochondria provide the energy from respiration to keep the tail beating. The acrosome contains proteases to digest a pathway through to the egg cell and deliver the haploid sperm nucleus.

▷ Human female reproductive system

In female mammals, the gonads are called the **ovaries**.
They produce the female gametes called **ova** or **eggs**.
The ovaries also make female hormones.

Each ovary is an oval structure about 4 cm long, attached
to the abdominal cavity by ligaments.
Eggs are formed from the **germinal epithelium** on the
outside of the ovary, which is made up of actively dividing
cells called **oogonia**.

Close to each ovary is an **oviduct** or **Fallopian tube**.
The funnel-like opening of this tube has a fringe of
finger-like **fimbriae**. This feathery fringe is lined with cilia,
which collect the **secondary oocytes** (which form the eggs)
when they are released from the ovary.

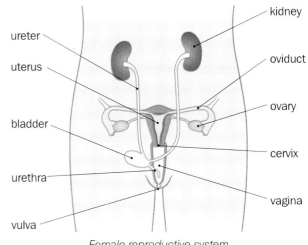

Female reproductive system

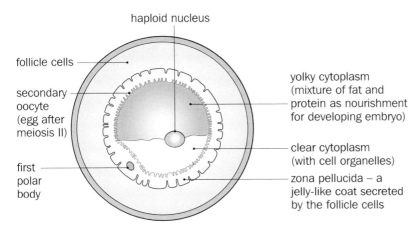

A human secondary oocyte (diameter approximately 120 μm)

The oviducts are two muscular tubes lined with cilia.
The egg is swept along the oviduct by a combination of
ciliary action and muscular contractions of the wall.
The oviducts open into the **uterus** or womb.
This is pear-shaped and is about 5 cm wide and 8 cm long.
Most of the uterus wall is composed of smooth muscle,
called the **myometrium**.
The lining of the womb is called the **endometrium**.
It is well supplied with blood and is the part of the womb into
which the embryo implants during pregnancy and which is
shed during **menstruation**.

The uterus opens into the **vagina** through a ring of muscle
called the **cervix**.
The vagina is a muscular tube, which opens to the outside
through the **vulva**.
The vulva consists of two outer folds of skin, the **labia majora**,
which surround two inner, more delicate folds, the **labia minora**.
Enclosed within the labia is a small body of erectile tissue
called the **clitoris**.
This is equivalent to the penis in a male. It is sensitive and swells
with blood when sexually stimulated.

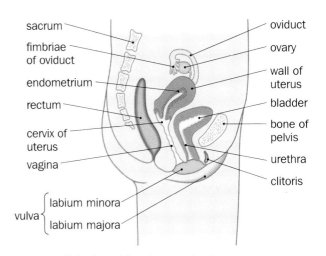

Side view of female reproductive system

▷ Gametogenesis

Gametogenesis is the term given to the production of gametes in the gonads.
Spermatogenesis is the formation of sperm in the testis
and **oogenesis** is the formation of eggs in the ovary.
Both of these processes involve meiosis to produce haploid gametes.
It is important that the gametes are haploid so that at fertilisation the normal
diploid number is re-established.

Spermatogenesis

Spermatogenesis is the process by which sperm are produced in
the seminiferous tubules.
The diploid spermatogonia in the germinal epithelium divide
many times by mitosis to produce **primary spermatocytes**.
These then undergo meiosis to form haploid **secondary
spermatocytes**.
The secondary spermatocytes develop into **spermatids**, which
eventually form mature sperm in the space inside the
seminiferous tubule.

In the wall of the seminiferous tubule there are large **Sertoli cells**.
These secrete a fluid, which nourishes the spermatids and
protects them from the immune system of the male as they
mature into sperm.

Around each seminiferous tubule are groups of **interstitial cells**.
Their function is to secrete **testosterone**, the male sex hormone.
Testosterone controls the development of secondary sexual
characteristics in a male at puberty.
The hormone is also important in stimulating the cells of the
seminiferous tubule, particularly Sertoli cells, during spermatogenesis.

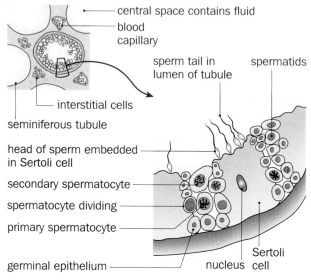

Stages in the development of human sperm

Oogenesis

Oogenesis is the process by which eggs are produced in the ovary.
The process starts in the fetus when the oogonia lining the
germinal epithelium divide to form **primary oocytes**.
The germinal epithelium also divides to form **follicle cells**,
which surround the primary oocytes forming **primary follicles**.
So at birth, a baby girl will already have about a million primary
follicles. The primary oocytes will have started to divide by
meiosis, but the process stops at prophase I.

At puberty, hormones produced by the pituitary stimulate
the follicles to develop further.
Each month, several follicles start to develop but usually only
one matures into a fully developed **Graafian follicle**.

First the primary oocyte completes its meiotic division to form
a **secondary oocyte** and a small **polar body**.
The follicle cells around the secondary oocyte grow and
a number of fluid-filled spaces form.
The mature Graafian follicle migrates to the surface of the ovary.
Eventually the follicle bursts and the secondary oocyte surrounded
by some follicle cells is released, a process known as **ovulation**.
The second division of meiosis to form a mature ovum will only
occur if a sperm penetrates the secondary oocyte.
After ovulation, the remaining follicle cells develop into the **corpus luteum**.
The corpus luteum is important in secreting the hormone **progesterone**.

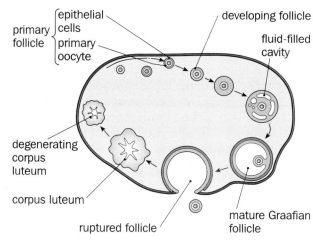

Development of a follicle in the human ovary

▷ The menstrual cycle

Human females usually produce one mature egg each month, from the start of puberty (around 12–14 years).
The menstrual cycle lasts about 28 days and is controlled by hormones.
It involves the production and release of an egg (**ovulation**) and the preparation of the uterus to receive the egg if it becomes fertilised (**implantation**).

Menstruation is usually taken as being the start of the cycle.
This is the breakdown of the lining of the uterus (the endometrium) and the release of blood and cells through the vagina.

The events of the menstrual cycle and its hormonal control can be summarised as follows:

- The anterior pituitary gland in the brain secretes **follicle stimulating hormone** (**FSH**).
  This is carried in the blood to the ovary, where it stimulates the development of one or more Graafian follicles.

- As the follicle matures, it starts to produce the hormone **oestrogen**.
  Oestrogen has two main effects.
  First, it causes the repair and thickening of the endometrium.
  Secondly, it inhibits the production of FSH by the anterior pituitary gland, preventing further follicles from ripening and causing it to secrete a second hormone, **luteinising hormone** (**LH**).

- The surge of LH into the bloodstream occurs on about day 12.
  This triggers ovulation, which is the release of a secondary oocyte from the Graafian follicle when it bursts, about 14 days into the cycle.
  LH also stimulates the remaining follicle cells in the ovary to form the corpus luteum.
  The corpus luteum secretes the hormone **progesterone**.
  The corpus luteum and the ovary still secrete a reduced amount of oestrogen.

- Progesterone, along with oestrogen, inhibits the production of both FSH and LH by the anterior pituitary, an example of negative feedback.
  Progesterone and oestrogen stimulate the further growth and blood supply of the endometrium.

- If a pregnancy occurs, the corpus luteum is stimulated by hormones released by the developing embryo.
  Progesterone and oestrogen levels remain high, the womb lining stays intact and FSH production is still inhibited.
  If there is no pregnancy, then the corpus luteum starts to degenerate and the levels of progesterone and oestrogen fall.
  FSH is no longer inhibited and starts to be secreted by the pituitary.
  The endometrium breaks down, resulting in menstruation, and the cycle starts again.

Why is it important that FSH is inhibited if a pregnancy occurs?
What are the two effects of the reduction in the secretion of oestrogen and progesterone by the corpus luteum?
Why is it important that the endometrium is at its thickest at the time of ovulation?

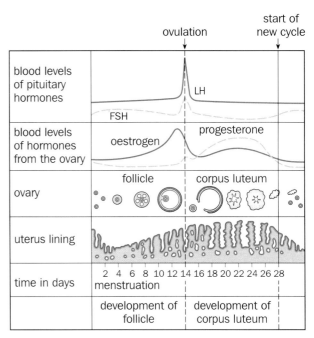

Changes occurring during the human menstrual cycle

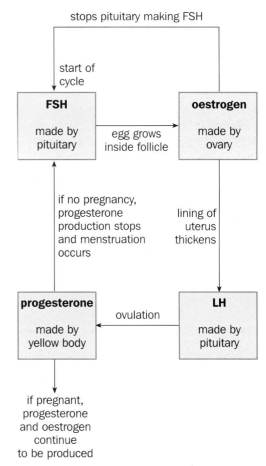

Hormonal control of ovulation and menstruation

▷ Fertilisation

In order that fertilisation can take place, the sperm has to travel from the seminiferous tubule of the male to the oviduct of the female.
The sperms are stored in the epididymis on the outside of each testis.
Here they are mixed with secretions that make them active.
They are moved by muscular contractions of the epididymis into the vas deferens.
As we have mentioned, other secretions from the seminal vesicles, Cowper's glands and the prostate gland are added to the sperm to eventually form semen.

Sexual arousal results in the penis of the male becoming erect.
This is the result of an increase in the blood supply to the spongy tissue of the penis.
In this condition the penis can be inserted into the female's vagina.
Sexual stimulation may eventually result in waves of intense pleasure for both partners, known as **orgasm**.
In the male, the semen is forced out of the penis by powerful contractions of the urethra. This is called **ejaculation**.
About 2–6 cm^3 of semen is ejaculated into the vagina of the female during copulation.

The sperm are deposited at the top of the vagina near the cervix. From here they use their tails to swim through the cervix and up through the uterus to the oviducts.
The sperm can remain viable for up to 2 days.
The alkaline semen helps to neutralise the acid fluid in the vagina and uterus.
The semen also contains hormones called **prostaglandins**, which stimulate the uterus and oviducts to contract and assist the sperm on their journey.
However, of the millions of sperm in one ejaculation, only a few hundred will complete the journey to the oviducts.

If ovulation has recently occurred, then there will be a secondary oocyte in the oviduct. This can remain viable for up to 24 hours.
The secondary oocyte is surrounded by the follicle cells and a clear membrane called the **zona pellucida**.
Proteases released from the acrosomes of a number of sperm digest a pathway through the follicle cells and the zona pellucida.
Eventually one sperm succeeds in passing through the outer layers and penetrating the cell surface membrane of the secondary oocyte.

Instantly the zona pellucida thickens and separates from the surface of the secondary oocyte.
It forms a barrier impenetrable to other sperm.
At the same instant, the secondary oocyte undergoes its second meiotic division to form the mature egg.
The male nucleus of the sperm fuses with the egg nucleus, producing a diploid **zygote** or fertilised egg, which will develop into the embryo and then into a fetus.

SEM of human sperms (× 2000)

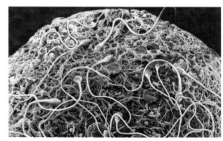

SEM of sperms on the surface of a secondary oocyte (× 1300)

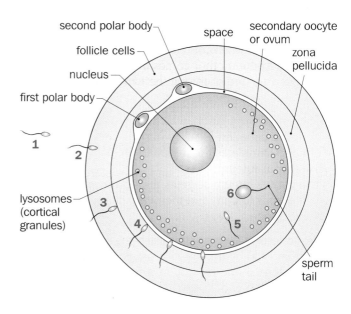

1 sperm approaches secondary oocyte

2 acrosome reaction releases enzymes that digest a pathway through to secondary oocyte

3 a second acrosomal enzyme digests a pathway through the zona pellucida

4 the membrane of the sperm head fuses with the membrane of the oocyte. The lysosomes release enzymes into the secondary oocyte. These enzymes cause the zona to thicken and separate from the oocyte. The zona now forms a barrier to the passage of any other sperms

5 only one sperm enters the oocyte. The nucleus of the secondary oocyte undergoes meiosis II and forms an ovum and a secondary polar body

6 the male nucleus fuses with the female nucleus to form a diploid zygote. This is fertilisation

136

▷ Implantation

After fertilisation, the zygote starts to divide by mitosis, forming a
ball of cells called the **blastocyst**.
It takes the blastocyst 3 days to reach the uterus.
The outer layer of cells of the blastocyst is known as the **trophoblast**.
This is able to embed in the endometrium, a process called **implantation**.

The trophoblast develops into two membranes – the **chorion** and the **amnion**.
The chorion grows a number of finger-like processes called **chorionic villi,**
which increase the surface-area for the absorption of nutrients from the uterine wall.
The chorion also secretes **human chorionic gonadotrophin** (**HCG**),
which prevents the degeneration of the corpus luteum.
Detection of this hormone in the urine is the basis of most pregnancy tests.

The chorionic villi eventually form part of the **placenta**, which is attached
to the fetus by the **umbilical cord**.
The amnion forms a complete sac around the developing fetus enclosing
amniotic fluid. This acts as a shock absorber, protecting the fetus from damage,
keeps its skin moist, provides room for movement, and acts as a heat buffer.

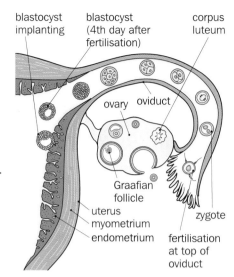

▷ The placenta

The placenta is a plate-like structure formed from the tissues
of both the mother and the fetus.
The chorionic villi project into blood filled spaces within the
endometrium of the mother's uterus.
The blood of the mother comes into close association
with that of the fetus without the two actually mixing.
This is important since the fetus is genetically different from the mother;
an immune response could be produced if the placental barrier were breached.
In addition, the relatively higher blood pressure of the mother's blood
could damage the delicate blood vessels of the fetus.

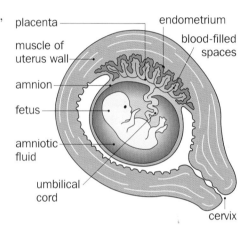

Section of the uterus to show fetus and placenta

The fact that the fetal blood and the maternal blood come
into such close contact means that rapid and efficient exchange of
materials can take place along diffusion gradients between the two.
The functions of the placenta include:

- The transfer of oxygen and soluble food, such as amino
  acids and glucose, from the mother to nourish the fetus.

- The transfer of carbon dioxide and nitrogenous waste
  products from the fetus to the mother so that they can
  be excreted by the mother.

- To act as a molecular filter to prevent toxins and
  disease-causing microbes getting into the fetal blood.
  Unfortunately viruses such as *Rubella* and HIV are
  able to cross the placenta and can damage the fetus.
  Toxic materials such as alcohol and nicotine are also
  potentially damaging.

- Some antibodies can pass from the mother to the fetus
  and provide immunity to certain diseases. This is called
  passive natural immunity since the antibodies are
  not actually produced by the fetus itself.

- The placenta must take over, from the corpus luteum,
  the role of secreting progesterone, which prevents
  ovulation and menstruation from occurring.

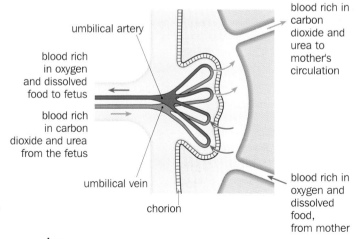

key
← diffusion pathway of oxygen and dissolved food
← diffusion pathway of carbon dioxide and urea

Diffusion pathways across the human placenta

137

▷ Birth

In humans, birth (or parturition) takes place about 40 weeks after conception. During the later stages of this development (gestation), the fetus normally moves to a position facing downwards inside the uterus, with its head just above the cervix.

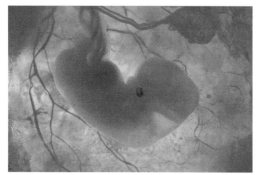
Human embryo at 7 weeks

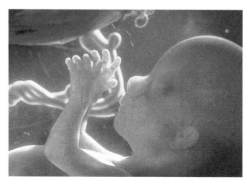
Human fetus at four months

The placenta continues to produce progesterone and oestrogen during pregnancy.
The level of progesterone production rises steadily until just before birth, when it falls dramatically.
This makes the myometrium increasingly sensitive to **oxytocin**.
Oxytocin is a hormone released by the posterior pituitary gland.
Together with prostaglandins secreted by the placenta, oxytocin stimulates the smooth muscle of the myometrium to contract.
The pressure on the muscle in the uterine wall and on the cervix stimulates more oxytocin to be released (this is a rare example of **positive feedback**).
As a result, the contractions increase in force and frequency during labour.

The contractions eventually force the fetus through the cervix and out through the vagina.
Continued contractions result in the placenta becoming detached from the uterus wall and being expelled as the 'afterbirth', along with the umbilical cord.

▷ Lactation

Lactation is the production of milk by the breasts.
The **mammary glands** develop during puberty under the influence of the sex hormones.
Each mammary gland is composed mainly of fat and contains a number of **lactiferous glands** that secrete milk.
Progesterone and oestrogen from the placenta stimulate the development of these glands during pregnancy.

At birth, the loss of the placenta stimulates an increase in the secretion of **prolactin** by the anterior pituitary.
Prolactin is a hormone that causes the lactiferous glands to secrete milk, which is then stored in the lactiferous ducts.
The baby sucking on the nipple initiates a reflex that results in the release of oxytocin, which stimulates the release of milk from the lactiferous ducts.
So the hormone prolactin stimulates the production of milk in the breasts and the hormone oxytocin stimulates the release of the milk in response to suckling.

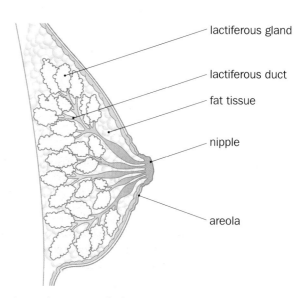
Internal structure of a human mammary gland

lactiferous gland

lactiferous duct

fat tissue

nipple

areola

▷ Biology at work: Human sub-fertility

One in six couples in the UK seek specialist help during their reproductive lives because of difficulty in getting pregnant.

Infertility is the complete inability to conceive a child and is very rare. Much research has focused on the causes of and treatments for **sub-fertility.** This is defined as difficulty in conceiving naturally for reasons affecting the man, woman, or both partners.

Many reproductive technology procedures are surrounded by considerable moral and ethical controversy.

Treatment centres are subject to regulation by the government 'watchdog', the Human Fertilisation and Embryology Authority (HFEA).

Causes of infertility

● **Ovulation failure** – the greatest cause of female infertility, usually associated with absence of, or irregular, menstrual periods. It can be caused by a failure in the feedback loop of the hormonal interactions between the hypothalamus, pituitary and ovaries.

● **Blockage of the Fallopian tubes** – any blockage in the passage of the egg from the ruptured follicle to the site of fertilisation in the Fallopian tubes will cause infertility.

● **Endometriosis** – a condition where small pieces of the endometrium are found outside the uterus attached to the ovaries. During menstruation these bleed, causing pain and infertility.

● **Mucus defects** – mucus that does not thin under the influence of oestrogen at ovulation may prevent sperm penetration or contain anti-sperm antibodies.

● **Polycystic ovary disease (PCOD)** is another common cause of ovulation failure caused by abnormal levels of male androgens

Treatments

● **Ovulation failure** – 95% of cases are treatable with the use of the anti-oestrogen drug **clomiphene citrate.** This mimics the action of oestrogen and is taken in preference to oestrogen by the brain.

● **Blockage of the Fallopian tubes** – microsurgery is often used to remedy the problem. If not then assisted reproduction methods will be required.

● **In-vitro fertilisation (IVF)** – male and female gametes are mixed in a glass petri dish in such conditions that fertilisation can occur. It is a complex and demanding treatment made up of several stages. The success rate as measured by the number of live births per treatment cycle is about 13% and rising.

● **Gamete intra-Fallopian transfer (GIFT)** – involves oocyte collection and immediate replacement into the Fallopian tube together with 2–300 000 sperm. It is less successful than IVF but simpler and cheaper.

● **Micromanipulation of individual sperm and oocytes** – The outer coat of the oocyte is difficult for sperm to penetrate, owing to their poor motility and structure. These outer cells can be easily dissected away by hand using a variety of novel techniques, allowing entry of the sperm.

● **Intracytoplasmic sperm injection (ICSI)** – involves the direct injection of the sperm into the oocyte cytoplasm. This technique has largely superseded **sub-zonal insemination (SUZI)** where a single sperm cell is injected between the zona pellucida and the oocyte surface membrane.

Relative frequency of the various causes of infertility

Cause	% Couples
ovulatory failure	21
tubal damage	14
endometriosis	6
mucus defect	3
sperm defect	24
other male factor	2
coital failure	6
unexplained	28

The total comes to more than 100% as some couples have more than a single cause.
Source: after Hull M.G.R. et al BMJ,291:1693

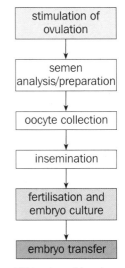

IVF treatment involves several stages

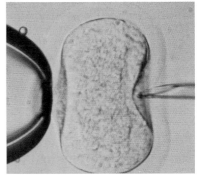

Sperm are injected directly into the oocyte cytoplasm during ICSI

▷ Biology at work: Hormones in domestic animals

Farmers are always looking for ways to increase the productivity of their livestock.
Efficient food production will increase profits but also helps meet the rising global need for food.
Farmers can increase meat production by making individuals grow faster or by rearing more animals.

Animals that grow faster are able to convert more of their feed into meat and have a higher **protein conversion efficiency** (PCE) value.
Cattle and sheep have a relatively low PCE due to their high cellulose diets. Until recently, it was common practice to use synthetic male sex hormones (**androgens**) or female sex hormones (**oestrogens**) to increase a cow's ability to retain nitrogen and build up protein levels.

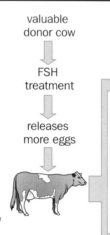

valuable
donor cow

↓

FSH
treatment

↓

releases
more eggs

embryo transfer
1. artificial insemination using sperm from a bull with the desired characteristics
2. embryos are taken out of the donor cow after 6–8 days
3. the embryos are transferred to the uterus of recipient cows under anaesthetic or are frozen for later use

in vitro fertilisation
1. eggs are collected and cultured in the laboratory for 5 days
2. the eggs are fertilised with sperm from a bull with the desired characteristics, cultured for 5–6 days and frozen until required
3. the eggs are are transferred to the uterus of recipient cows under anaesthetic

Embryo transplantation and MF techniques to increase productivity in cattle

Hormones can also be used to increase the reproduction rates of livestock. There are three main applications.

- **Embryo transplantation**
  The development of embryo transplantation techniques has increased the potential productivity of rearing livestock. A cow with the desired characteristics is treated with **follicle-stimulating hormone** (FSH). This hormone increases the growth of Graafian follicles and so more eggs are released. The donor cow is artificially inseminated and the resulting embryos are removed after 6—8 days. These are then transferred to a recipient cow's uterus under anaesthetic.

- **Control of the oestrus cycle**
  Animals with frequent periods of oestrus and short gestation, such as pigs, can produce several litters a year. Cows give birth to one calf at a time but can be re-mated as soon as they stop producing milk. Sheep have a short gestation period and can give birth to multiple offspring but only come into oestrus once a year. To overcome these differences, breeding can be synchronised using artificial hormones. This means the farmer can control when and how many of his livestock become pregnant. This coordination makes it easier to feed them on the same programme and reduces veterinary charges.
  There are two methods of control:
  i) increase **progesterone** levels in the blood,
  ii) injecting **prostaglandin F2α**.

- **Increasing milk production**
  The period during which a cow gives milk is called **lactation**. Several hormones control the length of lactation and the volume of milk produced per day. **Somatotrophin** is a naturally occurring growth hormone secreted from the pituitary gland, which causes a general increase in body size.
  In cows, increased growth leads to larger udders and hence greater milk production.
  The injection of a genetically engineered version of the hormone **bovine somatotrophin** (BST), causes a 21% increase in milk yield. The use of this hormone has caused concern about whether milk containing it is safe to drink.

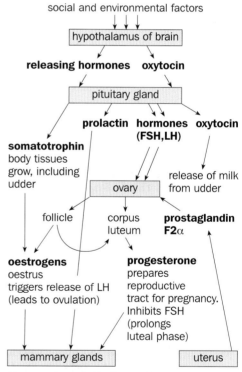

Hormonal control in livestock reproduction

Summary

- Sexual reproduction involves the production of haploid gametes, which fuse at fertilisation to produce a diploid zygote.
- Sexual reproduction results in offspring that show variation as a result of random segregation of chromosomes at metaphase I of meiosis, crossing over at prophase I of meiosis, random fertilisation of gametes, and random mating between individuals of the same species.
- The basic structure of a flower consists of the sepals, petals, stamens and carpels.
- Pollination is the transfer of pollen from the anther to the stigma of a plant of the same species.
- The two main methods of pollination are by insects and by the wind.
- Cross-pollination results in far greater genetic variation in a population than self-pollination.
- A double fertilisation occurs in flowering plants, since one male gamete fuses with the egg nucleus and the other fuses with the endosperm nucleus.

- The human testes produce spermatozoa and the male hormone testosterone.
- The human ovaries produce eggs and secrete the female sex hormones.
- Spermatogenesis is the production of sperm, and oogenesis is the production of eggs. Both of these processes involve meiosis to form haploid gametes.
- The menstrual cycle involves the production and release of eggs (ovulation) and the preparation of the uterus to receive the egg if it becomes fertilised (implantation).
- The placenta has a number of important functions involving the transfer of materials between the mother's blood and the baby's blood.
- The pituitary secretes hormones that have an important role in the onset of birth and lactation.

▷ Questions

1 The diagram shows the life cycle of a moss.

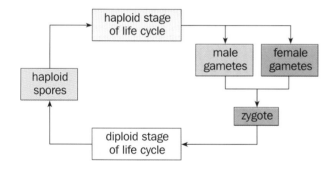

a) Copy the diagram and mark on it the place where meiosis occurs.
b) A spore from this moss contains 16 chromosomes. How many chromosomes would you expect there to be in:
   i) a female gamete,
   ii) a cell taken from the moss during the diploid stage of its life cycle?
c) Some DNA was extracted from cells during the haploid stage of the life cycle. It was found to contain 14% adenine.
   i) What percentage of thymine would you expect the sample to contain?
   ii) What percentage of cytosine would you expect the sample to contain?
d) Suggest two ways in which the male gametes of this organism are likely to differ from the female gametes.

2 The diagram shows the nuclei K–T found in the ovary of a pollinated flower with a diploid number of 12.

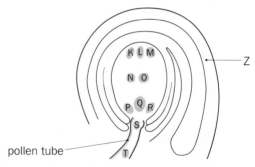

a) Copy and complete the table to show which of the nuclei K–R will fuse with S and T at fertilisation, the function of the fusion product, and the number of chromosomes that it will contain.

Nucleus with which it will fuse (K–R)	Function of fusion product	Number of chromosomes
S		
T		

b) After fertilisation the structure labelled Z swells.
   i) Name the structure that is produced.
   ii) Describe fully how this structure might help to ensure the survival of the species.

141

3 The diagram shows a section through part of one seminiferous tubule in the testis.

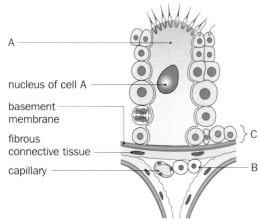

A

nucleus of cell A

basement membrane

fibrous connective tissue

capillary

C

B

a) Name:
   i) the cells labelled A and B in the diagram,
   ii) the layer of cells labelled C.
b) Write a detailed account describing the way in which sperm are produced and the part played by A, B and C in their production.

4 The diagram below shows a section of a human secondary oocyte.
   a) Name the structures labelled A, B, C, D, E and F.
   b) i) How does the nucleus of a secondary oocyte differ from that of a primary oocyte?
      ii) Describe how a secondary oocyte reaches the site where fertilisation may occur from the site in the ovary where it was produced.

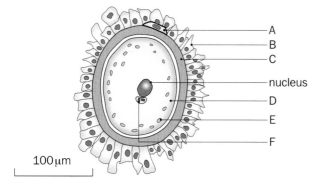

A
B
C

nucleus

D

E

F

100 μm

5 The drawings show the sperm and eggs of three different animals.

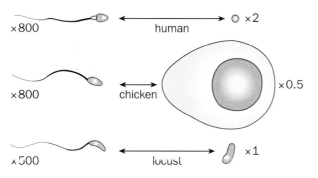

×800   human   ○ ×2

×800   chicken   ×0.5

×500   locust   ×1

a) i) How many times longer is the chicken egg than the chicken sperm?
   ii) Calculate the actual length of the chicken sperm in millimetres, showing your working.
b) What is the main advantage to the locust of producing eggs that are much larger than sperm?
c) Explain why human eggs are smaller than chicken eggs, even though adult humans are much larger than adult chickens.

6 Copy and complete the table to show the correct function(s) of luteinising hormone, oestrogen and progesterone by marking the appropriate box or boxes with a tick (✓). Some hormones may have more than one function.

Function	Luteinising hormone	Oestrogen	Progesterone
immediate cause of ovulation			
immediate cause of repair of the uterine lining after menstruation			
inhibits production of follicle stimulating hormone			
maintains the uterus for implantation			
stimulates formation of a structure that produces progesterone			

7 The graph shows the effect of the number of hours of daylight on the timing of oestrus in sheep. The graph refers to daylight conditions in northern Europe over a period of 21 months.

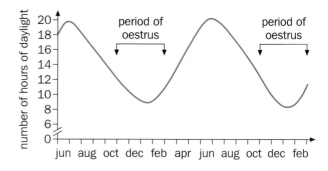

a) Comment on the relationship between hours of daylight and the periods of oestrus shown in the graph.
b) Why is it an advantage that the periods of oestrus in sheep occur at the times shown on the graph?

Gene technology enables scientists to manipulate DNA in many ways.
Individual genes can now be located in the DNA of an organism.
An individual gene can be isolated, removed and cloned.
The DNA of one organism can be combined with the DNA of another.
Genes can also be made from the RNA of an organism.
There are already many commercial applications of genetic engineering,
and future developments may well provide the means to alleviate
suffering and cure disease.
However, there are many reservations about the long-term effects
of a genetically modified world.

Technician at microscope injecting cells with DNA

▷ The basic principles of genetic engineering

Restriction endonucleases are enzymes that cut DNA
into small fragments.
This allows individual genes to be isolated.

A gene from one organism can be inserted into the DNA of another.
The gene that has been isolated for insertion is called **donor DNA**.
The donor DNA is inserted into the host DNA of another organism.
DNA that contains genetic material from *two* different organisms
is called **recombinant DNA**.

Restriction endonucleases are used to cut the donor DNA and
the host DNA into smaller pieces.
The enzymes make staggered cuts, called 'sticky ends', that allow
the donor DNA to be spliced into the host DNA.

Another group of enzymes, called **DNA ligases**, are used to join
the sticky ends of the donor DNA and the host DNA together.
The sticky ends are complementary.
For instance, an ATG end will 'stick' to a TAC end.

As you will see, host cells with recombinant DNA can be used
to clone genes or to produce important substances such as
antibiotics, hormones and enzymes.

An enzyme called **reverse transcriptase** can be used to make
a gene from RNA.
First, the RNA is extracted, which is a mirror image copy of the
desired gene.
Then reverse transcriptase is used to make a single strand of
copy DNA (**cDNA**) from the isolated RNA.

The single strand of cDNA can be used as a template to make the
second strand, so forming the double stranded DNA helix of the gene.

The cDNA coding for rennin has been spliced into a plasmid in
E. coli cells.
Non-animal rennin can then be produced by replication of the
bacterial cells in large industrial fermenters.

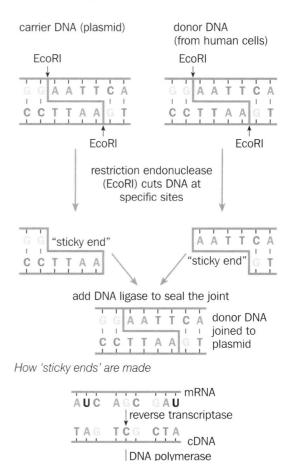

How 'sticky ends' are made

The use of reverse transcription and DNA polymerase to make double-stranded DNA

▷ Production of insulin

Some human diseases are caused by the inability of a person
to produce certain chemicals.
For instance, diabetics are unable to make their own insulin and
haemophiliacs are unable to produce Factor VIII.
Many of these chemicals are proteins coded for by DNA.
In the past, some of these diseases have been treated using chemicals
extracted from animals.
For example, diabetics were treated with insulin extracted from pigs.
Sometimes this resulted in side effects produced by the patient's
immune system.

Genetic engineering has now made it possible to use bacteria
to mass-produce human insulin.

First, the gene that codes for insulin is identified and isolated from
a healthy human cell.
Then the donor DNA is spliced into the host bacterial DNA.
The bacterial cells are grown in a nutrient medium in a large industrial
fermenter, which provides ideal conditions for growth.

The bacterial cells multiply rapidly and soon there are millions of cells
all carrying the insulin-producing gene.
The gene is transcribed and translated and the insulin produced.
This type of insulin does not have the side effects associated with
animal insulin.

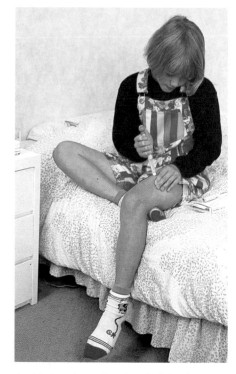

A girl gives herself an insulin injection

▷ Industrial fermentation

Fermentation involves the aerobic and anaerobic respiration of microbes.
Industrial fermentation is now widely used to culture cells such as bacteria
and yeasts.
Genetically altered cells can be produced on a large scale, producing
useful chemicals such as antibiotics, biogas and alcohol.
Strictly speaking, fermentation refers to anaerobic respiration but it
is generally accepted to include aerobic respiration as well.

There are many advantages in using micro-organisms such as bacteria
and yeasts in industrial fermentation:

- They have a very rapid rate of growth.

- They can be grown continuously on a large scale.

- Their cells have a high protein content.

- They can utilise waste products as substrates, for example
  agricultural waste.

- They usually produce products that are non-toxic.

- Because they are living organisms, their chemical reactions
  are controlled by enzymes.
  This means that fermentation can take place at lower temperatures
  and therefore the production is cheaper.

A large industrial fermenter

144

▷ Batch and continuous cultivation

One important use of large-scale industrial fermentation is the production of antibiotics such as penicillin.
The fermenter is inoculated with a culture of a suitable fungus, in this case *Penicillium chrysogenum*, which then proceeds to grow under the ideal conditions maintained inside the fermenter.

These include:

- **Adding nutrients** such as sugar or starch as a source of carbon for respiration.
  Ammonia or urea is added as a source of nitrogen to make proteins.
  Vitamin B complex is added for respiration.

- **Maintaining a constant temperature** of about 30 °C.

- **Maintaining a constant pH** of about 6.5.

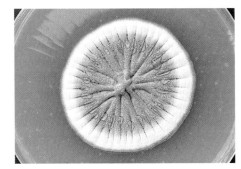

Penicillium *growing on agar*

Batch cultivation

It takes about 30 hours for penicillin production to start.
Penicillin is secreted into the surrounding liquid by the fungus.

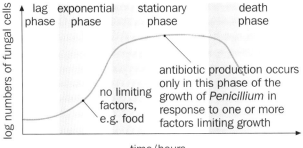

Look at the graph. You can see there is a delay.
This is because penicillin is a **secondary metabolite**, a substance which is not necessary for the growth of the fungus.
Secondary metabolites are not produced until *after* the exponential phase of growth is completed.
After about 6 days, the mixture in the fermenter is filtered, the penicillin is extracted using a solvent and purified into a crystalline salt.
This type of fermentation is known as **batch cultivation**.
After the 6 day period, the fermenter is emptied, cleaned and sterilised ready for the next batch.

Continuous cultivation

This type of cultivation allows production to continue for several weeks, since raw materials are added throughout the process and the products are continuously being removed.
This method is only suitable for products that are known as **primary metabolites**.
These are substances that are essential for the life of the micro-organism and, as a result, they are produced throughout the growth of the organism.

Industrial fermenters are huge tanks in which conditions are carefully controlled.
They may hold 500 000 dm^3 or more and allow the economic production of vast quantities of important products.

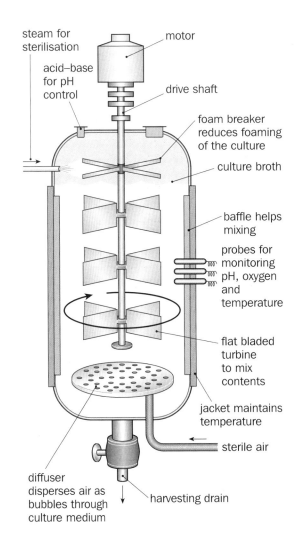

Continuous cultivation in an industrial fermenter

▷ Gene cloning using vectors

Sometimes large quantities of a particular gene are required.
As you will see on page 149, a possible treatment for cystic fibrosis
requires many copies of the appropriate healthy human gene.
Techniques in gene cloning allow this to be achieved.

The DNA fragment containing the wanted gene is inserted
into the DNA of a host cell.
The host cell is known as a **vector**.
The recombinant DNA acts as a carrier molecule for the gene
that is to be copied.
As the host cell reproduces and replicates its DNA, clones
of the required gene are made at the same time.

Bacteria, viruses and even some eukaryotic cells have all been
used as vectors.
Bacteriophages can be used as vectors since they are able to inject
the recombinant DNA into bacterial cells such as *E. coli*.
As you saw in Chapter 6, the host cell then replicates the virus many
times, making multiple copies of the recombinant DNA.

The most commonly used vector is the bacterial **plasmid**.
In addition to their single loop of DNA, bacterial cells also contain
small circles of DNA called plasmids (see page 29).
Plasmids are easy to work with since they can replicate very quickly,
producing many copies of the original gene.

Plasmids can be isolated and cut open by restriction endonucleases.
A human gene that has been cut out of a human chromosome by
restriction endonuclease can be spliced into the plasmid using
DNA ligase.
The recombinant plasmid is then inserted into the host bacterium.
The bacterial cells are grown in nutrient medium in industrial
fermenters.
In these conditions, the bacteria multiply rapidly, making many
copies of the human gene.
The human DNA is transcribed and translated by the bacterial
cells, so producing the human protein.
The protein is then separated and purified.

Eukaryotic cells have also been used as vectors to clone
recombinant DNA.
Yeast cells often have naturally occurring plasmids in them.
They can be used to make **yeast artificial chromosomes** (**YACs**).
These are used for cloning larger DNA fragments.

Sometimes **marker genes** are used to indicate that new genes have
been incorporated into host cells.
Marker genes are linked to the desired gene, so they give clear evidence
that the desired gene has been carried to the host cell.
Some of them may be radioactive so that the position of the labelled gene
can be easily located.
Bacterial cells containing genetically engineered plasmids can also
be identified by the use of marker genes that confer antibiotic resistance.
So the cells into which the gene has been inserted can be identified
by the fact that the host cell is now resistant to a certain antibiotic.

146

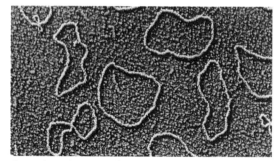
Scanning electron micrograph of bacterial plasmids

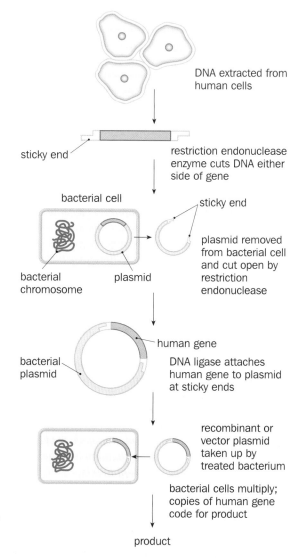

DNA extracted from human cells

sticky end — restriction endonuclease enzyme cuts DNA either side of gene

bacterial cell

sticky end

plasmid removed from bacterial cell and cut open by restriction endonuclease

bacterial chromosome

plasmid

human gene

bacterial plasmid

DNA ligase attaches human gene to plasmid at sticky ends

recombinant or vector plasmid taken up by treated bacterium

bacterial cells multiply; copies of human gene code for product

product

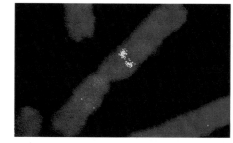
Radioactive marker genes on a chromosome

▷ Polymerase chain reaction

The **polymerase chain reaction** (**PCR**) allows gene cloning to take place in a test-tube.

The reaction enables many identical copies of double stranded DNA to be made without the use of bacteria.

Each strand is copied, producing two new strands, then each of these is copied and so on, doubling the amount of DNA at each cycle.

This is semi-conservative replication of DNA in a test-tube.

The raw materials

The original sample of DNA is dissolved in a buffer solution and mixed with the following:

● DNA polymerase (this is a heat-stable form of the enzyme extracted from the thermophilic bacterium *Thermus aquaticus*),

● the four different types of nucleotide containing the bases adenine, guanine, cytosine and thymine,

● short pieces of DNA called **primers**, which act as signals to the DNA polymerase enzyme to start copying.

Stages of the PCR cycle

1. **Strand separation**: the original DNA (called target DNA) is heated to 95 °C for 5 minutes and denatured.
   It separates out into two single strand lengths of DNA.

2. **Primer binding**: the solution is rapidly cooled to 55 °C to enable the primers to bind to the complementary base sequences on each of the single strands of DNA. This provides a starting point for the DNA replication.

3. **Strand synthesis**: the solution is heated to 70 °C. The thermostable DNA polymerase enzyme catalyses the synthesis of a complementary strand for each of the single strands of DNA using the supply of nucleotides. The DNA polymerase produces two identical double strands of DNA.

The process is then repeated by changing the temperature of the solution to 95 °C, then 55 °C and then 70 °C, so doubling the amount of DNA produced each time.

Many processes in DNA technology require large amounts of DNA, for example DNA sequencing and DNA fingerprinting. Often only small samples are available, so PCR can be used to create vast quantities.

It can be used to increase the tiny amount of DNA sample in a speck of blood.

This gives forensic scientists enough material to use for genetic fingerprinting, which may lead to the identification of a criminal. Apart from its use as a forensic tool, genetic fingerprinting has also been used to detect inherited diseases, to monitor bone marrow transplants, and to confirm animal pedigrees.

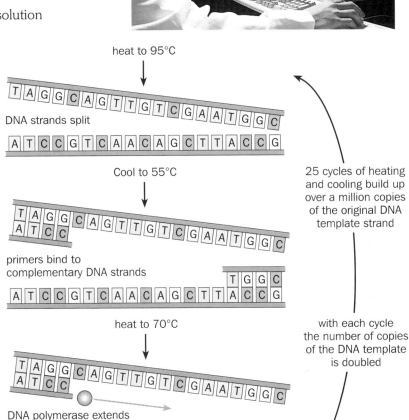

The polymerase chain reaction

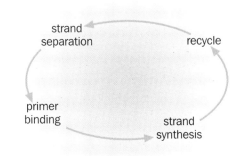

The PCR cycle

147

▷ Genetic fingerprinting

The DNA in your cells is as unique as your fingerprints.
Unless you have an identical twin, your '**genetic fingerprint**' or
DNA profile is different from everyone else's.
There are certain regions of chromosomes, called **introns**, that code for the
production of proteins, and certain non-coding regions, called **extrons**.
These regions of non-coding DNA contain a block of repeated nucleotides
called **short tandem repeats** (**STRs**).
It is the number of times that these blocks of STRs are repeated that
produces the variation in individuals.

The technique of genetic fingerprinting can be used to provide
forensic evidence and thus solve crimes.
Since body cells contain the same DNA, virtually any tissue can be used.
Only a small amount of, say, blood, hair root, skin cells or semen is needed.

Genetic fingerprints viewed on an autoradiogram

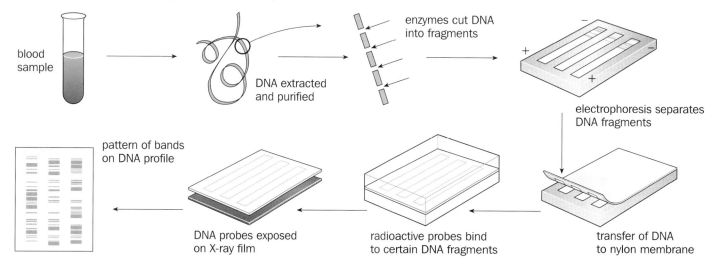

- The DNA is extracted from the sample and cut into millions of small fragments using restriction endonucleases, aimed at specific STRs. These enzymes are specific, making cuts in specific places for each particular individual.

- The DNA fragments are separated using **electrophoresis**.
  This involves exposing the fragments of DNA to an electric current in a trough of gel. The DNA fragments are negatively charged and so they move towards the anode (positive terminal) when an electric field is applied. The smaller the fragment, the faster it moves, so the DNA becomes separated into bands according to the size of the fragments.

- The DNA fragments are transferred to a nylon membrane by a process called **Southern blotting**. This does not alter the pattern of the fragments resulting from the electrophoresis.

- Radioactive DNA probes are used to attach to specific parts of the fragments.

- Any probe sequences that have not bound to the DNA fragments are washed off and the membrane is dried.

- The nylon sheet with DNA fragments attached is placed under X-ray film.

- The radioactive probes on the DNA fragments expose the film.

- This produces a visible pattern of light and dark bands (where a radioactive probe is present) rather like a bar-code. Everyone's bar-code is different.

Scientist working on DNA profiles

148

▷ Gene therapy

Cystic fibrosis (CF) is an inherited disease that affects
1 in 2000 people in the UK.
Sufferers of the disease produce thick, sticky mucus from the cells
that line particular passages in the body.
This can block the bronchioles and alveoli of the lungs, causing
congestion and difficulty in breathing.
The pancreatic duct can also become blocked with mucus so that
the reduced release of pancreatic juice results in inadequate digestion.

Patients are treated by vigorous chest physiotherapy.
The mucus is difficult to remove and is a breeding ground for germs.
Sufferers often get infections and have to be treated with strong antibiotics.
Each infection leaves the lungs further damaged and the patient's health
deteriorates progressively.
The physiotherapy, of course, does nothing to relieve the digestive disorder.

Cystic fibrosis is caused by a defective gene, resulting from the deletion
of a base triplet (see page 371 on gene mutations).
The deletion of the base triplet means that an amino acid is omitted
from the coded protein.
The gene is recessive, so to inherit the disease **both** alleles
have to code for CF.

The normal gene codes for the production of a protein found in the
cell membrane called **cystic fibrosis transmembrane
regulator** (CFTR).
CFTR transports chloride ions out of cells into mucus.
Sodium ions follow and water is drawn out of the cells by osmosis.
As a result, the mucus that lines the respiratory passages is a normal
watery consistency.

However, if you have CF, your CFTR protein lacks the amino acid
phenylalanine in just one place in the chain.
As a result, chloride ions are not transported out of the cell.
So instead of being watered down, the mucus remains thick
and sticky. This results in the air passages becoming blocked,
making it difficult to breathe properly.

Scientists are researching a genetic treatment for cystic fibrosis.
They hope that gene therapy will work like this:

● A non-defective gene is isolated and cut out by restriction
  enzymes.

● The gene is then cloned many times by PCR.

● The genes are encapsulated in tiny spheres of lipids called
  liposomes.

● An aerosol inhaler is used to add the non-defective gene to
  the epithelial cells of the lungs of a CF sufferer.

● The liposomes fuse with the phospholipid bilayer of the cell
  surface membrane and the DNA enters the affected cells,
  which then start to express the inserted gene by making the
  correct protein.

In the past, trials have been carried out using a type of virus called
an adenovirus as a vector to insert the CFTR gene into affected cells.
But these tended to produce reactions in damaged lung tissue.

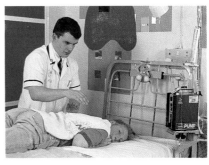

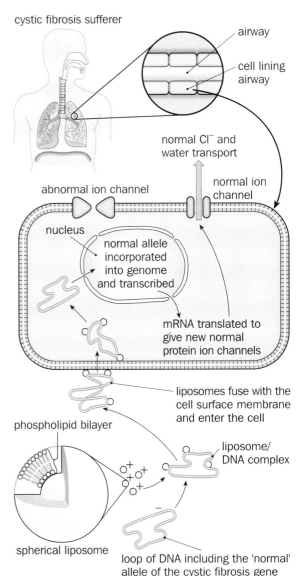

cystic fibrosis sufferer

airway

cell lining airway

normal Cl⁻ and water transport

abnormal ion channel

normal ion channel

nucleus

normal allele incorporated into genome and transcribed

mRNA translated to give new normal protein ion channels

liposomes fuse with the cell surface membrane and enter the cell

phospholipid bilayer

liposome/ DNA complex

spherical liposome

loop of DNA including the 'normal' allele of the cystic fibrosis gene

149

▷ Transgenic organisms

A **transgenic** organism has had the DNA from another organism
of another species transferred into it.
Its genotype has been altered, effectively producing a new strain of organism.
They are also called **genetically modified organisms**.

Tracey is a transgenic sheep. She is healthy and normal except in one respect:
she has had a human gene inserted into her DNA.
The gene codes for the production of a protein called alpha-1-antitrypsin (ATT).
The protein is secreted in Tracey's milk and from which it is extracted.
The protein is valuable since it may be part of a potential treatment for
human lung diseases such as emphysema and cystic fibrosis.

How do you think the human gene got into Tracey's cells?
The human gene for ATT was isolated and cloned.
It was then injected into a fertilised egg and 'adopted'
by one of the chromosomes.
The fertilised egg divided by mitosis, producing identical cells
each containing the ATT gene.
The early embryo was then transplanted into a surrogate mother
and Tracey was eventually born.

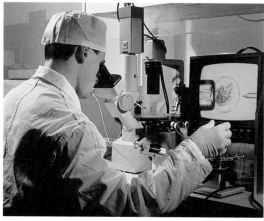

This technique has been used to make other valuable proteins
that cannot be synthesised by laboratory methods.
The blood-clotting protein Factor VIII has been extracted from the milk
of transgenic ewes into which the human gene was inserted.
This has been used as a treatment for haemophilia.

Genetic manipulation of a bovine embryo

▷ Bovine somatotrophin

Bovine somatotrophin (BST) is a natural hormone secreted by
the pituitary in a cow.
It has three physiological effects:

* It stimulates growth in young animals.
* It affects carbohydrate and fat metabolism.
* It increases milk production in cows.

Scientists inserted the gene that codes for BST into bacteria.
The bacteria replicated in large-scale industrial fermenters.
As a result, large amounts of BST hormone became available.
The hormone was injected into cows and was found to increase
milk production by as much as 20%.

A modern milking parlour

However, treated cows sometimes become infertile, either through
a lack of response to artificial insemination or by aborting developing embryos.
BST-treated cattle are also prone to **mastitis** (an inflammation of the udders)
and there is evidence that it increases the cow's susceptibility to disease
by depleting the immune system.
Health fears have arisen over drinking milk produced by cattle injected with BST,
because small quantities of BST appear in the milk and in the meat.
BST should not be a risk to most consumers, because it is a protein that will
be digested into its constituent amino acids in the human gut.

However, there is concern about its effect on pregnant and lactating mothers.
Critics argue that not enough is known about the long-term effects of drinking BST milk.
Others see its use as an unnatural and cruel way of extracting milk from cows.

▷ Transgenic plants

Foreign genes can be introduced into plant cells quite naturally.
The soil bacterium *Agrobacterium tumefaciens* is the cause of
'crown gall' infection in some plants.
The bacterium attacks wounds and causes the plant cells to
multiply and form a tumour.

It does this by inserting genes from its own plasmids into one
of the plant's chromosomes.
The plasmid gene links up with the plant's DNA and stimulates
the tumour growth.
Plant geneticists have been successful in replacing the
tumour-forming genes in the bacterial plasmids with useful genes.
These can be inserted into the plant's DNA by a vector.

For instance, this technique has been used to introduce into
potato plants genes that promote resistance to diseases such as potato
roll leaf virus, which can have a severe economic effect on crop yield.

Legume plants, such as peas, beans and clover, have nitrogen-fixing
bacteria in their roots.
The bacteria provide the plant with a source of nitrogen as nitrates
and obtain nutrients made by the plant in return.
Soon it may be possible to transfer the nitrogen-fixing genes
directly into other plants such as wheat and rice.
Such plants would no longer need artificial fertilisers,
as they would be able to fix their own nitrogen.

This may limit the use of fertilisers, which can have an adverse effect
on the environment.
So genetically modified plants may be able to reduce the impact
of modern crop production techniques on the environment
because fewer agrochemicals will be needed.
Such a view has to be balanced by the threat to environmental stability
that could come from the release of genetically modified organisms
into biological communities.

'Flavr Savr' tomatoes

Most tomatoes are picked when they are green so that they are still firm
on arrival at the shops.
The green tomatoes are treated with **ethene** gas to turn them red
(this does not affect their natural flavour).
Normally tomatoes produce an enzyme called **polygalacturonase**,
which breaks down the pectin in cell walls, making them mushy and
thus reducing their shelf life.

To stop the tomatoes from going soft, scientists have found a way of
blocking the production of polygalacturonase.
Polygalacturonase is coded for by a single gene, which produces a
mRNA molecule.
In *Flavr Savr* tomatoes this mRNA is blocked by a complementary
antisense mRNA produced by a reverse *Flavr Savr* gene.
The antisense mRNA binds to the polygalacturonase mRNA
and so prevents the translation of the polygalacturonase gene into
the sequence of amino acids that make up the enzyme.
The result is that *Flavr Savr* tomatoes are tastier and have a longer shelf life.

1. plasmid extracted from the bacterium
   A. tumefaciens

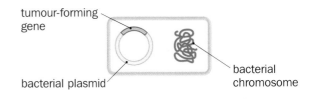

2. the useful gene replaces the tumour-forming gene
   in the plasmid

3. the modified plasmid is inserted back into the
   bacterium

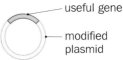

bacterial cell multiplies and so
does plasmid carrying new gene

4. when the bacterium infects the plant the useful
   gene is introduced to one of the plant's
   chromosomes instead of the tumour-forming gene

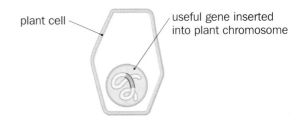

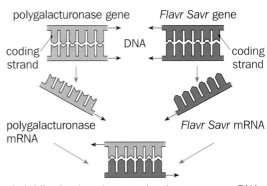

The treated tomatoes have not gone mouldy

hybridisation inactivates polygalacturonase mRNA

▷ Plant tissue culture

Plant tissue culture, or **micropropagation**, involves cloning plants.
Cloning results in the production of large numbers of genetically identical plants.
Clones are taken from stock plants that have desirable characteristics and that are commercially important.
They are grown in tissue culture under sterile conditions with controlled concentrations of nutrients and hormones.

Plant tissue culture is a form of vegetative propagation and has many advantages over the more traditional methods of propagation such as grafting or taking cuttings.

- It is very time-effective, since it dispenses with the need for pollination and seed production.

- It ensures that the good qualities of the stock plants are retained, for example resistance to disease and insects, or high fruit yield.

- It enables large numbers of new plants to be produced from a single parent.

- It is extremely cost effective.

- It is easy to transport or store large numbers of plants under sterile conditions.

- It has conservation use in the recovery programmes of endangered plants.

- It helps to eliminate plant diseases since only healthy stock are selected and sterile conditions are used.

- It eliminates the seasonal restrictions on germination.

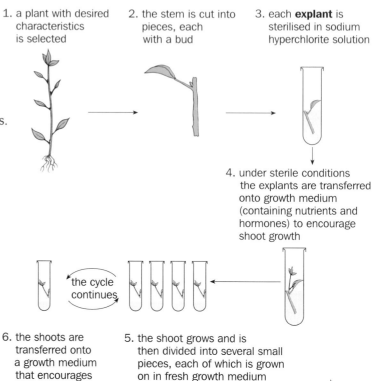

1. a plant with desired characteristics is selected

2. the stem is cut into pieces, each with a bud

3. each **explant** is sterilised in sodium hyperchlorite solution

4. under sterile conditions the explants are transferred onto growth medium (containing nutrients and hormones) to encourage shoot growth

the cycle continues

5. the shoot grows and is then divided into several small pieces, each of which is grown on in fresh growth medium

6. the shoots are transferred onto a growth medium that encourages root growth

7. after 3–4 weeks the plantlets are potted into sterile compost

Stages in micropropagation

▷ Cloning from protoplasts

Techniques have been developed by which complete plants can be grown from single cells.
A small piece of stock plant tissue is taken and treated with cellulase enzymes.
The enzymes remove the cellulose cell walls and split the cells up.
The naked cells are called **protoplasts**.

The protoplasts are then cultured under sterile conditions and grow to form an undifferentiated mass of cells called **callus**.
The callus tissue is then grown, using sterile culture techniques, to produce complete plants.
This technique is an effective way of producing large numbers of plants from one commercially valuable plant.
It has been used to produce high value ornamental plants such as orchids.

The protoplasts of closely related species can be fused.
This results in hybrid plants and induces variation.
By fusing protoplasts of different strains, it is possible to transfer genes, for example the gene for blight-resistance in potato plants.

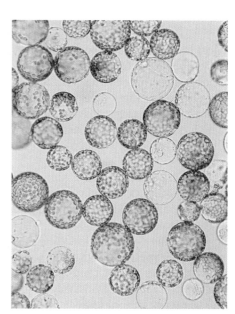

Tobacco leaf protoplasts

▷ Cloning farm animals

Embryo cloning

Embryo cloning has been used to produce many genetically identical individuals.

On average, a female sheep or cow will produce one offspring per pregnancy.
Embryo cloning has made it possible for farmers to rapidly increase their livestock numbers.

First, eggs taken from the best cows are fertilised in a petri dish by sperm from the best bulls.
This is known as **in-vitro fertilisation**.
The fertilised egg divides to form a ball of cells.
At this stage the young embryos are surgically split up to produce a number of separate embryos.
Each separate embryo is a genetically identical clone (though it does have half its genes from the father and half from the mother).

The embryos are then transplanted into other cows called **surrogates**.
They grow and are eventually born, producing several individuals with the same characteristics as the parents.

Cloning by nuclear transfer

This technique enables clones to be produced from **one** individual.
It has allowed the cloning of superior livestock such as cows with a high milk yield.
If the cow were to be mated with a bull, the resulting genotype might not give the same unique characteristics.
Cloning produces identical copies and preserves desirable features for future generations.

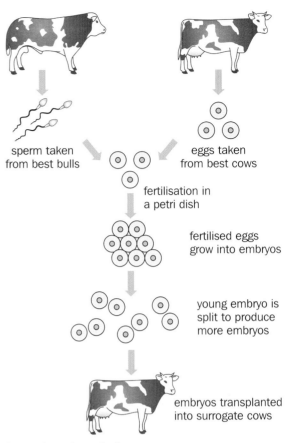

sperm taken from best bulls

eggs taken from best cows

fertilisation in a petri dish

fertilised eggs grow into embryos

young embryo is split to produce more embryos

embryos transplanted into surrogate cows

Stages in embryo cloning

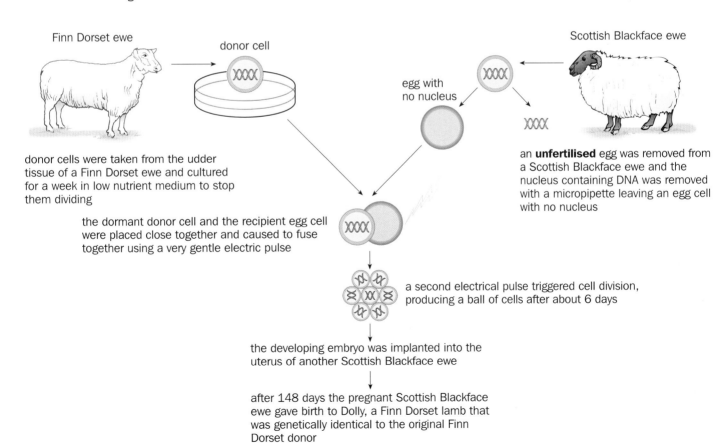

Finn Dorset ewe

donor cell

egg with no nucleus

Scottish Blackface ewe

donor cells were taken from the udder tissue of a Finn Dorset ewe and cultured for a week in low nutrient medium to stop them dividing

an **unfertilised** egg was removed from a Scottish Blackface ewe and the nucleus containing DNA was removed with a micropipette leaving an egg cell with no nucleus

the dormant donor cell and the recipient egg cell were placed close together and caused to fuse together using a very gentle electric pulse

a second electrical pulse triggered cell division, producing a ball of cells after about 6 days

the developing embryo was implanted into the uterus of another Scottish Blackface ewe

after 148 days the pregnant Scottish Blackface ewe gave birth to Dolly, a Finn Dorset lamb that was genetically identical to the original Finn Dorset donor

▷ Evaluation of genetic engineering

Like many beneficial scientific advances, for instance the discovery of antibiotics, the introduction of gene technology has brought with it the possibilities of misuse.

Body cell gene therapy brings the benefit of targeting a particular tissue. In the case of cystic fibrosis, the therapy would solve the problem of congested lungs.
Body cell gene therapy could be used to target the blood cells to cure **thalassaemia**, a disease caused by a recessive mutant gene resulting in severe anaemia.
With body cell gene therapy, the sex cells are not involved, so the cure is not passed on to the offspring.

Far more controversial is **germ-line gene therapy**.
This involves repairing the original gene inside the fertilised egg.
The resulting individual grows and develops with healthy genes functioning in *all body cells*.

This means that not only is the defective gene eliminated from the patient, but the risk of it being passed on to the offspring is also removed.
On the face of it, the ability to treat diseases such as cystic fibrosis and haemophilia in this way appears very attractive.

But ethical questions have to be raised as to whether we have the right to alter the genes of future generations.
We know very little about how genes function and control the development of human embryos.

Tampering with genes in the fertilised egg could result in unforeseen effects which are only discovered later in life or in subsequent generations.
Would we be only one step away from altering genes that code for skin colour, height or even intelligence?
This raises major ethical questions about the technique.
It is perhaps not surprising that research into germ-line gene therapy is currently banned in the UK.

The introduction of genetic engineering in the 1970s brought with it fears that new strains of microbes could escape from laboratories and cause outbreaks of disease.
In fact, scientists have worked with strains that are very poorly adapted to live inside the human body.
Work on potentially dangerous pathogens has been restricted to isolated laboratories with strict hygiene conditions, highly effective air filters and extensive monitoring of the atmosphere.

Worries that genetically modified organisms might escape into the environment and get into food chains have so far proved unfounded.
But the introduction of transgenic animals and plants is still viewed by many as interfering with nature. (See pages 156 and 157 on GM foods.)

On the one hand, gene technology may be able to provide the means to alleviate suffering and cure genetic diseases.
But on the other hand, there are justifiable reservations about the long-term effects that manipulation of the human genome and the production of genetically modified organisms may have.

ORGANIC FOOD AVAILABLE HERE

"...want to avoid eating food with pesticide residues."

"...are concerned about the preservation of British wildlife."

"...believe organic food has more flavour."

"...do not want to eat genetically modified food."

"...want to pay a fair price to farmers."

:...to guarantee strict animal welfare guidelines are adhered to."

"...like to eat seasonally."

Greenpeace activists removing GM maize in Norfolk. Twenty-eight of the Greenpeace volunteers were aquitted of criminal damage at Norwich Crown Court on 20th September 2000

154

▷ Biology at work: DNA fingerprinting

In 1998, the Russian Government confirmed that nine sets of bones unearthed near Yekaterinburg in the late 1970s were those of the last tsar and his family.
The Bolsheviks executed Tsar Nicholas II and his family after the Russian revolution in 1917.
The positive identification of the remains 80 years after their burial was only possible with the use of forensic techniques, including DNA fingerprinting.

For years, forensic scientists have used genetic markers in the form of blood groups to eliminate or include suspects in criminal investigations. However, a sufficient quantity of blood in good condition was necessary, and old and degraded samples were difficult to analyse accurately. Also, the use of blood groups could obviously not be used to identify actual individuals.
The first forensic use of DNA profiling occurred in the 1980s. This involved the successful conviction of a rape and murder suspect in Leicestershire.

In 1985 Professor Alec Jeffreys of Leicester University demonstrated that chromosomes had regions of non-coding DNA.
He termed these mini-satellites, and they can be used to identify individuals.
They are scattered throughout the chromosomes and consist of repeated blocks of nucleotides that do not code for any particular protein.
It is the number of times these blocks are repeated that produces the variation in individuals.
If enough regions of variation, or **loci**, are examined, it is possible to obtain a profile which is exclusive to an individual.

Polymerase chain reaction (PCR)

The PCR technique is now a common method for creating copies of specific fragments of DNA (See page 147).
PCR rapidly amplifies a single DNA molecule into many billions of molecules.
It detects repeating, very short sequences of nucleotides.
These very short pieces of DNA are known as Short Tandem Repeats (STRs).
Using STRs from the DNA in a single strand of hair at a crime scene, sufficient copies can be produced to carry out forensic tests.
This is a major advantage as it enables tests to be carried out accurately, quickly and regardless of the age of the sample.

It is for this reason that PCR was used in the identification of the bones of Tsar Nicholas II and his family.
The analysis confirmed that the bones came from a father, mother and three siblings.
Further analysis of mitochondrial DNA (mtDNA), which is inherited maternally, showed that the mother shared the same maternal line as the present Duke of Edinburgh.
This was not conclusive evidence and it was only after the known remains of the Tsar's brother were exhumed that it was shown that they shared the same mtDNA sequence.

The Russian Imperial Family in 1913

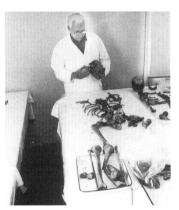

Skeletal remains of the tsarist family are examined by a forensic scientist

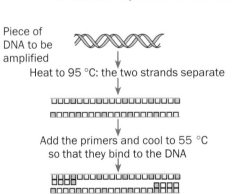

Piece of DNA to be amplified

Heat to 95 °C: the two strands separate

Add the primers and cool to 55 °C so that they bind to the DNA

Raise temperature to 70 °C. The thermostable polymerase enzyme copies each strand, starting at the primers

Enzyme — Enzyme

Repeat the process until enough DNA is made

▷ Biology at work: The GM food debate

Genetically modified (GM) food, in the form of tomato puree, vegetarian cheese or products containing genetically modified soya, has probably been eaten by most consumers already.

Consumer confidence in the increasing use of GM food and food products changed in early 1999.

Research on genetically modified potatoes and their effect when fed to laboratory animals prompted this change.

Much debate over the validity of this research followed, resulting in controversy and public concern over the safety of GM foods.

Consequently, many food producers and retailers banned GM ingredients from their own-brand products.

Lord Melchett arrested for destroying GM maize in Norfolk, July 1999

GM foods – the benefits

The scientific community and biotechnology companies were quick to stress the safety of GM foods and their benefits:

- **Solving global hunger** – genetic modification could feed the world through the development of crops that will tolerate drought, saline soils or frost, and thus increase food production in marginal areas.

- **Environmentally friendly** – genetic modification can confer resistance to insects, weeds and diseases. Together with genes that improve nitrogen uptake, these improvements should lead to a decrease in the use of chemicals.

- **Consumer benefits** – genetically modified food plants have already been produced which can provide food with an improved flavour and better keeping qualities, which are easier to produce, and which require fewer additives.

The GM food debate has raised questions about the ethics and scientific assumptions of such developments.

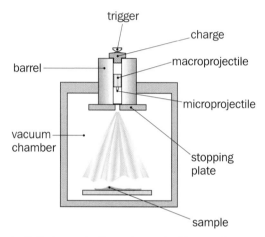

ballistic impregnation – is used with cereal crops and involves sticking DNA onto minute gold or tungsten particles, which are then fired into the plant tissue. The plant DNA then takes up some of these particles.

What is GM food?

Genetic engineering is the controlled modification of genetic material by artificial means and involves the isolation of specific regions of DNA using specialised enzymes, which cut the DNA at precise locations. Selected DNA fragments can then be transferred into plant cells. Food derived from such plants is referred to as **genetically modified**. There are several ways in which **gene transfer** can occur:

- **plasmid transfer** (see page 151),
- **ballistic impregnation**,
- **electroporation**.

With all these techniques, only a small proportion of the novel DNA is incorporated into the plant's DNA.

To check how successful gene transfer has been, **marker genes** are linked to the DNA fragments before transfer.

These marker genes are usually genes that allow the plant to grow in the presence of a specific antibiotic or herbicide.

Other techniques, for example **antisense technology**, are used to neutralise the action of specific undesirable genes, such as those involved in the excessive ripening of fruit.

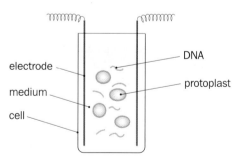

electroporation – works with plant cells that have no cell walls such as pollen tubes. Microsecond pulses of a strong electrical field cause minute pores to appear, allowing DNA to enter from a surrounding solution.

Examples of GM foods

Although some genetically modified food plants are approaching commercial use, very few have so far been approved.

- **Tomatoes** – research was aimed at gaining a better understanding of the ripening process using **antisense technology** (see page 151).

- **GM yeast** – micro-organisms have been genetically modified to yield **chymosin,** which is identical to the enzyme obtained from animal rennets.

- **GM maize** – maize grown in the USA has now been genetically modified to be resistant to an insect pest, the European corn borer.

- **GM soya** – the first herbicide-tolerant soya beans produced in the USA were approved for use in the European Union in 1996 as processed beans. More than 60% of all processed foods contain soya or soya products.

- **Processing aids** – current UK legislation requires that a food's ingredients should be listed. There are no such requirements to indicate those substances such as enzymes that are not found in the finished product.

GM foods – the concerns

Opposition to the increased use of GM foods revolves around five main areas of concern:

1. **Environmental safety** – there are worries that new GM food plants will become successful weeds, that they will transfer their new genes to wild relatives or similar crops nearby, and that those with insect-resistant genes will lead to the establishment of resistant populations of pests.

2. **Food safety** – concern focuses on the inclusion of marker genes for antibiotics and herbicides. In particular, the proteins these genes can produce, what levels should be acceptable and whether the genes are transferable to other organisms such as microbes in the intestine of the consumer. There is no recorded evidence currently of such transfer occurring between plants and microbes or humans.

3. **Changes in farming structure** – may occur which amplify the existing trends towards larger farms and more capital intensive systems. These tend to favour wealthy farmers in the northern hemisphere.

4. **Biodiversity** – fewer companies will increasingly control plant breeding, reducing the number of plant varieties available to farmers and leading to a reduction in the use of the old varieties and wild relatives. This could make plants more susceptible to attack by pests and diseases.

5. **Animal health** – developments in livestock production that affect animal welfare are increasingly unlikely to be accepted by regulatory authorities or the public. There are currently no products of animal biotechnology in food shops. In the future, such research could, however, benefit disease resistance in cattle in the Third World.

Whilst the biotechnology companies will continue to develop genetic modification techniques, public confidence and understanding is now seen as crucial to the acceptance of new GM food products.

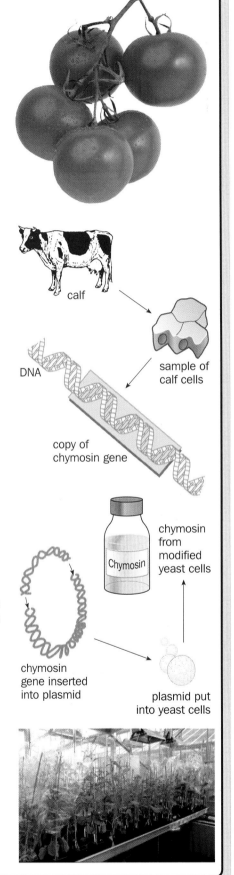

calf

DNA

sample of calf cells

copy of chymosin gene

chymosin from modified yeast cells

Chymosin

chymosin gene inserted into plasmid

plasmid put into yeast cells

Summary

- Genetic engineering involves the extraction of a gene or genes from one organism and their transfer into a host organism.
- DNA derived from two different organisms is called recombinant DNA.
- The manipulation of DNA involves the use of enzymes such as restriction endonucleases, ligases and reverse transcriptases.
- The polymerase chain reaction can produce large amounts of identical DNA from a small sample.
- Genetic fingerprinting can produce a DNA bar-code that is unique for each individual.
- A DNA fragment containing the wanted gene is inserted into a carrier DNA molecule known as a vector.
- Bacterial plasmids are the most commonly used vector and can reproduce the gene on a vast scale inside industrial fermenters.
- Bacterial plasmids can be labelled using marker genes. Some of these may be radioactive.
- It is hoped that gene therapy can be used to replicate non-defective genes to use in the treatment of diseases such as cystic fibrosis.
- Genetically modified organisms have the DNA of another species transferred into them.
- Cloning can be used to produce large numbers of genetically identical organisms in a relatively short period of time.

▷ Questions

1 Copy and complete the following:
The isolation of specific genes during genetic engineering involves the formation of DNA fragments. These fragments are formed using ___ enzymes, which make staggered cuts in the DNA within specific base sequences. This leaves single stranded 'sticky ends' at the ends of each fragment. The same enzyme is used to open up a circular loop of bacterial DNA, which acts as a ___ for the DNA fragments. The complementary sticky ends of the bacterial DNA are joined to the DNA fragment using another enzyme called ___. DNA fragments can also be made from a ___ template. Reverse transcriptase is used to produce a single strand of DNA and the enzyme ___ catalyses the formation of a double helix. Finally, the new DNA is introduced into ___ cells. These can then be cloned on an industrial scale and large amounts of protein can be harvested. An example of a protein currently manufactured using this technique is ___.

2 The polymerase chain reaction is a process that can be carried out in a laboratory to make large quantities of identical DNA from very small samples. The process is summarised in the flowchart.
   a) i) At the end of one cycle, two molecules of DNA have been produced from each original molecule. How many DNA molecules will have been produced from one molecule of DNA after five complete cycles?
      ii) Suggest one practical use to which this technique might be put.
   b) Give two ways in which the polymerase chain reaction differs from the process of transcription.
   c) The polymerase chain reaction involves semi-conservative replication. Explain what is meant by semi-conservative replication.

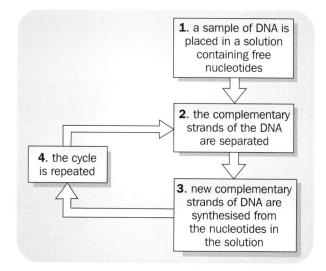

1. a sample of DNA is placed in a solution containing free nucleotides

2. the complementary strands of the DNA are separated

4. the cycle is repeated

3. new complementary strands of DNA are synthesised from the nucleotides in the solution

3 Penicillin is an antibiotic derived from the fungus *Penicillium chrysogenum*.
The antibiotic can be produced on a commercial scale as shown in the diagram.

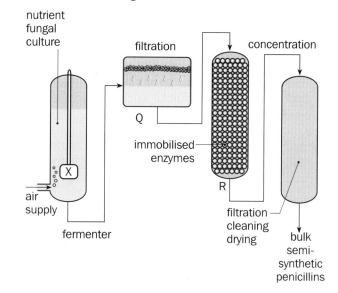

nutrient fungal culture

filtration

concentration

Q

immobilised enzymes

R

air supply

fermenter

filtration cleaning drying

bulk semi-synthetic penicillins

X

a) i) What is the purpose of structure X?
    ii) Why is air supplied to the fermenter?
b) Explain the purpose of the filtration carried out at Q.
c) i) Suggest one reason for using enzymes at R.
    ii) Suggest why *immobilised* enzymes are used.

4 The diagram shows how a gene from a human may be inserted into a bacterium to produce a genetically modified organism.

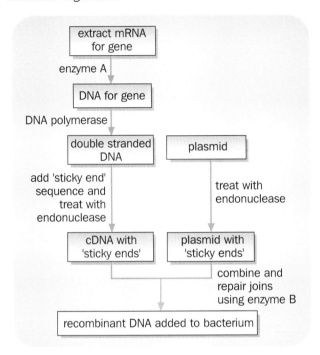

a) Name the enzymes A and B.
b) Describe how treating plasmids with endonuclease produces sticky ends, and explain their importance.
c) Suggest one way in which genetically modified organisms may be used.

5 a) i) In the DNA of a herring, 28% of the nucleotides contain adenine. What percentage of the nucleotides would you expect to contain guanine?
        ii) The percentage of nucleotides containing adenine is similar in both herring DNA and wheat DNA. Explain how organisms with the same proportion of adenine can be as different from each other as herring and wheat.
    b) In processed food products, cheaper varieties of fish may be substituted for more expensive varieties. Food inspectors have developed a DNA test to identify the species of fish used.
        i) In this test, a section of the DNA that codes for part of a protein known as cytochrome b was isolated. It was 351 base pairs in length. What is the maximum number of amino acids for which this section of DNA could code?

ii) The sequence of DNA was then cut into shorter pieces using a restriction endonuclease. The positions where the cuts were made depended on the species of fish from which the DNA came.
Explain why the restriction endonuclease cuts the DNA in different positions in different species of fish.

6 The diagram shows a method that has recently been used to clone sheep.

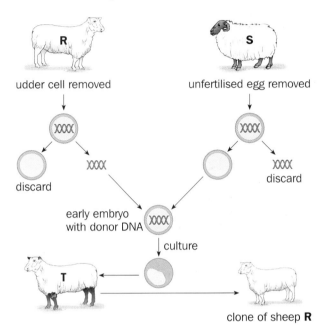

clone of sheep **R**

a) i) State the scientific term used to describe the developmental stage of the embryo transferred to the uterus of ewe T.
    ii) State the scientific term used to describe ewe T.
    iii) Name the first process that takes place in the uterus of ewe T after embryo transfer.
    iv) Name the hormone that is essential for this process to take place.
b) Scientists used ewes from different homozygous varieties in order to check that the procedure was successful at each stage and that the lamb produced was a clone of R. Suggest what could have been deduced about the procedure if the lamb had been born:
    i) with a black face,
    ii) with black legs.
c) i) Suggest one reason why scientists did not think that it would be possible to clone sheep from udder cells.
    ii) Some scientists did not regard sheep produced in this way as a pure clone. Suggest one reason for this.
d) Suggest one reason why it would be undesirable to produce all farm animals in this way.

Further questions on genes and genetic engineering

▷ **Nucleic acids and protein synthesis**

1 The diagram below shows part of a DNA molecule.

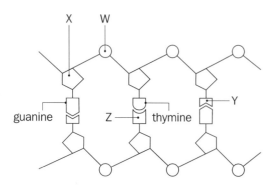

What do each of the following letters on the diagram represent?

W ; X ; Y ; Z ;

(*NEAB*) [4]

2 The diagram below shows the process of DNA replication.

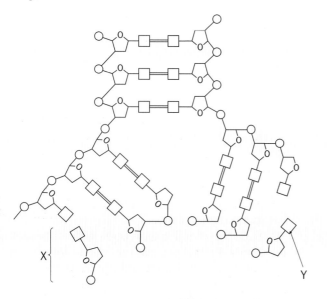

a) Name the parts labelled X and Y. [2]
b) Name *one* enzyme involved in DNA replication and state the type of reaction it catalyses. [2]
c) Suggest why DNA replication is described as *semi-conservative*. [1]
d) Name the stage of the cell cycle during which DNA replication occurs. [1]

(*Edex*) [6]

3 The diagram below shows the sequence of bases in one strand of the DNA from part of a gene. The base sequence is read from left to right.

DNA base sequence

A C C C C A T T T C A T C C A

The table below shows the anticodons of some tRNA molecules and the specific amino acids each would carry.

Amino acid	tRNA anticodon
Alanine	CGA
Glycine	CCA
Lysine	UUU
Proline	GGA
Tryptophan	ACC
Valine	CAU

a) Using this information, write down the amino acid sequence coded for in this part of the gene. [2]
b) The diagram below shows the same length of DNA after it has undergone a mutation.

A C C T C A T T T C A T C C A

Suggest how this mutation might affect the protein produced. [3]

(*Edex*) [5]

4 The diagram below shows the structure of a tRNA molecule.

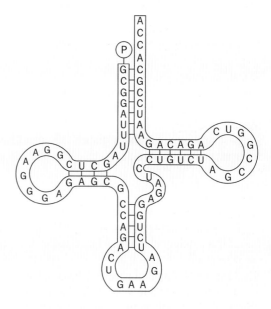

a) Give *two* ways in which the structure of a tRNA molecule differs from that of a DNA molecule. [2]
b) Explain how the specific shape of the tRNA molecule shown in the diagram is determined by the pattern of bonding. [2]
c) i) Give the base sequence of the anticodon of this tRNA molecule. [1]
   ii) Which mRNA codon would correspond to this anticodon? [1]

(*NEAB*) [6]

5 Copy and complete the table below to give correct functions of DNA, messenger RNA (mRNA) and transfer RNA (tRNA) during protein synthesis. Place a tick (✔) in the appropriate box if the statement is correct and a cross (✗) in the box if the statement is incorrect.

Statement	DNA	mRNA	tRNA
Attaches to ribosome			
Carries amino acid to ribosome			
Translated			
Transcribed but not translated			
Site of anticodon			
Site of codon			

(WJEC) **[6]**

6 The diagram below outlines protein synthesis in a cell.

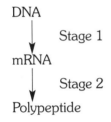

a) Name stages 1 and 2. [2]
b) Where does stage 2 take place within a cell? [1]
c) Describe the role of tRNA in stage 2. [3]

(Edex) **[6]**

▷ **Cell division**

7 The table below refers to the processes of mitosis and meiosis. Copy the table.
If the statement is true, put a tick (✔) in the appropriate box. If the statement is false, put a cross (✗) in the box.

Statement	Mitosis	Meiosis
Crossing over occurs		
Reduction in chromosome number from diploid to haploid		
Genetic uniformity of daughter cells		
Homologous chromosomes associate in pairs		

(AEB) **[4]**

8 The table above right refers to the first and second divisions of meiosis. Copy the table.
If the statement is correct, put a tick (✔) in the appropriate box and if the statement is incorrect, put a cross (✗) in the appropriate box.

Statement	First division of meiosis	Second division of meiosis
Pairing of homologous chromosomes occurs		
Chromosomes consist of pairs of chromatids during prophase		
Chiasmata are formed		
Chromatids are separated		
Independent assortment of chromosomes occurs		

(Edex) **[5]**

9 a) The diagrams below represent chromosomes in a cell during stages in the process of mitosis.

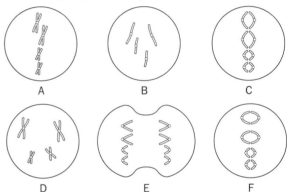

Write the letters in the order that represents the sequence in which these stages occur. [1]
b) State *two* ways in which meiosis differs from mitosis. [2]
c) Explain the significance of mitosis in living organisms. [3]

(Edex) **[6]**

▷ **Reproduction**

10 Graph A below shows the concentration of FSH and LH in plasma during a woman's menstrual cycle.
Graph B shows the concentration of two hormones, X and Y, produced in the ovary during the same menstrual cycle.

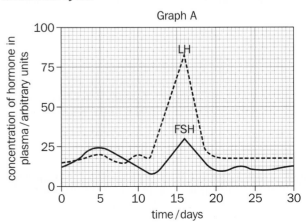

Further questions on genes and genetic engineering

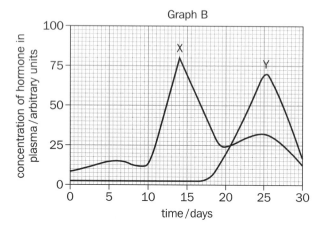

Graph B

a) Where are FSH and LH produced? [1]
b) Name hormones X and Y. [2]
c) On which day did ovulation occur in this woman's cycle? Explain the evidence for your answer. [3]
d) Describe an example of negative feedback involving two of these hormones. [2]

(NEAB) [8]

11 Records of human fertility for the period 1930 to 1990 have shown changes in the sperm counts of normal men.
The table below summarises the changing percentages of men with high or low sperm counts over the period of sixty years. High or low sperm counts are defined as follows:

High sperm count $> 100 \times 10^6$ sperm cm^{-3}
Low sperm count $< 20 \times 10^6$ sperm cm^{-3}

Time period	Men with high sperm counts (%)	Men with low sperm counts (%)
1930–1950	50	5
1951–1960	45	4
1961–1970	28	14
1971–1980	21	11
1981–1990	15	18

a) i) Comment on the changes in the percentage of men with high sperm counts during the period 1930 to 1990. [2]
   ii) Compare the figures for men with low sperm counts with those with high sperm counts over the same period. [3]
b) Explain why it is necessary for large numbers of sperms to be produced when only one sperm is required to bring about fertilisation. [2]
c) Exposure of pregnant women to high levels of certain oestrogens during early pregnancy can result in reproductive disorders in their male offspring. It appears that a number of compounds in the environment can mimic the action of oestrogens when ingested. Such compounds, termed oestrogenic chemicals, are found in pesticides, such as DDT and PCBs, and also in the

breakdown products of certain detergents. They accumulate in the fatty tissue and have the same effect as oestrogens, which play a major role in the menstrual cycle.
   i) Describe the normal role of oestrogens in the menstrual cycle. [3]
   ii) Suggest how the oestrogenic chemicals pass from the mother to the developing fetus. [3]

(Edexcel) [13]

▷ Gene technology

12 One of the processes in gene technology involves the synthesis of DNA, using messenger RNA (mRNA) as a template. This is shown in the diagram below.

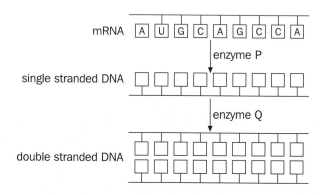

a) Name enzyme P. [1]
b) Copy the diagram above and write on the sequence of bases which would be present in the single stranded DNA. [2]
c) Name enzyme Q. [1]
d) The double stranded DNA can be inserted into a bacterial cell, which will then synthesise a protein which is coded for by this DNA.
   Name one protein which is produced in this way on an industrial scale. [1]

(Edexcel) [5]

13 The table opposite shows some restriction endonuclease enzymes and their binding and cleavage sequences. These enzymes can be used for making selective cuts in double-stranded DNA. Their binding sequences are mirror images on opposite strands. The asterisk (*) indicates the point of cleavage of the strands.
a) Some of these enzymes produce DNA fragments with 'sticky ends'. These are useful in preparing lengths of DNA for subsequent splicing.
   i) State what is meant by the term sticky end. [1]
   ii) Which of the enzymes in the table will generate DNA fragments with sticky ends? [2]
b) i) Name the enzyme used to join ends of DNA together. [1]
   ii) This enzyme can be used to join lengths of DNA with sticky or non-sticky (blunt) ends.

Name of restriction enzyme	Binding sequence
*Bal*I	TGG*CCA
*Eco*RI	G*AATTC
*Hpa*I	GTT*AAC
*Hae*III	GG*CC
*Not*I	GC*GGCCGC

Suggest why, in genetic engineering, it is preferable to use DNA with sticky ends when this reaction is carried out. [2]

c) Before using a restriction enzyme, an estimate is made of how useful it is likely to be. The formula below gives the probable number of cuts that might be made in a length of random sequence DNA by a restriction endonuclease.

$$\frac{\text{number of base pairs in the DNA module}}{4^n}$$

where n is the length of binding sequence. (The number 4 is related to the four possible bases found in DNA.)

   i) A bacterial plasmid (known as pBR322) has a length of 4300 base pairs. Calculate the expected number of cuts in this plasmid for the enzymes *Eco*RI and *Hae*III. [2]

   ii) Suggest which enzyme is likely to be most useful in inserting a gene into this plasmid. Explain your answer. [2]

(O&C) **[10]**

14 Glyphosate is a broad-spectrum herbicide. The diagram below shows stages in the production of a crop plant that is resistant to glyphosate. M represents the gene for glyphosate resistance.

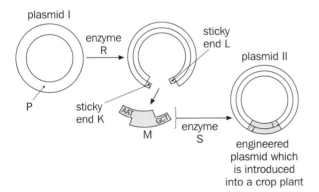

a) i) Name the molecule P which forms the plasmid. [1]

   ii) Name enzyme R and enzyme S. [2]

iii) The diagram shows detail of the sticky ends on M. Write down the base sequence you would expect to find on sticky ends K and L of the plasmid. [2]

b) i) Suggest *one* advantage to farmers of growing crops which are resistant to glyphosate. [1]

   ii) Suggest *one* disadvantage of using gene technology in this way to develop a crop plant with glyphosate resistance. [1]

(WJEC) **[7]**

15 Animals in which genes have been altered by the technique of recombinant DNA technology are referred to as *transgenic animals*.
This technique may be used, for example, to enable a sheep to produce milk which contains proteins normally produced by humans. A human gene for the required protein can be substituted for a similar gene in a sheep chromosome.
The diagram below shows the sequence of events in this process.

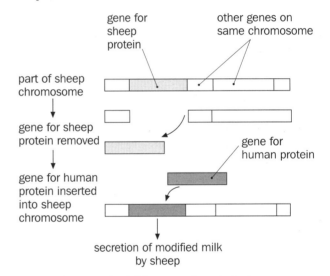

Adapted from Freeland, Microorganisms in Action

a) i) Name the enzyme which would be used to remove the gene for sheep protein from the sheep chromosome. [1]

   ii) Name the enzyme which would be used to attach the gene for the human protein to the sheep chromosome. [1]

b) Describe how the modified DNA might be re-introduced into a sheep. [2]

c) Suggest *two* advantages of using transgenic animals rather than microorganisms to produce human proteins. [2]

(Edexcel) **[6]**

How long can you hold your breath underwater?
Not as long as a seal can, that's for sure!
Seals can remain underwater for up to 48 minutes.

Divers continue to breathe underwater using air tanks.
The deeper they go, the greater the water pressure on their bodies.
The air in their lungs gets compressed and this forces nitrogen
as well as oxygen through the membranes of the lungs into the blood.
If a diver resurfaces too quickly, bubbles of nitrogen can form in the
tissues, causing blocked blood vessels, pain and even death.
This is known as the 'bends'.
A seal does not hold its breath at all when it dives. It actually breathes
as much air out of its lungs as it can.
Not only does this make the seal less buoyant, it also avoids the bends.

Many diving mammals, like seals, are able to store oxygen during a dive.
Their muscles contain a lot of myoglobin, which combines with oxygen
even more readily than haemoglobin.
Also, oxygenated blood is redirected away from regions such as the skin,
to critical areas such as the brain and the heart.

▷ Gas exchange and respiration

If cells are to stay active, grow and divide, they need a source of energy.
This energy comes from the oxidation of organic molecules such as
glucose in **respiration**.
As respiration involves oxidation reactions, all cells must have a constant
supply of oxygen.
As well as releasing energy, respiration also produces the waste products
carbon dioxide and water.

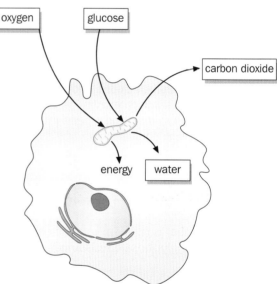

> **Respiration is a series of oxidation reactions taking place
> in all living cells. It results in the release of energy
> from organic compounds such as glucose.**

$$\underset{C_6H_{12}O_6}{\text{glucose}} + \underset{6O_2}{\text{oxygen}} \longrightarrow \underset{6CO_2}{\text{carbon dioxide}} + \underset{6H_2O}{\text{water}} + \underset{2880 \text{ kJ}}{\text{energy}}$$

Gas exchange is not the same as respiration. It is the process by which
oxygen gets to the cells and carbon dioxide is removed.
Respiration is the release of energy in cells.
Respiration creates a constant demand for oxygen and a constant release
of toxic carbon dioxide, which must be removed.

Animals and plants have evolved special **gas exchange surfaces**, which
allow the exchange of oxygen and carbon dioxide with the environment.

> **Gas exchange involves the diffusion of gases into and out
> of cells in order that respiration can take place.**

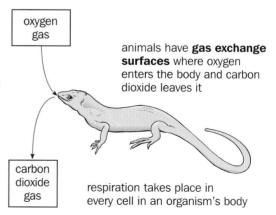

animals have **gas exchange
surfaces** where oxygen
enters the body and carbon
dioxide leaves it

respiration takes place in
every cell in an organism's body

What is the difference between gas exchange and respiration?
How would you describe the function of a gas exchange surface
such as the gills of a fish?

▷ Gas exchange surfaces

What do the gills of a fish, the alveoli (air sacs) in the lungs of a mammal and the spongy mesophyll cells in the leaves of a plant have in common?

They are all excellent gas exchange surfaces.
They allow quick and efficient gas exchange between the cells of the organism and its environment.

What features do these gas exchange surfaces have in common?

- They have a large surface area relative to the volume of the organism, over which gas exchange can take place rapidly.

- They are thin, so there is a short diffusion pathway over which gases can diffuse rapidly.

- They have a moist surface where gases can dissolve first before they diffuse in or out.

- They are able to maintain a concentration gradient down which gases can diffuse.

Humans and other mammals have a high metabolic rate.
This means that they have high oxygen requirements.
To make gas exchange even more efficient, they have developed:

- a blood transport system with red blood cells containing the pigment haemoglobin,

- a means of ventilation to get gases to and from the gas exchange surface.

▷ Gas exchange in unicellular organisms

In unicellular organisms, the gas exchange surface is the cell surface membrane.
These unicells have a high surface area/volume ratio.

Look back to page 52 to see how the surface area/volume ratio decreases as the volume of a cell increases.

The smaller the organism, the greater its surface area/volume ratio and the greater the efficiency of diffusion of gases through the membrane.

What happens when a unicellular organism uses up oxygen in respiration?

Oxygen diffuses down a concentration gradient into the cell as the oxygen inside the cell is quickly used up in respiration.
The build-up of carbon dioxide inside the cell sets up another concentration gradient and gas diffuses out of the cell.

The cell surface membrane of a unicellular organism is moist, allowing gases to dissolve, and thin, allowing rapid gas exchange.

The external gills of this Axolotl allow for efficient gas exchange

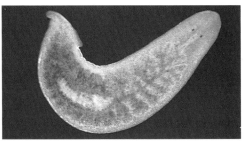
This flatworm's body has a large surface area/volume ratio

1 cm³ 'cell'
surface area/volume ratio = 6:1

8 cm³ 'cell'
surface area/volume ratio = 3:1

27 cm³ 'cell'
surface area/volume ratio = 2:1

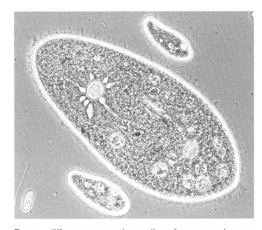
Gases diffuse across the cell surface membrane of this Paramecium

▷ Different gas exchange systems

Look at the photographs of the animals on this page.
Each has evolved a method of gas exchange that adapts it for life in a particular environment.
What special gas exchange surface does each animal have?
What features of this surface assist in the diffusion of gases?

A sea anemone

A nematode worm

A flatworm

A lugworm (Arenicola marina)
showing gills

A nudibranch (sea slug)
with obvious external gills

A tadpole with external gills

Copy and complete the table using your observations of each animal.

Name of animal	Gas exchange surface	Ways in which it makes gas exchange efficient

▷ Gas exchange in animals

Worms

What is the gas exchange surface of a worm?
Oxygen and carbon dioxide diffuse across the skin surface.
Worms do not have any special gas exchange organs.
But they have developed a tubular shape.
Why do you think this is?

Look at the 'tubular animal' and the 'cube-shaped animal'.
Calculate the surface area and volume for each 'animal'.
Then work out the surface area/volume ratio for each.

Can you see that they have the *same* volume (8 cm^3)?
But the surface area of the elongated animal is 34 cm^2
and that of the cube-shaped animal is 24 cm^2 .
The elongated animal has a greater surface area/volume ratio
than the cube-shaped animal (4.25 cm^{-1} compared with 3.0 cm^{-1}).

The tubular shape of the earthworm and other **annelids**
is efficient for the exchange of gases.
The skin is moist for gases to dissolve, and thin so
there is only a short distance between the air and
the blood capillaries beneath the skin surface.
The blood system maintains a diffusion gradient
by constantly removing oxygen and taking it to the cells
and bringing carbon dioxide back.
Some types of worm have evolved a flattened shape.
Why do you think this is?

Insects

Insects have evolved a system of **tracheal tubes**
throughout their bodies.
Openings at the side of the body called **spiracles** open
into a branching system of tubes that supply the tissues with air.
The spiracles can open and close like valves, allowing
gas exchange but also reducing water loss.

The smallest of the branching tubes are called **tracheoles**
and are in contact with the tissues.
The end of each tracheole contains a small amount of fluid
in which the gases dissolve.
When tissues such as muscle are active, the fluid is drawn into
the tissue, supplying oxygen.
The fluid is released back into the tracheole when the muscle
is at rest, so removing the waste carbon dioxide.

- The tracheal system provides the insect with a large surface
  area for exchange of gases.

- Small insects can rely on diffusion through the tracheal
  system alone to get gases in and out of the tissues.

- Larger or more active insects ventilate their tracheal system
  by rhythmical body movements that pump air in and out.

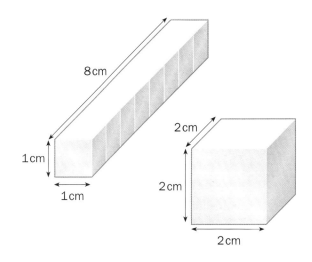

Gas exchange occurs across the earthworm's skin

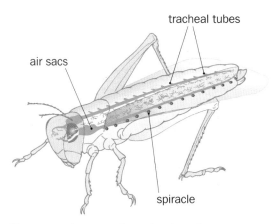

The gas exchange system of an insect

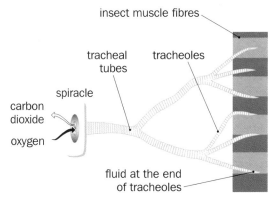

Insect tracheal system

167

▷ Gas exchange in fish

Fish use water as a gas exchange medium instead of air.
This brings problems, as you can see from the table.

	Water	Air
oxygen content (%)	0.7	20
oxygen diffusion rate	low	high
density (kg per litre)	1.0	0.0013
viscosity	1.0	0.02

Water contains far less oxygen than air and the rate of diffusion
of gases in water is slower.
Water is denser and more viscous, so it does not flow as freely as air.

Specialised gas exchange organs are needed: the **gills**.
Gills are made up of numerous folds, providing a huge surface area
over which water can flow and gases can be exchanged.

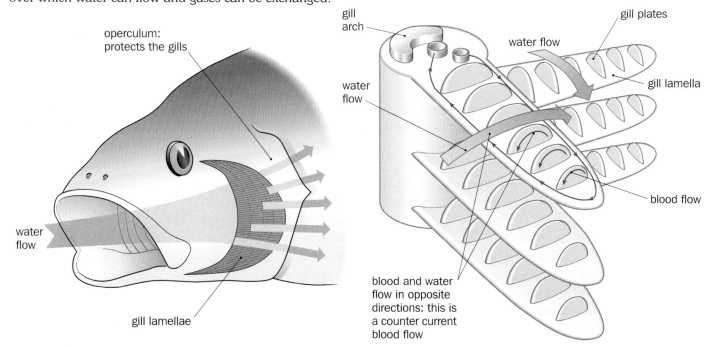

operculum:
protects the gills

water flow

gill lamellae

gill arch

water flow

water flow

gill plates

gill lamella

blood flow

blood and water flow in opposite directions: this is a counter current blood flow

In bony fish there are four pairs of gills in the **pharynx** (throat).
Each gill is supported by a bony **gill arch**.
Along each gill arch is a double row of **gill lamellae**.
These thin flaps lie on top of each other like the pages in a book.
When surrounded by water they give a large surface area for
gas exchange.
Out of water, the lamellae stick together and the gill collapses,
so the fish suffocates.

Can you see from the diagram that each gill lamella has **gill plates**
along each of its sides?
The gill plates are the gas exchange surfaces.

Blood vessels bring deoxygenated blood to the gill lamellae.
The blood then passes through tiny capillaries present
in each of the gill plates.
Oxygen passes through the gill plates into the capillaries
and carbon dioxide passes out into the water.
Blood vessels carry oxygenated blood away.

▷ Ventilation of the gills

Bony fish have evolved a ventilation mechanism that allows water to pass across the gill more or less continuously.

To take in water:

- The mouth opens.
- The **operculum** (gill cover) closes the opening at the back of the pharynx.
- The floor of the mouth cavity is lowered.
- The volume inside the mouth cavity increases and so the pressure inside the cavity falls.
- This allows water to rush in through the mouth.

For water to pass out:

- The mouth closes.
- The floor of the mouth cavity is raised.
- The volume inside the mouth cavity decreases and so the pressure inside the cavity rises, forcing water back over the gills.
- The operculum opens and water flows out.

A counter current system

Bony fish have gills that use a **counter current principle**. In the lamellae, the blood in the capillaries flows in the **opposite** direction to the water flowing over the surface.

Can you see from the diagram that the blood is flowing forward in the capillaries of the gill plate?
At the same time water passes over the gill plate in the opposite direction.

This means that a diffusion gradient is maintained between the blood and the water right across the gill plate.

Can you see in this diagram that:

- blood with a relatively high oxygen concentration meets water with a lot of oxygen in it?
  So there is still a diffusion gradient for oxygen **into** the blood.

- blood with a relatively low oxygen concentration meets water which has had most of its oxygen removed?

The counter current system allows the gills of a bony fish to achieve an 80% extraction of oxygen from water. That's three times the rate of extraction of human lungs from air!
This helps to overcome the problem of there being less oxygen in water.

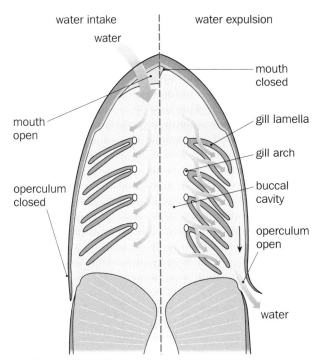

Ventilation of fish gills

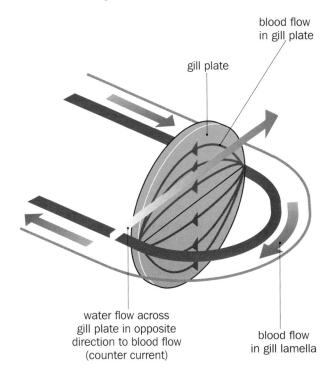

the counter current system maintains a diffusion gradient along the whole length of the gill plate

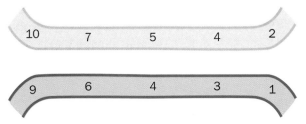

(numbers represent relative oxygen concentrations)

▷ Gas exchange in humans

Do you remember learning about the lungs at GCSE?
The lungs are specialised *internal* gas exchange surfaces.
They are found in your chest, either side of your heart.
The lungs are protected by the **rib cage**, which is also
involved in breathing.
A muscular **diaphragm** separates the
lungs from the organs below.

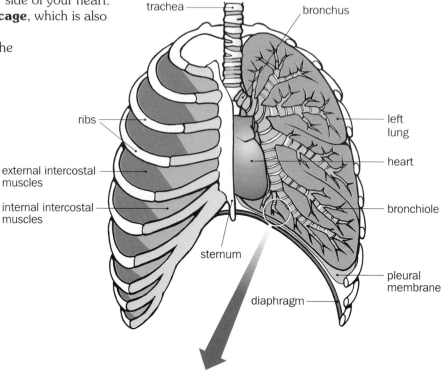

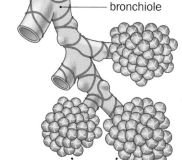

The human respiratory system

Why are the lungs so efficient at exchanging gases?

- The exchange surfaces are **alveoli** (air sacs),
  which provide a large surface area relative to
  the volume of the body.
  (If you unfolded all the alveoli from a human
  lung, it would give an area of about 80 m² –
  that's nearly the size of a tennis court!)

- The surfaces of the alveoli are moist for gases to
  dissolve.

- The alveoli are very thin, which helps diffusion
  by providing a very short diffusion pathway.

- Each alveolus is surrounded by a capillary network.
  This good supply of blood helps to maintain concentration
  gradients, because the blood is always taking oxygen
  away from the alveolus and returning with carbon dioxide.

- Ventilation of the lungs ensures that the air in the air passages
  is changed.
  This again helps to maintain the gas concentration
  gradients between the air in the alveoli and that in the blood.

Where *exactly* in the lungs does gas exchange occur?

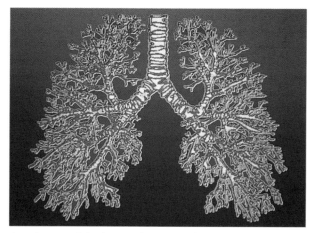

A resin cast of the human lungs

170

▷ Breathing

Your lungs contain elastic tissue – they have no muscle.
So how are you able to breathe in and out?

Air is drawn into the lungs by reducing the pressure inside
them to below atmospheric pressure.
Air is blown out of the lungs by increasing the pressure
inside them to above atmospheric pressure.
Movements of the ribcage and diaphragm produce
these pressure changes.

Inspiration (breathing in)

If air is to enter the lungs, then the pressure inside them
must be lower than atmospheric pressure.

- The external intercostal muscles **contract** and the
  internal intercostal muscles **relax**, raising the ribs upwards
  and outwards.

- At the same time, the muscular diaphragm **contracts** and
  flattens.

- Both these actions **increase** the volume inside the thorax,
  causing the pressure inside the thorax to **decrease**.

- Since atmospheric pressure is greater, air rushes
  into the lungs and they inflate.

Expiration (breathing out)

Breathing in is an active process but breathing out is usually passive.
Inspiration stretches the elastic tissue of the alveoli.
When the inspiratory muscles relax, this elastic tissue recoils,
pushing the air out.

- The internal intercostal muscles **contract** and
  the external intercostal muscles **relax**.
  This lowers the ribs downwards and inwards.

- The diaphragm **relaxes** and bulges upwards due to
  pressure from the organs below, for example the liver.

- Both these actions **decrease** the volume inside the thorax,
  causing the pressure inside the thorax to **increase**.

- Air is forced **out** of the lungs as the elastic tissue
  of the alveoli recoils.

Around each lung and lining the thorax are the
pleural membranes.
Between these two membranes is a space called the
pleural cavity, which contains **pleural fluid**.
During breathing the pleural fluid acts as a lubricant.

This allows friction-free movement of the lungs against the
inner wall of the thorax.
The alveoli do not collapse when we breathe out because
they have an anti-sticking chemical called a **surfactant**
covering their surfaces.
This chemical acts by reducing the surface tension and
so keeps the alveoli open.

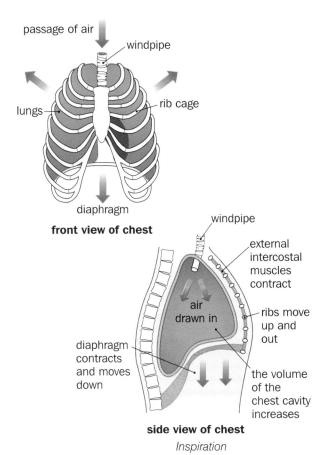

front view of chest

Inspiration

side view of chest

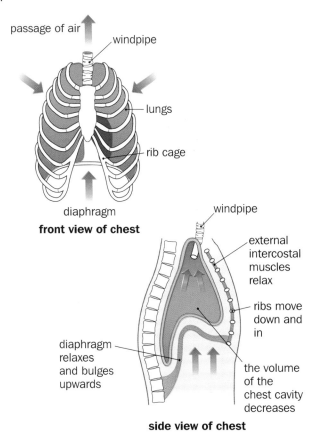

front view of chest

side view of chest

Expiration

▷ Gas exchange at the alveolus

Gas exchange takes place in the lungs at the tiny air sacs or alveoli. As you have seen, these provide a huge surface-area for the respiratory gases to pass across.

Ventilation ensures that air is moved into and out of the air passages of the lungs regularly.
This helps to maintain the necessary concentration gradients of oxygen and carbon dioxide.

The capillaries around the alveoli provide efficient blood transport of gases.
This prevents a build-up of oxygen and carbon dioxide and maintains gas concentration diffusion gradients.
In addition, the red blood cells contain the respiratory pigment haemoglobin.
This has a high affinity for oxygen, making the removal of oxygen from the alveoli even more efficient.

Look at the diagram.
Deoxygenated blood enters the capillaries around the alveolus.
This blood has less oxygen and more carbon dioxide than the air inside the alveolus.
So oxygen diffuses out of the alveolus into the blood in the capillary.
Carbon dioxide diffuses out of the capillary into the air in the alveolus.

Can you see that by the time the blood leaves the alveolus, the concentration of oxygen and carbon dioxide in the alveolus and in the blood are balanced?

The lining of the alveolus is moist and gases diffuse in solution.
The walls of the alveolus and blood capillary are each only one cell thick, making it easy for diffusion to take place.

Look at the table.

Why is the percentage of oxygen in the alveolus **less** than that in inspired air?
The answer is because the inspired air mixes with air already in the lungs (residual air), which has a lower percentage of oxygen.

Explain the differences in carbon dioxide concentration between inspired and expired air.
Why does the percentage of nitrogen hardly change?
Why is expired air saturated with water?

▷ Air conditioning

The first part of the respiratory system treats the air that you breathe in.
As you breathe in through your nose, the air is warmed, moistened and filtered.

The trachea, bronchi and bronchioles are lined with ciliated epithelial cells.
There are also **goblet cells**, which secrete slimy mucus.
The mucus traps dust particles and some germs that you breathe in.
Then the cilia beat to move a stream of mucus up to your throat.
This removes the dust and germs.

Tobacco smoke temporarily anaesthetises the cilia and stops them beating.
What effect does this have on the accumulation of mucus in the lungs?

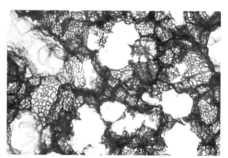

A photomicrograph of lung tissue

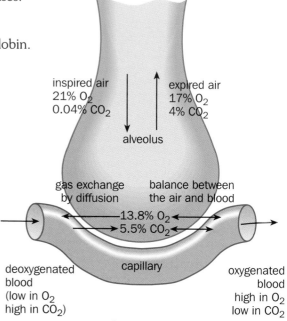

inspired air
21% O_2
0.04% CO_2

expired air
17% O_2
4% CO_2

alveolus

gas exchange by diffusion

balance between the air and blood

13.8% O_2
5.5% CO_2

deoxygenated blood
(low in O_2
high in CO_2)

capillary

oxygenated blood
high in O_2
low in CO_2

Percentage composition of inspired, alveolar and expired air			
Gas	Inspired	Alveolar	Expired
O_2	20.95	13.80	16.40
CO_2	0.04	5.50	4.00
N_2	79.01	80.70	79.60
H_2O	variable	saturated	saturated

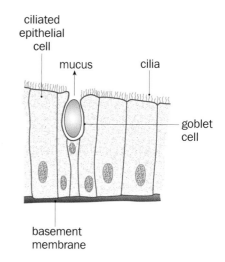

ciliated epithelial cell

mucus

cilia

goblet cell

basement membrane

▷ Control of breathing

You can exercise voluntary control over your breathing muscles.
You do this when you shout, sing, sigh or play the saxophone.
But you do not usually think about breathing – it's automatic.

Regular breathing

The basic rhythm of breathing is controlled by part of the brain
called the **medulla**.
There is a group of nerve cells in the medulla that make up
the **respiratory centre**.

During quiet breathing, nerve impulses from the respiratory centre
travel along nerves to the external intercostal muscles and the
diaphragm.
The muscles then contract and you breathe in.

As air enters the lungs, **stretch receptors** in the walls
of the bronchi and bronchioles send impulses back to the medulla.
When the lungs are sufficiently inflated, the increased feedback
from the stretch receptors causes the respiratory centre
to stop sending out impulses for about 3 seconds.
The external intercostal muscles and the diaphragm relax and
expiration takes place.

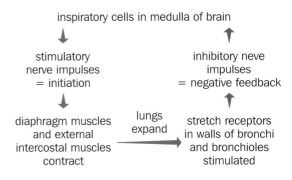

Varying your breathing

Your breathing rate alters when you exercise.
Greater muscular action means you need more energy from respiration.
More oxygen is needed in the muscles and extra carbon dioxide
must be removed quickly. So,

- the **depth** of breathing must be increased,
- the **rate** of breathing must be increased.

During exercise the rate of respiration increases in your cells.
So more oxygen is used up and more carbon dioxide is produced.
It is the **rise in carbon dioxide** that triggers the changes in
your breathing.

Chemoreceptors are cells that are sensitive to changes in the
presence and concentration of specific chemicals in the blood.
Some are able to detect very small changes in pH.
The most sensitive chemoreceptors are located in the medulla itself.
A rise in carbon dioxide concentration results in more carbonic acid.
This dissociates, increasing the hydrogen ion concentration and
producing a more acidic pH.

$$CO_2 + H_2O \rightleftharpoons H_2CO_3 \rightleftharpoons H^+ + HCO_3^-$$

There are chemoreceptors in areas lining the carotid arteries and aorta.
These areas are called the **carotid bodies** and **aortic bodies** respectively.
These are sensitive to changes in carbon dioxide and pH,
and can also detect changes in oxygen.

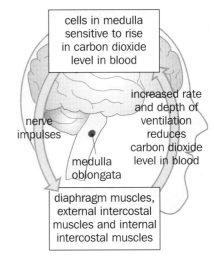

When the chemoreceptors detect any of these changes, they send
nerve impulses to the respiratory centre in the brain.
The respiratory centre sends more frequent impulses to
the external intercostal muscles and the diaphragm.
As a result, breathing becomes faster and deeper until carbon dioxide
levels return to normal.

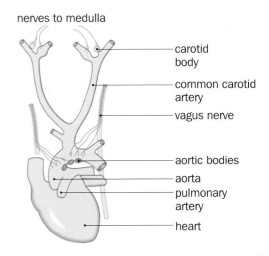

▷ Gas exchange in plants

All plant cells need a supply of oxygen because they carry out respiration all the time.

Some plant cells also carry out photosynthesis, so they need a supply of carbon dioxide.

Carbon dioxide produced during plant respiration may be used by photosynthesising cells.

And oxygen produced during photosynthesis can be used by cells for respiration.

Oxygen enters root tissue by diffusion from air spaces between soil particles.

Respiration keeps the oxygen concentration in the cells below that in the soil,

so maintaining a diffusion gradient.

The root system is extensive, giving a large surface-area, and the thin root hairs provide little barrier to diffusion.

However, most gas exchange in plants occurs in the leaves.
Leaves are thin and have a large surface area/volume ratio.
They also have an extensive internal system of air spaces.
Gases are able to diffuse in and out of these air spaces through tiny pores called **stomata**.

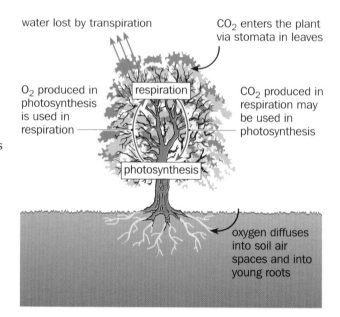

water lost by transpiration

CO_2 enters the plant via stomata in leaves

O_2 produced in photosynthesis is used in respiration

respiration

CO_2 produced in respiration may be used in photosynthesis

photosynthesis

oxygen diffuses into soil air spaces and into young roots

▷ Leaf structure

The **palisade mesophyll** is the main photosynthetic tissue. The cells are deep and packed full of chloroplasts. The chloroplasts are able to move and so arrange themselves in a position that gives maximum light absorption.

The **upper epidermis** is a single layer of cells. It is transparent since no chloroplasts are present and this means that light can pass straight through to the tissues below. There are not many stomata in the upper epidermis (if any at all) since the heat from direct sunlight would cause excessive evaporation.

The upper surface of a leaf is covered by a waxy **cuticle**. This reduces water loss significantly.

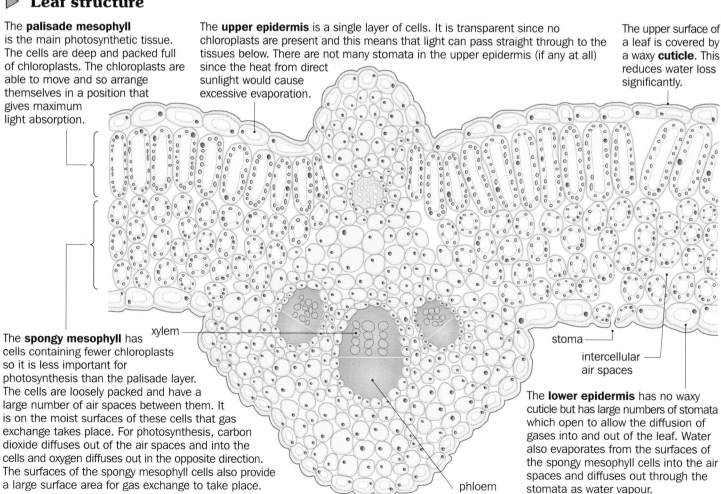

xylem

stoma

intercellular air spaces

phloem

The **spongy mesophyll** has cells containing fewer chloroplasts so it is less important for photosynthesis than the palisade layer. The cells are loosely packed and have a large number of air spaces between them. It is on the moist surfaces of these cells that gas exchange takes place. For photosynthesis, carbon dioxide diffuses out of the air spaces and into the cells and oxygen diffuses out in the opposite direction. The surfaces of the spongy mesophyll cells also provide a large surface area for gas exchange to take place.

The **lower epidermis** has no waxy cuticle but has large numbers of stomata which open to allow the diffusion of gases into and out of the leaf. Water also evaporates from the surfaces of the spongy mesophyll cells into the air spaces and diffuses out through the stomata as water vapour.

174

▷ Stomata

Stomata are the tiny pores found on the underside of a leaf.
Each stoma is bordered by two **guard cells**.
These guard cells have chloroplasts, unlike other epidermal cells.
The stomata allow exchange of gases to occur between the air
and the internal tissues of the leaf.
About 90% of water evaporation from a plant takes place
through the stomata.

The opening of the stomata depends upon environmental conditions.
The guard cells have thickened inner walls.
When the guard cells take up water by osmosis, they swell and
become turgid.
The thickened inner walls of the guard cells become more curved
and the stoma pore opens.
When the guard cells lose water they become flaccid.
Their thickened inner walls spring back and close the stoma.
By opening and closing, the stomata control the amounts
of gases diffusing into and out of the leaf.
They also control the amount of water vapour evaporating.
(The mechanism of stomatal opening and closing is covered
in Chapter 12.)

Opening and closing

The most important environmental factors affecting the opening
and closing of stomata are light, carbon dioxide and water.

The stomata tend to open during the day and close at night.
Increased light intensity results in more photosynthesis, which
reduces the carbon dioxide concentration in the cells.
Low carbon dioxide stimulates the stomata to open.

Low light intensity reduces photosynthesis.
Carbon dioxide accumulates in the cells since it is not being used up.
High carbon dioxide stimulates the stomata to close.

Lack of water also causes the stomata to close because
the guard cells lose their turgor and become flaccid.

Water stress can also cause an increase in **abscissic acid** (**ABA**)
in the leaves, which stimulates the stomata to close.

Why do floating water plants only have stomata on the upper
surface of their leaves?

▷ Lenticels

The protective layer of bark in woody plants prevents gas exchange.
But underneath the bark are respiring cells, so how can they get oxygen?
A **lenticel** is a small area of bark where the cells are loose.
The lenticels allow oxygen to diffuse into the living stem tissue
and carbon dioxide to diffuse out.

SEM of a stoma with two guard cells

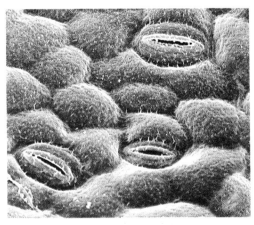

SEM of lower leaf epidermis showing stomata

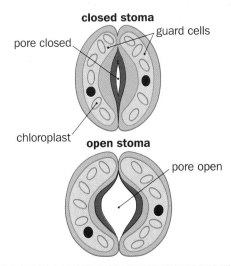

Photomicrograph of a section of a lenticel

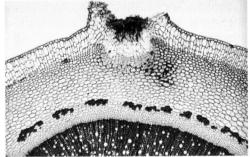

▷ Biology at work: Asthma

Asthma is a common ailment in children.
The symptoms include attacks of breathlessness, which
can vary from quite mild to very severe.
Asthma affects about one in 20 of the overall population
and it is estimated that around 150 000 school children
in the UK suffer from the condition.

Asthmatic attacks occur due to inflammation of the bronchioles.
These are the air passages in the lungs that lead to the alveoli,
and their obstruction means that more effort is required
to deliver sufficient air to the lungs.
The obstruction is made worse by increased secretion of phlegm
due to the inflammation, and sufferers develop a dry cough in
an attempt to clear the airways.

There are many possible causes of asthma, including air pollution,
respiratory infections, exercise in cold air and allergies.
The most common allergens are pollen, house dust, house dust
mites, fur and feathers.

Where asthma occurs for only a few months of the year, the cause is
likely to be pollen or spores, and this is known as seasonal asthma.

More than half the children with asthma grow out of it
by the time they reach 21.
Prior to this they will probably receive very effective
treatment in the form of drugs.

Bronchiodilators (which are often related to adrenaline)
give quick relief by causing the smooth muscle
lining the bronchioles to relax – so widening the airways.
Steroids may be taken to reduce the amount of inflammation
of the bronchioles.

Both these drugs can be taken in aerosol form
using an inhaler.
When used correctly, these devices deliver the
correct dose directly to the inflamed tissue,
so allowing a speedy response.

Asthma should not be confused with emphysema, which
has some common symptoms, such as breathlessness and
a shortage of oxygen.
Emphysema is a disease in most cases caused by cigarette
smoking and is due to permanent lung damage.
The alveoli burst and blend together to form a greatly
reduced surface area for gas exchange, combined
with a loss of elasticity.

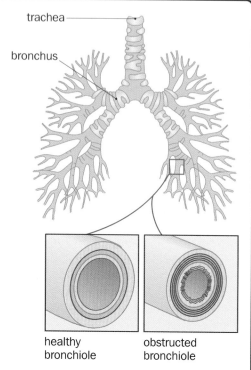

The effect of asthma on the lungs

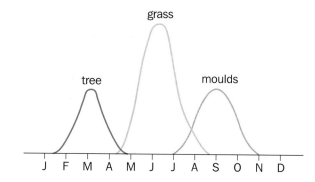

Seasonal variation in pollen and spore counts

A sportswoman using an inhaler

▷ Biology at work: Everest without oxygen

On 8th May 1978 Rienhold Messner and Peter Habeler were the first to climb Mount Everest (8848 metres) without an additional supply of oxygen.
At the time this was commonly believed to be an impossible feat. Their success was made possible by a careful and slow process of **acclimatisation.**

This involved a gradual exposure to an atmosphere where the air contained less than a third the amount of oxygen present in air at sea level.
This reduction in oxygen has severe consequences on the body.

A reduction in blood oxygen levels causes a condition known as **hypoxia**.
If allowed to continue, hypoxia may lead to acute mountain sickness or more life-threatening conditions, including cerebral oedema (swelling of the brain) and pulmonary oedema, leading to excess fluid in the lungs.
Death can result from these conditions unless the climber descends rapidly.

The body's response to hypoxia depends on a number of factors, including the speed and severity of exposure to low oxygen levels.
In general, the following responses occur.

- Rate and depth of breathing increase to increase oxygen uptake and carbon dioxide removal.

- Heart rate increases to transport more oxygen-laden red blood cells from the lungs to the tissues.

- Concentration of the blood increases owing to water reabsorption into the tissues.

- Production of red blood cells from bone marrow increases after the first week, due to an increased secretion of a hormone called **erythropoietin**, which is made in the kidneys.

- Growth of more blood capillaries to the tissues, allowing a quicker diffusion of oxygen to the cells.

- The number of mitochondria per cell increases, so oxygen is used up quickly and a steep diffusion gradient is maintained.

There is a limit to how much oxygen can be extracted from the air at such altitudes because of the above responses.
For instance, the heart can only beat so fast before it has an inadequate amount of time to refill between contractions.
A few hundred metres higher and Everest would be impossible to climb without supplemental oxygen.
It is for this reason that the area above 8000 metres on the world's highest mountains is referred to as the 'Death Zone'!

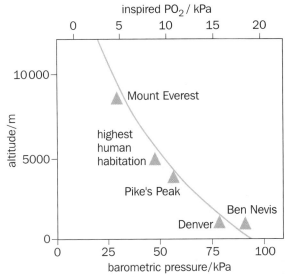

The relationship between altitude and inspired oxygen pressure

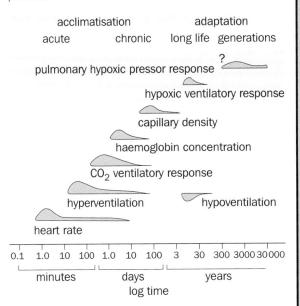

The time scale for acclimatisation and adaptive changes. The curve of each response shows rate of change

In the 1968 Olympics, athletes who were used to training and competing near sea level experienced a significant reduction in performance.
This was because the games were held in Mexico City, which is at an altitude of 2242 metres.
The athletes who normally lived at a high altitude did well and won many of the endurance races, such as the 10 000 metres.

The lower oxygen levels at altitude mean that less oxygen is delivered to the muscles.
The body's immediate response is to release red blood cells stored in the spleen.
Within 12 hours there is also an increase in the rate at which red blood cells are formed.
The hormone erythropoietin is responsible for this increase.
These changes lead to a total increase in circulating haemoglobin by as much as 50–90%.
Consequently, the capacity of the blood to carry oxygen is also increased.

Other changes include an increase in phosphate substances inside the red blood cells.
These combine with the haemoglobin to reduce its affinity for oxygen.
This means the haemoglobin will give up its oxygen more easily when it reaches the muscle tissue.
At altitudes of 2000–2500 metres, it takes about 2 weeks for the body to acclimatise and bring about these changes.

Recent developments have tried to reproduce the benefits of altitude training but at sea level.
These range from crude and uncomfortable breathing apparatus worn by athletes, to complex hypoxic training rooms.

An obvious benefit of this is a reduction in travel cost.
Others benefits include:

- no air pressure change,

- no exposure to higher levels of ozone and UV light,

- no tissue enlargement,

- no accelerated dehydration,

- better oxygen supply to peripheral tissues,

- longer maintenance of improvements such as drop in heart rate.

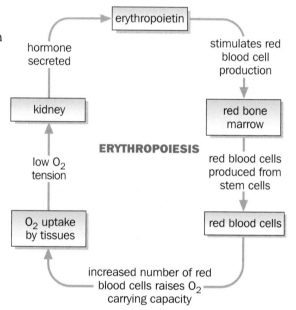

Summary

- Gas exchange is needed for respiration to take place. Oxygen has to be taken up and carbon dioxide released.
- Efficient gas exchange surfaces:
    have a high surface area/volume ratio,
    are thin and permeable,
    are moist so that gases can diffuse in solution.
- In unicellular organisms the cell surface membrane has enough surface area relative to the volume of the cell to act as a gas exchange surface.
- In larger organisms, structures such as gills, tracheal tubes and alveoli have evolved to enable efficient gas exchange to take place.
- Many fish use a counter current system to increase the rate of gas exchange across the gills.
- Insects have evolved a system of air tubes called tracheoles to carry air directly to the tissues.
- Mammals have internal lungs and a method of ventilation to change the air in them.
- Some animals have an efficient respiratory pigment, such as haemoglobin.
- The spongy mesophyll cells of a leaf provide the main gas exchange surfaces in a plant.
- Gases pass into and out of plant tissues through stomata and lenticels.
- Both animals and plants have developed gas exchange systems that enable them to overcome their reduced surface area/volume ratio.

▷ Questions

1 a) Unicellular organisms such as *Amoeba* have no special organs for gas exchange. Large, multicellular organisms such as mammals have complex internal systems for gas exchange. Explain why a mammal needs such a system when a single-celled organism does not.

   b) How does a molecule of carbon dioxide in the atmosphere reach the palisade mesophyll cells of a leaf?

2 The rate of diffusion of a molecule across a membrane depends on the relative concentration of the molecule on either side of the membrane, the membrane's thickness and its surface area.

$$\text{Rate of diffusion} = \frac{\text{surface area} \times \text{difference in concentration}}{\text{thickness of the membrane}}$$

   a) For maximum diffusion to take place, which factor should:
      i) be as large as possible,
      ii) be as small as possible?
   b) Use the equation to explain how the following are adapted for efficient gas exchange:
      i) a single-celled *Amoeba*,
      ii) the human lungs.

3 *Arenicola* is a marine worm that lives in a burrow in the mid-shore.
   It has gills along its body that extract oxygen from the seawater that it pumps through its burrow.
   a) The diagram shows a cross-section through the body and gills of *Arenicola*. How do you think that the structure of the gill makes it efficient for gas exchange?

   b) What is the advantage to the worm of pumping seawater through its burrow?

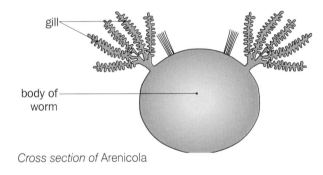

Cross section of Arenicola

4 a) What are the essential features of a good respiratory surface?

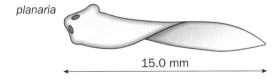

   b) This aquatic animal is able to carry out gas exchange by diffusion.
      Explain how this occurs taking into account size and shape of the animal, its environment, metabolic activity and maintenance of diffusion gradients.
   c) Outline how a continuous supply of oxygen reaches all tissues of an earthworm.

5 The data in the table shows that the carbon
   dioxide concentration in the alveoli of the lungs
   affects the amount of air taken in by breathing
   movements.

Carbon dioxide concentration in the alveoli (arbitrary units)	40	42	44	46	48	50	52
Air taken in (dm³ min⁻¹)	8	15	22	29	36	43	50

   a) If the lowest carbon dioxide concentration is
      increased by 5%, calculate (showing your
      working)
       i) the new carbon dioxide concentration,
       ii) the percentage increase in ventilation rate.
   b) In what two ways do the respiratory movements
      change to bring about this effect?

6 Describe the pathways and mechanisms in the
   movement of oxygen in a mammal from:
   a) the air to the alveolus,
   b) the alveolus to the lung capillary,
   c) the lung capillary to the tissues.

7 The diagram shows the way in which water flows over
   the gills of a bony fish.

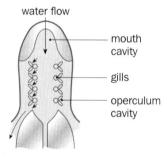

water flow — mouth cavity — gills — operculum cavity

The graph shows the changes in the mouth cavity and
operculum cavity during ventilation.

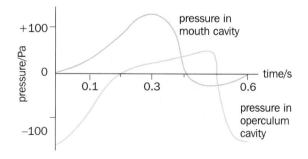

   a) Use the graph to calculate the ventilation rate in
      cycles per minute.

b) During ventilation, water flows over the gills in one
   direction.
   What evidence is there in the graph that supports
   this statement?
c) How does the counter current principle make the
   diffusion of oxygen across the gills more efficient?

8

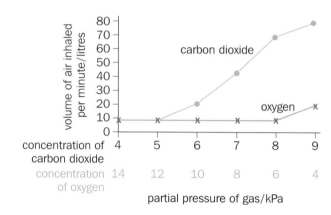

The graph shows the effects of changing the
concentration of oxygen and carbon dioxide in the air
on the volume of air inhaled in 1 minute by a person.
a) Calculate the percentage increase in the volume of
   air inhaled per minute when the partial pressure of
   carbon dioxide rises from 5 kPa to 8 kPa.
b) Describe the effect of changing oxygen
   concentration on the volume of air breathed in per
   minute.
c) The volume of air breathed in per minute is
   regulated by the respiratory centre. Where in the
   brain is the respiratory centre located?

9 The drawing shows the 24-hour cycle of stomatal
   opening and closing for a plant.
   Explain how this cycle of opening and closing is
   advantageous to the plant.

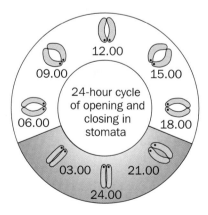

Marathon runners have great endurance.
They are able to maintain intense exercise for long periods, up to 26 miles!
But they have to train to achieve this level of fitness.
Training improves the efficiency of both the respiratory system and the **cardiovascular** system.

The cardiovascular system is made up of the heart, the blood vessels and the blood.
Endurance training can bring about the following changes.

- The heart size increases, particularly the left ventricle. Its muscular wall becomes thicker and the space inside becomes larger.

- This means that the volume of blood pumped with each heartbeat increases (this is called the **stroke volume**).

- So the resting heartbeat rate decreases.

- The volume of blood in the body increases.

- Recovery of the breathing and heartbeat rates is quicker after exercise.

If we look more closely at our transport system, you will be able to see why these changes improve an athlete's performance.

▷ Mass flow transport

Animal cells need a constant supply of oxygen and nutrients.
They also need to get rid of waste products such as carbon dioxide.

Simple, small animals, such as sea anemones, flatworms and nematodes, can do this by *diffusion* across their moist body surfaces.
But in larger animals, diffusion is too slow to supply all the body cells efficiently.
They need a **transport system** to carry oxygen, nutrients, carbon dioxide, waste products and hormones to and from the special exchange surfaces.

Our own circulatory system transports large volumes of fluid to all parts of our bodies.
It is an example of a **mass flow system**.

Our circulatory system consists of:

- **blood** – the fluid that is transported through the system,
- **blood vessels** – the tubes that carry the blood,
- a **heart** – to pump the blood through the network of blood vessels.

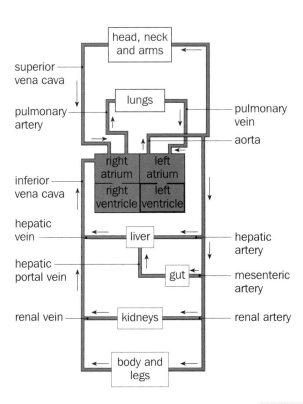

▷ Closed or open?

Animals such as snails and insects have **open blood systems**.
The blood does not flow through blood vessels.
It is pumped out of the heart into large spaces
in the body cavity.
The blood comes into close contact with the tissues
and exchange of materials takes place.
The blood then returns to the heart.

The blood of an insect does **not** transport oxygen.
Can you remember how oxygen gets to the tissues of an insect?

In a **closed circulation system**, the blood flows through vessels.

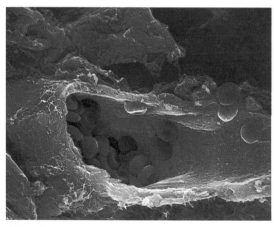

SEM of a vein (× 1400)

▷ Single or double?

Fish have a **single circulation system**.

The heart pumps deoxygenated blood to the gills.
Oxygenated blood is then carried to the tissues.
Deoxygenated blood returns to the heart.

So how many times does the blood pass through the heart
of a fish in **one** circuit of the body?

You can see from the diagram that the blood passes
through the heart only **once** in one circuit of the body.
That's why it is called a **single circulation**.

We have a **double circulation system**.

The right side of the heart pumps deoxygenated blood to the lungs.
Oxygenated blood then returns to the left side of the heart.
The left side of the heart pumps the oxygenated blood to the tissues.
Deoxygenated blood then returns to the right side of the heart.

So blood passes through the heart **twice** in each circuit
of the body: once through the right side and once through
the left side.
This is called a **double circulation**.

In mammals, the flow of blood is maintained by:

● a muscular heart, which pumps blood out through the arteries
to the capillaries,

● rhythmical contractions of the muscle in the thick-walled arteries,
which can be felt as a pulse,

● contraction of the body muscles during normal movements,
which help to squeeze blood along the thin-walled veins.
Veins also have **semi-lunar valves** to prevent the blood
from flowing backwards.

● breathing in creates a negative pressure inside the thorax,
which helps to draw blood towards the heart.

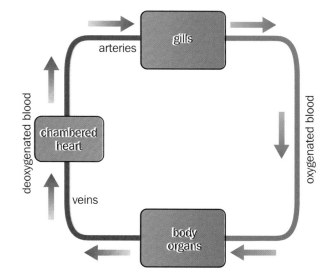

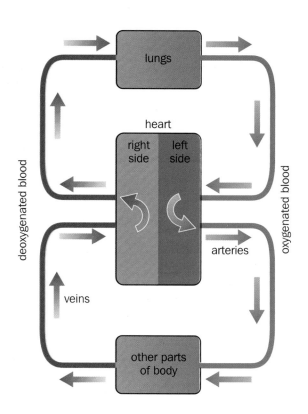

▷ Blood vessels

There are three main types of blood vessels:
arteries, **veins** and **capillaries**.

Arteries carry blood **away** from the heart. They branch to form smaller **arterioles**.
Arterioles sub-divide into tiny, thin-walled capillaries. Capillaries form a branching
network through a tissue. They allow rapid diffusion of materials between the
blood and the cells. Capillaries join up to form **venules**.
Venules then join up to form larger veins.

The walls of arteries and veins are made up of three main layers:

- a thin inner lining of epithelial cells,
- a middle layer made up of elastic tissue and smooth muscle,
- an outer layer of collagen fibres and elastic tissue.

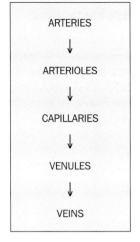

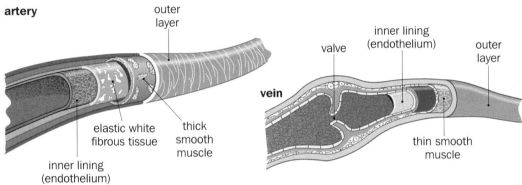

Arteries	Veins	Capillaries
a)	b)	c)
carry blood away from the heart thick muscular walls	carry blood back to the heart thin muscular walls	link up arteries and veins in the tissues no muscle: wall made up of one cell thick **endothelium**
lots of elastic tissue in wall relatively small lumen	little elastic tissue in wall relatively large lumen	no elastic tissue present small lumen — just large enough for a red blood cell to squeeze through
blood under high pressure blood flow is rapid blood flows in pulses no valves	blood under low pressure blood flow is slow no pulse valves prevent backflow of blood	pressure falls as blood passes along capillary blood flow is slowing down no pulse no valves

- The elastic tissue in the artery wall allows
  the vessel to 'give' as blood surges through.
  So the artery wall first stretches as a result of the
  high blood pressure, before an elastic recoil
  of the wall pushes the blood on its way.
  This swelling can be felt as a pulse where
  arteries travel near the surface of the skin.

How the semi-lunar valves work in a vein:

- The blood has enough pressure to force the valves
  open as it flows towards the heart.
- Backflow of blood causes the valves to close.

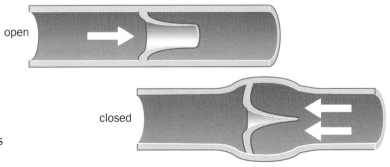

The action of semi-lunar valves

▷ Heart structure

Your heart is made up of mainly **cardiac muscle**.
Cardiac muscle tissue is made up of muscle fibres.
Each muscle fibre is made of interconnecting muscle cells.
Each muscle cell is joined to the next by **intercalary discs**.
These allow the rapid spread of impulses through the tissue
from cell to cell.
The heart is often described as being 'myogenic'.
This means that it can rhythmically contract and relax
of its own accord throughout a person's life.

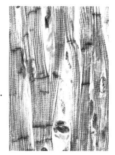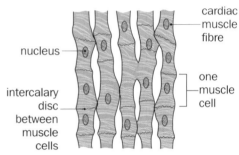

The structure of cardiac muscle

The heart is really two pumps side by side.
The right side of the heart pumps deoxygenated blood to the lungs.
The left side of the heart pumps oxygenated blood to the rest of the
body.
Each side of the heart is kept completely separate and so
the deoxygenated blood and the oxygenated blood do not mix.

On each side of the heart there are two chambers.
The upper chambers are called **atria** (singular **atrium**).
The **right atrium** receives blood from the **vena cava**.
The **left atrium** receives blood from the **pulmonary veins**.

When the atria contract, blood passes into the lower
chambers, called **ventricles**.
When the **right ventricle** contracts, it pumps blood out
into the **pulmonary arteries**.
When the **left ventricle** contracts, it pumps blood out into the **aorta**.

The thickness of the walls of each chamber of the heart
is related to the distance that it has to pump blood.

Why do you think that the atria have less muscular walls
than the ventricles?

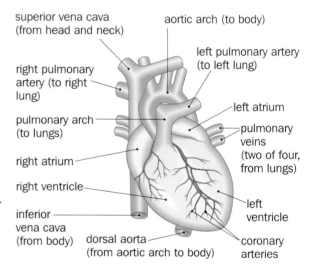

External structure of the heart

The two atria only have to pump blood a short distance
down to the ventricles.
The ventricles have much thicker walls because they have to
develop enough pressure to force the blood further.

Why do you think the left ventricle has a more muscular
wall than the right ventricle?

The right ventricle has only to force blood to the lungs,
which are either side of the heart.
The left ventricle has to pump blood all round the body.

Two sets of valves are present in the heart to keep the
blood flowing in one direction.

● The **atrio-ventricular valves** are found on each side,
  between the atria and the ventricles.
  They prevent the backflow of blood into the atria when the
  ventricles contract.
  On the right side, the **tricuspid valve** has three flaps.
  On the left side, the **bicuspid valve** has two flaps.

● The **semi-lunar valves** are found at the base of the
  pulmonary artery and the **aorta**.
  These valves close to prevent the backflow of blood into
  the ventricles when they relax.

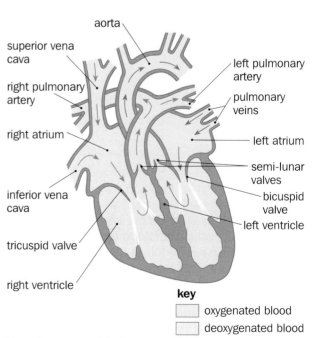

Internal structure of the heart

184

▷ The cardiac cycle

The **cardiac cycle** describes the sequence of events in one heartbeat. It is described in terms of alternate contractions (**systole**) and relaxations (**diastole**).

How long would each cardiac cycle last for a heart beating 75 times a minute?
Each cardiac cycle would last 60/75 = 0.8 seconds.

The valves in the heart respond to pressure changes during a cardiac cycle.
The noise of the blood when the valves open and close makes the sound of your heartbeat (lub-dub).

There are **_three_** main stages to the cardiac cycle.

Atrial systole

- The heart is full of blood and the ventricles are relaxed.
- Both the atria contract and the blood passes down to the ventricles.
- The atrio-ventricular valves open due to the pressure of blood against them.
- 70% of the blood flows **_passively_** down to the ventricles so the atria do not have to contract a great amount.

Ventricular systole

- The atria relax.
- The thick muscular walls of the ventricles contract, forcing blood out of the heart into the pulmonary artery and the aorta.
- The pressure of blood against the atrio-ventricular valves causes them to shut, preventing blood going back into the atria.
  This produces the first part of the heart sound 'lub'.
- The pressure of blood against the semi-lunar valves opens them.
- The pulmonary artery then carries deoxygenated blood to the lungs and the aorta carries oxygenated blood to the different parts of the body.

Diastole

- The ventricles relax.
- The pressure inside the ventricles drops below that in the arteries.
- Blood under high pressure in the arteries causes the semi-lunar valves to shut, preventing blood from going back into the ventricles.
  This produces the second part of the heart sound 'dub'.
- During diastole, all the muscle in the heart relaxes.
- Blood from the vena cava and pulmonary veins enters the atria. The whole cycle starts again.

Look at the graph showing the pressure changes in the left atrium, the left ventricle and the aorta during a cardiac cycle.
a) Calculate how many complete cardiac cycles there would be per minute.
b) Match the letter on the graph with the following events:
  i) semi-lunar valves open,
  ii) atrio-ventricular valves close,
  iii) semi-lunar valves close,
  iv) atrio-ventricular valves open.

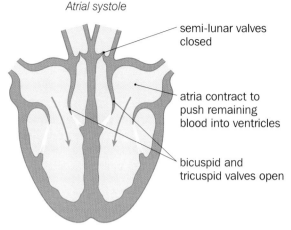

Atrial systole

semi-lunar valves closed

atria contract to push remaining blood into ventricles

bicuspid and tricuspid valves open

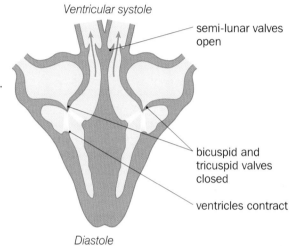

Ventricular systole

semi-lunar valves open

bicuspid and tricuspid valves closed

ventricles contract

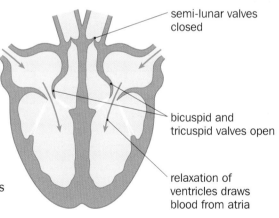

Diastole

semi-lunar valves closed

bicuspid and tricuspid valves open

relaxation of ventricles draws blood from atria

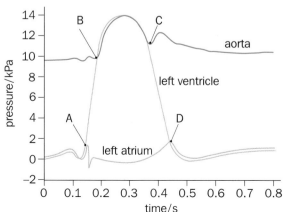

▷ Control of the heartbeat

As you know, the heart is myogenic: that is, it can contract and relax without having to receive impulses from the nervous system.

The cardiac cycle is started by specialised cardiac muscle tissue in the wall of the right atrium called the **sino-atrial node** (**SAN**).
You may have heard it called the '**pacemaker**'.
The cells of the SAN set the rhythm at which all the other cardiac muscle cells beat and so can control the speed of the cycle.

The SAN sends out electrical impulses to the rest of the atria.
These impulses spread out in a wave of electrical activity (depolarisation) over the atrial walls.
The cardiac muscle in the walls of both atria contract in rhythm with the impulses from the SAN.
So both right and left atria contract at the same time.

The electrical impulses do not pass down to the ventricles.
It is important that the muscles of the ventricles do not start to contract until the muscles of the atria have finished contracting.
Collagen fibres prevent the electrical signals from passing through the heart wall from atria to ventricles.
The delay ensures that the ventricles do not start to contract before they fill with blood.

So what causes the ventricles to contract?

A second node, the **atrio-ventricular node** (**AVN**), picks up the impulses that have passed through the atrial muscle.
The AVN responds by generating its own electrical impulses, which travel along specialised muscle fibres called **Purkinje fibres**.
The fibres in the right and left ventricle walls are together known as the **Bundle of His**.
The impulses are carried rapidly to the apex of the ventricles.
This causes the cardiac muscle in each ventricle to contract simultaneously, from the bottom up.
So blood is squeezed up and out through the arteries.

An electrocardiogram (ECG) can be used to detect changes in the electrical activity of the cardiac cycle.
Electrodes are taped to the patient's chest and connected to a monitor that produces the ECG trace.
You can find out more about ECGs and pacemakers on page 195.

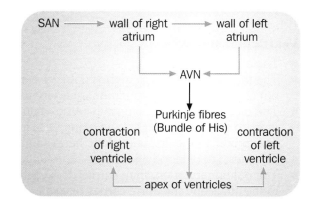

Controlling the heartbeat

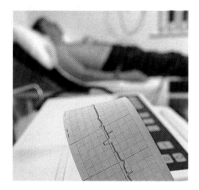

An electrogardiogram producing an ECG trace

▷ Modifying the heartbeat

You have seen that the heartbeat is started off and controlled by the heart itself.
But what happens when you exercise?
Cardiac output can be adjusted to meet the varying needs of the body.

cardiac output = heartbeat rate × stroke volume

(Stroke volume is the volume of blood forced out of the heart by each muscular contraction.)

Changes in cardiac output are controlled by the **autonomic nervous system**.
There are **two** distinct parts to the autonomic nervous system:
the **sympathetic** (**SNS**) and the **parasympathetic nervous systems** (**PNS**).

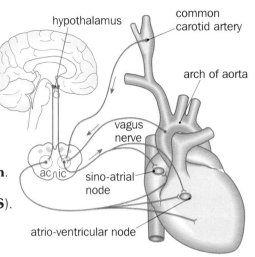

Stimulation of the heart by the sympathetic nervous system
increases cardiac output by:

● increasing the heartbeat rate,
● increasing the stroke volume.

Stimulation of the heart by the parasympathetic nervous system
decreases cardiac output by:

● decreasing the heartbeat rate,
● decreasing the stroke volume.

These two opposing systems work on a negative feedback principle,
involving two centres in the medulla of the brain:

● The **cardiac acceleratory centre** is linked by the sympathetic
nervous system to the sino-atrial node.
● The **cardiac inhibitory centre** is linked by the **vagus nerve**
of the parasympathetic nervous system to the sino-atrial node,
atrio-ventricular node and the Bundle of His.

So what determines which of these cardiac centres is stimulated?
Well, carbon dioxide concentration and pH certainly have an effect.

During vigorous exercise, the carbon dioxide level in the blood
increases as a result of increased respiration.
This causes a lowering of blood pH (it becomes more acidic).

Sensory receptors in the **carotid body**, located on the carotid artery,
detect this change.
They send nerve impulses to the cardiac acceleratory centre,
resulting in an increase in cardiac output.
Blood flow to the lungs increases and so the extra carbon dioxide is removed.

If a fall in carbon dioxide level (a rise in pH) is detected by the
carotid receptors, they send impulses to the cardiac inhibitory centre,
resulting in a decrease in cardiac output.

Stretch receptors and **pressure receptors** in the walls of the
aorta and carotid artery can detect changes in the blood flow to
them, due to increased blood pressure.
If the blood pressure in the arteries is high, the stretch receptors
are stimulated and send impulses to the cardiac inhibitory centre.
This sends impulses along the vagus nerve to the heart to reduce cardiac output.
If blood pressure is low, the stretch receptors trigger impulses to the cardiac
acceleratory centre, increasing cardiac output.

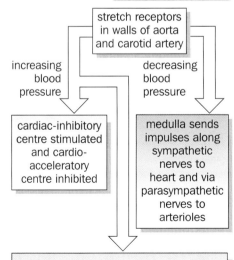

▷ The blood

The blood is the main transport medium in your body.
But it has several other functions as well.

- It defends the body against disease.

- It maintains diffusion gradients. For instance, it transports respiratory gases to and from the alveoli and it removes absorbed food from the villi of the small intestine.

- It acts as a buffer. Many of the blood proteins are able to neutralise excess acid or alkali and so keep the pH of the blood constant.

- It provides pressure for such processes as the formation of tissue fluid and filtration by the kidneys.

- It distributes heat around the body.

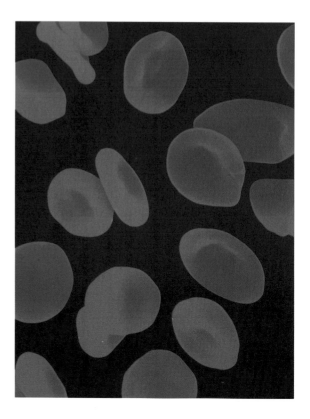

Blood plasma

About 55% of your blood is a liquid and about 45% is made up of cells.
The pale yellow liquid fraction is called **plasma**.
The composition of the plasma (its pH and salt concentration) is regulated by the kidneys.

Plasma contains:

- *plasma proteins*, such as albumins (for the osmotic balance of the blood), antibodies (for immunity) and clotting factors such as fibrinogen,
- *absorbed food molecules*, such as glucose, amino acids and fatty acids,
- *excretory waste products*, such as carbon dioxide, urea and uric acid,
- *hormones*, *salts* and *heat*.

White blood cells

These are sometimes called **leucocytes** and there are at least five different types.
What they have in common is that they protect the body from disease-causing organisms as part of the immune system.

White blood cells are larger but much less abundant than red blood cells.
They all have a nucleus and they are spherical or irregular in shape.

The two best known types are **lymphocytes** (made in the lymph nodes and responsible for antibody production) and **neutrophils** (phagocytic cells made in the red bone marrow that are able to engulf microbes and cell debris).

White blood cells and their role in the immune system are dealt with in greater detail in Chapter 15.

If you leave a sample of blood to stand the cells separate from the plasma

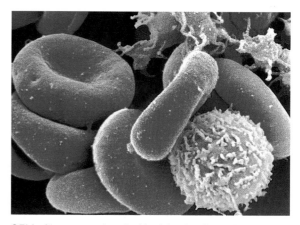

SEM of human red and white blood cells and platelets

Red blood cells

Red blood cells are also known as **erythrocytes**.
They transport oxygen from the lungs to the tissues.
Red blood cells contain the pigment **haemoglobin**, which combines with oxygen to give **oxyhaemoglobin**.

Packaging the haemoglobin inside red blood cells rather than dissolving it in the plasma means that the solute potential of the blood is not affected.

Unlike white blood cells, red blood cells do not have a nucleus.
This makes more room for the haemoglobin in the cell and so increases the amount of oxygen that each red blood cell can carry.

Red blood cells are shaped like biconcave discs, a bit like doughnuts that have not had their centres taken out.
This disc shape gives a large surface area/volume ratio.
This means that there is a lot of membrane over which gas exchange can occur when loading and unloading oxygen.
Imagine a red blood cell with the same volume but in the shape of a sphere.
It would provide a far lower surface area/volume ratio.

Red blood cells are quite small (roughly half the size of white blood cells).
This means that no molecule of haemoglobin is far from the cell surface membrane and its source of oxygen.
In fact red blood cells can just about squeeze through a capillary.
This slows down the flow of red blood cells, making gas exchange in the capillaries more efficient because the red blood cells are there longer.
In the embryo, red blood cells are made by the liver, but this function is taken over by the red bone marrow soon after birth.
The average red blood cell only lasts for about 120 days, because it lacks a nucleus and other organelles needed to maintain the cell.

Platelets

Platelets are small cell fragments consisting of cytoplasm surrounded by the cell surface membrane.
They do not have a nucleus and are only about 3 μm in diameter.
They are made in the bone marrow and last about 6 or 7 days.

The main role of platelets is in blood clotting.
Injury to the lining of a blood vessel exposes collagen fibres.
The platelets stick to these and swell up, releasing chemicals called **thromboplastins.**

The thromboplastins attract several plasma proteins called **clotting factors** to the site of the injury.
These set off a cascade effect in the presence of calcium ions.
The inactive plasma protein **prothrombin** changes to **thrombin**.
Thrombin converts another plasma protein, **fibrinogen**, to its insoluble form, **fibrin**.
Fibrin forms a mesh of threads, which trap the red blood cells, so helping to block the cut.
These dry to form a clot, preventing entry of bacteria and further loss of blood, and allowing the wound to heal.

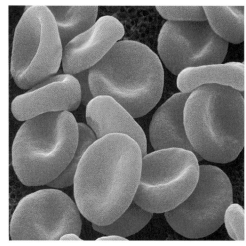

SEM of red blood cells

haemoglobin in solution in cytoplasm
(no nucleus or mitochondria)

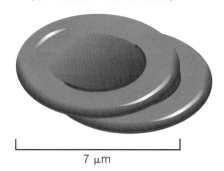

7 μm

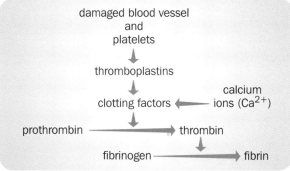

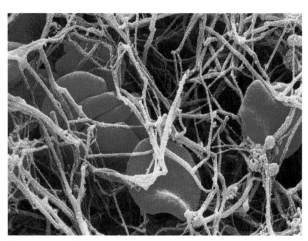

Red blood cells caught up in a mesh of fibrin threads

189

▷ Oxygen transport

Red blood cells contain the pigment haemoglobin.
You should remember that haemoglobin is a conjugated protein,
because it is attached to a prosthetic group.
In this case the prosthetic group is called haem, and it contains iron.
There are four haem groups in each haemoglobin molecule
and each one can bind to an oxygen molecule.

$$\text{Hb} + 4O_2 \underset{\text{in tissues}}{\overset{\text{in lungs}}{\rightleftharpoons}} \text{HbO}_8$$

haemoglobin   oxygen   oxyhaemoglobin

The **partial pressure** of oxygen (pO_2) is a measure of the
oxygen concentration.
The greater the concentration of dissolved oxygen, the higher
its partial pressure.

Red blood cells pick up oxygen in the dense network of capillaries
that cover the alveoli of the lungs.
Here the partial pressure of oxygen is high and the haemoglobin
becomes **saturated** with oxygen.
The cells carry the oxygen as oxyhaemoglobin to the respiring tissues.
Here the partial pressure is low, since oxygen is continually
being used up in respiration.
Under these conditions, oxyhaemoglobin gives up its oxygen to
the respiring cells. We say that it **dissociates**.

So the properties of haemoglobin ensure that at high partial pressures
of oxygen, it combines with large amounts of the gas.
And at low partial pressures of oxygen, it combines with very little.

Samples of haemoglobin can be exposed to different partial pressures
of oxygen.
The amount of oxygen combining with haemoglobin at the different
partial pressures can then be estimated.
The percentage saturation of each sample can be plotted against
the partial pressure to give an **oxygen dissociation curve**.

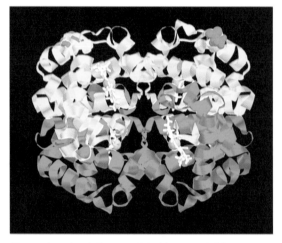

Computer simulation model of haemoglobin

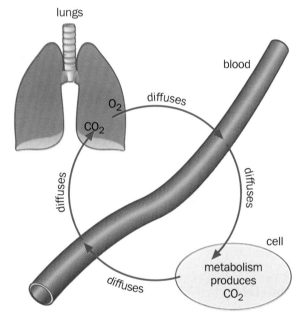

Gas exchange and transport

Look at the graph.
Can you see that haemoglobin becomes almost fully saturated
with oxygen at high partial pressures (like the conditions in the lungs).
Oxyhaemoglobin dissociates under conditions of low partial pressures
(like the conditions in the respiring tissues, which are using up
oxygen in respiration).

So why are oxygen dissociation curves S-shaped?
Remember that each molecule of haemoglobin has
four haem groups.
When the first oxygen molecule combines with the first haem group,
the shape of the haemoglobin molecule becomes distorted.
This makes it easier for the other three oxygen molecules to
bind with the other haem groups.

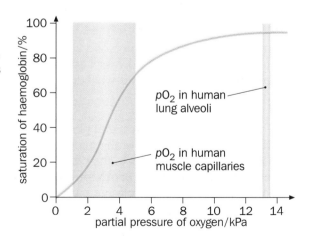

▷ The Bohr effect

Haemoglobin picks up oxygen in the lungs and delivers it to the tissues.
In fact, it is even more efficient than the dissociation curve suggests,
because the amount of oxygen carried by haemoglobin depends
not only on the partial pressure of oxygen but also
on the **partial pressure of carbon dioxide**.

Look at the graph.
Can you see that, at higher carbon dioxide partial pressures,
the oxygen dissociation curve moves to the **right**?
This is known as the **Bohr effect**.
Higher partial pressures of carbon dioxide increase the
dissociation of oxyhaemoglobin.
So, when oxyhaemoglobin reaches the tissues, the high
partial pressure of carbon dioxide resulting from respiration
makes oxyhaemoglobin respond by giving up its oxygen
even more readily.
So oxyhaemoglobin releases its oxygen where it is most needed:
to the actively respiring tissues.

> **The further a dissociation curve moves to the right,
> the more readily haemoglobin gives up its oxygen.
> The further a dissociation curve moves to the left,
> the more readily haemoglobin picks up oxygen.**

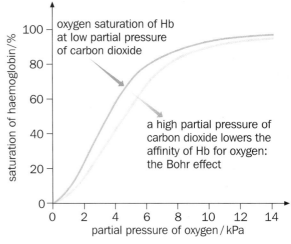

▷ Fetal haemoglobin

The developing fetus obtains oxygen from its mother.
The fetal blood and the mother's blood flow closely side by side
in the placenta but never mix.
This allows materials to diffuse from the blood of the mother into
the blood of the fetus and vice versa.

Look at the oxygen dissociation curve for fetal haemoglobin.
Can you see that it is to the **left** of that for adult haemoglobin?
How do you think this could be an advantage to the fetus?
The fetal haemoglobin combines with oxygen more readily than
adult haemoglobin does.
We say that if has a **higher affinity** for oxygen.
So at the placenta the fetal haemoglobin can 'steal' oxygen
from the mother's haemoglobin.

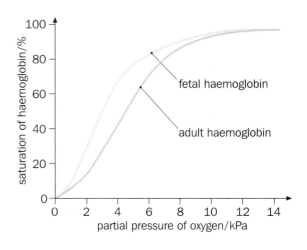

▷ Myoglobin

There is an oxygen-binding molecule in muscle called **myoglobin**.
Oxymyoglobin is far more stable than oxyhaemoglobin.
It will only give up its oxygen at very low oxygen partial pressures.

Look at the dissociation curve for myoglobin.
Can you see that it is to the left of the haemoglobin curve?
This means that at each partial pressure of oxygen, myoglobin
has a higher percentage oxygen saturation than haemoglobin.

This enables myoglobin to act as an oxygen store.
Usually the respiring muscle gets its oxygen from oxyhaemoglobin.
But if the oxygen partial pressure becomes very low (as a result of
exercise),the oxymyoglobin gives up its oxygen.

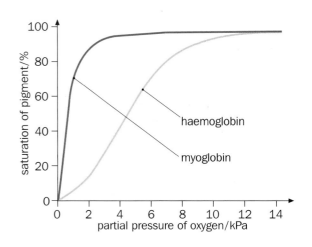

▷ Carbon dioxide transport

Carbon dioxide is carried in the blood in **three** ways.

- About 5% is carried **in solution** in the plasma as carbon dioxide.

- About 10% combines with amino groups in the four polypeptides that make up the haemoglobin molecule. The compound formed is called **carbamino-haemoglobin**.

- About 85% is carried in the form of **hydrogen carbonate**.

The sequence of events in which hydrogen carbonate is formed is significant for a number of reasons and is worth looking at in detail.

- Carbon dioxide produced by the respiring tissues diffuses into the red blood cells in the tissue capillaries.
  As you have seen, some of it combines with amino groups to form carbamino-haemoglobin.

- The red blood cells contain an enzyme called **carbonic anhydrase**, which catalyses a reaction between the rest of the carbon dioxide and water to form carbonic acid.

- The carbonic acid dissociates into negatively charged hydrogen carbonate ions and positively charged hydrogen ions.
  The hydrogen ions tend to increase the acidity.

- The hydrogen ions combine with haemoglobin to give **haemoglobinic acid (HHb)**.
  The hydrogen ions bind to amino acid side-chains in the haemoglobin molecule.
  This brings about a distortion of the molecule, which decreases its affinity for oxygen.
  So more oxygen is released to the tissues.
  (Remember the Bohr effect, where oxygen is given up under high partial pressures of carbon dioxide?)

- The build-up of hydrogen carbonate ions causes them to diffuse out of the red blood cell, leaving the inside of its membrane positively charged.

- In order to balance the electrical charge, chloride ions diffuse into the red blood cell from the plasma.
  This is known as the **chloride shift**.

Can you see that haemoglobin is acting as a buffer? It helps to maintain the blood pH by removing hydrogen ions from solution.

When the blood reaches the lungs, all the reactions described above are reversed.
Carbamino-haemoglobin breaks down to release carbon dioxide.
The hydrogen carbonate and hydrogen ions recombine, forming carbon dioxide molecules as the chloride shift is reversed.
The carbon dioxide diffuses out of the blood into the air in the alveoli.
The haemoglobin molecules are now free to pick up more oxygen and form oxyhaemoglobin.

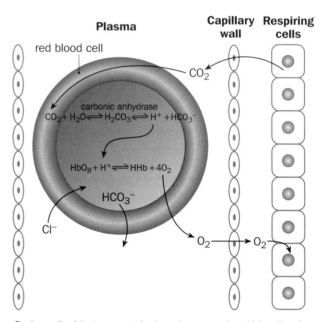

Carbon dioxide transport in the plasma and red blood cell

'OK folks, let's do the chloride shift!'

▷ Exchange across capillaries

Capillaries are adapted to allow the exchange of materials between the blood and the cells.

- They have very thin, permeable walls, only one cell thick.
- They provide a huge surface area for exchange, because there are so many of them.
- Blood flows through them very slowly.
- The body cells are never far from a capillary.

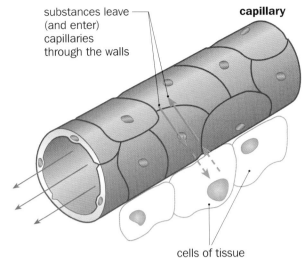

substances leave (and enter) capillaries through the walls

capillary

cells of tissue

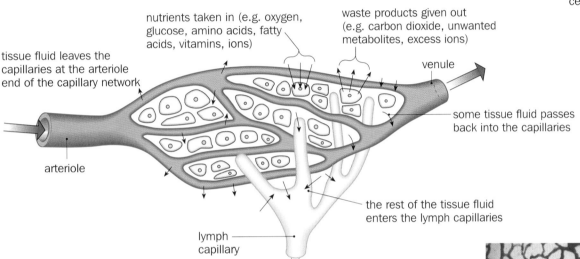

nutrients taken in (e.g. oxygen, glucose, amino acids, fatty acids, vitamins, ions)

waste products given out (e.g. carbon dioxide, unwanted metabolites, excess ions)

tissue fluid leaves the capillaries at the arteriole end of the capillary network

venule

some tissue fluid passes back into the capillaries

arteriole

the rest of the tissue fluid enters the lymph capillaries

lymph capillary

▷ Formation of tissue fluid

As blood flows through the capillaries, some of the plasma passes out into the tissues.

This **tissue fluid** consists of plasma without the large plasma proteins, which are too big to pass through the capillary wall.

The tissue fluid 'bathes' the cells, supplying them with glucose, amino acids, fatty acids, salts and oxygen.

The tissue fluid removes carbon dioxide and other waste materials from the cells.

As blood enters the narrow capillaries from the arterioles, a build-up of blood pressure occurs.

This forces water through the capillary walls into the cells.

Other components of tissue fluid enter the cells from the capillary by diffusion or by active transport.

As fluid leaves the capillary, the blood pressure starts to fall.

As the blood has lost much of its solute cargo, it now has a higher concentration than the tissue fluid.

So water passes back into the capillary by osmosis.

Waste products leave the cells and enter the capillary by diffusion.

This **net** movement of tissue fluid back into the capillary can only happen when the pressure of the blood has dropped and is countered by the osmotic effect.

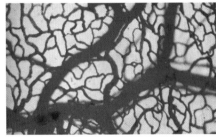

Capillaries in a frog's foot

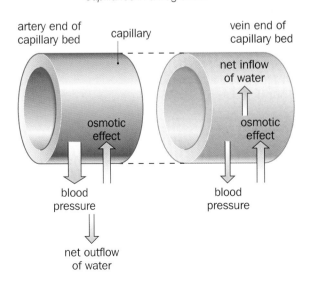

artery end of capillary bed

capillary

vein end of capillary bed

net inflow of water

osmotic effect

osmotic effect

blood pressure

blood pressure

net outflow of water

▷ Lymph

Not all of the tissue fluid returns to the blood capillary.
About one-tenth of it enters a separate system of capillaries
called the **lymph capillaries**.
The lymph capillaries are part of the **lymph system**.

Lymph capillaries have tiny valves that allow the tissue fluid
to enter but won't let it leak out again.
Once inside the lymph system, the tissue fluid is called **lymph**.

So what's the difference between tissue fluid and lymph?

They both consist of plasma minus the large plasma proteins,
but it's largely a matter of where they are found.

> **Tissue fluid surrounds the tissues.**
> **Lymph is found only in the lymph system.**

The tiny lymph capillaries join up to form **lymph vessels**.
These have a structure very similar to veins.
They are thin-walled and contain semi-lunar valves.

Perhaps not surprisingly, the flow of lymph is very slow.
It relies upon pressure from nearby muscles, the action of valves,
and the negative pressure created in the chest when we
breathe in, which helps to draw the lymph along.

Unlike blood, lymph is transported in one direction only,
from the tissues towards the heart.
The smaller lymph vessels join up to form two large lymph vessels.
These empty the lymph into the **subclavian veins**, under
the collar bones.
Here the lymph mixes with blood before joining the **vena cava**
just before it enters the heart.

Lymph is a milky looking fluid.
It contains fats absorbed by the lymph capillaries in the villi
of the small intestine.
These lymph capillaries are called **lacteals**.
The walls of lymph vessels are more permeable than the walls of
blood capillaries, so large molecules such as fats can pass
through them.

At intervals along the length of the lymph vessels are
structures called **lymph nodes**, which are an important part of
your defence system.

Lymphocytes are produced in the lymph nodes.
They have an important role in producing antibodies.
Lymphocytes are released from the lymph nodes and
eventually find their way into the blood.
So the lymph system is an important part of the body's
immune system (see chapter 15).
Your lymph nodes often swell up if you have an infection.

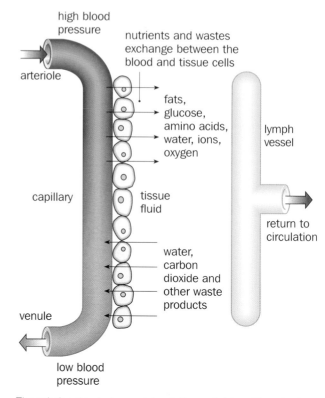

*The relationship between blood, tissue fluid and lymph at a
capillary network*

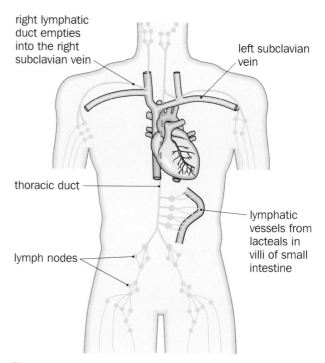

The lymph system

▷ Biology at work: Pacemakers

As you know, the cardiac cycle is controlled by a specialised group of cells in the wall of the right atrium known as the sino-atrial node (SAN). This is often called the **pacemaker** of the heart and it works by sending out an electrical signal which causes the atria to contract.

If the sino-atrial node is not working properly or the conductive tissue of the heart is damaged, then a patient may be fitted with an artificial pacemaker. These devices are designed to deliver an electrical stimulus to the heart muscle when they sense that a spontaneous heartbeat has not occurred.

As a temporary measure, the pacing unit (containing the power supply) may be worn externally on a belt. Most pacemakers, however, are designed for long-term use and the pacing unit is inserted underneath the skin.

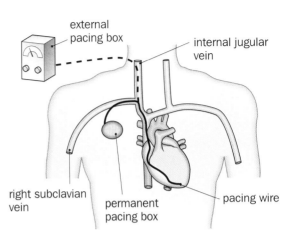

The position of an artificial pacemaker

Pacemakers may stimulate just one chamber (the right ventricle) or, in the case of dual chamber pacemakers, the right atrium may be stimulated as well.
Rate responsive pacemakers can be fitted, which adjust their output in response to changes in the patient's level of physical activity.

▷ The electrocardiogram (ECG)

As you have already seen, the control of the heartbeat depends upon electrical activity. A variety of cardiac disorders can produce irregularities in this activity. The electrocardiogram, or ECG, is a useful diagnostic tool in that it can detect these irregularities.

Electrodes are taped at various positions on the body and the electrical activity of the heart is then displayed on a monitor.

The resultant trace can be compared with a normal ECG with its characteristic P, QRS and T waves.
The P wave shows the atrial contraction, the QRS 'spike' immediately precedes the contraction of the ventricles, and the T wave represents the relaxation of the ventricles.

ventricular fibrillation
the contractions of the ventricles are extremely irregular

complete heart block
the atria and ventricles are beating independently

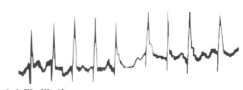

atrial fibrillation
caused by the atria beating fast and irregularly

Some abnormal ECG traces

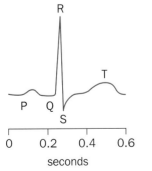

A normal ECG trace

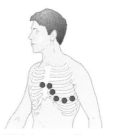

ECG lead positions

195

▷ Biology at work: Treatment of hypertension

Constant high blood pressure, or **hypertension,** is harmful. It makes the heart work harder and causes the arteries to narrow. For enough blood to reach the body's tissues and organs, blood pressure needs to increase still further. This increases the chances of fatty deposits forming in the arteries. If these form in the coronary arteries, it may cause a heart attack or heart failure. Hypertension can also cause damage to the kidneys, eyes and brain.

Blood pressure categories for adults over 18		
Category	Systolic (mmHg)	Diastolic (mmHg)
normal	<130	<85
high normal	130–139	85–89
high blood pressure		
stage 1	140–159	90–99
stage 2	160–179	100–109
stage 3	180–209	110–119
stage 4	>210	>120

The categories are for those not on a high blood pressure drug and with no short-term serious illness.

The risk of high blood pressure increases after the age of 35, with more than 25% of men and women over 55 suffering from hypertension. Hypertension is often referred to as a 'disease of affluence'. This is because the risk factors are:

- *obesity* – a loss of 3 kg in weight reduces blood pressure,
- *salt* – a reduction in salt lowers blood pressure,
- *alcohol* – drinking the equivalent of 4 pints a day increases blood pressure,
- *smoking* – this is a particularly high risk factor.

Hypertension can be reduced by changes in lifestyle, such as a healthy diet, regular exercise, relaxation and stopping smoking. If hypertension continues, a series of different drugs are given until the condition is under control.

Beta blockers are antihypertensive drugs that are in common usage today. James Black, who received the Nobel Prize for medicine in 1988, discovered them in the late 1950s. They were originally developed to treat **angina.** It was discovered that they were also very effective at lowering blood pressure by relaxing the smooth muscle cells that control the size of the blood vessels. Beta blockers work by **competitively inhibiting** the action of the hormones **adrenaline** and **noradrenaline.** These bind with **receptors** on the cell surface membranes of the heart muscle and smooth muscle lining blood vessels to bring about:

- narrowing of the blood vessels,
- an increase in the rate and strength of the heartbeat.

Both these actions serve to increase blood pressure. There are different kinds of beta blockers. Some act only on those receptors specific to the heart, the β_1 **receptors**, while others act on both the β_1 and the β_2 **receptors** found in the blood vessels.
The blocking of noradrenaline causes a reduction in impulses from the **sino-atrial node,** and this leads to a reduction in the heartbeat rate. The overall effect of these drugs, then, is to lower the blood pressure by reducing the output of the heart, causing the blood vessels to dilate.

DISCOVERY and DEVELOPMENT of a MEDICINE

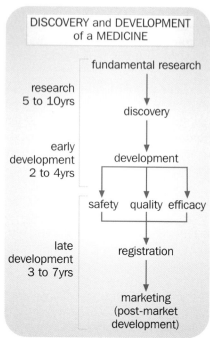

The research and development cycle of a new drug can take 12 or more years and may cost in excess of £150 million

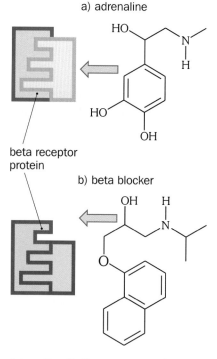

Adrenaline fits the receptor and activates it. Beta blocker also fits the receptor but blocks the access for adrenaline

Summary

- The blood transports oxygen, carbon dioxide, dissolved food, waste materials and hormones around the body. The blood also provides immunity, distributes heat around the body and acts as a buffer.
- Arteries contain a lot of muscle and elastic tissue to maintain the flow of blood under high pressure.
- Veins have relatively thin walls. They have semi-lunar valves to prevent the backflow of blood.
- Capillary walls are only one cell thick, allowing exchange of materials to take place easily.
- Plasma and some white blood cells are forced out of the capillaries under pressure to form tissue fluid. Most tissue fluid passes back into the capillaries; the rest enters the lymph system.
- Blood is made up of liquid plasma, red blood cells, white blood cells and platelets.
- The red blood cells contain haemoglobin, which combines with oxygen in the lungs to form oxyhaemoglobin.
- The oxygen dissociation curve for haemoglobin shows that it becomes fully saturated with oxygen in the lungs and releases oxygen to the tissues.

- At high concentrations of carbon dioxide, oxyhaemoglobin responds by releasing more oxygen.
- Fetal haemoglobin and myoglobin have a greater affinity for oxygen than adult haemoglobin.
- Carbon dioxide is mainly carried in the form of hydrogen carbonate ions in the plasma.
- The heart consists of two muscular pumps. One pumps deoxygenated blood to the lungs where it picks up oxygen; the other pumps the oxygenated blood all around the body.
- There are three main phases of the heartbeat: atrial systole, ventricular systole and diastole.
- The heartbeat is initiated by the heart itself (myogenic). This involves the sino-atrial node, the atrio-ventricular node and the Bundle of His.
- The heartbeat can be modified by the cardiac acceleratory and cardiac inhibitory centres in the brain, which respond to sense receptors in the carotid body and stretch receptors in the large arteries.

▷ Questions

1 Copy and complete the following passage.
Blood consists of a pale yellow liquid called ___, in which are found a number of different kinds of cells. The plasma contains various proteins, such as albumins, which help to maintain the ___ ___ of the blood; ___, which are antibodies; and ___, which are involved in blood clotting. The red blood cells, or ___, transport ___, which combines with the conjugated protein ___. White blood cells, or ___, are of two main types: ___, which engulf bacteria and cell debris, and ___, which produce antibodies as part of the body's ___ response. ___ are cell fragments involved in the ___ of blood.

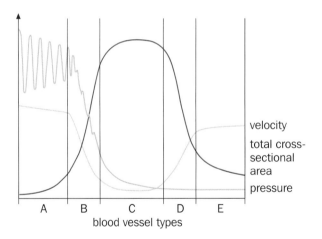

2 The graph shows the blood pressure, blood velocity and cross-sectional area of different types of blood vessels.
   a) Name the blood vessels A, B, C, D and E.
   b) Which of these vessels has the highest proportion of muscle tissue in its wall?
   c) i) Explain the variations in blood pressure shown in vessel type A.
      ii) What is the reason for the rapid drop in blood pressure in vessel type B?
   d) What are the advantages of the relationship between blood velocity and cross-sectional area of vessel type C?

   e) Suggest two reasons for the increase in blood velocity in vessel types D and E when the blood pressure is low.

3 Look at the diagram at the top of the next page of the blood of a mammal, magnified about 1000 times.
   a) What are the cells labelled A, B and C called?
   b) Approximately how many red blood cells are there for every white blood cell?
   c) Describe the main functions of cell types A, B and C.
   d) In what process is structure D involved?
   e) Outline the main stages of this process.

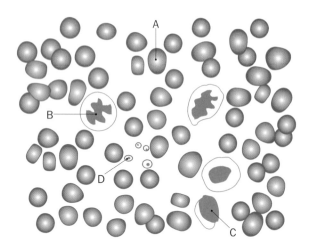

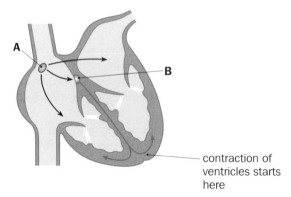

contraction of ventricles starts here

a) Name structure A.
b) Explain why each of the following is important for pumping blood through the heart:
   i) There is a slight delay in the passage of electrical activity that takes place at point B.
   ii) The contraction of the ventricles starts at the base.
c) Describe how stimulation of the cardiovascular centre in the brain may result in an increase in heart rate.

4 a) Explain how increased haemoglobin concentration can lead to increased performance in endurance events.
   b) The graph shows the oxygen dissociation curve for haemoglobin as blood passes through capillaries in the lungs and skeletal muscle of an athlete. Explain how features of the oxygen dissociation curves for haemoglobin in the lungs and skeletal muscle benefit the athlete.

6 The diagram shows some nerves associated with the heart and the blood system.
   a) In which part of the brain are the cardiac inhibitory and acceleratory centres found?
   b) Give two stimuli, detected in the aorta and carotid body, that may result in a change of heart rate.
   c) Suggest two ways in which stimulation of the heart by nerve X leads to an increase in the amount of blood pumped out of the ventricles.

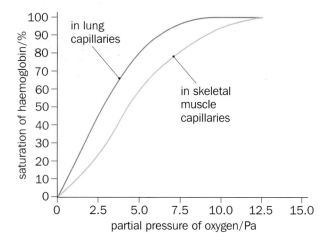

5 The diagram shows a vertical section through the human heart. The arrows indicate the direction of movement of electrical activity, which starts muscle contraction.

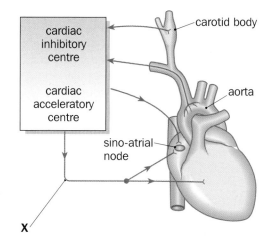

These North American redwoods can grow to a height of 60 metres.
So how does water get up to such a height from the roots?
And how are the products of photosynthesis transported away
from the leaves?

Try to imagine one of these giant redwoods on a summer's day.
The leaves will be photosynthesising and will need carbon dioxide,
water, nutrients and light.

As you have seen, carbon dioxide is able to diffuse into the leaves
from the atmosphere through the stomata.
Water and mineral nutrients have to reach the leaves from the roots.
Photosynthetic products, such as sugars and amino acids, need to be
transported away from the leaves to maintain concentration gradients.

In simple photosynthesising organisms such as algae,
these processes take place by diffusion.
Spirogyra, for example, has most of its cells close to
the surrounding water.

But in complex, multicellular plants, a **mass flow system** is needed.
In larger plants diffusion would simply be too slow to supply:

- carbon dioxide for photosynthesis during daylight,

- oxygen for respiration,

- inorganic nutrients, such as nitrates and phosphates,

- sugars made during photosynthesis for those plant cells
  that cannot photosynthesise, such as root cells.

Plants are able to develop good transport tissue as they are
made from a column of plant cells with strong, supporting
cellulose cell walls.
If these cells lose their end-walls, they form **tubes**.
And this is exactly what happens.

Simple **parenchyma** cells either lose their end-walls altogether
or the end-walls become perforated to form a system of tubes.
There are two such systems:

- the **xylem** tissue, which transports water and mineral salts
  up the stem from the roots to the leaves,

- the **phloem** tissue, which transports the materials made in
  photosynthesis, for example sugars and amino acids, to all
  other parts of the plant.

In each case the walls of the tubes are further thickened by the addition
of cellulose and **lignin**, a woody material.

So in plants there are *two* distinct transport tissues.

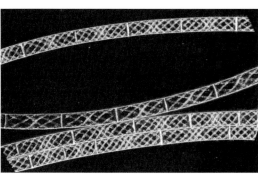

Spirogyra: *a simple filamentous green alga*

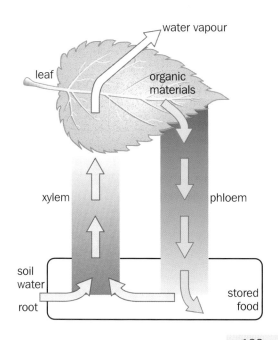

▷ Tissues inside the stem

On page 174, we looked at the different tissues that make up
the internal structure of a leaf.
A transverse section of a stem reveals a ring of **vascular bundles**.
Each vascular bundle consists of:

- a cap of **sclerenchyma** fibres for mechanical support,
- outer phloem tissue for transporting organic materials,
- inner xylem tissue for transporting water and mineral salts and also for
  mechanical support,
- a thin layer of tissue called the **cambium**, between the phloem and xylem.

Cambial cells divide to cut off new phloem cells (secondary phloem) to the **outside**
and new xylem cells (secondary xylem) to the **inside**.
A region of dividing cells like this in a plant is called a **meristem**.
In older stems a complete ring of secondary xylem and secondary phloem forms
to give additional mechanical support.

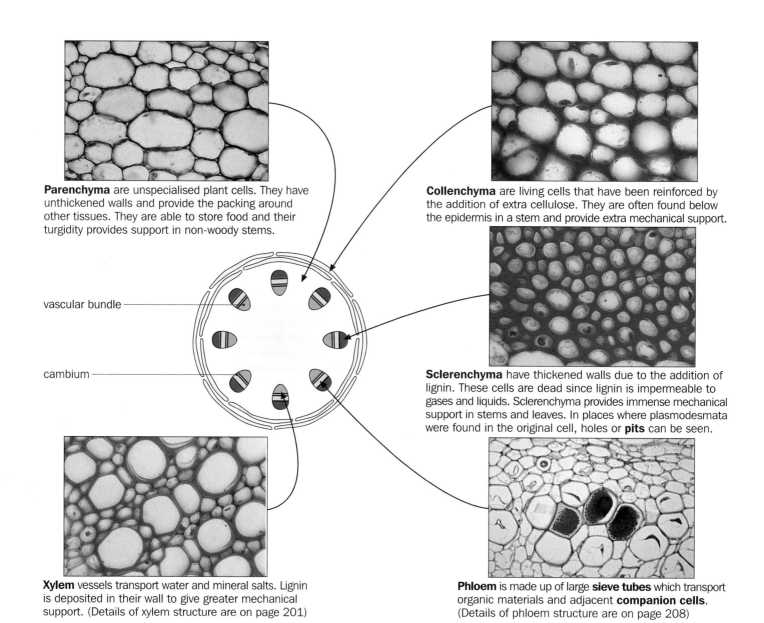

Parenchyma are unspecialised plant cells. They have
unthickened walls and provide the packing around
other tissues. They are able to store food and their
turgidity provides support in non-woody stems.

Collenchyma are living cells that have been reinforced by
the addition of extra cellulose. They are often found below
the epidermis in a stem and provide extra mechanical support.

vascular bundle

cambium

Sclerenchyma have thickened walls due to the addition of
lignin. These cells are dead since lignin is impermeable to
gases and liquids. Sclerenchyma provides immense mechanical
support in stems and leaves. In places where plasmodesmata
were found in the original cell, holes or **pits** can be seen.

Xylem vessels transport water and mineral salts. Lignin
is deposited in their wall to give greater mechanical
support. (Details of xylem structure are on page 201)

Phloem is made up of large **sieve tubes** which transport
organic materials and adjacent **companion cells**.
(Details of phloem structure are on page 208)

▷ Structure of xylem tissue

There are two main types of water-conducting tissue:
vessels and **tracheids**.

Xylem vessels form when a column of parenchyma cells
lose their end-walls.
The walls of these tubes become strengthened
by the addition of lignin.
This increased mechanical strength is important if the vessels
are to withstand the strong pressures that occur during
water transport.
As lignin is impermeable, materials cannot pass into xylem cells
and so the protoplasm dies.
This means that the cells are hollow and there are no cell contents
to restrict the flow of water.

No lignin is laid down where plasmodesmata were present
in the original cell walls.
These non-lignified areas are known as **pits** and they allow
water to pass sideways between one xylem vessel and the next.

Primary xylem is the first xylem tissue in a young stem, root or leaf.
There are two types of primary xylem: **protoxylem** and **metaxylem**.

Protoxylem is the first xylem to develop behind root and shoot tips.
Lignin is added in rings or spirals to form annular vessels (rings)
and spiral vessels (spirals).

Metaxylem is more mature and the walls are fully lignified
(with the exception of pits).

Secondary xylem is formed from the ring of cambium in a stem.
Each year woody plants are able to increase their girth in this way as
new secondary xylem is formed.
This is known as **secondary thickening**.

The seasonal growth of the xylem shows up as **annual rings**.
A ring formed in the previous year transports little water, its main
function being to support the plant's increasing biomass.

How do you think that you could find out the age of a tree?

Tracheids are elongated cells with tapering ends.
They also conduct water but are less well adapted than vessels.
Unlike large vessels, tracheids do not have open ends so
that water has to pass from cell to cell via the pits.
Tracheids are usually found in the finest branches of the xylem
tissue in the leaves and in the roots.

Other xylem tissue includes:

● **fibres**, which are similar to sclerenchyma fibres.
Their function is solely support; they have no role in water transport.

● **xylem parenchyma**, the packing tissue that keeps
the other xylem elements in place.

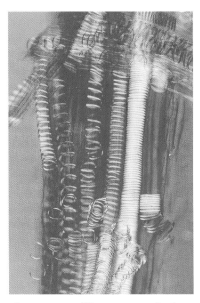

*Can you see different types of xylem
vessel in this micrograph?*

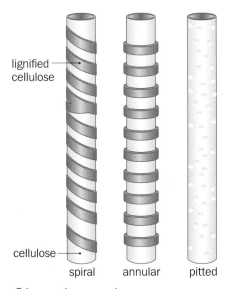

lignified
cellulose

cellulose

spiral   annular   pitted

Primary xylem vessels

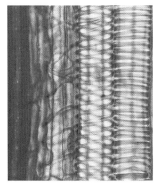

LS xylem tissue

▷ Transpiration

Transpiration is the loss of water from the surface of land plants. About 99% of the water that a plant absorbs from the soil is lost in transpiration.

- Most water passes out through the stomata of the leaves.
- Only a small amount is able to pass out through the cuticle.
- A very small amount is lost through the lenticels in woody stems. The water is lost as water vapour to the air.

Water loss through the stomata is a consequence of gas exchange. If gases are to diffuse in and out of the internal tissues of the leaf, they pass through stomata on the lower leaf surface. Inevitably, water vapour will escape when the stomata are open. Since plants are able to open and close the stomata, they are able to exercise some control over this loss of water. The sun provides the energy that evaporates the water.

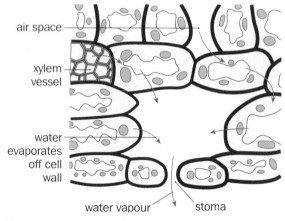
Water evaporates out of a stoma pore

Diffusion pathway

As you have seen, the spongy mesophyll of a leaf consists of loosely packed cells with many air spaces between them. Water evaporates from their moist cell walls into the air spaces. So the air spaces soon become saturated with water vapour. Connecting the air spaces to the atmosphere are the stomata. If the water potential of the air outside is **lower** than that in the air spaces, then water will diffuse along the gradient in water potential, out of the leaf.

Measuring the rate of transpiration

You have probably used a potometer before. It actually measures the **rate of water absorption**, but this is virtually the same as the rate of transpiration, since nearly all the water taken in is lost. A very small amount of water is used in the leaf for photosynthesis.

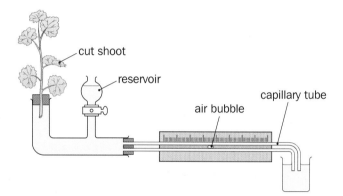
A simple potometer

- A leafy shoot is cut under water to prevent air bubbles from entering the xylem vessels.
- The cut shoot is attached by means of a rubber bung. Vaseline is used to ensure an air-tight seal.
- The inside of the apparatus is flooded with water.
- An air bubble is introduced at the end of the capillary tube.
- The distance moved by the air bubble per unit time is measured.

A potometer can be used to investigate the rate of transpiration under different conditions.

What do you think would happen to the rate of transpiration under these conditions?

- high humidity,
- high wind speed,
- high temperature,
- high light intensity.

In each case, say how you could simulate these environmental conditions in a laboratory situation.

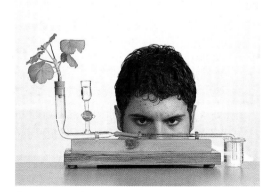
A potometer in use

▷ Factors affecting the rate of transpiration

Anything that changes the gradient in water potential between
the air spaces inside the leaf and the air outside will affect
the rate of transpiration.

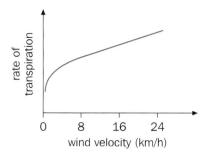

Humidity

When the atmosphere is humid, it contains a lot of water molecules.
This reduces the water potential gradient between
the air spaces and the atmosphere.
So the rate of transpiration will decrease.
Low humidity will increase the rate of transpiration.

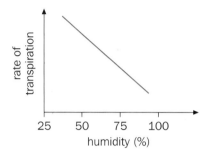

Wind speed

If the air is still, water vapour diffusing out of the leaf will tend to
accumulate around the stomata pores.
This reduces the water potential gradient and slows down the rate of transpiration.
But windy conditions disperse this water vapour,
increasing the gradient in water potential and thus increasing
the rate of transpiration.

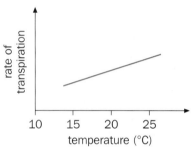

Temperature

Increasing temperature increases the kinetic energy of water molecules
so their rate of diffusion through the stomata pores increases.
In addition, the air is able to hold more water molecules at higher temperatures.
We say that the relative humidity of the air is lower.
Both these effects result in an increase in the rate of transpiration.

Light

As you will see, light influences the opening and closing of the stomata,
so it has an indirect effect upon the rate of transpiration.

▷ How do the stomata open and close?

You know that stomata open during the day and close at night.
Closing the stomata will of course reduce the transpiration rate.
Two guard cells lie either side of the stoma pore.
They control the size of the stoma pore by changing their shape.
As you saw in Chapter 10:

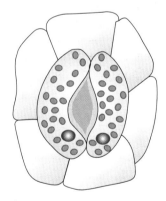

- If water enters the guard cells, they swell up and the stoma pore opens.
- If water leaves the guard cells, they become flaccid and the stoma pore closes.

Guard cells turgid: stoma opens

These changes are thought to be due to a reversible uptake and loss
of potassium ions by the guard cells.

- During the day, the chloroplasts inside the guard cells photosynthesise.
- As a result they produce ATP, which fuels an active transport mechanism
  that takes up potassium ions from the surrounding epidermal cells.
- This lowers the water potential in the guard cells and water enters
  by osmosis, the guard cells become turgid and the stoma pore opens.
- At night, the chloroplasts in the guard cells do not photosynthesise.
- Less ATP is available for the active uptake of potassium ions, which
  then start to leave the guard cells by diffusion.
- This loss of potassium ions raises the water potential in the guard cell, water
  passes out into the epidermal cells, which have a more negative water potential.
- The guard cells become flaccid and the stoma pore closes.

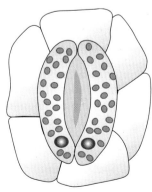

Guard cells flaccid: stoma closes

▷ Water uptake by roots

If you look at a transverse section of a root, you will be able
to see many of the plant tissues that are found in a stem but
they are arranged in a different way in a root.

Can you see that the transport tissue (the xylem and phloem)
is concentrated into a central core in a root?
Roots are subjected to *vertical* stresses; that is, they have
to be able to resist being pulled out of the soil.
A central core of strong xylem tissue gives ideal resistance to
being up-rooted and at the same time gives economy of space.

Behind the root tip are numerous tiny **root hairs**.
Water enters the root hairs from the soil and passes across
the root cortex and into the xylem tissue.
From here, water passes up the xylem vessels in the stem to
the leaves.

Root hairs are well adapted for absorbing water and mineral ions.
They have very thin walls, giving a short diffusion pathway, and their
shape provides a large surface area volume ratio for absorption.

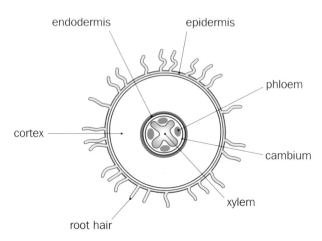

Transverse section through a young root

Routes through the root

The water in the soil contains a very weak solution of mineral
salts, so it has a high water potential (near to zero).
Inside the root hair vacuole, there is a relatively strong solution
of sugars and other dissolved substances, giving the contents
of the vacuole a low water potential (more negative).
So water passes into the root hair cell down a water potential
gradient, from a region of high water potential (in the soil) to
a region of lower water potential (in the root hair vacuole)
by osmosis.

The water potential in the xylem is lower than that in the root hairs.
So water taken in by the root hairs passes across the cortex and
enters the xylem tissue in the centre of the root.

There are *two* main pathways along which water travels:

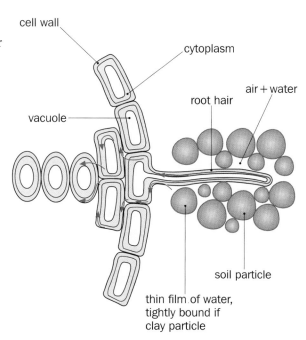

Absorption of water by a root hair

- The **apoplast** pathway involves water passing through
  the **cell walls** of the cortex cells.
  The cell walls are made up of minute cellulose fibres and
  water is thought to pass along the spaces between them,
  a bit like soaking up water with a paper towel.
  As the water seeps along the micro-spaces between the fibres,
  the cohesive forces between the water molecules mean
  that more water is pulled along the apoplast route.

- The **symplast** pathway suggests that water passes along
  through the **cytoplasm** of the cortex cells.
  There will be a gradient in water potential across the cortex.
  The cytoplasm in the cells nearest the xylem will have a
  lower water potential than those nearer the outside of the root.
  Between adjacent cells there are strands of cytoplasm
  called **plasmodesmata**.
  These connections allow water molecules to pass between the
  cytoplasm of one cortex cell and the next.

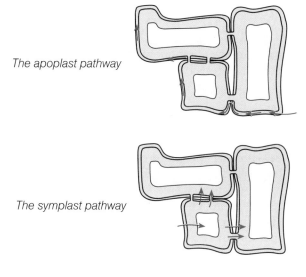

The apoplast pathway

The symplast pathway

The endodermis

Around the central core of transport tissue in a root
is a layer one cell thick called the **endodermis**.
It is here that the apoplast pathway becomes blocked.

The cell walls of the endodermis are impregnated with
a waxy material called **suberin**.
This forms a band of wax around the cells called the
Casparian strip.
Suberin is waterproof, so the Casparian strip effectively
stops water passing along the cell walls (apoplast route).
The only way that water can pass across the endodermis
is by the symplast route, by crossing the cell membrane and
passing through the cytoplasm.

It is thought that, as the water passes through the cytoplasm of
the endodermal cells, they actively secrete mineral salts into
the xylem tissue.
This lowers the water potential in the xylem, causing water
to be drawn through the endodermis.
This 'pulling' of water into the xylem from the surrounding cells
is thought to produce a positive hydrostatic pressure inside
the xylem, forcing water upwards.
This positive pressure is known as **root pressure**.
Root pressure can be demonstrated by cutting the stem of a potted
plant near the base. Water can be seen to seep out of the cut.
Root pressure is thought to be a minor force in the movement
of water up the stems of plants.

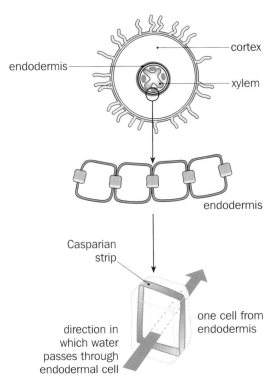

▷ Mineral uptake

As you saw in Chapter 1, many mineral ions are needed
for plant metabolism.
Mineral ions enter through the root hairs either passively or actively.

- Mineral ions enter the root hair by simple *diffusion* provided
  their concentration is greater outside the root hair than inside.

- If the concentration of mineral ions in the soil is lower than it is
  inside the root hair, then energy from ATP is required to enable
  active transport to take place.

Active transport (as you saw in Chapter 3) enables cells to selectively
take up ions against a concentration gradient, into the symplast pathway.
It is thought that most ion uptake by roots occurs in this way.

Any active transport mechanism requires energy from respiration.
Consequently, anything that affects the rate of respiration
will affect the rate of ion uptake by the roots.
Such factors include temperature, oxygen supply and the presence
of respiratory inhibitors such as cyanide.
Once inside the root hairs, mineral ions may move across the cortex
by the apoplast route (by diffusion or mass flow in solution).
Otherwise, ions pass via the symplast route (by diffusion or active transport).
Either way, mineral ions have to pass across the endodermis by the
symplast pathway and are then thought to enter the xylem by a
combination of active pumping and diffusion.

A demonstration of root pressure

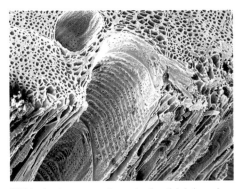

*SEM of xylem vessels: note the thick bands
of lignin*

▷ How water passes up the stem

So how is water able to reach the tops of 60 metre high Californian redwoods?

To find the answer we need to look at what goes on in the leaf.
● Water evaporates from the walls of the spongy mesophyll cells and the air in the air spaces becomes saturated with water.
● Usually the air outside the stomata is not saturated with water. So water diffuses from a region of high water potential (in the air spaces) to a region of lower water potential (in the air outside).

As more water evaporates from the spongy mesophyll walls, more water is drawn in to replace it.
Water passes from the xylem through the spongy mesophyll cells in *two* ways, which we have already looked at.
● Water can pass from cell to cell along the cell walls by the **apoplast** pathway.
● Water can pass along a water potential gradient in the cytoplasm of the cells by the **symplast** pathway.

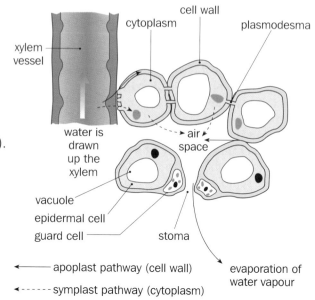

The route by which water passes out of the leaves

▷ Cohesion-tension theory

As molecules of water are removed from the xylem, more water molecules are 'pulled up' to replace them.
This pulling force is known as **transpiration pull**.
The negative pressure produced is rather like sucking a fluid up through a straw.
When a fluid is sucked up a straw, it is under a tension; and it is the same with the water inside the xylem vessel.

This mass flow of water through the xylem relies upon *two* important properties of water.
● **cohesion** – the water molecules tend to stick together,
● **adhesion** – the water molecules also tend to stick to the inside of the xylem vessel.

This drawing of a continuous column of water up the xylem vessel is known as the **cohesion-tension theory**.
The force needed to break the water column is very great.
The walls of the xylem vessels have to be thickened in order to withstand the tension in the water column, otherwise they would collapse.
The cohesion-tension theory is regarded as the main way in which water reaches the leaves of plants from the roots.

As you have seen, **root pressure** is thought to contribute a positive pressure, or push, to the water column.
Capillarity is a third force that is also thought to contribute to the rise of water in the xylem.
Water tends to rise inside narrow tubes by capillary action.
In plants, capillarity relies upon the tendency of water molecules to stick to the walls of xylem vessels by adhesion.
This force may be important in the upward movement of water in small plants but it is of little relevance in large trees.

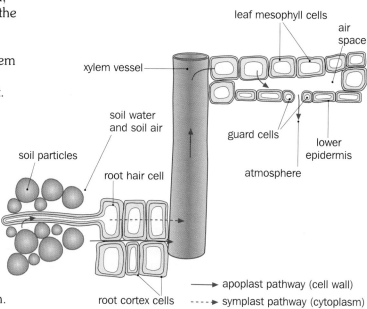

The cohesion-tension mechanism accounts for the passage of most water up a stem

▷ Reducing water loss

All plants have to balance water uptake with water loss.
It is important that they maintain the turgor in their cells,
or they will wilt.
Excessive transpiration can lead to the death of a plant
if it passes its **permanent wilting point** and cannot
regain its turgor.

Xerophytes are plants that live in conditions where water is scarce.
These will of course include hot, dry, desert conditions.
But not all xerophytes live in these sorts of regions.
Many plants can be deprived of water in winter when
the soil water freezes.
They can experience *water stress* because they continue
to transpire but cannot take up water from the soil.
Xerophytic plants are also found in exposed, windy areas.

Xerophytic adaptations enable a plant to reduce its
water loss in number of different ways.

- A **very thick waxy cuticle** cuts down evaporation from the upper
  epidermis, as in the leaves of evergreen shrubs such as *Oleander*.

- Having **smaller leaves** reduces the surface area/volume
  ratio, so there is less area over which water is lost, as in *Pinus*.

- **Rolling up** of leaves so that the lower surface faces inside and
  traps humid air next to the stomata reduces the rate of
  evaporation from the leaf surface, as in marram grass (*Ammophila*).

- **Sunken stomata** can be found in grooves in some xerophytic
  leaves, for example marram. Humid air accumulates in the
  grooves above the stomata, reducing the rate of diffusion of
  water molecules.
  Sunken stomata have the effect of reducing the amount of air
  movement over the surface of the stomata.

- **Leaf hairs** are outgrowths of the epidermal cells of leaves.
  They are also able to trap damp air close to the leaf surface,
  reducing the amount of air movement and cutting down
  transpiration, as in marram and *Oleander*.

- Some plants have **succulent leaves** in which they are able
  to store water, for example *Bryophyllum*.

- Other plants have **succulent stems** for water storage,
  for example cacti.
  These stems also take over the role of photosynthesis from the
  reduced leaves.

- Some plants have the ability to **close their stomata during
  daylight** to significantly reduce transpiration, for example
  most cacti and pineapple.

- Many xerophytes have **shallow, extensive root systems** to
  quickly absorb water from rain and overnight condensation,
  for example most cacti.

- The **development of sclerenchyma** tissue in the leaf prevents
  it from collapsing in times of drought, as in the case of *Hakea*.

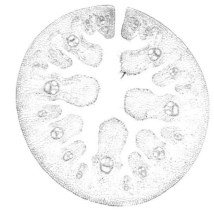

Transverse section through a leaf of marram grass

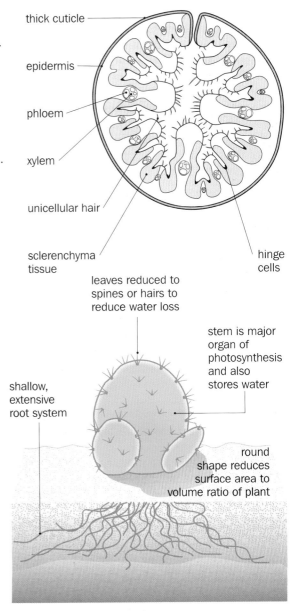

thick cuticle

epidermis

phloem

xylem

unicellular hair

sclerenchyma tissue

hinge cells

leaves reduced to spines or hairs to reduce water loss

stem is major organ of photosynthesis and also stores water

shallow, extensive root system

round shape reduces surface area to volume ratio of plant

▷ Structure of phloem tissue

As you have seen, transport of water through the xylem
is a **passive** process and the cells that make up
the xylem vessels are dead.

The transport of materials such as sugars and amino acids
made in photosynthesis is an **active** process, that is, it requires
energy for it to work.
Not surprisingly then, phloem is living tissue.
The movement of substances such as sugars and ions
through the phloem is called **translocation**.

The most important phloem tissues in terms of transport
are **sieve tubes** and **companion cells**.

Sieve tubes

Phloem tissue is made from columns of parenchyma cells.
Each parenchyma cell is adapted to form a **sieve element**.
A column of sieve elements joined together forms a sieve tube.
Sieve tubes allow the mass flow of materials.
But they are very different to the xylem vessels.

The sieve tube is alive, though as it matures it loses several
of the usual plant cell organelles.
The nucleus, ribosomes and Golgi bodies all degenerate.
So the sieve element ranks with the red blood cell as
one of the few cells that does not contain a nucleus.
Presumably, the loss of these structures allows materials
to flow more easily through the cells.

The sieve elements **do** have a cell wall, a cell surface membrane,
and cytoplasm containing endoplasmic reticulum and mitochondria.
There is, in fact, only a small amount of cytoplasm lining the inside
of the cellulose wall.

The end-walls, where two sieve elements meet, together
form the **sieve plate**.
Here the end-walls are perforated by a number of large pores,
unlike in xylem vessels where the end-walls completely break down.
It is through these pores that materials have to pass during
translocation.

Companion cells

Each sieve element has at least one companion cell
adjacent to it.
Companion cells have a more typical plant cell structure,
with all the usual components.
However, they have many more mitochondria and ribosomes
than the usual plant cell.
This reflects the fact that they are metabolically very active.

Companion cells are linked to sieve elements by numerous
plasmodesmata.
The fact that the sieve element has lost so many of its organelles
means that it needs a companion cell with a nucleus to help
it to survive.

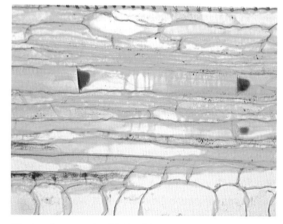

Photomicrograph of L.S. phloem

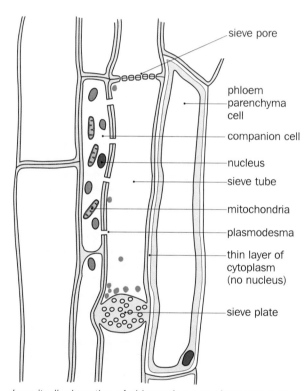

Longitudinal section of phloem tissue to show structure

sieve pore

phloem parenchyma cell

companion cell

nucleus

sieve tube

mitochondria

plasmodesma

thin layer of cytoplasm (no nucleus)

sieve plate

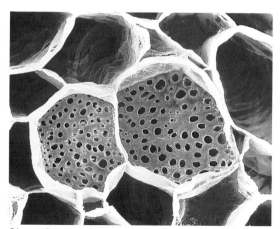

*Sieve plates and sieve tubes are clearly visible in this
transverse section of phloem*

▷ Transport of substances in the phloem

Organic substances, such as sucrose (30%), amino acids, minerals and hormones, are transported along the sieve tubes.
The speed at which these substances move through the sieve tubes is far too rapid to be explained by diffusion alone.

Movement of water through the xylem is due to a water potential gradient between the soil water and the air. The process is purely **passive**.
The mass flow of materials through the sieve tubes is an **active** process.

The mass flow theory

Areas in a plant where sucrose is loaded into the phloem are called **sources**.
The usual source of sucrose is the photosynthesising leaf.
Areas where sucrose is removed from the phloem are known as **sinks**.
A lot of sucrose is removed from the phloem to form starch in the root.
Look at the mass flow model.

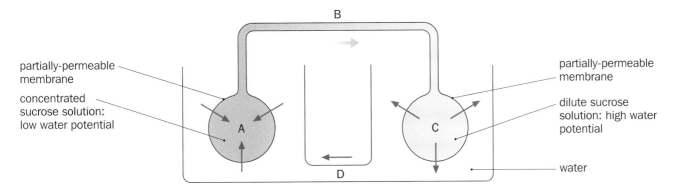

Region A represents a source.
Sugar is added at A and so the solution in A has a low water potential.
Region C represents a sink.
Sugar is removed from the solution at C, so it has a higher water potential.

There will be a tendency for water to pass into both A and C by **osmosis.**
But this tendency will be far greater in A, since is has a much lower water potential than C.

As water enters A, hydrostatic pressure builds up, forcing the solution out into B.
Mass flow of solution occurs along a hydrostatic gradient along B into C.
This forces water out of C into D.

In our model, A represents the leaf cells, a source of sugar made in photosynthesis.
C represents a sink, an area where sugar is removed.
This could be the roots, where sucrose is converted to starch for storage.
Channel B, joining the source to the sink, would be the phloem.
Channel D, bringing water back to the leaves, represents the xylem.

The use of radioactive tracers has shown that materials can move up and down in the phloem, depending upon the needs of the plant.
For instance, sugars made in older leaves (sources) can be transported to young leaves (sinks) nearer to the shoot tip.
We need to look at the nature of the sources and sinks to establish the **active** mechanism involved in translocation.

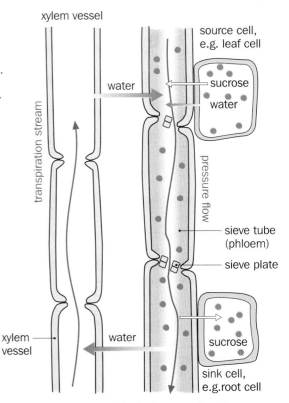

Possible sources and sinks in the mass flow theory

▷ The loading and unloading of sucrose

If our mass flow model is to work, then sucrose must be
- constantly **added** at A, and
- constantly **removed** at C.

Otherwise the set-up would eventually come to equilibrium.

Loading sucrose

Sucrose is produced in the leaf mesophyll cells as a result
of photosynthesis. These are the sources.
But how does the sucrose get into the phloem sieve tubes?

It may move by the apoplast pathway, passing along the cell walls.
It can also travel by the symplast pathway, moving from cell to cell
via the plasmodesmata.
It is thought to be a combination of these two methods.

The sucrose is loaded into sieve tube elements using an
active transport mechanism.
Specialised donor **transfer cells** are responsible for this.
The transfer cells are modified parenchyma cells with very
folded inner walls.
This folding increases the surface area of cell surface membrane
over which active transport can take place.
The transfer cells contain large numbers of mitochondria,
which provide the ATP needed for the active transport of sucrose.

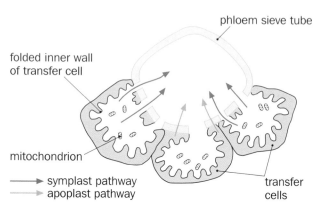

Transfer cells load sucrose into sieve tubes by active transport

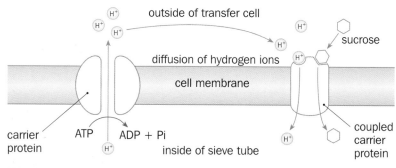

ATP from respiration is used to pump sucrose into the sieve tube
element against a concentration gradient.
To enter, the sucrose has to cross the cell membrane.
Once inside, the sucrose molecules are too large to diffuse out
passively, so they stay inside.

Unloading sucrose

Unloading of sucrose will occur anywhere in the plant where
sucrose is needed (at the sinks).
This could be in the root or at the stem apex and flower buds.
So phloem transport may be up or down the stem, unlike xylem
transport which is only in one direction, from the roots up to the leaves.

At these sinks, there will be a low concentration of sucrose.
But sucrose molecules are too large to diffuse across the cell membrane
out of the sieve tube.
So transfer cells are again involved in the active transport of sucrose
out of the sieve tubes into the surrounding tissue.
As soon as sucrose enters the tissue it is converted to something else,
for example starch in the roots, or cellulose in the cells of the stem apex.

'Sucrose sir? At your service'

▷ Biology at work: Aphids and plant viruses

Aphids such as greenfly and blackfly are probably
the most common pests in British gardens.
Viral diseases such as **tobacco mosaic virus** (**TMV**)
are also all too familiar to plant growers.

What is the connection between these tiny,
often wingless, insects and diseases that can cause
considerable economic loss ?

The link lies in the feeding mechanism of the aphid.
Aphids feed from the phloem tubes in plant stems.
They have specially adapted mouthparts that are formed
into a narrow tube called a **stylet**.

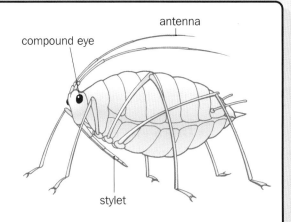

The aphid uses the stylet to pierce the phloem sieve tube cells.
It then feeds on the sugary sap that is forced under pressure
up the stylet.
Scientists have used this feeding method to study the composition
of the sap. A feeding aphid is anaesthetised and its body
removed, leaving the stylet in place.
The stylet acts as a handy micropipette from which sap
can be collected.

Although plant viruses can enter through wounds caused
when planting or pruning, the main transmitters (vectors)
of viruses between plants are aphids.

The tiny viral particles live in the salivary glands of the insects.
In the act of piercing the plant tissue, saliva is introduced
into the plant cells.
Once inside the cells, the viral particles proceed to reproduce.
Within about 24 hours of infection, it has been found that
viral particles can start to spread throughout a plant,
carried by the phloem vessels.

Tomato plant affected by tobacco mosaic virus

Once a plant is infected by a virus, the only solution
is to dig it up and burn it.
Aphids themselves can be eliminated by a variety
of chemicals, including systemic pesticides that enter
the phloem and kill the insect when it feeds.
Alternatively, a **biological control** could be used, whereby
a predator is introduced, which feeds on the aphid.
(See page 413).

Aphids feeding

▷ Biology at work: Dutch elm disease

Dutch elm disease (DED) is a wilt disease caused by a fungus called *Ophiostoma ulmi*. It is one of the most devastating tree diseases in Europe and North America. DED is transmitted by bark beetles carrying spores on their bodies. After over-wintering in the bark of an elm tree, the beetle emerges in mid-April to mid-May and begins to feed on new elm trees. It is during this feeding period that the majority of DED infections occur.

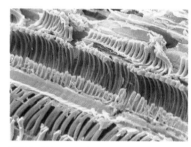
SEM of large xylem vessels

What causes Dutch elm disease?

After an elm tree is infected with only a few spores of the DED fungus, the spores rapidly reproduce in the vascular system of the tree. They begin to block the tree's **xylem vessels**, which transport water, and the elm tree starts to show visible signs of wilting. As more xylem vessels are blocked, the elm tree begins to die back and eventually dies.

Initially, fungal growth is sustained by nutrients available in the xylem sap. Eventually, damage arises from the interaction of fungal enzymes and toxins with the host plant's physiology. This takes a number of forms:

- The fungus produces enzymes that digest cell walls, releasing monosaccharides from the cellulose. This leads to the death of **parenchyma** cells. The partially hydrolysed cell wall and parenchyma cell contents can block the vessel, impeding the transport of water through the plant.

- The same enzymes penetrate the **pits** of vessel walls or **end-plates**, further advancing the spread of the fungus through the plant.

- Fungal toxins such as glycoproteins plug the **pores** of the **pit membranes** of vessels, reducing water flow.

- The secretion of oxalic acid by the fungus reduces the cohesive forces in the water column, which lowers surface tension. This leads to the formation of a **cavitation** bubble of water vapour. The replacement of water by air forms an **embolism**, which reduces the transpiration pull.

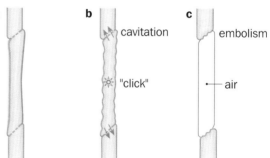

Pathogen-induced cavitation and embolism in a xylem vessel.
a) Under extreme low pressure as a result of cell wall damage, walls are strained inwards from dotted line.
b) A cavitation bubble forms and the walls vibrate causing an audible 'click'. Water exits to the adjoining vessels.
c) The evacuated vessel gradually becomes air-filled causing an embolism to form.

Combating DED

A research team at the University of Toronto has developed a vaccine which 'elicits', or activates, the elm tree's own natural immune response system.

The elm elicitor is unique because, unlike synthetic chemicals and fungicides, it does not attack the DED fungus. There are two types of DED fungus, an aggressive and a non-aggressive group of strains. Most elm trees can successfully defend themselves against the non-aggressive strains of the disease, because the tree's natural defence response is rapid enough to shut down the spread of the disease. This includes:

- the production of fungicidal compounds called **phytoalexins,**

- the production of rings of the impermeable compound **tylose,** which seal off the xylem vessels to localise the infection,

- **barrier zones** of starch-filled parenchyma, which act as a shield between infected xylem and healthy cambium.

This response alone is insufficient to combat the aggressive strain of the DED fungus. Here the elicitor is injected into the tree and activates a natural defence response early enough for the tree to respond even to the rapid activity of the aggressive strain of the disease.

Hedgerow elms in an area severely attacked by Dutch Elm Disease.

Summary

- Water is transported through the plant in one direction — from the roots, up the stem, to the leaves.
- This is a passive process and water passes down a water potential gradient from the soil water to the air.
- Water enters the root through root hairs, which are thin and have a large surface area/volume ratio.
- Water passes across the root cortex by the apoplast and symplast pathways.
- The endodermis prevents passage by the apoplast route, so water has to pass through the cytoplasm of the epidermal cells.
- Salts are actively added to the water in the xylem, which lowers the water potential and draws in more water. This produces a positive pressure known as root pressure.
- Loss of water by evaporation from the leaves is called transpiration.
- Most transpiration takes place through the stomata, which tend to open during the day and close at night.
- When water vapour is lost from the leaves, a water potential gradient is set up that draws water out of the xylem vessels.
- Transpiration pull is the main method by which water rises in the xylem: it is dependent upon a water potential gradient between root and leaf, cohesive forces between water molecules, and adhesive forces between water molecules and the inside of the xylem vessel walls.
- Xylem vessels have developed lignified walls to withstand the pressures involved in water transport.
- Xerophytes are plants that live in environments short of water. They have developed many adaptations to reduce water loss, particularly adaptations of the leaves.
- Translocation of organic materials takes place in the phloem sieve tubes. This is an active process involving the use of energy from ATP.
- The mass flow theory explains how materials are transported from sources to sinks.
- Sucrose is loaded into companion cells by active transport.

▷ Questions

1 a) What are the main cell types that make up xylem tissue?
   b) Explain how the structure and distribution of xylem in a stem is related to:
       i)   transportation of water and mineral salts,
       ii) mechanical support.
   c) Explain how movement of materials in the xylem takes place.

2 Describe how water transport in a flowering plant takes place:
   a) from its uptake from the soil by root hairs,
   b) its transport up the stem to the leaves,
   c) its evaporation from the leaves into the atmosphere.

3 Diagrams A and B show transverse sections through the stem and root of a flowering plant, to show the distribution of tissues.

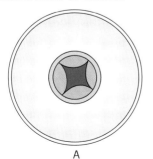

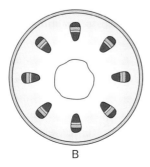

A   B

   a) Which diagram (A or B) is a stem? Explain your choice.
   b) Copy and complete the section of the stem indicating the tissue *most* involved in the following processes:
       i)   upward transport of water (W),
       ii)   transport of sugars (S),
       iii) cell division (D).

4 Copy and complete the table, which refers to xylem and phloem tissue.
   If you think that the statement is correct, put a tick (✓) in the appropriate box.
   If you think that the statement is incorrect, put a cross (✗) in the appropriate box.

Statement	Xylem	Phloem
may contain tracheids		
contains cells with living contents		
contains lignified cells		
transports organic products of photosynthesis		
unidirectional transport		
transport inhibited by metabolic poisons		

5 a) Copy and complete the table, which compares the xylem and phloem.

Feature	Xylem	Phloem
name of conducting cells		
direction in which materials are transported		
one possible mechanism by which materials are transported		

b) Briefly describe one way of demonstrating the movement of fluid in the phloem.

c) The table shows the concentrations of two chemicals in the phloem and xylem sap of the white lupin, *Lupinus albus*.

Chemical	Xylem (mg litre^{-1})	Phloem (mg litre^{-1})
sucrose	not detected	154000
magnesium	27	85

Why do you think that the concentration of sucrose and magnesium differs in xylem and phloem?

6 *Phaseolus* has leaves with a thin cuticle and hairless epidermis.
Pelargonium has leaves with a thicker cuticle and hairy epidermis.
These plants were used to carry out an investigation into water loss from detached leaves, measuring the change in the mass of leaves over several hours.
The results of the investigation are shown in the graph.

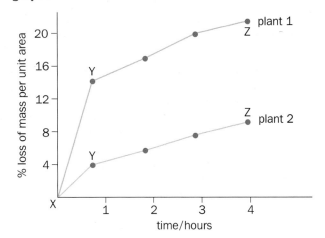

a) Describe how you would carry out this investigation.
b) i) Suggest why percentage loss of mass was rapid from both plants between X and Y.
   ii) Why does the rate of loss decrease between Y and Z?
   iii) Deduce, giving reasons, whether you think *Pelargonium* was plant 1 or plant 2.

7 The diagram shows details of phloem structure in transverse section (TS) and longitudinal section (LS).

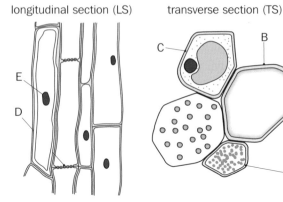

longitudinal section (LS)   transverse section (TS)

a) i) Name the cell types labelled A to C.
   ii) Name the structures labelled D and E.
b) i) The phloem tissues translocate organic materials from 'sources' to 'sinks'. Explain the meaning of the terms 'sources' and 'sinks', giving an example in each case.
   ii) Give two ways in which the phloem sieve tubes are adapted for translocation.

8 The diagram shows structures found on the lower epidermis of a leaf.

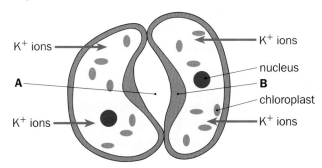

a) What are the structures labelled A and B?
b) One theory suggests that the space labelled A becomes larger as a result of the influx of potassium ions into the cells shown in the diagram.
   i) Name the process that results in the movement of these potassium ions.
   ii) Describe how this influx of potassium ions results in an increase in the size of A.

▷ Gas exchange

1   a) State *three* characteristic features of gas exchange surfaces. [3]
    b) Describe how the process of inspiration (breathing in) takes place in mammals. [3]
    (London) **[6]**

2   The drawings below illustrate the size and shape of *Amoeba* (a protoctist) and *Planaria* (a platyhelminth).

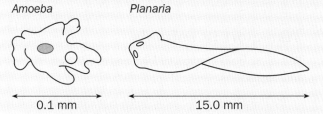

Amoeba   Planaria

◄——►   ◄—————————►
0.1 mm   15.0 mm

For each animal, explain why simple diffusion provides adequate gas exchange between the organism and its environment. [4]
(WJEC) **[4]**

3   The drawing below shows structures in the breathing system of an insect.

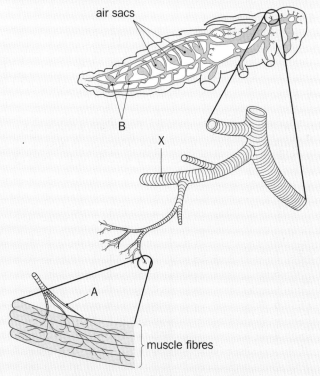

air sacs

B

X

A

muscle fibres

a) Name the structures labelled A and B. [2]
b) Describe the mechanism by which the respiratory surfaces of an insect are ventilated. [2]
c) Suggest the function of the bands of thickening in structure X. [1]
d) Give *two* features which are common to the respiratory surfaces of an insect and of a mammal. [2]
(NEAB) **[7]**

Further questions on gas exchange and transport

4   a) The diagram below shows part of the human airway system.

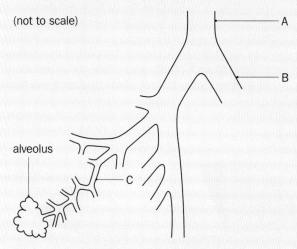

(not to scale)

A

B

alveolus

C

Name the parts labelled A, B and C, and for each part, give *one* distinctive feature. [6]
b) The table below shows how different types of breathing affect ventilation.
The headings of the 5 columns of data (A, B, C, D and E) are given below.
   A Tidal volume / cm^3 $breath^{-1}$
   B respiration rate / breaths min^{-1}
   C dead space volume / cm^3
   D pulmonary ventilation / cm^3 min^{-1}
   E alveolar ventilation / cm^3 min^{-1}
The breathing types are all at rest.

Breathing type	A	B	C	D	E
Quiet	500	12	150	6000	4200
Deep, slow	1200	5	150	6000	5250
Shallow, rapid	150	40	150	6000	0

   i)   Suggest what is meant by the term *dead space volume*. [1]
   ii) **Pulmonary ventilation**
        = Tidal volume × Respiratory rate
        Using the data above, derive a similar word equation to show how the rate of alveolar ventilation has been calculated. [1]
   iii) Explain why alveolar ventilation decreases with shallow rapid breathing. [1]
   iv) What will happen to a person who continues to ventilate by shallow, rapid breathing? [2]
        (O&C) **[11]**

5   Mountaineers often experience problems with gaseous exchange when they climb to high altitudes. This is because of the low pressure, low temperature and low humidity of the air.
    a) How is the diameter of the trachea maintained at low pressures? [1]

215

b) Air is inhaled through the trachea, bronchi and bronchioles. As it passes along these tubes, the air is warmed and humidified (unless it is already at body temperature and saturated with water vapour).

The diagram below shows the partial pressures of oxygen, water vapour and other gases entering the lungs at sea level and at 8000 m above sea level.

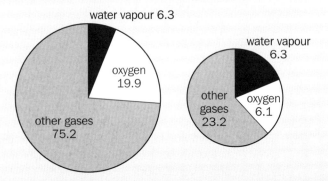

partial pressures of gases at sea level /kPa   partial pressures of gases at 8000 m above sea level /kPa

i) Comment on the differences in the air entering the lungs at sea level compared with that at 8000 m above sea level. [3]
ii) Suggest how oxygen absorption by the lungs at sea level would differ from that at 8000 m. [2]
iii) Suggest how the concentration of carbon dioxide in the blood at sea level would differ from that at 8000 m. [2]

(*Camb*) **[8]**

6 The concentrations of potassium ions were measured in sections taken through closed and open stomata on the leaves of a bean plant. The results are shown in the diagram below.

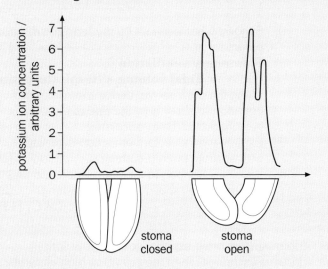

a) There is an increase in the concentration of potassium ions in the guard cells when the stomata are open. Where do these potassium ions come from? [1]

b) Explain how the increase in potassium ion concentration affects the water potential of the guard cells and how it causes the stomata to open. [3]
c) When stomata are open, the increase in potassium ion concentration involves active transport. If the guard cells were treated with a respiratory poison, how would this affect the stomata? Explain your answer. [2]

(*NEAB*) **[6]**

▷ Transport in animals

7 The table below refers to features of arteries, veins and capillaries.

Copy the table. If the statement is correct, place a tick (✓) in the appropriate box and if the statement is incorrect place a cross (✗) in the appropriate box.

Feature	Arteries	Veins	Capillaries
Walls permeable			
Collagen fibres present in walls			
Endothelium present			
Series of valves present			

[4]

(*London*) **[4]**

8 The bar chart below shows the relative thickness of parts of the walls of two blood vessels A and B. One of these blood vessels is an artery, the other is a vein.

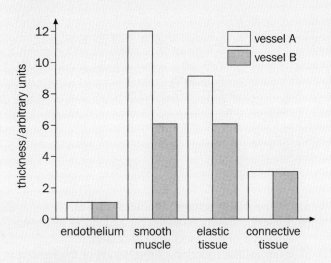

a) Which blood vessel is the artery? Explain the reasons for your answer. [2]
b) Explain how the structure of veins ensures the flow of blood in one direction only. [2]

(*NEAB*) **[4]**

9 The diagram below shows the pathways for the conduction of *electrical impulses* during the cardiac cycle.

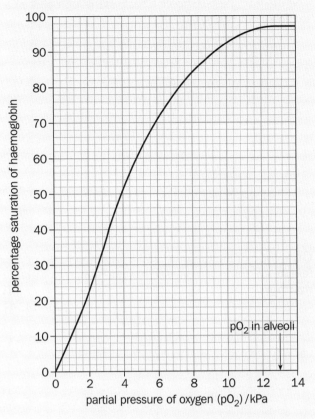

X

conductive pathways

a) i)   Name the structure labelled X.   [1]
    ii) In the wall of which chamber of the heart is structure X located?   [1]
    iii) Describe the role of structure X in the control of the cardiac cycle.   [2]
b) The table below shows the pressures in the left atrium, left ventricle and aorta during a single cardiac cycle.

Stage	Pressure/kPa		
	Left atrium	Left ventricle	Aorta
1	0.5	0.4	10.6
2	1.2	0.7	10.6
3	0.3	6.7	10.6
4	0.4	17.3	16.0
5	0.8	8.0	12.0

Give the name of *one stage* for each of the following.
   ii) Blood flows into the aorta   [1]
   iii) The valve between the atrium and the ventricle (bicuspid valve) is open   [1]
   (*NEAB*) **[6]**

10 Copy and complete the table below which gives information about *three* types of mammalian blood cell.

Appearance of blood cell	Name of blood cell	Function
A		
B		Makes antibodies
C		Phagocytosis

[4]
(*AEB*) **[4]**

11 The graph below shows the dissociation curve for oxyhaemoglobin in the blood of a person at rest.

percentage saturation of haemoglobin

pO$_2$ in alveoli

partial pressure of oxygen (pO$_2$) /kPa

a) i)   A typical partial pressure of oxygen in resting skeletal muscle is 2.5 kPa. Use the graph to determine percentage saturation of haemoglobin with oxygen in the blood leaving the resting muscle.   [1]
    ii) Blood leaving the lungs contains 20 cm^3 of oxygen per 100 cm^3 of blood. Calculate the volume of oxygen released per 100 cm^3 of blood as it passes through the resting muscle.   [2]
b) i)   Copy the graph. Sketch the dissociation curve expected when the person is exercising.   [1]
    (ii) Give *two* changes in the blood of the exercising person which would have caused the change in the dissociation curve you sketched in (i).   [2]
   (*AEB*) **[6]**

▷ Transport in plants

12 The diagram below shows a section through part of a single xylem vessel.

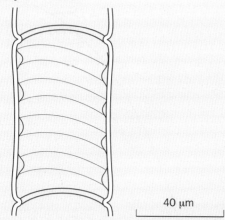

40 μm

On a copy of the diagram, label *four* structural features of the xylem vessel that are related to water transport. [4]

(Camb) **[4]**

13 The uptake of water by a leafy shoot can be investigated using a potometer, as shown in the diagram below.

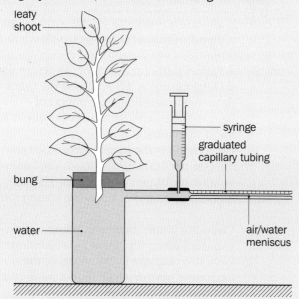

leafy shoot

syringe

graduated capillary tubing

bung

water

air/water meniscus

a) i) What assumption is made when this apparatus is used to investigate the rate of transpiration? [1]
   ii) State *two* precautions which must be taken when setting up and using this apparatus. [2]
b) Using this apparatus, four experiments were carried out with the same shoot in the order given below.
   A Still air, leaves untreated
   B Moving air, leaves untreated
   C Still air, lower surface of leaf covered with grease
   D Moving air, lower surface of leaf covered with grease

Temperature and light intensity were kept constant during the investigation.
The results are shown in the graph below.

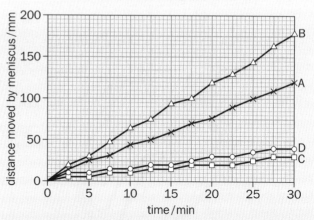

The mean rate of water uptake during experiment A was 3.2 mm³ per minute.
The cross-sectional area of the bore of the capillary tube is 0.8 mm². Calculate the mean rate of water uptake by the shoot during experiment B. Show your working. [3]
c) i) Describe and explain the effect of moving air on the rate of water uptake in experiment B. [3]
   ii) Suggest an explanation for the different effects of moving air in experiments B and D. [3]

(London) **[12]**

14 The diagram below shows some cells from a plant root.

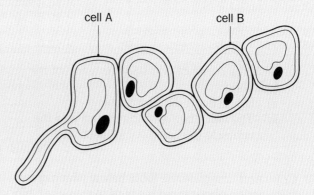

cell A   cell B

a) In terms of water potential, explain how water moves from the soil into cell A. [2]
b) Draw a line on the diagram to show the apoplastic pathway through these root cells. [1]
c) Describe how oxygen reaches cell B. [1]
d) The table below shows the concentration of certain mineral ions in the soil and in cell A.

	Concentration/mmol dm⁻³		
	Potassium	Sodium	Chloride
Soil	0.1	1.1	1.3
Cytoplasm of cell A	93	51	58

From this table, what is the evidence that uptake of mineral ions from the soil is (i) by active transport and (ii) selective? [2]

(*AEB*) **[6]**

15 The drawing below shows three pathways along which water can pass from the soil into the xylem of a root.

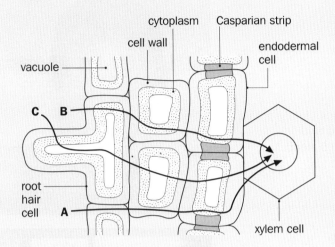

a) Name the pathway labelled B. [1]
b) The Casparian strips shown in the endodermal cells are made of a waterproof material. Suggest the importance of the Casparian strip in the movement of water through the root. [2]
c) Explain in terms of water potential how water enters a root hair cell. [2]

(*NEAB*) **[5]**

16 The diagram below shows a longitudinal section of two cells of phloem tissue in a plant stem.

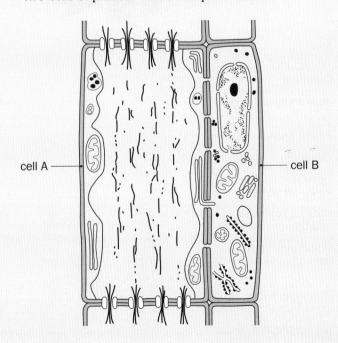

a) Name the cells labelled A and B in the diagram. [2]
b) (i) State the function of phloem in a plant. [1]
   (ii) Describe how aphids can be used to investigate the function of phloem. [3]

(*London*) **[6]**

17 The diagram below shows a transverse section of a leaf of *Ammophila arenaria*, which is a xerophyte. The photomicrograph shows the details of the area indicated by the box on the diagram.

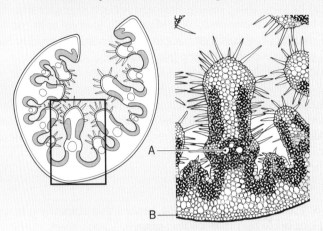

a) Name the parts labelled A and B. [2]
b) Describe *two* xeromorphic features shown in this leaf and, in each case, indicate how the feature helps to reduce transpiration. [4]

(*London*) **[6]**

13 Diet and health

What do we mean by the word **health**?
Health has been described as
'the state of complete physical, mental and social well-being'.
Being healthy, then, means that you feel good physically,
you have a positive outlook and are able to cope with the social
and mental pressures that people experience in everyday life,
and you do this without any great difficulty.
Being healthy is far more than just being free from disease.

To sustain a healthy lifestyle, a person needs to have a balanced and
varied diet, should take exercise, have proper shelter and enough sleep.
In addition, good hygiene will reduce the likelihood of infection.

▶ What is disease?

To most of us the word 'disease' means that something is wrong
with our body and that we feel unwell.
A disease is usually due to a malfunction of the body.
A doctor is able to diagnose what a disease is by looking at
the **symptoms**. These may be physical, mental or both.

Diseases such as influenza are described as **acute**, because their
effects come on suddenly and affect the body quickly.
The symptoms often disappear as quickly as they appeared.
Other diseases are more long-term, with the symptoms lasting
for months or years.
Such diseases are referred to as **chronic**; their symptoms
persist for a much longer time.
The table shows the major categories of disease and their causes.

Category of disease	Cause of disease	Examples
physical	temporary or permanent damage to part of the body	bone fractures, leprosy
infectious	invasion of the body by other organisms	rabies, malaria, influenza
deficiency	inadequate diet	kwashiorkor, scurvy, rickets
inherited	defective genes passed on from parents	cystic fibrosis, haemophilia, sickle cell anaemia
degenerative	organs and tissues 'wear' and do not work so well with age	arthritis, poor sight and hearing defects
mental	a wide range of disorders from psychological to those resulting from brain damage	depression, paranoia, schizophrenia
social	social interactions with family, friends, strangers	drug dependence, agoraphobia, alcoholism
self-inflicted	damage to the body as a result of the person's own actions	sun-related skin cancer

▶ Infectious diseases

Many organisms are able to live inside the human body.
Organisms that do so and cause disease are called **pathogens**.
Bacteria and viruses are probably the best known pathogens but
many fungi, protists and parasites can also cause disease.

Diseases are said to be **infectious** or **communicable** if these
pathogens can be passed from one person to another.
This can occur during normal social contact.
For instance, we may breathe in airborne viruses such as influenza,
measles or chickenpox when someone sneezes or coughs close to us.
Contaminated food or water can carry infectious diseases such as
salmonella, cholera and typhoid.
Sexually transmitted diseases (STDs) include gonorrhea and syphilis.
Any break in the skin surface reduces the barrier to infection and can
allow pathogens such as tetanus and gangrene to enter the body.
Some parasites have adaptive features that allow them to penetrate
the skin surface.
Some pathogens and parasites are transmitted between hosts by **vectors**.
For instance, mosquitoes act as vectors in the spread of malaria.
When the mosquito takes a blood meal, the malarial parasite *Plasmodium*
may be injected into the person's blood along with the insect's saliva.

Kibumba camp, Zaire during the Rwanda Crisis

▶ Non-infectious diseases

In developed countries, far fewer people die of infectious diseases because
they have better medical services and improved housing and hygiene.
In these countries people tend to die as a result of **non-infectious diseases**.
This category includes the diseases that are not caused by pathogens.

- **Physical diseases** result from damage to parts of the body,
  for example bone fractures, concussion and spinal injuries.

- **Mental diseases** may be anxiety **neuroses,** such as claustrophobia,
  or **psychoses**, as in the case of schizophrenia and manic depression.
  Such neuroses and psychoses can drastically affect a person's behaviour.

- **Deficiency diseases**, such as marasmus, and obesity are linked to
  malnutrition.

- **Degenerative diseases** are associated with ageing. As we age our
  bodies tend not to work as well as they did. Diseases such as arthritis,
  motor neurone disease, Alzheimer's disease, heart disease and cancers
  increase in incidence with age.

- **Social diseases** are associated with lifestyle. For instance, smoking
  can result in cancer and emphysema.
  Alcohol abuse and the misuse of drugs can lead to dependence.

- **Inherited diseases** are caused by the passing on of defective alleles.
  Such diseases include cystic fibrosis and multiple sclerosis.

- **Self-inflicted diseases** result in people putting their health at risk
  as a result of their own decisions. This broad grouping can include
  everything from sunburn to smoking and drug-related diseases.

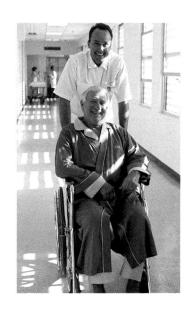

*Kirt Cobain, the lead singer of Nirvana,
was a known drug user and
committed suicide*

▶ Patterns of disease

Epidemiology is the study of patterns of disease and the ways in which diseases spread through human populations.
Information about the distribution of a particular disease can enable us to identify its cause.
Such information can also be used to identify the ways in which infectious diseases are transmitted.
In the case of non-infectious diseases, the data collected may help to establish a link with a possible cause. An example of this was establishing the link between smoking and lung cancer in the 1950s.

Epidemiologists collect data from a particular target population.
For instance, the numbers of deaths from lung cancer per 100 000 population aged between 18 and 65 in London.
Data expressed in this way allows fair comparisons to be made over time.
The type of data collected on the spread of disease includes:

An epidemiologist processing data

- **incidence** – the number of new cases occurring over a particular time,
- **prevalence** – the number of people who have the disease over a particular time,
- **mortality** – the number of deaths from a certain disease over a particular time.

Such data can be used to assess the nature of a disease, which may be:

- **endemic** if an infectious disease is always present in a population; diseases such as measles, mumps and tuberculosis are endemic in the UK,
- **epidemic** if an infectious disease spreads rapidly through a population, such as the epidemics of new strains of influenza that can occur,
- **pandemic** if the disease spreads over a wide area, such as a continent or the whole world. TB and AIDS are pandemic diseases.

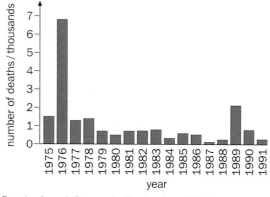

Deaths from influenza in England and Wales 1975–91

Worldwide disease

In developing countries in Africa and Asia, about 40% of people die from infectious diseases.
Each year more than 14 million children under the age of 5 years die from diseases associated with poor medical aid, poor housing and malnutrition.
These diseases include diarrhoea, dysentery and measles.

Contrast this situation with the developed countries (eg Europe, Japan, USA).
Here there is better medical care and few people die from infectious diseases.
Instead, illnesses in these countries tend to be linked to affluence.
Overnutrition (leading to obesity), smoking and drinking too much alcohol are among the unhealthy lifestyles that can lead to the onset of diseases such as cancers and coronary heart disease.

In developed countries, the low level of infectious disease means that a very high percentage of infants survive to become adults and that people live to an old age.

By contrast, in developing countries, life expectancy is shorter and infant mortality rates are higher, and this is linked to the incidence of infectious disease and a relatively poor diet.

Despite this gap, progress has been made and the **World Health Organisation** (**WHO**) has targeted a life expectancy of 60 and an infant mortality rate of less than 50 deaths per 1000 births for the year 2000.
Improved education, good medical services, improved living conditions and the relief of poverty are essential if these goals are to be achieved.

Contaminated water supply

▷ A balanced diet

A **balanced diet** is one that provides an adequate intake of the nutrients and energy needed to sustain the body and ensure health and growth.

A **nutrient** is a substance in food that provides a benefit to the body.

Each type of nutrient carries out one or more of three basic functions.

- **To provide energy** – this is mainly the role of carbohydrates and fats (proteins are only used as respiratory substrates if carbohydrates and fats are in short supply).
- **To allow growth and repair** of body cells and tissues. Proteins in the diet provide a source of amino acids with which cells can make their own proteins.
- **To regulate the body's metabolism.** These nutrients include vitamins and minerals that are needed in very small amounts in our diet. These are called **micronutrients**.

Carbohydrates, proteins and fats have to be supplied in large quantities in the diet every day, so these are called **macronutrients**.

▷ Nutrients and their role in the body

Carbohydrates

As you saw in Chapter 1, there are three main groups of carbohydrates:

- **monosaccharides** – single sugars, for example glucose, fructose and galactose,
- **disaccharides** – double sugars, for example maltose, sucrose and lactose,
- **polysaccharides** – chains of sugars, for example starch, glycogen and cellulose.

The major functions of carbohydrates in the body are as energy sources, energy stores or structural substrates.

Lipids

Lipids are composed of carbon, hydrogen and oxygen, but with less oxygen than carbohydrates.
Triglycerides are made up of three **fatty acid** molecules and one molecule of **glycerol**. Their main function is as an energy store.

Some foods rich in carbohydrates

Phospholipids make up a major constituent of the cell surface membrane.

Proteins

Proteins are composed of carbon, hydrogen, oxygen and nitrogen (some also contain sulphur and phosphorus).
They are made up of **amino acids**, which form chains, helices and folded structures, giving each protein its particular property. (Remember, there are 20 different amino acids.)

Many proteins have a structural function but **enzymes** and **hormones** which control metabolism are globular proteins.

Some protein-rich foods

▶ Differences in energy needs

There are a number of reasons why different people have different energy requirements.

The most important factors determining the energy requirements of an individual are metabolic rate and physical activity.

- **Basal metabolic rate (BMR)** is the rate at which energy is used up when the body is at rest.
  It is the rate of respiration that the body needs to keep 'ticking over' during periods of inactivity.
- **Diet-induced thermogenesis (DIT)** is the increase in the body's heat production by cellular respiration after food is eaten. This increase is greater if pure protein is consumed rather than carbohydrates and fats, but of course most diets are mixed.
- **Physical activity** is the factor that varies most in determining a person's overall energy requirements.
  The effect of physical activity varies according to body size and the duration and intensity of the activity.

The energy needs of people also vary according to age, gender, activity, pregnancy and lactation.

- **Age**
Children have a greater energy requirement than adults.
They have a larger surface area to volume ratio than an adult and therefore a greater heat loss.
A young child will weigh less than an adult but has a higher BMR because the child is still growing.

- **Gender**
Women have a relatively higher body fat content than men.
Fat tissue has a lower metabolic rate than muscle.
So women generally have a lower energy requirement than men.

- **Activity**
As we have said, physical activity uses up energy.
The more active you are, the more energy you need.
The type of activity and its duration will affect the amount of energy needed.

- **Pregnancy**
During pregnancy, the growth of the fetus uses up extra energy.
A pregnant woman may require about 0.8 MJ more than the 9 MJ per day recommended for a non-pregnant woman.

- **Lactation**
During breast-feeding, the production of milk is a drain upon the energy reserves of the mother.
Some energy will have been stored by the mother as fat during pregnancy.
But she will also need to eat more each day to get the extra energy that she needs.

▶ Differences in nutrient needs

Many of the factors that affect energy requirements also
affect the body's need for other nutrients.

● Age

Infants and young children require more protein per unit of body mass
than adults because they are still growing and need protein to make
new cells.

Each tissue and organ has its own **critical period** when growth is rapid.
For instance, the critical period for the brain is during fetal
development and the first year after birth.
There are two critical periods for muscle development –
infancy and adolescence.

Elderly people sometimes pay too little attention to their diets.
Lack of fresh fruit and vegetables makes vitamin C deficiency
quite common in this age group.

Osteoporosis or decalcification of the bones can also be a problem
in old age.
Minor falls can easily result in bone fractures.
The condition is more prevalent in women (after the menopause)
than in men.
It is caused by low vitamin D intake, although vitamin D levels can
be raised by exposure of the skin to sunlight, which enables the body
to make its own vitamin D.

Why do you think that small doses of vitamin D (5–10 mg per day)
are recommended for housebound people who spend a lot of
their time indoors?

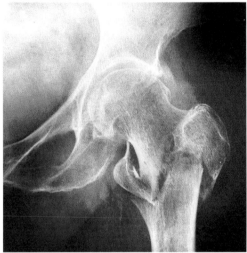

X-ray of an elderly woman's hip showing a
fractured femur due to osteoporosis

● Gender

A poor diet can lead to anaemia, which can be a problem in adolescent
girls.
Anaemia is due to iron deficiency, which may be caused by the onset of
menstruation.
A dietary supplement of iron tablets corrects the condition.

● Activity

Physical exercise can increase the body's protein requirement, for example
activities such as body-building where greater development of muscle occurs.

● Pregnancy

There is a general need for increased nutrients during pregnancy.
This is especially true for vitamins A and C and for calcium which
is needed for bone formation.
However, care should be taken not to exceed recommended doses of
supplementary nutrients such as vitamins A and D as they can be toxic.

● Lactation

The demand for extra nutrients is greater during lactation than it is
during pregnancy.
This is particularly true of protein, vitamin D and iron.
Since the milk-producing cells of the mother's breasts use nutrients derived
from her diet, whatever she eats affects the composition of her milk.
So mothers should have a varied and balanced diet to produce
healthy nutritious milk.

▶ Dietary reference values and nutritional requirements

Each nutrient has a particular function in the body.
Some nutrients are needed in greater quantities than others.
For example, we need about 75 grams of protein per day but only a few milligrams of vitamin C.
Each person's nutrient and energy requirements are related to their age, gender, level of physical activity and state of health.
Some people absorb nutrients more efficiently than others and so have lower than average nutritional requirements.

In the UK, the estimated requirements for particular groups of the population are based on the advice given by the Committee on Medical Aspects of Food and Nutrition Policy (COMA).

The COMA panel reviews scientific evidence and then makes proposals that are used by the government to formulate policy.
In 1991, a new COMA report was published, called *Dietary Reference Values for Food Energy and Nutrients for the United Kingdom*.
The scientific evidence was examined by various groups within the UK population.

The Balance of Good Health

Dietary reference values

The COMA report introduced the term **dietary reference values (DRVs)**.
This attempted to avoid the idea that *everyone* should be eating the *same* quantities of nutrients irrespective of age, gender, fitness, etc.

DRVs	The nutrient and energy requirements for a particular group with reference to age, gender, fitness, etc.
EAR	An estimate of the average energy or nutrient requirements needed by 50% of the population
RNI	The amount of nutrients required to meet the needs of 97.5% of the population
LRNI	The amount of nutrients that meet the needs of 2.5% of the population

There are two groups of DRVs.
The first refers to COMA's recommendations on energy and nutritional requirements and the second to vitamins and minerals.
The graph here shows you how DRVs are used.

Estimated average requirement (EAR) is an estimate of the average requirement of energy or nutrients.
50% of the population will need more than the EAR for energy and nutrients and 50% of the population will need less.
Reference nutrient intake (RNI) is the amount of a particular nutrient that ensures that the needs of nearly all the population (97.5%) are met.
Lower reference nutrient intake (LRNI) is the amount of a nutrient that is enough for only a small number of people (2.5%).
Most people will need more than this.
Note that RNI and LRNI apply *only* to nutrients.
The only DRV that refers to energy is EAR.
It is important to realise that these are not recommended intakes for an *individual*, but a reference standard against which a comparison can be made for a *population* or *group* of people.

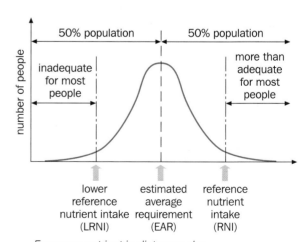

Energy or nutrient in diet every day

Safe intakes

The second group of DRVs refers mainly to vitamins and minerals.
The *safe intake* is the amount judged to be sufficient for everyone.

Levels of nutrient intake *below* the safe intake could risk deficiency.
But there is no evidence to suggest that intake above this level will
give any further benefits.
Indeed some micronutrients are toxic in large quantities.
Consequently, safe intakes are set well below levels that would be *unsafe*.

How should DRVs be used?

As well as varying between different age groups, the requirements
for energy and nutrients vary with gender, and, for females,
during pregnancy and lactation.

The RNI should be used when assessing the dietary intake of
a group.
The nearer the average intake of the group to the RNI,
the less likely it is that any individual will have a deficient intake.
The nearer the average to the LRNI, the greater the probability
that some individuals are not getting enough.
When planning a diet for a particular group, the aim should be
to provide the RNI.

Age	Protein/ g day^{-1}	Calcium/ mg day^{-1}	Iron/ mg day^{-1}	Zinc/ mg day^{-1}	Vitamin A/ μg day^{-1}	Folic acid μg day^{-1}	Vitamin C/ mg day^{-1}
0–3 months*	12.5	525	1.7	4.0	350	50	25
4–6 months	12.7	525	4.3	4.0	350	50	25
7–9 months	13.7	525	7.8	5.0	350	50	25
10–12 months	14.9	525	7.8	5.0	350	50	25
1–3 years	14.5	350	6.9	5.0	400	70	30
4–6 years	19.7	450	6.1	6.5	500	100	30
7–10 years	28.3	550	8.7	7.0	500	150	30
males:							
11–14 years	42.1	1000	11.3	9.0	600	200	35
15–18 years	55.2	1000	11.3	9.5	700	200	40
19–50 years	55.5	700	8.7	9.5	700	200	40
50+ years	53.3	700	8.7	9.5	700	200	40
females:							
11–14 years	41.2	800	14.8	9.0	600	200	35
15–18 years	45.0	800	14.8	7.0	600	200	40
19–50 years	45.0	700	14.8	7.0	600	200	40

*Formulated
All the values assume a well-balanced diet in which DRVs for energy and all other nutrients are met.
(μg = microgram 1000 μg = 1 mg)

*Reference Nutrient Intakes (RNIs) for protein and six
micronutrients.*

Calculating EARs for energy

EARs for energy are based upon the present lifestyles and
activity levels of the UK population.
As with nutrient requirements, the energy requirements are
related to age, gender, body size and levels of activity.

EARs are estimated by multiplying the **BMR** by the person's
current **physical activity level (PAL)**.

$$EAR = BMR \times PAL$$

This overall ratio of energy used to BMR is determined by the
lifestyle of a person.
A PAL factor of 1.4 reflects the lifestyle of most adults in the UK.
This factor is suitable for adults who do little physical activity at
work or in their leisure time.

For more active people, larger PAL values are used.
For example, a PAL of 1.9 is appropriate for very active adults.

Calculate the EARs for energy for:

i)   a 16-year-old male with a BMR of 8.15 MJ day $^{-1}$
    at the following PALs: 1.1, 1.4 and 1.9,

ii) a 19-year-old female with a BMR of 5.78 MJ day $^{-1}$
    at the following PALs: 1.2, 1.4 and 1.8.

Compare each of these values with the figures for EARs
given in the table for PALs at 1.4.

Age	EAR/MJ day^{-1}	
	males	females
0–3 months (formula fed)	2.28	2.16
4–6 months	2.89	2.69
7–9 months	3.44	3.20
10–12 months	3.85	3.61
1–3 years	5.15	4.86
4–6 years	7.16	6.46
7–10 years	8.24	7.28
11–14 years	9.27	7.92
15–18 years	11.51	8.83
19–49 years	10.60	8.10
50–59 years	10.60	8.00
60–64 years	9.93	7.99

The EARs for adults (over 19 years) given here are based on low activity levels (PAL of 1.4 – see text).

EARs for energy for different age groups and sexes

▶ Essential amino acids

Proteins have a number of functions in the human body:

- they make up body protein such as muscle,
- all enzymes are proteins and so they control metabolic pathways,
- many hormones, for example insulin, are proteins.

All these proteins are made inside cells from a pool of amino acids.

There are 20 different amino acids. As you have seen in Chapter 1, they all have the same basic structure, but each one has a different R group.

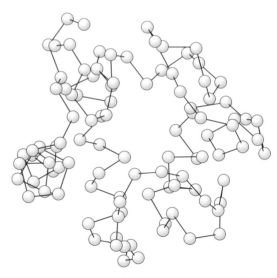

The tertiary structure of the protein cytochrome C

Amino acids can be divided into two main groups.

- **Non-essential amino acids**, which the body is able to make itself.
There are eight of these, which we can synthesise from simpler compounds.
For instance, the amino acid alanine can be synthesised from the compound pyruvate.

- **Essential amino acids**, which can only be obtained in our food.
There are 12 amino acids that cannot be synthesised from existing organic compounds in the body.
These essential amino acids (EAAs) must be supplied in the diet as we need them to make particular proteins.

Some essential amino acids are used to synthesise non-essential amino acids.
This takes place by the process of **transamination.**
For instance, the essential amino acid phenylalanine can be converted to the non-essential amino acid tyrosine.
This means that if we are short of phenylalanine, then we may also be short of tyrosine unless it is present in the diet.

As we have said, cells assemble proteins from a '***pool***' of available amino acids in the cell.
This pool is stocked with amino acids derived from protein that we have eaten.

As a general rule, any animal protein that we eat contains all the essential amino acids.
But proteins in plant material contain only ***some*** of the essential amino acids.
So if you are a vegetarian, you may need to supplement your diet to ensure that you have the full range of amino acids.

Your cells are continually drawing on their pool of amino acids to make new structural proteins, enzymes and hormones.

If you are short of protein in your diet, the amino acid pool may be topped up with amino acids from the breakdown of body protein such as muscle.

A vegetarian meal

▷ Essential fatty acids

Lipids in the diet consist of fats, oils and waxes.
Most of our lipid intake (about 95%) consists of **triglycerides**.

You should remember from Chapter 1 that a triglyceride is made up of one molecule of glycerol and three molecules of fatty acids.

The other 5% of our lipid intake consists of **phospholipids**, which form an important part of our cell surface membranes, and **cholesterol**.

Animal products generally have a high lipid content, since fats act as the main energy stores in the bodies of many animals.
Animal products with high lipid contents include dairy products, fatty meats and fish such as herring and mackerel.
The lipid contents of many plants is quite low, except for seeds, nuts and olives.
This is because their main energy store is carbohydrate, such as starch.

The body can synthesise many of the fatty acids it needs itself.
The few that it cannot make are called **essential fatty acids (EFAs)** and they must be supplied in our diet.
Examples include linoleic acid and linolenic acid.
They are vital for the formation of the phospholipids that make up the cell surface membrane of plant and animal cells.

The liver has an important role in the conversion of essential fatty acids such as linolenic acid into a form that can be used to make hormones such as prostaglandins.
These compounds are important in triggering the actions of the immune, renal and circulatory systems.

We need only very small amounts of these EFAs in our diet.
In fact, people with a healthy diet probably have a year's supply of EFAs in their fat stores.

However, if there is a deficiency of essential fatty acids in the diet, it can reduce growth in infants, affect the healing of wounds, and cause hair loss and scaly skin in adults.

Remember that, where possible, your diet should contain unsaturated fats, as these carry far fewer health risks.

glycerol

fatty acid
fatty acid
fatty acid

a simple
diagram of a
triglyceride

The structure of a triglyceride

Many animal products have a high content of saturated fatty acids

A fast food outlet

▶ Vitamins

Vitamins are a group of unrelated organic compounds.
They cannot be synthesised by the body and therefore
they are *essential* to the diet.
They are needed only in small amounts but if they are lacking
in the diet they can result in **deficiency diseases**.
This is because many vitamins are needed by the body
to make **coenzymes**, such as NAD^+, FAD and NADP.

A coenzyme is a non-protein that needs to be present
if an enzyme is to work.

So, without coenzymes, enzymes fail to function and
biochemical pathways become blocked.
For instance, the vitamin **niacin** is needed for the formation
of NAD and without it many of the energy-releasing reactions
of the cell cannot take place.

Vitamin A

Vitamin A is also called **retinol** and is found in only a few foods.
It is present in milk, eggs, liver and fish liver oils.
It is also present in fruits such as mangoes and papaya.
Retinol can be synthesised from carotene, a photosynthetic pigment
found in vegetables such as carrots, spinach and cabbage.

Children deficient in vitamin A often develop dry skin and hair.
They become prone to infections of the ear, urinary and
digestive systems.
Most noticeable, however, is an inflammation of the eyes leading
to a drying and ulceration of the cornea called **xerophthalmia**.
The ability to see in dim light is diminished, a condition known as
night blindness.
Light-sensitive cells in the retina called **rods** are able to
detect light of low intensity.
They convert vitamin A into the light-absorbing visual pigment
rhodopsin.
A lack of retinol in the diet means that not enough rhodopsin
is synthesised and rod cells are unable to function (see page 337).

Vitamin D

Vitamin D has been called 'the sunshine vitamin' because
if the skin receives enough sunlight, the body is able to
synthesise enough vitamin D without it being needed in the diet.

However, given our climate, we rely upon a dietary intake of vitamin D.
Dark-skinned people living in Britain produce little vitamin D themselves.
So they need to ensure that their diet includes sufficient amounts.

Sources of vitamin D in the diet include fish liver oils, egg yolk and milk.
Vitamin D is necessary for the small intestine to absorb calcium.
It is also needed to regulate the deposition of calcium in bone cells.
So deficiency symptoms include the lack of calcium in bones,
causing **rickets** in children.
In adults, deficiency gives rise to the condition known as **osteomalacia**,
which leads to a softening of the bones and an increased chance of fractures.

Maintaining vitamin and mineral intake

'He must be fond of carrots'

▶ Malnutrition

Malnutrition is nutrition that deviates from the normal.
When these deviations are large, then clinical symptoms appear.

Undernutrition is often associated with underdeveloped nations.
We are accustomed to seeing news programmes on the television
showing starving people in famine-hit countries.
Yet it is ironic that one of the most serious health problems, **coronary
heart disease**, is most common in affluent, industrialised societies.
Coronary heart disease is associated with **overnutrition** and **obesity**.

No more food, Berdale, during the Somalia famine

Undernutrition

Undernutrition can be general (starvation) or specific, as in the case
of the deficiency of a particular vitamin, mineral or food type.
One of the more common deficiency diseases in the world is
xerophthalmia, caused by a deficiency of vitamin A.

During starvation, the **basal metabolic rate** (**BMR**) is reduced.
BMR is the rate at which energy is used when the body is at rest.
It is the rate of respiration that the body needs to keep 'ticking over'
during periods of inactivity.
People can survive for many weeks without food, provided they have
access to water, because during periods of starvation, the body draws
upon its stores of carbohydrate, fat and protein for energy.

Worldwide, the most common form of undernutrition is **protein
energy malnutrition** (**PEM**).
As the term suggests, this is caused by a lack of dietary energy and
protein.
In its extreme forms it can lead to **kwashiorkor** and **marasmus**.
In both conditions the child is underweight, though this is more
extreme in a child with marasmus.

A child showing the symptoms of kwashiorkor

The clinical signs of kwashiorkor are **oedema** (a swelling of the legs),
sparse, dry hair, a flaky appearance to the skin and a bloated 'moon
face' appearance.
The 'moon-faced' child is apathetic, showing little interest in its
surroundings.
There is an accumulation of fat in the liver which can lead to **cirrhosis**
(permanent damage due to the replacement of healthy liver cells with
scar tissue).

A child with marasmus has a very low weight for its age and thin arms
and legs, with little muscle or fat.
The face has a wizened appearance, referred to as 'old man's face'.
There are fewer biochemical changes and in this respect the child with
marasmus has adapted to its poor diet better than one with kwashiorkor.

In either case, the child is in danger and any feeding should involve
the frequent serving of very small amounts of food.
This is because PEM causes pancreatic and intestinal cells to die.
So fewer digestive enzymes are secreted and the surface area for
the absorption of digested food is much reduced.

A child suffering from marasmus

Starvation

Dietary survey data for poor communities in developing nations has shown energy intake to be much lower than the DRV. The significance of this is that protein that should be used for growth and repair of cells has to be used as an energy source. So children showing the symptoms of protein deficiency, as in the case of kwashiorkor, are really suffering from insufficient energy intake.

A food drop during an Ethiopian famine

Most aid programmes that supply food to famine-stricken areas aim to increase the energy intake of the population.
Staple foods such as wheat and rice will satisfy energy intake and also provide enough protein.
However, tropical crops such as cassava (a root crop) and sweet potato, whilst having a high energy content, are low in protein, so they need to be supplemented with other protein foods.

The body adapts to progressive starvation by

- quickly using up **glycogen** stored in the liver,
- drawing upon the body's **fat** stores (this may last for between 4 and 6 weeks depending on the amount of fat stored),
- using **protein** as an energy source, which results in a wasting of the muscles and other tissues.

Anorexia nervosa

Anorexia nervosa is a wasting disease and its symptoms are very similar to that of marasmus.
In contrast though, it is usually found in developed countries and can be brought on by psychological distress.
Anorexia is most common in teenage girls from middle to high income families.

Sufferers of anorexia nervosa lose their appetite, eat little food and become dangerously thin. The symptoms include:

- wasting, as muscle tissue is used as a source of energy once the body's fat reserves have been used up,
- a decrease in body temperature, metabolism and heart rate,
- slowing of growth and sexual development (the normal menstrual cycle stops),
- a greater susceptibility to infections,
- depression, so that the affected person's thoughts are dominated by food and eating less and less.

The causes of anorexia are complex, but tend to involve low self-esteem and anxiety about growing up and sexuality. It often develops from a desire to diet, but anorexics who have lost a great deal of weight still see themselves as being too fat.

People with anorexia often fail to see that they are starving themselves.
Treatment focuses on building up their self-esteem and if this is achieved, then normal eating patterns and weight gain usually follow.

The model Kate Moss: a role-model for many teenage girls

Obesity

In Britain and other affluent countries, more people suffer from overnutrition than from undernutrition.

If a person takes in more energy in food than required, then the surplus respiratory substrates are converted to storage fat. This particular form of malnutrition is caused by a combination of factors:

- high intake of fatty foods and refined foods containing a lot of added sugar,
- too little exercise,
- social and emotional stress, leading to 'comfort eating',
- physiological problems such as an underactive thyroid gland, although these tend to be rare.

There are two ways in which people can identify being obese:

- being 20% above the recommended weight for his or her height,
- having a **body mass index (BMI)** greater than 30.

$$\text{body mass index} = \frac{\text{body mass (in kg)}}{\text{height (in metres)} \times 2}$$

A person with a BMI of less than 20 is underweight, between 25 and 30 is overweight, and more than 30 is obese. If you are 20–24, then you are just right!

Waistband measurements are easier than calculating the BMI. Scientists have shown that women with waistband measurements of over 80 cm (31.4 inches) and men with waistband measurements greater than 94 cm (36.9 inches) are twice as likely to develop cardiovascular diseases.

Obesity can cause or lead to an increased incidence of

- coronary heart disease (CHD),
- high blood pressure (hypertension),
- angina (blood flow to the heart muscle is sufficient, but the coronary arteries cannot deliver the additional oxygen needed for exercise, so any physical effort results in chest pains),
- varicose veins (the walls of the veins become stretched due to the accumulation of blood from poor circulation),
- diabetes, gall bladder disease, osteoarthritis and some cancers.

Which of the following actions would be best for an obese person to lose weight?

- cut down on all carbohydrates,
- cut down on fat,
- cut down on starchy and fibrous foods.

Which of these would be the least helpful?
Give reasons for your answers.

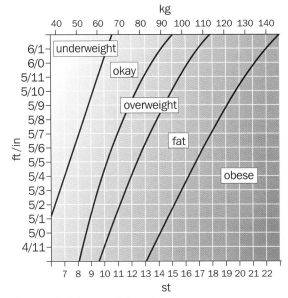

Average height to weight ratios

The 'fattest man in the world' from the film Monty Python's Meaning of Life

Coronary heart disease

CHD is one of the main causes of death in Britain and many other developed countries.
A blockage or constriction of the coronary arteries results in heart failure.

The smooth lining of healthy blood vessels allows blood to flow through them easily.
But the lining can be damaged by the build-up of a fatty deposit called **atheroma**.

This narrowing of the arteries is gradual.
It cuts down the flow of blood and the first signs are often noticed during exercise.
Because of the restriction of blood flow, blood pressure increases and the heart has to beat faster than usual to deliver blood to the tissues.
This can cause pains in the chest and arms known as **angina**.
Someone with angina is more likely to suffer a heart attack.

A heart attack occurs when there is a sudden and severe blockage of the coronary artery.
This cuts off the blood supply to the heart muscle.
The affected part of the heart muscle becomes damaged due to lack of oxygen and the heart may stop beating altogether.
A victim of cardiac arrest will die unless the heart starts to beat again within a few minutes.

Risk factors

CHD is not caused by any one particular factor but by a combination of things.
Age, gender, weight, amount of exercise, blood pressure, diet, smoking and inherited genes are all risk factors.
High levels of blood cholesterol have been shown to increase the risk of CHD.

- A diet high in saturated fat results in high cholesterol levels.
- Our bodies need some cholesterol (see page 17) although the body cells are able to manufacture some of this themselves.
- The intake of polyunsaturated fats results in lower blood cholesterol so these are recommended in the diet instead of saturated fats.

Regular exercise increases fitness, reduces body fat, lowers blood pressure and reduces the risk of heart disease.
But diet, as you have seen, is also important in the reduction of the incidence of CHD.

Use the information about diet in this chapter and in Chapter 1 to explain how the following dietary recommendations act to decrease CHD:

- eating less fat,
- eating less sugar,
- eating more fibre,
- eating less salt.

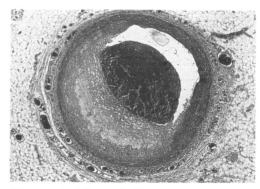

Atheroma building up inside an artery

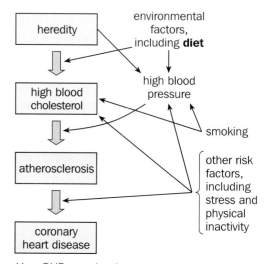

How CHD can develop

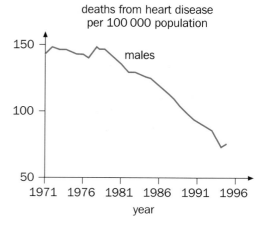

deaths from heart disease per 100 000 population

Deaths from heart disease in the U.K. between 1971 and 1995
(Source: Office for National Statistics)

▶ Biology at work : Biotechnology and food production

You have already seen how fermentation on an industrial scale can produce useful products such as penicillin. Microorganisms can also play a significant role in food production.

Microorganisms are very efficient producers of protein, and in the 1960s the food producers Rank Hovis McDougall (RHM) began a research programme that led to the production of **mycoprotein**.

This is a high protein material produced by a filamentous fungus called *Fusarium*.
RHM found this fungus growing in the soil in a field in Buckinghamshire.
They realised it had great potential as a food material because it was fibrous, high in protein and didn't have an unpleasant taste.

Mycoprotein is produced on an industrial scale in fermenters by a process known as **continuous culture.**
This involves the continuous addition of growth medium and the removal of the protein product at the same time.

At the end of the cycle, the fungus and culture medium are removed from the fermenter for **downstream processing.**
This involves filtration to separate the growth medium from the brown, fibrous 'filter cake'.
The filter cake is frozen quickly to prevent it from becoming a fertile growth medium for other microbes.
The 'cake' can then be used as the base material for a number of food products.
Downstream processing can actually increase the percentage of protein by some 40-45%.
This occurs when the material and some of its original mass is lost due to the evaporation of water.

Due to its fibrous nature and high protein content, mycoprotein makes an ideal meat substitute and since the mid-1980s it has been actively used in this way. Marketed under the name '**Quorn**', it has appeared in a variety of meat dishes such as savoury pies and curries.

In theory, mycoprotein offers the potential for famine relief if it can be produced cheaply and in sufficient quantities. However, at the moment, its major attraction is that it is a healthy, low-fat alternative to meat.

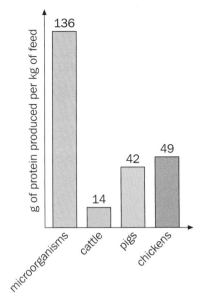

Protein production by microorganisms outstrips most other organisms

Fusarium *growing on a cereal*

Some food products derived from mycoprotein

▶ Biology at work: Carbo-loading and performance

Athletes have always tried to find ways to improve their performance.
With the exception of illegal drug use, this has mainly been
through the adoption of specialised diets and training regimes.
Improved knowledge and understanding of sports physiology has
led to the development of many commercial products.
These are often endorsed by successful athletes and claim to enhance
performance.
They claim to work by 'super-charging' **glycogen** stored in muscle fibres.
Are these claims mere sales hype, or do the products actually work?

Carbohydrates and fats are both used to supply the glycogen necessary
for all forms of physical exercise. However, it is the type of muscular
activity that determines which nutrient is used for fuel:

- **exercise duration** – intermittent or prolonged,
- **exercise intensity** – light or heavy.

'After taking Maxerol
I felt full of energy …
Mark Hylton
European
Championships 4 ×
400 m relay Gold
Medallist

Athletes often
endorse
performance-
enhancing products

With increasing duration and intensity of exercise, there is a
reduction in the dependence on carbohydrate as a fuel source
and an increase in the reliance on fat. The concept of a glycogen-loaded
diet, or **carbo-loading,** was first devised in the 1960s. It is achieved
by the following steps.

- 7 days prior to a major event, an intensive training run depletes muscle glycogen levels.
- For the next 3 days the athlete eats mainly fats and proteins to deprive the muscles of
  carbohydrate and increase the activity of the enzyme **glycogen synthase.**
- Training is reduced during this period to prevent total glycogen depletion and possible injury.
- The final 3–4 day period utilises a carbohydrate-rich diet, restricted intake of fats and
  proteins, and high fluid intake, together with low intensity training.

Fuel and exercise

Exercise intensity	Exercise duration	Fuel used
maximal sprint	short	carbohydrate
low to moderate	moderate – up to 2 hours, e.g. jogging	carbohydrate and fat equally
severe	prolonged, e.g. cycling	less carbohydrate, more fat

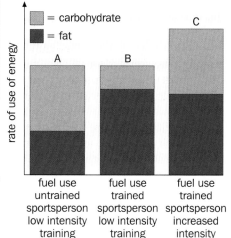

Increased carbohydrate together with the increased glycogen synthase levels
results in increased muscle glycogen storage with the overall effect of
improved performance. There are some disadvantages with this regime:

- increased body weight due to increased intake of water to store glycogen,
- weakness, depression and irritability during the depletion phase.

Other methods have developed from this approach.
Following glycogen depletion, athletes have reduced the low carbohydrate
period to a day, or ignored it altogether.
The main beneficial effect arises from the reduction in training linked to
an increased carbohydrate intake.

On the competition day the best time for the athlete to eat is 2–3
hours before the event. Meals should be of low volume, contain
carbohydrates and plenty of fluids to allow for the topping up of liver glycogen.
It is this effect which most commercial products seek to boost, not the longer
term build-up of glycogen stores, which takes several days to effect through carbo-loading.

▶ Biology at work: Herbal medicine and free radicals

Herbal medicines have increased in popularity recently.
Is this due to their proven effectiveness, or are they just the latest lifestyle fad?
Current interest is based on their beneficial effects on life-threatening diseases such as coronary heart disease (CHD).
This is due to the **antioxidant** vitamins and non-nutrient phytochemicals, such as **flavonoids**, which are found in herbs.

CHD is caused by many risk factors such as raised blood pressure, high blood cholesterol levels, smoking and lack of exercise.
Atherosclerosis or 'furring-up' of the arteries with fatty, cholesterol deposits, is a condition common to CHD sufferers.
Low density lipoproteins (LDLs) transport cholesterol from the liver to the body cells.
High density lipoproteins (HDLs) remove cholesterol from the arteries for disposal in the liver and hence exert a protective effect compared to LDLs.

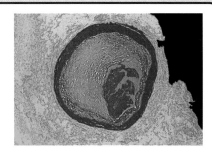

An artery blocked by cholesterol deposits

The **antioxidant hypothesis** provides a new insight into the development of atherosclerosis.
LDLs are susceptible to oxidation by highly reactive **free radicals** (e.g. hydrogen peroxide) to form oxidised LDLs (ox-LDLs).
These are not recognised by the cell receptors and are taken up by white blood cells, which migrate from the bloodstream to damage arterial walls.

Free radicals are produced as part of normal metabolism.
They are prevented from causing damage to the cell and DNA by enzyme control systems.
These systems weaken with age and free radicals from external sources, such as poor quality food and tobacco smoke.
Antioxidant vitamins such as C, E and provitamin A, beta-carotene, provide support for these enzyme systems.
LDL particles lack antioxidant enzymes and so antioxidant vitamins are their only source of protection against ox-LDL formation and eventual **atheromas**.

The treatment of CHD with herbal medicine often involves the use of several herb extracts with each containing many active substances.
Yarrow has at least 20 active constituents and is usually prescribed for hypertension but is also used to treat urinary infections and for wound healing.
Acting together in this way, the effect is termed **synergism** and an example includes the way vitamin C is involved in the regeneration of used vitamin E.

A diet high in fruit and vegetables, which contain nutrient antioxidant vitamins, is recommended to combat **oxidative stress** and help prevent atherosclerosis.
Oxidative stress caused by free radical damage is thought to be the main cause of ageing and the determination of life span in mammals.

A level of 200 mg day^{-1} of vitamin C is thought to be ideal for protection and can be easily obtained from fruit.
Taking vitamin supplements can be an important source of antioxidant vitamins to help a diet low in fruit and vegetables but is not a total substitute.

Yarrow is prescribed for hypertension

These foods also contain a wide range of non-nutrient antioxidant components such as flavonoids.
These act in support of vitamin C in maintaining the integrity of the blood capillaries and contribute to the antioxidant status of the cell.
Studies have shown that diets high in flavonoids lower the risk of CHD.

Summary

- Health can be described as the state of complete physical, mental and social well-being.
- Disease is usually due to a malfunction of the body and can be diagnosed by symptoms.
- Infectious diseases are caused by pathogens, which may be passed from one person to another.
- Epidemiology is the study of the patterns of diseases and how they are spread.
- A balanced diet has an adequate intake of nutrients and energy needed to sustain the body and ensure health and growth.
- Different people have different energy requirements and different nutrient needs.
- Dietary reference values outline the nutrient and energy requirements for a particular group of people with reference to age, gender and fitness.
- Essential amino acids can only be obtained from food and cannot be synthesised from existing organic compounds in the body.
- Similarly, there are some essential fatty acids that need to be present in the diet.
- Vitamins are a group of organic compounds that are essential to our diet and, if lacking, can cause deficiency diseases.
- Undernutrition due to lack of dietary energy and protein can result in kwashiorkor and marasmus.
- Obesity can occur if a person takes in more energy in food than is required.
- Coronary heart disease can bring about a blockage of the coronary arteries, resulting in heart failure.

▶ Questions

1. b) Describe the likely long-term effects that an excessive fat intake can have upon the blood vessels.
   b) Why do some nutritionists consider that it is more healthy to eat plant fats rather than animal fats?

2. Evaluate the different energy needs and nutrient requirements of each of the following groups:
   i) a very active man,
   ii) a breast-feeding woman,
   iii) a girl aged 12–14,
   iv) a pregnant woman,
   v) a child aged 6,
   vi) a child aged 1.

3. Define each of the following terms and explain their use in dietary health:
   i) dietary reference values (DRVs),
   ii) estimated average requirement (EAR),
   iii) reference nutrient intake (RNI),
   iv) lower reference nutrient intake (LRNI).

4. a) Describe and explain the likely effect on health of changing to a lower fat and higher fibre diet.
   b) Explain why the amount of salt eaten should be reduced.
   c) Suggest why medical opinion favours a combination of exercise and diet, rather than diet alone in order to lose weight.

5. Diet and lifestyle are factors that affect the likelihood of a person developing cardiovascular disease. Explain how each of these factors can influence the development of cardiovascular disease.

6. The body mass index is one measure of obesity:

$$\text{body mass index} = \frac{\text{body mass in kg}}{2 \times \text{height in metres}}$$

   The normal range for the body mass index is 20 to 25. A person with a BMI of 30 is considered to be obese.
   a) Calculate the BMI for a man with a mass of 85 kg and who is 180 cm tall.
   b) What advice would you give this man about his weight. Give reasons for your advice.
   c) Explain how the balance between energy intake and energy expenditure affects obesity.
   d) Regular exercise increases the basal metabolic rate (BMR).
      i) What is meant by the basal metabolic rate?
      ii) Explain how an increase in basal metabolic rate could decrease the chance of heart disease.

14 Exercise and health

Endurance is the ability of the body to carry out exercise. Weightlifters need to have good muscular endurance to be able to lift very heavy weights and support them for a short time. Other sports that require high muscular endurance but relatively low cardiovascular endurance are boxing, wrestling and sprinting.

In contrast, high levels of cardiovascular and respiratory endurance are needed to run a marathon.
This sort of exercise takes place over a longer period of time and requires far less muscular endurance.
Sports requiring high levels of cardiovascular and respiratory endurance include distance running, swimming and cycling.

▶ Breathing and exercise

Gas exchange is considered in Chapter 10.
You should remember that we breathe in more oxygen than we breathe out and this maintains the concentration gradient that allows oxygen to diffuse from the alveoli into the blood. Similarly, we need to breathe out carbon dioxide to maintain the concentration gradient that allows carbon dioxide to diffuse out of the blood capillaries and into the alveoli.

Air is exchanged between the lungs and the atmosphere when we breathe. The volume of air exchanged depends upon the depth of each breath and the breathing rate.
At rest, only about 0.35 dm³ of air is exchanged with each breath. This represents only about one-seventh of the alveolar air, so the changes in gas composition are relatively small.

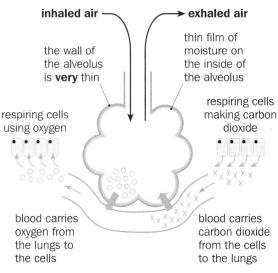

Gas exchange at the alveolus

We cannot empty our lungs completely.
With forced breathing we can exhale about 3 dm³ of air, although about 1dm³, known as the **residual volume**, remains in the lungs and cannot be breathed out.
At rest, our residual volume is much larger, with about 2.5 dm³ of air remaining in the lungs.
With strenuous exercise, the **depth** of breathing increases and breathing **rate** increases.
This enables us to cope with the greater demands that exercise places on our bodies.

Ventilation rate is the total volume of air taken into the lungs in 1 minute (expressed in dm³ min⁻¹).
It enables us to measure the effect that exercise has on our breathing.

ventilation rate = breathing rate × tidal volume
(Tidal volume is the volume of air moved in and out of the lungs in a single breath.)

Athletes at the peak of their fitness are able to increase their ventilation rate by increasing their tidal volume.
There is only a small increase in their rate of breathing.

239

▶ Measuring human lung volumes

A **spirometer** is used to measure the volume of air
that moves in and out of the lungs.
It is basically a clear, plastic box, filled at the bottom with water.
The space inside the spirometer contains oxygen.

When you breathe out the box moves up, and when you breathe
in the box moves down.
These changes can be recorded as a trace on a revolving drum,
called a **kymograph**.
With most spirometers the exhaled air passes through a container of soda lime,
a chemical that absorbs carbon dioxide, although this is not always the case.

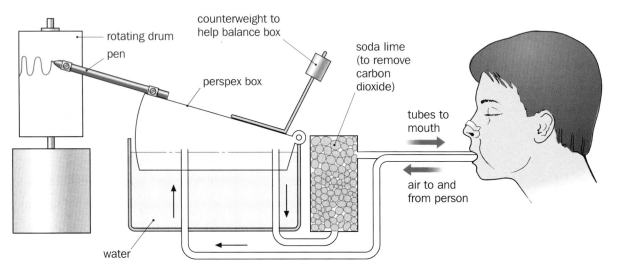

In the first experiment, there was no soda lime in the container.
A person was asked to breathe normally through the mouthpiece.
The first trace records the person's **tidal volume**.

> **Tidal volume is the volume of air breathed in and out**
> **during a single breath.**

Look at the trace and read the tidal volume.

The person was then asked to breathe in as hard as possible and
then breathe out as hard as possible to give the **vital capacity**.

> **Vital capacity is the maximum volume of air that can**
> **be breathed in or breathed out of the lungs.**

Now try to read the vital capacity from the trace.

In a second experiment, soda lime was place in the container.
The person was asked to breathe normally and the second trace
was obtained.

Why do you think the trace falls with time?

What was the breathing rate of the person in breaths min⁻¹?

What was the total amount of air breathed in and out of the
lungs in 1 minute?

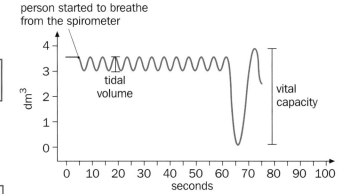

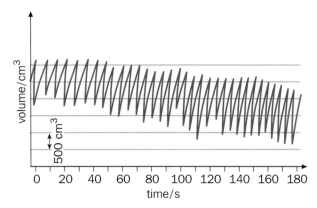

A trace from a spirometer containing soda lime

▷ Pulse rate

As you saw in Chapter 11, each time the heart contracts it forces blood out into the aorta and pulmonary arteries.

> **The volume of blood pumped out with each heartbeat is called the stroke volume.**

This surge of blood from each heartbeat causes a bulge in the walls of the arteries, which travels along the arteries.
Where arteries are near the body surface, you can feel (or even see) each bulge travelling as a **pulse**.
One pulse is equivalent to one heartbeat.

You have probably taken someone's pulse by feeling an artery at the wrist or at the neck.

The **pulse rate** is the same as the heart rate.
Pulse rate is usually counted as the number of pulses recorded in 30 seconds, which is then doubled to give the pulse rate in beats per minute.

The **resting pulse rate** gives a good indication of a person's fitness.
The fitter you are, the lower your resting pulse rate.
The same volume of blood is being passed out of the heart per minute, but with fewer heartbeats.

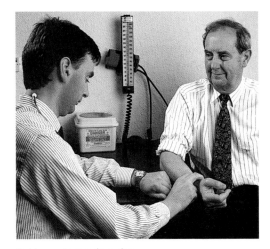

Taking a person's pulse

Pulse rate	Level of fitness
less than 50	outstanding
50–59	excellent
60–69	good
70–79	fair
80 and over	poor

General relationship between resting pulse rate and levels of fitness

Physically fit people tend to have a larger stroke volume as a result of their increased heart size, particularly the left ventricle.
As much as 5 dm^3 of blood can be pumped out of the heart every minute.
As their stroke volume is greater, their hearts do not have to beat as quickly during exercise.
When the exercise is over, their pulse rate returns to normal far more quickly than for unfit people.
Athletes who compete in endurance events such as the pentathalon tend to have a low pulse rate and a large heart.

The normal resting pulse rate for a person is between 60 and 100 beats per minute.
The pulse rate tends to fall with increasing age.
The average pulse rate for a healthy, fit young adult is about 70.

Pulse rate is affected by certain risk factors.
Some of these are the result of a person's lifestyle.
For instance, higher pulse rates would be recorded for people who

- smoke,
- take little exercise,
- have a diet high in saturated fats.

An accident waiting to happen.

▶ Blood pressure

As you saw in Chapter 11, the cardiac cycle describes the sequence of events that take place during one heartbeat.
There are alternate contractions (**systole**) and relaxations (**diastole**) of the heart.

During ventricular systole, both ventricles contract at the same time to force blood out of the heart.
At this point the *maximum* arterial pressure is achieved.

> **Systolic pressure is the pressure at which blood leaves the heart through the aorta from the left ventricle.**

After ventricular systole, the ventricles relax and the pressure in the ventricles drops.
The semi-lunar valves in the aorta close to prevent backflow of blood into the left ventricle.
A steady flow of blood through the arteries is then achieved by the pulse.

Diastole is when the ventricles relax.
At this time the pressure inside the left ventricle drops below that in the arteries.

> **Diastolic pressure is the minimum blood pressure in the aorta.**

Diastolic pressure gives an indication of the *resistance* of the arteries to blood flow.
If resistance to blood flow is low, then the diastolic pressure will be low.
If resistance to blood flow is high, then the diastolic pressure will be high.
Atherosclerosis, or 'hardening of the arteries', occurs when fatty deposits line the artery wall, increasing the resistance to blood flow.
The heart then has to work harder to force oxygenated blood through to the tissues.

Measuring blood pressure

Blood pressure can be measured with a **sphygmomanometer**, which gives readings for both systolic and diastolic blood pressure.
The first figure (systolic pressure) is put over the second figure (diastolic pressure) to give a fraction.
A healthy young adult's blood pressure is about 120/75 mmHg.

Hypertension

Hypertension is the harmful condition of having a constantly high blood pressure.
The causes and treatment of hypertension are explained on page 196.
A person can lower their blood pressure, reducing hypertension, by

* taking regular exercise,
* reducing their intake of alcohol,
* reducing the amount of salt in their diet,
* losing weight,
* not smoking.

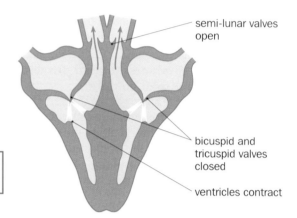

semi-lunar valves open

bicuspid and tricuspid valves closed

ventricles contract

Ventricular systole

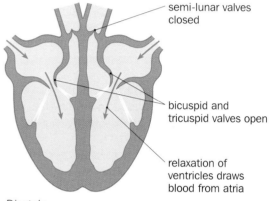

semi-lunar valves closed

bicuspid and tricuspid valves open

relaxation of ventricles draws blood from atria

Diastole

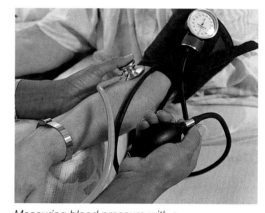

Measuring blood pressure with a sphygmomanometer

Category	Blood pressure/mmHg	
	systolic	diastolic
below normal	< 100	< 60
normal	100–139	60–89
borderline	140–159	90–94
hypertension	> 159	> 94

The World Health Organisation classification of adult blood pressures

▷ Energy and exercise

Active people make more use of their muscles.
In order to function, muscles need a source of energy
called **adenosine triphosphate (ATP)**.
ATP is made in the cells during respiration.

All muscular contractions require ATP, but exercise puts
increased demands on the body to synthesise more of
this important compound.
Only a limited amount of ATP is present in muscle cells,
enough in fact to allow you to run as fast as you can
for only a few seconds.
After this time you rely on the re-synthesis of ATP.

There are three basic pathways for this replacement.
Which pathway operates at any given time depends on
how intense the activity is, how immediate the energy
requirement is and whether or not sufficient oxygen
is present.

These athletes will be using the ATP/CP and anaerobic glycolysis system

The **ATP/CP (creatine phosphate)** pathway provides
an almost instant replenishment of ATP. The creatine
phosphate is broken down and the energy released is
used to add a phosphate to ADP to re-form ATP.
This system is especially useful during the initial stages
of very intense activity such as sprinting.
However, creatine phosphate supplies (like ATP) are
limited, and after around 10 seconds ATP re-synthesis
by this pathway will fail.

The body then depends on glycogen (its store of
carbohydrate) for the re-synthesis of ATP.
Glycogen is broken down into glucose, which is
then converted into pyruvate.
In the absence of oxygen, the glucose is converted
into **lactic acid** (or **lactate**).
This process is technically known as **anaerobic glycolysis**
or the **lactic acid system**.
It only releases about 5% of the energy in a molecule of
glycogen.
However, it is released quickly.
Therefore it is useful for short-term, high intensity exercise,
such as a 100 metre swim.
It is most effective in events lasting around 1 minute.

The remaining 95% of the energy available in the
glycogen molecule is released via the **aerobic system**.
This is the route that involves the Krebs cycle and
the electron transport chain.
It can take up to 3 minutes to complete this final stage of
respiration but the advantage is that this has the potential
to release the relatively vast amount of energy that is
available.
As a result, this system is most important for endurance
events, such as 10,000 metre runs and cycle races.

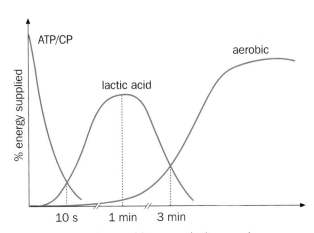
The 3 pathways that provide energy in the muscles

243

▶ Fuels for the re-synthesis of ATP

The most abundant fuel stored in the body is fat.
However, glycogen stored in the liver and muscle
will be the first energy source used during exercise.
Contrary to popular belief, it is these glycogen stores
that are of most importance for muscle contraction
and not blood glucose, which is used mainly to supply
the brain and nervous system.

Glycogen is used in preference to fats partly because
it requires less oxygen for its break-down.
However, once again glycogen is in limited supply, and
in endurance events the body will need to use some
fat in order to conserve glycogen.
When athletes talk of 'hitting the wall' in endurance
events, this is the point at which all the glycogen
reserves are gone.
Training programmes for endurance athletes help the
body to become increasingly reliant on fat reserves,
although the body can never rely on fat alone.

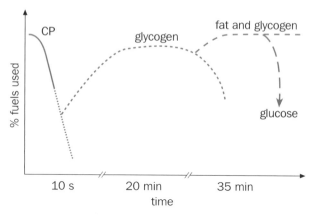

The relationship between the duration of exercise and the type of fuel used

▶ Glycogen loading

Glycogen loading or **supercompensation** is a dietary
technique often practised by endurance athletes.
The idea is to increase the athlete's muscle glycogen
stores to such an extent that by the time of a race
they may be at twice the normal levels.

So how does this technique work?
Seven days prior to a race, an athlete will deplete
his or her glycogen stores with the aid of endurance
training.
For the next 3 days, carbohydrates are omitted
from the diet.
In the remaining days leading up to the race,
lots of high carbohydrate meals, for example pasta
dishes, are consumed to boost the glycogen stores.

This technique has been shown to be effective in
maximising aerobic energy production, although
research has also shown that with trained athletes the
initial glycogen depletion is usually not necessary.

The start of a London Marathon

▷ The oxygen debt

As you have seen, during short-term, high intensity exercise, such as sprinting, the muscles revert to anaerobic respiration to re-synthesise ATP.
This causes an accumulation of lactate in the muscles.

During the recovery period just after vigorous exercise, breathing continues faster and deeper.
Extra oxygen is needed to break down the lactate and restore oxygen levels in the body.
This is called the **oxygen debt**.

Sprinters often hold their breath during a 100 metre race and quickly build up lactate in their muscles.
Afterwards they need up to 7 litres of oxygen to get rid of it and have to breathe in deeply to pay back their oxygen debt.

Distance runners could not stand such a build up of lactate. They run at a much slower speed and although they build up some lactate in the early stages of a race, they are able to get rid of this while they are running.
You can find out more about lactate formation in muscle on page 291.

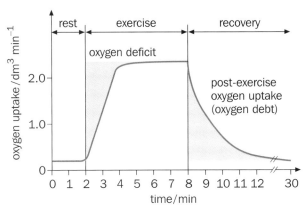

Oxygen uptake before, during and after strenuous exercise. The post-exercise oxygen uptake (oxygen debt) is that amount over and above the resting uptake (unshaded area) during recovery.

▷ Aerobic exercise

Your body adapts to regular exercise and becomes more efficient at carrying it out.

Aerobic exercise makes full use of both your gaseous exchange and cardiovascular systems.
The type of exercise can vary from marathon running, swimming or team sports to jogging or just a brisk walk.

Aerobic exercise improves ventilation of the lungs and makes the circulatory system more efficient at delivering oxygenated blood to the tissues.

Regular aerobic exercise has been found to

- increase heart muscle (particularly the left ventricle),
- increase the stroke volume (the volume of blood pumped out with each heartbeat),
- decrease the resting heartbeat rate,
- lower systolic and diastolic blood pressures, so reducing hypertension,
- increase both tidal volume and vital capacity of the lungs,
- increase the utilisation of fat, so reducing a person's weight,
- increase muscle size and enhance the amount of glycogen and fat stored in muscle,
- decrease blood cholesterol levels,
- improve a person's resistance to disease.

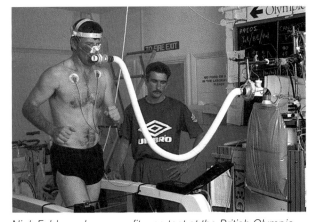

Nick Faldo undergoes a fitness test at the British Olympic Medical Centre

▶ Tobacco smoke

Cigarette smoke contains thousands of harmful chemicals
that pose a threat to human health.
The three most hazardous chemicals are tar, nicotine and carbon
monoxide.

- **Tar** collects in the lungs as the tobacco smoke cools.
  It is a mixture of many toxic chemicals.
  Some of these are **carcinogens** (substances that cause cancer).
  These carcinogens affect the DNA in the cells of the alveoli,
  resulting in mutations.
  Normally genes control cell division, so that it stops when enough
  cells have been produced for growth and repair of lung tissue.
  But the gene mutations form **oncogenes**, and normal cell division
  goes out of control.
  This can eventually lead to the formation of a malignant tumour.

Tumour suppressor genes normally inhibit cell division.
Carcinogens in tobacco tar can also cause them to mutate, so that
they become inactive and this can also lead to cell division running out
of control.

Oncogenes and mutated tumour suppressor genes can both
lead to lung cancer.
The developing tumour cells can find their way through the epithelial
cells and into the lymph capillaries of the lung.
From here they may circulate around the body forming **metastases**
(secondary tumours) in other organs such as the liver and the brain.

- **Nicotine** is one of the most powerful poisons known.
  It is the substance that makes tobacco addictive and its absence
  results in the withdrawal symptoms that people experience when
  they try to give up smoking.

Nicotine stimulates the release of the hormone **adrenaline**
into the bloodstream.
Adrenaline has many effects on the body, but significantly it
causes an increase in heart rate and raises blood pressure.
Many long-term smokers develop raised blood pressure and
this can lead to other problems with the cardiovascular system,
including atherosclerosis, coronary heart disease and strokes.

- **Carbon monoxide** is a gas that combines more readily than
  oxygen with haemoglobin in the red blood cells.
  This causes a reduction in the amount of oxygen in the blood
  and so the heart has to work harder to supply the body with
  the oxygen it needs.

Smokers inevitably have raised carbon monoxide levels and
this affects the oxygenation of the tissues.
In the short term, this means that the smoker is unable to participate
in physical activity.
However, in the long term, high levels of carbon monoxide
can lead to a hardening of the arteries, especially the
coronary arteries supplying oxygen to the heart muscle.

Scanning electron micrograph of a cancer in a bronchus

Cause	Total
heart disease	40,000
lung cancer	38,000
chronic bronchitis emphysema	26,000
total smoking related deaths	104,000

Estimated numbers of smoking related deaths in the UK in 1990

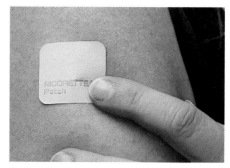

A nicotine patch

▷ Diseases of the lungs

Chronic bronchitis

The tar in tobacco smoke produces two reactions in the lungs.

- The goblet cells in the epithelium of the air passages are stimulated to secrete more mucus.
- The ciliated cells of the epithelium which waft the mucus out of the air passages do not work and may even be destroyed.

Both these actions result in an accumulation of mucus in the bronchial passages.
Therefore the mucus remains stuck in the lungs.
Bacteria and viruses accumulate and breed in the mucus.

The result is **chronic bronchitis** and 'smoker's cough'.
Large amounts of **phlegm** (a mixture of mucus, bacteria and some white blood cells) are produced, which the sufferer attempts to cough up.

Ciliated cells lining the air passages

Emphysema

This disease often develops from bronchitis in smokers.
Substances in tobacco smoke stimulate **mast cells** to secrete protein-digesting enzymes.
These enzymes destroy the elastin in the walls of the alveoli, which means they do not stretch and recoil as the lungs inflate and deflate.
As a result the bronchioles can collapse, and air trapped in the alveoli can cause them to burst.
So the surface area of the lungs available for gas exchange is much reduced.
The loss of elastin also makes it more difficult to force air out of the lungs when breathing out.
A person with healthy lungs should be able to expire 4 dm³ of air after a deep breath, whereas a person with emphysema may only be able to force out about 1.2 dm³ of air.

This means that a person suffering from emphysema exchanges far less gas with the atmosphere.
As a result their blood is not as well oxygenated and they have to breathe more rapidly.
Breathlessness becomes more frequent as the disease progresses.
Eventually the sufferer may become bed-bound and have to resort to a face mask in order to get a sufficient supply of oxygen.

A smoker may breathe in only 15% of the smoke produced from a cigarette, while the remaining 85% is released into the room.
Evidence suggests that non-smokers suffer from the effects of this smoke, a condition known as **passive smoking**.
Because of this, smoking is being banned from more and more public places.
People in restaurants, theatres and on public transport are showing less tolerance to the risks to their health that come from an increasing minority of smokers.

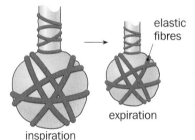
Normal alveoli stretch and recoil as lungs inflate and deflate

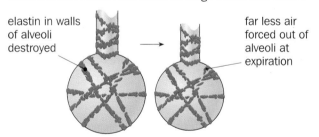
The development of emphysema

Passive smoking: somebody else's problem

▶ Smoking and heart disease

The correlation between smoking and lung cancer was established as long ago as the 1950s.
It was some time later that smoking was identified as a risk factor in coronary heart disease (CHD) and other cardiovascular disorders.

People of all ages who smoke are at a greater risk of dying from CHD than non-smokers of the same age.
There is also a link between the number of cigarettes that a person smokes per day and their chances of dying from CHD.
In the UK about 110 000 people die prematurely each year due to the effects of cigarette smoking.
About half of the preventable, early deaths are due to diseases of the heart and blood vessels.

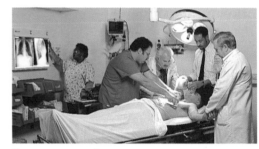
Emergency cardiac treatment

Atherosclerosis

This is the result of a build-up of fatty deposits (plaque) on the inner walls of arteries, forming atheroma.
The arteries become thicker and less flexible.
This leads to a narrowing of the vessels, which inevitably reduces the flow of blood.
As a result, the heart has to pump harder to get the blood through.

Initially this may result in **angina**, with the symptoms of severe chest pains brought on by physical exertion.
The pain is caused by a shortage of oxygenated blood to the heart muscle, but the muscle tissue does not die.

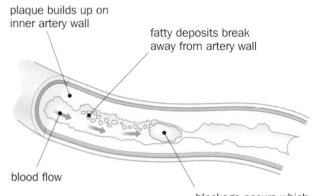

plaque builds up on inner artery wall

fatty deposits break away from artery wall

blood flow

blockage occurs which can stop blood flow

Heart attack

Atherosclerosis in one of the two coronary arteries that supply the heart muscle can be potentially fatal.
The build-up of fatty tissue may result in an artery becoming completely blocked by a blood clot (**thrombosis**).
The heart muscle becomes starved of oxygen and dies.
This is called a **coronary heart attack**.
If the damage to the heart tissue is extensive, then the person may die.
However, many people survive heart attacks, with treatment followed by adjustment of their lifestyles.
This means reducing risk factors by giving up smoking, taking exercise and eating a more appropriate diet.

Strokes

Atherosclerosis can also affect the blood supply to the brain.
Again, atheroma may form in an artery supplying the brain.
Part of the brain becomes starved of oxygen and dies, and the person is said to have had a **stroke**.
This can result in a loss of function or sensation associated with the part of the brain that is affected.
Smoking causes increased blood pressure and so makes the chance of a stroke occurring more likely.

Stroke victim 'learning' to walk again

▷ Links between smoking and disease

Linking smoking and lung cancer

Cigarette smoking became really popular amongst men during the First World War.

It became fashionable with women later in the 1940s. Epidemiologists soon found a correlation between smoking cigarettes and the incidence of lung cancer.

Not surprisingly, when doctors first saw the evidence, many of them gave up smoking.
As a result, the number of deaths from lung cancer amongst doctors decreased dramatically.

From the graph above, you can see the sort of data that helped scientists establish the link between smoking and lung cancer.
In the early part of the 20th century, deaths from lung cancer were low but these increased dramatically as the habit of cigarette smoking became more widespread.
In contrast, deaths from other lung diseases such as tuberculosis were falling, as a result of improved medical care and better housing.

Statistics also demonstrated a link between the number of cigarettes that a person smokes and the risk of dying from lung cancer.
The second graph clearly shows that the more cigarettes smoked, the greater the risk of a premature death from lung cancer.

Direct evidence linking smoking and lung cancer have come from two different sources.

- **Experimental animals** were used in the 1960s to investigate the effects of cigarette smoke on the lungs. Tumours similar to those that occurred in humans were found in the lungs of dogs exposed to cigarette smoke.

- **Chemical analysis** was carried out on the tar extracted from cigarette smoke.
  A number of carcinogenic substances were found in the tar.

Evidence such as this clearly establishes the link between the smoking of cigarettes and the incidence of lung cancer.

Linking smoking and heart disease

We have already looked at the effects of smoking on the cardiovascular system.
Atherosclerosis makes it harder for the heart to pump oxygenated blood to the tissues.
This can result in angina, a coronary heart attack or a stroke.
Again epidemiological evidence, such as this graph from the Royal College of Physicians, shows a clear link between the number of cigarettes smoked each day and the risk of dying from heart disease.

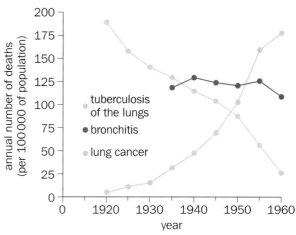

Deaths from lung disease in England and Wales 1920–60

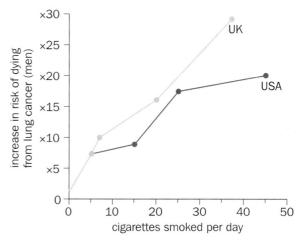

The relationship between male deaths from lung cancer and the number of cigarettes smoked daily

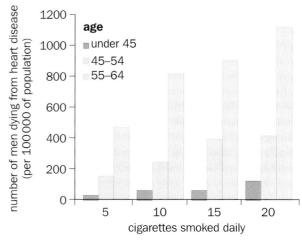

Smoking and the risk of death from CHD amongst men

▶ Global distribution of coronary heart disease

Epidemiological evidence has shown that there are differences in the death rates from CHD across the world.
As you can see from the data, death rates from CHD are highest in northern Europe and lowest in Japan.

In Britain, the incidence of CHD is higher in Scotland, Northern Ireland, northern England and north-west England than it is in other parts of the country.
It is also greater amongst men than women, particularly amongst manual workers.
The incidence of CHD also varies between different ethnic groups, being higher in people of south Asian origin.

This sort of data can help in the identification of the **risk factors** that contribute to CHD.

- **Smoking**
As you have seen, smoking accelerates the development of atherosclerosis and increases the risk of CHD.

- **Heredity**
People who inherit a tendency for high blood cholesterol levels suffer increased incidence of CHD.

- **High blood lipid levels**
A diet rich in saturated fat can lead to high levels of low density lipoproteins and cholesterol, which can be deposited as plaque on the lining of arteries.

- **Obesity**
Obesity is often linked to CHD but this could be due to other risk factors such as high cholesterol intake.

- **Alcohol**
A high intake of alcohol raises the blood pressure (hypertension) and increases the risk of atherosclerosis.

- **Diabetes**
Diabetics are more likely to develop CHD and at an earlier age.

- **Exercise**
Lack of exercise makes the heart less healthy, increases atherosclerosis and increases blood pressure.

Additional risk factors contributing to CHD appear to be ageing, being male and lifestyle.
Obviously we have no control over some of these risk factors, as is the case with a person who inherits high blood cholesterol or diabetes.
But some risk factors are **preventable**.
We can reduce the risk of CHD by leading a healthier lifestyle. Eating a diet low in saturated fat, reducing alcohol intake, giving up smoking and taking more exercise can all significantly reduce the risk of a person getting CHD.

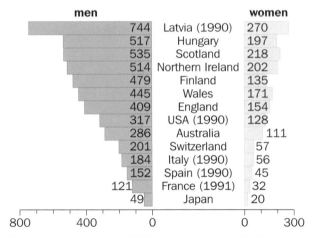

men		women
744	Latvia (1990)	270
517	Hungary	197
535	Scotland	218
514	Northern Ireland	202
479	Finland	135
445	Wales	171
409	England	154
317	USA (1990)	128
286	Australia	111
201	Switzerland	57
184	Italy (1990)	56
152	Spain (1990)	45
121	France (1991)	32
49	Japan	20

Number of deaths from CHD of people aged 35–74 per 100 000 population. Unless stated otherwise, the figures are for 1992.

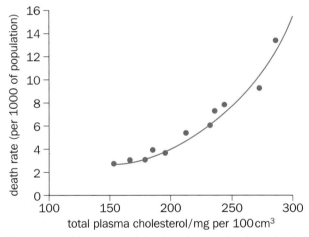

The relationship between blood cholesterol levels and risk of death from CHD

▷ Biology at work: Coronary artery bypass.

The coronary artery bypass operation is a very common and successful procedure in the western world, where one-quarter of all deaths are attributed to heart disease.

The purpose of a bypass operation is to relieve patients of the symptoms of **coronary heart disease (CHD)**.
This condition results from the narrowing and possible blockage of the coronary arteries that supply the heart muscle with oxygen and nutrients.
The arteries become narrowedby deposits of cholesterol-rich deposits called **atheroma.**
If blood clots form on the rough surface of these deposits, then complete blockages may occur.

A common symptom of heart disease is **angina** – a pain in the chest that may spread up the neck and down the left arm.
This pain occurs during physical exertion.
Complete blockage of an artery will result in the death of a portion of the heart muscle, and this leads to what is commonly referred to as a heart attack.
If a large area of heart muscle is affected, then an attack can be fatal.

A bypass operation is carried out when the symptoms of heart disease have not been reduced by drugs and a change in lifestyle, such as stopping smoking or adopting a more sensible diet.

In the operation, lengths of vein (often from the leg) are attached from the aorta to a point below the blockages, so bypassing them and restoring an adequate blood supply to the muscle.

The sites of blockage are identified by an X-ray technique known as **angiography**, whereby a substance opaque to X-rays is injected into the arteries.
The surgery requires two surgeons to carry out the procedure, and typically might last for 5 hours.
During this time, the heart will be stopped and the circulation and oxygenation of the blood will be taken over by a heart-lung machine.

Although bypass is considered to be a successful surgical technique, it only treats the symptoms of the disease.
Studies have shown that more than half the bypass grafts are still functioning after 10 years, but it is quite possible for these grafts themselves to ultimately become affected by the disease.
One of the key changes in lifestyle necessary to reduce the incidence of heart disease is to give up cigarette smoking.

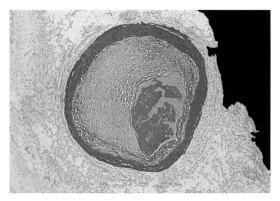

A microscopic section of a blocked artery

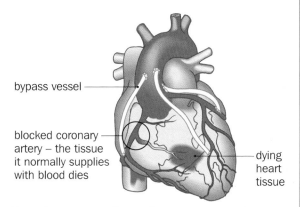

bypass vessel

blocked coronary artery – the tissue it normally supplies with blood dies

dying heart tissue

How a bypass operation works

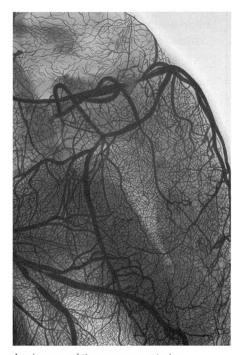

Angiogram of the coronary arteries

251

▶ Biology at work: X-rays and CT scanning

X-rays were discovered as far back as 1895.
Ever since then they have been used in medicine
as an important diagnostic tool.

Low doses of X-rays are used to produce images
of body tissues.
Dense tissues such as bone absorb X-rays more than
soft tissues like skin and muscle.
As a result, when a leg, for example, is X-rayed,
it casts a shadow either onto a screen or
more commonly onto a photographic plate.
Damage such as a hairline fracture can easily be seen.

Parts of the body comprised largely of soft tissue,
such as the digestive system, can be studied using a
special X-ray technique.
A liquid that is opaque to X-rays is introduced into the
intestines and when an X-ray is taken, a clear image
is revealed.
In the case of the digestive system this is known as having
a barium meal because the opaque liquid contains a
barium compound.

Computed tomography (CT) scanning builds on the
value of X-rays to produce clearer and more detailed images.
Tomography is the technique of using X-rays to obtain
an image of a section through part of the body.
These sections can be taken at any angle required and
a computer is used to construct images of the tissues
being studied.
These images can be viewed and manipulated on a TV
screen and they are especially useful for studying tumours
and haemorrhages (internal bleeding) of the brain and
other soft tissues.

3D CT scanning can take adjacent sections and build
them up into 3D images of an area of the body such as a
damaged joint.

When using both traditional X-raying and CT scanning,
it is important that only very low doses of X-rays are
used, because X-rays can increase the rate of mutations
in cells.
As a result, X-rays will not be taken if there is any risk
of pregnancy.
Radiographers and radiologists operate the machinery
from behind a protective screen and wear a film badge
to monitor their exposure to the X-rays.

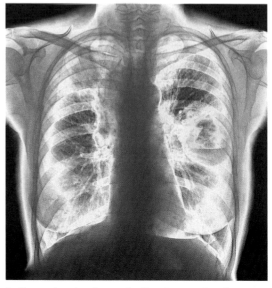

*An X-ray showing the red/yellow tumour in a lung
cancer victim*

CT scanning set up

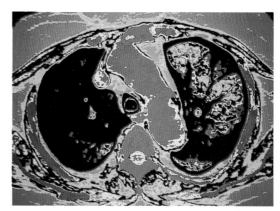

*CT scan through the thorax showing one lung
(black) diseased with pulmonary emphysema*

▶ Biology at work: Exercise – putting life into your years

Recent surveys in the UK and USA indicate that over 75% of the population believe that exercise is good for their health.
In contrast, few individuals actually participate in regular physical exercise. Consequently, a substantial proportion of the adult population is in poor physical condition. They suffer a reduced quality of life and even loss of independence, increasing the risk of certain diseases linked to a sedentary lifestyle.
All of this may be preventable with sensible and realistic advice.
The promotion of physical exercise is based on a number of health benefits:

- reduced risk of certain diseases such as cardiovascular disease,
- enhanced physical capacity,
- reduction in the decline associated with ageing,
- promotion of mental health, stress reduction and enhanced self-esteem.

Manchester United training in Brazil

The evidence for these benefits is assumed but the exact details are less clear. There are two complicating factors that account for this lack of clarity.

- **Human lifestyle** – genetics, diet, stress, smoking, the environment and socio-behavioural factors are all contributory factors to the cause of disease.
- **Exercise** – is a very general term to describe a wide range of activities from aerobics to weight-training, all of which have varying effects.

Moderate exercise may not produce the same fitness improvements as vigorous exercise, but this does not mean that it will not have beneficial health effects.
Indeed, over-exercising can lead to problems in a minority of athletes:

- over-use injuries,
- hormonal imbalances,
- suppression of the immune system,
- mental staleness.

'Take more exercise' is too simple a statement for a doctor to make. Exercise is something that requires gross muscular activity and is associated with an increase in metabolism. There are three broad categories.

- **Aerobic** – involves a significant increase in cardiovascular activity using the major muscle groups in a sustained and rhythmic way. Exercise of this type is usually recommended for 30 minutes continuously, three times a week.
  Health benefits can be gained from much lower doses.

- **Muscle strengthening** – strengthening exercises require the muscles to work against a resistance, which can be provided by weights, exercise machines or a person's own body weight. Benefits from moderate exercise include improved posture, less fatigue, reduced musculo-skeletal problems.

- **Flexibility and mobility** – this kind of exercise helps maintain mobility in the joints through slow controlled actions and muscle stretching. It reduces the risk of poor posture and over-extending of muscles, strains and sprains.

For the individual, regular exercise of an appropriate intensity, frequency and duration can promote health.
More realistic advice in the future may be for exercise that is moderate in intensity, reduced in duration and of increased frequency.

Summary

- Ventilation rate is the total volume of air taken into the lungs in 1 minute.
- Tidal volume is the volume of air breathed in and out during a single breath.
- Vital capacity is the maximum volume of air that can be breathed in or breathed out of the lungs.
- The volume of blood pumped out with each heartbeat is called the stroke volume.
- The pulse rate is the same as the heart rate and the resting pulse rate is a good indication of a person's fitness.
- Systolic pressure is the pressure at which blood leaves the heart through the aorta from the left ventricle.
- Diastolic pressure is the minimum blood pressure in the aorta.
- The ATP/CP (creatine phosphate) pathway provides an almost instant replenishment of ATP in muscle cells.
- After vigorous exercise, more oxygen is needed to break down lactate and repay the 'oxygen debt'.
- Tobacco smoke contains many harmful chemicals including tar, nicotine and carbon monoxide.
- Diseases of the lungs include chronic bronchitis, emphysema and lung cancer.
- Smoking is a high risk factor that can lead to coronary heart disease.

▶ Questions

1 Fitness can be defined as the capacity to do physical work at a particular constant heart rate. Describe and explain how each of the following affects fitness:
   a) emphysema, b) regular exercise.

2 The graph shows the effect of smoking on life expectancy.
   Use information from the graph to calculate how the chances of living to 85 are affected for someone smoking 15-24 cigarettes a day compared with someone who never smoked regularly.

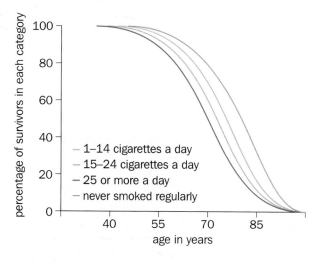

b) The incidence of both bronchitis and emphysema is increased by smoking cigarettes.
   i) Describe the symptoms of bronchitis.
   ii) Explain why patients suffering from emphysema can often walk only a few metres before having to stop for a rest.

3 a) Give two differences that can be seen between healthy lung tissue and lung tissue from a person with emphysema.

b) Explain why people suffering from severe emphysema may find it difficult to climb stairs or walk up hills.

c) i) Emphysema is a common industrial disease of people who have worked in mining and quarrying industries. Suggest one feature that these industries have in common that could increase the risk of emphysema.
    ii) Suggest one way in which workers in these industries could be protected from exposure to this factor.

4 The graph shows the death rates of non-smokers and ex-smokers from lung cancer.
   a) Suggest one reason why the risk of cancer decreases only slowly for a number of years after a person has stopped smoking.
   b) Suggest why people who smoke have a higher risk of lung cancer than non-smokers.
   c) i) Describe how the effects of smoking increase the risk of one **named** respiratory disease other than cancer.
      ii) Give one of the symptoms of the disease that you have named.
   Describe one method by which respiratory diseases can be diagnosed.

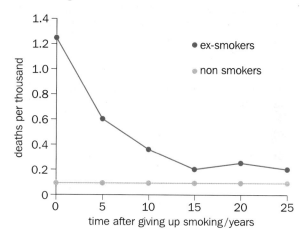

15 Infectious disease and immunity

▷ Millennium bugs

Bacteria and viruses are constantly changing their genetic make up.
The antibiotics and antiviral drugs used to treat diseases caused by
bacteria and viruses are becoming increasingly ineffective.
Resistance to antibiotics is growing as a result of their over-use.

MRSA (methicillin-resistant *Staphylococcus aureus*) is of great concern
to experts in infectious diseases.
There is an increasing possibility that if you go into hospital for an operation,
or if you develop an open wound, MRSA will be there, ready and waiting
to cause infection and delay healing.
This bacterium was 95% controlled by penicillin in the 1940s, but now
less than 10% responds to penicillin.

In Scotland in 1997, a new strain of *E. coli 0157* caused an outbreak of
food poisoning which affected 500 people and killed 20.
This food poisoning could have been avoided by good hygiene, but this new
strain got into the human food chain and existing antibiotics proved useless.
The emerging pattern is that more and more strains are becoming
resistant to an ever-growing list of antibiotics.

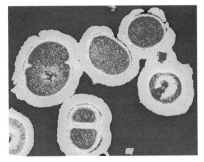

MRSA

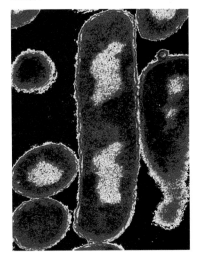

TEM E.coli bacterium (×20 000)

▷ White blood cells and defence

As mentioned in Chapter 11, the function of white blood cells, or **leucocytes**,
is to defend the body against **pathogens** (disease-causing organisms).
Their are five kinds of white blood cells. They all originate in the bone
marrow from the division of **stem cells** (which also make red blood cells
and platelets).

- **Neutrophils**, have a characteristic lobed nucleus and are the largest.
  They are concerned with phagocytosis (see page 188).
- **Lymphocytes** are relatively small with a large, round nucleus.

There are two types of lymphocytes, both of which play a major role
in the **immune system**.
B-lymphocytes produce antibodies to counter pathogens and their toxins.
T-lymphocytes are involved in **cell-mediated immunity**.
Both types of lymphocytes migrate, in the bone marrow, to the lymph nodes
and spleen where they mature.
On their way, the T-lymphocytes pass to the **thymus** (a gland in the neck).
Here they become 'sensitised' and are able to recognise specific **antigens**
(chemicals on the surface of microorganisms and foreign matter).
Together, neutrophils and lymphocytes account for 90% of the
white blood cells in the body. The other 10% are made up of **monocytes**,
eosinophils and **basophils**.

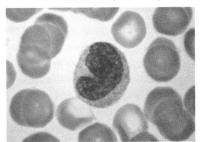

White blood cell: a monocyte

- Monocytes are large cells, with a kidney-shaped nucleus.
  They develop into **macrophages,** which are phagocytic.
- Eosinophils stain red and are associated with allergies.
- Basophils stain with basic dyes, such as methylene blue, and are able
  to release chemicals such as histamines that cause inflammation.

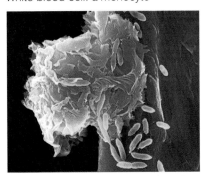

*SEM of alveola macrophage attacking
E. coli bacteria*

▷ Bacterial growth

Bacteria are a major group of pathogens against which white blood cells defend us. Basically there are four main phases of growth.

- The **lag phase** when the cells are active but there is little growth as they are taking up water and starting to produce enzymes.
- The **exponential** or **log phase** where the population increases rapidly. There is a doubling of the bacterial cells at each **generation time**. With optimum conditions, plenty of nutrients and ample space, subsequent generation times get shorter because there are no limiting factors. Eventually the **carrying capacity** is reached. This is the maximum population that an environment can support.
- The **stationary phase** sees bacterial cells dying more or less at the same rate as they are produced. The population encounters limiting factors in the form of nutrient depletion and a fall in pH as carbon dioxide and other wastes accumulate.
- The **death phase** occurs when more bacterial cells are dying than are being produced, so the population declines. Causes of death may be shortage of nutrients, lack of oxygen, or the accumulation of toxic waste products.

rapid growth: the population increases by doubling. Little environmental resistance

increasing environmental resistance means as many bacterial cells are dying as are being produced

carrying capacity

number of organisms

population declines because of effects of limiting factors

time

lag phase | exponential (log) phase | stationary phase | death phase

lag phase: bacterial cells take up water and synthesise enzymes

▷ Factors affecting growth

Temperature

Bacteria can be classified into three groups according to the range of temperature at which they grow best.

- **Thermophiles** have an optimum temperature of above 40 °C. They grow in hot springs, compost heaps and hot water heaters. One species has been found growing in the hot water escaping from thermal vents on the ocean floor at a temperature of 250 °C!
- **Mesophiles** have an optimum temperature between 20 and 40 °C. They include most bacteria, including those pathogenic to humans.
- **Cryophiles** grow best at temperatures below 20 °C. These bacteria live in the Arctic and Antarctic Oceans, but also in fridges and freezers.

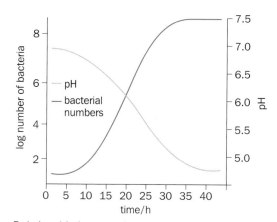

Thermophiles thrive in piles of manure

pH

Most bacteria have enzymes that ensure optimum growth at a neutral pH of 7, but can tolerate a range of pH from 6 to 8.
Very few bacteria can tolerate a pH of less than 4.
(Most bacteria are killed in the human stomach at a pH of 2.)
As you have seen, bacteria produce waste products that lower the pH of the medium and can lead to death of the bacterial population.

Oxygen

Oxygen is needed by aerobic bacteria for respiration to produce ATP for growth and reproduction but not by anaerobic bacteria.
The oxygen may come from the water in the culture medium.
Obligate anaerobes are killed if oxygen is present.

Nutrients

Nutrients are essential for growth and usually include carbon, hydrogen, oxygen, nitrogen, sulphur and phosphorus.
For instance, nitrogen is needed for amino acid and protein synthesis.
Lack of a particular nutrient can lead to decline and death.

log number of bacteria

— pH
— bacterial numbers

pH

time/h

Relationship between bacterial numbers and pH with time.

▷ Culturing bacteria

All bacterial cultures should be regarded as potentially dangerous. Certain safety precautions should be taken and aseptic techniques used whenever you work with microorganisms.

- Any cuts should be covered with a clean, waterproof dressing before any work is attempted.
- Do not eat or drink during practical work and avoid sucking pens or pencils.
- Windows and doors should be closed to avoid the possibility of airborne contamination.
- Wash your hands with anti-bacterial soap before and after working with microorganisms.
- Wipe down the bench with disinfectant such as 10% sodium chlorate(I) before and after working.
- Report any spillages of cultures to your teacher immediately.
- Tape petri dishes securely after inoculation and label them.
- Never remove the lid of a sealed petri dish.
- Never incubate cultures of microorganisms above 30 °C.
- Sterilise all media and containers by autoclaving after use.
- Dispose of all cultures in plastic petri dishes after use by placing them in an autoclavable plastic bag and autoclaving them at 103 kPa (121°C) for 20 minutes.

Step 1

- Before you start to work with microbes:
  - wash your hands and
  - swab the bench with disinfectant.

Step 2

- You will be given a sterile agar plate. Keep the lid on the petri dish.
- Label the lid with your name.

Step 3

⚠ wear eye protection

- Heat an inoculating loop in a Bunsen flame until it is red hot.

Step 4

- Unscrew the bottle and hold the opening of it in a flame for *2 seconds.*

Step 5

- Dip the sterile loop into the microbe sample and then replace the cap on the bottle.

Step 6

- Slightly lift the lid. Gently streak the loop over the surface of the agar. Replace the lid.

Step 7

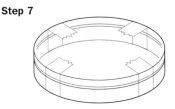

- Seal the petri dish with sellotape. Put the dish upside down in an incubator at 25°C for 2–3 days.
  Never open a sealed petri dish.

Step 8

- Swab the bench with disinfectant.
- Wash your hands.

▶ Monitoring the growth of bacteria

An understanding of how microorganisms grow is important. Biotechnologists using microorganisms in fermenters need this information, as do environmental health officers testing food or water samples.
Therefore being able to count the microorganisms in a sample is an important skill.

There are a number of techniques used, one of which is the **haemocytometer**.

The haemocytometer is basically a modified microscope slide that was originally designed to count red blood cells.

The central section of the slide is 0.1 mm lower than the outer sections and has a ruled area engraved on it.

The middle area has a grid 1 mm square and is called the type A square.
This is further sub-divided into 25 type B squares, each with an area of $0.04 \, mm^2$.

Finally, each of these squares is divided into 16 type C squares, each with an area of $0.0025 \, mm^2$

Using all these dimensions, we can calculate the volume of liquid in each square beneath a coverslip.
For example, the volume of the type C square will be $0.00025 \, mm^3$.

The haemocytometer has a special coverslip.
If this is correctly positioned then a rainbow pattern (called Newton's rings) will be visible where it touches the surface of the haemocytometer.

If a sample of culture medium is placed on the haemocytometer and viewed under a microscope, the number of cells in any particular type of square can be counted.
Any cells touching the bottom or right hand side are ignored, but those touching the top and left hand side are included.

Given that we know the volume of a medium in a square and bearing in mind any dilution of the original sample, we can calculate the number of cells per mm^3.

This count can be carried out at specified time intervals using replicates for accuracy.

With practice, cell counts with the haemocytometer can be made very quickly.
However there are a number of disadvantages with this method:

- cell counts can be unreliable due to the small volume of sample on the slide.
- it is possible to count dead cells as well as living ones leading to inaccurate totals.
- living cells may be obscured by debris in the sample.

Collecting river water samples for microbiological examination

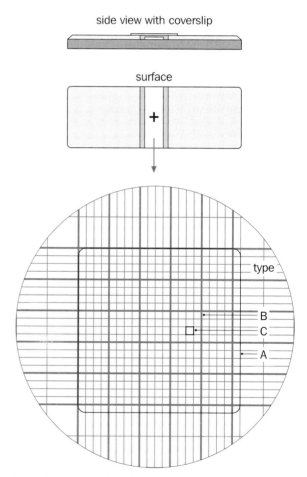

Use of a haemocytometer

▶ Dilution plating and turbidimetry

The haemocytometer will give a **total cell count**, not distinguishing dead cells from those that are **viable**, that is, capable of growth and reproduction.

Dilution plating

A total viable cell count can be made using the **dilution plate** technique.

A culture medium is subjected to a series of dilutions.
A small sample of each dilution is streaked onto a sterile agar plate.
The plates are then incubated at 25-30 °C for 2-5 days.

After this time, the plates are examined, the aim being to find a dilution at which colonies of bacteria can be easily seen and counted as separate and not overlapping.

The assumption is made that each colony arises from a single cell from the original medium.

Therefore to find the total viable cell count, the number of colonies is simply multiplied by the appropriate dilution factor.

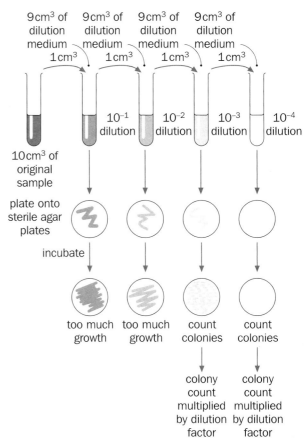

Dilution plating techniques

Turbidimetry

A third technique, known as **turbidimetry**, involves using a **colorimeter** to measure the cloudiness (turbidity) of the culture medium.

A colorimeter shines a light beam through the sample and the amount of light absorbed is measured.
As cells grow and divide, more light is blocked.
The absorbance figures can be compared to a calibration curve.
This is a graph prepared by using known concentrations of cells and recording their absorbance.

This technique is clearly less time-consuming than the other two but it does depend upon the assumption that the turbidity is solely caused by the microorganisms.
The culture mixture must be continually stirred to prevent settling.

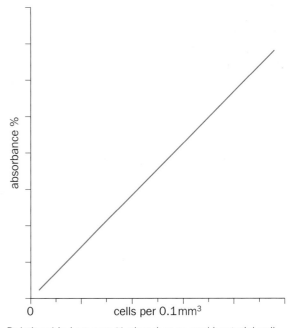

Relationship between % absorbance and bacterial cell numbers

▶ Bacterial disease

The ability of bacteria to produce disease is affected by a number of factors.

- **Pathogenicity** is simply how ill an infection can make you.

Many bacteria are not pathogenic at all. For instance, the millions of bacteria normally found in your large intestine do you no harm.
In fact, many of them are beneficial to you.
On the other hand, bacteria such as those causing tuberculosis, bubonic plague and typhoid can lead to diseases that are fatal.

Pathogenicity is the result of toxins produced by the bacteria.
Some of these are released as waste products and are known as **exotoxins**, for example tetanus.
Other toxins, called **endotoxins**, are part of the bacterial cell itself.
When bacterial cells die, they break up and these endotoxins are released.

- **Infectivity** is the number of bacteria needed to cause infection.

This varies from one disease to another, but most require large numbers of bacteria, as in the case of *Salmonella* food poisoning.
In contrast, typhoid fever is far more infective and requires only a small number of bacteria to be present. The fewer the bacteria required to trigger illness, the more **virulent** the disease is.

- **Invasiveness** is the ability of bacteria to spread within the body of the host from the point of entry to other tissues where they multiply.

This is not easy for bacteria to do since they have to overcome the body's defence system and avoid phagocytosis.
The bacteria also have to penetrate the tough connective tissue and fibres found around tissues.
They do this by secreting enzymes that break down the tissues.
Fortunately, not many bacteria have evolved the ability to do this.
Those that have, such as bubonic plague and anthrax, are highly invasive.

Salmonella food poisoning

Food poisoning caused by *Salmonella* comes on suddenly as a result of the presence of large numbers of bacteria (it is not very virulent).
The symptoms, which usually occur within 12–24 hours of eating contaminated food, include fever, vomiting, diarrhoea and abdominal pain.
It can occasionally prove fatal.

Salmonella bacteria from an animal's gut may contaminate other parts of the animal's body during slaughter and processing.
If the meat is then chilled or frozen, little bacterial growth will occur until defrosting.
Bacteria may be transmitted during defrosting if any water drips onto other foods and contaminates them. Similarly, the bacteria can be transmitted by handling raw chicken. Inadequate cooking can accelerate bacterial growth.
Salmonella may be passed on in eggs and unpasteurised milk.
A sufferer may also act as a *carrier* since the bacteria colonise the small intestine and may be egested in the faeces for up to 4 months.

Precautions include the adequate thawing of frozen food and thorough cooking.
Raw and cooked foods should be stored separately in fridges, and the transfer of bacteria from raw to cooked foods via hands, utensils and work surfaces should be avoided.

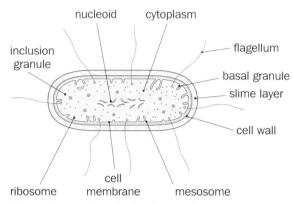

The basic structure of a bacterial cell

Food bug outbreak shuts wards to others

A HOSPITAL has been closed to all GP-arranged admissions except suspected cases of the *E. coli 0157* food poisoning outbreak. Monklands Hospital in Airdrie is using a third ward to deal with the outbreak. It will be used as an intensive care unit.

Thirty-two adults and a child were being treated yesterday in the hospital, where the Lanarkshire Infectious Diseases Unit is based. The number giving cause for concern rose from ten to 15 over the weekend and the number showing symptoms rose from 189 to 209

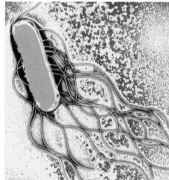

TEM of Salmonella bacterium

Cholera

Cholera is a water-borne disease caused by the bacterium *Vibrio cholerae*.
It tends to occur in areas where there is a lack of proper sanitation, an unclean water supply or contaminated food.
Water supplies become contaminated when infected people pass out large numbers of the bacteria in their faeces.
Many of these people may not actually suffer from the disease and are called **symptomless carriers**.

Transmission can occur by drinking contaminated water or by infected people handling food or cooking utensils without washing their hands.
The bacterium multiplies in the small intestine and secretes a toxin which prevents the normal absorption of salts and water.
The symptoms are severe diarrhoea and loss of fluid.
Dehydration can cause death if the condition is not treated within 24 hours.

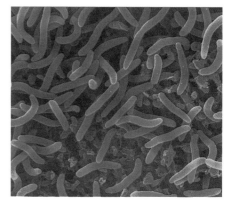

SEM Vibrio cholerae

Cholera can be treated by giving the patient a solution of salts and glucose intravenously.
If the sufferer is able to drink, then **oral rehydration therapy** can be given.
Treatment is often effective since the glucose takes salts with it as it is absorbed into the blood in the small intestine.

Effective treatment of sewage and the chlorination of drinking water mean that cholera is virtually unknown in developed countries.
In many developing countries, overcrowding, poor sanitation and the lack of clean water encourages the spread of the disease.
These countries do not have the financial resources to solve the problems of poor housing, lack of proper sanitation and untreated water supplies.

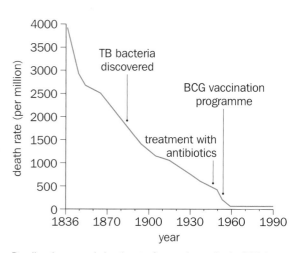

Oral rehydration therapy given to Rwandan refugee during cholera epidemic

Tuberculosis

Tuberculosis (TB) is a bacterial disease that was once thought to be nearly eradicated.
However, in recent years it has shown a resurgence and is estimated to kill two million people a year worldwide.

Pulmonary TB is the most common form and is caused by the bacterium *Mycobacterium tuberculosis*.
It attacks the lungs and the lymph nodes, especially those in the neck.
Sufferers have a persistent cough and fever and lose weight through lack of appetite.
The bacterium is transmitted in airborne droplets and can spread rapidly where people live in overcrowded conditions.
The bacteria may remain in the lungs or the lymph system for years before becoming active.

The introduction of the antibiotic streptomycin along with improved housing conditions brought about a large decrease in the incidence of TB in the UK in the 1940s.
This was the case in many other developed countries too and it was hoped that the disease could be completely eradicated.
However, TB is now showing a worldwide increase due to some strains of the bacterium becoming resistant to drugs.
Poor housing and an increase in homeless people has also contributed to the increased incidence of TB in developed countries.

Overcrowded street in Jaipur, India

Decline in annual death rate from tuberculosis (TB) in England and Wales

▷ Viral disease

We looked at the structure and reproduction of viruses on page 39.
You should remember that they are extremely small (0.02–0.3 µm),
and are made up of DNA or RNA surrounded by a protein coat.

Viruses are intracellular parasites which are only capable of
reproducing inside living host cells.
They cause disease by

- damaging the host cells that they invade,
- producing toxins as they invade cells and reproduce.

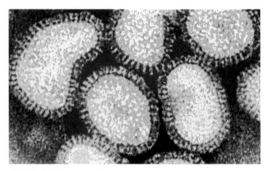

TEM of influenza virus

▷ Influenza

Influenza is an RNA virus with a spiky protein coat consisting of
two types of antigen which bind specifically with the host cell.

There are three main types of influenza virus: A, B and C.
Only influenza type A causes serious epidemics.
Deaths can occur due to secondary respiratory infections by
bacteria causing bronchitis and pneumonia.
Type B usually causes milder, more local outbreaks. Type C
produces minor cold-like symptoms and is not very common.

Transmission of influenza is by droplet infection (coughing and
sneezing).
These droplets may be inhaled directly or may evaporate to
give airborne virus particles that can survive dry conditions
for some time.
Transmission is more likely in crowded and poorly ventilated places.

The virus affects the respiratory passages, especially the nose
and throat.
The **incubation period** (the time between infection and the
symptoms developing in a person) is about 2 days.
The symptoms may last up to 4 days and include headache,
sore throat, backache and fever, with the body temperature rising
to 40 °C with shivering and sweating.
The virus attacks the epithelial lining of the trachea, bronchi and
bronchioles, and, as mentioned above, secondary infections by bacteria
may also occur. A person rarely remains infective for more than 6 days.

Treatment of viral infections is difficult because the virus is inside the cells
of the host.
Drugs may not penetrate these cells and if they did they may even
damage them further. Antibiotics are ineffective against viruses so for
the main part we have to rely upon the body's own defence system.
Rest, aspirins or paracetamol to reduce temperature, and plenty of fluids
help to relieve some of the symptoms of influenza.

Vaccination helps to protect particularly susceptible individuals.
But protection is short-lived and mass vaccination is not recommended.
Use of tissues and handkerchiefs cuts down the spread of droplets by
sneezing and coughing.
Better ventilation and less overcrowding in work places also helps.
The spread of influenza would be much restricted if affected people
stayed isolated instead of going to work and transmitting it to others.

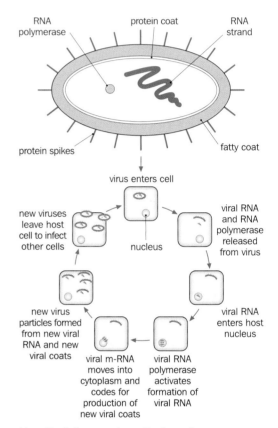

How the influenza virus attacks cells

▷ Acquired immune deficiency syndrome (AIDS)

AIDS is caused by the human immunodeficiency virus (HIV).
The virus attacks **helper T-cells** in the body's immune system.
HIV resembles the influenza virus in appearance with its
outer lipid envelope with glycoprotein spikes.
The protein core contains two RNA molecules instead of one.

HIV is a **retrovirus**. This means that it uses the RNA to produce
a single strand of DNA, called **copy DNA (cDNA)**, inside the
host's cell.
The enzyme **reverse transcriptase** catalyses this reverse
transcription of DNA from an RNA template.

The virus can remain latent for many years before being activated,
when it will start to replicate and destroy the host cell.
By reducing the number of helper T-cells, HIV weakens the body's
ability to fight disease.
Eventually the person infected with HIV can succumb to any
of a number of other infections because of their weakened
immune system.
So AIDS (acquired immune deficiency syndrome) is actually
the name given to a collection of diseases brought on by the
weakening of the body's immune system.

Replication of HIV

1   The HIV retrovirus attaches to a receptor site on the surface
    of the host cell.
2   The envelope of the virus fuses with the host cell surface
    membrane.
3   The viral RNA, under the action of reverse transcriptase,
    acts as a template to make a single strand of DNA (cDNA).
4   It then forms a second complementary DNA strand.
5   The resulting double strand of DNA inserts itself in the
    chromosomal DNA of the host cell, forming a **provirus**.
6   The viral DNA is transcribed into mRNA.
7   The mRNA directs the synthesis of viral proteins.
8   New viruses are made from the protein and RNA and leave
    the host cell to infect other cells.

So eventually each infected helper T-cell bursts open to release
thousands of new viruses which can infect other helper T-cells.
As the number of viruses increases, so the number of helper
T-cells is reduced.
Eventually the immune system can become so weakened that
the symptoms of AIDS begin to appear.

It is important to realise that HIV does not necessarily result
in AIDS.
Some infected people remain symptomless and are
therefore carriers.
They make antibodies against the virus, which can be detected
in a blood test.

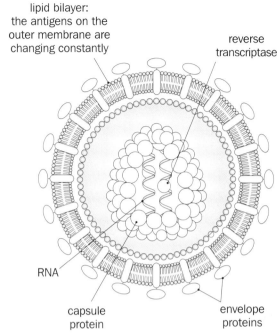

The structure of HIV

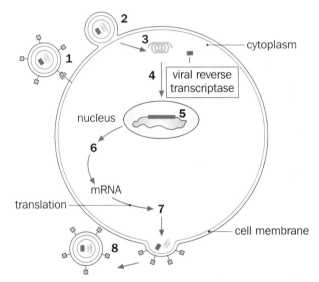

The replication of HIV

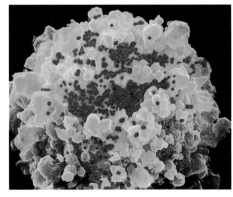

*SEM of a T-lymphocyte infected with HIV virus
(red) (×5000)*

▶ Signs, symptoms and transmission of AIDS

For every 100 people infected with HIV per year, about 12 develop the signs and symptoms of full-blown AIDS.
This can take up to 7 or 8 years to develop.

Initially after infection, short-lived symptoms of flu-like illness may appear.
These may include swollen lymph glands and a raised temperature.
This is followed by a period of months or even years when there are no signs of illness.
As the immune system weakens, infections that would normally be held in check start to take hold.

Symptoms of these **opportunistic infections** include a rare form of skin cancer called **Kaposi's sarcoma**.
Other types of cancer may appear and the sufferer may experience weight loss, fever, diarrhoea and deteriorating brain function leading to dementia.
The most common cause of death in AIDS patients is a rare type of pneumonia.

Transmission

HIV is mainly transmitted in the blood or in semen.
The virus enters the body through slight abrasions that may occur during sexual contact or via hypodermic needles contaminated with infected blood.

Early in the history of the disease, the transfusion of infected blood placed haemophiliacs at risk since they required regular injections of Factor VIII.
Developed countries soon introduced sterilisation and screening of blood and blood products prior to transfusion.

Sexual transmission of HIV can occur between male homosexual partners.
Damage to the lining of the rectum during anal intercourse can cause bleeding and infection by contaminated blood or semen.
Either partner may infect the other.

Heterosexual transmission of HIV is much rarer since the walls of the vagina are much tougher and do not bleed as easily.
People who have a large number of sexual partners are more at risk.
Secretions from the vaginal wall may carry HIV to the male partner via his penis.
Alternatively, HIV from infected semen may get across the lining of the vagina, especially if any ulceration has occurred.

The second highest risk group is those drug users who inject intravenously.
In 1986, HIV spread alarmingly through drug addicts in Edinburgh who shared needles and syringes.

Needles were in short supply in Edinburgh after pharmacists stopped their sale in 1982 in a bid to curb drug mis-use.

Unborn babies are at high risk of infection from HIV if the pregnant mother carries the disease since it can pass across the placenta to the fetus.
A lactating mother can also pass the virus to her infant in breast milk.

Diana, Princess of Wales meeting AIDS patients

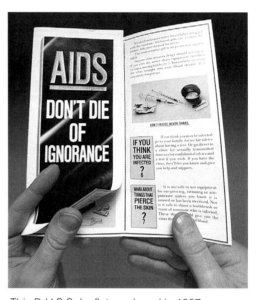
This D.H.S.S. leaflet produced in 1997 was distributed to every household in the UK

A drug addict injecting

▶ Treatment and prevention of HIV

The World Health Organisation has estimated that 30 million adults have become infected since the pandemic started. In 1998 there were 2.6 million deaths and 5.8 million new cases of AIDs recorded.

Treatment

There is no cure for AIDS and as yet no vaccine for HIV.

- Scientists are trying to develop drugs that will inactivate HIV, but as we mentioned earlier, the problem is that the drugs may damage the host lymphocytes.

If drugs do reduce the number of T-lymphocytes in the blood, the patient is open to opportunistic infections.
The best known drug so far developed is **zidovudine (AZT)**. This stops HIV replicating by binding with reverse transcriptase and blocking its action.
But this can result in harmful side effects, such as anaemia.

- The development of a vaccine offers the best hope of attacking the HIV virus and preventing AIDS.

However, the virus is able to change its surface proteins so it is hard to produce a vaccine that can counter this.

HIV is a retrovirus and retroviral genes can cause cancer. So any vaccine based on an attenuated (killed) whole virus could cause cancer.

Prevention

Precautions that can be effective in reducing the spread of HIV include the following:

- The use of condoms to provide a physical barrier to the transmission of the virus during heterosexual and homosexual intercourse.

- Setting up free needle exchange schemes for those people who inject drugs. This reduces the risk of transmission from the use of shared needles and syringes.

- Screening donated blood for HIV antibodies and eliminating any contaminated blood being used for transfusion.

- Education programmes make people aware of the methods of transmission of the HIV virus and how they can be prevented.

- **Contact tracing** is important in the control of the spread of HIV in the UK. Any person diagnosed as HIV positive is asked to identify people who they may have put at risk, either as a result of sexual intercourse or by sharing needles. These people are then offered an HIV test, which reveals the presence of HIV antibodies in their blood. However, these antibodies will only appear several weeks after the person has become infected.

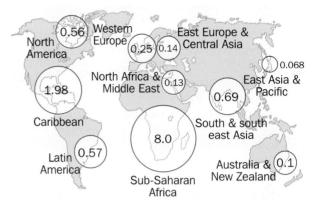

Percentage of adults (15–49 years) living with HIV/AIDS, 1998

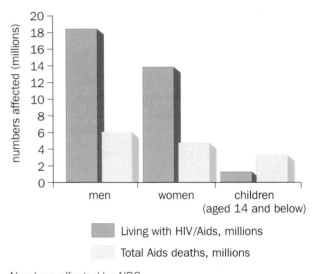

Living with HIV/Aids, millions

Total Aids deaths, millions

Numbers affected by AIDS

▶ Malaria

Malaria is not caused by a bacterium or a virus.
The microorganism responsible is the protoctist *Plasmodium*.
This malarial parasite infects liver cells and red blood cells.

Plasmodium is carried from one person to another by the female *Anopheles* mosquito.
The mosquito is called a **vector** because it transmits the disease.
The protist has a complex cycle of transmission which includes both sexual and asexual stages.
When the mosquito bites an infected person, it takes up red blood cells that contain the gametes of *Plasmodium*.
These gametes fuse in the gut of the mosquito, producing the infective form of the protist which then migrates to the insect's salivary glands.
When the mosquito bites an uninfected person, *Plasmodium* is transmitted into the blood together with an anticoagulant in the saliva.
Plasmodium then invades the red blood cells and liver cells of the newly infected person where it multiplies asexually producing many more of the parasites.

The most dangerous species is *Plasmodium falciparum*.
P. falciparum can cause red blood cells to stick together, leading to the blockage of blood vessels to the brain, lungs and kidneys.
Symptoms of malaria include high fever, chills and heavy sweating, and if untreated the sufferer may die within a few days.

Malaria flourishes in some of the warmer regions of the world.
Poorer countries are at risk since they do not have the resources or expertise to combat the disease.
Mosquito control programmes have often been disrupted by civil wars.

Treatment and prevention

Most efforts to control malaria are directed at destroying the mosquito vector and so breaking the cycle of transmission.
Control measures have included:

- draining ponds and ditches where the mosquito lays its eggs and where the larvae develop but this is expensive and it is impossible to drain all breeding areas,
- stocking ponds and lakes with fish that eat mosquito larvae,
- spraying insecticides on the surfaces of ponds and lakes to kill the larvae and pupae,
- using nets treated with insecticide around people's beds to protect them from mosquitoes.

Treatment of malarial victims has included:

- anti-malarial drugs such as quinine and chloroquinine to prevent the parasite spreading within the human body; however, the over-use of such drugs has resulted in resistant strains of *Plasmodium* appearing,
- development of vaccines to attack different stages of the parasite inside the body,
- insect repellents sprayed on the skin to prevent the mosquito from landing.

You can see how the allele for sickle cell anaemia can give people protection from malaria on page 378.

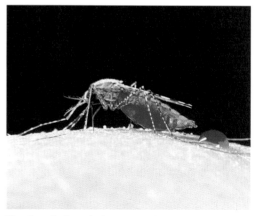

The female Anopheles *mosquito transmits malaria*

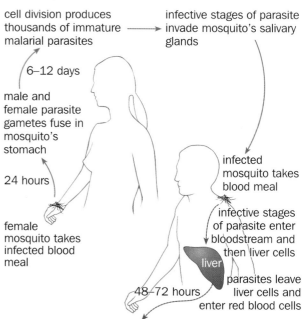

cell division produces thousands of immature malarial parasites → infective stages of parasite invade mosquito's salivary glands

6–12 days

male and female parasite gametes fuse in mosquito's stomach

24 hours

female mosquito takes infected blood meal

infected mosquito takes blood meal

infective stages of parasite enter bloodstream and then liver cells

liver

parasites leave liver cells and enter red blood cells

48–72 hours

maturation and production of parasite's male and female sex cells (gametes)

The life cycle of the malaria parasite

Healthworker fumigates homes to remove mosquitoes

▶ Natural defence barriers

Most microorganisms find it difficult to get inside the body. If they did not experience resistance from the body's defences, then we would become constantly ill and would eventually die.

There are four main ways in which the body prevents potential pathogens from entering.

Physical defence

The skin provides a physical barrier to the entry of pathogens. The tough, outer layer of dead cells contains keratin and very little water, which microorganisms need for growth.
If we keep our skin healthy, it is rarely penetrated by microorganisms.
The skin also secretes various chemicals which inhibit the growth of bacteria such as

- tears – the lachrymal glands secrete tears which dilute and wash away microorganisms and irritant chemicals from the eyes,
- sebum – secreted by the sebaceous glands contains fatty acids that have an antimicrobial action,
- mucus – a sticky secretion produced by goblet cells that line the air passages. The mucus traps many airborne pathogens.

Mechanical defence

Nasal hairs filter the air that is drawn into the nasal passages. Bacteria and other particles trapped in the mucus are swept away from the lungs by **cilia**.
Cilia are tiny hairs that beat with a wave-like motion.

Chemical defence

Tears, mucus, saliva and sweat all contain chemicals that inhibit the growth of microorganisms.
Lysozyme is an enzyme found in many of these secretions. It catalyses the hydrolysis of molecules in the cell walls of bacteria.
In addition to lysozyme, sweat contains lactate, which also slows bacterial growth.

Hydrochloric acid present in gastric juice kills most microorganisms that get as far as the stomach.

The vagina contains harmless bacteria that convert carbohydrate to lactate, which kills off pathogenic bacteria.

Biological defence

There are natural populations of harmless bacteria living on the skin and mucous membranes that inhibit the growth of many pathogenic microbes.
They protect us by competing with pathogenic bacteria for nutrients.
Wide-spectrum antibiotics can destroy these useful bacteria and so remove some of the body's defences.

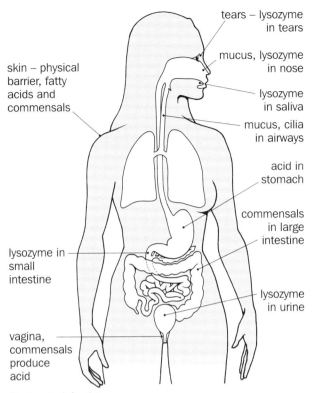

skin – physical barrier, fatty acids and commensals

tears – lysozyme in tears

mucus, lysozyme in nose

lysozyme in saliva

mucus, cilia in airways

acid in stomach

commensals in large intestine

lysozyme in small intestine

lysozyme in urine

vagina, commensals produce acid

Barriers to infection

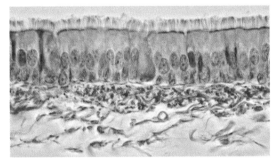

Cilated cells of the respiratory pathway waft mucus along

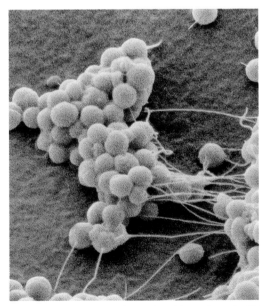

SEM of symbiotic bacteria on the skin surface (×2000)

267

▶ Immune response

An immune response is the way in which the body responds to invasion by a specific pathogen or antigen.
This response involves the production of cells and chemicals designed to defend the body against the pathogen.

Antigens are substances that can produce an immune response. Antigens trigger the production of **antibodies** by the immune system. Each type of antibody is specific to a particular antigen and reacts with it to make it harmless.

Self antigens are part of the cell surface membrane of body cells. They do not activate an immune response, except in the case of auto-immune disease, because our bodies recognise them as being part of us.
Non-self antigens are found on the cell walls and cell membranes of bacteria, viruses, fungi, animal parasites, pollen and incompatible blood cells. Toxins released by some bacteria and viruses may also act as antigens. These do produce an immune response as our bodies recognise them as being foreign.

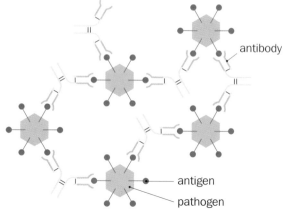
Pathogens immobilised by the formation of an antigen-antibody complex

Antigens are large complex molecules that take the form of a protein, polysaccharide or glycoprotein.
They have two distinct characteristics:

- they stimulate the formation of specific antibodies,
- they react specifically with these antibodies.

▶ The nature of antibodies

Antibodies are glycoproteins which belong to a special group of blood proteins known as **immunoglobulins.**

The basic structure of an antibody consists of two pairs of polypeptide chains.
Two of the chains are long and are referred to as **heavy (H) chains**. The other two shorter chains are referred to as **light (L) chains**. The chains are held together by disulphide (S-S) bridges.

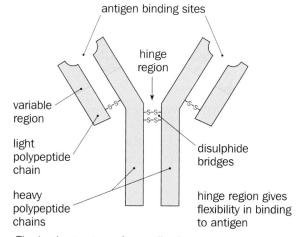
The basic structure of an antibody

Each antibody molecule has two identical antigen binding sites. These are different for each kind of antibody, which allows the antibody to recognise and attach *specifically* to a particular antigen. It is the sequence of amino acids at the antigen binding sites that makes the three-dimensional shape that fits with the specific antigen. It's like the lock and key mechanism in which an enzyme binds to its specific substrate.
In this case, an **antibody–antigen complex** is formed.

The antigen attachment site is known as the *variable* region and is specific to each antigen.
The rest of each polypeptide chain is termed the *constant* region, as it is common to other antibodies too.

Some antibodies act by immobilising the antigens so that they can be destroyed by phagocytosis.
Others, known as **antitoxins**, are able to neutralise the toxins released by bacteria such as those that cause cholera, diphtheria and tetanus.

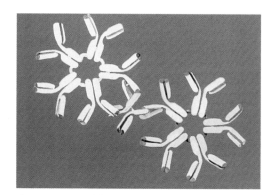
Computer graphic representing two antibodies bound to an antigen.

▷ Cell-mediated immunity

There are many different types of white blood cells involved in immunity.
Cell-mediated immunity involves **T-lymphocytes** and **macrophages.**

Macrophages

Macrophages are phagocytic (see page 188).
Although macrophages are non-specific in their response to pathogens –
they engulf and digest all types of foreign cells and viruses – some of the
antigen molecules become embedded in the macrophage cell membrane.
This can alert T- and B-lymphocyte cells to the fact that the body has
been invaded by a particular pathogen.

Lymphocytes

Lymphocytes are white blood cells that recognise and react
with antigens.
There are two main types: **T-lymphocytes** and **B-lymphocytes**.
These develop from **stem cells** in the bone marrow.
They eventually migrate to the **spleen** and **lymph nodes** where
they mature.

T-lymphocytes initially pass to the **thymus** (a lymph gland in
the neck) where they are activated.
These activated, or **competent**, T-lymphocytes then also pass to
the lymph nodes and spleen.
There are millions of types of T-lymphocytes, each recognising
and attacking a particular type of antigen.
This is known as **cell-mediated immunity**.
It takes place like this:

- Macrophages engulf the pathogens bearing the antigens.

- Binding sites on the surface of particular T-lymphocytes
  recognise and fit with the molecular structure of the antigen.

- The T-lymphocytes become activated and start to multiply rapidly.
  They produce a large clone of identical cells, all of which can
  recognise the antigen as being foreign.
  This clone differentiates (sub-divides) into the following cell types:

- **cytotoxic T-cells** (killer cells) destroy the antigen directly by
  attaching to them and releasing the chemical **perforin** to
  kill them,

- **helper T-cells** attract and stimulate macrophages and
  promote the activity of other T- and B-cells to increase antibody
  production,

- **memory T-cells** have no action but multiply very fast if a
  second invasion of the antigen occurs, producing an even bigger
  clone of T-lymphocytes and resulting in rapid destruction of
  the antigen,

- **suppressor T-cells** slow down the vigorous response of the
  T-cytotoxic cells and the T-helper cells, so slowing down and
  stopping the immune response.

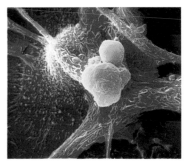

Macrophage attacking cancer cell

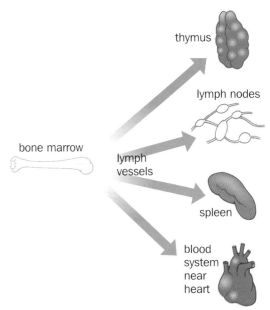

The origin and circulation of lymphocytes

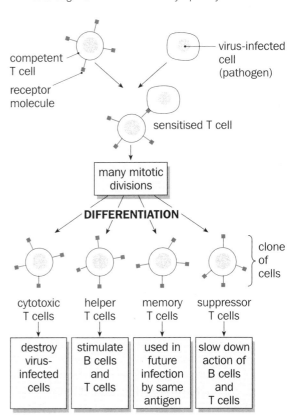

269

▶ Antibody-mediated immunity

Sometimes known as the **humoral response**, **antibody-mediated immunity** involves the production of B-lymphocytes, which are activated by antigens attached to the macrophage membrane.
B-lymphocyte activity is also stimulated by helper T-cells.

The B-lymphocytes attack and destroy the antigen on the surface of microorganisms and other foreign (non-self) material by producing antibodies that circulate in the blood, lymph and tissue fluid.

There are *three* different types of B-lymphocytes.

- **Plasma B-cells** which secrete antibodies into the circulation.
  Each antibody is specific to the pathogenic antigen.
  Plasma cells produce antibodies very quickly (as many as 2 000 per second for each cell).
  An active plasma cell can live for 4–5 days.
- **Memory B-cells** live for a long time in the blood.
  They do not produce antibodies, but are programmed to remember a specific antigen and respond very rapidly to any subsequent infection.
- **Dividing B-cells** produce more B-lymphocyte cells.

Stages in antibody-mediated immunity

- Macrophages engulf the foreign material of the pathogen.
  Antigens from the pathogen embedded in the macrophage cell membrane are recognised by B-lymphocytes.
- B-lymphocytes are activated when specific binding sites on their surface membrane attach to the antigens.
- The activated cells either enlarge to form plasma cells, which produce antibodies, or multiply to form a clone of memory B-cells. Dividing B-cells continue multiplication to produce a large clone.
- The antibodies circulate and bind with any material with the specific antigen and destroy it.
- Any further invasion by a pathogen with the same antigen will trigger the same events to happen, since there is a large clone of memory cells specific to that antigen.
  These can be activated to produce plasma B-cells very quickly and so produce vast quantities of a specific antibody.

What do you think is meant by the **primary** and **secondary responses** of antibody production?

Compare
  i)   the length of the latent period and
  ii) the amount of antibody produced in the primary and secondary responses.

From what you have learnt about the action of B-lymphocytes, explain:
  i)   the differences in the rate of response,
  ii) the increasing production of antibodies in both responses.

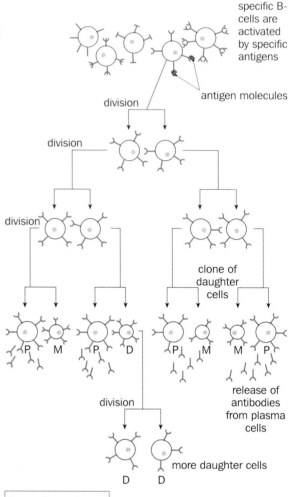

P = plasma B-cell
M = memory B-cell
D = dividing B-cell

Antibody-mediated immunity

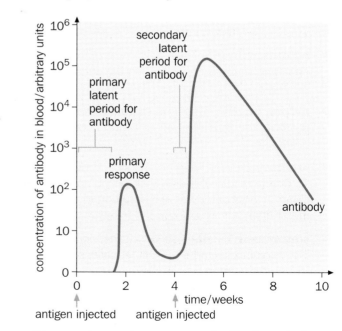

Primary and secondary responses of antibody production

▶ The reaction between antibody and antigen

The antibody becomes attached to the antigen at the antigen binding site like a key in a lock (though neither is an enzyme).

This causes the antibody to change from a T shape to a Y shape. This exposes part of the antibody molecule to substances in the plasma that are together known as **complement.**

It is the combined effect of antibody and complement that determines the action of the antibody.

For instance the antibody may

- cause the antigens to stick together – **agglutination**,
- stimulate **phagocytosis** by neutrophils,
- act as an **antitoxin** and cause the precipitation of soluble bacterial toxins,
- prevent pathogenic bacteria attaching to cell membranes.

Some of these methods of antigen destruction are shown in the diagram.

▶ Immunity and immunisation

So far we have looked at the type of immunity that occurs during the course of an infection.

The pathogen invades the body, which responds by stimulating the production of T-lymphocytes and B-lymphocytes which are involved in the immune response.

Memory cells are formed which provide long-term immunity to the antigen.

This type of immunity is termed **active** because the lymphocytes are **activated** by antigens present on the surface of the pathogen. Since this activation takes place during the natural course of an infection, we call it **natural active immunity**.

But the immune response can also be triggered **artificially**. This involves the injection of antigens into the body. We call this **artificial active immunity**, although it is more commonly referred to as **vaccination**.

Passive immunity occurs when an individual becomes temporarily immune to an antigen by receiving ready-made antibodies from someone else.

- **Natural passive immunity** occurs when pre-formed antibodies pass naturally from mother to baby across the placenta and in breast milk.
  Immunity is only temporary since the baby's body does not 'know' how to make more antibodies. But it provides the baby with protection until it develops its **own** immune system.

- **Artificial passive immunity** occurs when pre-formed antibodies extracted from one individual are injected into another as a **serum**. This only produces short-term immunity because the injected antibody will possess 'non-self' antigens and so the body will produce antibodies against it.
  However, this sort of immunity can provide a 'quick fix' and is given to people who have been bitten by poisonous snakes or rabid dogs.

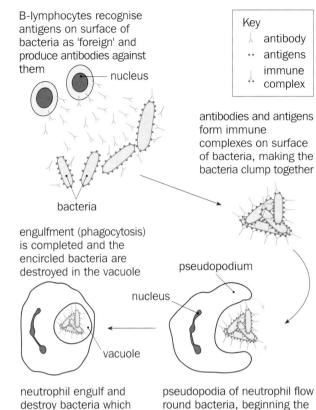

B-lymphocytes recognise antigens on surface of bacteria as 'foreign' and produce antibodies against them

nucleus

bacteria

Key
ʎ antibody
·· antigens
immune complex

antibodies and antigens form immune complexes on surface of bacteria, making the bacteria clump together

engulfment (phagocytosis) is completed and the encircled bacteria are destroyed in the vacuole

pseudopodium

nucleus

vacuole

neutrophil engulf and destroy bacteria which have been attacked by antibodies

pseudopodia of neutrophil flow round bacteria, beginning the process of engulfment (phagocytosis)

Lymphocytes and neutrophils at work

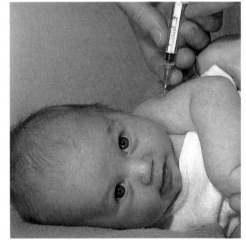

▶ Vaccination

As you have seen, a **vaccine** is an antigen that is injected or swallowed, which causes the development of active immunity in the patient. The small quantities of antigen introduced into the person's body stimulate the production of antibodies as if infected by the disease. This type of immunity is long-term since the body is able to produce memory cells in the normal way.

Antigens are treated before being introduced to the body of the patient, in order to make them relatively harmless.

Most vaccines are made in one of the following ways.

'Don't worry you'll only feel a little prick'

- **Killed virulent organisms** such as whooping cough bacteria. The microorganism is killed by heat or by use of chemicals, which denature its enzymes.
  So the dead pathogen will not cause the disease, but it will possess antigenic sites on its surface that will be recognised by T- and B-lymphocytes, and result in the production of antibodies in the recipient. But there is no chance of the pathogen replicating and causing infection.

- **Live non-virulent strains** such as in the virus causing rubella. Vaccines made in this way are often called **attenuated** vaccines. The pathogen is deliberately weakened to ensure it does not cause severe infection. Other examples are BCG vaccine used against tuberculosis and the Sabin vaccine used against poliomyelitis, which is taken orally.

- **Modified toxins** such as the vaccine used against diphtheria and tetanus. In this type of vaccine, the **toxoids** (toxic substances) produced by the bacteria are made harmless.
  They are used to stimulate antibody production, but there is no risk of infection by the pathogen.

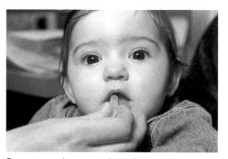

Some vaccines can be taken orally

- **Isolated antigens** separated from a pathogen, such as influenza. The important antigens are separated from the microorganism, in this case by breaking up the pathogen's structure and obtaining glycoproteins. The 'flu vaccine' contains a mixture of antigens from various strains of influenza virus, in an attempt to combat the great variation that exists. This **antigenic variation** occurs in microorganisms that have a high mutation rate.

- **Genetically engineered antigens** as in the case of hepatitis B. Restriction endonucleases are used to extract from the pathogen the genes that code for a particular antigen.
  As you saw in Chapter 9, the genes can then be inserted in a harmless plasmid vector using a ligase enzyme.
  The bacterial cells then replicate to produce large amounts of antigen.

The active immunity that vaccines produce can give protection for a long time.
However, several more vaccinations, called **boosters**, may be needed after the initial one.
Boosters stimulate quicker production of antibodies and prolong protection. In the case of diphtheria, the first injection lasts 1 year, whereas a second 'booster' injection provides protection for 10 years.

ABO blood groups

All red blood cells may look the same, but they have different antigens on their cell surface membranes.

People can be put into one of four blood groups under the **ABO system**. These blood groups are called **A**, **B**, **AB** and **O**.

They are determined by which antigens are present on the red blood cells. There are two main antigens: **A** and **B**.

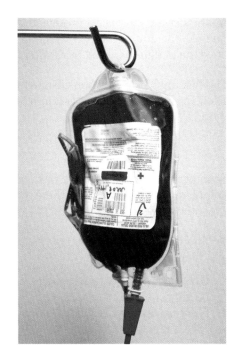

- People in blood group **A** have only **A** antigens on their red blood cells.
- People in blood group **B** have only **B** antigens.
- People in blood group **AB** have both **A** and **B** antigens.
- People in blood group **O** have neither **A** nor **B** antigens.

The plasma will not contain antibodies that will attack its own antigens. So depending upon the blood group, the plasma may contain just **anti-A** antibodies or just **anti-B** antibodies, both of them or neither of them.

Antigen on red blood cells	Antibody in plasma	Blood group	% of UK Caucasian population
A	anti-B	A	46
B	anti-A	B	8
A and B	none	AB	2
neither A nor B	anti-A and anti-B	O	44

- The anti-B antibodies in blood group A plasma do not attack the A antigens of blood group A red blood cells. But they will attack the B antigens of blood group B red blood cells.
- The anti-A antibodies in blood group B plasma do not attack the B antigens of blood group B red blood cells. But they will attack the A antigens of blood group A red blood cells.
- There are no anti-A and anti-B antibodies in blood group AB plasma to attack the A or B antigens of blood group AB red blood cells.
- Blood group O plasma contains both anti-A and anti-B antibodies but there are neither A nor B antigens on their red blood cells.

Blood transfusion

When people have a blood transfusion it is important that they receive blood that is compatible with their own.

If a transfusion of incompatible blood is given, then the body will produce antibodies that will unite with the antigens on the surface of the introduced red blood cells resulting in them clumping together.

These clumped red blood cells can block small vessels and cause kidney failure and other potentially lethal reactions.

Look at the table which shows blood transfusion compatibility between the donor and the recipient.

- Group O people are called **universal donors**.
  Why are they able to give their blood to anybody?

- Group AB people are said to be **universal recipients**.
  Why are they able to receive blood from any donor?

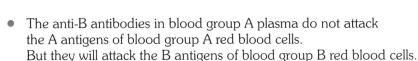

		recipient			
		A	B	AB	O
d o n o r	A	✓	✗	✓	✗
	B	✗	✓	✓	✗
	AB	✗	✗	✓	✗
	O	✓	✓	✓	✓

✓ = safe transfusion
✗ = unsafe transfusion

▶ Antibiotics

Antibiotics are chemicals produced by microorganisms (mainly bacteria and fungi) which *at low concentrations* have the ability to inhibit or destroy pathogens.

The first antibiotic was penicillin, which was developed in the 1940s in response to the need to treat soldiers in the Second World War.
(You can read about the large scale production of penicillin on page 145.)

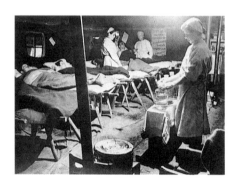

Several species of fungi have been used to produce antimicrobial chemicals and there are now 50–100 commercially available antibiotics.

Antibiotics are characterised by their range of effectiveness and their mode of action.

- **Broad spectrum antibiotics** kill a wide range of bacteria.
- **Narrow spectrum antibiotics** are effective against only a few types of bacteria.

To kill a specific pathogen, you need to use a narrow spectrum antibiotic which is specific for the disease.

All antibiotics must have **selective toxicity.**
This means they should kill or inhibit the growth of bacteria or fungi, but cause little or no damage to the host.

Antibiotics interfere with the growth or metabolism of the pathogen in a variety of ways.

- **Penicillin** inhibits the enzymes that are involved in the formation of the bacterial cell wall.
  Bacteria with weak cell walls die due to leakage of the cell contents.

- **Streptomycin** binds to the bacterial ribosomes, so preventing protein synthesis, including the synthesis of enzymes.
  The lack of protein affects bacterial growth and results in its death.
  Fortunately, bacterial ribosomes are different from human ones.
  So streptomycin does not interfere with the synthesis of proteins in the cells of the patient taking the drug.
  Tetracyclines also work by interfering with bacterial ribosomes.

- **Polymyxines** damage bacterial cell membranes even in resting cells.

Antibiotics tend to be used against bacterial infections more than fungal infections.
This is because fungal cells work in a similar way to human cells.
Consequently, many antifungal agents are highly toxic to humans.

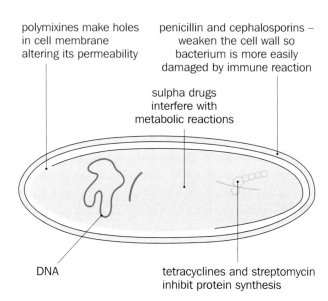

Some antibiotics and the way they work

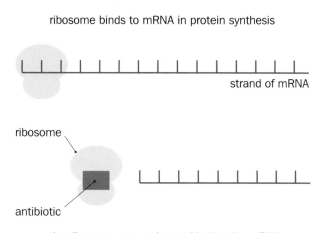

▶ Antibiotic resistance

Many bacteria that were once susceptible to antibiotics have become resistant due to random mutations.
This is the case with penicillin-resistant bacteria which are able to synthesise **penicillinase**.
This enzyme is able to break down the antibiotic.

Repeated exposure to antibiotics has led to more bacteria surviving and passing on resistant genes.
Antibiotic-resistant genes are often carried by plasmids in bacteria and can be passed on to different strains.
This method of transferring genetic information is called **conjugation**.
For example, gonorrhea-causing bacteria that can no longer be killed by high doses of penicillin can pass on their resistance to other strains.
Some bacteria have become resistant to two or more antibiotics as a result of conjugation.

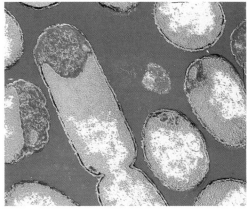

Bacterial cells pass on genetic information during conjugation

Perhaps surprisingly, resistant microorganisms often occur in hospitals where antibiotics are used most often, especially to prevent infections occurring from surgery.
This has been the case with MRSA, 90% of which are now unaffected by penicillin.
Even more worrying is the emergence of more strains of MRSA that are resistant to a growing list of antibiotics.

The inappropriate and widespread use of antibiotics should be avoided.
In the past, antibiotics have probably been prescribed too readily by many GPs.
Reducing the number of antibiotics in use means that fewer bacteria are exposed to them and reduces the chances of resistant strains appearing.

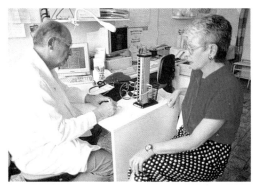

Many doctors have over-prescribed antibiotics in the past

▶ Screening antibiotics

It is important that, if an antibiotic is used, it should be the most effective one for a particular strain of bacteria or fungus.
This can be achieved by **screening**.

Samples of the microorganism are taken from the sufferer, or from contaminated food or water, or from faeces.
The microorganism is grown on agar plates.
Different antibiotics absorbed onto filter paper discs are then placed on the surface of the agar and the plate incubated.

The antibiotic diffuses out of each filter paper disc, killing the microbe and producing a clear area: the **inhibition zone**.

The greater the diameter of the inhibition zone, the more effective the antibiotic is against the microorganism.

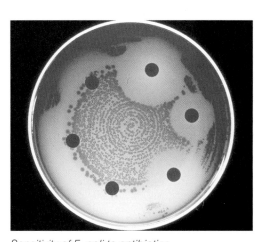

Sensitivity of E. coli to antibiotics

Which antibiotic do you think is most effective against the bacteria tested here?

▶ Biology at work: Antibodies and pregnancy testing

The testing of urine samples for signs of pregnancy goes back to ancient Egyptian times, but the reliable and sensitive tests we have today are a recent innovation.

These tests were developed in the 1960s. They involve the detection of **human chorionic gonadotrophin** or **HCG.**

HCG is a hormone produced by the placenta in early pregnancy.
It stimulates the ovaries to produce oestrogen and progesterone.
These hormones are needed to maintain a healthy pregnancy.
HCG is excreted in the urine and high levels act as confirmation of pregnancy.

Pregnancy tests make use of the fact that antibodies will be manufactured by the immune system that bind to the large HCG molecules.
This then causes the HCG molecules to bind together and produce a visible change in the test apparatus.

The most common pregnancy test involves a dipstick. This is basically a strip of absorbent material (the wick) on a plastic backing, impregnated with antibodies.

The application area is dipped into a sample of early morning urine, which moves up the wick.
As it moves up, HCG in the urine binds to HCG antibodies (which are combined with coloured latex beads) built into the test kit.

This combination of HCG, antibodies and beads progresses up the wick to an area containing immobilised HCG antibodies.
Here the HCG/antibody complex becomes concentrated, and the beads form a coloured band visible through a plastic window.

This represents a positive result.

There is a second window which confirms that the test is actually working properly.
Beneath this window is a third row of antibodies which will combine with the antibodies attached to the coloured beads if no HCG is present.

So a negative pregnancy test should still show a result, that is, a coloured band but in a different window.

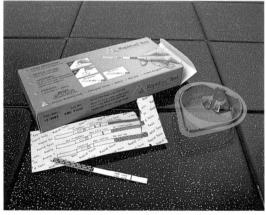
Commercial pregnancy testing kit

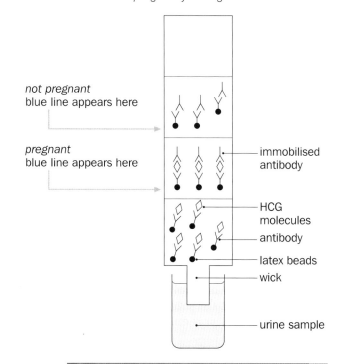

not pregnant
blue line appears here

pregnant
blue line appears here

immobilised antibody

HCG molecules

antibody

latex beads

wick

urine sample

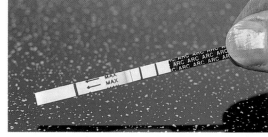
Test stick showing a positive result

276

▶ Biology at work: Meningitis

In November 1999, the UK government launched its official **meningitis** vaccination programme, first targeting 15–17 year olds and then babies. Public concern over the increasing incidence of the disease and associated deaths in these age ranges led to this move.

What is meningitis?

Meningitis is an infection of the brain's membranes (**meninges**) caused by both viruses and bacteria. Viral infection is most common but is rarely life-threatening – most people make a full recovery.

There are two types of bacterial meningitis: meningococcal and pneumonococcal, the former being most common.

One in 20 people who contract bacterial meningitis die and one in seven are left with a permanent disability, including brain damage.

It is now the biggest killer of children under the age of 4.

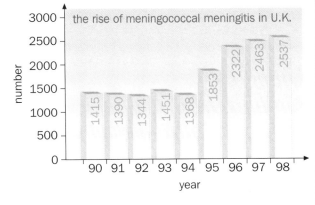

How is it caught?

The disease is cyclic and peaks in incidence occur every 10–15 years.

In 1999, the incidence of over 2500 cases was the highest for over 50 years.

Airborne droplets spread the disease and it can be transmitted through coughing, sneezing and kissing. Once breathed in, the bacteria colonise the tissues lining the nose and throat and rarely invade further.

What are the symptoms?

Most people have a natural resistance to meningococcal meningitis: at any one time, about 5,000,000 people in the UK may be carriers. There are, however, small risks of complications arising from the symptoms, which develop within 2–10 days of contact:

- raised temperature,
- headache,
- aches and pains,
- vomiting.

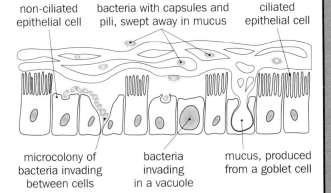

Bacteria on the epithelial surface of the nose or throat membranes. Their presence is natural; it is when they invade non-ciliated cells or are phagocytosed that symptoms occur.

Many of these are similar to other common infections, which is a problem since delays in diagnosis can prove fatal once symptoms specific to meningitis emerge.

Bacterial invasion of the mucosal linings in the respiratory tract and eventual passage into the bloodstream leads to capillary leakage and the characteristic red spots that do not fade under pressure when a drinking glass is applied. Once in the blood of the meninges, bacteria pass into the cerebro-spinal fluid, causing inflammation, which then irritates nerve endings. This leads to the reaction to bright light, and muscle spasms that cause a stiff neck. Swelling of the brain causes headaches, vomiting, drowsiness and eventual coma, seizure and death. The polysaccharide **capsule** on the outer surface of the bacterium enhances its **pathogenicity**. This has the effect of neutralising the host's non-specific and specific immune responses.

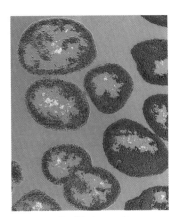

SEM meningitis bacteria (×18 000)

Summary

- White blood cells (leucocytes) defend the body against pathogens.
- Bacterial growth can be affected by temperature, pH, oxygen and nutrients.
- Certain safety precautions should be taken and aseptic techniques used when working with microorganisms.
- The growth of bacteria can be monitored by a number of methods, including the use of a haemocytometer, dilution plating or turbidimetry.
- The ability of bacteria to produce disease is affected by pathogenicity, infectivity and invasiveness.
- Viruses are intracellular parasites that cause disease by damaging the host cells that they invade and producing toxins as they invade cells and reproduce.
- AIDS is caused by human immunodeficiency virus (HIV), which attacks the body's immune system.
- Our bodies provide physical, mechanical, chemical and biological defence against microorganisms.
- An immune response is the way in which the body responds to invasion by a specific pathogen or antigen.
- Antibodies bind to specific antigens forming an antibody–antigen complex.
- Cell-mediated immunity involves the activities of T-lymphocytes and macrophages.
- Antibody-mediated immunity involves the production of B-lymphocytes, which are activated by antigens that become attached to the macrophage membrane.
- Active immunity may be triggered naturally or artificially. Passive immunity occurs when a person receives ready-made antibodies from someone else.
- Vaccines can be made from killed virulent organisms, live non-virulent strains, modified toxins, isolated antigens or genetically engineered antigens.
- Antibiotics are chemicals produced by microorganisms, which, at low concentrations, can destroy pathogens.
- There is an increasing tendency for bacteria to become resistant to antibiotics as the result of random mutations.

► Questions

1 For each of the following infectious diseases, describe the method of transmission, the symptoms of the disease and the methods by which the incidence of the disease can be reduced:
   a) influenza,
   b) *Salmonella* food poisoning,
   c) AIDS.

2 a) i) Describe how influenza is transmitted from one person to another.
      ii) Suggest one reason why epidemics of influenza, such as the one in 1999/2000, tend to be more common in the winter.
   b) The incidence of influenza and the death rate from it vary considerably from year to year.
      i) In one year the death rate from influenza in the United States was 0.3 per 100 000. The population of the United States is about 250 million.
         How many people died from influenza in the United States in this year?
      ii) Every few years, major outbreaks of influenza occur as a result of the emergence of a new variety of the influenza virus. Explain how a new variety causes a major outbreak.
   c) Describe how viruses such as influenza virus cause the signs and symptoms of disease.

3 The diagram shows some of the events that occur when a particular virus infects a cell in the human body.
   a) Describe how viral proteins are produced within the infected cell.
   b) Describe how the activated T-lymphocytes respond to the viral infection and prevent further spread of the virus.
   c) Explain why a particular type of virus activates only the receptors on the surface of specific T-lymphocytes.

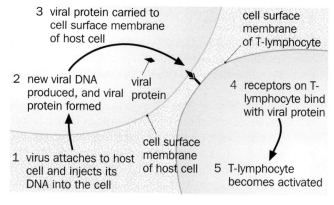

3 viral protein carried to cell surface membrane of host cell

cell surface membrane of T-lymphocyte

2 new viral DNA produced, and viral protein formed

viral protein

4 receptors on T-lymphocyte bind with viral protein

1 virus attaches to host cell and injects its DNA into the cell

cell surface membrane of host cell

5 T-lymphocyte becomes activated

4 a) Describe two ways in which healthy human skin protects the body against invading pathogens.
   b) The body has two ways of protecting itself from invading pathogens once they have entered — antibody-mediated immunity and cell-mediated immunity.

278

i) Name one group of microorganisms against which:
   1) antibody-mediated immunity is most effective,
   2) cell-mediated immunity is most effective.
ii) In each case, name the cell that is activated first in response to a pathogen to which the body is constantly exposed and state the response of each cell type to the pathogen.

5 The graph shows the response of a person to the use of a live vaccine.
a) i) Explain why the response to the secondary injection was much greater than the response to the primary injection.
    ii) Suggest why a 'booster' injection of the vaccine may need to be given every few years.
b) i) Give one example of a live vaccine.
    ii) Describe briefly how a live vaccine may be produced.
    iii) Suggest one possible risk of using a live vaccine.

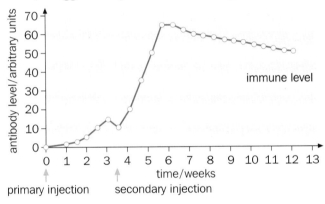

6 a) Give three factors that may determine the ability of bacteria to produce disease in the body.
b) Give two ways in which antibiotics affect the functioning of bacteria.
c) Explain one way in which antibiotic-resistant strains of bacteria counteract the effects of antibiotics.
d) Scientists researching ways of dealing with antibiotic-resistant bacteria have found that certain carbohydrates are effective against bacteria that infect epithelial cells lining the throat and lungs. These carbohydrates work by competing with the bacteria for receptor sites on the membranes of the epithelial cells.
   Suggest what is meant by 'competing for receptor sites'.

7 a) i) Draw a simple labelled diagram to show the main features of a virus.
    ii) State one way in which viruses differ from all other groups of microorganisms.

b) HIV (human immunodeficiency virus) can reproduce within human helper T-lymphocytes. The graph shows three phases in the relationship between the concentration of HIV in blood plasma helper T-lymphocytes in an affected individual.
   i) Use the information in the graph to describe fully the relationship between helper T-lymphocytes and HIV:
      1) during phase I,
      2) during phase II,
      3) during phase III.
   ii) Suggest a full explanation for:
      1) the initial rise in HIV during phase I,
      2) the initial fall in helper T-lymphocytes during phase I.
   iii) Suggest one function of B-lymphocytes during phase I.

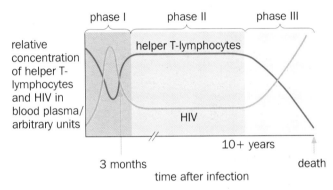

8 The graph shows the primary and secondary immune response when a child is vaccinated.
a) The vertical axis on the graph is labelled 'immune response'.
   Suggest what might have been measured to reflect this.
b) One difference between the result of the two vaccinations is that the peak height of the second immune response is much higher than the first. Give a full biological explanation for this observation.
c) Describe two other differences between the results of the first and second vaccination.

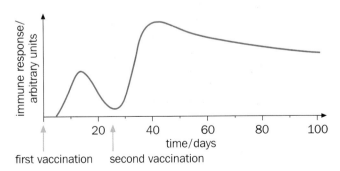

► Diet and health

1 The table below gives data about changes in energy intake from food eaten in the home over a period of 20 years from 1970 to 1990 in the United Kingdom. The figures show the mean intake per person per day.

Intake	Year				
	1970	1975	1980	1985	1990
Total energy/kJ	10 750	9620	9370	8480	7860
Total fat/g	119	107	106	96	86
Saturated fatty acids/g	52.6	51.7	46.8	40.6	34.5
Proportion of total energy derived from – fat – saturated fatty acids (%)	42 19	42 20	43 19	43 18	42 17

a) Comment on the figures for total energy and their relationship to fat in the food intake. [3]

b) i) Calculate the percentage change in total energy from 1970 to 1990. Show your working. [2]

   ii) Suggest *two* reasons for the change in energy intake during the period shown. [2]

c) The Government recommendation in the United Kingdom is that not more than 35% of energy should be derived from fat and that saturated fatty acids should not provide more than 11%. Suggest changes which could be made to the diet shown in the table to help meet these recommendations. [2]

d) Give *two* reasons why it is recommended that fresh fruit be used as snacks instead of chocolate or biscuits. [2]

(*London*) **[11]**

2 The tables below are nutrition information labels from cartons of skimmed and whole milk.

Skimmed milk

Nutrition	Typical values	
	per 100 ml (3½ oz)	per 500 ml
Energy	3.5 k calories 145 k joules	175 k calories 725 k joules
Protein	3.4 g	17.0 g
Carbohydrate	5.0 g	25.0 g
Total fat	0.1 g	0.5 g
Vitamins/minerals: % of recommended daily amount		
Thiamin (vitamin B_1)	3.0%	15%
Riboflavin (vitamin B_2)	11.2%	56%
Vitamin B_{12}	10.0%	50%
Calcium	24.4%	122%

Whole milk

Nutrition information		
Typical values	per 100 ml (3.5 fl oz)	per 500 ml
Energy	68 k calories	340 k calories
	284 k joules	1420 k joules
Protein	3.3 g	16.5 g
Carbohydrate	4.7 g	23.5 g
sugars	4.7 g	23.5 g
starch	0.0 g	0.0 g
Fat	4.0 g	20.0 g
saturates	2.5	12.5 g
monounsaturates	1.1 g	5.5 g
polyunsaturates	0.1 g	0.5 g
Fibre	0.0 g	0.0 g
Sodium	less than 0.1 g	0.3 g
Vitamins/minerals: % of recommended daily amount		
Vitamin A	7.0%	36%
Riboflavin (B_2)	11.0%	56%
Niacin	4.0%	21.0%
Vitamin B_{12}	32.0%	160%
Calcium	15.0%	74.0%

a) Calculate the percentage change in energy content when whole milk is converted into skimmed milk. [2]

b) Give *two* reasons why it may be considered better for a person's health to drink skimmed milk instead of whole milk. [2]

c) Suggest why no vitamin A (retinol) is recorded in the nutritional information for skimmed milk. [1]

d) Suggest *one* reason for the difference in the calcium content of skimmed milk and whole milk. [1]

(*London*) **[6]**

3 The table below refers to features of certain vitamins. Copy the table. If a feature is correct place a tick (✓) in the appropriate box and if the feature is not correct, place a cross (✗) in the appropriate box.

Feature	Vitamin A	Vitamin B
Fat soluble		
Present in wheatgerm		
Present in green vegetables		
Promotes collagen formation		
Can be synthesised from carotene in the intestine		

[5]

(*London*) **[5]**

4 Vitamin C is a water-soluble vitamin which is found in foods of plant origin. It is unstable and easily destroyed. An investigation was carried out into the effects of boiling on the vitamin C content of some vegetables. The vitamin C content of each of the vegetables was determined in their raw state and after boiling. The results are shown in the table below.

Vegetable	Vitamin C content/mg per 100 g		Percentage loss in vitamin C
	In raw vegetables	In boiled vegetables	
Cabbage	49	20	?
Fresh peas	24	16	33
Green beans	18	10	44

a) Calculate the percentage loss of vitamin C for boiled cabbage. Show your working. [2]

b) (i) Describe how the vitamin C content of the fresh vegetables could be determined. [4]

  ii) State *three* precautions which would need to be taken when carrying out the investigation you described in b)(i). [3]

c) Suggest *two* ways, other than boiling, in which vitamin C may be lost from fresh fruit and vegetables. [2]

(London) [11]

5 It is thought that the intake of salt (sodium chloride) in the human diet has an effect on blood pressure. An investigation was carried out into the effect of different intakes of sodium in the form of sodium chloride on the systolic blood pressure of different groups of people. Communities from developed and developing countries were investigated separately. Data were collected from three different age groups in each of the communities studied. The results are shown in the graphs below.

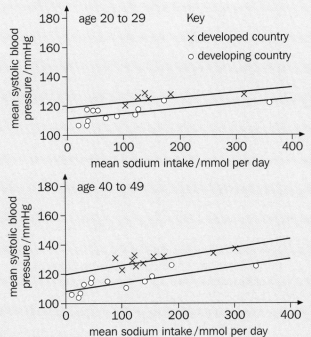

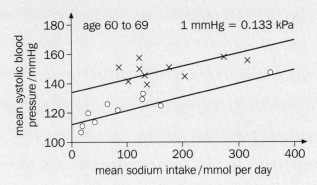

a) i) Compare the data shown in the graphs for people from developed and from developing countries for each of these age groups. [4]

  ii) Suggest *two* reasons for the differences in the data for developed and developing countries. [2]

b) i) Increased blood pressure is a risk factor for coronary heart disease. Describe the effects of constriction of the coronary arteries. [3]

  ii) Give *two* factors in the diet, other than sodium intake, that are risk factors for coronary heart disease. [2]

(London) [11]

▶ **Exercise and health**

6 a) The table below shows the results of an investigation into the effects of five minutes standard exercise on the pulse rate of four men who were of the same age and mass.

Individual	Pulse rate / beats per minute	
	Resting	Immediately after exercise
John	64	82
David	70	105
Anthony	78	135
Neil	68	98

  i) Calculate the mean percentage increase in pulse rate for these men. Show your working. [2]

  ii) Explain why it is an advantage for the pulse rate to increase during exercise. [2]

b) John plays football regularly. His resting pulse rate is lower than that of the other men and increases only by 28% after five minutes standard exercise. His blood pressure is lower than that of the other men.

  i) Explain how regular exercise has brought about these effects. [3]

  ii) Explain why John has a lower risk of developing cardiovascular disease. [1]

(NEAB) [8]

Further questions on human health and disease

7 The table below shows measurements taken from two men, both 45 years of age, on attendance at a health clinic.

Measurement	Man A	Man B
Height / cm	175	160
Body mass / kg	65	83
Systolic blood pressure / mm Hg	130	162
Diastolic blood pressure / mm Hg	87	106
Plasma cholesterol / mg 100 cm^{-3}	207	241

a) Explain briefly how blood pressure measurements are taken using a sphygmomanometer. [3]
b) What broad conclusions can you draw from the measurements given in the table? [2]
c) From the table, it appears that one of the men is more likely to develop cardiovascular problems than is the other. What advice should this man be offered to enable him to improve his cardiovascular health?

[3]
(O&C) **[8]**

8 The breathing movements of an athlete were recorded before, during and after a two minute period of strenuous exercise. The breathing movements were recorded by means of a stethograph, which monitors chest movements. The graph below shows the recording over a seven-minute period. The exercise period was during the third and fourth minutes.

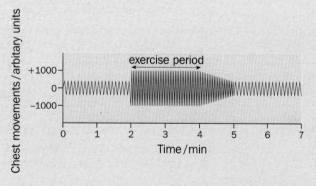

a) Describe the changes in chest movements which occurred with the onset of exercise. [2]
b) Explain the chest movements during the minute following the exercise period. [2]
(NICCEA) **[4]**

9 Chronic bronchitis is more common in the United Kingdom than in any other country in the world.
a) Describe *two* risk factors that could account for the high incidence of chronic bronchitis in the United Kingdom. [2]

b) i) Explain how chronic bronchitis affects the efficiency of breathing. [3]
   ii) The bronchioles (air passages) in the lungs have muscle cells in their walls. The cells are stimulated to contract by acetylcholine produced by nerve endings. The acetylcholine molecules fit into protein receptors on the muscle cell membranes.
   Anticholinergic drugs have molecules that fit the same receptors. Explain how these drugs may be useful in the treatment of chronic bronchitis. [3]
(NEAB) **[8]**

▶ Infectious diseases and immunity

10 a) *Bacillus subtilis* is a bacterium commonly used in laboratory investigations. In the space below, draw the shape of this bacterium. [1]
b) Give *three* environmental factors which could influence the growth of microorganisms. Explain the effect of each. One example is given for you.
Factor: oxygen
Explanation: This is required for use in respiration to provide energy for growth. [3]
(NEAB) **[4]**

11 a) A student investigated the growth of a culture by counting the number of cells in samples removed at hourly intervals. Each sample was prepared for counting in a standard way. A haemocytometer was used to count the number of cells. The results are shown in the graphs below.

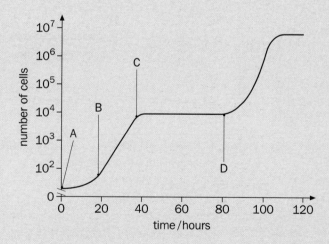

i) Explain the shape of the curve between the following.
A and B ; B and C ; C and D ; [3]
ii) Suggest why the population increased at point D. [1]

b) One haemocytometer observation taken during the experiment is shown in the diagram below.

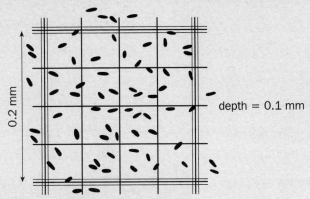

0.2 mm

depth = 0.1 mm

Calculate the number of bacteria in 1 cm³ of the sample. Show your working. [3]

c) Suggest why the use of dilution plating would give a lower estimate of the number of bacteria present, compared with counting with a haemocytometer. [1]

(*NEAB*) **[8]**

12 a) State the meaning of each of the following terms, which are applied to large scale fermentation processes.
  i) Batch culture [2]
  ii) Continuous culture [2]
 b) i) Give *one* example of a process using *each* type of culture. [2]
  ii) What factors might determine whether an industrialist should employ a batch rather than a continuous culture process? [4]

(*O&C*) **[10]**

13 a) In the United Kingdom, vaccination against the following diseases is available through the National Health Service during the first few years of life: measles; mumps; tetanus; whooping cough (pertussis); polio; rubella; diphtheria; meningitis (Hib);
  i) Give *three* diseases against which children may be vaccinated during the first six months by a single injection, containing all three vaccines. [1]
  ii) At what age is the MMR (measles, mumps and rubella) vaccination usually given? [1]
 b) Outline the vaccination schedule against tuberculosis in the United Kingdom. [2]
 c) The table below shows the results of a number of surveys (A, B, C and D) into the vaccination of children against whooping cough.

	A	B	C	D
Percentage of children vaccinated	55	75	85	95
Number of cases of disease	560	325	74	0

  i) Use the information in the table to explain the effectiveness of vaccination in preventing an epidemic of whooping cough. [2]
  ii) Suggest *one* reason why parents may choose not to have their children vaccinated against whooping cough. [1]

(*NEAB*) **[7]**

14 The diagram below shows an antibody molecule.

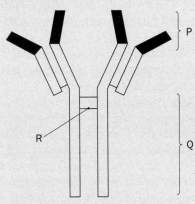

P

R

Q

 a) i) Name the region labelled P and state its function. [2]
  ii) Name the region labelled Q and state its function. [2]
  iii) Name the type of bond labelled R. [1]
 b) Shortly after a microorganism, such as a bacterium or a fungus, enters the human body for the first time, the blood contains many different antibody molecules, each produced by a different group of cells. This is known as a polyclonal response.
  i) Name the type of cells that produce antibodies and releases them into the blood. [1]
  ii) Explain why different groups of cells respond to an infection by a bacterium or a fungus to give a polyclonal response. [3]

(*Camb*) **[9]**

15 a) Antibiotics, antiseptics and disinfectants are all used to help prevent the spread of human disease. For each of the following situations, which is the most appropriate type of substance to use? Explain your choice.
  i) Cleaning a graze on the skin caused by fall on gravel. [2]
  ii) Treating an internal fungal infection. [2]
 b) Interferons are chemicals, produced in the body, which give protection against a specific group of microorganisms.
  i) Which group of organisms do interferons give protection against? [1]
  ii) How do interferons limit the spread of these microorganisms? [1]

(*NEAB*) **[6]**

16 Respiration

One of the great mountaineering mysteries of all time neared its resolution with the remarkable discovery of George Mallory's body on Mount Everest. On 8th June 1924, Mallory and his partner, Andrew Irvine, disappeared whilst attempting to be the first climbers to reach the summit. Mallory's perfectly preserved body was located on the upper slopes on 1st May 1999 and shows that he fell and died whilst descending. The fate of Irvine and whether the two actually reached the summit before perishing remains a mystery.

So how did an experienced climber like Mallory fall?
The majority of fatalities, which involve falls above 8000 metres, are indirectly attributable to a lack of oxygen and its effects on the brain. Near the summit, climbing is limited by the maximum oxygen consumption rate, which is low. The brain's capacity to think clearly and make simple judgements is then limited. A momentary lapse in concentration can lead to a stumble resulting in a fatal fall.

North face of Everest from Base Camp, 1924

▶ The need for energy

Living organisms need a constant source of energy to drive the metabolic reactions that take place inside their cells. These metabolic reactions include the following.

- **Movement.**
Energy is needed for various types of movement in cells, including
– movement of cilia and flagella,
– muscle contraction,
– movement of chromosomes in cell division.

- **Maintaining a constant body temperature**.
Endotherms, which include mammals and birds, need heat energy to keep their body temperature stable and so provide the optimum internal environment for their enzymes to function.

- **Anabolic processes.**
These are the processes in which large, complex molecules are built from smaller, simple molecules.
This *synthesis* involves an input of energy since new chemical bonds have to be made within the molecule.
Examples of anabolic processes include the synthesis of polysaccharides from sugars, synthesis of proteins from amino acids and DNA replication.

Mallory and Irvine prepare to leave Camp V on 6th June, 1924

- **Active transport.**
Energy is needed to move some molecules and ions across the cell surface membrane against a concentration gradient.

- **Bioluminescence.**
Some organisms are able to convert chemical energy into light.
Examples include 'glow worms', some phytoplankton and some bacteria.

- **Secretion.**
The packaging and transport of secretory products into vesicles in cells such as those in the pancreas requires energy.

Bioluminescence in Astronesthes, *a deep water fish*

▶ Cellular respiration

All living cells and organisms get their energy from respiration.
This usually involves the oxidation of glucose to release energy
and produce carbon dioxide and water.
It is important not to confuse respiration with gas exchange.
Let's remind ourselves of the difference.

> **Gas exchange is the diffusion of gases into and out of cells,
> which allows respiration to take place.**

So gas exchange involves taking oxygen in for respiration and
then removing the carbon dioxide produced during the process.

> **Respiration is a series of oxidation reactions taking
> place inside living cells, which results in the release of
> energy from organic compounds such as glucose.**

Autotrophs are able to make complex organic molecules, using
an energy source such as sunlight, during photosynthesis.
The sunlight energy is transformed into chemical bond energy,
which is stored in molecules such as carbohydrates, fats and proteins.
These energy-rich molecules are called **respiratory substrates**,
since they can be broken down in respiration.

Most living organisms respire **aerobically**, using oxygen which
releases a relatively large amount of energy.

> **Aerobic respiration is respiration that uses oxygen.**

Some organisms respire **anaerobically**.
They do not use oxygen to carry out respiration.

> **Anaerobic respiration occurs in the absence of oxygen.**

Some anaerobic cells switch to aerobic respiration if oxygen becomes
available, because aerobic respiration releases far more energy.
However, there are some species of bacteria that carry out only
anaerobic respiration and are actually poisoned by the presence of
oxygen. These are called **obligate anaerobes.**

▶ Releasing energy

The chemical bond energy in your food could be released
by combustion (burning).
The glucose would be converted to carbon dioxide and water
but the energy would be released in an uncontrolled way and
the increase in temperature would be fatal for living cells.

Respiration involves the gradual release of energy in small steps,
rather than the rapid release of energy all at once.
The glucose is broken down in a step-by-step manner, with the
controlled release of small amounts of energy at each stage.
It is these reactions that provide the energy to make a molecule
called **adenosine triphosphate**, or **ATP**.
When a molecule of glucose is respired aerobically, it releases
enough energy to make 38 molecules of ATP.

$$C_6H_{12}O_6 + 6O_2 \longrightarrow 6CO_2 + 6H_2O + 38 \text{ ATPs}$$

Gas exchange increases with exercise

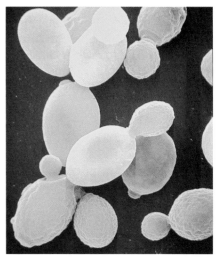
*These yeast cells can respire aerobically
or anaerobically*

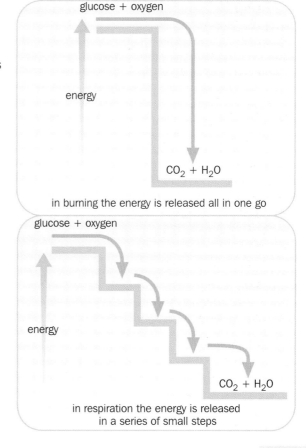

glucose + oxygen

energy

$CO_2 + H_2O$

in burning the energy is released all in one go

glucose + oxygen

energy

$CO_2 + H_2O$

*in respiration the energy is released
in a series of small steps*

▶ The role of ATP

ATP is the short-term energy store of the cell.
It is often called the 'energy currency' since it picks up energy
from food in respiration and passes it on to power cell processes.

If you look at the diagram you can see that ATP is made up of

- a base (adenine),
- a pentose sugar (ribose),
- three phosphate groups.

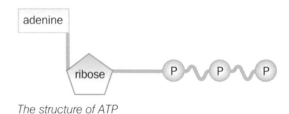

The structure of ATP

The three phosphate groups are joined together by two **high energy bonds**.
ATP can be hydrolysed to release a large amount of energy.
When hydrolysed, ATP produces **adenosine diphosphate** (**ADP**) and phosphate (Pi).
The hydrolysis of ATP to ADP is catalysed by the enzyme ATPase.
The third phosphate group is removed from ATP releasing 30 kJ mol^{-1} of free energy.
This energy is used to drive reactions within the cell, such as active transport.

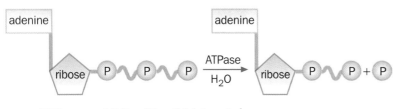

$$ATP \longrightarrow ADP + Pi + 30 \text{ kJ mol}^{-1}$$

The hydrolysis of ATP

It is also possible to remove the second phosphate group from ADP
by breaking another high energy bond.
The hydrolysis of ADP to **adenosine monophosphate** (**AMP**)
releases a similar amount of energy.

AMP and ADP can be converted back into ATP by the addition of
phosphate molecules.
Since the hydrolysis of ATP is **exergonic** (energy is released),
the production of ATP must be **endergonic** (energy is used up).

The production of ATP is called **phosphorylation**.
This can take place in two main forms.

- **Photophosphorylation**, takes place on the membranes of the
  chloroplasts during photosynthesis.
- **Oxidative phosphorylation**, takes place on the membranes
  of the mitochondria during aerobic respiration.

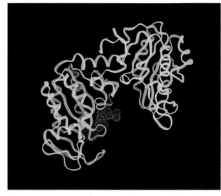

*Computer simulation of an ATP molecule
bound to an enzyme*

Just as 30 kJ mol^{-1} of energy are released when ATP is hydrolysed,
so 30 kJ mol^{-1} of energy are needed to add each phosphate molecule
to make ATP.
This energy is released from various enzyme-controlled reactions at
different stages of aerobic respiration.

ATP is the universal energy carrier, but it cannot be transported from
cell to cell.
It has to be used inside the cell in which it has been made.

▶ Stages in aerobic respiration

There are four main stages in the breakdown of glucose during aerobic respiration:

- **glycolysis**,
- **the link reaction**,
- **Krebs cycle**,
- **electron transport chain**.

▶ Glycolysis

Glycolysis is the splitting (**lysis**) of glucose. It takes place in a number of enzyme-controlled reactions, starting with the breakdown of the six-carbon glucose molecule into two molecules of **pyruvate** (3C).
The process yields little energy since most is still 'locked up' in the molecules of pyruvate.

Glycolysis takes place in the cytoplasm of cells.
Glycolysis does not need oxygen.
It is the first stage of aerobic respiration and is, in fact, the **only** stage of anaerobic respiration.

- Initially, the glucose is phosphorylated to make **glucose phosphate** (6C).
The phosphate comes from a molecule of ATP.
(Glucose does not react easily, so the ATP raises its energy level, making the subsequent reactions easier.)

- Glucose phosphate is then phosphorylated to **fructose bisphosphate** (6C) using up another ATP.

- Fructose bisphosphate (6C) splits into two molecules of **glycerate-3-phosphate** (3C)

- The glycerate-3-phosphate (3C) is converted to pyruvate (3C).
Hydrogen is removed and transferred to the hydrogen acceptor **NAD** (**nicotinamide adenine dinucleotide**). Enough energy is released at this stage to make two molecules of ATP.

Important: Since **two** molecules of glycerate-3-phosphate are formed, there will be two molecules of $NADH_2$ formed and $2 \times 2 =$ four molecules of ATP.

So from one molecule of glucose, glycolysis produces the following:

- two molecules of ATP (four ATPs are produced but two ATPs are used up),

- two molecules of $NADH_2$ (reduced hydrogen acceptor),

- two molecules of pyruvate, which enter the link reaction in aerobic respiration.

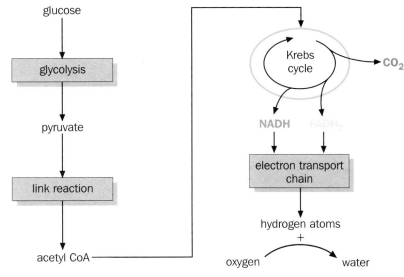

Summary of aerobic respiration

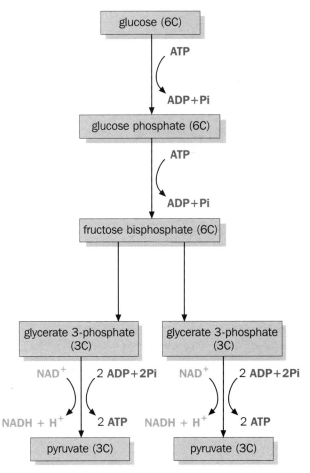

two molecules of pyruvate are produced from each molecule of glucose

Glycolysis

▶ The link reaction

The link reaction links glycolysis to Krebs cycle, the next stage of aerobic respiration. It is sometimes treated as part of Krebs cycle.

- Pyruvate (3C) enters the matrix of the mitochondria from the cytoplasm.
- In the presence of oxygen, three things happen:
  1. The pyruvate is **decarboxylated** (a molecule of carbon dioxide is removed).
  2. The pyruvate is also **dehydrogenated** (hydrogen is removed).
     The hydrogen is transferred to the hydrogen acceptor NAD^+ to form $NADH + H^+$.
  3. The resulting **acetate** (2C) combines with coenzyme A (CoA) to form the two-carbon molecule **acetyl coenzyme A**, which then enters Krebs cycle.

The overall reaction is

$$pyruvate + CoA + NAD^+ \longrightarrow acetyl\ CoA + CO_2 + NADH + H^+$$

- Since **two** molecules of pyruvate are formed from each glucose molecule, there will be also be **two** acetyl coenzyme A molecules formed.

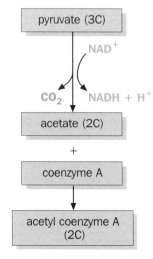

The link reaction

▶ Krebs cycle

This series of reactions was discovered by Sir Hans Krebs in 1937. It is also known as the **citric acid cycle** or the **tricarboxylic acid cycle (TCA cycle)**.
Krebs cycle takes place in the matrix of the mitochondria and includes the following reactions.

- Acetyl coenzyme A (2C) combines with a four-carbon compound (**oxaloacetate**) to form a six-carbon compound (**citrate**).

- A series of reactions take place where the citrate (6C) is both decarboxylated and dehydrogenated.

Carbon dioxide is released as a waste product and the hydrogen atoms are picked up by hydrogen acceptors NAD and **FAD (flavine adenine dinucleotide)**.

- As a result, oxaloacetate (4C) is regenerated to combine with more acetyl coenzyme A.
- So after **one** turn of the Krebs cycle, we have:
  - three molecules of NADH,
  - one molecule of $FADH_2$,
  - one molecule of ATP,
  - two molecules of CO_2.

But don't forget that two molecules of acetyl coenzyme A enter Krebs cycle for each molecule of glucose.
So the cycle turns **twice** for each glucose molecule, so giving $6 \times NADH$, $2 \times FADH_2$, $2 \times ATP$ and $4 \times CO_2$.

The most important role of Krebs cycle is to provide hydrogen that can be used in the **electron transport chain** to provide energy for the formation of ATP.

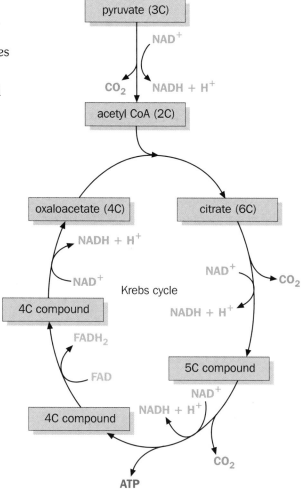

Krebs cycle

▶ The electron transport chain

The electron transport chain provides the means by which the energy from the hydrogen atoms removed from compounds in Krebs cycle, glycolysis and the link reaction can be used to make ATP.

Oxygen is required for this final stage of aerobic respiration. The reactions take place on the inner membrane of the mitochondria.

The electron transport chain involves a chain of carrier molecules along which hydrogen atoms and electrons are passed.

- The hydrogen atoms are passed on to other carrier molecules from the hydrogen carriers reduced NADH and $FADH_2$.
- NADH is the first carrier in the chain.
  It passes its hydrogen on to FAD.
- The hydrogen atoms split into hydrogen ions (H^+) and electrons.

The electrons are transferred along a series of **electron carriers**. The hydrogen ions stay in solution in the space between the inner and outer membranes of the mitochondria.

- Finally the electrons recombine with the hydrogen ions to form hydrogen atoms and are passed on to oxygen to form water. Oxygen is therefore the final electron acceptor, the reaction being catalysed by the enzyme **cytochrome oxidase**.
- The transfer of electrons along the chain releases sufficient energy to make ATP from ADP and Pi.

If you look at the diagram, you can see that this occurs at three points along the chain.
So for each NADH entering the chain, three ATP molecules are made. You should remember that reduced FAD is also produced by Krebs cycle. This can enter the chain at stage 2 but in this case only two ATP molecules will be generated.

- The formation of ATP in this way is called **oxidative phosphorylation**.

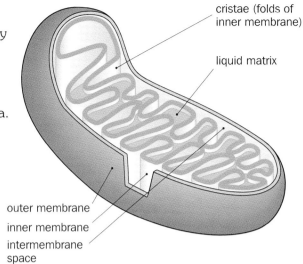

cristae (folds of inner membrane)

liquid matrix

outer membrane
inner membrane
intermembrane space

Three dimensional structure of a mitochondrion

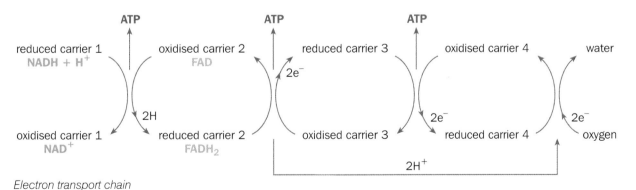

Electron transport chain

Stage	Site in cell	Number of ATPs made
glycolysis	cytoplasm	two (four made, two used) per glucose
link reaction	matrix of mitochondrion	none
Krebs cycle	matrix of mitochondrion	two (one per turn) per glucose
Electron transport chain	inner membrane of mitochondrion	34 per glucose

289

▶ Chemiosmotic theory

In Chapter 2 we looked at the detailed structure of the mitochondrion.

Do you remember that it has a double membrane and that the inner membrane is folded to form cristae?

These cristae give the inner membrane a large surface area, so there is more room for electron carriers and ATP formation.

The cristae are lined with stalked granules.

These stalked granules contain **ATP synthetase** enzymes.

The **chemiosmotic theory** provides a model to explain the synthesis of ATP in oxidative phosphorylation.

- The energy released by the electron transport chain is linked to pumping hydrogen ions from the matrix into the space between the two membranes of the mitochondrion.
- This results in a higher concentration of hydrogen ions in the intermembrane space than in the matrix of the mitochondrion: an electrochemical gradient is set up.
- The hydrogen ions pass back into the matrix through the stalked granules, along the electrochemical gradient.
  As they do so, their electrical potential energy is used to make ATP from ADP and Pi.
  ATP synthetase catalyses the reaction.

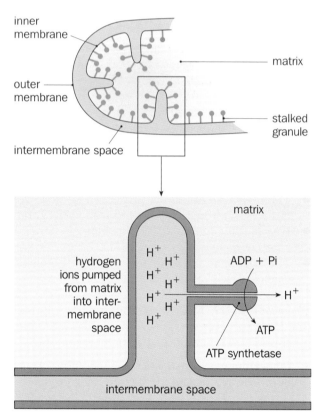

hydrogen ions diffuse back into matrix through stalked granules and their energy is used to make ATP

Part of a mitochondrion

▶ ATP balance sheet

How many ATP molecules are made from each glucose molecule?

First, let's count the number of ATP molecules made *directly*.

Glycolysis makes two ATPs (four made but two used up).
Krebs cycle makes two ATPs (one per turn).
Total = four ATPs.

Now let's see how many NADH and FADH₂ molecules are made

Glycolysis makes two NADH.
Link reaction makes two NADH.
Krebs cycle makes six NADH (three per turn) and two FADH₂ (one per turn)
Total = ten NADH and two FADH₂

You know that each NADH can produce three ATP molecules, so that gives $10 \times 3 = 30$ ATPs.
You know that each FADH₂ can make two ATP molecules, so that gives $2 \times 2 = 4$ ATPs.
Now add on the ATPs made directly in glycolysis and Krebs cycle = 4 ATPs.

So that gives a grand total of 38 molecules of ATP produced from each glucose molecule.

So you can see that most ATP is made in the electron transport chain by oxidative phosphorylation.

▶ Anaerobic respiration

Anaerobic respiration is respiration in the absence of oxygen. Some organisms carry out aerobic respiration if oxygen is available but are able to change to anaerobic respiration in its absence. Most **anaerobes** fall into this category, but there are some bacteria, such as *Clostridium welchii*, which causes gangrene, that thrive in the absence of oxygen. These are called obligate anaerobes.

In the absence of oxygen, only glycolysis can operate. As a result, the energy yield in anaerobic respiration is low and the pyruvate is converted into waste products.

Fermentation

This type of anaerobic respiration takes place in **yeast**.

The pyruvate is converted to **ethanol** and carbon dioxide. The problem is, where does the hydrogen, passed on to NAD in glycolysis, go to?
As you can see in the diagram, it is used to reduce ethanal to ethanol.

> glucose ⟶ ethanol + carbon dioxide + 2ATP

Each ATP molecule can release about 60 kJ mol^{-1} if it is broken down to AMP, so this is pretty small compared to the 2880 kJ mol^{-1} produced in the aerobic respiration of one glucose molecule.

It represents an efficiency of $\frac{60}{2880} \times 100 = 2\%$

The ethanol becomes toxic to the yeast if it accumulates. Ethanol cannot be broken down to yield any additional energy.

Lactate formation in muscle

As you know, if, during vigorous exercise, we can't get enough oxygen to our muscles, the muscle cells can revert to anaerobic respiration.
In this case, glycolysis again takes place, but the pyruvate is converted into lactate instead of ethanol.
The reduced NAD made in glycolysis again passes its hydrogen on to pyruvate, this time reducing it to lactate.

> glucose ⟶ lactate + 2ATP

Again, the efficiency of energy release is low at about 2%.

The build-up of lactate in the muscle causes fatigue and cramp. When oxygen becomes available again, the lactate is broken down.
First, it is carried in the bloodstream to the liver where it is converted back to pyruvate.
About one-fifth is used to release energy in aerobic respiration and the rest is converted into glycogen.
The oxygen required to break down the lactate is called the **oxygen debt**.
At the end of the activity, the oxygen debt is repaid by continuous deep and rapid breathing.

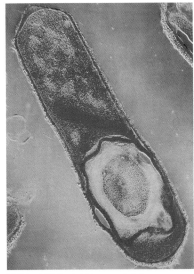

TEM of Chlostridium welchii

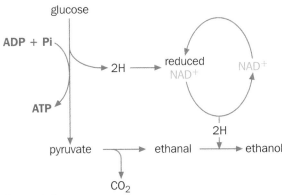

Fermentation

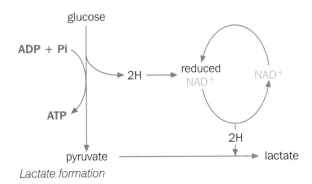

Lactate formation

▶ Other respiratory substrates

Glucose is not the only substance that can be oxidised to release energy in cells. Other organic molecules can also be used as respiratory substrates to produce ATP, in certain circumstances.

Lipids

Fats provide a store of energy in the body which can be drawn upon when carbohydrate levels are low.

- First, the fats are hydrolysed to fatty acids and glycerol.
- The fatty acids are broken down in the matrix of the mitochondria to form two-carbon acetyl fragments that combine with coenzyme A to form acetyl coenzyme A. This then enters Krebs cycle.
- The glycerol is phosphorylated and converted into glyceraldehyde 3-phosphate. This compound is an intermediate in glycolysis and so can enter the pathway and subsequently be broken down in Krebs cycle.

The oxidation of fats produces large amounts of hydrogen ions, as each triglyceride consists of one molecule of glycerol and three fatty acids molecules. These hydrogen ions can be picked up by hydrogen carriers and used in the electron transport chain to make ATP.
In fact, 1 gram of fat releases more than twice as much energy as 1 gram of carbohydrate.

Protein

Protein is another potential respiratory substrate, but is only used in cases of starvation.

- First, the protein is hydrolysed to its constituent amino acids.
- The amino acids are **deaminated** in the liver, with the removal of the amine (NH_2) group from the rest of the molecule.
- This leaves an organic acid that can be fed into Krebs cycle and respired.

A malnourished woman and child collecting spilt grain in Thiekthou during a famine in Sudan

▶ Respiratory quotient

The **respiratory quotient** (**RQ**) is the ratio of carbon dioxide given off to oxygen used up during respiration.

$$RQ = \frac{CO_2 \text{ given off}}{O_2 \text{ used up}}$$

The respiratory quotient gives information about the type of organic molecule being respired.

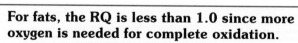

For carbohydrates, the RQ is 1.0	For fats, the RQ is less than 1.0 since more oxygen is needed for complete oxidation.
$C_6H_{12}O_6 + 6O_2 \longrightarrow 6CO_2 + 6H_2O$ $RQ = \dfrac{6CO_2}{6O_2} = 1.0$	$C_{18}H_{36}O_2 + 26O_2 \longrightarrow 18CO_2 + 18H_2O$ $RQ = \dfrac{18CO_2}{26O_2} = 0.7$

Proteins have an RQ of between 0.8 and 0.9.
In practice, living organisms respire more than one type of substrate, so results for RQ can vary.
Also, substrates are not always fully oxidised.

▶ Respirometers

A simple respirometer can be used to measure the RQ of germinating seeds or even small animals such as woodlice and mealworms.
A respirometer measures the changes in gas pressure inside the apparatus.

- Potassium hydroxide solution is placed in the left-hand tube.
  Potassium hydroxide absorbs carbon dioxide.
- An equal volume of water is placed in the right-hand tube to ensure that the barometric pressure in each tube is equal.
- A wire basket containing the living organisms is positioned inside the left-hand tube.
- Both tubes are then placed in a water bath at 20 °C with the taps open.
- The taps are then closed and the apparatus is left for 15 minutes.
- As the organisms respire, they take up oxygen from the air in the apparatus and give out carbon dioxide.

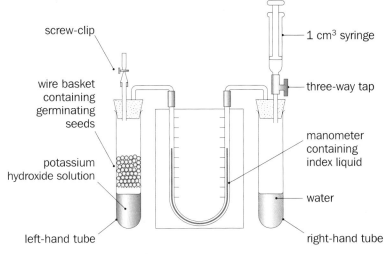

A simple respirometer

The carbon dioxide is absorbed by the potassium hydroxide solution, causing the gas pressure in the left-hand tube to fall. The fluid in the left-hand limb of the manometer rises as a result.

- The rise in the fluid is recorded after 15 minutes.
  Provided that the internal diameter of the manometer is known, how could you calculate the volume of oxygen used up by the organisms?
- The potassium hydroxide is then removed from the left-hand tube and replaced with water. The experiment is repeated and any increase or decrease in the gas volume is recorded.
  This gives a measure of the amount of carbon dioxide produced.
- If the volume of carbon dioxide produced is the same as the volume of oxygen absorbed, then there will be no change in the levels of liquid in the manometer.
- However, if more carbon dioxide is produced than oxygen used up, the level of liquid in the left-hand tube will fall.

Worked example

Uptake of oxygen = 0.50 cm³ (as measured in the first experiment, when potassium hydroxide is present in the apparatus).
Carbon dioxide produced – oxygen absorbed = 0.25 cm³
(as measured in the second experiment when water is present).
Total carbon dioxide produced = 0.25 + 0.50 = 0.75 cm³.

$$RQ = \frac{\text{carbon dioxide produced}}{\text{oxygen absorbed}}$$

$$RQ = \frac{0.75}{0.50}$$

$$= 1.50$$

▶ Biology at work: Brewing

The basic techniques involved in brewing are centuries old.
Alcoholic fermentation is carried out by yeast and relies
upon anaerobic conditions inside the fermenter.
The most common form of yeast to be used is *Saccharomyces
cerivisiae*, though *Saccharomyces carlsbergensis* is used in
the production of lager.

Over time, the most desirable yeast strains have been
selected.
These can now be improved by the use of genetic
engineering to produce more alcohol.

The initial source of carbohydrate in brewing is barley,
although the yeast cannot digest the starch until the barley
has been **malted** and **mashed.**
These processes allow the starch to be digested into simple
sugars by enzymes found in the sprouting barley.
Hops are also added for flavour and a sugary liquid called
wort is created.
It is this liquid that undergoes fermentation.

Yeast is added to the wort and uses maltase enzymes
to break down maltose into glucose.
Initially the yeast grows aerobically, using oxygen from
the air that cools the wort.
However, this oxygen is soon used up and anaerobic
fermentation begins.

In the absence of oxygen the yeast uses the glucose as its
substrate in glycolysis, resulting in the formation of ethanol.
When the yeast has used up all the available carbohydrate,
fermatation ceases and the beer is removed.

This is the so-called **batch culture process**.
To brew more beer in the same fermenter, a new wort and
batch of yeast must be added.
Continuous culture has been attempted with brewing
but although it saves time, it yields a poorer quality
product.

Downstream processing of beer to improve the product
involves clarification to give a clear liquid, conditioning
(storage) to allow the natural removal of unpleasant
tasting compounds, and pasteurisation to remove bacteria.

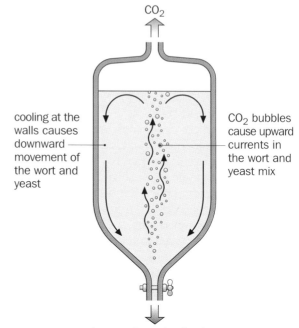

CO_2

cooling at the walls causes downward movement of the wort and yeast

CO_2 bubbles cause upward currents in the wort and yeast mix

beer and yeast collection

A modern beer fermenter

Hops being added in 'coppers' to make wort

Cask conditioning – part of the downstream process

▶ Biology at work: Biofuels

Biofuels are literally fuels that are biological in origin.
They exist in a variety of forms, for example
alcohol, methane gas, and oil substitutes such as biodiesel.
Biofuel production often involves making use of 'waste'
biomass.
In other words, using the considerable energy locked up in
plant and animal material that is neither fully digested
nor assimilated in food chains.

Biogas (principally methane) is used on a small scale
to power generators in many parts of the developing world.
Cattle dung is digested by anaerobic bacteria in
underground vessels, producing a roughly 60:40 mix of
methane and carbon dioxide.
When the CO_2 is removed, the methane is a clean and
efficient fuel that can be used for both heat and power.
The need to remove CO_2 and the relatively slow gas
production are two drawbacks to this process.

In some parts of the world, fermentation of carbohydrate-
rich crops, such as sugar cane, is used to produce ethanol,
which can then be used as a petrol substitute in cars.
It has the advantage of being far less polluting.
As with brewing, the fermentation of sugar cane involves
yeast respiring the sugars under anaerobic conditions to
produce ethanol.

The drawback to ethanol production becoming a worldwide
biofuel is the need to pre-treat the tough cellulose found in
much 'waste' biomass before it can be fermented.

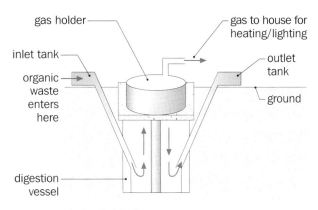

A simple biodigester

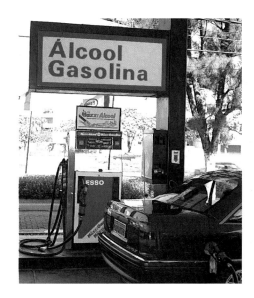

Biodiesel is an oil substitute manufactured from oil
seed rape.
300 kg of oil can be extracted from 1 tonne of rape
and then converted into **rape methyl ester** (**RME**).
Although currently around 90% of rape seed oil is used
in the food industry, biodiesel represents an attractive
biofuel owing to the absence of oxides of sulphur and
the low emissions of particulates, both of which are
major drawbacks with diesel of petroleum origin.

Fuels using the energy in biomass may play an
important role in replacing finite fossil fuels, as well as
being less polluting to the environment.

Oil seed rape is the basic raw material for the production of
biodiesel

295

Summary

- Respiration is a series of oxidation reactions taking place inside living cells, which results in the release of energy from organic compounds such as glucose.
- Aerobic respiration takes place in the presence of oxygen; anaerobic respiration takes place in the absence of oxygen.
- Respiration releases energy to drive the metabolic activities that take place in cells.
- ATP is the short-term energy store in the cell, made from ADP and Pi by phosphorylation.
- Glycolysis involves the splitting of glucose and the conversion of glycerate-3-phosphate to pyruvate, with the production of ATP and NADH.
- The link reaction involves the conversion of pyruvate to acetyl coenzyme A, which enters Krebs cycle.
- Krebs cycle is a series of reactions that results in the formation of NADH, FADH$_2$, ATP and CO$_2$.
- The electron transport chain converts the energy in NADH and FADH$_2$ into molecules of ATP.
- The chemiosmotic theory involves proton pumps and the formation of ATP by ATP synthetase.
- Anaerobic respiration involves the conversion of pyruvate to ethanol or to lactate. In either case, the amount of energy released is far less than in aerobic respiration.
- Lipids and proteins can also be respired; lipids release far more energy than carbohydrates do.
- Respiratory quotient (RQ) is the amount of carbon dioxide released divided by the amount of oxygen used up. RQ can be measured using a respirometer.

▶ Questions

1 Copy and complete the following account of aerobic respiration.
   The first stage in the breakdown of glucose is a process called ...., which takes place in the........... of the cell and eventually results in the production of two molecules of .... from each molecule of glucose. In most organisms, this product enters the stage of respiration called .... cycle. This cycle occurs in ...... conditions inside organelles called .... During these two stages, hydrogen atoms are removed from the substrate and passed on to coenzymes such as ... and ....The final stage of the process is called the .... and involves the formation of energy-rich molecules of ....

2 ATP can be used as a temporary energy store and supplies energy to cells for a number of processes. During aerobic respiration, ATP is mainly produced in the mitochondria.
   a) What is the term given to the production of ATP in respiration?
   b) Draw a simple diagram to show the structure of ATP.
   c) Describe how ATP is used in processes within cells.

3 Describe the roles of each of the following in Krebs cycle and in the electron transport chain:
   a) coenzyme A,
   b) NAD$^+$,
   c) oxygen,
   d) ADP.

4 Copy and complete the table putting a tick (✓) if the statement i) to iii) applies to the process or a cross (✗) if it does not apply.

	Glycolysis	Krebs cycle	Oxidative phosphorylation
i) produces ATP			
ii) involves the production of carbon dioxide			
iii) occurs in mitochondrion			

5 The diagram shows the structure of a mitochondrion.

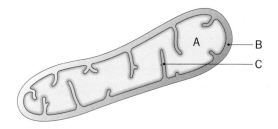

   a) Name the parts of the organelle indicated by the letters A, B and C.
   b) Describe where in the mitochondrion
      i) the electron transport chain is found,
      ii) the reactions of Krebs cycle occur.
   c) List the products formed in Krebs cycle.
   d) By what process do hydrogen ions flow out of space B into space A?

6 The diagram below represents an outline of stages in aerobic respiration.

a) Name the compounds represented by P, Q, R and S.

b) Which letter represents the stage at which most ATP is produced?

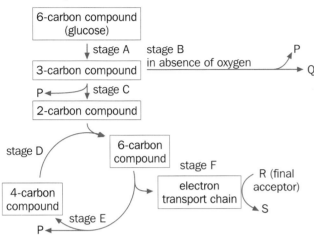

c) Which two letters represent separate stages where ATP is not produced?

d) Indicate the nature of the reactions in stage F.

7 The diagram shows the series of reactions that take place in Krebs cycle.

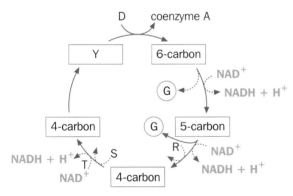

a) Where exactly in the cell do these reactions take place?

b) Give the general name for reactions such as T.

c) Name the compounds labelled D and G.

d) Write down the equations for the reactions labelled R and S.

How many carbon atoms are found in compound Y?

Describe the role of NADH + H$^+$ in respiration.

8 a) In the process of glycolysis, the formation of pyruvate involves this reaction:

$NAD^+ + 2H = NADH + H^+$

What happens to the NADH in

i) an animal cell respiring anaerobically,

ii) a yeast cell respiring anaerobically?

b) Compare aerobic and anaerobic respiration in terms of energy release.

9 a) What is meant by the term respiratory quotient, RQ?

b) What can you conclude about the respiratory substrates that produce the following RQs:

i) 0.7

ii) 1.0

iii) 0.9?

c) Describe in detail, how you would use a respirometer to obtain the RQ of castor oil seeds.

10 The diagram below shows apparatus that can be used to measure the rate of anaerobic respiration in yeast cells. The tube contains a yeast suspension in 1% glucose solution and a redox indicator†. The pyrogallol solution absorbs oxygen.

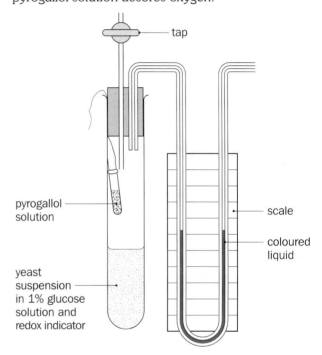

a) i) Name *one* suitable redox indicator which could be used in this experiment.
[1]

ii) Give *one* change you would expect to observe during the experiment as the yeast respires and give a reason for your answer.
[2]

b) Describe how you could use the apparatus to investigate the effect of temperature on anaerobic respiration of glucose by yeast.
[3]

(London) **[6]**

† *An artificial hydrogen acceptor can be used as a redox indicator to indicate progress of oxidation-reduction (redox) reactions.*

▶ Producing superweeds

Scientists have predicted that the increased levels of CO_2 in the atmosphere will result in greater crop yields, because crop plants will be able to convert more CO_2 into carbohydrate during photosynthesis. Some plant physiologists have predicted lush plant growth resulting from the beneficial conditions for photosynthesis.

However, other scientists have been examining the possible effect of increased CO_2 levels on the growth of weeds.

As global warming increases, weeds could become a growing menace to farmers. The effectiveness of glyphosphate, a widely used weedkiller, is being reduced by increased levels of atmospheric carbon dioxide. Subjecting different types of weed to doses of glyphosphate under current atmospheric CO_2 levels resulted in the herbicide stopping weed growth. However, in a CO_2-rich atmosphere, some weeds were able to resist the herbicide.

These weeds were 'C_3' plants whose biochemical pathways become far more efficient if more CO_2 becomes available.

With CO_2 levels expected to double in the next 50 years, it may be that farmers will have to find alternative ways of controlling weeds other than chemical herbicides.

Spraying with chemical herbicides may become a thing of the past

▶ Autotrophic nutrition

Autotrophic nutrition is about making your own food.

Autotrophs are able to use a source of energy to make complex organic molecules from inorganic raw materials. In effect, the energy from the source is transferred into chemical bond energy in organic foodstuffs.

Chemoautotrophs (mainly bacteria) are able to harness the energy released in exergonic chemical reactions to synthesise their organic food.

Photoautotrophs, which include green plants and algae, are able to use light energy to synthesise their own organic materials.

The overall equation for photosynthesis is as follows:

$$\textbf{carbon dioxide} + \textbf{water} \xrightarrow{\text{light energy}} \textbf{glucose} + \textbf{oxygen}$$

$$\mathbf{6CO_2 + 6H_2O} \xrightarrow{\text{light energy}} \mathbf{C_6H_{12}O_6 + 6O_2}$$

The raw materials for photosynthesis are carbon dioxide, water and light energy. If you look at the reaction, do you think photosynthesis is an exergonic or an endergonic reaction? Does it involve reduction or oxidation? The simple equation conceals the fact that photosynthesis is, in fact, a series of complex biochemical pathways, catalysed by specific enzymes. The two main stages are:

- **The light-dependent stage involving the photoactivation of chlorophyll and the transfer of energy to produce ATP and NADPH.**
- **The light-independent stage involving the fixation of carbon dioxide and the use of ATP and reduced NADPH to convert it into carbohydrate.**

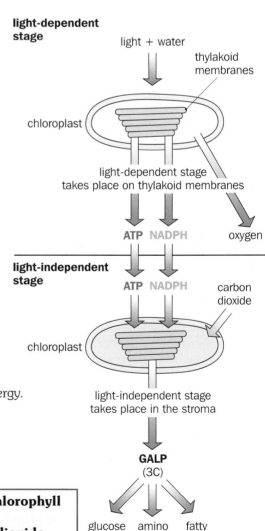

light-dependent stage

light + water

thylakoid membranes

chloroplast

light-dependent stage takes place on thylakoid membranes

ATP NADPH oxygen

light-independent stage

ATP NADPH carbon dioxide

chloroplast

light-independent stage takes place in the stroma

GALP (3C)

glucose amino acids fatty acids

▶ The site of photosynthesis

We looked at the structure of a leaf in Chapter 10 and the detailed structure of a leaf palisade cell and a chloroplast in Chapter 2.
Look at the diagram to remind yourself of the exact site of photosynthesis.

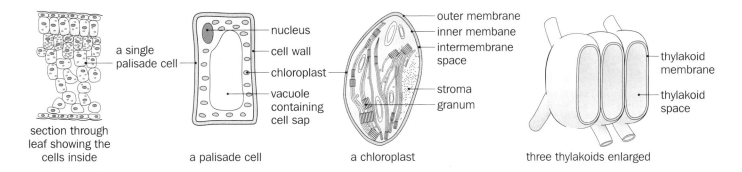

section through leaf showing the cells inside

a palisade cell

a chloroplast

three thylakoids enlarged

- **The reactions of the light-dependent stage of photosynthesis take place on and across the thylakoid membranes of the chloroplast.**
- **The reactions of the light-independent stage of photosynthesis take place in the stroma of the chloroplast.**

Detecting the site of photosynthesis

As long ago as 1883, the German botanist T. W. Engelmann was able to demonstrate the site of photosynthesis in cells.
He carried out an ingenious series of experiments using a filamentous green alga.
In each of these giant cells there is a ribbon-like chloroplast with a spiral shape.

Engelmann used the fact that oxygen is given off during photosynthesis to identify the site of the reactions.
He used the motile, oxygen-sensitive bacterium, *Pseudomonas*, which tends to cluster around areas where oxygen concentration is highest.
When the alga was put on a slide and illuminated, the bacteria were seen to cluster around the edge of the cells close to the chloroplast.

Further work was done using this same technique.
This time, the alga was illuminated with light of different wavelengths.
Engelmann noticed that the bacteria clustered in greatest concentration near to the chloroplasts when wavelengths of 450 nm (blue) and 650 nm (red) were used.
These wavelengths resulted in increased photosynthesis, which produced more oxygen and so attracted more of the *Pseudomonas* bacteria.

It has since been shown that green plants photosynthesise most rapidly when illuminated with blue and red light.

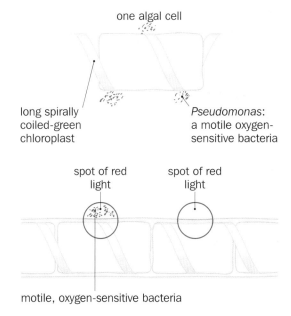

one algal cell

long spirally coiled-green chloroplast

Pseudomonas: a motile oxygen-sensitive bacteria

spot of red light

spot of red light

motile, oxygen-sensitive bacteria

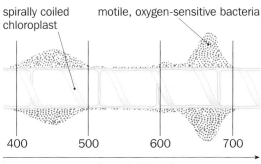

spirally coiled chloroplast

motile, oxygen-sensitive bacteria

wavelength of light /nm

Engelmann's experiments on the part played by chlorophyll in photosynthesis

▶ Photosynthetic pigments

Different wavelengths of light are trapped by different photosynthetic pigments.
There are two main groups of photosynthetic pigments in green plants: the **chlorophylls** and the **carotenoids**.

There are a number of different forms of chlorophyll, with **chlorophyll *a*** and **chlorophyll *b*** being the most common. The chlorophylls absorb light in the blue–violet and the red parts of the spectrum.

Why do you think that green plants look green?
It's because they reflect green light instead of absorbing it.

All chlorophylls have a complex ring structure with a long hydrocarbon tail.
Can you see the magnesium atom at the centre of the molecule?
Plants look yellow when they are short of magnesium because they cannot produce enough chlorophyll. This condition is called **chlorosis**.

The structure of chlorophyll should remind you of haemoglobin, another molecule with a ring structure.
Can you remember which metal is at the centre of the ring in a molecule of haemoglobin?

The carotenoids are often referred to as **accessory pigments**.
They include **carotene** and **xanthophyll**, and they absorb light from the the blue–violet part of the spectrum.

The **absorption spectrum** is a graph that shows how much light a particular pigment absorbs at each wavelength.
Can you see from the graph that the photosynthetic pigments absorb light mainly from the blue–violet and red parts of the spectrum?

The **action spectrum** is a graph that shows the rate of photosynthesis at different wavelengths of light.

Can you see that the action spectrum of photosynthesis corresponds closely to the absorption spectrum of the chlorophylls and carotenoids?

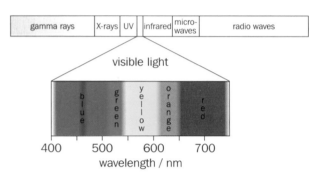

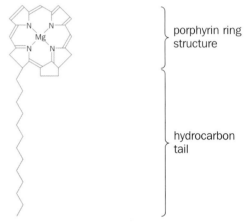

The shape of a chlorophyll molecule

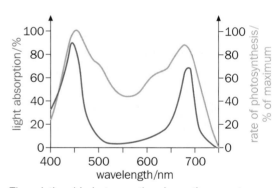

The relationship between the absorption spectrum and the action spectrum (green line)

▶ Separating photosynthetic pigments

Photosynthetic pigments can be separated by **chromatography**.

- First, the pigments are extracted by grinding up a leaf, using a pestle and mortar, with a solvent such as propanone.
- The extract is then 'spotted' onto the origin line of a piece of chromatography paper.
- The chromatogram is placed into a glass tank containing a solvent.
- The solvent gradually rises up the chromatography paper and the different pigments separate out depending upon their relative solubility in the solvent and their adhesion to the chromatography paper.
- When the solvent front comes close to the top, the paper is taken out and dried.
- The Rf value for each pigment can then be worked out, and the pigment can be identified. Work out the Rf value of each pigment.

$$Rf\ value = \frac{distance\ travelled\ by\ pigment}{distance\ travelled\ by\ solvent\ front}$$

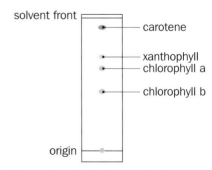

Separation of plant pigments by chromatography

▶ Harvesting light

The chlorophylls and the accessory pigments
are found in the thylakoid membranes of the chloroplast.
They are grouped in clusters of several hundred molecules.
Each group is called an **antenna complex**.

Within each antenna complex, there are special proteins which
help the pigment molecules to pass absorbed light energy
from one molecule to the next.
So photons of light are transferred through the antenna complex
until they reach molecules of chlorophyll *a* in the **reaction centre**.

There are *two* types of reaction centre:

Photosystem I is arranged around a chlorophyll *a* molecule
with an absorption peak of 700 nm.
So the reaction centre of photosystem I is called **P700**.

Photosystem II is arranged around a chlorophyll *a* molecule
with an absorption peak of 680 nm.
This reaction centre is called **P680**.

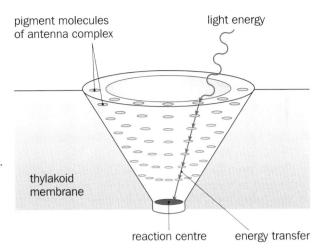

A single antenna complex

▶ Light-dependent stage of photosynthesis

The reactions of the 'light stage' of photosynthesis take place in
the thylakoids of the chloroplast.
They involve:

- The synthesis of ATP from ADP and Pi.
  Remember that this is called **phosphorylation**.
  In this case it is called **photophosphorylation**,
  as light energy is involved.

- The splitting of water molecules by **photolysis**
  to produce hydrogen ions and electrons.

The hydrogen ions are picked up by the carrier molecule **NADP**
(nicotinamide adenine dinucleotide phosphate).
The addition of a hydrogen ion reduces $NADP^+$ to $NADPH + H^+$.

So the products of the light-dependent stage are ATP and NADPH
and these molecules are needed for the light-independent stage.

There are two different ways in which ATP can be synthesised by
photophosphorylation:

- **non-cyclic photophosphorylation,**
- **cyclic photophosphorylation.**

Bioluminescence of chlorophyll

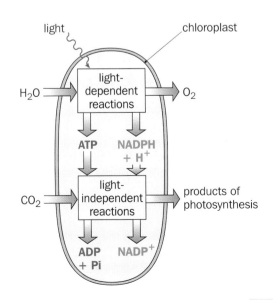

▶ Non-cyclic photophosphorylation

Non-cyclic photophosphorylation involves both photosystem I and photosystem II.
Can you see from the diagram, why the pattern of electron flow in non-cyclic photophosphorylation is often referred to as the **Z-scheme**?

- Light is absorbed by photosystem II and passed on to chlorophyll *a* (P680).
- The irradiated chlorophyll *a* (P680) molecule emits two electrons.
  These energised electrons are raised to a higher energy level and are picked up by an electron acceptor.
- The electron acceptor passes the electrons along a chain of **electron carriers** to photosystem I.
  The energy released from the electrons is used to make ATP from ADP and Pi.
- Light is absorbed by photosystem I and passed on to chlorophyll *a* (P700).
  It emits two electrons.
- The energised electrons rise to a higher energy level and are picked up by a second electron acceptor.
- Since both chlorophylls (P680 and P700) have now lost electrons, they will both be positive and unstable.
- The two electrons released from the chlorophyll *a* (P680) of photosystem II go to replace the two that have been lost by chlorophyll *a* (P700) of photosystem I.
- P680 of photosystem II receives its replacement electrons from the splitting of water (**photolysis**).
- During photolysis, the water molecule dissociates into electrons, hydrogen ions and oxygen. As we have said, the electrons go to photosystem II. The oxygen is released as a waste gas.
- The hydrogen ions combine with electrons held by the second electron acceptor to give NADPH.
  This passes to the reactions of the light-independent stage.
- So the products of the light-dependent stage are NADPH, ATP and waste oxygen gas.

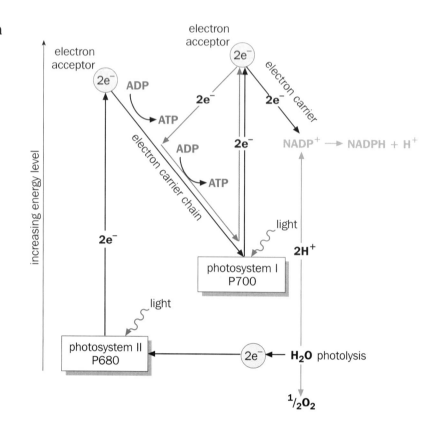

▶ Cyclic photophosphorylation

Cyclic photophosphorylation involves photosystem I only.
Light is absorbed by photosystem I and passed on to chlorophyll *a* (P700).
This causes the chlorophyll *a* molecule to emit an electron.
This 'energised' electron is raised to a higher energy level and is picked up by an **electron acceptor**.
The electron is then passed along a chain of **electron carriers** before it is returned to the chlorophyll *a* molecule (P700).
As the electron passes along the electron carrier chain, enough energy is released to make ATP from ADP and Pi.
This ATP is needed for the light-independent stage.
No NADPH is made during cyclic photophosphorylation.

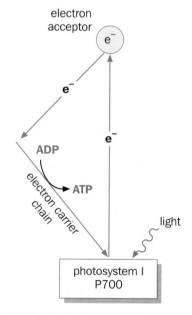

Cyclic photophosphorylation

302

▶ Chemiosmosis in the chloroplast

As you have seen, the reactions of the light-dependent stage of photosynthesis take place in the thylakoid membranes of the chloroplast.

In the 'Z-scheme', electrons flow along the chains of electron carriers from photosystem II and photosystem I.
As they do so, they provide energy to pump hydrogen ions from the stroma, across the thylakoid membrane, into the thylakoid space.
This sets up an electrochemical and a concentration gradient, since there are more hydrogen ions inside the thylakoid space than there are outside in the stroma.
Hydrogen ions diffuse along this gradient out across the thylakoid membrane through protein channels.
This drives the formation of ATP by **ATP synthetase**.
This process is very similar to the formation of ATP that we came across in respiration in Chapter 16.

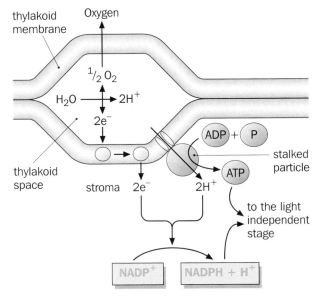

ATP production in the chloroplast by chemiosmosis

▶ The light-independent stage

This cyclic pathway is sometimes called the **Calvin cycle**.
The diagram shows a simplified version of the cycle. In reality there are many enzyme-controlled reactions involved.
The important stages are:

● Carbon dioxide combines with a five-carbon compound, **ribulose bisphosphate (RuBP)**.

The reaction is catalysed by the enzyme **RuBP carboxylase**, the most common enzyme in the world.

● The product is an unstable six-carbon compound that breaks down to form two molecules of three-carbon **glycerate 3-phosphate (GP)**.
● ATP is used to phosphorylate the two molecules of GP to form two molecules of three-carbon **glycerate biphosphate**.
● The next stage involves the use of NADPH to reduce each molecule of glycerate biphosphate to **glyceraldehyde 3-phosphate (GALP)**.
● For every six molecules of GALP formed, five are used in a series of reactions to regenerate ribulose bisphosphate, which can then combine with more carbon dioxide.
● One of the six GALP molecules is converted to glucose and other carbohydrates, amino acids and lipids.

Can you see where the products of the light-dependent stage (ATP and NADPH) are used in the light-independent stage?

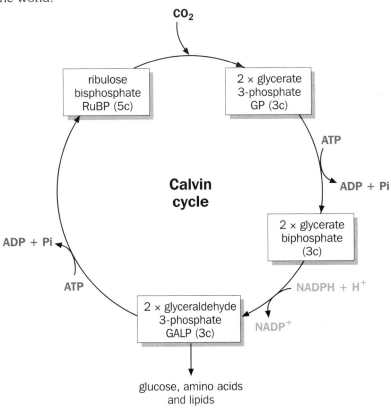

▶ The use of isotopes

The Hill reaction

$$6CO_2 + 6H_2O \xrightarrow{\text{light energy}} C_6H_{12}O_6 + 6O_2$$

How do we know that the oxygen released in photosynthesis actually comes from the water molecule and not from the carbon dioxide?
In 1939, the British biochemist Robert Hill showed that isolated chloroplasts give off oxygen in the presence of a hydrogen acceptor.

Then, in 1941, he placed cells of the green alga *Chlorella* into water containing the heavy isotope ^{18}O.
(^{18}O is an isotope of oxygen with a mass number of 18 rather than 16.)
By using a mass spectrometer, he was able to show that the oxygen given off in photosynthesis was the isotope ^{18}O, which must have come from the water.

$$CO_2 + H_2{}^{18}O \longrightarrow (CH_2O) + {}^{18}O_2$$

When Hill repeated the experiment with carbon dioxide containing the heavy ^{18}O instead, the oxygen given off was 'normal' ^{16}O, so confirming his earlier results.
The splitting of water or photolysis is sometimes called the **Hill Reaction**.

A scientist working with a mass spectrometer

The Calvin cycle

The events of the light-independent stage of photosynthesis are also known as the **Calvin cycle**, after the American biochemist Melvin Calvin.
In the 1940s he was able to make use of the newly available radioactive isotope of carbon, ^{14}C (normal form is ^{12}C).

Calvin grew cultures of the unicellular alga *Chlorella* in flat glass containers called 'lollipops'.
He exposed *Chlorella* to carbon dioxide labelled with the radioactive isotope $^{14}CO_2$, for varying periods of time.
They were then killed by dropping them into hot methanol.
The products of photosynthesis were extracted and separated by two-way chromatography.
X-ray film, which is sensitive to $^{14}CO_2$, was then placed over the chromatograms, and left to develop for a few days.
When the X-rays were developed, the radioactive compounds showed up as a patterns of dark spots on the sheets.
This technique is known as **autoradiography**.
The radioactive spots were cut out and analysed to identify the compounds present.
The first product formed was **glycerate 3-phosphate**.

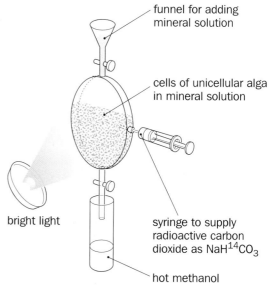

funnel for adding mineral solution

cells of unicellular alga in mineral solution

bright light

syringe to supply radioactive carbon dioxide as $NaH^{14}CO_3$

hot methanol

Calvin's 'lollipop' apparatus

The table shows the subsequent compounds that were formed after further periods of time.

The technique enabled Calvin to piece together a pathway showing the reactions that take place in the light-independent stage.

Substances in Chlorella extract labelled with radioactive carbon after different periods of photosynthesis in the presence of $^{14}CO_2$

Time of exposure to light after isotope added/s	Substances containing ^{14}C
5	glycerate 3-phosphate (GP)
15	GP, hexose phosphates
60	GP, hexose phosphates, sucrose, amino acids
300	GP, hexose phosphates, sucrose, starch, amino acids, proteins, lipids

▶ Measuring the rate of photosynthesis

There are a number of ways of measuring the **rate** of photosynthesis.
If you look at the equation for photosynthesis, you can get some ideas.

$$\text{carbon dioxide} + \text{water} \xrightarrow{\text{light energy}} \text{glucose} + \text{oxygen}$$

You could find out how fast photosynthesis is taking place by measuring

- the rate at which carbon dioxide is used up,
- the rate at which glucose is produced,
- the rate at which oxygen is produced.

The most convenient method is collecting the bubbles of gas given off
by pondweed over a given time and then measuring the total volume of
gas produced. This can be done accurately using an apparatus known
as a **photosynthometer**.

- A piece of well illuminated Canadian pondweed (*Elodea*), about 10 cm
  long, is cut underwater and fixed into the flared end of the capillary tube.
- Depending upon which environmental variable you decide to investigate,
  you need to make sure the other factors are kept constant.

For instance, if you are investigating the effect of light intensity
on the rate of photosynthesis, it is important to keep
- the concentration of carbon dioxide in the water in
  the boiling tube constant,
- the temperature of the water in the water bath constant.

- The apparatus is flooded with water and a bench lamp placed
  at various distances away from the plant in order to change the
  light intensity.
- Bubbles of gas collect in the flared end of the capillary tube and
  are collected for a set time (usually 5 minutes).
- After this time, the gas collected can be drawn into the capillary tube
  by gently pulling the plunger on the syringe, and the volume measured.
- The light intensity is inversely proportional to the distance of the lamp
  from the plant, $I \alpha \dfrac{1}{d^2}$ (where I is the light intensity and d is the distance
  between the light source and the plant).
- After taking readings of the length of the bubble collected from the
  plant when the lamp is at different distances away, you can draw a graph
  showing the amount of gas produced per unit time against light intensity.

The variables that you can investigate using this technique include
light intensity, temperature, carbon dioxide concentration and
light quality (wavelength).

How would you vary the temperature, CO_2 concentration, and light quality?

The graph shows the effect of increasing light intensity on the rate of
photosynthesis. As you can see, the rate increases with increasing
light intensity but only up to a certain point.
At this point, the **law of limiting factors** means that one of the **other** factors,
such as CO_2 or temperature, must be limiting the rate of photosynthesis .
This factor must be increased if the rate of photosynthesis is to increase further.

> **When a process (for example photosynthesis) is influenced by
> several factors, the rate at which the process proceeds
> is determined by the factor in shortest supply.**

. . . . . *101, 102, 103*

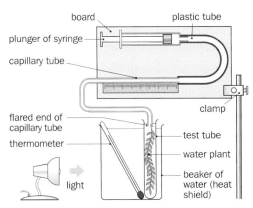

*A photosynthometer set up to measure the
effects of light intensity on photosynthetic rate*

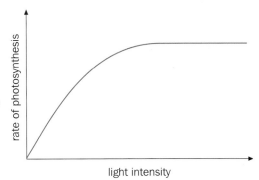

*The relationship between light intensity and
photosynthetic rate*

▶ Biology at work: Manipulating photosynthesis

To obtain the best possible yield from a crop, a grower needs photosynthesis to proceed at its maximum rate. The rate of photosynthesis is limited by three key factors: **light** in terms of both **intensity** and **wavelength**, **temperature** and the **carbon dioxide concentration.**

Manipulating these so-called **limiting factors** is only really feasible in a glasshouse situation.
Artificial lighting can be used when natural light intensity is low, although in the summer months, even in the UK, the natural light intensity is often above 10,000 lux, which is the maximum useable intensity for photosynthesis.

Carbon dioxide is often a limiting factor for crop growth because the atmospheric level of 0.03% is lower than the optimum for photosynthesis.
Over long periods, the optimum CO_2 level is around 0.1%.
An increase in CO_2 levels in a glasshouse can be achieved by burning high-quality fuel like paraffin.
Paraffin burns without producing unwanted fumes and it also increases the temperature at the same time.

The importance of temperature is related to the fact that photosynthesis is an enzyme-controlled process.
If other factors are not limiting then a 10 °C rise in temperature (within the range 10–35 °C) will lead to a doubling of the rate of photosynthesis.
A temperature of around 25 °C is often quoted as an optimum for photosynthesis.
Paraffin heaters, for example, can provide this environment in winter but in summer additional heating is rarely required.

Glasshouse cultivation can provide increased yields and 'out of season' crops.
However, it is not simply a matter of increasing light, heat and CO_2 levels indefinitely.
For example, very intense light can damage chloroplasts, and CO_2 levels of 0.5% over long periods can cause stomatal closure.
Therefore glasshouses require adequate shading and ventilation systems to ensure that the potential limiting factors are maintained at an **optimal** level.

In large-scale commercial operations, these parameters can be closely monitored and controlled by computer.
Close control is important because the cost of manipulating the environment must not outweigh the potential increase in profit.

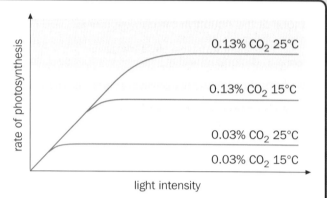

The effect of light intensity on photosynthetic rate at different carbon dioxide concentrations and at different temperatures

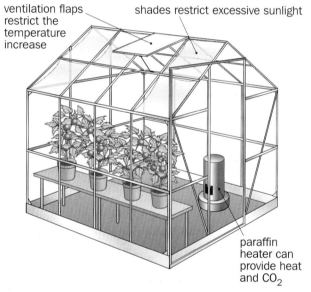

ventilation flaps restrict the temperature increase

shades restrict excessive sunlight

paraffin heater can provide heat and CO_2

Large scale conventional glasshouses

Biology at work: Feed the world

By the year 2020, enough food will have to be produced to feed the extra 2.5 billion people who will be living in the developing countries. Today more than three-quarters of a billion people in the developing world remain undernourished.

The simple answer is to produce more food, but new land for agricultural development is limited. Yields are also restricted by the deteriorating quality of the agricultural environment.

- Soils are being eroded and are losing fertility as micronutrients are exhausted.
- Water supplies are being used up and wasted.
- Grassland for stock animals is being overgrazed.
- Excessive use has been made of fertilisers and pesticides, which can cause health problems.

Greater food production will come from targeting local agricultural systems by:

- making the most of local resources, knowledge, and analysis,
- seeking the participation of local farmers.

Country	Grain consumption
USA	860
Australia	503
China	292
Brazil	277
Bangladesh	176
Kenya	145

To survive, a person needs an energy input equivalent to 286 kg per year. The table shows the average grain consumption per person in 1990. Kenya and Bangladesh do not meet the basic needs of their people.

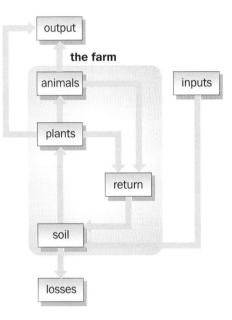

The use of nutrients on a farm can be represented as a balance sheet of inputs and outputs

In Kenya, the production of maize and beans requires the replacement of depleted nutrients such as nitrogen and phosphate, to avoid soil degradation and erosion. The beans are inter-cropped with the maize since they are legumes, which fix atmospheric nitrogen for use by the maize. This technique has spread to semi-arid areas as the population has increased. But research has shown that under these semi-arid conditions, beans do not fix atmospheric nitrogen. The whole agricultural system is now under threat.

A possible solution involves using the cowpea legume. This is a local legume species more suited to the semi-arid environment. It can fix substantial amounts of nitrogen even in very dry soils. Cowpeas can be inter-cropped with maize and supplemented by small amounts of nitrogen fertiliser. The use of energy intensive inputs such as fertiliser can be justified to save the soil before it becomes too exhausted. Greater plant biomass leads to greater levels of humus being deposited. This integration of traditional and new technologies is called **fertiliser-augmented soil enrichment** (**FASE**).

The progress of sustainable agricultural development in developing countries cannot rely on advances in genetic engineering and applied ecology. The active participation of local farmers and the integration of traditional and alternative practices are equally important to being able to feed the world.

Building small stone walls around land contours can reduce soil erosion and conserve water

Summary

- Photosynthesis involves the use of light energy to synthesise organic molecules.
- The light-dependent stage involves the photoactivation of chlorophyll and energy transfer to produce ATP and NADPH.
- The light-independent stage involves the fixation of carbon dioxide and the use of ATP and NADPH to convert it into carbohydrate.
- The light-dependent stage takes place on and across the thylakoid membranes of the chloroplast.
- The light-independent stage takes place in the stroma of the chloroplast.
- The photosynthetic pigments include chlorophylls a and b, carotene and xanthophyll.
- The absorption spectrum is a graph showing how much light a pigment absorbs at each wavelength.
- The action spectrum is a graph showing the rate of photosynthesis at different wavelengths.
- Chlorophylls and accessory pigments are grouped together to form antenna complexes. They funnel photons of light to the reaction centre.
- There are two types of reaction centre, photosystem I (P700) and photosystem II (P680).
- Both cyclic and non-cyclic photophosphorylation involve the synthesis of ATP from ADP and Pi.
- The products of the light-dependent stage, NADPH and ATP, are used in the light-independent stage, when carbon dioxide is fixed and then reduced to carbohydrate.
- The rate of photosynthesis can be measured using a photosynthometer.
- The rate at which photosynthesis proceeds is determined by the factor that is in shortest supply. These factors include light intensity, light quality, temperature and carbon dioxide concentration.

▶ Questions

1   Copy and complete the following account.
Photosynthesis is a type of .... nutrition involving the synthesis of organic molecules from inorganic materials. The process involves two types of reactions, light-dependent and .... In the light-dependent reactions, light energy is absorbed by molecules of .... located on the .... of the chloroplasts;............and ....are produced and oxygen is given off as a waste product. In the light-independent reactions,................accepts molecules of carbon dioxide, which together with the products of the light-dependent reactions results in the formation of ....This compound can be converted to .... or used to regenerate the carbon dioxide acceptor molecule.

2   a) Draw a fully labelled diagram of a chloroplast.
    b) Where in the chloroplast do the following take place:
        i)   photoactivation of chlorophyll,
        ii) regeneration of ribulose bisphosphate?
    c) i)   Explain what is meant by the photoactivation of chlorophyll.
        ii) Explain how, as a result of photoactivation, ATP and NADPH are formed in the chloroplast.
        iii) What is the other product of the light-dependent stage?

3   The following account contains **eight errors.** The first has been circled.
Copy and complete the account, substituting the **correct** terms in place of the errors.

The third stage of (respiration) occurring in the light is the oxidation of carbon dioxide to the phosphorylated three-carbon sugar. This conversion is brought about in part of a cyclic series of enzyme reactions known as the Hill cycle. ATP and reduced NAD produced during the light harvesting and energy transduction are essential components. The primary carboxylation reaction is between a two-carbon compound and carbon dioxide. The reaction is catalysed by a hydrolase enzyme. The first stable product is a six-carbon compound, which is phosphorylated and reduced using ADP and reduced NADP to form a different three-carbon compound. For every three molecules of carbon dioxide and three molecules of the five-carbon compound, six molecules of this three-carbon compound are synthesised. One of these six is the net production of photosynthesis, the other five molecules being used in the regeneration of three molecules of the five-carbon acceptor, which re-enters the cycle.

4   a) Chlorophyll a is found in all plants that can photosynthesise. What is its function?
    b) The graph at the top of the next page shows the absorption spectra of three types of pigment found in the leaf of a plant.
        i)   State the wavelength that is most effectively absorbed by chlorophyll a.
        ii) Name the technique you would use to isolate chlorophyll a.

iii) Use the information in the graph to explain why it is an advantage for a leaf to contain more than one pigment.

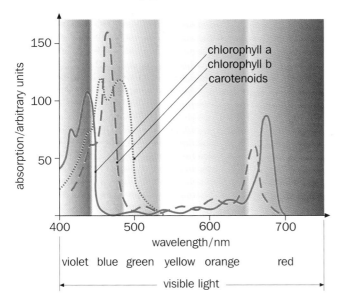

5 Copy and complete the diagram of the light-dependent stage of photosynthesis by
  a) drawing four arrows to show the flow of electrons,
  b) indicating with a letter 'P' the site of non-cyclic photophosphorylation,
  c) writing, in the appropriate boxes, equations to show
     i) the photolysis of water,
     ii) the formation of reduced NADP.

6 The diagram shows the structure of a chloroplast as seen with an electron microscope.
  a) Name the features labelled A, B, C, D and E.

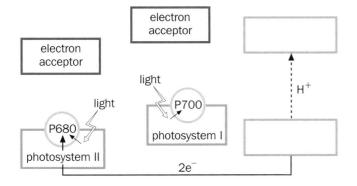

b) Which of the following values best describes the magnification of the diagram ×150, ×1500, ×15 000, ×150 000?
c) i) State the exact region of the chloroplast where chlorophylls *a* and *b* would be found.
   ii) Name two other pigments that may be found inside a chloroplast.

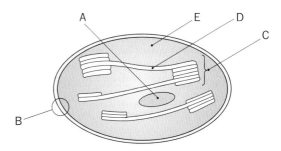

7 The graph shows the effect of light intensity on the rate of photosynthesis of an aquatic plant measured at two different carbon dioxide concentrations.
  a) i) Describe the effects of increasing the carbon dioxide concentration on the rate of photosynthesis.
     ii) Explain why the curve for low carbon dioxide concentration flattens out above a light intensity of 6 arbitrary units.
     iii) Suggest how the rate of photosynthesis might have been measured.
  b) Describe briefly how amino acids may be produced from the products of photosynthesis.

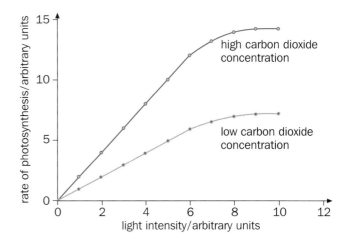

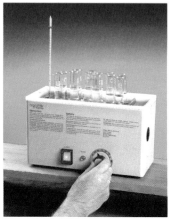

Have you ever used a thermostatically controlled water bath?
Perhaps in an investigation into enzyme activity, you needed
to keep your reacting mixtures at a constant temperature.
You set the dial on the water bath to the temperature that you need.
When the water in the water bath reaches that temperature, it
will stay constant throughout the experiment.
You don't have to keep re-adjusting the temperature.

How do you think this happens?

Inside the water bath is a thermostat that detects
changes in temperature.
Once the required temperature is reached, the thermostat
signals the heating element to switch off.

The temperature of the water bath starts to fall. If it falls too low,
then this is detected by the thermostat, which switches the heater
back on, so the temperature of the water rises again.

The heating element is switched on or off depending on
the temperature of the water detected by the thermostat.
In other words, the system relies on **feedback**.
And since the change in water temperature results in the heater
producing an *opposite effect*, this is known as **negative feedback**.

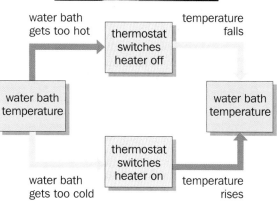

The enzymes that control the chemical reactions in our cells operate
best within fairly narrow limits of temperature, pH, substrate and
product concentration.
In a mammal, the immediate environment of the cells is the tissue fluid.
So if cellular enzymes are to work to their optimum, then it is important
that the composition of tissue fluid is kept as stable as possible.

> **Homeostasis is the maintenance of a constant internal
> environment within a living organism.**

You have already seen examples of homeostatic control systems
operating for blood pressure and gas composition of the blood.
At GCSE, you probably looked at how blood sugar and body
temperature were controlled and maintained within narrow limits.

Each control system must have

- a **receptor** (sensor), which detects a **stimulus**.
  A stimulus is a change in the level of the factor being regulated.
  This detectable change is called the **input**.

- a **coordinator,** which receives and controls information from
  the receptor and triggers the action that will correct the change.

- an **effector,** which carries out the action that brings about the
  change (often called **the corrective mechanism**).

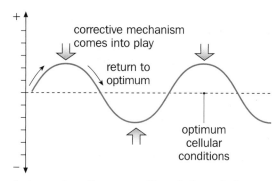

*A change in optimum conditions in the cells is
detected by receptors. Corrective mechanisms are
activated which restore conditions to the optimum*

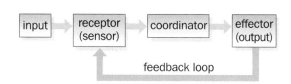

▷ Heat gain and loss

Living organisms exist in habitats where the temperatures range from 115 °C in volcanic vents to −40 °C at the poles. An organism's temperature varies according to the amount of heat it gains and the amount of heat it loses.
If heat gain is greater than heat loss, then the temperature of the organism will rise, and vice versa.
To maintain a stable body temperature, an organism needs to balance its heat gain with its heat loss.
This regulation of body temperature is called **thermoregulation**.

Organisms gain heat as a waste product of respiration and from their environment, if it is warmer.
There are three ways in which heat can be transferred to and from an organism.

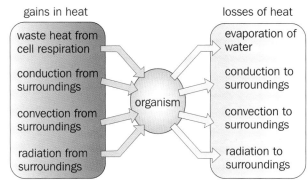

How an organism gains and loses heat

- **Radiation** accounts for most of the energy that is lost and gained by organisms. Heat can be radiated to and from the air, water and ground.

- **Conduction** is the transfer of energy by contact from molecule to molecule.
  Air does not conduct heat as well as liquids and solids, because the molecules are spread out.
  So conduction is greatest when an organism is in contact with water or with solids such as the ground.

- **Convection** transfers heat energy by currents of air or water. Heated water and air rise and cooled water and air sink.
  This sets up convection currents around the organism.
  Heat can also be lost from an organism when water evaporates from a surface, for example during sweating.

▷ Thermoregulation in ectotherms

Ectotherms are animals that do not generate much body heat.
All animals are ectothermic except for birds and mammals.
In many ectotherms, such as fish and amphibians, their body temperature fluctuates more or less with that of their environment.
However, other ectotherms, such as lizards, control their body temperature by their behaviour or by increased activity.

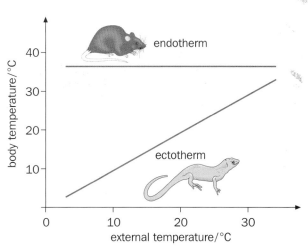

Many lizards live in habitats that are hot during the day but cold at night.
Lizards spend the night under cover of rocks or in a burrow.
When they emerge in the morning, their body temperature will be well below that needed for normal activity.
During this time, the lizard's movements will be slow and this means it is less efficient than normal at avoiding predators or catching prey.
So it basks in the sun, positioning itself at right angles to the sun's rays, to raise its body temperature.
Soon the lizard is fully active and able to hunt for food.
During the hottest part of the day, the lizard finds shade under a rock to prevent itself from overheating.
Towards the end of the day, the lizard again basks in the sun.
It then returns to its burrow, and its body temperature again drops to nearer that of its surroundings.

▶ Thermoregulation in endotherms

Endotherms are animals that generate their own body heat. They are able to regulate their body temperature and keep it relatively constant.

Mammals and birds are endothermic, deriving heat from metabolic processes taking place inside the body, mainly waste heat from respiration.

You are able to maintain your **core body temperature** at about 37 °C even though the environmental temperature varies.

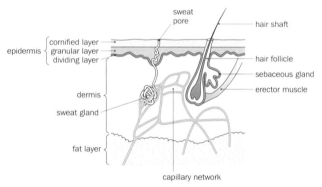

Section of human skin

The role of the skin in thermoregulation

Most heat exchange occurs through the skin and it has an important role in controlling body temperature.

If you look at the section of the human skin, you can see that it has a complex structure.

The structures involved in thermoregulation are found in the dermis.

Capillaries provide the cells of the epidermis and dermis with food and oxygen but they are also involved in regulating heat loss. The more blood that flows through the capillaries, the greater will be the amount of heat lost from the skin.

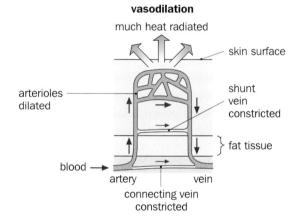

There are many capillary networks in the dermis, often forming loops.

As you know, capillaries have no muscle in their walls, but the arterioles that bring blood to them do.

When this muscle contracts, it causes the arteriole to **constrict**, that is, it becomes narrow, reducing the blood supply to the capillary.

Blood is diverted along a **shunt vessel**, so less blood gets into the capillary network and less heat is lost.

This is called **vasoconstriction**. The skin becomes paler.

When the muscle in the arteriole relaxes, it **dilates**, becoming wider and allowing more blood into the surface capillaries.

This **vasodilation** allows more heat to be lost from the capillaries.

When do you think vasoconstriction and vasodilation happen?

Sweat glands each have their own capillary blood supply. A salty solution of sweat is secreted along the sweat duct and passes out of the sweat pore to lie on the skin surface. The skin becomes flushed.

As the sweat evaporates, it takes heat out of the skin, so cooling it.

Connected to each hair follicle is an **erector muscle**. When this contracts, it causes the hair to stand upright, trapping a stationary layer of air close to the skin surface.

Since air is a good insulator of heat, this reduces heat loss. This is of little use to humans, but is effective in mammals that have thick fur.

Birds effectively do the same thing on a cold day when they fluff up their feathers and trap air close to the skin.

On hot days, the erector muscles relax and the hairs lie flatter against the skin surface, reducing the insulating layer of air so that it has far less effect upon reducing heat loss from the skin.

Robin on a cold day

▶ Controlling body temperature

No matter what the environmental temperature is, your core body temperature stays at around 37 °C (unless you have a fever or hypothermia).
How is this homeostatic control achieved?

Your body temperature is controlled by the **hypothalamus**, a small structure at the base of the midbrain.
The hypothalamus acts as the body's thermostat, along with its other functions.
The hypothalamus monitors the temperature of the blood passing through it.
If the blood temperature is high, the hypothalamus sends out nerve impulses that switch on 'cooling mechanisms', such as increased sweating and vasodilation.
If the temperature of the blood is low, then the hypothalamus sends out nerve impulses that switch on 'warming mechanisms'.
In addition, the hypothalamus receives nerve impulses from hot and cold temperature receptors in the dermis of the skin.
These respond to changes in environmental temperature.

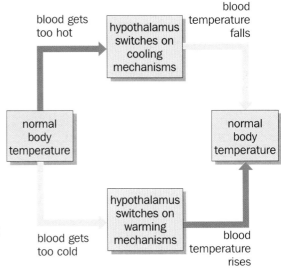

Overcooling

When the surrounding environment is cold, the hypothalamus detects a decrease in the temperature of its blood supply and receives impulses from the skin's cold receptors. It send out nerve impulses that bring about the following responses.

- **Vasoconstriction** of arterioles diverts blood away from the skin surface, so less heat is lost by radiation.
  That's why you look pale when you are cold.
- **Sweating** is reduced, or stops altogether.
- **Erector muscles** contract, raising your hairs and trapping a stationary layer of insulating air close to the skin surface.
- **Shivering** is the rapid, involuntary contraction and relaxation of muscles, which results in increased heat production.

These responses have the effect of conserving body heat and producing more heat.

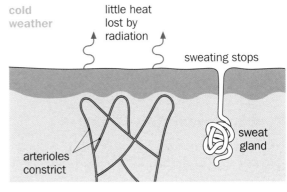

Overheating

When the environment is hot, the hypothalamus detects an increase in the temperature of its blood supply and receives nerve impulses from the skin's heat receptors.
It sends out nerve impulses that bring about the following responses.

- **Vasodilation** of arterioles allows more blood to reach the capillaries near the skin surface, so more heat is lost by radiation.
  That's why you look flushed when you are hot.
- **Sweating** increases, so more sweat lies on the skin surface. Evaporation of this sweat cools the skin.
- **Erector muscles** relax and the hairs lie flatter against the skin. This reduces the stationary layer of insulating air.

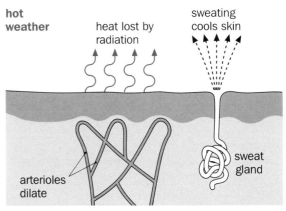

In addition, **_behavioural adaptations_** play a part in thermoregulation. Desert mammals avoid high daytime temperatures by being nocturnal.
Some animals hibernate during the hottest months, a process called **aestivation**.
In cold areas, animals are active during the day, often huddling together in groups to reduce heat loss, as in the case of penguins.

Time for a bit of aestivation

▶ The pancreas

The **pancreas** is both an exocrine and an endocrine gland.
Exocrine glands release secretions along ducts or tubes.
The pancreas secretes pancreatic juice down the pancreatic duct into the duodenum.
Endocrine glands secrete hormones directly into the bloodstream.
A **hormone** is a chemical that coordinates certain activities in the body.

The pancreas secretes the hormones **insulin** and **glucagon** into the blood to regulate the blood sugar level.
The pancreas plays a central role in the control of blood glucose.
If you look at the photomicrograph of a section through the pancreas, you can see that scattered amongst the cells that produce digestive enzymes are groups of different cells called **islets of Langerhans**.
The islets of Langerhans are made up of two different types of cells.

- The **alpha cells** (α-cells) are sensitive to low levels of glucose in the blood and secrete the hormone **glucagon**.
- The smaller **beta cells** (β-cells) detect increases in blood glucose levels above the normal and secrete a different hormone called **insulin**.

Glucagon and insulin act in opposite ways to maintain a constant blood glucose level.

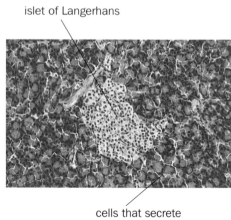

islet of Langerhans

cells that secrete pancreatic enzymes

Section of the pancreas

▶ Control of blood glucose

The blood of a normal person contains between 80 and 90 mg of glucose per 100 cm^3. Blood glucose levels will rise due to the following.

- The absorption of carbohydrates from the alimentary canal.

- The conversion of stored **glycogen** to glucose by a process called **glycogenolysis**. Glycogen is stored in the liver and muscles and can be quickly converted into glucose to meet the body's needs.

- The conversion of amino acids and glycerol to glucose by a process called **gluconeogenesis**.

Excess amino acids are broken down in the liver by **deamination**.
The amino part of the molecule is excreted, but the remainder can be converted into glucose.
During fasting, the blood glucose level is maintained by the conversion of lipid stores.
Animals do not store proteins.
So starvation may lead to proteins being used, resulting in muscular wastage.

Glucagon

If the blood glucose level gets too low, the α-cells of the islets of Langerhans detect the change and secrete glucagon.
This hormone fits into **receptor sites** on the cell membranes of liver cells and leads to the activation of the enzymes inside to

- convert glycogen to glucose,
- increase the rate of gluconeogenesis (the conversion of amino acids and glycerol into glucose).

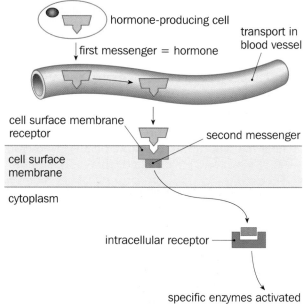

hormone-producing cell

first messenger = hormone

transport in blood vessel

cell surface membrane receptor

second messenger

cell surface membrane

cytoplasm

intracellular receptor

specific enzymes activated

The role of a hormone in activating specific enzymes

Insulin

If the level of glucose in the blood gets too high, the β-cells of the islets of Langerhans detect the change and secrete insulin. This hormone circulates around the body in the bloodstream and attaches to receptor sites on the cell membranes of liver, muscle and adipose (fat-storing) cells.

This changes the permeability of these cell membranes to glucose, by increasing the activity of a carrier molecule which transports glucose across the cell membrane.

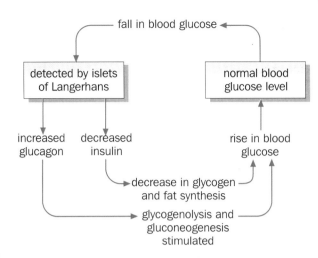

The secretion of insulin results in the following changes.

- The rate of respiration in the cells increases, since there is now more of the respiratory substrate, glucose, available.
- The rate of conversion of glucose to glycogen increases. The glycogen is stored in the liver and muscles (**glycogenesis**).
- The rate at which glucose is converted to fat and stored in adipose tissue increases.

Diabetes

Some people are unable to control their blood glucose level properly because they are unable to produce sufficient insulin. This clinical condition is called **diabetes mellitis**.

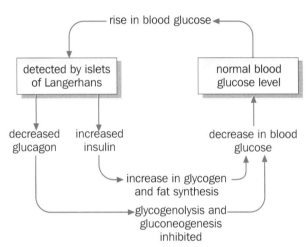

After a carbohydrate meal, the blood glucose level rises. In diabetics there is insufficient insulin to increase the permeability of the cell membranes to glucose, so the cells are starved of their fuel, even though the blood glucose level is high. The cells have to respire using proteins and fats instead, which results in the patient losing weight.

Another symptom is thirst, caused by the increased water potential of the blood.
The patient needs more water to dilute the blood and so lower its water potential.
One indicator of diabetes is the presence of glucose in the urine. This is because the kidneys are unable to reabsorb the high levels of glucose filtered into the tubules.

Diabetes can vary in severity and there are thought to be a number of different causes.

- The insulin receptor sites on the cell membranes of liver, muscle and adipose cells fail to recognise insulin.
  So despite the fact that insulin is produced, its effects are blocked.
- The β-cells of the islets of Langerhans are destroyed by the body's own autoimmune system and so are no longer able to secrete insulin.

Child injecting insulin

Some diabetics can control their blood glucose levels by carefully regulating their carbohydrate intake.
Others may need daily injections of specific amounts of insulin.
For many years, this insulin came from slaughtered pigs or cows.
Since this was different from human insulin, it gradually built up an immune response in the patient, causing problems in later life.
As you saw in Chapter 9, human insulin can now be produced on a large scale by genetic engineering, eliminating the problems associated with animal-derived insulin.

An insulin dosage for injection

▶ Excretion

Many of the metabolic reactions that take place inside the bodies of living organisms produce waste products which can be toxic if they are allowed to build up.

> **Excretion** is the removal from the body of waste products made in the cells during metabolism.

In humans these **excretory products** include

- carbon dioxide from respiration, which is excreted by the lungs,
- **nitrogenous waste products**, formed from the breakdown of excess amino acids and nucleic acids, such as urea, uric acid and ammonium salts,
- bile pigments, which are made in the liver and excreted in the bile via the small intestine. They are formed from the breakdown products of haemoglobin from old red blood cells. Any useful iron is removed and used to make new haemoglobin before the bile pigments are excreted.

Excreting nitrogenous waste

Different animals deal with the excretion of nitrogenous waste in different ways, depending upon the environment which they inhabit.

- **Fish** release their nitrogen as **ammonia**, a small, highly toxic molecule.
  Ammonia is extremely soluble and quickly diffuses out across the gills, at no energy cost to the fish. The ammonia is diluted down to non-toxic levels.

- **Birds and insects** excrete their nitrogen as **uric acid**, which is made from ammonia at a large energy cost to the animal.
  Uric acid is almost insoluble in water and is non-toxic.
  Very little water is needed to excrete uric acid and it is removed from the bodies of birds and insects as a white paste. This is important in conserving body water and allows them to inhabit arid environments.

- **Mammals** excrete their waste nitrogen as **urea**.
  If more protein is eaten than the body needs, any excess protein or amino acids cannot be stored in the body.

Excess amino acids are broken down in the liver by **deamination**. The amino group is removed from the amino acid and the rest of the molecule is used in respiration.
The nitrogenous waste product of deamination is ammonia.
Urea is made in the liver by combining two molecules of ammonia with one molecule of carbon dioxide.
The synthesis of urea requires a lot of energy, but its advantage is that it is far less toxic than ammonia and so the tissues are able to tolerate it in higher concentrations.

Urea is the main nitrogenous waste product in humans.
It is carried from the liver to the kidneys in the bloodstream, where it is filtered out and excreted in the urine.

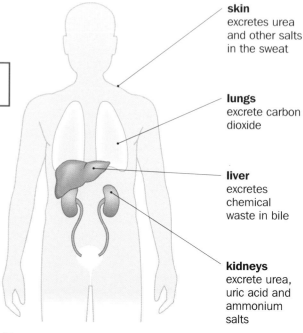

skin
excretes urea and other salts in the sweat

lungs
excrete carbon dioxide

liver
excretes chemical waste in bile

kidneys
excrete urea, uric acid and ammonium salts

Human excretory organs

Fish release ammonia across their gills

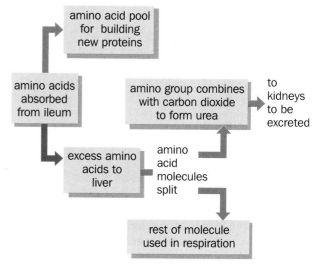

The process of deamination

In the diagram: amino acid pool for building new proteins; amino acids absorbed from ileum; amino group combines with carbon dioxide to form urea; to kidneys to be excreted; excess amino acids to liver; amino acid molecules split; rest of molecule used in respiration

316

▶ The kidneys

You have two **kidneys** positioned at the back of your abdomen.
If you put your hands on your hips, your kidneys should be where your thumbs are.

The kidneys are the main organs in the **urinary system**.
They filter waste products out of the blood.
Each kidney receives its blood supply from a branch of the aorta called the **renal artery**.
The kidney consists of millions of filtering units called **nephrons**.
Blood comes to the kidney under high pressure to make filtration efficient.
The filtered blood leaves the kidneys along the **renal veins**.

The filtered waste products are excreted by the kidney as **urine**.
The urine passes down a muscular tube called the **ureter**.
There is a ureter connecting each kidney to the **bladder**.
The bladder is a muscular sac that stores the urine.
When **urination** occurs, a ring of muscle called the **sphincter muscle** relaxes and urine passes out of the body along the **urethra**.
In females, the urethra is relatively short, whilst in males it is longer and acts as the passage for both urine and semen at different times.

Each day the kidneys filter about 180 litres of fluid, but, as you will see, most of this is reabsorbed.
On average, about 1 litre of urine is produced each day.

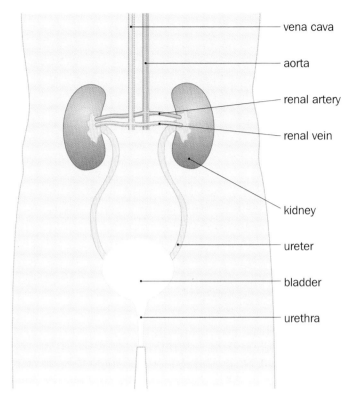

Human urinary system

▶ Kidney structure

Each kidney is surrounded by a layer of adipose (fat) tissue and a layer of fibrous connective tissue.
These keep the kidneys in position and protect them from mechanical damage.
If you cut a section through the kidney, three main areas can be seen.

- The dark, outer region is called the **cortex**.
  It is here that filtration is carried out by the nephrons.
  It has a dense capillary network which receives blood from the renal artery.

- The lighter, inner region is called the **medulla**.
  Each nephron extends across the medulla to form structures called **renal pyramids**.

- The renal pyramids project into a central space called the **pelvis**.
  Urine passes out into the pelvis before it passes down the ureter.

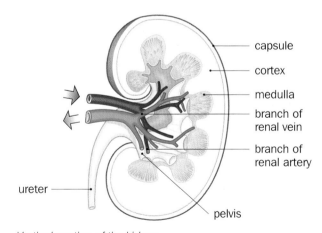

Vertical section of the kidney

The kidneys have a major homeostatic role in the body.
They remove nitrogenous waste products, and they also help to control the water content and pH of the blood.

▶ Structure of the nephron

The **nephron** is the functional unit of the kidney.
Under the microscope, kidney tissue can be seen to be made up of thousands of these tiny tubes.
At one end of the nephron, in the cortex, is the cup-shaped **Bowman's capsule**.
Immediately below the capsule is a twisted region called the **proximal convoluted tubule**.
This leads into the long, hairpin-like **loop of Henle,** which runs deep into the medulla and then back out to the cortex, where it forms another twisted region called the **distal convoluted tubule**.
This is joined to a **collecting duct**, which carries urine through the medulla to the pelvis of the kidney.

Each nephron has a rich blood supply.
Blood is brought to the kidney by the renal artery, which branches many times to form arterioles. Each Bowman's capsule is supplied with blood by an **afferent arteriole**.
This branches inside the Bowman's capsule to form a knot of capillaries called the **glomerulus**.
These join up again to form the **efferent arteriole**, which takes blood away from the Bowman's capsule.
Can you see from the diagram that the afferent arteriole is much wider than the efferent arteriole? This means that more blood is carried to the glomerulus than is carried away from it.

▶ Ultrafiltration

Ultrafitration involves the filtering (under pressure) of small molecules out of the blood and into the Bowman's capsule.
To understand how ultrafiltration works, it is necessary to know about the microstructure of the Bowman's capsule.
The blood entering the glomerulus is separated from the space inside the Bowman's capsule, by two cell layers and a basement membrane.

- The first cell layer is the wall or **endothelium** of the capillary.
  In the glomerulus, this single layer of cells has thousands of gaps.
- The **basement membrane** between the two cell layers is composed of glycoprotein and collagen fibres.
  Its mesh-like structure acts as the filter during ultrafiltration.
- The second cell layer makes up the wall of the Bowman's capsule.
  The epithelial cells in this wall are called **podocytes**.
  They have foot-like processes and, like the cells of the capillary, they do not fit tightly together, so there are gaps between them.

The gaps in the capillary endothelium and in the Bowman's capsule wall will allow most molecules to pass through.
But the basement membrane prevents large molecules, such as proteins and also blood cells, from passing through and so acts as the filter.
Only small, soluble molecules can pass through the basement membrane.
The blood pressure in the kidney is higher than in other organs.
This high pressure is maintained in the glomerulus because the afferent arteriole has a wider diameter than the efferent arteriole.

More blood goes to the glomerulus than comes away. A hydrostatic pressure builds up, forcing substances through the endothelial pores, across the basement membrane and into the Bowman's capsule.

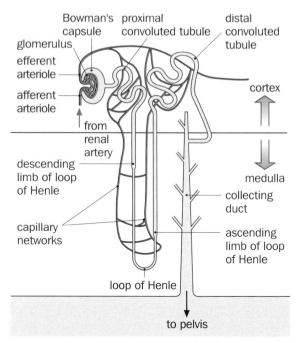

The structure of a nephron and its blood supply

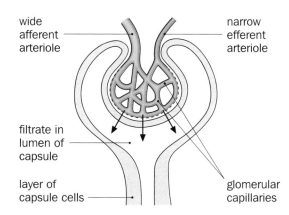

Ultrafiltration in the Bowman's capsule

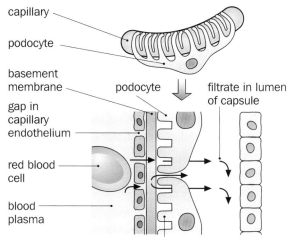

podocyte cell of Bowman's capsule wall

Microstructure of glomerulus and Bowman's capsule

▶ Reabsorption

Ultrafiltration is so efficient that up to 20% of the water and solutes are removed from the plasma as it passes through the glomerulus. If you look at the table you can see that the filtrate in the renal capsule is identical to the blood plasma, apart from containing no plasma proteins. These are too large to pass through the basement membrane.

You can also see that useful substances such as amino acids and glucose are filtered out of the blood.
These are needed by the body and so they are reabsorbed back into the blood as the filtrate flows along the nephron.
This process is called **selective reabsorption** since only certain molecules are reabsorbed.
All the glucose, amino acids, vitamins and many sodium and chloride ions are actively transported out of the proximal convoluted tubule and back into the blood.

If you look at the structure of the cells making up the wall of the proximal convoluted tubule, you will see many of the adaptations associated with active transport:

- microvilli provide a large surface area for absorption,
- numerous mitochondria provide ATP for active transport.

The uptake of these substances means that the blood in the capillaries surrounding the nephron now has a relatively high solute concentration.
So a large amount of water passes out of the filtrate in the proximal convoluted tubule and back into the blood by *osmosis*.

▶ The loop of Henle

The **loop of Henle** is a hairpin loop that runs deep into the medulla and then turns and goes back to the cortex again.
The first part of the loop is called the **descending limb** and the second part of the loop is called the **ascending limb**.

The function of the loop of Henle is to create an area of high solute concentration deep in the medulla.
The collecting ducts of each nephron pass through this area and so a lot of water can be reabsorbed from the collecting ducts by osmosis. A concentrated urine can be produced as a result.

The diagram shows you how the loop of Henle works.
The ascending limb is more permeable to salts and less permeable to water.
As the filtrate moves up, sodium and chloride ions move out passively at first and are then actively pumped out into the surrounding tissue.
This causes water to pass out of the descending limb by osmosis.
As a result the filtrate becomes more concentrated as it passes down the descending limb of the loop.
The net result is that the solute concentration at any part of the loop is lower in the ascending limb than it is in the descending limb.
This mechanism is called the **countercurrent multiplier mechanism**.
As the collecting ducts pass through the medulla to the pelvis, they pass through this region of high solute concentration.
So water is drawn out of the collecting ducts by osmosis, resulting in a far more concentrated urine.

Molecule or ion	Approximate concentration/g dm^{-3}	
	Plasma	Filtrate
water	900.0	900.0
protein	80.0	0.0
glucose	1.0	1.0
amino acids	0.5	0.5
urea	0.3	0.3
inorganic ions	7.2	7.2

Mean composition of human plasma and filtrate

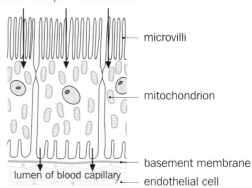

reabsorption of useful materials by active transport and diffusion

Cells of the proximal convoluted tubule

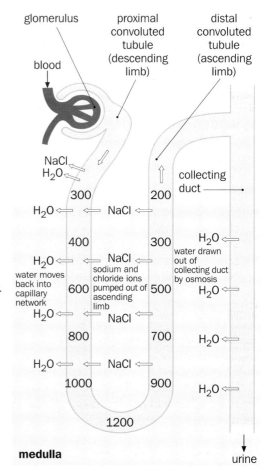

The countercurrent multiplier mechanism

▶ The distal convoluted tubule and collecting duct

The distal convoluted tubule is made up of cells with a similar structure to those of the proximal convoluted tubule.
They have microvilli on their surfaces and have many mitochondria.
These cells can actively pump sodium ions out of the nephron and into the blood.
Hydrogen carbonate ions dissociate from carbonic acid and then also pass into the blood.
This raises the pH of the blood when necessary.
So the distal convoluted tubule is able to control the acid/base balance of the blood.

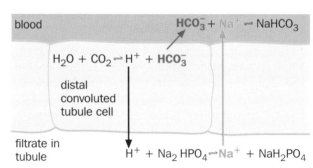

$$HCO_3^- + Na^+ \rightharpoonup NaHCO_3$$

$$H_2O + CO_2 \rightharpoonup H^+ + HCO_3^-$$

distal convoluted tubule cell

filtrate in tubule

$$H^+ + Na_2HPO_4 \rightharpoonup Na^+ + NaH_2PO_4$$

Acid/base balance controlled in the distal convoluted tubule

The second part of the distal convoluted tubule acts as the collecting duct.
The permeability of the walls of both the distal convoluted tubule and the collecting duct is affected by hormones.
This regulates how much water passes out into the medulla, and consequently how concentrated the urine will be.

▶ Water balance in desert animals

As you have seen, the loop of Henle is concerned with water reabsorption.
The longer the loop of Henle, the greater the solute concentration set up in the medulla. So the more water is reabsorbed and the more concentrated the urine becomes.
Mammals that inhabit arid areas such as deserts, have particularly long loops of Henle, since they need to conserve as much water as possible.

The thicker the medulla, the longer the loop of Henle that passes through it.
So the thicker the medulla, the more concentrated the urine is.
The kangaroo rat (*Dipodomys deserti*) lives in desert regions and can produce urine that is ten times more concentrated than the beaver.
The kangaroo rat is well adapted to desert conditions and is able to survive with little or no water intake. How does it do this?

- If you look at the table you can see that most of its water gain comes from its food.
  The food may be completely dry, but 'metabolic water' is produced from it during respiration in the cells.
  So all the water needs of the kangaroo rat are satisfied directly or indirectly from its food.

- Kangaroo rats remain underground during the day.
  The air in their burrows is cooler and more humid, so less water is lost from the body by evaporation.

- The kangaroo rat is able to conserve body water by producing a highly concentrated urine.
  It is also able to produce very dry faeces.

- Its nasal passages are adapted to cool the air before it is breathed out.
  So respiratory moisture condenses in the nasal passages before it can be exhaled.

Mammal	Relative thickness of medulla	Maximum urine concentration/ arbitrary units
beaver	1.0	52
pig	1.3	110
human	2.6	140
rat	5.2	300
kangaroo rat	7.8	550

The kangaroo rat

Water gain (cm³)	
metabolic water	54.0
water in dried food	6.0
Total water gain	60.0

Water loss (cm³)	
urine	13.5
faeces	2.6
evaporation (mainly breath)	43.9
Total water loss	60.0

▶ Osmoregulation by the kidney

Osmoregulation is the homeostatic control of body water.
We need to balance our water intake with our water loss.
As you can see from the pie-charts, we get most of our water from drinking and from the food we eat.
We get a small proportion from metabolic reactions such as respiration.

Most of the water we lose is lost as urine. The amount lost as sweat depends upon environmental temperature and our activities.
Since gas exchange surfaces need to be moist, water will inevitably be lost when we breathe out.
Some water is also lost in the faeces.

Controlling body water

Control of body water is another example of homeostasis operating on a principle of negative feedback.
In this case, the receptors responsible for detecting changes are located in the **hypothalamus** of the brain.
These **osmoreceptors** react to changes in the solute concentration of the blood as it flows through the hypothalamus.

If you haven't had a drink for a while, your blood will have a low water potential (it becomes more concentrated).
This is detected by the osmoreceptors in your hypothalamus, which stimulates your pituitary to release **antidiuretic hormone** (**ADH**).
The release of ADH into the bloodstream brings about the following.

- ADH makes the distal convoluted tubule and the collecting duct *more* permeable to water.
- This allows more water to be reabsorbed from the distal convoluted tubule and the collecting duct into the region of high solute concentration in the medulla.
- This produces a smaller volume of more concentrated urine.

So the action of ADH is to *conserve* body water.

What happens if you drink lots of fluids?
Your blood will have a high water potential (it becomes more dilute).
This is detected by the osmoreceptors in your hypothalamus and results in a decrease in the amount of ADH secreted by the pituitary.
This decrease in the amount of ADH in the bloodstream results in the following.

- Lack of ADH makes the distal convoluted tubule and the collecting duct *less* permeable to water.
- Less water is reabsorbed into the medulla.
- Larger quantities of dilute urine are produced.

In addition to stimulating the release of ADH when the blood is concentrated, the hypothalamus also activates your **thirst centre** in the brain. As a result, you feel thirsty and take in additional water to dilute the blood. Drinking stops the stimulation of your thirst centre almost immediately. This is thought to be due to the thirst centre responding to the stomach filling with water.

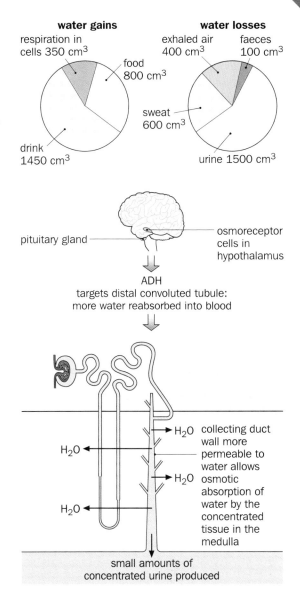

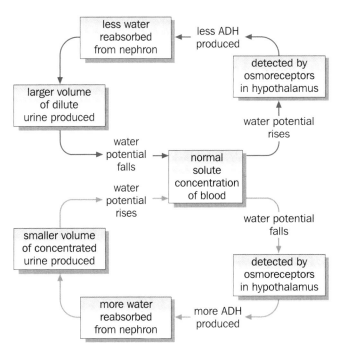

Biology at work: Kidney dialysis

The kidneys have an important role in homeostasis. They maintain the salt and water balance of the body fluids, as well as excreting waste products.

When the kidneys are damaged by injury or disease, this balance is affected and wastes accumulate in the blood. In severe cases, the function of the kidneys needs to be taken over by the process of **dialysis.** This will be necessary until the kidneys recover, or until a kidney transplant is available, or possibly for the rest of a patient's life.

There are two methods of kidney dialysis, **haemodialysis** and **peritoneal dialysis**.

Haemodialysis is where the blood is passed through an artificial kidney machine, either in hospital or at home. Each haemodialysis session lasts between 2 and 6 hours and a patient may need two or three sessions a week.

Access to the bloodstream is obtained using a **shunt**, which is a special tube that connects an artery to a vein. Blood flows from this tube into the machine and back to the patient.

Inside the machine, the blood flows over the surface of the partially permeable dialysis membrane. This membrane separates the blood from the dialysis fluid.

The dialysis fluid has the same composition as that desired in the blood plasma. As a result, wastes, toxic molecules and excess fluid pass (by diffusion) from the blood into the dialysis fluid. To aid this process, the blood and dialysis fluid flow in opposite directions. This so-called **countercurrent principle** ensures that a fairly constant diffusion gradient is maintained between the blood and the fluid.

The 'purified' blood is returned to the patient and the dialysis fluid is discarded.
Being connected to the machine is clearly restrictive but at least for this period of time the patient can eat and drink more or less what they want.

Peritoneal dialysis makes use of natural filtering within the abdomen (the peritoneum) and is usually carried out at home.

Peritoneal dialysis involves inserting dialysis fluid into the peritoneal cavity using a catheter.
Waste products and excess water pass through the peritoneal membrane into this cavity.
After several hours, the fluid is drained out and discarded. During this period of time the patient can carry on with normal activities.

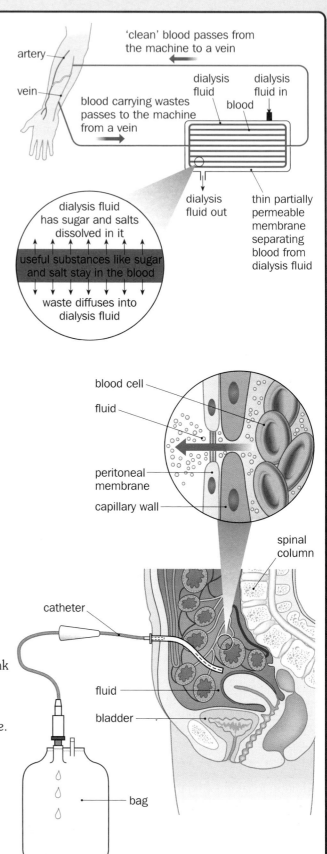

322

▶ Biology at work: Kidney transplantation

Kidney transplantation

Inevitably, the health of patients with long-term kidney failure suffers, and many doctors look upon a kidney transplant as preferable to long-term dialysis.

Only one functional donor kidney is needed to restore the health of a patient, and a kidney transplant is the most common and straightforward type of transplant operation.

To prevent the recipient's immune system rejecting the kidney, the tissue type and blood group of recipient and donor must be a close match.
This will often be the case where a close relative donates a kidney.
Often though, kidneys come from people who have consented to the medical use of their organs after death.

Rushing a transplant organ to a recipient

An operation has a reasonable chance of success as long as the transplant is completed within 48 hours of the removal of the donor kidney.
During this time, a machine passes a cool saline solution through the kidney to keep it viable.

The operation involves the donor kidney being placed into the pelvis of the recipient.
Often the renal artery and vein are joined to the **iliac** blood vessels in this region.
The ureter is connected directly to the bladder of the recipient.

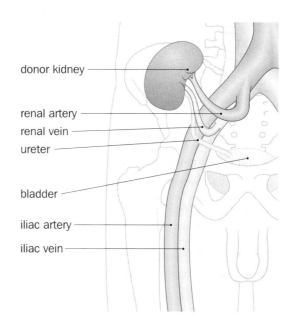

The general rate of success with kidney transplantation is around 80% and even higher when the donor is a close relative.

However, if the kidney is rejected, then the patient must return to dialysis before further transplants are undertaken.

Usually, all kidney transplant patients take special drugs to reduce the risk of rejection.
These are called **immunosupressants** and they usually have to be taken for the rest of a patient's life.

Thereare about 2000 kidney transplant operations carried out in the UK each year.
But there are approximately twice as many people waiting for a suitable donor for the operation.

Why do you think that kidney transplantation is a better option for a patient than kidney dialysis?

Kidney transplantation is more expensive than kidney dialysis in the short term, but less expensive in the long term.
Try to explain this statement.

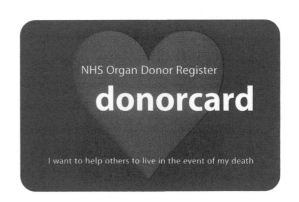

323

Summary

- Homeostasis is the maintenance of a constant internal environment within a living organism.
- Many homeostatic systems rely upon negative feedback to produce an opposing change.
- Some ectotherms are able to control their body temperature by their behaviour.
- The skin has a major role in maintaining a constant core body temperature.
- In mammals, the hypothalamus monitors body temperature and switches on a number of corrective mechanisms if the body temperature rises or falls too much.
- The pancreas secretes glucagon to raise the blood glucose level, and insulin if the blood glucose level needs to be reduced.
- Diabetes can be treated by moderating carbohydrate intake or injecting genetically engineered insulin.
- Excretion is the removal from the body of waste products made in the cells during metabolism.
- Fish, birds, insects and mammals produce different excretory products.
- The kidneys are the main organs of the urinary system and are composed of numerous nephrons.
- The Bowman's capsule of each nephron is well adapted for ultrafiltration of the blood.
- Useful substances are reabsorbed into the blood as the filtrate passes along the nephron.
- The loop of Henle creates a region of high solute concentration deep in the medulla by the countercurrent multiplier mechanism. This enables water to be reabsorbed back into the blood.
- Osmoreceptors in the hypothalamus monitor the solute concentration of the blood.
- The secretion of ADH by the pituitary increases the reabsorption of water from the nephron.
- Desert-living mammals, such as the kangaroo rat, have adaptations for conserving their body water.

▶ Questions

1 a) i) What is meant by the term 'homeostasis'?
       ii) Why is homeostasis important to the functioning of the human body?
   b) Hill walkers often encounter extreme changes in environmental conditions.
       Describe the changes involved in thermoregulation when a walker responds to a rapid fall in environmental temperature.

2 a) What is meant by
       i) an ectotherm,
       ii) an endotherm.
   b) Explain how ectothermic animals try to prevent their bodies from overheating.
   c) How does an endotherm prevent its body from overheating?

3 The diagram shows the main blood vessels going to and coming from the liver.
   a) In a healthy person, the blood glucose level in the hepatic vein fluctuates much less than that in the hepatic portal vein. Explain why this is so.
   b) Blood glucose level is more or less constant, even if a person has not eaten for several days.
       How does gluconeogenesis help to maintain this constant blood glucose level?

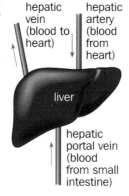

hepatic vein (blood to heart)
hepatic artery (blood from heart)
liver
hepatic portal vein (blood from small intestine)

   c) Suggest why people suffering from diabetes are advised to eat their carbohydrate in the form of starch rather than in the form of sugars.

4 The chart shows the sources of energy for 1 hour of cycling.
   a) What percentage of the energy comes from carbohydrates?
   b) Glycogenolysis and gluconeogenesis both contribute to the formation of respiratory substrates during exercise.
       What is meant by
       i) glycogenolysis,
       ii) gluconeogenesis?

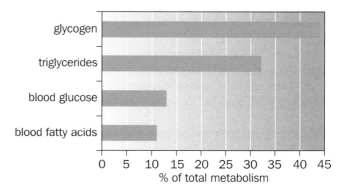

glycogen
triglycerides
blood glucose
blood fatty acids

0 5 10 15 20 25 30 35 40 45
% of total metabolism

5 a) i) What is the end product of nitrogen metabolism excreted by terrestrial insects?
       ii) What is the advantage to terrestrial insects of excreting this substance?

iii) Explain why fish are able to excrete ammonia, which is highly toxic.
b) Describe how urea is formed from surplus amino acids in the mammalian liver.

6 The diagram shows a Bowman's capsule.

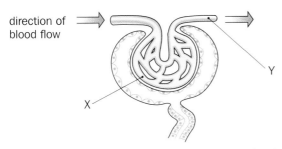

direction of blood flow

a) i) What is the name given to the network of capillaries labelled X?
   ii) State **three** consequences of constricting the diameter of blood vessel Y.
b) Much of the water in the filtrate is reabsorbed from the collecting duct.
   i) Name the part of the nephron which provides the osmotic gradient for reabsorption.
   ii) Suggest **one** way in which this section of the nephron might be modified in desert animals.

7 The diagram shows a cell from the proximal convoluted tubule of a nephron.

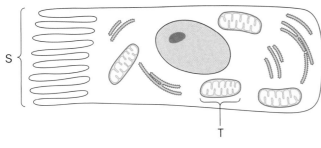

a) State **three** ways in which this cell may differ from a prokaryotic cell.
b) Explain fully the part played by S and T in the functioning of the proximal convoluted tubule.

8 a) i) Name the structure that detects changes in the water potential of the blood.
      ii) Name the gland that secretes ADH into the blood.
   b) The diagram represents the parts of a nephron. Use the appropriate letters to show the region where
      i) the epithelium is relatively impermeable to water,
      ii) the epithelium is freely permeable to water,
      iii) ADH increases the permeability of the epithelium to water.

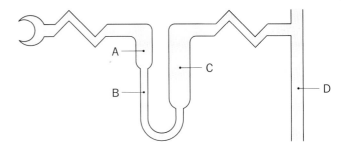

9 The table shows the volumes of fluid filtered by the glomerulus and the urine excreted under three different conditions. The total amount of solute excreted is the same in each case.
   a) i) In A, calculate the percentage of water reabsorbed.
      ii) State whether A, B or C leads to the most concentrated urine.
      iii) Which condition, A, B or C, would you expect to find in a person who has taken strenuous exercise on a hot day?
      iv) What effect would ADH have on the water potential of plasma?
   b) i) Name the structure found in *Amoeba* which regulates the water potential of the cytoplasm.
      ii) Suggest why the structure is absent from
         1. marine and parasitic Protozoa,
         2. freshwater algae.

Condition	Glomerular filtration rate (dm^3 day^{-1})	Volume of urine (dm^3 day^{-1})
A urine isotonic to plasma	180	2.4
B ADH increased	180	0.5
C ADH absent	180	23.3

10 The diagram shows part of the nephron and collecting duct of a mammal.
   a) Why does the solute concentration of the fluid in the loop of Henle increase between points A and B?
   b) Why do the cells in the ascending limb of the loop of Henle have many mitochondria?
   c) Small desert mammals are able to exist in arid conditions. Explain the advantage to these mammals of
      i) high levels of ADH in their blood,
      ii) nephrons with very long loops of Henle.

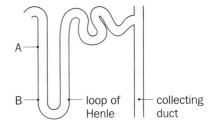

loop of Henle   collecting duct

19 Control and coordination

▶ Brain transplants

Once damaged, brain cells, unlike most cells, never regenerate.
But a new transplant operation pioneered in the United States
could change all that.

Three years ago, Don Fitch suffered a stroke. A tiny blood clot
in an artery leading to the brain cut off the blood supply. Don's left arm was
paralysed and the whole of the left side of his body was severely weakened.
Don is only the fourth person in the world to have the operation.

At the University of Pittsburgh Medical Centre, Douglas Kondziolka
is leading a team of neurosurgeons.
The surgery was fast, taking just 15 minutes, and done under local anaesthetic.
Dr Kondziolka and his team drilled a small hole into Don's skull and then, using
a syringe, injected about 2 million new human brain cells into the damaged area.
It is hoped that these cells will link up with the live brain tissue around them.
The brain cells transplanted into Don's skull were taken
from a tumour in a 22 year old man. Researchers discovered that
immature cells from the brain tumour could be treated to develop
into mature nerve cells suitable for transplanting into the brain.

It will take up to 6 months to see if the implanted brain cells survive
and 'wire up' into Don's existing brain circuitry.
If the brain transplants are successful, the technique could be used
to treat many forms of brain damage, including Parkinson's disease
and spinal cord injuries.

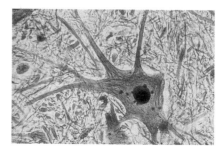

*Human brain cell of the type injected
into Don Fitch's skull*

▶ The nervous system

The nervous system controls and coordinates our actions by

- detecting changes (**stimuli**) inside and outside our bodies,
- processing the information received about these stimuli and
  deciding what to do, often as a result of previous experience,
- initiating responses to these stimuli by coordinating the body's actions.

The information about our internal and external environment is detected
by **receptors**, for example eyes and ears.

Responses are brought about by organs called **effectors**.
Effectors are usually muscles or glands.

Processing sensory information, deciding what to do and initiating
a response is the role of the **central nervous system** (**CNS**).
The central nervous system is made up of the **brain** and the **spinal cord**.

Many nerves are paired, joined to the brain or spinal cord, bringing
information to the CNS and taking other information away.
These nerves make up the **peripheral nervous system** (**PNS**).

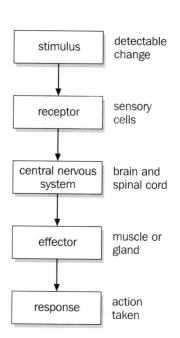

Neurones are the basic functional unit of the nervous system.
Neurones are highly specialised cells that are able to generate and
transmit nerve impulses.
They link up to form nervous pathways around the body.

There are different types of neurone, but basically their structure is
the same.
The diagram shows a **motor neurone**, which carries nerve impulses
from the brain or spinal cord to a muscle or a gland (the effector).

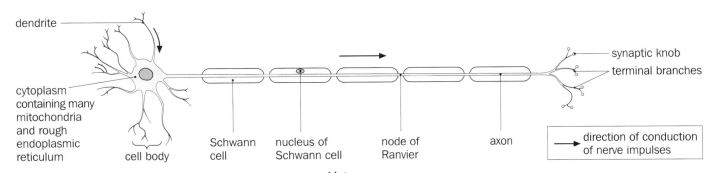

Motor neurone

The motor neurone consists of a **cell body**, which contains a nucleus,
a nucleolus and other organelles such as mitochondria and ribosomes.
Many thin cytoplasmic extensions carry impulses *towards* the cell body.
These **dendrites** are relatively short and are able to communicate
with other neurones.
One particularly long extension carries impulses *away* from the cell body.
An **axon** can travel from your spinal cord all the way to your big toe.
The axons of motor neurones form connections with a muscle or a gland
at structures called **motor end plates**.
Mitochondria are particularly numerous in the branched ends of the axon
where they are involved in the formation of transmitter substances.

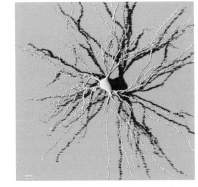

A multipolar neurone

The axon may have a fatty sheath of **myelin** wrapped around it.
If so, it is said to be a **myelinated** axon.
The sheath is formed when **Schwann cells** wrap themselves around
the axon along its length.
This results in several layers of fatty myelin surrounding the axon.
Between adjacent Schwann cells are small gaps called **nodes of Ranvier**.
At these points the axon is exposed as there is no myelin present.
The myelin sheath has the effect of increasing the rate of transmission
of impulses along the axon.

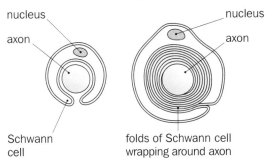

T.S. axon showing myelin sheath formation

The structure of a **sensory neurone** is similar to that of a motor neurone,
the main difference being that a sensory neurone has one long dendrite
bringing information to the cell body rather than a long axon taking
information away.
The sensory neurone carries impulses from receptor cells towards the brain
or spinal cord.

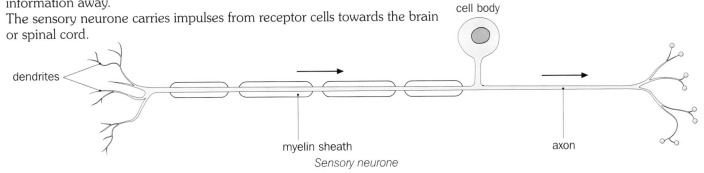

Sensory neurone

▶ Transmission of nerve impulses

Neurones transmit impulses as a series of electrical signals.
These electrical signals pass rapidly along the cell surface
membrane surrounding the axon as a nerve impulse.
This is not the same as an electric current passing along a wire,
which is a great deal faster.
Nerve conduction is a specialised development of the excitability
that is common to all animal cells.
This mechanism is the same throughout the animal kingdom.

Resting potential

Experiments have been carried out using squid axons.
These are large enough to have microelectrodes inserted
into them to measure changes in electrical charge.
The piece of squid axon is placed into a bath of saline solution
and two microelectrodes are connected to a voltmeter.
One microelectrode is placed on the outside of the cell surface
membrane of the axon and one is inserted into the axon.
This demonstrates that, in a resting axon, the inside of the
membrane has a negative electrical potential compared to
the outside.
The difference between the two potentials is called the
resting potential and is about -65 mV.
So the electrical potential on the inside of the axon is 65 mV
lower than that on the outside.
In this resting state the axon is said to be **polarised**.

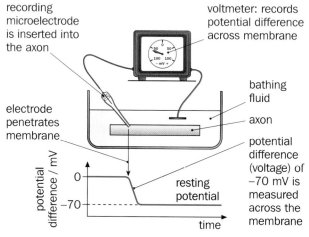

How is the resting potential produced and maintained?
As with most cells, the neurone can maintain an internal
composition which is different from the outside.
In the case of neurones, sodium ions, Na^+, and potassium ions, K^+,
are transported across the membrane against their concentration
gradients by **active transport**.

Carrier proteins in the membrane pick up Na^+ ions and transport
them to the outside.
At the same time, K^+ ions are picked up from the outside and brought
across the membrane into the cytoplasm of the axon.
This is known as the **sodium–potassium pump** and, like every
active transport system, it relies upon ATP from respiration.

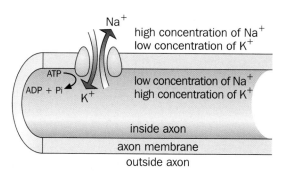

How the resting potential is maintained

But how does the outside of the membrane end up being positive
compared with the inside?
The Na^+ ions are passed out faster than the K^+ ions are brought in.
Approximately three Na^+ ions leave for every two K^+ that enter.
Also, K^+ is able to diffuse back out quicker than Na^+ can diffuse back in.
So the net result is that the outside of the membrane is positive
compared to the inside.
The resting potential is established and the axon is polarised.

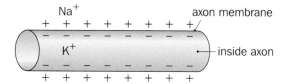

Part of the axon of a resting neurone

328

The action potential

A nerve impulse can be initiated in a neurone by mechanical, chemical, thermal or electrical stimulation.
Experiments have tended to use electrical stimuli since their strength, duration and frequency can be controlled and the axons are not damaged.

When a small electrical current is applied to the axon, the resting potential changes.
It switches from –65 mV inside the membrane to +40 mV.
So, for a very brief period, the inside of the axon becomes positive and the outside negative.
This change in potential is called the **action potential** and lasts about 3 milliseconds.
If the electrodes from the previous experiment are connected to a cathode ray oscilloscope, then it is possible to see the action potential as a peak, before the resting potential is returned.
When an action potential occurs, the axon is said to be **depolarised**.
When the resting potential is re-established, the axon membrane is said to be **repolarised**.

Depolarisation

So what happens to the membrane when it becomes depolarised?
Changes occur in the permeability of the axon membrane to both Na^+ ions and K^+ ions.
When the axon is stimulated, channels open in its cell surface membrane which allow Na^+ ions to pass through.
Since there is a higher concentration of Na^+ ions outside the axon membrane, they flood in by diffusion.
The Na^+ ions create a positive charge of +40 mV inside the membrane, reversing the resting potential and causing the action potential.

Potassium channels open in the membrane and K^+ ions diffuse out along a concentration gradient, starting off **repolarisation**.
At the same time, sodium channels in the membrane close, preventing any further influx of Na^+ ions.
This re-establishes the resting potential, since the outside of the membrane will become positive again compared with the inside.
We say that the membrane is **repolarised**.
In fact, so many K^+ ions leave that the charge on the inside of the membrane becomes more negative than it was originally.
This shows up as an 'over-shoot' on the oscilloscope.
The potassium channels close and the sodium-potassium pump starts again, restoring the normal concentration of sodium and potassium ions either side of the membrane.
This re-establishes the resting potential.

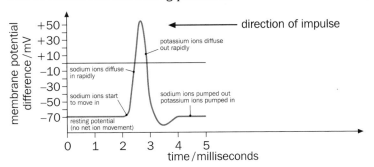

Ion movements during passage of an action potential

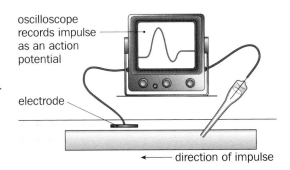

oscilloscope records impulse as an action potential

electrode

direction of impulse

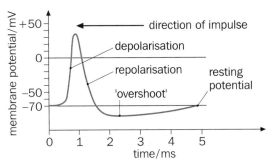

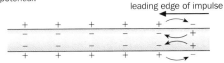

a). In the resting axon, there is a high concentration of sodium ions outside and a high concentration of potassium ions inside. But the net effect is that the outside is positive compared to the inside giving the resting potential.

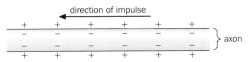

b). The axon is stimulated producing an action potential, setting up local circuits on the axon membrane.

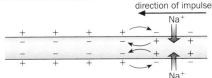

c). Sodium ions rush into the axon along a diffusion gradient depolarising the membrane and causing an action potential.

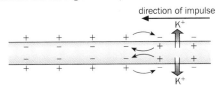

d). As the action potential passes along the axon potassium ions diffuse out along a concentration gradient, starting off the process of repolarisation.

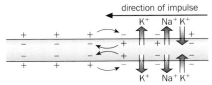

e). The sodium-potassium pump is re-established, fully repolarising the membrane.

Transmission of an impulse

▶ Progress of an impulse

You have seen how an action potential can be started.
But how does it travel *along* an axon from one region to the next?

As you have seen, when a nerve impulse reaches any point
on the axon, an action potential is generated.
Small local circuits occur at the leading edge of the action potential.
Sodium ions move across the membrane towards negatively
charged regions.
This excites the next part of the axon and so the action potential
progresses along its length.
The local circuits effectively change the potential of the axon
membrane, creating a 'new' action potential *ahead* of the impulse.

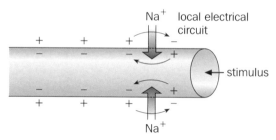

The passage of an impulse

The all or nothing law

One of the properties of neurones is that an action potential can only
be generated if the stimulus reaches a certain **threshold intensity**.
Below this threshold, no action potential can be created.
Once the threshold level is reached, the size of an impulse is
independent of the intensity of the stimulus.
So a more intense stimulus will not give a greater action potential.

So how is it that we can distinguish weak and strong stimuli?
The answer is that a strong stimulus produces a greater *frequency*
of action potentials.
So more action potentials are fired off as the intensity of stimulation
increases.
For a weak stimulus, fewer action potentials would be generated.
Also, a strong stimulus is likely to result in action potentials occurring
in more neurones than a weak stimulus.

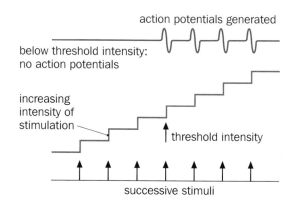

The refractory period

Following the passage of one action potential, there is a time delay
before the next one can pass.
This is called the **refractory period** and it lasts a few milliseconds.
During this time the sodium channels in the membrane are closed,
preventing the inward movement of Na^+ ions.
This is known as the **absolute refractory period** and another
impulse cannot be conducted, no matter how intense the stimulus.
The absolute refractory period lasts about 1 millisecond.

After this, the membrane starts to recover as potassium channels open.
Even though it is not fully repolarised, an action potential can occur if
the stimulus is more intense than the usual threshold level.
This time of reduced excitability can last a further 5 milliseconds and
is known as the **relative refractory period**.

The importance of the refractory period is that it ensures that

* impulses can only flow in one direction along an axon, since the
  region of axon behind the impulse cannot be depolarised,
* it limits the frequency at which successive impulses can pass
  along an axon.

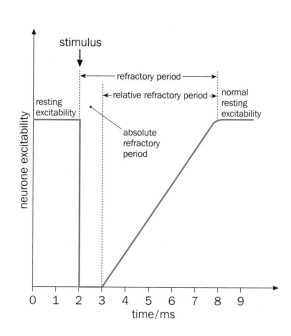

▶ Speed of transmission

Myelinated neurones are able to transmit action potentials at a speed of up to 100 metres per millisecond.
In unmyelinated neurones, the transmission rate is much slower at 1–3 m ms^{-1}.

The speed of transmission of an impulse depends upon the axon diameter and the myelin sheath.

● Axon diameter

The thicker the axon, the faster the rate of transmission of an impulse.
This is thought to be due to the greater surface area of axon membrane over which exchange of ions can occur.
Giant axons are found in a number of invertebrates, including earthworms, marine annelids and crustaceans.
They are thought to be associated with rapid escape responses, since rapid transmission of impulses is needed between receptors and muscles to withdraw the animal from danger.

● The myelin sheath

Myelin speeds up the rate of transmission by insulating the axon.
Myelin is a fatty substance which does not allow sodium ions or potassium ions to pass through it.

So depolarisation and action potentials cannot occur in those areas of the axon that are myelinated.
They can, however, occur at the **nodes of Ranvier**, so in myelinated axons, the action potential 'jumps' from one node to the next.
This can increase the speed of transmission by up to 100 times.

This is known as **saltatory conduction** and is only found in the myelinated axons of vertebrates.
Saltatory comes from the Latin *saltare*, which means to leap.

Saltatory conduction has the advantages of

● increasing the speed of impulse transmission (human myelinated axons transmit impulses over a 100 times faster than unmyelinated axons),

● myelinated axons also have the effect of conserving energy. As the sodium–potassium pump operates only at the nodes, fewer ions have to be transported across the membrane to restore the resting potential.

Metabolic poisons have been used in experiments on nerve axons.
Dinitrophenol inhibits the sodium–potassium pump and prevents transmission of an impulse along a nerve.
However, after washing, the poisoned axons transmit impulses if treated with ATP.
This is clear evidence that restoring the resting potential is an energy-requiring process, relying upon ATP from respiration.
Anything that affects the rate of respiration, such as temperature, will affect the transmission rate in a nerve.

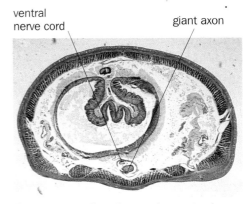

Transverse section of an earthworm to show ventral nerve chord

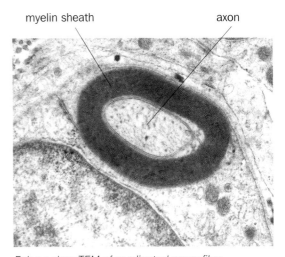

False colour TEM of myelinated nerve fibre

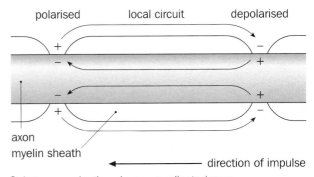

Saltatory conduction along a myelinated axon

▶ The synapse

A **synapse** is where two neurones *functionally* meet.
When two neurones meet, they do not touch.
There is a small gap, about 20 nm wide.
The gap is called the **synaptic cleft**.
The neurone that carries the impulse to the synapse is called the **presynaptic** neurone.
The neurone that carries the impulse away from the synapse is called the **postsynaptic** neurone.

So how is information transferred across the synapse from one neurone to the next?
Chemicals known as **neurotransmitters** are released by the presynaptic cell and diffuse across the synaptic cleft to trigger an action potential in the postsynaptic cell.

Motor neurones have specialised synapses with muscles called **neuromuscular junctions**.

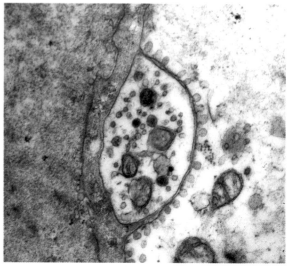

TEM of a synapse showing the synaptic cleft and synaptic vesicles

Structure of the synapse

The axons of neurones end in swellings called **axon terminals** or **synaptic bulbs**.
The surface of the synaptic bulb is called the **presynaptic membrane**.
It is separated by the synaptic cleft from the **postsynaptic membrane** of the cell body or dendrite of the next neurone.
The postsynaptic membrane contains many channels through which specific ions can pass.
The postsynaptic membrane has a number of large protein molecules on its surface, which act as receptor sites for the neurotransmitter substance.

If you look at the diagram showing the structure of a synapse, you will see that a number of mitochondria are present in the synaptic bulb.
This should suggest to you that active transport is involved in synaptic transmission.
Also present in the synaptic bulb are a number of **synaptic vesicles**.
These vesicles contain the neurotransmitter substance, which is released into the synaptic cleft on the arrival of an impulse.

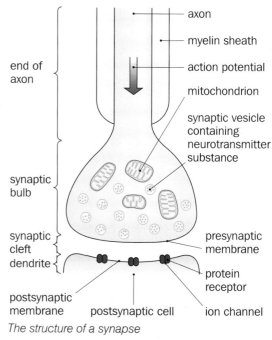

The structure of a synapse

A number of different neurotransmitters are produced by the nervous system.

Dopamine and **serotonin** are neurotransmitters that are active in the brain.
We need only be concerned with the main two neurotransmitters that occur in the body, **acetylcholine** and **noradrenaline**.
Neurones that release acetylcholine are said to have **cholinergic** synapses.
Neurones releasing noradrenaline have **adrenergic** synapses.

Whilst looking at the mechanism of synaptic transmission, we will concentrate on cholinergic synapses and the transmitter acetylcholine.
You can find out the effects that different chemicals have on synaptic transmission on page 340.

In 1969, Dr. Malcolm Sayer used a dopamine-derived drug to successfully treat post-encephalitis patients. Unfortunately the effects were only temporary.

The story provided the basis for the film 'Awakenings'.

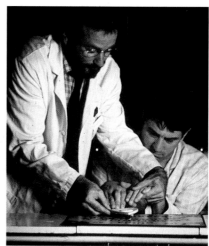

Robin Williams and Robert De Niro in the film 'Awakenings'

▶ Synaptic transmission

The following description shows how acetylcholine brings about transmission at a synapse.

- When an action potential arrives at a synaptic bulb it causes calcium channels to open in the presynaptic membrane. Since the concentration of calcium ions is many times greater in the synaptic cleft than inside the synaptic bulb, the calcium ions rush in.
- This influx of calcium ions causes vesicles containing acetylcholine to move towards the presynaptic membrane. The vesicles fuse with the presynaptic membrane, releasing the neurotransmitter into the synaptic cleft.
- The released acetylcholine diffuses across the synaptic cleft and attaches to specific receptor sites on the postsynaptic membrane. These protein receptor sites have a complementary shape to that of acetylcholine but the binding is only temporary.
- The binding of the neurotransmitter to the receptor sites opens up sodium channels in the postsynaptic membrane. Sodium ions flood in, depolarising the membrane and creating an action potential.
- If acetylcholine stayed bound to the receptor sites on the postsynaptic membrane, then the sodium channels would remain open, continually producing action potentials.
  To prevent this happening, the enzyme **acetylcholinesterase** is present in the synaptic cleft.
  This splits acetylcholine into acetate and choline.
  The choline is taken up by the presynaptic cell and combined with acetyl coenzyme A to reform acetylcholine.
  Hence the need for mitochondria in the synaptic bulb.

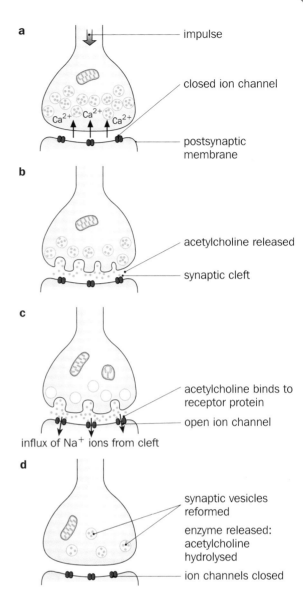

▶ Functions of the synapse

- Each action potential that arrives at the presynaptic membrane will cause a number of vesicles to release their transmitter.
  A number of action potentials are required before there is enough transmitter (**the threshold level**) to initiate an action potential in the postsynaptic cell. This is called **temporal summation**.
- A number of presynaptic neurones may form synapses with one postsynaptic neurone. Action potentials arriving in each presynaptic neurone will release transmitter, which builds up to the threshold level and triggers a postsynaptic impulse. This is called **spatial summation**.
- Since synaptic vesicles are present only in the synaptic bulb of the presynaptic neurone, then impulses can only pass across a synapse in *one* direction.
- The events at the cholinergic synapse described above show what happens at an **excitatory synapse** in a nervous response. But some synapses respond to the neurotransmitter by opening potassium channels and keeping sodium channels closed. Potassium diffuses out and this makes it more difficult for the postsynaptic membrane to be depolarised.
  These are called **inhibitory synapses**.
  Inhibitory synapses are involved in the stretch reflex.
  In this case, motor neurones controlling muscles that are antagonistic to the one being stimulated are inhibited.

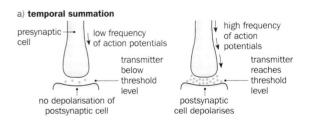

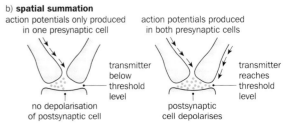

▶ Receptors

Animals are able to detect internal and external changes.
They have specialised cells that are sensitive to particular stimuli.
These **receptor** cells are able to convert stimuli into electrical impulses in nerve cells.
This process of converting one form of energy, such as light or sound, into the electrochemical energy of an action potential is known as **transduction**.

There are five main categories of receptor, depending on the nature of the stimulus:

- **chemoreceptors** detect chemical stimuli when we taste or smell a particular substance,
- **photoreceptors** detect light rays,
- **thermoreceptors** detect changes in temperature,
- **mechanoreceptors** detect pressure, movements and vibrations,
- **electroreceptors** detect electrical fields and occur mainly in fish.

So receptors are only able to respond to *specific* stimuli.
Let's look at an example of a mechanoreceptor and a photoreceptor.

Which receptors are being stimulated here?

▶ The Pacinian corpuscle

The Pacinian corpuscle is a mechanoreceptor found in the dermis of the skin.
It consists of the ending of a single sensory neurone, surrounded by several layers of connective tissue that make up the **capsule**.
When pressure is exerted on the capsule, it becomes squeezed out of shape.
This deforms the sensory nerve ending inside it, causing sodium channels in the membrane to open up.
An influx of sodium ions into the sensory nerve ending causes its membrane to depolarise and create a **generator potential**.

The greater the pressure applied to the Pacinian corpuscle, the greater is the deformation and the more stretch-mediated sodium channels open up and the greater the depolarisation.

Once the generator potential reaches a certain **threshold level**, an action potential is generated and transmitted along the axon.

Below the threshold level, only local depolarisation occurs and this is insufficient to create an action potential.
This has the effect of cutting out minor mechanical stimuli.
The threshold level is exceeded when summation of generator potentials occurs and this triggers an action potential.
Greater pressure upon the Pacinian corpuscle results in an increase in the frequency of the action potentials produced.

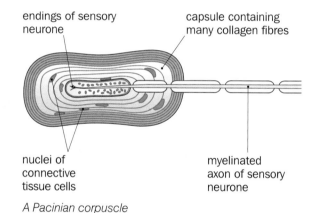

endings of sensory neurone

capsule containing many collagen fibres

nuclei of connective tissue cells

myelinated axon of sensory neurone

A Pacinian corpuscle

Exceeding the threshold level!

▶ The eye

The human eye is a complex organ containing photoreceptors. It is able to

- control the amount of light that enters it,
- refract (bend) light rays in order to focus them,
- transduce light energy into action potentials.

Structure of the eye

The eye is a spherical structure held in a protective, bony socket in the skull called the **orbit**.
It can be rotated in the orbit by two pairs of **rectus muscles** and one pair of **oblique muscles**.
These muscles are attached to the tough, opaque outer layer of the eye, the **sclerotic**.
The main role of the sclerotic is protection and to keep the eye in shape, under the pressure of its fluid contents.
At the front of the eye it forms the transparent **cornea**, which refracts the light rays entering.
Over the surface of the cornea is the thin, transparent **conjunctiva**.
This is continuous with the eyelids and helps to protect the cornea.
Tears produced by the **lachrymal gland** lubricate these two layers.

Inside the sclerotic is the highly pigmented **choroid**, which prevents internal reflection of light.
The choroid has a rich blood supply to nourish the layer of light-sensitive cells of the retina, which is attached to it.
At the front of the eye, the choroid forms the **iris**.
This contains involuntary muscle with both radial and circular fibres.
If you look at the diagram, you can see how the antagonistic action of these two sets of fibres controls the size of the **pupil** and so regulates the amount of light entering the eye.

Behind the pupil is the **lens**, which is made out of transparent protein enclosed in a capsule attached to the **suspensory ligaments**.
The **ciliary muscles** control the tension on the suspensory ligaments and so are able to change the shape of the elastic lens.
This focuses rays of light onto the light-sensitive **retina**.

The retina is the innermost layer of the eye.
It contains the light-sensitive **rods** and **cones**, which convert light rays into nerve impulses that leave the eye along the **optic nerve**.
The **fovea** or yellow spot is a focal point on the retina which contains only cones.
The **blind spot** is the point where the optic nerve leaves the eye and there are no light-sensitive cells here.

The eye is divided into two chambers. The one in front of the lens contains a transparent liquid called **aqueous humour**.
The second chamber lies behind the lens and is filled with transparent, jelly-like **vitreous humour**, which helps to maintain the eye's shape.

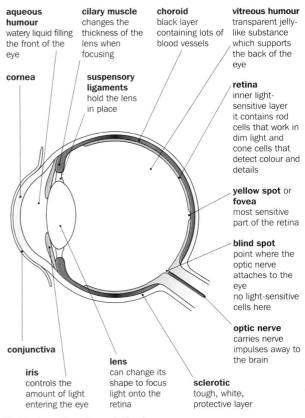

aqueous humour
watery liquid filling the front of the eye

cornea

cilary muscle
changes the thickness of the lens when focusing

suspensory ligaments
hold the lens in place

choroid
black layer containing lots of blood vessels

vitreous humour
transparent jelly-like substance which supports the back of the eye

retina
inner light-sensitive layer it contains rod cells that work in dim light and cone cells that detect colour and details

yellow spot or **fovea**
most sensitive part of the retina

blind spot
point where the optic nerve attaches to the eye
no light-sensitive cells here

optic nerve
carries nerve impulses away to the brain

conjunctiva

iris
controls the amount of light entering the eye

lens
can change its shape to focus light onto the retina

sclerotic
tough, white, protective layer

Vertical section through the human eye

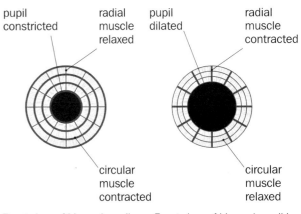

pupil constricted

radial muscle relaxed

pupil dilated

radial muscle contracted

circular muscle contracted

circular muscle relaxed

Front view of iris and pupil in bright light

Front view of iris and pupil in dim light

▶ Focusing light onto the retina

If you don't focus your camera correctly, you end up with
a blurred photograph.
Your *eye* also has to focus incoming light rays if it is to produce
a clear image on the retina.
As light rays enter the eye, they are **refracted** (bent) to focus
them onto the retina.
Most of the refraction is carried out by the cornea.
But the amount of refraction needed varies depending on
how far away the object is from the eye.
Light rays from an object close to the eye need to be refracted
more than distant objects.
The elastic lens changes its shape to focus close objects
onto the retina. This process is called **accommodation**.

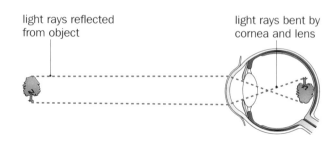

light rays reflected
from object

light rays bent by
cornea and lens

When viewing close objects, the lens becomes more biconvex
and bulges. This is because the ring of ciliary muscle contracts to
close the aperture around the lens.
The suspensory ligaments anchoring the lens to the ciliary muscle
slacken, so the lens assumes a more spherical shape under its own
elasticity. This shape of lens focuses close objects onto the retina and
the *eye* is said to be **accommodated**.

When viewing distant objects, the lens is thin (elliptical).
In this condition, the ring of ciliary muscle relaxes, widening the
aperture around the lens.
This tightens the suspensory ligaments,which pull the lens out
into a thinner shape.
A thin lens focuses distant objects clearly onto the retina and
the *eye* is said to be **unaccommodated.**

looking at a near object

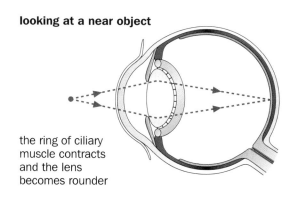

the ring of ciliary
muscle contracts
and the lens
becomes rounder

▶ The retina

This delicate inner layer of the *eye* contains the **photoreceptor** cells.
There are two types: the **rods** and the **cones**.

Both transduce light energy into chemical energy.
Each contains a photochemical pigment in its outer segment.
The cones are high light intensity colour receptors that are located
mainly in the yellow spot.
There are no rods here and the fact that the cones are so closely
packed together (about 125,000 per mm^3) gives them high definition.

looking at a distant object

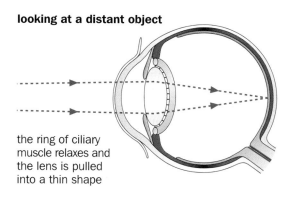

the ring of ciliary
muscle relaxes and
the lens is pulled
into a thin shape

If you look at the diagram, you will see that each cone has its own
single connection with the optic nerve.
So for each cone stimulated, an impulse passes to the brain.
This gives cones **high visual acuity**.
On the other hand, you will see that many rods connect with a single
bipolar neurone. A bipolar neurone has *two* extensions coming out
of the cell body. One is a dendrite and the other is an axon.
So impulses from a number of rods summate before triggering
an impulse in the bipolar neurone, giving **low visual acuity**.
This characteristic of rods is called **retinal convergence**.
Rods are distributed more or less evenly over the rest of the retina,
though they are highly concentrated in the periphery.

Notice that light rays have to pass through the nerve network before
reaching the photoreceptors, producing an **inverted retina**.

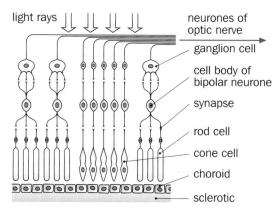

light rays

neurones of
optic nerve

ganglion cell

cell body of
bipolar neurone

synapse

rod cell

cone cell

choroid

sclerotic

Structure of the retina

▷ Photoreception

Rods and cones are composed of an inner and an outer segment.
The outer segment is made up of numerous membranes stacked on top of each other, rather like the thylakoids in the granum of a chloroplast.

These membranes carry a photosensitive pigment: **rhodopsin** in the case of rods and **iodopsin** in cones.

The inner segment of each photoreceptor cell contains the cell's nucleus and many mitochondria.

Rods are sensitive to low light intensity.
Their photochemical pigment rhodopsin, or **visual purple**, is made up of a protein, **opsin**, and a light-absorbing component, **retinine**. Retinine is derived from vitamin A.
When light strikes a molecule of rhodopsin, it splits into opsin and free retinine.
This process is called **bleaching** and results in depolarisation of the membrane of the rod.
A generator potential is created and an impulse passes to the brain.

Before it can be stimulated again, a rod has to resynthesise rhodopsin. The mitochondria provide energy in the form of ATP to resynthesise rhodopsin from opsin and retinine.

Cones are high light intensity colour receptors.
Their visual pigment, iodopsin, is less easily broken down and takes longer to be resynthesised.
In bright light, most of the rhodopsin in the rods is bleached and the eye is said to be **light adapted**.
Vision is poor if the retina is exposed to dim light, as it takes time for the rods to resynthesise rhodopsin and regain their response. This is why your eyes need time to adjust if you enter a cinema on a sunny day.
Once your rods have resynthesised rhodopsin, your retina is said to be **dark adapted**.

▷ Colour vision

The **trichromatic theory** of colour vision suggests that there are three different types of iodopsin located in three different types of cone.
Each distinct type of cone responds to one of blue, green or red light.
The graph shows the extent of stimulation of each type of cone at different wavelengths of light.
Can you see that the graphs overlap?
So light with a wavelength between blue, green and red stimulates a combination of cones.
For instance, yellow light stimulates equal numbers of red and green cones and the brain interprets the impulses as yellow.
Orange light stimulates more red than green cones and the brain interprets these impulses as orange.

Deficiency of one or more cone types produces **colour blindness**.
Because the graphs overlap, absence of red cones means that it is still possible for green cones to detect green, yellow, orange and red.
But the brain cannot distinguish between these colours properly as there are no impulses from red cones with which to contrast impulses from green cones.
This **red–green colour blindness** is relatively common.

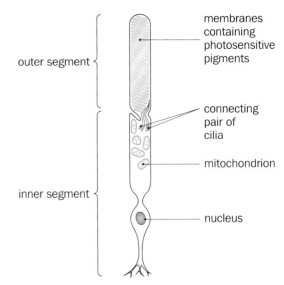

The structure of a rod

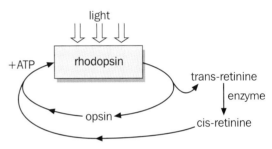

The breakdown and regeneration of rhodopsin

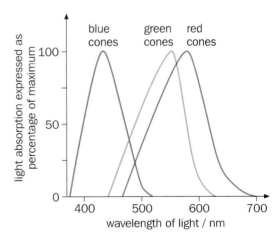

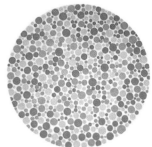

Can you see the numbers …?

▶ The spinal cord

The **spinal cord** is a hollow tube running from the base of the brain to the end of the spine.

Together with the brain it makes up the central nervous system (CNS). The spinal cord is protected by the vertebrae which make up the backbone.

Pairs of **spinal nerves** branch off the spinal cord in the gaps between neighbouring vertebrae.

Each pair of spinal nerves contain sensory neurones bringing impulses to the CNS and motor neurones carrying impulses away.

When viewed in section, the spinal cord can be seen to consist of two distinct areas.

- The central **grey matter** containing the cell bodies of relay and motor neurones.
- The outer **white matter** containing myelinated axons, which run up and down the spinal cord to and from the brain.

In the centre of the grey matter is the **spinal canal**, through which the nutritive **cerebrospinal fluid** circulates.

Spinal nerves join and leave the spinal cord through the dorsal and ventral roots.

Sensory neurones enter the spinal cord via the dorsal root and the concentration of their cell bodies forms a swelling called the **dorsal root ganglion**.

Motor neurones leave the spinal cord via the ventral root.

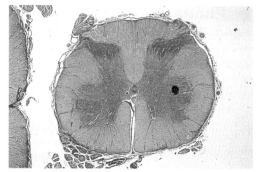

Photomicrograph of T.S. of the spinal cord

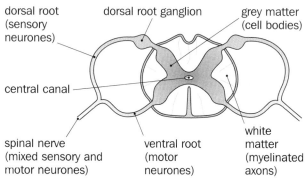

T.S. of the spinal cord

▶ Spinal reflexes

A **reflex** is an automatic, rapid response to an adverse stimulus. For instance, when you remove your hand from a hot object. The action is involuntary in that the brain is not involved in the actual response, though it may be informed of the event. Many reflexes are protective, but as you have seen in earlier chapters, complex actions such as swallowing, coughing and blinking are also coordinated by reflexes.

The neurones that are involved in a reflex make up a **reflex arc**.

Let's look at a withdrawal reflex arc.

A simplified reflex arc

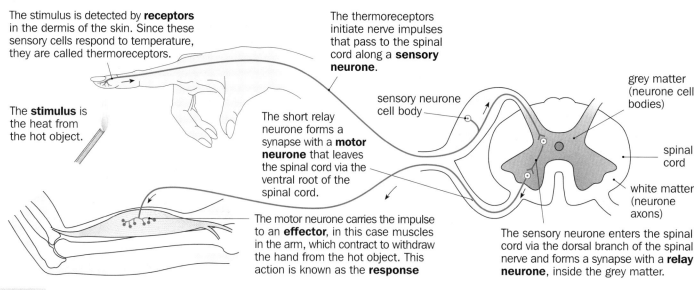

The stimulus is detected by **receptors** in the dermis of the skin. Since these sensory cells respond to temperature, they are called thermoreceptors.

The thermoreceptors initiate nerve impulses that pass to the spinal cord along a **sensory neurone**.

The **stimulus** is the heat from the hot object.

The short relay neurone forms a synapse with a **motor neurone** that leaves the spinal cord via the ventral root of the spinal cord.

The motor neurone carries the impulse to an **effector**, in this case muscles in the arm, which contract to withdraw the hand from the hot object. This action is known as the **response**

The sensory neurone enters the spinal cord via the dorsal branch of the spinal nerve and forms a synapse with a **relay neurone**, inside the grey matter.

▶ The brain

Like the spinal cord, the brain is made up of grey and white matter. In this case, the white matter is on the inside and the grey matter, made up of cell bodies, is located in the outer **cortex**.
The brain has spaces continuous with that in the spinal cord. These cavities are called **ventricles** and contain cerebrospinal fluid.

During the development of the CNS, the brain forms as a swelling at the end of the spinal cord.
This swelling soon forms three distinct regions: the **forebrain**, the **midbrain** and the **hindbrain**.
It is not easy to see this division in humans because the roof of the forebrain (the **cerebrum**) has grown massively to completely cover the midbrain and the hindbrain.

The brain is surrounded by three protective membranes called **meninges**, and is of course encased by the skull.

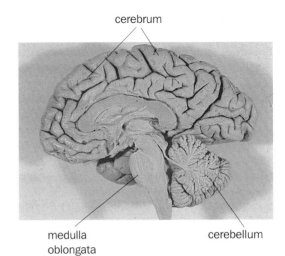

Vertical section through the human brain

Functions of the brain

The brain is a complex organ to study, and we will only look at the major parts and their associated functions.

The **medulla oblongata** is part of the hindbrain that controls many reflex actions of the body.
The **vagus nerve** leaves the medulla, carrying impulses that affect heart rate (see Chapter 11), breathing rate (see Chapter 10), blood pressure and peristalsis of the gut.
The medulla also controls such reflexes as swallowing, coughing and the secretion of saliva.

The **cerebellum** is also part of the hindbrain. It receives sensory information from muscles and the ears.
It is concerned with posture, body movement and balance.
The cerebellum coordinates smooth body movements such as walking, dancing and riding a bike.

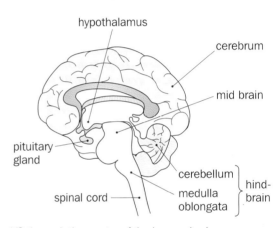

VS through the centre of the human brain

The **hypothalamus** is found at the base of the forebrain.
It is the main controlling centre for the **autonomic nervous system**.
As you have seen, the hypothalamus monitors the blood passing through it and so regulates body temperature and blood composition.
The hypothalamus also regulates the activities of the pituitary gland, which itself influences the actions of other endocrine glands.

The hypothalamus therefore provides an important link between the nervous system and the endocrine system.

The **cerebral hemispheres** form the cerebrum, or roof, of the forebrain.
The cerebral hemispheres receive sensory information, interpret it in terms of previous experience and send out motor information to bring about the appropriate responses.
In this way, all the voluntary actions of the body are coordinated.
The cerebral hemispheres are the site of such complex faculties as learning, reasoning, intelligence, personality and memory.
War injuries and operations on brain tumours have enabled scientists to map out many of the sensory areas and motor areas of the cerebral cortex.

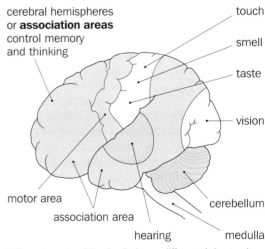

Different parts of the brain have different jobs to do

▶ The effectors: muscles

There are three types of muscle.

Cardiac muscle is found only in the heart. As you saw in
in Chapter 11, it is **myogenic** – that is, it initiates its own contractions.

Smooth muscle is often called **involuntary muscle**, because
it is not under conscious control.
It is under the control of the autonomic nervous system and is found in
the walls of the gut, blood vessels, ureters, bladder, urethra and uterus.

Skeletal muscle is often called **voluntary muscle,** since it is under
conscious control, or **striated muscle**, because of its appearance.
It is this type of muscle that we shall be looking at in detail.

As its name suggests, skeletal muscle is attached to the skeleton
by non-elastic tendons.
Contraction of skeletal muscle enables us to carry out movements.

Muscle structure

An individual skeletal muscle is made up of hundreds of **muscle fibres**.
Within each muscle fibre are numerous **myofibrils**, which are thin
threads that run the length of a muscle fibre and have a characteristic
striped appearance along their length.

You can see how skeletal muscle gets its striped appearance by using an
electron microscope.
Each myofibril is made up of alternating light and dark bands, because
each myofibril is composed of overlapping strands of contractile
protein called **myosin** and smaller protein strands called **actin**.

Each contractile unit within the myofibril is called a **sarcomere**.
It is the way in which the myosin and actin filaments overlap that gives
each sarcomere its banded appearance.

If you look at the diagram you will see that there is a region where the
actin and myosin filaments overlap, giving a dark **A band**.

Between the dark bands are lighter bands where only actin is present.
This region is called the **I band**.

Within each dark A band you can see that there is a region made up
of only myosin filaments. This is called the **H zone**.

As we have said, the regions where only actin is present look lighter.
We have called these the I bands.
In the centre of each I band is the **Z line**.
The Z line marks the end of one sarcomere and the beginning of the
next. The sarcomere is the basic unit of muscle contraction.

Around each myofibril is a network of small tubes containing calcium
ions.
These have a major part to play in the contraction of skeletal muscle.

Actin filaments also contain two other proteins that are involved
in the mechanism of muscle contraction.
These are called **troponin** and **tropomyosin**.

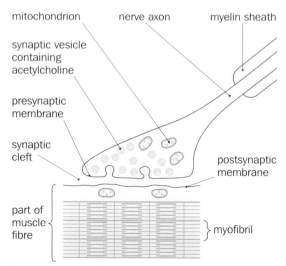

A neuromuscular junction

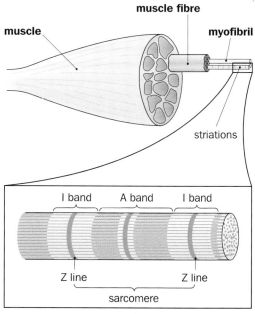

The detailed structure of a muscle

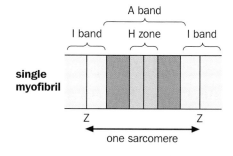

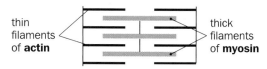

▶ How do muscles contract?

When a muscle contracts, the actin filaments slide over the myosin filaments.
This brings about the following changes that can be observed in a sarcomere under the electron microscope:

- the I bands become shorter,
- the A band does not change in length,
- the Z lines become closer together, so the sarcomere shortens,
- the H zone becomes narrower.

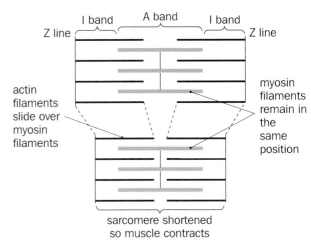

Changes in a sarcomere during muscle contraction

The sliding filament theory of muscle contraction

So how do the actin filaments slide over the myosin filaments when a muscle contracts?

- A nerve impulse reaches the neuromuscular junction.
- Synaptic vesicles are released (in the same way as in a synapse), and the transmitter (acetylcholine) diffuses across and depolarises the membrane of the muscle fibre, producing an action potential.

1. When the muscle is relaxed, the binding sites on the actin are covered by tropomyosin.

- Calcium ions are released from the system of tubes into the muscle fibres.
- The calcium ions bind with troponin and alter its shape.
- Troponin is now able to displace tropomyosin, which has been blocking its binding site on the actin filaments.

2. When the membrane of the muscle is depolarised calcium ions are released from the tubes and bind with the troponin which displaces tropomyosin from the binding site.

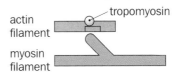

- This enables the myosin heads to attach to the actin filaments, using energy provided by ATP.
- As the myosin heads attach to the actin binding sites, they tilt, causing the actin filaments to slide past the myosin filaments.
- As the actin filaments move, the myosin heads become detached, and then attach to the next binding site on the actin filaments.
- Calcium ions are actively absorbed back into the system of tubes.

3. The myosin head binds to the actin, using energy from ATP and forming an actomyosin bridge.

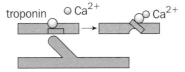

4. As the myosin heads attach to the actin filaments they tilt causing the actin filaments to slide past.

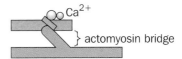

- Troponin changes back into its original shape and so allows tropomyosin to once again block the binding sites on the actin filaments.
- The way in which the muscle contracts is known as the **ratchet mechanism**.

5. As the actin filaments move past, the myosin heads become detached and attach to the next binding site. Troponin reverts to its original shape and once again tropomyosin blocks the binding site on the actin filaments.

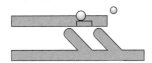

▶ Biology at work: The effect of drugs on synaptic transmission

Most drugs that affect the nervous system do so
by influencing the transmission of nerve impulses
across synapses.
In some cases (for example, amphetamines) the drug affects
the release of the neurotransmitters. Other drugs
(for example, beta-blockers) modify the effects that the
neurotransmitters have on the postsynaptic membrane.

Drugs affecting the nervous system can also be categorised
as either **excitatory** or **inhibitory** in their effects.
Excitatory drugs amplify synaptic transmission whilst
inhibitory drugs decrease the process.

Excitatory drugs

Amphetamines are a group of excitatory drugs which also
suppress the appetite. Their original medical use was in treating
obesity but they are much less widely prescribed now because
patients may develop a dependency. Amphetamines stimulate the
release of neurotransmitters such as **noradrenaline.** This has the
effect of increasing brain activity, making a person more alert.
Due to this stimulant effect, amphetamines are liable to abuse
and their prescription is controlled by legislation.
Caffeine also leads to the release of more noradrenaline.

Ecstasy – the designer drug of the 90s – is related to
amphetamines. Its effects are similar in that it makes
people feel lively and alert. As with amphetamines,
though, excessive use can cause adverse side effects,
such as high temperatures and convulsions.

Inhibitory drugs

Beta-blockers are an example of inhibitory drugs.
They are principally used to treat heart disease,
although they can also be used to reduce the physical
symptoms of anxiety, such as palpitations and tremors.
They work by blocking the so-called **beta receptors**.
These are specific sites where neurotransmitters bind.
The beta-1 receptors are found in heart muscle and the
beta-2 receptors in tissues such as the lungs and blood vessels.

By blocking these receptors, beta-blockers inhibit the binding of
neurotransmitters such as **adrenaline** and **noradrenaline**.
The normal effect of these chemicals is to increase cardiac output,
increase airflow in the lungs and dilate blood vessels.

Drugs such as beta-blockers are known as **antagonists**
because they interfere with the normal action of a transmitter.
Drugs that produce a similar effect to a transmitter are known
as **agonists**.

▶ Biology at work: Motor neurone disease

Motor neurone disease (MND) is a fatal disease, which arises as a result of degeneration of **motor neurones** in the spinal cord and brain. MND is characterised by the following progressive symptoms:

- twitching and cramping of muscles in the hands and feet,
- impairment of the use of the arms and legs,
- 'thick speech' and difficulty in projecting the voice,
- shortness of breath, and difficulty in breathing and swallowing, which eventually results in death.

Intellect and memory are usually not affected, nor are the senses, which are dependent on **sensory neurones** to relay impulses. Diagnosis of the disease is difficult and requires a range of tests to eliminate other conditions.
Often an **electromyograph** (**EMG**) is used, in which a needle is inserted into various muscles to measure electrical activity. The incidence of the disease is between 1.5 and 2 per 100,000 population per year. About 50% of patients die within 3 years of the first symptom. Some patients may survive longer, with a few rare cases exceeding 10 years.

The cause of MND is not known and there is no known treatment to halt or reverse its progression.
In the last 5–10 years, much research has been carried out and two possible mechanisms for the cause of MND have been found:

- free radical effects,
- excitotoxic effects.

In 1993, a research team identified a defective gene which codes for the **superoxide dismutase** enzyme (SOD).
SOD helps to protect motor neurones from **free radical** damage, by inactivating the superoxide radical.
Free radicals are highly unstable, very reactive chemicals, which contain an unpaired electron. They react with and damage key biological molecules such as nucleic acids.

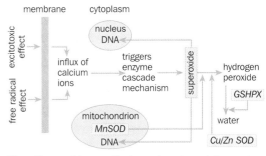

The effects of free radicals and excitotoxicity on the membranes of motor neurosis are linked

Chemical neurotransmitters can become toxic if their concentration exceeds the normal physiological amount, in which case they are said to be **excitotoxic**. Excitotoxic damage affects membranes, causing an excessive influx of calcium ions into the cell.
This triggers a cascade mechanism involving a number of enzymes, which results in the death of the motor neurone.
A well-studied excitotoxic neurotransmitter substance is the amino acid **glutamate**. This shows an increase in concentration in the cerebrospinal fluid of MND sufferers.
Both mechanisms may in fact be interlinked in bringing about the destruction of motor neurones.

The recently licensed drug **riluzole** is effective at minimising the impact of glutamate on motor neurones by inhibiting its release. The effects, however, are slight, with an average gain in life expectancy of only 2 months.
This may seem negligible compared with the cost of the treatment for a 50 mg/day dose for this period, which is £1600. Such apparently modest gains are the norm initially with medical research, where any progress has to be seen as encouraging both for the patient and the research teams.

Professor Stephen Hawking, the world famous physicist, has had MND for 30 years

▶ Plant growth substances

Growth in plants is coordinated by **plant growth substances** (**PGS**).
These are produced in certain areas of the plant and transported
to other parts where they can affect cell division, cell elongation and
cell differentiation.
Plant growth substances are not specific and can affect different tissues
and organs in contrasting ways.
Different PGS may interact to increase each other's effects, in which
case they are said to be **synergic**.
Alternatively PGS may act to decrease each other's effects, in which
case they are said to be **antagonistic**.

▶ Auxin

Auxin was the first growth-promoting substance to be isolated.
As long ago as 1880, Charles Darwin noticed that grass **coleoptiles**
grew towards the direction of a light source.
A coleoptile covers and protects the embryo leaves and stem apex.
The response of part of a plant to light is called **phototropism**.
Shoots respond by growing towards the light, so are
positively phototropic.
Roots respond by growing away from the light, so are
negatively phototropic.

Regions of actively dividing cells are known as **meristems**.
Apical meristems are found at the tips of shoots and roots.
Experiments have shown that when shoots are exposed to light from
one direction, auxin is transported to the shaded side.
Here it stimulates cell elongation and the elongated cells cause
the shoot to bend towards the light.

Geotropism is the response of a shoot or root to gravity.

If a shoot or root is placed in a horizontal position, then auxin tends
to accumulate on the lower side.
In shoots, the auxin stimulates more cell elongation on the lower side
and as a result, the shoot bends upwards. It is **negatively geotropic**.
However in roots, high concentrations of auxin inhibit cell elongation.
So when auxin accumulates on the lower side of a root it slows down
the degree of cell elongation compared to the upper side of the root.

The result is that there is greater cell elongation on the upper surface
and so the root bends downwards. It is **positively geotropic**.

At high concentrations, auxins prevent the growth of lateral shoots.
Many gardeners remove the shoot tips of a plant to make it grow
bushier. This is because the uppermost (apical) bud produces auxin,
which is transported down the stem and inhibits the growth of lateral
buds.
This is known as **apical dominance**.
Normally the auxin produced by the apical bud, passes down
the stem and stimulates elongation in the cells just behind
the apical meristem, but inhibits the growth of lateral buds.
Removal of the apical bud means that the growth of lateral buds
is no longer inhibited and so a bushier plant is produced.
This effect occurs every time a hedge is clipped.

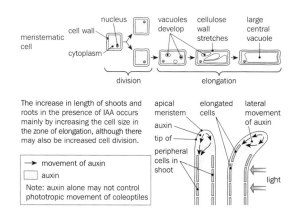

The increase in length of shoots and
roots in the presence of IAA occurs
mainly by increasing the cell size in
the zone of elongation, although there
may also be increased cell division.

→ movement of auxin
☐ auxin
Note: auxin alone may not control
phototropic movement of coleoptiles

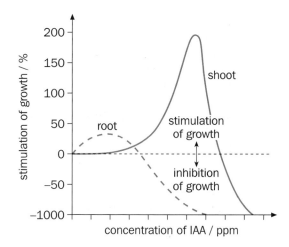

▶ Gibberellins

Gibberellins were first discovered by Japanese scientists studying a plant disease caused by a fungus.
The active growth substances were isolated from the fungus *Gibberella fujikuroi* in 1935 and called gibberellins after the fungus.

Gibberellins are produced in seeds, young leaves and young apical tissues, particularly in root apices.
In cereal grains, gibberellins stimulate the production of α-amylase.
After water has been absorbed by the seed, gibberellins diffuse from the seed embryo to a layer where the enzyme α-amylase is made.
The enzyme hydrolyses the seed's food store, mobilising food that the embryo uses to grow.
Dormancy, a period of low metabolic activity, is broken and germination begins.

Gibberellins also affect stem elongation in dwarf plants.
Normal growth is prevented because the gene controlling gibberellin production is switched off.
But if gibberellins are sprayed onto the surface of dwarf plants, they grow to their normal height.

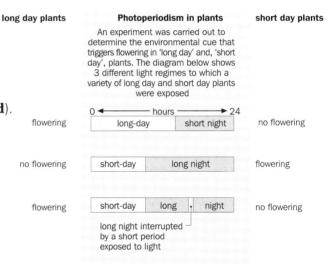

The role of gibberellin in seed germination

▶ Photoperiodism

Photoperiodism is the response of a plant to the relative lengths of daylight and darkness.
Flowering is affected by the period of illumination (**photoperiod**).
Flowering plants can be classified according to the photoperiod in which they flower.

Day neutral plants, such as snapdragons, flower whenever they have grown sufficiently. The photoperiod has no effect.

Long day plants, such as spinach and poppy, only flower if the number of hours of light to which they have been exposed is *above* a certain critical level (or alternatively, the number of hours of darkness is *below* a critical level).

Short day plants, such as chrysanthemums and strawberries, only flower when the number of hours of light to which they are exposed is *below* a certain critical level (or alternatively, the number of hours of darkness is *above* a critical level).

The photoreceptor involved in photoperiodism is the light-sensitive pigment called **phytochrome**, which exists in two forms:
phytochrome 660 (P_r) absorbs red light, and
phytochrome 730 (P_{fr}) absorbs far-red light.
On absorbing light of a particular wavelength, each form of phytochrome is converted to the other form.
Sunlight contains much more light of wavelength 660 nm than 730 nm, so during daylight, P_r is converted to P_{fr}, which accumulates.
P_{fr} is unstable and, during the hours of darkness, slowly reverts back to P_r, which accumulates.
The plant measures day length (or rather night length) by the amount of phytochrome existing in each of the two forms. In daylight, P_{fr} predominates.
Flowering in plants is thought to be initiated by a hormone 'florigen'.
In long day plants, a high concentration of P_{fr} is needed for the release of florigen.
In short day plants, a high concentration of P_r elicits the release of florigen.

Photoperiodism in plants

An experiment was carried out to determine the environmental cue that triggers flowering in 'long day' and, 'short day', plants. The diagram below shows 3 different light regimes to which a variety of long day and short day plants were exposed

long day plants		short day plants
flowering	long-day / short night (0 → 24 hours)	no flowering
no flowering	short-day / long night	flowering
flowering	short-day / long night (long night interrupted by a short period exposed to light)	no flowering

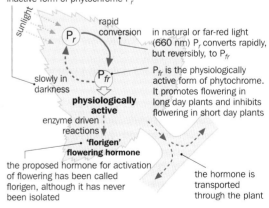

in the dark, or in far-red light (730 nm), P_{fr} reverts spontaneously, but slowly, back to the physiologically inactive form of phytochrome P_r

rapid conversion — in natural or far-red light (660 nm) P_r converts rapidly, but reversibly, to P_{fr}

P_{fr} is the physiologically active form of phytochrome. It promotes flowering in long day plants and inhibits flowering in short day plants

slowly in darkness

physiologically active
enzyme driven reactions ↓
• **'florigen' flowering hormone**

the proposed hormone for activation of flowering has been called florigen, although it has never been isolated

the hormone is transported through the plant

▶ Biology at work: Commercial applications of plant hormones

Plant hormones are commonly referred to as **plant growth substances** because they are chemicals that modify plant growth.
They can affect cell division, cell elongation or cell differentiation or indeed any combination of these stages of growth.

Plant growth substances, or more commonly their synthetic derivatives called **plant growth regulators**, are widely used in horticulture and agriculture.
They are used to increase both the yield and quality of a crop, as well as to increase the efficiency of harvesting.

The yield of a crop can be significantly reduced by competing species

Synthetic auxins such as 2,4-D are very effective as **selective weed killers**.
Important cereal crops are narrow leaved (monocotyledonous), whereas most of their competing weeds are broad leaved (dicotyledonous).
Concentrations of auxins that have a significant effect on broad leaved plants have little effect on the narrow leaved crops.
The auxin increases the growth rate of the affected plants, probably through interfering with protein production.
The plants cannot sustain this rate of growth and they soon die.

Synthetic auxins are also used in rooting powders because they stimulate the growth of side roots from cut stems.

Ethene is another plant growth substance with important commercial applications.
Its main effect is the stimulation of flowering and the ripening of fruit.
It is used with crops such as pineapples to synchronise fruiting.
This makes harvesting a much more efficient process.
It is also widely used to induce ripening of fruit prior to its appearance on supermarket shelves.

Other plant growth substances also have commercial applications.
Cytokinins, for example, are used to extend the life of leafy crops like lettuce.
They achieve this by delaying leaf senescence (ageing).

Some of these chemicals can be used in combination with each other (synergistically).
Cytokinin together with auxin and gibberellin can be used to promote **parthenocarpy**.
This is fruit formation without fertilisation.
The seedless fruits it produces are very popular with consumers.

Ethene can induce ripening of bananas

Summary

- The nervous system controls and coordinates our actions by detecting stimuli, processing the information and initiating responses.
- The stimuli are detected by receptors and the responses are brought about by effectors.
- Neurones are the basic functional units of the nervous system. Sensory neurones carry impulses to the brain and spinal cord, passing their impulses on to relay neurones, which in turn pass their impulses on to motor neurones.
- At rest, the nerve axon is polarised. The sodium-potassium pump makes the outside of the axon positive and the inside of the axon negative.
- An action potential results in the inside of the axon becoming positive and the outside negative.
- Changes in the permeability of the axon membrane result in an influx of sodium ions and depolarisation before the sodium-potassium pump is re-established and the axon is repolarised.
- An action potential can only be generated if the stimulus reaches a certain threshold intensity.
- Following the passage of an impulse, there is a time delay, or refractory period, before another action potential can be created.
- The speed of transmission of an impulse is affected by the axon diameter and the presence of a myelin sheath.
- A synapse is where two neurones functionally meet. The transfer of information from one neurone to the next relies on the secretion of neurotransmitters such as acetylcholine and noradrenaline.
- The Pacinian corpuscle is a mechanoreceptor found in the dermis of the skin.
- The human eye is a complex organ containing photoreceptors, and able to control the amount of light that enters it, refract light rays in order to focus them, and transduce light energy into action potentials.
- The trichromatic theory of colour vision suggests that there are three distinct types of iodopsin located in three different types of cone.
- A spinal reflex consists of a receptor, a sensory neurone, a relay neurone, a motor neurone and an effector.
- The sliding filament theory provides the basic mechanism for muscle contraction.
- Plant growth substances have various commercial applications, including rooting powders, selective weed killers and stimulating the ripening of fruit.

▶ Questions

1   a) Name the type of neurone shown in the diagram.
   b) Name the structures labelled X and Y.
   c) A nerve impulse can be initiated by stimulation with a microelectrode.
      What would be the effect of stimulation at point Z?
   d) The synaptic bulbs release a chemical transmitter, acetylcholine. Nerve gases prevent the breakdown of this chemical. From this information suggest
      i) one early symptom of nerve gas poisoning,
      ii) one reason for this observed symptom.

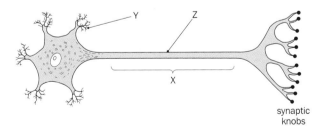

synaptic knobs

2   a) Name the regions X and Y on the diagram of the nerve axon.
   b) What effect does X have on the part of the axon that it covers.
   c) What is the main chemical present in the region labelled X?

   d) What effect does the distribution of this chemical have on the transmission of impulses along the neurone?

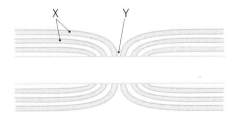

3   The graph shows the change in potential difference at a point in a neurone during the propagation of a nerve impulse.

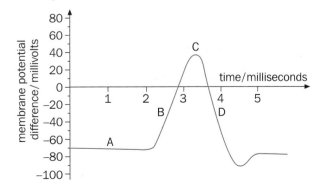

a) From the graph give the value of
   i) the resting potential of the neurone,
   ii) the maximum change which occurs in the potential difference across the membrane.
b) Explain, in terms of ion movements, the change in potential difference that takes place between
   i) points A and B,
   ii) points C and D.

4 a) Name the following structure in the synapse:
   i) structure A,
   ii) structure B,
   iii) the contents of structure B.

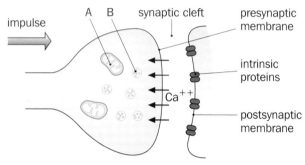

b) The arrival of an impulse changes the permeability of the presynaptic membrane, allowing calcium ions to rapidly diffuse in as shown by the arrows on the diagram.
   Describe the effect caused by this influx of ions.
c) Sodium ions also play a vital part in this process.
   i) Use the diagram to name the parts of the synapse that can act as a channel for sodium ions.
   ii) Suggest how these channels are opened.
d) i) Describe the effect that their opening has on the postsynaptic membrane.
   ii) Explain fully why structure A is found abundantly in the presynaptic region.

5 When the back of the hand accidentally touches a hot surface, the biceps muscle contracts and the hand is rapidly removed. This is an example of a reflex action involving three neurones.
a) i) Explain what is meant by a reflex action.
   ii) Name the effector involved in the above reflex action.
b) The diagram shows a cross-section through the spinal cord.
   Copy and complete the diagram, labelling the neurones involved in the reflex action.

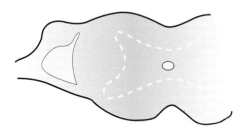

6 a) Describe the trichromatic theory of colour vision.
b) It is possible to measure the light-absorbing properties of the pigments in the colour-sensitive cells of the retina. The graphs show the results obtained from two people.
   Suggest and explain how the colour vision of these two people would be different.

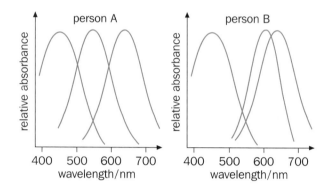

7 The diagram shows the appearance of a sarcomere from a relaxed muscle microfibril, as seen through a light microscope.
a) Use your knowledge of the sliding filament theory to explain the appearance of each of the bands P, Q and R.
b) Draw a similar diagram to show the appearance of the sarcomere when the microfibril is contracted.
c) Explain what has happened to cause the effect shown in your diagram.

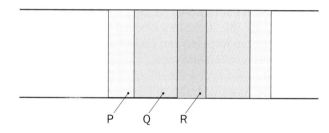

8 The graph shows the effect of applying different concentrations of auxin to the roots and shoots of a plant. Use the graph to describe three ways in which the response of the roots to auxin differs from the response of the shoots.

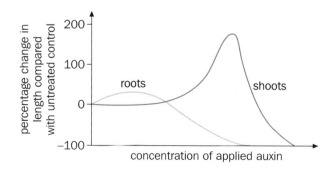

▶ Respiration

1 The passage below is a description of cellular respiration. Copy and complete the passage by writing the correct number in each of the spaces provided.

In the conversion of 1 molecule of glucose to 2 molecules of pyruvate, ... molecule(s) of ATP are first used up. Overall, the net production from glycolysis is . . . . . molecule(s) of ATP and . . . . . molecule(s) of reduced NAD.
At the beginning of the Krebs cycle, the 2 carbon acetyl group from acetyl coenzyme A combines with a molecule containing . . . . . carbon atoms.
Each turn of the Krebs cycle produces . . . . . molecule(s) of carbon dioxide, 1 molecule of reduced FAD and . . . . . molecule(s) of reduced NAD.
Oxidation of a molecule of reduced NAD results in the production of . . . . . molecule(s) of ATP by the electron transport chain. [7]

(WJEC) **[7]**

2 The diagram below shows the main stages of aerobic respiration.

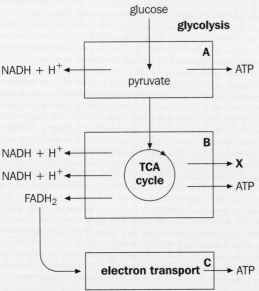

a) State precisely where the reactions in boxes A, B and C occur in the cell. [3]
b) Name substance X. [1]
c) A total of 38 molecules of ATP are formed during the complete breakdown of one molecule of glucose. State how many molecules of ATP are formed at each of the stages A, B and C. [2]
d) If glucose is burned, the energy transferred as heat and light is 2881 kJ mol^{-1}. In the reactions described above, some of the energy is retained in the form of ATP. The energy 'trapped' in ATP is 50 kJ mol^{-1}. Calculate the percentage of the energy made available from the breakdown of one molecule of glucose which is retained for biological reaction in the cell. Show your working. [3]

(O&C) **[9]**

3 The diagram below shows part of the respiratory pathway. The broken arrows represent intermediate stages.

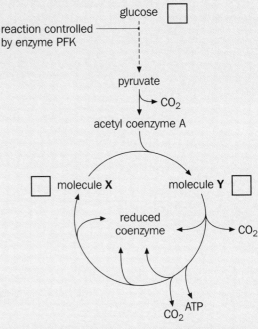

a) Copy the diagram and in each of the boxes write the number of carbon atoms in the named molecules. [1]
b) Give *two* different chemical processes which are involved in the conversion of molecule Y to molecule X in the Krebs cycle. [2]
c) Describe how the reduced coenzyme produced from the Krebs cycle may be used to produce ATP. [3]
d) ATP regulates its own production in respiration by affecting the activity of the enzyme PFK. Suggest how this regulation may be achieved through negative feedback. [2]

(NEAB) **[8]**

4 The diagram below shows some of the processes that occur within a mitochondrion and some of the substances that enter and leave it.

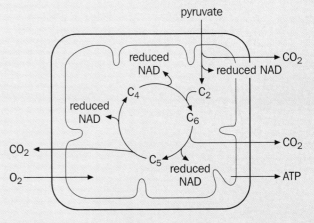

a) i) Name the process that produces pyruvate in the cytoplasm. [1]

ii) Name the process that produces reduced NAD and carbon dioxide in the matrix of the mitochondrion. [1]

b) Describe how ATP is produced from reduced NAD within the mitochondrion. [3]

(NEAB) **[5]**

▶ Photosynthesis

5 The diagram below summarises the biochemical pathways involved in photosynthesis.

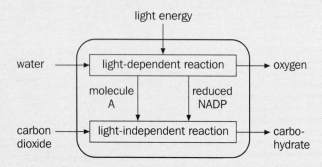

a) Name molecule A. [1]

b) i) Describe how NADP$^+$ is reduced in the light-dependent reaction. [2]

ii) Describe the part played by reduced NADP in the light-independent reaction. [2]

a) Suggest why, in a young plant, you would expect the rate of photosynthesis to be greater than the rate of respiration over a 24-hour period. [1]

(NEAB) **[6]**

6 The diagram below shows some of the processes which occur in the light-independent reaction of photosynthesis.

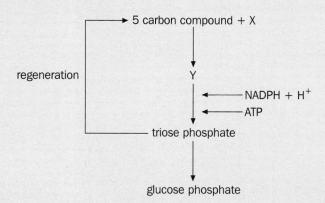

a) Name substances X and Y. [2]

b) State the origin of the NADPH + H$^+$ and the ATP used in the light-independent reaction. [1]

c) Where in the chloroplast does the light-independent reaction occur? [1]

(London) **[4]**

7 The graph below shows how the wavelength of light affects the rate of photosynthesis.

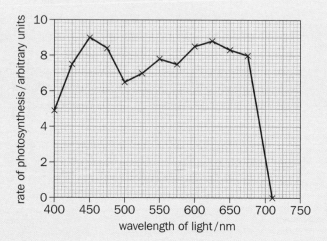

a) i) What name is given to the relationship between wavelength of light and the rate of photosynthesis, as shown in this graph? [1]

ii) From the graph, state the optimum wavelength of light for photosynthesis. [1]

iii) Explain the effect on the rate of photosynthesis of varying the wavelength of light from 550 to 700 nm. [2]

b) i) Name the stage of photosynthesis that produces oxygen. [1]

ii) State where in a chloroplast this stage would occur. [1]

(London) **[6]**

8 Copy and complete the following account of photosynthesis by selecting appropriate answers from the list below. Not all the answers are needed. Each answer selected should be used once only.
ATP; cyclic phosphorylation; hydrogen; light-dependent; light-independent; NAD$^+$; NADP$^+$; non-cyclic phosphorylation; oxygen; photosystem I; photosystem II; pyruvic acid; ribose bisphosphate; ribulose bisphosphate; water; phosphoglyceraldehyde;

Photosynthesis consists of two major stages. In the first stage, known as the . . . . . stage, molecules of . . . . . are broken down liberating . . . . . gas. Photosynthetic pigments, collectively known as . . . . ., absorb light at a wavelength of 680 nm and the energy is used to raise an electron to a higher energy level. This electron may be involved in the reduction of a carrier called . . . . . or it may be involved in the synthesis of . . . . . in a process called . . . . . . These compounds are used in the second stage of photosynthesis called the . . . . . stage. Carbon dioxide combines with . . . . . to form . . . . . and this is used to form sugars and starch. [10]

(O&C) **[10]**

9 The graph below shows the rate of photosynthesis in two crop plants, A and B, at different light intensities.

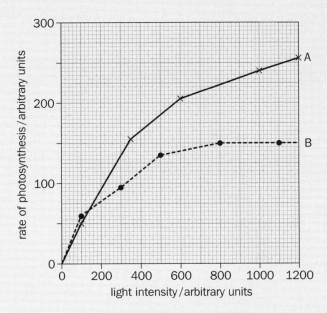

a) Describe the ways in which increasing light intensity has similar effects on the two crops. [2]
b) Suggest the most likely limiting factor for crop B at a light intensity of (i) 100 arbitrary units and (ii) 1000 arbitrary units [2]
c) From these data, suggest, with reasons, which crop is better suited for growth in tropical conditions. [2]
(NEAB) [6]

▶ **Homeostasis**

10 The table below shows the core temperatures of two camels at various times on a hot, sunny day.
Animal A was allowed to drink but animal B was deprived of water.

Time of day	Core temperature / °C	
	Animal A (allowed to drink)	Animal B (deprived of water)
9.00	36.0	34.8
12.00	37.5	38.6
15.00	39.2	40.1
24.00	35.8	37.0

a) Explain why the body temperature of animal A does not rise as high as that of animal B. [2]
b) Explain how the body temperature of animal B is controlled. [2]
(AEB) [4]

11 *Liolaemus* is a reptile which lives at a high altitude in the mountains of South America.
In an investigation, the air temperature and the body temperature of this lizard were measured at intervals during one morning. The results are shown in the table below.

Time of day (24 hour clock)	Air temperature / °C	Body temperature of lizard / °C
07.10	−3.0	2.5
07.20	−1.0	10.0
07.30	−2.0	19.0
08.00	1.0	31.0
08.20	1.5	33.0
08.45	5.0	34.0
10.00	9.0	35.0
11.00	13.0	36.0

a) Describe the changes in air temperature and body temperature during the following time intervals.
  i) 07.10 to 08.00 [2]
  ii) 08.00 to 11.00 [2]
b) Suggest how the lizard increases its body temperature during the early morning. [2]
c) Suggest how the lizard controls its body temperature between the hours of 08.45 and 11.00. [2]
d) Explain why it may be an advantage for this lizard to be able to control its body temperature. [2]
(London) [10]

12 A person fasted overnight and then swallowed 75 g of glucose. The graph below shows the resulting changes in the concentrations of insulin and glucose in the blood.

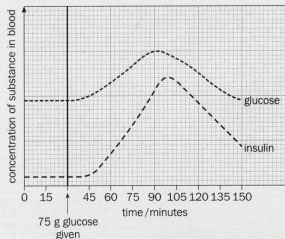

a) i) Explain the relationship between the concentrations of glucose and insulin in the blood in the first 30 minutes after the glucose was swallowed. [2]
  ii) Use information from the graph to explain what is meant by the term *negative feedback*. [1]
b) Explain why the concentration of glucagon in the blood rises during exercise while that of insulin falls. [2]
(AEB) [5]

351

13 An experiment was carried out to investigate the relationship between the concentrations of glucose and insulin in the blood of healthy people. At the start of this experiment, 34 volunteers each ingested a syrup containing 50 g of glucose. The concentration of glucose and insulin was determined in blood samples at intervals over a period of 2 hours. The results shown in the graph below are mean values for the group of volunteers.

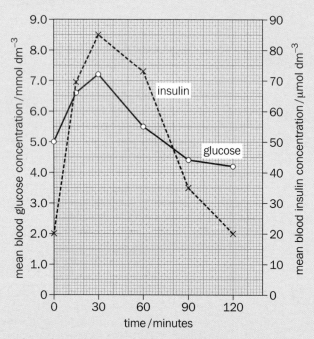

a) From the graph, find the mean concentration of insulin 100 minutes after the start of the experiment. [1]
b) Comment on the changes in the concentration of glucose during the following time intervals.
   i)   0 to 30 minutes [2]
   ii) 30 to 120 minutes [2]
c) Comment on the relationship between the concentrations of glucose and insulin as shown by this graph. [3]
d) Name *one* hormone, other than insulin, which is involved with the regulation of blood glucose and state its effect on blood glucose concentration. [2]
   (*London*) **[10]**

14 Copy the following account of kidney function, then write on the dotted lines the most appropriate word or words to complete the account.

In the kidney, the renal artery branches to form many smaller arterioles, each of which divides further to form a knot of capillaries, called a . . . . . . Here, small molecules such as . . . . . and . . . . . are forced into the cavity of the Bowman's (renal) capsule by the process of . . . . . . Selective reabsorption takes place in the

nephron. In the proximal convoluted tubule all the . . . . . is reabsorbed. In the ascending limb of the loop of Henle, ions are actively pumped out of the nephron. This causes . . . . . to be drawn out of the collecting duct. [6]
   (*London*) **[6]**

15 a) The kidney has a number of important functions which include excretion and homeostasis. Explain the meaning of the terms (i) *excretion* and (ii) *homeostasis*. [2]
   b) The table below shows the composition of some fluids from the body of a healthy individual under normal conditions.

Fluid	Concentration as percentage of total volume		
	Protein	Glucose	Urea
Blood plasma	8.1	0.1	0.3
Region of nephron (kidney tubule) Renal capsule			0.03
End of first convoluted tubule			0.03
Urine			1.9

   Copy and complete the table to show the values that you would expect for (i) protein and (ii) glucose. [2]
   c) i) Which region of the nephron is responsible for establishing a gradient of ions across the medulla? [1]
      ii) Explain how this gradient of ions leads to the production of concentrated urine. [2]
   (*NEAB*) **[7]**

▶ Control and coordination

16 The diagram below shows a neurone and some of the structures associated with it.

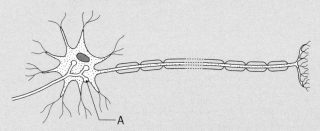

a) i) Name the type of neurone shown in the diagram. [1]
   ii) Give *one* reason for your answer. [1]
b) i) Name the part labelled A. [1]
   ii) Describe how A is involved in the passage of nerve impulses to the cell body of the neurone. [4]
   (*London*) **[7]**

17 The diagram below shows some of the events which occur in a synapse after the arrival of an impulse at the presynaptic membrane.

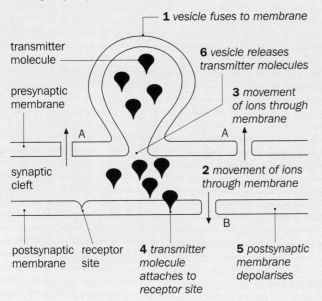

- **1** vesicle fuses to membrane
- transmitter molecule
- **6** vesicle releases transmitter molecules
- presynaptic membrane
- **3** movement of ions through membrane
- A
- A
- synaptic cleft
- **2** movement of ions through membrane
- B
- postsynaptic membrane
- receptor site
- **4** transmitter molecule attaches to receptor site
- **5** postsynaptic membrane depolarises

a) Put the events 1 to 6 on the diagram in the correct sequence. [1]

b) Name the ions labelled A and B. [2]

c) Name *one* transmitter molecule released by synaptic vesicles. [1]

(*NEAB*) **[4]**

18 The flow chart below shows some of the events which take place at a neuromuscular junction.

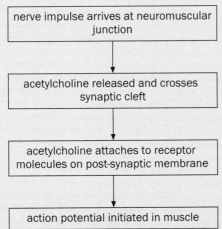

nerve impulse arrives at neuromuscular junction

↓

acetylcholine released and crosses synaptic cleft

↓

acetylcholine attaches to receptor molecules on post-synaptic membrane

↓

action potential initiated in muscle

a) By what process does acetylcholine cross the synaptic cleft? [1]

b) Molecules of the drug curare are very similar in shape to those of acetylcholine. Explain the following statements.

   i) Curare can be used to stop muscles from contracting during a surgical operation. [2]

   ii) Curare has no effect on an adrenergic synapse. [2]

(*NEAB*) **[5]**

19 The diagram below shows rod cells from the retina of a human eye.

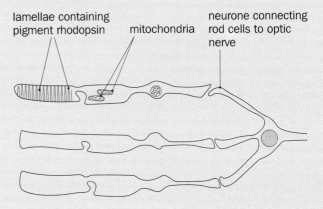

- lamellae containing pigment rhodopsin
- mitochondria
- neurone connecting rod cells to optic nerve

a) Describe the effect of light on rhodopsin. [2]

b) i) What is the function of mitochondria? [1]

   ii) Suggest why there are large numbers of mitochondria in a rod cell. [1]

c) Explain how the connections between the rod cells and the neurones in the optic nerve enable the eye to be sensitive to low light intensities. [2]

(*NEAB*) **[6]**

20 Copy the following passage, which refers to the structure and function of striated muscle, then write on the dotted lines the most appropriate word or words to complete the account.

A striated muscle fibre contains many strands, called . . . . ., which run the length of each fibre. Within these strands there are thick filaments made of the protein . . . . ., and thin filaments which contain the protein . . . . . . When a muscle contracts, the two kinds of filament slide past each other. Energy to enable the sliding filaments to move is provided by molecules of . . . . ., attached to the head of each thick filament. [4]

(*London*) **[4]**

21 a) Name the main plant growth substance involved in each of the following:
rooting powders; growth of seedless grapes; delaying fruit drop; induction of flowering in pineapples; [4]

b) When a leaf is detached from a plant it will normally turn yellow and lose protein and RNA very rapidly. In an investigation into this process, a spot of plant growth substance X was placed on a recently detached leaf. A green area of active tissue remained where substance X had been placed. The rest of the leaf became yellow.

   i) Identify plant growth substance X. [1]

   ii) Suggest the probable mode of action of substance X. [2]

(*NEAB*) **[7]**

353

20 Inheritance

Gregor Mendel (1822–84) was an Austrian monk and teacher.
He was the first person to work out the ways in which genes are inherited.
He worked with pea plants to study their patterns of inheritance.
He chose plants with easily observable features, such as
plant height, flower colour and seed shape.
To some extent Mendel was lucky, since he chose characteristics
that are controlled by single genes.
He was painstaking in his methods, meticulously collecting and
recording his results. He built up sufficient amounts of accurate data
to enable him to come to sound scientific conclusions.
The amazing thing about Mendel's work is that he worked out
the underlying rules of inheritance before any knowledge
of DNA, genes or chromosomes became available.

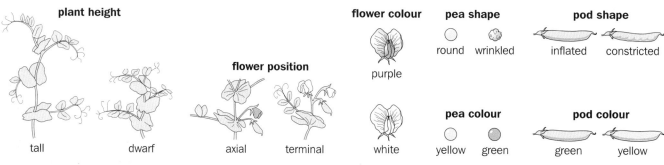

▷ Alleles

As you saw in Chapter 7, nearly all organisms that reproduce
sexually have homologous pairs of chromosomes: they are **diploid**.
One of each pair comes from the father and one from the mother.
At each particular position, or **locus**, along each chromosome pair,
there will be equivalent copies of a gene.
Different versions of a gene can be found in a population and
these are called **alleles**.

Some alleles are **dominant** and are able to mask the effect
of other **recessive** alleles. For instance, the allele for tall plant,
T, is dominant to the allele for dwarf plant, **t**, which is recessive.

If the two alleles are the same, we say they are **homozygous**.

They can be **homozygous dominant**, for example **TT**.
They can be **homozygous recessive**, for example **tt**.

We say that an individual is **heterozygous** if they have two
alleles that are different, for example **Tt**.

The alleles that an individual has forms their **genotype**.
So the genotype of a tall plant could be **TT** or **Tt**.
The **phenotype** is the way the alleles are expressed in an individual.
For instance, the genotype **TT** or **Tt** would result in a tall
phenotype and the genotype **tt** would result in a dwarf phenotype.
The phenotype is the result of the interaction of the genotype and
the environment.

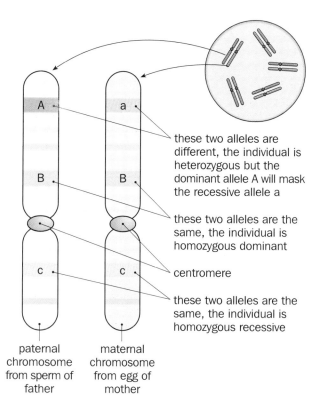

▷ Monohybrid inheritance

Monohybrid inheritance concerns the inheritance of a *single* characteristic, such as plant height or flower colour.
It involves the inheritance of two alleles involving a single gene.
The best way to understand how genes are passed on is to use examples.
For instance, there is one gene for height in pea plants.
The gene for plant height has two alleles: tall (**T**) and dwarf (**t**).
Notice that we always show the dominant allele as a capital letter and the recessive allele as a small letter.
There will be three possible genotypes for plant height:

TT = homozygous tall
Tt = heterozygous tall
tt = homozygous dwarf.

Let's cross a homozygous tall plant with a homozygous dwarf plant.
Can you see that, as a result of meiosis, all the gametes from the tall plant contain the dominant allele **T** and all the gametes from the dwarf plant contain the recessive allele **t**?

When fertilisation occurs, the new plant receives one dominant **T** allele and one recessive **t** allele.
So it will be heterozygous and have the genotype **Tt**.
Its phenotype will be tall, because the **T** allele is dominant to the recessive **t** allele.
The first generation is known as the **F₁**, and in this particular genetic cross, all the F_1 are heterozygous tall (**Tt**).

What happens if we cross two of these F_1 plants?

This time half of the gametes of *each* plant will have the dominant (**T**) allele and half will have the recessive (**t**) allele.
This time when fertilisation occurs, there are three possible combinations of alleles in the **F₂**, or second, generation:
TT (homozygous tall), **Tt** (heterozygous tall),
tt (homozygous dwarf).
So the ratio of phenotypes will be 3 tall:1 dwarf because homozygous tall and heterozygous tall look the same.
This cross enabled Mendel to formulate his first law of inheritance.
The **law of segregation** states that:

> **The characteristics of an organism are determined by alleles which occur in pairs.**
> **Only one of a pair of alleles can be present in a single gamete.**

In Mendel's time, genes and chromosomes had not been discovered.
Instead of 'alleles' he used the term 'factors'.
Remember that *pairs* of chromosomes separate during meiosis.
If the alleles are present on the homologous chromosome pair, then they must also separate into different gametes.
We say that alleles **segregate** into different gametes during meiosis.
Look back to page 119 and read about how meiosis produces gametes with half the normal chromosome number and half the normal number of alleles.

Variation in sweet pea plants

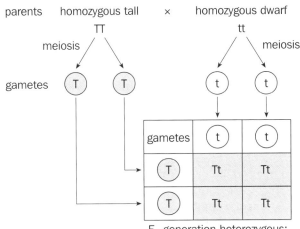

F_1 generation heterozygous:
all tall plants

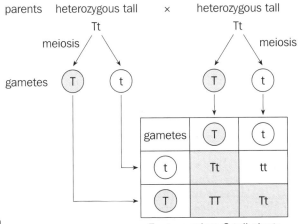

F_2 generation: 3 tall plants
(1 homozygous + 2 heterozygous)
1 dwarf plant

Genetic crosses

As mentioned above, Mendel was fortunate in his choice of characters, because he chose ones that are controlled by single genes.
Most characters are controlled by a number of genes, for instance height in humans.
There are not just tall and short people but a whole range of heights.
This is an example of **continuous variation**.
The differences are not clear-cut and often have to be measured to tell different phenotypes apart.

Mendel chose characters that were clear-cut and easy to tell apart, for instance flower colour. These characters are controlled by a single gene. Where these type of differences occur, we call it **discontinuous variation**.

Questions on single-gene inheritance do not often come up in advanced examinations, because they are fairly easy.
But you need to be able to understand them if you are to be able to do more demanding genetic crosses.
The best approach is to do as many examples as possible.
Here is a monohybrid cross involving animals.

Coat colour in guinea pigs is controlled by a single gene for which there are two alleles: black and white.
Since black is the dominant allele, we will give it the symbol **B**.
Since white is recessive, we will give it the symbol **b**.
You may not be given these symbols in an examination, in which case choose the first letter of the dominant character and make it a capital (as with **B** for black here).
Then choose the **same** letter for the recessive allele but make it small case (so white is **b** in our example **not w**).

As you can see, if we cross a homozygous black guinea pig with a homozygous white one, all the F$_1$ are black.
Then crossing two of these individuals from the F$_1$ gives us an expected ratio of 3 black to 1 white.
The 3:1 ratio is sometimes called a **Mendelian ratio** for a monohybrid cross.

Test cross

If you look at the last cross, you will see that the recessive alleles are hidden in the F$_1$ generation but reappear in the F$_2$.

But how can we tell if a black guinea pig is homozygous or heterozygous? They both look identical.
What we do is to take the individual and cross it with a homozygous recessive individual. This is called a **test cross**.

The diagrams explain what happens.

If our tall plant is homozygous (**TT**), then crossing it with a dwarf plant (**tt**) gives *all* tall plants (**Tt**).
If, however, our tall plant is heterozygous (**Tt**), then crossing it with a dwarf plant (**tt**) will give *half* tall plants (**Tt**) and *half* dwarf plants (**tt**).

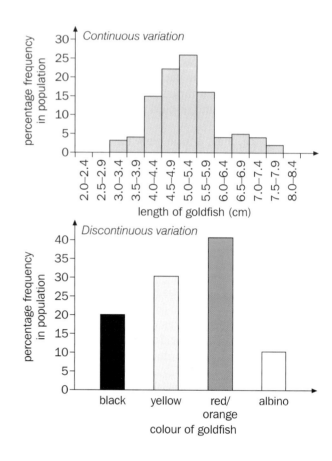

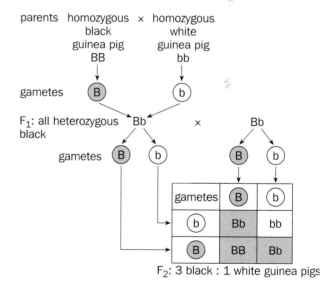

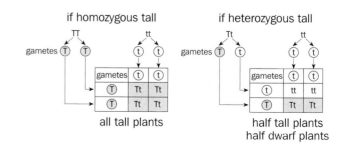

356

▷ Monohybrid inheritance in humans

Some 'faulty' alleles can be passed on from one generation to the next.

Cystic fibrosis

Cystic fibrosis is an inherited disease caused by a gene mutation. In Britain it affects one child in *every* 2000.
The condition is caused by a recessive allele (**c**).
So to have cystic fibrosis, a person must have *two* recessive alleles (**cc**).

Heterozygous individuals (**Cc**) do not suffer from the condition but are **carriers** and may pass the defective allele on to their children. What would be the chances of a child inheriting cystic fibrosis if both parents were carriers (**Cc**)?

As you can see from the diagram, there would be a 1 in 4 chance of the child inheriting the disease.

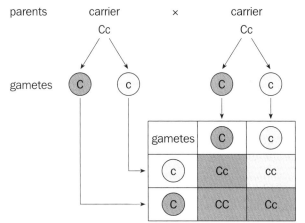

F_1 : 1 normal : 2 carriers : 1 cystic fibrosis

We dealt with the possible future treatment of cystic fibrosis by gene therapy in Chapter 9.
Another disease caused by the inheritance of two recessive alleles is **thalassaemia,** which results in severe anaemia.

Huntington's chorea

Huntington's is a rare inherited condition which affects about 1 in 20 000 people in Britain. The symptoms are particularly distressing. The cells of the brain degenerate and the patient's coordination is affected.
The 'chorea' refers to the clumsy and jerky movements that are symptomatic in the sufferer.
The patient becomes moody and depressed, memory becomes affected, they eventually become totally disabled and ultimately die. The most sinister aspect of Huntington's is the fact that the symptoms only become apparent when patients are in their 30s or 40s. By this time the person may well have had a family and so unintentionally passed the defective allele on to the next generation.

Huntington's chorea is caused by a dominant allele.
So only *one* allele is necessary to give the disease.
So all heterozygous people are sufferers.

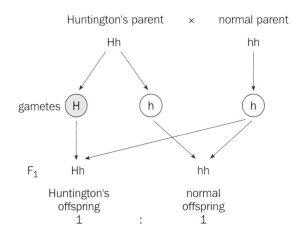

Sickle cell anaemia

Sickle cell anaemia is a human blood disease caused by the inheritance of a recessive allele.
The red blood cells are malformed, taking on a crescent or sickle shape. The sickle cells get stuck in capillaries and inhibit the circulation of oxygen to the tissues. This can lead to death at an early age.

Sickle cell anaemia is due to the recessive gene not coding for the correct form of haemoglobin.
A sufferer must have inherited two recessive alleles from its parents. Carriers or heterozygous individuals have some normal red blood cells and some sickle cells, so they are not so badly affected.
You can find out more about sickle cell anaemia on page 378.

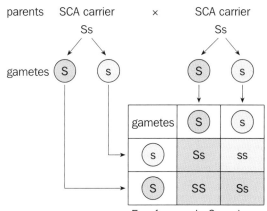

F_1 : 1 normal : 2 carriers : 1 sickle cell anaemia

▷ Dihybrid inheritance

For GCSE, it is unlikely that you studied more than monohybrid inheritance.

Dihybrid inheritance involves the inheritance of *two* separate genes. In one experiment, Mendel looked at how seed colour and seed shape were inherited.

There are two alleles for seed shape: round (**R**) and wrinkled (**r**). There are two alleles for seed colour: yellow (**Y**) and green (**y**).

Mendel knew from doing monohybrid crosses that round seed shape was dominant to wrinkled, and that yellow seed colour was dominant to green.

Mendel decided to cross homozygous pea plants with the two dominant characters (round and yellow seeds) with homozygous plants with the two recessive characters (wrinkled and green).

He found that *all* the F_1 generation had round yellow seeds. He then self-pollinated flowers from the F_1 (sometimes called '**selfing**'). When he collected and counted the seeds he found the following:

	round yellow	round green	wrinkled yellow	wrinkled green
	315	108	101	32
approx. ratio	9 :	3 :	3 :	1

We can show the cross in a diagram.

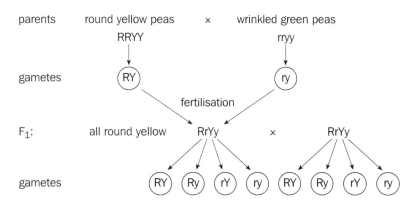

gametes→	RY	Ry	rY	ry
RY	RRYY	RRYy	RrYY	RrYy
Ry	RRYy	RRyy	RrYy	Rryy
rY	RrYY	RrYy	rrYY	rrYy
ry	RrYy	Rryy	rrYy	rryy

F_2 ratio: round yellow: 9
round green: 3
wrinkled yellow: 3

358

▷ Questions on dihybrid inheritance

Dihybrid crosses often appear in advanced examinations.
If you are not careful, especially with the layout of the cross,
you can make mistakes.
Here are some useful tips.

- As you see in our example, there are *two* genes involved,
  each with *two* alleles.
  So this time we write *four* letters, one for each of the four alleles.
  For example, **RRYY** and **rryy**.

- Always put the alleles for the same characteristic together.
  For example, **RrYy** never **RYry**.
  This looks clearer and will help you to show segregation better.

- At segregation, remember Mendel's first law still applies, so
  only show *one* allele of each gene in the gamete.
  For example, **RY**, **Ry**, **rY** or **ry**.
  It is always a good idea to *circle* the gametes so you don't
  get them mixed up with the F_1 or the F_2 generations, and
  remember – an individual that is heterozygous for both
  characteristics can produce four different types of gametes.

- To keep things neat, use a **Punnett square**.
  If you are crossing two individuals that are heterozygous for
  both characteristics, you'll need to show $4 \times 4 = 16$
  individuals in the F_2.

same sequence of gametes →

gametes	RY	Ry	rY	ry
RY				
Ry				
rY				
ry				

same sequence of gametes ↓

- Always write the gametes down in the same sequence on
  each axis of the Punnett square, starting with the two
  dominant alleles and ending with the two recessive alleles.
  If you do this, you can almost anticipate the position of
  each of the genotypes within the square.

- Try drawing out a Punnett square for a cross between
  RrYY and **RRYy.**

The results of the dihybrid cross led Mendel to formulate his
second law of inheritance: the **law of independent assortment**.

> **Either of a pair of alleles may combine randomly with**
> **either of another pair.**

So in our example, we don't just get **RR** and **YY** together, or
rr and **yy** together.
We can get *either* of each pair of alleles combining to give any
of the following:

RRYY, RRYy, RRyy, RrYY, RrYy, Rryy, rrYY, rrYy and **rryy.**

- Another important hint is to make sure that you convert the correct
  number of genotypes into the correct ratio of phenotypes if asked.
  Remember that there are 16 individuals in the Punnett square.
- In some examination questions, they give you the ratios or
  even the raw numbers of the phenotypes of the F_2 and expect you
  to work backwards to the correct genotypes of the F_1 and parents.
- Remember that practice makes perfect and that you can gain full
  marks for genetic crosses. They are **always** examined.

Either of a pair of alleles can combine with either
of another pair

▷ A dihybrid test cross

Mendel wanted to cross F_1 plants from his dihybrid cross.
He wanted to be sure that the heterozygous plants could
produce four different types of gametes.
As with a monohybrid test cross, he crossed the F_1 plants with
homozygous recessive plants that produced wrinkled green seeds.
These plants were **double recessive** because they were
recessive for both characters.
Here are Mendel's results:

gametes	(RY)	(Ry)	(rY)	(ry)
(ry)	RrYy	Rryy	rrYy	rryy

- round yellow 57
- round green 51
- wrinkled yellow 49
- wrinkled green 53

The results were close to the ratio of 1:1:1:1 that we would
expect to get from the cross.

▷ Chi-squared test (χ^2) of the dihybrid test cross

Our expected result for this test cross is 1:1:1:1 and Mendel's results
(the observed results) seem pretty close to the expected.
We can use the chi-squared test to compare the observed results with
those that we expected to get.
The test is a way of estimating the probability that differences between
observed and expected results are due to chance.

Chi-squared is calculated as follows:
1. Calculate the expected values (E). In our example, this is the
   total number of seeds divided by the number of possible
   types $= \dfrac{210}{4} = 52.5$
2. Work out the differences between the observed (O) and
   expected results.

3. The differences are then squared, because some values will be
   negative.
4. Now work out the value of chi-squared using this formula:

$$\chi^2 = \Sigma \frac{(O - E)^2}{E}$$

In practice, it is best to use a table like the one below.

Phenotype	Observed (O)	Expected (E)	Difference (O − E)	Difference squared (O − E)²	$\dfrac{(O-E)^2}{E}$
round yellow	57	52.5	4.5	20.25	0.38
round green	51	52.5	−1.5	2.25	0.043
wrinkled yellow	49	52.5	−3.5	12.25	0.233
wrinkled green	53	52.5	0.5	0.25	0.00048
					$\Sigma = 0.66$

Next we need to find the number of **degrees of freedom**.
This is a measure of the *spread* of the data and is always one
less than the number of classes of data.
So in this case, it is four classes minus one, which equals three
degrees of freedom.

Now look at the table of chi-squared values for three degrees of
freedom.
Our result of 0.66 corresponds to a probability just below 0.9, so
we can conclude that the deviation from the expected 1:1:1:1
ratio is not significant.

Degrees of freedom	Probability (p)						
	0.90	0.50	0.20	0.10	0.05	0.02	0.01
1	0.02	0.46	1.64	2.71	3.84	5.41	6.64
2	0.21	1.39	3.22	4.61	5.99	7.82	9.21
3	0.58	2.37	4.64	6.25	7.82	9.84	11.34
4	1.06	3.36	5.99	7.78	9.49	11.67	13.28

▷ Linkage and recombination

Linkage occurs when two different genes are located on the *same* chromosome.

For this reason, they are usually inherited together, because they move together during meiosis and end up in the same gamete.

Under normal circumstances, the linked genes on the same chromosome pass into the gamete and then into the offspring *together*.

This is contrary to Mendel's law of independent assortment.

If genes **A** and **B** had been on separate chromosomes, then there would have been more genetic variation in the gametes and in the offspring. Independent assortment would have allowed parent **AaBb** to produce four types of gametes, (AB)(Ab)(aB)(ab), instead of just two.

How many types of offspring could have been produced then?

Draw a Punnett square and work it out.

Recombination occurs when alleles are exchanged between homologous chromosomes as a result of *crossing over* (see page 122 to remind yourself).

If you look at the example below, you will see that, due to some crossing over, *some* alleles **A** and **B** end up on different chromosomes and so are no longer linked.

Recombination allows Mendel's second law of independent assortment to operate and so increases the genetic variation in the gametes and hence in the offspring.

The further apart two genes are on a chromosome, the more chance there is of crossing over occurring.

This has been used to determine where a gene **locus** (position) is on a chromosome and so produce **chromosome maps** (see more about the applications of chromosome mapping on page 367).

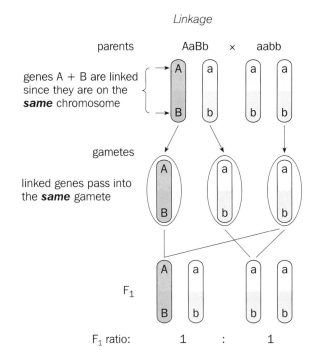

Linkage

Recombination

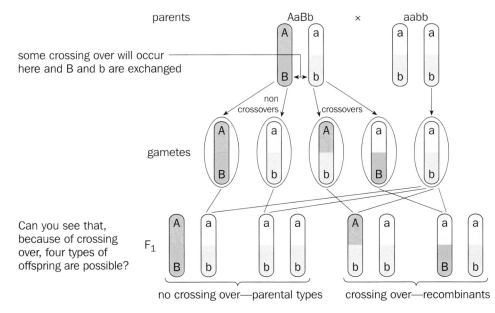

▷ Codominance

Up to now the examples that we have looked at involve alleles that are either dominant or recessive.
In these cases the effect of the recessive allele is masked by the dominant one in the heterozygous condition.
Sometimes, however, both alleles seem to be expressed and neither seems to dominate the other.
So the phenotype is often a mixture of the effects of each allele. This condition is known as **codominance**.

Snapdragon plants can produce red flowers or white flowers. But if you cross the two homozygous plants, the offspring are all pink. The two parents produce heterozygous offspring that are intermediate between them.

What happens if we self-pollinate the pink plants of the F_1? You can see from the diagram that we end up with red, pink and white flowered plants in the F_2, in a ratio of 1:2:1.

Notice that the ratio of the phenotypes is the same as the ratio of the genotypes in a codominant cross.
Notice also that each allele is represented as a capital, so red flower = C^R and white flower = C^W. This is to reflect that neither allele is recessive and that they both exert an equal effect on the phenotype.

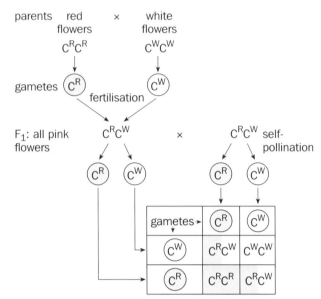

F_2 ratio: 1 red : 2 pink : 1 white

▷ Multiple alleles

So far, we have looked at examples where a gene has only two alternative alleles. There are examples where a gene may have three or more alleles. For instance, the four common blood groups of the human ABO blood system are determined by one gene, **I**, with three different alleles. But remember, a gene can only be represented twice, with one allele on the locus of each homologous chromosome.

The three alleles are I^A, I^B and I^O.
The alleles I^A and I^B are codominant and code for slightly different antigens on the surface of red blood cells.
The allele I^O is recessive to both I^A and I^B and codes for no antigens.
Look at the table. You can see the possible genotypes for each blood group.

Genotype	Blood group
$I^A I^A$	A
$I^A I^O$	A
$I^B I^B$	B
$I^B I^O$	B
$I^A I^B$	AB
$I^O I^O$	O

A cross between a blood group AB person and one with blood group O can produce offspring with neither of the parental blood groups.
A cross between a heterozygous blood group A person and a heterozygous blood group B person can give offspring of any of the four blood groups.

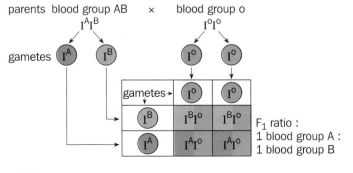

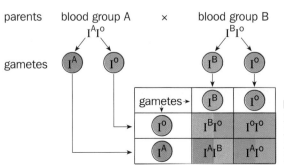

▷ Gene interaction

The examples of dihybrid inheritance that we have
looked at have involved genes that control different characters.
Sometimes the alleles of more than one gene affect each other.
This is known as **gene interaction**.

Bateson and Punnett studied the interaction between two
genes, found on different chromosomes, which affect comb
shape in poultry. If you look at the diagram, you can see that
there are different forms of comb.

Bateson and Punnett crossed homozygous 'pea' combed
fowls with homozygous 'rose' combed fowls.
The F_1 individuals all had a different comb form called 'walnut'.

When the F_1 'walnut' combed birds were interbred, four types
of comb occurred in the F_2: pea, rose, walnut and a new form
of comb called 'single'.

Bateson and Punnett suggested that two genes were involved.
For one gene, the dominant allele **P** gave pea comb.
For the other gene, the dominant allele **R** gave rose comb.
But when both dominant alleles **P** and **R** appeared together,
they interacted to produce a walnut comb phenotype.
And if neither of the two dominant alleles were present, then
it gave a single comb.

The genotype of the homozygous pea comb parent = **PPrr**.
The genotype of the homozygous rose comb parent = **ppRR**.
The genotype of the F_1 heterozygous walnut comb birds = **PpRr**.
And the genotype of the F_2 single comb birds = **pprr**.
The results can be shown in the following diagram.

pea comb

walnut comb

rose comb

single comb

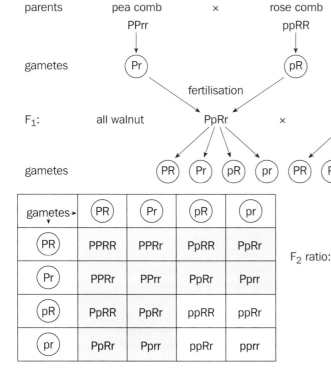

F₂ ratio:

rose comb: 3

▷ Sex linkage

You should remember from Chapter 7 that humans have 46 chromosomes that can be arranged into 23 pairs. The first 22 homologous pairs of chromosomes are referred to as **autosomes**. The last pair of chromosomes are the sex chromosomes. Females have two X chromosomes that look alike. Males have one X chromosome and one much shorter Y chromosome.

The diagram shows how sex is inherited.
All the female's eggs contain an X chromosome.
Half the male's sperm contain an X chromosome and the other half contain a Y chromosome.

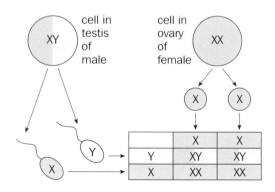

At fertilisation, an egg may fuse with either an X sperm or a Y sperm. So there is an equal chance of the child being a boy or a girl. So it seems that the presence of a male determining allele present on the Y sex chromosome confers maleness.

Linkage occurs when genes are located on the **same** chromosome. **Sex linkage** occurs when genes are carried on the sex chromosomes. These genes may have nothing to do with sex determination; they just happen to be carried on the X or Y chromosomes.

A Y chromosome is a bit like an X chromosome with a bit missing.
As the Y chromosome is smaller, it carries fewer alleles.

This part is missing from the Y chromosome

The allele for colour vision is carried on the part of the X chromosome that is missing from the Y chromosome. This means that a male will only have one allele for colour vision.
There is a defective, recessive allele of the colour vision gene which can lead to colour blindness, particularly of red and green light.
Let **C** = the allele for normal colour vision
and **c** = the allele for colour-blindness.
What happens if we cross a normal-sighted female with a colour-blind male?

Female with two alleles for colour vision ✗✗

Male with one allele for colour vision ✗Y

All the offspring are normal-sighted. The females have the allele for colour-blindness on one of their X chromosomes. We say that they are **carriers**. They have the colour-blind allele but do not show it in their phenotype.
Now let's cross a normal-sighted male with a carrier female.

There is a 1 in 4 chance that the carrier female will pass on the colour-blind allele to one of her children and it will **always** be a boy.

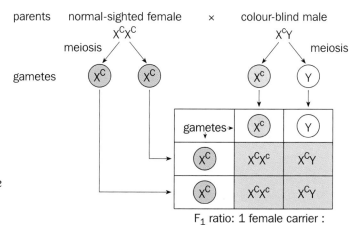

F_1 ratio: 1 female carrier :
1 normal-sighted male

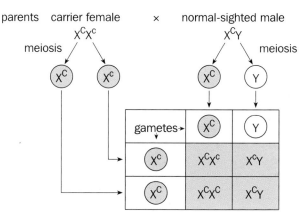

F_1 ratio: 1 normal-sighted female : 1 carrier female :
1 normal-sighted male : 1 colour-blind male

▷ Haemophilia

Haemophilia is a sex-linked disease, caused by a recessive allele on the X chromosome.
The gene that codes for Factor VIII, an important protein involved in blood clotting, is a sex-linked gene found on the X chromosome.

A defective, recessive allele of the gene can lead to haemophilia. Haemophiliacs are unable to make Factor VIII and can lose a lot of blood from even small injuries or bruises.
In the past this meant that most sufferers died in childhood, but now it can be treated by regular injections of Factor VIII.

Here is a cross between a normal male and a carrier female.
Can you see that the male only has to have **one** recessive allele to get haemophilia?
This is because its effect cannot be masked by a dominant, normal allele on the Y chromosome.

Haemophiliac females occur very rarely.
Why do you think that the onset of menstruation at puberty can often prove fatal for female haemophiliacs?

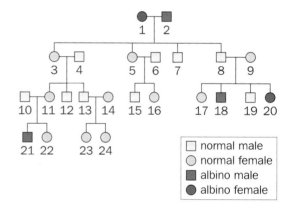

H = normal allele and h = haemophiliac allele

parents   normal male   ×   carrier female
$X^H Y$ $X^H X^h$

gametes

F_1 ratio: 1 normal female :
1 carrier female : 1 normal male :
1 haemophiliac male

▷ Pedigree analysis

Pedigree diagrams can be used to show how a condition such as haemophilia has been passed on from generation to generation.
They are like a family tree showing information that can be looked up in medical records.
The females are shown as circles and the males as squares.
A solid or coloured symbol is used to highlight the condition.
Here is a pedigree diagram showing the inheritance of albinism through four generations.

Other single gene conditions that can be illustrated using pedigree diagrams are thalassaemia, cystic fibrosis and Huntington's chorea.

The inheritance of haemophilia in the British royal family can be traced from Queen Victoria, who was a carrier. Look at the pedigree diagram.

How many of Queen Victoria's children were haemophiliac and how many were carriers?
How many of her granddaughters were carriers?
How many of her great-grandsons were haemophiliacs?

Explain why the allele for haemophilia has not been passed on to the present day royal family.

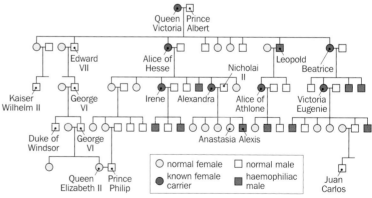

The transmission of haemophilia from Queen Victoria

- ☐ normal male
- ○ normal female
- ■ albino male
- ● albino female

▷ Biology at work: African cassava mosaic virus

Cassava is an important subsistence crop in sub-Saharan Africa, second only to maize.
Close to 200 million people, or 40% of the sub-Saharan population, rely on cassava.

African cassava mosaic disease (ACMD) is the most widespread disease of cassava in tropical Africa.
Total losses due to ACMD are difficult to estimate, but yield losses within individual cultivars have been reported to range from 16% to 100%.
Viruses of the genus *Begomovirus* (family Geminiviridae) cause ACMD.
Of the three species involved, **African cassava mosaic virus** (ACMV) is the most studied. All three species are transmitted by the whitefly *Bemisa tabaci*.

Healthy cassava tubers

Conventional breeding programmes to control ACMV have met with limited success, as all cultivars remain susceptible to infection.
However, researchers at The John Innes Centre, Norwich, have developed novel strategies to control the disease using genetic engineering.
In one approach, the researchers have engineered the expression of an antiviral, ribosomal-inactivating protein (dianthin) specifically in virus-infected cells.
Dianthin expression greatly reduces virus proliferation, allowing only sporadic and mild systemic infection of the laboratory host *Nicotiana benthamiana*.

The AC2 gene of ACMV is expressed early in infection.
It was discovered that the AC2 gene product activates **transcription** of the virus coat protein gene.
In the absence of the AC2 gene product, the coat protein is not produced.
The AC2 gene product activates transcription of the coat protein gene by interacting with the coat protein promoter and the host's transcription machinery.

Dianthin, a protein isolated from carnation, disrupts protein synthesis, causing cell death.
Plants transformed with the dianthin gene under the transcriptional control of the virus coat protein promoter show resistance to ACMV infection.
In healthy cells, the dianthin **transgene** is not expressed.
When the virus enters a host cell, however, the AC2 gene is expressed.
The AC2 protein activates transcription of the dianthin gene from the coat protein promoter.

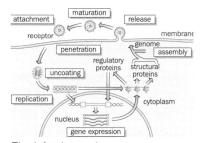

The infective cycle

Production of dianthin causes localised cell death, preventing the spread of the virus.
The use of the dianthin protein as an antiviral agent has been limited by its toxicity in plant cells (dianthin is not toxic when ingested by humans as it is degraded by digestive enzymes).
Using the dianthin gene with a **virus inducible promoter** is a particularly useful resistance strategy because only those cells infected with the virus produce dianthin, leaving the rest of the plant unharmed.

The next step is to transfer this technology to cassava in order to investigate its effectiveness in controlling cassava mosaic disease.

▷ Biology at work: Genetic Mapping

There are over 4000 human diseases caused by the inheritance of defective genes.
There are two types of genetic maps, linkage and physical maps.
Both are used to identify the genes associated with genetic diseases.

Linkage maps

These maps show the arrangement of genes or other recognisable segments of DNA called **markers** along the chromosome.
Linkage occurs where genes on the same chromosome are inherited together. When the frequency of **crossing over** is worked out, a map is put together to indicate the relative positions of genes on a chromosome.

- Crossing over occurs during meiosis when homologous chromosomes pair up and exchange small sections of DNA in a random fashion.
- This means that genes may not always be inherited together as they would end up on different chromosomes.
- The chance of two genes being separated is related to the distance between them.
- The further apart two genes are on a chromosome, the greater the chances that crossing over can occur between them.

The extent of **recombination** between two genes on the same chromosome can be used as a measure of their relative locations.

Inherited diseases can be located on the map by following the inheritance of a DNA marker.
This must be present in affected individuals but absent in unaffected individuals.
Genetic maps have been used to find several important disease genes including cystic fibrosis, sickle cell disease, fragile X syndrome and Duchenne muscular dystrophy.

Physical mapping

Physical maps provide a more powerful tool than linkage maps. They determine the actual distance between genes and markers on the chromosome. There are two general types.

- **Cytogenetic maps**, based on the distinctive banding patterns observed by light microscopy of stained chromosomes.
  They provide the lowest resolution physical map.
- **Contig maps** involve producing cloned pieces or fragments of DNA that can be sequenced, together with information about the order of the cloned pieces. The fragments are contiguous to each other in the chromosome.
  They provide a highly detailed map of the entire nucleotide sequence.
  This enables the actual distance between markers to be worked out using **gel electrophoresis.**

If the pieces are long, it would take more than 1000 pieces arranged end to end to complete the map of the shortest chromosome.
This problem has been overcome by the use of **yeast artificial chromosomes** (YACs).
These have allowed larger DNA fragments to be cloned and sequenced.

The efforts of the **Human Genome Project** have greatly facilitated searching for disease-causing genes by providing detailed genetic maps of the genome.

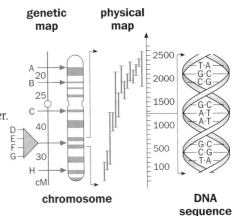

This model of a genetic map shows the location of 8 markers (A–H) along the chromosome. Physical maps are not representations but overlapping collections of DNA fragments.

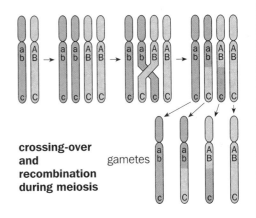

crossing-over and recombination during meiosis

gametes

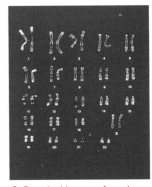

G-Banded human female chromosomes

Summary

- A gene is a section of DNA that codes for a particular character. It is found at a particular position (the locus) on a pair of homologous chromosomes. There may be different forms of the same gene called alleles.
- If both alleles are the same, the organism is homozygous. If the alleles are different, the organism is heterozygous.
- During meiosis, only one of a pair of alleles can be passed into a gamete (this is Mendel's first law).
- A dominant allele expresses itself in the heterozygous state, masking the recessive allele.
- The phenotype is what is presented to the environment. It may be the physical appearance but can include biochemical characteristics.
- The genotype is the genetic make-up of an individual.
- A monohybrid cross is the study of one gene; a dihybrid cross involves the inheritance of two separate genes.
- In dihybrid inheritance, either of a pair of alleles may combine randomly with either of another pair (this is Mendel's second law).
- A test cross is carried out to see whether an individual is homozygous or heterozygous.
- Codominance is where the heterozygous individual has a phenotype intermediate between the two homozygous parents. Both alleles are expressed and contribute to the phenotype.
- Genes present on the same chromosome are said to be linked and are inherited together. Crossing over in prophase I of meiosis can separate linked genes.
- Genes carried on the same sex chromosome are said to be sex linked.

▷ Questions

1 A red-flowered plant with the genotype **TtRr** is tall but self-pollination gives rise to seed which produces tall, red-flowered; tall, white-flowered; short, red-flowered; and short, white-flowered plants in the ratio of 9:3:3:1 respectively. The short, white-flowered plants have the genotype **ttrr**. The following cross was carried out: **TtRr × ttRr** and can be represented in this diagram.

	TR		tR	tr
tR	TtRR			ttRr
tr	TtRr		ttRr	

a) Copy and complete the diagram of the genetic cross.
b) Give the phenotypes of all the genotypes from the cross, in their correct ratio.

2 Mendel's first law states that the characteristics of an organism are determined by internal factors which occur in pairs and that only one of a pair of such factors can be represented in a single gamete.
a) Give the modern name for
    i) an internal factor controlling part of an organism's characteristics,
    ii) a pair of such factors.
b) Explain why these factors occur in pairs rather than singly.
c) Explain why only one of a pair of such factors can be represented in a single gamete.

3 In guinea pigs, the allele for black coat **B** is dominant to the allele for albino **b**, and the allele for rough coat **R** is dominant to the allele for smooth coat **r**.

A heterozygous black, smooth-coated guinea pig is mated with a heterozygous rough-coated, albino guinea pig. Show the cross diagrammatically and give the ratio of the phenotypes of the offspring.

4 In maize, the allele for coloured grain **C** is dominant to the allele for colourless **c**, and the allele for rounded grain **R** is dominant to the allele for wrinkled grain **r**.
a) Explain what we mean by
    i) a gene,
    ii) an allele.
b) Maize plants heterozygous for both characteristics were crossed and the following phenotypes were obtained:
    83 coloured, smooth
    38 coloured, wrinkled
    29 colourless, smooth
    8 colourless, wrinkled
    Why do you think that the results are not an exact 9:3:3:1 ratio?
c) Some of the colourless, rounded grain would have the genotype **ccRr** and some would be **ccRR**. Explain how you would use a test cross to distinguish between the two genotypes.

5 Two genes in a mouse interact to control *three* possible coat colours: grey, black and chocolate. The two genes are located on different chromosomes (autosomes). Each gene has two alleles: **A** is dominant to **a** and **B** is dominant to **b**. Examples of four genotypes and their phenotypes are shown in the table:

Genotype	Phenotype
AABb	grey
Aabb	grey
AaBb	black
aabb	chocolate

a) What colour coat would you expect each of the following genotypes to give:
   i) **AABB**,
   ii) **AaBb**,
   iii) **AAbb**,
   iv) **aaBB** ?
b) An **AABB** male was crossed with an **aabb** female.
   i) Give the genotype of the F_1.
   ii) Give the phenotypes of the F_2 and their ratio.
c) A female from the F_1 in b)i) was crossed with a chocolate male.
   What would be the ratio of the phenotypes for this cross?

6 In a breed of domestic fowl, pea comb is dominant to single comb, but feather colour shows codominance. Black feathers and white feathers are homozygous, i.e. **BB** and **WW** respectively, whereas the heterozygous condition **BW** gives the intermediate 'blue' feathers.
a) Show the cross between birds that are heterozygous for both alleles.
b) What proportions of the offspring would be
   i) pea-combed,
   ii) black-feathered,
   iii) blue-feathered,
   iv) pea-combed and blue-feathered,
   v) single-combed and white-feathered?

7 The inheritance of coat colour in cats is influenced by a gene present on the X chromosome but not on the Y. The allele for black coat colour can be represented by the symbol **B** and that for ginger coat colour by **G**. These alleles are codominant and the hairs of heterozygous cats show bands of both black and ginger, called tortoiseshell.
a) Define the terms
   i) gene,
   ii) allele,
   iii) codominant.
b) Use a diagram to show a cross between a ginger male and a tortoiseshell female.

8 a) State two reasons why female haemophiliacs are rarely found in a population.
b) Use suitable symbols to draw a genetic diagram to show the cross between a carrier female and a haemophiliac male.

9 Pituitary dwarfism is an inherited condition in humans in which affected individuals have very short limbs. The allele for pituitary dwarfism **d** is recessive to the allele for normal limbs **D**, and its locus is situated on the X chromosome. The pedigree diagram shows part of one affected family.

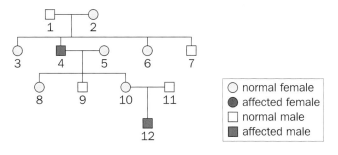

- normal female
- affected female
- normal male
- affected male

a) Identify and explain one piece of evidence from the diagram to show that the allele for pituitary dwarfism is recessive to the allele for normal limb length.
b) Explain why the genotype of
   i) individual 10 must be $X^D X^d$
   ii) individual 11 must be $X^d Y$

10 The pedigree diagram shows some of the descendants of two of the nine children of Queen Victoria and Prince Albert. Four of the male descendants suffered from the disease haemophilia, and these are shown shaded in.
a) Draw a genetic diagram to show how the gene for haemophilia was transmitted from Queen Victoria to Viscount Rupert.
b) Explain what is meant by a carrier.
c) There are four known carriers in the diagram. Name these carriers.
d) Name four other **possible** carriers in the diagram.

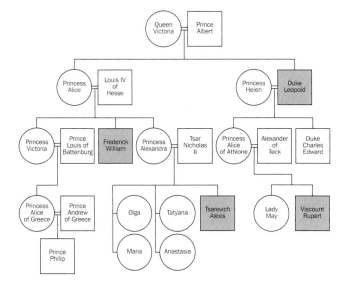

21 Selection, evolution and classification

▷ *Hallucigenia*

Peripatus looks a bit like a caterpillar. It is an invertebrate with stout, fleshy legs and belongs to a small, obscure animal group called the Onychophora.

In 1911, fossils of ancient soft-bodied onychophorans were discovered in the Burgess Shale in British Columbia.

In 1977, Conway Morris described many of the weird organisms found in the Burgess Shale.

He named one particular animal *Hallucigenia*, because of its 'bizarre and dream-like appearance'.

It had a tubular body supported by seven pairs of long, pointed spines, and had a row of fleshy tubes running along its back.

It did not seem to fit into any existing animal group.

How could the creature move around on seven pairs of rigid spikes?

There was much debate and in 1991 Ramskold and Hou suggested that *Hallucigenia* would make more sense if it were turned upside down.

The spines, which made no sense as walking appendages, could now function as protection.

The fleshy tubes now looked like the fleshy legs of *Peripatus*.

So by inverting *Hallucigenia*, Ramskold and Hou had turned the animal into an onychophoran! As you will see later in this chapter, the huge variety of life forms can make classification a tricky business.

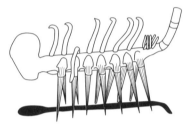
Hallucigenia

Hallucigenia *inverted*

▷ Variation

Phenotypic variation results from the effect of environmental factors on the genotype.

Phenotypic variation (V_p) = genetic variation (V_g) + environmental variation (V_e).

These environmental factors may include the following:

- Diet – in many countries, children now grow taller and heavier.
- Genetically identical plants are affected by light, temperature and nutrients.
- Physical training can result in improved athletic performance.

But of course such changes are not passed on to the next generation.

More important to natural selection and evolution is inherited variation.

Genetic variation is caused by:

1. **the random distribution of chromosomes during metaphase I of meiosis,**
2. **crossing over between chromatids of homologous chromosomes during prophase I of meiosis,**
3. **random mating between organisms of the same species,**
4. **random fertilisation of gametes,**
5. **mutations.**

The first four result in a ***reshuffling*** of genes in the population.

New ***combinations*** of alleles are created in the offspring that are different from the parents and different from each other.

Mutations are different in that they do more than merely reshuffle existing genes. They create completely new alleles.

This isn't the genetic reshuffle.

▷ Mutations

A **mutation** is a change in the DNA of an organism.
There are two types of mutation:

- a **gene** or **point mutation** – affecting a single gene,
- a **chromosome mutation** – affecting a single chromosome or set of chromosomes.

Both can occur in normal body cells or in the production of gametes.
Mutations that occur to body cells cannot be passed on to the offspring.
Cancers can develop if mutations occur in the genes that control cell division.
This can result in haphazard, unchecked growth leading to a tumour.
Often tumours turn out to be harmless, or **benign**, and may be
destroyed by the body's own defence system.
But sometimes tumour cells can spread around the body and invade
other tissues. This type of tumour is **malignant**.
A mutation can occur in the formation of an egg cell or a sperm cell.
If fertilisation occurs, the mutation will be passed on to all the cells
of the new individual through repeated cell divisions.

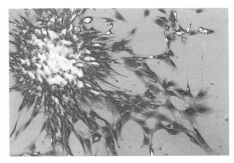

Cancerous cells breaking away from a malignant tumour

▷ Gene or point mutations

Gene or point mutations result from a change in the base
sequence of the DNA of a gene.
As you know, a gene codes for the formation of a particular
protein. So if the sequence of bases is changed, a ***different***
protein is produced. This new protein may have different
properties from the first. Since ***all*** enzymes are proteins, and
enzymes control metabolic pathways, a change in an enzyme may
block such a pathway. So a change in the sequence of DNA bases
can lead to a change in an enzyme.

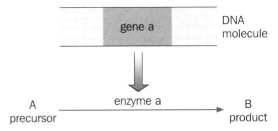

If gene a mutates it no longer codes for enzyme a and the pathway will be blocked

Let's say that one strand of DNA has the following 'normal' base sequence:
CCT AGT ATT CGC TGA GGC TAA TG
A **substitution** has occurred in the following strand, can you spot it?
CCT AGA ATT CGC TGA GGC TAA TG
An **inversion** has occurred in this strand:
CCT AGA TTA CGC TGA GGC TAA TG

Can you see that substitutions and inversions only alter one or two DNA codons?
The result is that only one or two amino acids in the protein are changed.
In some cases, the new amino acid does not alter the structure of the protein
a great deal, so the mutation may not matter at all.

Now see if you can spot the **deletion** in this DNA strand:
CCT AGT TTC GCT GAG GCT AAT G
or the **insertion** in this strand:
CCT AGT AGT TCG CTG AGG CTA ATG

Only one base may be added or removed but this causes a shift in
the whole sequence of bases and all the codons are changed after that point.

This is known as a **frame shift**. Such mutations can result in a completely
different primary protein structure from the original. The three-dimensional
shape of the protein also becomes altered and the protein is no longer able
to do its job. So insertions and deletions can be far more damaging than
substitutions or inversions.

Frame shifts are caused by deletions or
insertions of a base. Every base triplet
occurring after the mutation will now be
changed. We can use sentences as an
analogy.

THE CAT ATE THE BIG FAT RAT

The insertion of 'S' after CAT throws the
whole sentence

THE CAT SAT ETH EBI GFA TRA T

A deletion also makes nonsense of the
sentence.

THC ATA TET HEB IGF ATR AT

In a similar way, the sequence of base
triplets coding for specific amino acids can
be disrupted.

▷ Chromosome mutations

Chromosome mutations involve changes in entire chromosomes and are of two types:
- changes in the structure of a chromosome,
- changes in chromosome number.

Changes in chromosome structure

As you know, during prophase I of meiosis, homologous chromosomes pair up and exchange of chromosome material takes place at chiasmata. Perhaps it is not surprising that mistakes can occur, leading to major changes in the chromosome structure. There are four main types of changes:

- **Deletion** occurs when the chromosome breaks and a fragment of it is lost.
  The two ends join up to give a shorter chromosome.
  Since this involves the loss of genes, it can be lethal.
- **Inversion** – a deletion occurs but this time the chromosome fragment becomes reattached in an inverted position.
  So the correct genes are present but in the wrong order, so they will probably code for an incorrect protein.
- **Translocation** – a fragment of the chromosome becomes deleted and rejoins at a different position on the same chromosome.
  Reciprocal translocation occurs when the deleted section attaches to a different chromosome, as shown here.
- **Duplication** is when a portion of a chromosome is copied twice. As a result, the gene sequence is repeated.
  In our example, an extra length of chromosome has been added.

Whole chromosome mutations can be very disruptive because they involve entire blocks of genes.
Often the homologous chromosomes end up with a different gene sequence, which makes pairing up in meiosis impossible.

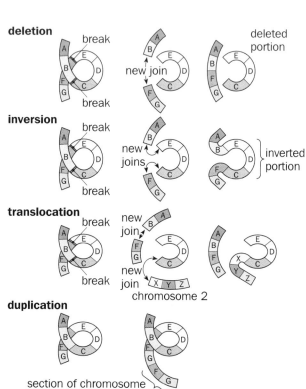

Changes in sets of chromosomes

Sometimes a mutation can affect whole sets of chromosomes. This is known as **polyploidy**.

A defect in meiosis may lead to a gamete getting two sets of chromosomes (diploid number).
When it is fertilised by a haploid gamete, the organism will be **triploid** (have three sets of chromosomes).
If two diploid gametes fertilise, then a **tetraploid** individual with four sets of chromosomes will be produced.
Tetraploidy can also happen after fertilisation if, during mitosis, the two sets of chromosomes double but fail to separate.
Tetraploids can be fertile, since there are two complete sets of homologous chromosomes that can pair up during meiosis.
Triploids cannot form complete homologous pairs, since one set is left isolated, so triploids are usually sterile.
Polyploidy is common in flowering plants and is associated with beneficial characters such as hardiness and disease-resistance.
Many important commercial crops, such as tomatoes, sugar beet, wheat and tobacco, are polyploids.

Chrysanthamums are polyploids

▷ Changes in chromosome number

Changes in the number of individual chromosomes can also occur.
Normally in humans the 23 homologous pairs of chromosomes form in meiosis I and then assort independently to give gametes each with 23 chromosomes.
But if just one of the 23 homologous pairs should fail to separate, then both chromosomes travel into one gamete.
This can result in one of the gametes having 24 chromosomes, and this is known as **non-disjunction**.

So what happens if the gamete with 24 chromosomes fuses with a normal gamete of the opposite sex with 23 chromosomes?

The resulting offspring will have 47 ($2n + 1$) chromosomes, in other words, *three* versions of the chromosome in question.
This condition is known as **polysomy**.

Down's syndrome is a well known example of polysomy.
Chromosome 21 fails to segregate from its homologous partner so the gamete produced has 24 chromosomes with two copies of chromosome 21. When fertilised with a normal gamete, the offspring has 47 chromosomes.
So the individual has three copies of chromosome 21.

Non-disjunction in most chromosomes is usually fatal.
Children with Down's syndrome are able to survive, though with varying degrees of disability.
In the case of Down's syndrome, the non-disjunction seems to occur in the ovary of the mother during egg production.
The incidence of the condition can be linked to the age of the mother.
At the age of 20 years the risk is 1 in 2000 but by the age of 40, this has risen to 1 in 100. After 45 years, the incidence is three times greater than at 40.

Can you find the extra chromosome for this Down's female?

▷ Mutagens

Mutations continually occur in nature at random.
The average rate at which a mutation occurs is about 1 in 100 000.
This is known as the spontaneous rate.
However, the spontaneous rate of a gene or chromosome mutation can be greatly increased by factors in the environment called **mutagens**.

Certain types of radiation, including ultraviolet light, X-rays and gamma rays, act as mutagens.
Emissions from radioactive substances are able to damage DNA.
High energy particles such as α and β particles are particularly dangerous.

Many Down's children surprise people with their achievements

A number of chemicals can act as mutagens.
These include **colchicine**, which can be extracted from crocuses.
It inhibits spindle formation during cell division, so the chromosomes fail to separate at anaphase and this leads to polyploidy.

Not all mutations are harmful. As you will see, some can be beneficial and produce an improvement in the phenotype.
Beneficial mutations are extremely rare, but they can give an advantage to an organism upon which natural selection can operate.

Nuclear waste dump site

373

▷ Charles Darwin and the theory of evolution

Charles Darwin (1809–1882) was the naturalist on *HMS Beagle*,
which sailed to South America and Australia on a scientific survey in 1832.
The voyage was a revelation to Darwin because he was able to study
vast numbers of animals and plants that he never knew existed.
He collected fossils in the rocks which showed him that different
life-forms had gone through many changes.
What impressed Darwin most of all were the variations that existed
between the species in a small group of volcanic islands about
600 miles off the coast of Ecuador.
These were the **Galapagos Islands**.
There was no life on these islands when they were originally formed
by volcanic activity, so any life-forms must have reached the Galapagos
by sea or air from the mainland.

HMS Beagle

▷ Darwin's finches

Among the many animals that Darwin studied on
the Galapagos Islands were the finches.
Darwin observed 13 different species of finch.
He suggested that one ancestral species of finch
had reached the islands with the help of the
prevailing south-east trade winds.
Since there were no other birds on the Galapagos,
the original finches found many food sources not
being eaten by other species.
Darwin noticed how individual finches differed
from one island to the next.
One of the main differences was in the size and
shape of their beaks.
Some had short, strong beaks with which they
could crack open seeds.
Others had long, thin beaks for catching insects.
There was even one species, the woodpecker
finch, which was able to use a cactus spine to
probe insect larvae out of the bark of trees.
It seemed that on each island, the characteristics
that best suited a particular finch to its environment
were passed on to the offspring.

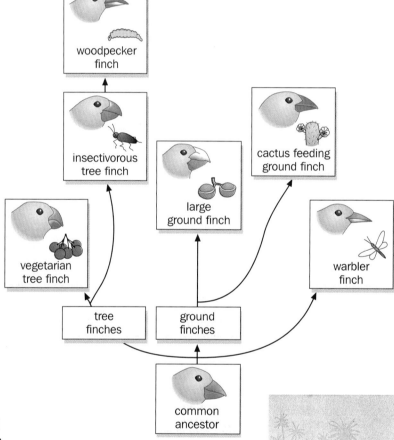

Darwin suggested that the finches had all developed
from a common ancestor and that each type of finch
had, over time, developed a type of beak adapted
to exploit a particular food supply.
This is a classic example of **adaptive radiation**.

This led Darwin to draw conclusions about how evolution came about.
At the same time, the British scientist **Alfred Wallace** had come to similar
conclusions about the theory of evolution.
For some time, Darwin was reluctant to publish his ideas, but eventually,
persuaded by Wallace, they jointly published their findings in a paper
to the Linnaean Society in 1858.
Soon after, Darwin published his famous book '*The Origin of Species*'.
At the time it caused consternation, suggesting as it did that humans
and apes could have evolved from a common ancestor.
With the passage of time, more and more scientists came to accept Darwin's ideas.

*Darwin's ideas on
the decent of man
were ridiculed at the
time*

▷ Natural selection

Darwin and Wallace jointly proposed that species evolve
by a process of **natural selection**.
The basic principle behind natural selection is that those organisms
that are better adapted to their environment are more likely to survive
and reproduce to produce successful offspring.

Natural selection can be summed up in a series of observations (O)
and deductions (D).

- All organisms produce far more offspring than are needed
  to simply replace the parents (O).

- Despite this tendency to increase, most populations maintain
  fairly constant numbers (O).

- There must be a 'struggle for existence' between individuals of the
  same species. They compete with each other for the means of survival.
  A number do not live long enough to reproduce (D).

- There is variation among the offspring of any species (O).

- Those individuals that are best adapted to their environment will be
  more likely to survive than others – 'survival of the fittest' (D).

- The survivors will be able to pass on the favourable characteristics
  to their offspring (D).

- Over successive generations, the characteristics of the population
  will slowly change (D).

Charles Darwin, the great British naturalist

Alfred Russell Wallace (1823–1913)

Overproduction

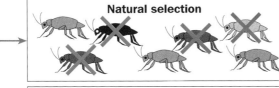

Populations tend to produce far more offspring than are needed
to replace the parents. Since most populations have stable
numbers, there must be a certain number that do not survive.

Variation

Sexually produced offspring show variation. Since their phenotypes vary, so must their genotypes. The individuals that are best
suited to their environmental conditions will survive to breed.

Natural selection

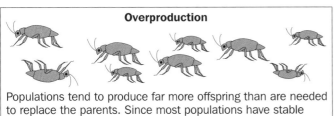

There is a struggle for survival as
individuals **compete** for scarce
resources. Those individuals that
are best adapted will survive to
reproduce.

Inheritance

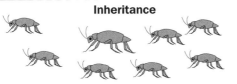

Variations are inherited. Each
new generation will have a
greater proportion of descendants
from individuals with successful
combinations of alleles that
produce favourable characteristics.

successful
combinations
of alleles

Darwin was unable to explain the origin of variation or how it was passed on
from one generation to the next, since there was no knowledge of genetics at that time.
The theory of evolution by natural selection is still generally accepted today.
The modern interpretation takes into account advances in modern genetics
and is called **neo-Darwinism**.
The modern definition of evolution refers to changes in the gene frequencies
of a population, which may or may not lead to the formation of a new species.

▷ Types of selection

You may have gained the impression from the first part of this chapter that natural selection is just a mechanism for change. More often than not, the opposite is true: an organism that has a 'good' phenotype may well produce descendants very similar to itself. Sharks, crocodiles and ferns are examples of 'successful' organisms that have remained virtually unchanged for millions of years, in relatively unchanging environments.

There are **three** different types of natural selection.

Crocodiles have changed very little over millions of years

● Stabilising selection

Stabilising selection tends to eliminate extreme variations from the population.
In a stable environment that does not change a great deal, the middle phenotypes tend to be **selected for** in greater numbers than the extreme ones.
Because it favours the average, stabilising selection tends to act to prevent change.
In our example, the light and dark beetles tend to be eliminated, since they are more conspicuous to preditors, leaving medium shaded beetles.
A good example of stabilising selection is human birth weight. Studies have shown that particularly small or particularly large babies have a higher mortality rate than average-sized ones.

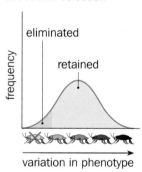
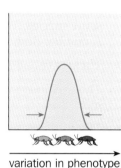

● Directional selection

Directional selection can occur if an environmental change takes place. It may be that the change in the environment favours the organisms at one extreme of the phenotypes.
In our example, the darker beetles are selected because their environment has become darker.
There is a selection pressure on the lighter beetles. May be they now have less camouflage and are more easily seen by predators. So there is a shift in the 'average' for the population.
A good example of directional selection is the peppered moth. As we shall see later in this chapter, there was an increase in the frequency of dark forms of the moth at the expense of the lighter forms as a result of industrial pollution darkening the environment.

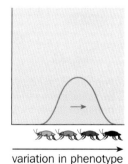

● Disruptive selection

Disruptive selection is the opposite to stabilising selection. Instead of favouring the mean, the extremes of the population are selected.
In our example, the light and dark beetles would be favoured at the expense of those with an intermediate shade.
This could happen if the beetles migrated to a new environment with a contrasting light and dark background.
This would probably result in selection of the light and dark beetles, since it would offer them better camouflage from predators.
Disruptive selection is uncommon compared with the other two forms. But it can be important in achieving evolutionary change, resulting in the formation of a new species.

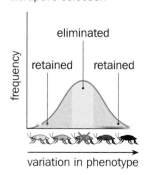
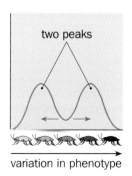

▷ Selection in action

The peppered moth

The process of evolution is generally slow, but there are examples of natural selection operating over a person's lifetime.
The peppered moth (*Biston betularia*) exists naturally in two forms:

- a pale, speckled form,
- a dark, melanic form, which arose as a mutation.

The moths feed at night and rest on trees during the day.

The light form is well camouflaged against the lichen-covered bark of trees in unpolluted areas.
This helps to prevent it from being seen by predatory birds.

The dark form is at a disadvantage in such areas as it tends to stand out against the light background.
Insect-eating birds such as robins and hedge sparrows eat dark individuals before they can reproduce and pass on the allele for dark colour.

Owing to the Industrial Revolution in the 1800s, the environment changed fairly rapidly in industrial areas.
The air quality declined and sulphur dioxide in smoke emissions killed the lichens that covered the tree bark.
The bark also became blackened by soot from the smoke.

Against the black background, the dark form was now better camouflaged than the light form.
The light moths were more easily seen against the dark background and were more frequently taken by birds before they could reproduce.
Before 1850, the dark variety of moth was rare.
By 1895, almost the entire population of moths in industrial centres, like Manchester and Birmingham, was dark.

Studies using the 'release and recapture' technique have been carried out in Birmingham and rural Dorset. (See page 417.)
They confirm that the change in gene frequency for light or dark shading in the moth population is the result of natural selection.

Clearly the darker moth has a selective advantage over the light moth in industrial areas, whereas in non-polluted areas this advantage is with the light moth.

In the 1950s, coal-burning in industrial areas was still commonplace.
However, between 1960 and 1980 the environment changed again.
There was a decline in the number of coal-burning factories and the Clean Air Act was introduced.

Can you see what has happened to the levels of sulphur dioxide and smoke in the industrial centres?
In what two ways will this affect the environment?
How has this affected the frequency of light and dark moths in industrial areas?
Is this an example of stabilising, directional or disruptive selection?

The pale and dark forms of the peppered moth

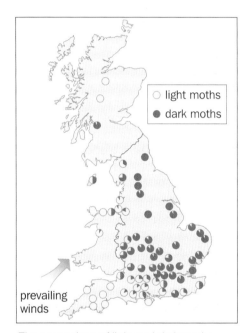
The proportions of light and dark moths found in Britain today

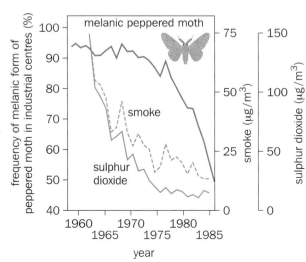

Sickle cell anaemia

Sickle cell anaemia (SCA) is a genetic disease resulting from a gene mutation.
The normal allele is partially dominant to the mutated allele for SCA,
so only individuals with **two** SCA alleles will have the disease.
Such individuals produce abnormal haemoglobin, which causes
red blood cells to become sickle-shaped.
This can prove fatal if the distorted red blood cells block blood vessels
or if the spleen destroys the abnormal sickle cells at a greater rate,
so causing anaemia.
Heterozygotes who carry one SCA allele develop a much milder form
of the disease called **sickle cell trait**.
The way in which gene mutation causes sickle cell anaemia is shown
in the diagram.
Can you see that the replacement of just one amino acid in the
haemoglobin molecule is responsible for the mutant gene?

Clearly, the possession of two SCA alleles puts a person at a great
selective disadvantage.
The frequency of the SCA allele is much higher in some human populations,
for instance in east Africa.

Malaria is a disease that leads to severe fever, convulsions and coma.
It can be fatal within a few days of the appearance of the first symptoms.
The cause is a unicellular parasite, *Plasmodium falciparum*, which enters
the red blood cells and multiplies inside them.
Plasmodium is spread from person to person by female mosquitoes
when they bite to take a blood meal. (See page 266.)

Look at the two maps of Africa.
The sickle cell allele is most common in those parts of Africa
where malaria is found.

Sickle cells have low potassium levels, which kill off the *Plasmodium*
parasite when it enters the cells.
Heterozygotes with sickle cell trait have sufficiently reduced potassium
levels to protect them against the parasite and are less likely to suffer
from malaria than people with two normal alleles.

Natural selection is in operation in this situation.
- There is strong selection pressure against people who are homozygous
  for sickle cell anaemia, **Hb^s Hb^s**, because they may die from anaemia.
- There is strong selection pressure against people homozygous for
  the normal allele, **Hb Hb**, because they could die from malaria.
- But, in areas where malaria is common, there is a strong selective
  advantage for heterozygous individuals, **Hb Hb^s**, since they do not
  suffer badly from anaemia and they are protected from malaria.

So the sickle cell allele remains in the population in areas where malaria
is an important **selective agent**.

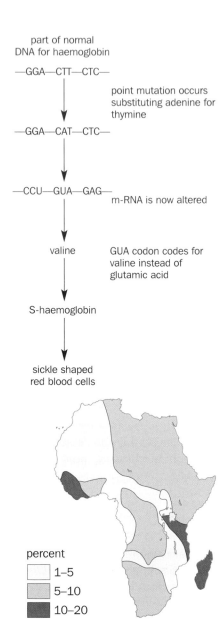

part of normal
DNA for haemoglobin

—GGA—CTT—CTC—

point mutation occurs
substituting adenine for
thymine

—GGA—CAT—CTC—

m-RNA is now altered

—CCU—GUA—GAG—

valine — GUA codon codes for
valine instead of
glutamic acid

S-haemoglobin

sickle shaped
red blood cells

percent
☐ 1–5
▦ 5–10
■ 10–20

*Distribution of people with at least one sickle
cell allele*

▦ present

Distribution of malaria

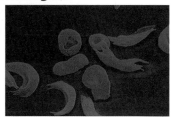

Sickle-shaped red blood cells

Antibiotic resistance

Antibiotics are chemicals that kill bacteria or inhibit their growth.
Soon after the introduction of antibiotics in the 1940s, certain bacteria were already developing a resistance to their effects.

If a population of bacteria, say *Staphylococcus*, were exposed to an antibiotic such as penicillin, most would be killed off.
But there may be just one or two individuals that by chance have a mutation that makes them resistant to the antibiotic.
The mutant bacterial cells are able to make an enzyme, in this case penicillinase, which breaks down the antibiotic.
These individuals have great selective advantage as they are unaffected and survive to reproduce very rapidly, passing on their resistant allele.
There is a constant search for new antibiotics as bacteria relentlessly develop resistance to existing ones. (See page 275.)

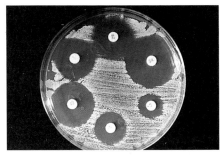

The effect of different antibiotics on the growth of E.coli. The clear areas around each disc show how much each antibiotic has inhibited bacterial growth.

Drug resistance

Resistance to pesticides such as DDT has occurred in a similar way.
DDT was introduced to control insect crop pests and to kill those that spread diseases such as malaria and yellow fever.
But within 2 years of its introduction, many insects had become resistant to DDT.
In many such cases of pesticide resistance, the presence of the chemical switches on a gene that codes for an enzyme that inactivates the pesticide.

Another example comes from the use of warfarin as rat poison.
Warfarin is an anti-coagulant. It kills the rat by inducing internal bleeding.
Mutant rats have an enzyme that allows their blood to clot in the presence of warfarin. The mutants survive to breed, so increasing the frequency of the resistant allele in the population.

Some rat colonies have developed resistance to warfarin

Myxomatosis

When the European rabbit was introduced to countries like Britain and Australia, its numbers soared owing to the lack of predation and competition.
The myxomatosis virus is spread by fleas and, when introduced into this country, it succeeded in killing 99% of the rabbit population.
Resistance in the remaining 1% was the result of one or two mutant genes.
In the first case, the mutant gene coded for an enzyme that made the myxomatosis virus inactive.
More interestingly, the second mutant gene affected the rabbits' behaviour.
They spent more time above ground, out of the congested burrows in which the fleas were more likely to spread the virus.

Copper tolerance

Copper is a toxic metal that can prevent plants growing on spoil heaps.
Resistant strains of the grasses *Festuca* and *Agrostis* have appeared.
The resistance seems to be linked to the plant's ability to transport copper out of the cell into the cell wall, so that it has less effect on cell metabolism.
These copper-tolerant grasses have a strong selective advantage at the sites of old mine workings and have been used to reclaim land from spoil tips where previously no plants could grow.

All the examples on this page illustrate directional selection.

Parys Mountain, the former copper mining centre in Anglesey, Wales

▷ Species and speciation

Populations are groups of interbreeding individuals of the same species, occupying the same habitat at the same time.

But within each population there are breeding subunits called **demes**. Individuals within a deme tend to breed with each other more often than they do with individuals of other demes.

Although they remain part of the same gene pool, the flow of genes between separate demes slows, or may even cease.

Each deme may evolve along separate lines so that eventually the demes may become so different that, even if they were to be reunited, they would not be able to breed successfully with each other.

They would become separate species, each with their own gene pool. This process is known as **speciation**.

Allopatric speciation

Allopatric speciation is the development of a new species as a result of populations being physically separated.

A **physical barrier**, such as a river, mountain range or stretch of sea, prevents populations of the same species from interbreeding. Let's look at an example.

1. The parent population of a single species occupies an environment that does not alter a great deal.
   The population is able to move into new areas of the environment – we say it 'expands its range'.
   The population has a single gene pool and individuals are able to interbreed freely – we say that there is regular 'gene flow'.

2. Geological processes cause the environment to change.
   Physical barriers appear, such as a mountain range and a stretch of ocean.
   These barriers cut off parts of the population and gene flow is prevented.
   This partition of a population by such physical barriers is known as **geographical isolation**.

3. The isolated populations may be subjected to different selective pressures. For example, the more northern population B will live in a colder climate. So selection will favour animals that are larger and that have longer fur.
   The southern population lives in a warmer, drier climate so smaller individuals with shorter fur will have a selective advantage.
   Because of the effects of natural selection on each gene pool, the two populations may become genetically different enough to be reproductively isolated, so producing new species.

4. Geological forces act to break down the barriers dividing the two sub-species.
   They are able to mix, but by now each sub-species has established a different gene pool and they are no longer capable of interbreeding. Two different species have evolved.

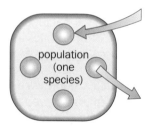

deme (a group of interbreeding members of one species)

If the members of a deme are isolated to such an extent that their capability to interbreed with other demes is lost, it will lead to the formation of a new species

1.

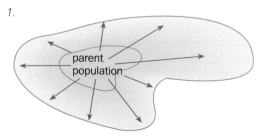

The parent population expands its range as it disperses to occupy new parts of the environment

2.

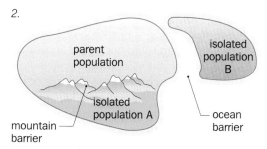

Geological processes cause the formation of physical barriers that prevent gene flow between the populations

3.

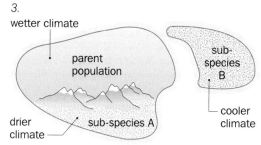

Each of the separated populations is subjected to different selection pressures by the environment

4.

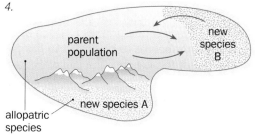

Oceanic barrier breaks down and the population of the new species B is able to mix directly with the parent population again, but no interbreeding takes place

380

Sympatric speciation

Sympatric speciation is when new species are formed when there are no physical barriers.

It is usually caused when **reproductive isolation** occurs between individuals of a population. It can have a number of causes.

- **Behaviour**

  Animals attract mates with elaborate courtship displays. Calls, rituals, colour, markings, dances and body language may be used to attract the opposite sex.
  Speciation may result if the mating routine of one sub-species fails to trigger a response in a potential partner of another sub-species.

- **Structure**

  The sex organs of individuals in the population may not be compatible and so mating is prevented.
  For instance, many insects have a 'lock and key' arrangement for their genitalia.
  In the plant kingdom, pollen transfer can be affected by differences in flower structure.

- **Gamete mortality**

  Gametes may be prevented from meeting. In animals, the sperm may fail to survive in the reproductive tract of another sub-species.
  In plants, pollen may fail to grow on the stigma of a potential partner.

- **Hybrid inviability**

  Mating between two different sub-species may result in a zygote which fails to divide. This may be because the chromosomes no longer match each other, as is the case with polyploidy.

- **Hybrid sterility**

  Mating between two species results in a hybrid, but the species is reproductively isolated if the hybrid is sterile.
  A well known example is when a zebra is mated with a donkey. The resulting 'zebronkey' is sterile because of the failure at meiosis to produce viable gametes. The zebronkey has 53 chromosomes that are unable to form homologous pairs at prophase I of meiosis.

- **Polyploidy**

  Polyploidy can be due to a malfunction occurring during meiosis when the chromosomes fail to separate (see page 372). This can result in 'instant speciation' and the new polyploid species, though still in contact with the 'parent species', is reproductively isolated from it.
  Animals are rarely able to develop into a new species in this way, because they are usually sterile.
  Plants, however, can often self-pollinate or reproduce vegetatively. A successful example can be found in the cord grass *Spartina*. The diagram shows how this polyploid hybrid was formed. Its vigorous growth and tolerance of varying salinities mean that it has been able to colonise estuarine mudflats. The cord grass fringes many harbours and estuaries in the UK, and if left unchecked can reach pest proportions.

Reproductive isolation can be important in preserving the uniqueness of a gene pool. It can prevent diluting effects of gene flow into the pool from other populations, which might be detrimental to existing good combinations that have resulted from natural selection.

Courtship in the great crested grebe

chromosomes contributed by zebra father ⅄ (Y)
chromosomes contributed by donkey mother ⋏ (X)

Zebra stallion (2n = 44) Donkey mare (2n = 62)
Karyotype of zebronkey offspring (2n = 53)

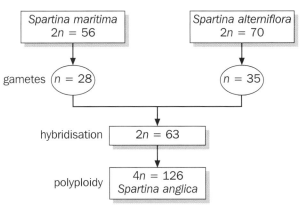

Spartina maritima 2n = 56		*Spartina alterniflora* 2n = 70

gametes (n = 28)   (n = 35)

hybridisation   2n = 63

polyploidy   4n = 126 *Spartina anglica*

Evolution of Spartina anglica, *a new species of cord grass*

Cord grass colonising parts of an estuary

▷ Artificial selection

Artificial selection (or selective breeding) is the process by which animals or plants with characteristics useful to humans are allowed to breed.
The aim is to produce offspring in which these characteristics are further enhanced.

In genetic terms, man rather than the environment determines which alleles pass to successive generations and which are lost.

Artificial selection has been practised for centuries and has been used to develop our modern crop plants, farm animals and domestic pets from their wild ancestors.

Cattle, for example, have been bred by artificial selection for two reasons.
Breeds such as the Hereford and Aberdeen Angus have been selected for the quantity and quality of their meat, whereas other breeds, such as the Jersey and Guernsey, have been selected for their milk yield.

Techniques such as artificial insemination and embryo transplantation have increased the success of selective breeding in animals.
However, more work has been carried out on breeding improved varieties of plants, as they have a greater potential for providing food.
Increasing the yield of crops such as wheat, as well as breeding for disease resistance, are two important areas of research.

A very familiar example of artificial selection is the domestic dog.
There are many different breeds of dog but they all belong to the species *Canis familiaris*.
The dog was selectively bred from the wolf (*Canis lupus*) around 13 000 years ago.
The many breeds that exist have been selected for a whole host of characteristics such as speed, agility and the ability to follow scent.

A danger with artificial selection in animals is excessive inbreeding.
This involves selective reproduction between closely related organisms, for example offspring of the same species.
This is common in pedigree 'show' dogs and the danger is that there will be a reduction in the variation of alleles in the population.
This then increases the risk of homozygosity, and harmful recessive alleles being expressed in the phenotype.

There is also the danger that the selection of characteristics that humans find appealing might prove to be harmful to the organism.

Hereford cattle are bred for their meat

Guernsey cattle are selected for their milk yield

The wolf is the wild ancestor of many domestic breeds of dog

The bloodhound, bred for its tracking ability

The German shepherd, bred for speed and agility

▷ Classification

Estimates of the number of different species in the world
vary from 3 to 30 million.
So far, over 2 million different kinds of organism have been
described and identified.
The sorting of this vast array of living organisms into groups
is known as **classification** or **taxonomy**.

Taxonomists look for differences and similarities between organisms.
Similarities between organisms may occur because they have evolved
along the same lines.
For instance, the limb bones of mammals follow a similar pattern.
There is one upper limb bone, two lower limb bones and an
arrangement of five digits.
These shared features are called **homologous structures**.
They can suggest how different organisms are related and the pattern
of their evolution, a study called **phylogeny**.

The system of classification that we use is based on the ideas of
a Swedish botanist called Carl Linnaeus.
In the early 18th century, he decided that he could place
animals and plants into **natural groups** based on their shared
similar features.
He was the first person to produce an ordered system of classification.
Since then, his system of classification has been greatly modified.

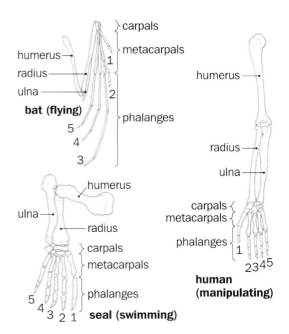

The variations on the pentadactyl limb

A hierarchical system

In any system of classification, taxonomists attempt to place
similar organisms closely together and dissimilar ones further apart.
Large groups of organisms can be divided into successively
smaller groups until you get to the smallest group: the **species**.
Such a classification that is ranked in ascending order is said to
be **hierarchical**.
Starting with the smallest group we have:

- **species** – a group of similar individuals that can breed freely
  to produce fertile offspring, for example *Homo sapiens* (humans),

- **genus** – a group of species that are very closely related,
  for example *Canis latrans* (the coyote) and *Canis lupus*
  (the timber wolf),

- **family** – a grouping of similar genera (plural of genus),
  for example the Ranunculaceae family includes buttercup,
  columbine and larkspur,

- **order** – a grouping of related families, for example
  Falconiformes (the falcons),

- **class** – a grouping of similar orders, for example Pisces (fish),

- **phylum** – a large grouping of all the classes that share some
  common features, for example the Arthropoda includes crabs,
  spiders and insects,

- **kingdom** – the largest taxonomic grouping, for example
  plants and animals.

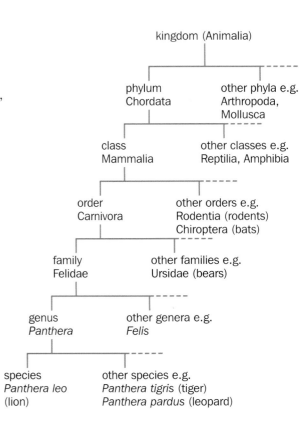

▷ The name game

Living organisms often have common names. For instance, wall pepper, pennywort, roseroot and houseleek all belong to the same family of plants.

But some things have more than one name: the ox-eye daisy is also called dog daisy and Marguerite in different parts of the country.
It can get very confusing, especially if you want to describe a particular species to a person from another country.
Luckily, there is a system of naming living things that is universally understood by biologists, that is the **binomial system**.

The binomial system was first used by Linnaeus and was based upon Latin, a language widely used by educated people at that time.
It involved giving each organism *two* names: the name of its genus and the name of its species.
For instance, *Quercus rubra* is the red oak, and *Fagus sylvatica* is the common beech.

By using these 'scientific names', it is possible for a scientist in Germany to communicate accurately with a scientist in Japan about a particular species that they may both be working on. Furthermore, it allows biologists to be precise when talking about species of mosses, toadstools, beetles and worms, many of which do not have common names.

The binomial system is successful because each particular organism has its own unique scientific name and because we can often see straight away that two species are closely related.
For instance, *Gibbula umbilicalis* and *Gibbula cineraria* are the purple top-shell and the grey top-shell, both common on rocky shores.

Rules of the game

Any universally used system of classification, such as the binomial system, has to have rules so that people are consistent in using it. Here are some of them.

- The generic (genus) name is the first word and is always given a capital letter.
  Several species may share the same generic name, but each has its own unique specific name.

- The specific (species) name comes second and always starts with a small letter.

- Both names should either be written in italics (in printed text) or be underlined (if using hand-writing).

- The scientific name should be written out in full the first time it is used, for example *Culex pipiens*.
  But after that it can be abbreviated, for example *C. pipiens*.

- If the particular species is unknown, then the abbreviation 'sp' can be used, for example *Ectocarpus sp*.

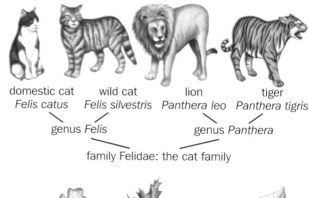

domestic cat	wild cat	lion	tiger
Felis catus	*Felis silvestris*	*Panthera leo*	*Panthera tigris*

genus *Felis*   genus *Panthera*

family Felidae: the cat family

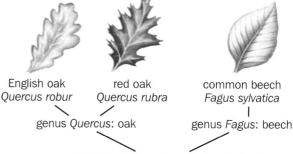

English oak	red oak	common beech
Quercus robur	*Quercus rubra*	*Fagus sylvatica*

genus *Quercus*: oak   genus *Fagus*: beech

family Fagaceae: the oak–beech family

The purple top-shell (Gibbula umbilicalis)

Your classification is:

Kingdom: Animalia
Phylum: Chordata
Class: Mammalia
Order: Primates
Family: Hominidae
Genus: *Homo*
Species: *Homo sapiens*

▷ The five kingdoms

Older systems of classification tended to be based on a two kingdom plan: the plants and the animals.
Problems arose when groups of organisms could not fit into either category. For instance, into which group does the single-celled *Amoeba* fit?
The five kingdom classification has gained general acceptance.
It recognises two basic cell types: prokaryote and eukaryote.
The Prokaryotae includes all the bacteria and the cyanobacteria.
The Eukaryota includes the Protoctista, an odd grouping including algae, amoebae, flagellates and ciliates.
Also in the Eukaryota are the fungi, plants and animals.

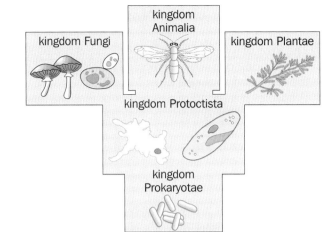

Main features of the five kingdoms

Prokaryotae
The bacteria and cyanobacteria have prokaryotic cells.
The cell has no distinct nucleus enclosed by a nuclear membrane.
Neither do they have membrane bound organelles such as mitochondria and chloroplasts.

Salmonella *bacteria are prokaryotes*

Protoctista
A collection of eukaryotic organisms including the algae (photosynthetic but not plants) to which the seaweeds belong.
Other protoctists include protozoans such as *Amoeba* and *Plasmodium*, ciliates such as *Paramecium*, and flagellates such as *Euglena*.
The protoctists seems to be a group in which organisms end up if they are not monerans, fungi, plants or animals.
Many have eukaryotic cell features such as chloroplasts.

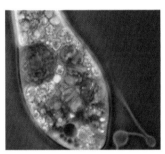

Euglena has chloroplasts but it is a protoctist not a plant

Fungi
Fungi are not able to photosynthesise.
Their cell walls are made not of cellulose, but of another polysaccharide called chitin.
Their bodies are composed of masses of filaments called **hyphae**, which are not divided up into separate cells.
Most are **saprobiont**, obtaining their food by the extra-cellular digestion of dead organic material. Some, however, are parasitic.
Fungi have membrane bound organelles.

This bracket fungus grows from the bark of the tree

Plants
Plants are multicellular.
They have chlorophyll and are photosynthetic.
Their cells have a cellulose cell wall and a sap-filled vacuole.
Many have proper stems, roots and leaves.
Primitive plants reproduce by spores; more advanced forms, such as conifers and flowering plants, produce seeds.

Animals
Animals are multicellular.
They are heterotrophic – they are unable to make their own food and need a supply of organic food material.
They have nervous systems and are able to move about.
Growth occurs throughout the body.

Vervet monkeys

▷ Biology at work: Natural selection on the underground

The idea of what a separate species is, is not as simple as we may think. Perhaps one of the best accepted definitions has been put forward by the respected zoologist Ernst Mayr:
'A species is a group of actually or potentially interbreeding natural populations that is reproductively isolated from other such groups.'

Recent research has indicated that a new species of mosquito could be well on the way to developing in the tunnels of the London underground.

It is thought that one way a new species can develop is when part of a population becomes isolated from the rest of the population. The two populations live in different environments and are acted on by natural selection in different ways. Eventually, genetic differences build up to such an extent that members of the two populations can no longer interbreed.

The London Underground, home to a new species of mosquito?

When the underground tunnels were being constructed around a 100 years ago, a population of the bird-biting mosquito *Culex pipiens* found its way underground. Subsequently, a new form of the mosquito, *Culex molestus,* evolved in its new environment. For example, it now feeds on rats and mice, although during the Second World War it plagued Londoners sheltering from bombs.

Apart from the obvious behavioural differences, *C. molestus* has been found to differ genetically from *C. pipiens* to a degree that would normally be expected only after thousands of years of separation.

Perhaps the biggest indicator of *C. molestus* becoming a new species is that attempts to cross-breed it with its surface-living relative have failed.

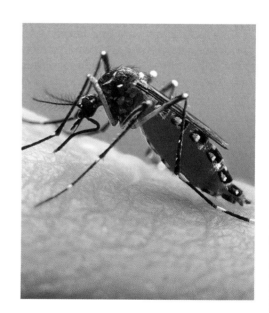

Further research has also found genetic differences between *C. molestus* mosquitoes on different underground lines. This may be due to the separation imposed by draughts blowing along and not between different tunnels.

Look back over the page on allopatric speciation.
What is the physical barrier that separates the two populations in this example?
How does this example differ from the often quoted examples of geographical isolation by mountain ranges and oceans?

In this example, the speciation seems to have taken place over a far shorter time scale.

How well do you think *C. molestus* fits Ernst Mayr's definition of a species?

▷ Biology at work: Recreating dinosaurs

In the film *Jurassic Park* and its sequel *The Lost World*, dinosaurs
were recreated from fragments of their DNA.
This came from the stomachs of ancient blood-sucking insects,
which had been mummified inside amber.

Recently, American scientists claimed they had managed to extract insect DNA
from amber that was up to 120 million years old.
It was thought that DNA could not last more than 100 000 years.
Scientists from the Natural History Museum in London spent over 2 years
searching for fossil DNA from museum specimens.
They could not find any DNA in their insect specimens but did
find DNA from modern fungi and themselves!
This contamination of DNA samples explained the American's findings.
Molecular techniques are routinely used in the identification and
classification of organisms.

A fly encased in Baltic amber

Systematics (or taxonomy as it is sometimes referred to) is
the study of classifying or grouping organisms, both living and fossil.
It is concerned with:

- discovering and describing biological diversity,
- investigating evolutionary relationships between organisms,
- classifying so as to reflect these relationships.

Many biologists mistakenly think that all organisms have
been classified and species identified.
The estimated number of species in the world is between
3 and 30 million.
Only 2 million have so far been identified.

Red wolf   *Coyote*

The use of museum collections to identify and classify
species is on the increase. An example is the status of
the red wolf, which is extinct in the wild.
Comparing mitochondrial cytochrome b genes from
museum skins with the gene sequences of the grey wolf
and the coyote enabled its status to be re-assessed.
This suggests that the red wolf was genetically very similar
to the coyote and may not have been a separate species.

*The anti-viral drug casteanospermine is found in the
Moerton Bay chestnut (left). A related genus Alexua
contains more of the drug.*

Correct identification and classification has important applications.

- **Agriculture** – the control of the cassava mealy bug in Africa failed
  initially because of incorrect identification of the pest.
- **Medicine** – the anti-viral casteanospermine is a potential new drug
  found in an Australian plant. A closely related Amazonian genus was identified
  and found to have greater quantities and less toxic forms of the drug.
- **Industry** – because fermentation products vary according to the strain
  of microbe involved, correct identification is essential for reliable production.
- **Forensic science** – sequencing the stages of corpse decomposition relies
  on the succession of decomposer communities. This is essential to reconstruct the
  events surrounding the cause of death.
- **Environmental assessment** – bio-indicators are used in pollution assessment.
  These include the use of diatoms to measure surface water acidification, the use of
  lichens for air pollution and freshwater invertebrates for river pollution.

The mayfly Ecdyonurus *is an
indicator of clean water*

Jurassic Park and the resurrection of dinosaurs remain science fiction.

Summary

- Variation is a result of both genetic change and environmental factors.
- Genetic change can be a result of the random distribution of chromosomes at metaphase I of meiosis, crossing over, random mating, random fertilisation of gametes and mutations.
- Gene or point mutations result from a change in the base sequence of DNA.
- Chromosome mutations result from a change in the chromosome structure or changes in the number of whole sets of chromosomes or individual chromosomes.
- Mutations can be induced by mutagens. These are certain types of radiation and certain chemicals.
- Natural selection results in individuals better adapted to surviving and passing their genes for beneficial characteristics on to the next generation.
- There are three main types of selection: stabilising, directional and disruptive selection.
- The separation of two populations as a result of geographical isolation or as a result of reproductive isolation can result in the formation of a new species. This process is called speciation.
- Artificial selection is the process of cross-breeding plants or animals with useful characteristics.
- The sorting of living organisms into groups is called classification or taxonomy.
- Phylogeny is the study of how different organisms are related and the pattern of their evolution.
- The five kingdom system classifies organisms into prokaryotes, protoctists, fungi, plants and animals.

▷ Questions

1 Explain the process of natural selection in relation to each of the following:
   a) melanic moths,
   b) heavy metal tolerance,
   c) bacterial resistance to antibiotics.

2 There are 64 chromosomes in each body cell of a horse and 62 chromosomes in each body cell of a donkey.

Animal	Number of chromosomes in one of the nuclei formed at the end of		
	mitosis	first division of meiosis	second division of meiosis
horse			
donkey			

   a) Copy and complete the table to show the number of chromosomes in the nuclei of these animals at the end of various stages of cell division.
   b) A mule is the offspring of a cross between a horse and a donkey.
      i) How many chromosomes would there be in a body cell from a mule? Give a reason for your answer.
      ii) Suggest why a mule is unable to produce fertile gametes.
      iii) Explain why a horse and a donkey are regarded as different species.

3 The graphs show three different types of selection. The shaded areas marked with arrows show the individuals in the population which are being selected against.

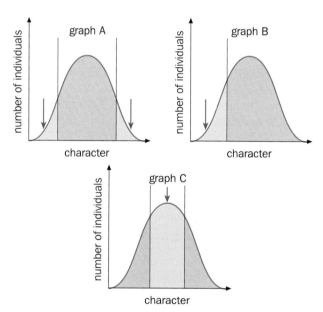

   a) What name is given to the type of selection shown in graph A?
   b) Describe one specific example of the type of selection shown in graph B. Be sure to name the organism and describe the character selected.
   c) What will happen to the modal class in subsequent generations as a result of the type of selection shown in:
      i) graph B,
      ii) graph C?

4 The dog-whelk lives on rocky shores around Britain. The graphs show the variation in shell height in two different populations, one from a rocky shore exposed to strong wave action and the other from a sheltered rocky shore. Shell height was measured as shown in the diagram.

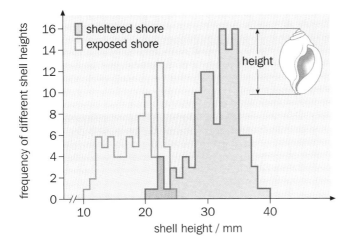

a) What type of variation is shown in the graphs?
b) Describe two differences shown in the graphs between dog-whelks from the exposed shore and dog-whelks from the sheltered shore.
c) In a follow-up investigation, it was found that dog-whelks on the sheltered shore had much thicker shells than those on the exposed shore. On the sheltered shore, there were more crabs, which are predators of dog-whelks. Describe how natural selection could account for this difference in shell thickness.

5 'The Chatham Islands lie 850 kilometres from mainland New Zealand. In 1980 the number of black robins, *Petroica traversi*, which live there dropped to 5. Today there are 200, all descended from a single breeding pair. DNA fingerprints from blood samples revealed that, for the genetic sequences used in the test, the robins appeared to be genetically identical. The robins are now prospering. Just over 70% of their young survive to fledgling state, compared with only 42% for their mainland cousin the bush robin, *Petroica australis*.
    Adapted from *New Scientist*, 31st May 1997
a) i) State the information conveyed in the scientific names about the taxonomic relationship between Chatham Islands black robins and mainland bush robins.
    ii) From the information in the paragraph above, name the factor that may have been responsible for the divergence between the two populations of robin.
b) Suggest
    i) the only way in which all robins on Chatham Islands may not be genetically identical,
    ii) two reasons why low genetic diversity might be a disadvantage in the long-term survival of Chatham Islands robins,
    iii) one reason for the difference in survival of young robins to fledgling stage in the two populations.

6 *Ectocarpus siliculosis* is a marine alga found growing on the shore and on the hulls of ships. Two populations of *Ectocarpus siliculosis*, A and B, were sampled. Samples of population A were collected from an unpolluted shore. Samples of population B were collected from the hull of a ship painted with antifouling paint, which slowly releases copper into the water. The diagram shows the percentage increase in algal samples collected from populations A and B and cultured, for identical periods of time, in media containing different concentrations of copper.

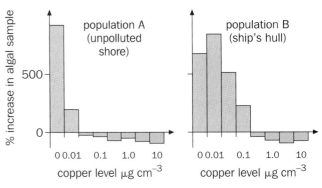

a) i) Describe two ways in which the data for the two populations differ.
    ii) Explain how copper tolerance observed in this population may have evolved.
b) Despite thorough cleaning and repainting with antifouling paint, the hull of the ship rapidly recolonised. Suggest why shipping companies are prepared to spend money to prevent this recolonisation.

7 The classification system for living organisms is a hierarchy of phylogenetic groupings.
a) Explain what is meant, in this context, by
    i) a hierarchy,
    ii) phylogenetic.
b) Copy and complete the table to show the classification of the ocelot.

Kingdom	Animalia
	Chordata
Class	Mammalia
	Carnivora
Family	Felidae
	Leopardus
	pardalis

Ecology is the study of how living organisms *interact* with each other and with their environment.

By *interaction* we mean the relationships that an organism has with its physical surroundings and with individuals of the same species and individuals of other species.

By *environment* we mean not only the physical (**abiotic**) conditions, such as light and temperature, but also the biological (**biotic**) conditions under which an organism lives.

▷ Habitats and niches

The **habitat** is the place where an organism lives.

It is the physical (abiotic) environment, which provides the conditions that the organism needs to survive, such as the right amount of light, oxygen and water, and a suitable temperature.

The habitat of a trout is a fast-flowing stream, and the habitat of wild garlic is a woodland.

Most habitats are made up of a patchwork of *microhabitats*.

For instance, in an oak tree, insects can live in or on the leaves, in cracks in the bark, inside an acorn or amongst the roots.

These are all examples of microhabitats.

The **niche** is the *role* that an organism plays in its environment.

It is quite simply the *way of life* of an organism in its natural surroundings.

For instance, the winter moth feeds on the buds of oak trees.

At the same time, it is the food of insectivorous birds and parasites.

This is the role or niche of the winter moth.

If two organisms occupy the same niche, they will **compete**.

In Britain, the North American grey squirrel and the native red squirrel seem to be competing for the same niche.

They both need the same food and nesting sites in the same kind of habitat.

How many habitats can you spot in this photograph?

Competing for the same niche

▷ Populations, communities and ecosystems

Ecology can be studied at a number of different levels.

A **population** is a group of individuals of the *same* species, living in the same habitat. For example, a population of tawny owls in a woodland, or a population of banded snails in a hedgerow. Since they are of the same species, the members of a population are able to interbreed.

A **community** consists of all the living things in a particular habitat.

For instance, all the inhabitants of a lake or a salt marsh.

A community is made up of the different populations of species that live in the habitat.

An **ecosystem** is made up of the community (biotic component) and the habitat (abiotic component).

An ecosystem is a major ecological unit. For instance, a pond ecosystem consists of all the living organisms in the pond *as well as* the water, dissolved oxygen, suspended materials and pond bed.

Coral reef ecosystem

▷ Feeding relationships

The individuals in a community can be classified by their method of feeding.

Living organisms can be classed as:

- **autotrophs** – those that can make their own food, or
- **heterotrophs** – those that cannot make their own food.

Autotrophs are able to make their own organic food from inorganic substances, using a source of energy.
Green plants are autotrophs. They use light energy to convert carbon dioxide and water into sugars by photosynthesis.
Algae and many types of bacteria can also photosynthesise using light energy.

Other autotrophic bacteria use the energy from chemical reactions to synthesise organic food. This is called **chemosynthesis**.
Since autotrophs are the only living things that can produce organic food substances, they ultimately provide all the food for other members of the community.
For this reason we call autotrophs **producers**.

Heterotrophs cannot make their own organic food – they have to take it into their bodies ready-made.
In other words, they eat it or consume it.
All animals are **consumers** and ultimately they all depend upon producers for food.

Light penetrating the tree canopy

- **Primary consumers** are herbivores. They eat producers.
- **Secondary consumers** are carnivores. They feed on primary consumers.
- **Tertiary consumers** are carnivores that eat other consumers. They are sometimes called top carnivores.

Each of these feeding categories is known as a **trophic level**.
'Trophic' comes from the Greek word meaning 'to feed'.
But how do you know which trophic level an animal belongs to?
You can get clues about what it eats from its teeth and by studying its feeding behaviour.

▷ Decomposers and detritivores

Secondary consumer and primary consumer

These two groups of consumers are important since they feed on dead animals and plants. They release organic and inorganic nutrients, which may be used again.

- **Detritivores** are primary consumers that feed on fragments of dead organic material called **detritus**. They shred the detritus up into smaller particles. Detritivores include small animals like earthworms and woodlice in the soil and freshwater shrimps and hog-lice in rivers and streams.

- **Decomposers** include microbes such as fungi and bacteria. They also obtain their energy from dead and decaying organic material. They complete the process of decomposition started by detritivores. Decomposers fulfil an important role by releasing nutrients from dead organic matter, which can be recycled and used for new plant growth.

Detritivores at work

▷ Chains and webs

Food chains show what eats what in a community.
They show the transfer of food energy from one trophic level to another.
Look at the food chain below:

oak leaves → caterpillar → blue tit → sparrow hawk

Notice that the arrows show the direction in which food energy is transferred.
Food chains always begin with a producer, usually a photosynthetic plant.
Here is a detritivore food chain:

dead leaves → woodlouse → carabid beetle → shrew → owl

We can use food chains to show feeding relationships in any community.
Here is a food chain for a lake community:

phytoplankton → water fleas → stickle back → perch → pike

If all the water fleas died:
What would happen to the number of sticklebacks?
What would happen to the number of phytoplankton?
A food chain seldom has more than five links. Why do you think this is?

▷ Food webs

Food chains give only a limited impression of the feeding relationships in a community.
They only ever show a consumer feeding on **one** type of animal or plant.
In reality, an animal will feed upon a variety of other organisms.

A **food web** gives a more complete picture of the feeding relationships in a community.
A food web consists of all the food chains in a community linked together.

Look at this simple grassland food web.

Suppose all the field voles were killed by disease.
Why might the number of dandelions increase?
Why might the number of foxes decrease?
Explain why the numbers of wood mice might either increase or decrease.

Look at the food web for a woodland community and give one example of:
  i) a decomposer,
  ii) a tertiary consumer,
  iii) an omnivore,
  iv) a producer,
  v) an invertebrate predator.
    Try to draw a pyramid of number for the food chain
    oak tree → winter moths → blue tits → weasels
    How might a pyramid of biomass look different from the pyramid that you have drawn?

A major drawback of food webs is that they do not tell you **how many** living organisms are involved.
Many food webs are just too complex to complete.

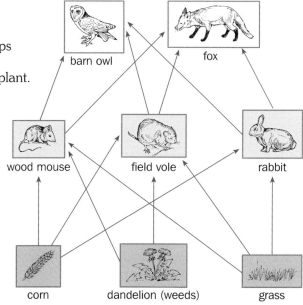
Food web for a grassland community

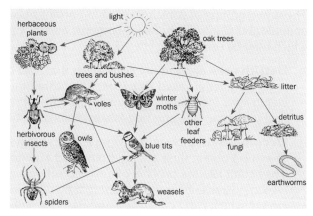
Food web for a woodland community

392

▷ Pyramids of number

Food webs describe the feeding relationships
that exist within a community but they give no information
about the numbers or **quantities** of organisms involved,
or their mass, or the energy involved.

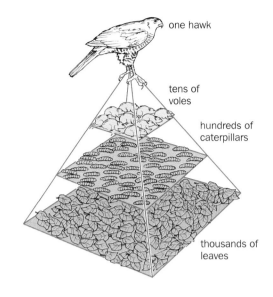

You can see from the diagram that it may take many plants
to feed one herbivore and many herbivores to sustain
just one carnivore.

Here are some numbers for this food chain:

hawk	1
voles	10
caterpillars	100
groundsel plants	600

We can display this information in a **pyramid of number**.
This is essentially a bar chart that is plotted horizontally.
The area of each bar is proportional to the number of
individuals at that trophic level.
The producers are placed at the base of the pyramid and
each successive consumer level is placed above them.

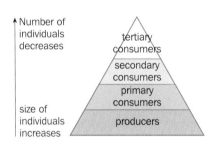

- What happens to the **numbers** of individuals as you go
  up this pyramid?
- What happens to the **size** of each individual organism as
  you go up the pyramid?

To construct a pyramid of number for a particular community,
you must first randomly sample the organisms.
This may involve quadrat analysis, the use of nets or
humane trapping.

The sample is divided up into each trophic level and
the numbers of individuals counted.
The units for pyramids of number are usually expressed as
individuals per square metre.

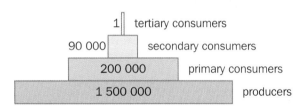

*Pyramid of number for a grassland community
in 0.1 hectare*

Problems with pyramids of number

Pyramids of number are an improvement upon food chains
and food webs since they do give **quantitative** information.
However, their major drawback is that they do not take into
account the **relative mass** of organisms at each trophic level.

For instance, both an oak tree and a grass plant each count as
just **one** organism.
But clearly one oak tree can support many more herbivores than
one grass plant can.
This limitation in the technique can result in some unusual
shaped pyramids, as you can see here.

In this pyramid of number, the tertiary consumers are parasites.
Many of them are able to feed on just one ladybird.
This top-heavy pyramid is said to be inverted.

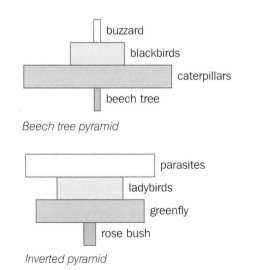

Beech tree pyramid

Inverted pyramid

▷ Pyramids of biomass

One way to overcome this problem of the size of the organism is to measure the **biomass** at each trophic level instead of the number of organisms present.

Biomass is the mass of living material present at a given time. So a biomass pyramid will show the mass of living organisms, at a particular trophic level, per unit area or volume, at a particular time (often expressed in $kg\,m^{-2}$).
This is also referred to as the **standing crop**.

To construct a biomass pyramid, you first need to collect some data.
You need to take random samples, usually harvesting all the organisms within a quadrat.
Then divide the organisms up into their respective trophic levels and weigh them. This is known as **wet mass** or **fresh mass**.
Find the average mass for each trophic level.
Then multiply the average mass by the estimated number of organisms to give the biomass at each trophic level.
Some scientists prefer to use **dry mass**, since the water content of organisms (especially plants) can vary a great deal.
However, obtaining dry mass data involves heating the sample in an oven at 110 °C to remove all the water.
This is neither practicable nor desirable since it inevitably kills the plants and animals that have been sampled.

Drawbacks with biomass pyramids

● The biomass recorded at any one instance is just a 'snap shot' in time. Biomass pyramids give no indication of the *rate* at which organisms grow. **Productivity** is the rate at which organic materials are produced per unit area or volume per unit time. Biomass data cannot take into account how fast organic materials are produced. For example, the grass in a field grows fast, it has *high productivity*. However, because it is grazed by herbivores such as sheep or cattle, its biomass at any one point in time will be low.

● Phytoplankton are tiny producers that grow very quickly in the sea. They grow and divide every 3 or 4 days.
We say that they have high productivity or that they have a high **turnover rate**. But they are constantly harvested by the primary consumers present in the habitat.
So their total biomass at any particular time is relatively small. But over a period of, say, a year, their biomass will be huge.
So this particular biomass pyramid looks inverted because it reflects only a few days of phytoplankton growth.

● Biomass can also vary with the seasons.
The biomass of a beech tree will be far greater in summer than it is in winter. Why do you think this is?

In the winter the tree will have shed the leaves, flowers and fruits that develop in the summer.

Pyramids of biomass overcome the problem of size of individuals but they do not take productivity into account.

Biomass is the weight of living material

Biomass sampling on a rocky shore

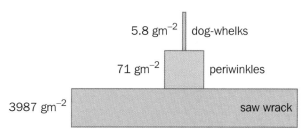

5.8 gm⁻² | dog-whelks
71 gm⁻² | periwinkles
3987 gm⁻² | saw wrack

Biomass pyramid for a rocky shore community

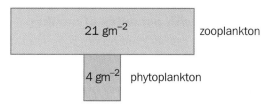

21 gm⁻² | zooplankton
4 gm⁻² | phytoplankton

Biomass pyramid for a plankton community

▷ Pyramids of energy

The most accurate way to represent the feeding relationships in a community
is to use an **energy pyramid**.
An energy pyramid shows the amount of energy transferred from one trophic
level to the next, per unit area or volume, per unit time.

This energy pyramid shows that 87 000 kJ m^{-2} year^{-1} is transferred to the
tadpoles (primary consumers) from the water plants (producers).
The tadpoles then pass 14 000 kJ m^{-2} per year to the small fish
(secondary consumers) and so on.

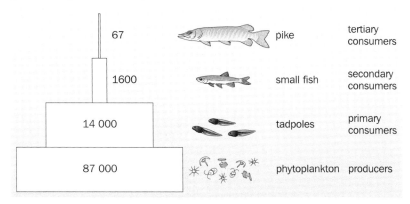

67	pike	tertiary consumers
1600	small fish	secondary consumers
14 000	tadpoles	primary consumers
87 000	phytoplankton	producers

A pyramid of energy for a lake community (figures are in kJ m^{-2} year $^{-1}$)

However, if the tadpoles gained 87 000 kJ m^{-2} year^{-1} from the water
plants but only passed on 14 000 kJ m^{-2} year^{-1} to the small fish, then
where did the other 73 000 kJ m^{-2} year^{-1} go to?

What have the tadpoles done with all that energy?
They will have used up a lot in respiration, using energy to swim around.
They will also have passed out some energy in waste materials.
The only energy that the tadpoles do pass on is that which
they have used to make new body cells as they grow.

A large proportion of energy is always 'lost' between trophic levels
in these ways.
Of the 87 000 kJ m^{-2} year^{-1} of energy that we started off with, only
67 kJ m^{-2} year^{-1} will end up in biomass as part of the pike's body.

The larva of the great diving beetle also predates upon tadpoles

Since only some of the energy is passed on, energy pyramids
are never inverted.
The pyramid's shape is not affected by the size of the organisms
nor their numbers, it simply reflects the amount of energy
that is passed on.

Unlike pyramids of number or biomass, energy pyramids make it
easy to compare the efficiency of energy transfer from one
trophic level to the next in different communities.
They reflect the productivity at each trophic level.

Although energy pyramids give a better representation of
the transfer of food energy between trophic levels than
pyramids of number or pyramids of biomass, the data is difficult
to obtain.
It requires incineration of the sample in a calorimeter to estimate
energy content.
This destructive sampling is seldom practicable nor desirable.

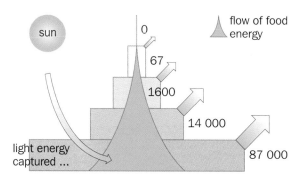

A pyramid of energy for the lake ecosystem in kJ m^{-2} year $^{-1}$

395

▷ Shortening the food chain

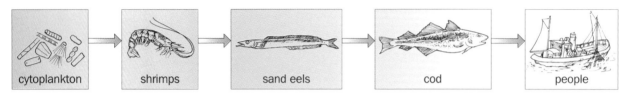

cytoplankton → shrimps → sand eels → cod → people

Look at the pyramid of number on the right.
It shows the estimated number of individuals that could
be supported by 1000 tonnes of phytoplankton per year.
Humans are at the top of this pyramid.
How many cod would one human eat in a year?
It works out at about 1 cod a day.

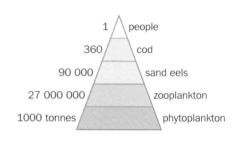

1	people
360	cod
90 000	sand eels
27 000 000	zooplankton
1000 tonnes	phytoplankton

What if the food chain is shortened and people ate
sand eels instead of cod?
Thirty people could be supported in this way,
that's assuming that each person could get by on
about 10 sand eels a day.

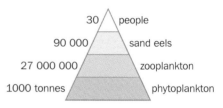

30	people
90 000	sand eels
27 000 000	zooplankton
1000 tonnes	phytoplankton

What if the food chain is shortened again?
People now feed on zooplankton such as shrimps.
How would you fancy 100 shrimps a day?
If so, the food chain could support 900 people a year.

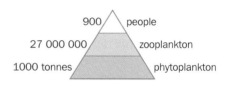

900	people
27 000 000	zooplankton
1000 tonnes	phytoplankton

What if we were to remove the last animal link in the food chain
and become vegetarian?
Feeding upon 2 kg of phytoplankton a day may not appeal to you.
But this could sustain 2000 people per year!

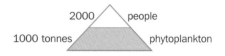

| 2000 | people |
| 1000 tonnes | phytoplankton |

What is the message for us from this simple exercise?
Quite simply, a vegetarian diet can support far more people.
By eliminating links in the food chain, more people at the end
of the food chain can be fed.
This is because we are reducing the 90% 'wastage' of energy
that occurs between one trophic level and the next.
The energy that is uneaten, undigested or used in respiration
at each trophic level.
Quite simply, the longer the food chain, the more energy will
be lost.

Why do you think that people living in under developed
countries tend to have vegetarian diets?
In western developed countries, people have a varied diet
including poultry, fish, lamb, beef and pork.
What does this tell you about the economies of these countries?

The human population is increasing at an alarming rate.
How do you think this will affect the future price of meat?

The rising price of food will inevitably push us down the
food pyramid towards a vegetarian diet.

Food distribution in Somalia

▷ Energy flow through producers

The energy in all ecosystems comes originally from sunlight.
This energy can be transferred from one form to another
but cannot be created or destroyed.
Solar energy enters the food chain at producer level during photosynthesis.
Some of this energy is then passed on to consumers, but eventually
all of it will leave the system as heat.

All living organisms depend directly or indirectly upon **primary production**.
Primary production is the production of organic materials by producers.
Green plants (and algae and some bacteria) are able to transfer solar
energy into the chemical energy in sugar during photosynthesis.

Photosynthesis is far less efficient than we may imagine.
Most of the sunlight that falls on a plant is not even absorbed.
Only light within the wavelengths 380 nm (red) and 720 nm (blue)
can be absorbed by chlorophyll and other plant pigments.
This light is called **photosynthetically active radiation**, or **PAR**.
This is the only light that can be used in photosynthesis.
But not all PAR will be absorbed by chlorophyll.
Some will be reflected and some will pass straight through the leaf
(in which case, we say that it is transmitted).

Photosynthetic efficiency is a measure of how well
a plant is able to capture light energy.

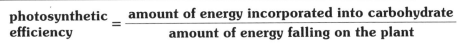

$$\text{photosynthetic efficiency} = \frac{\text{amount of energy incorporated into carbohydrate}}{\text{amount of energy falling on the plant}}$$

Even in ideal conditions the overall efficiency of energy
conversion in photosynthesis is less than 8%.
In reality, ideal conditions seldom prevail, due to daily and
seasonal fluctuations in light and temperature, lack of nutrients
and water stress.

The light energy captured by chlorophyll is used to make ATP.
The plant uses most of this ATP to carry out its own metabolic
processes.
The sugars made in photosynthesis accumulate as **gross
primary production** (**GPP**).
A great deal of this is used up in respiration, providing energy to
drive the plant's life processes.
What is left over is called **net primary production** (**NPP**).

$$\text{net primary production} = \text{gross primary production} - \text{respiration}$$

NPP represents the potential food available to primary consumers.
By eating plants, herbivores are, in effect, receiving light energy in
the form of organic molecules such as carbohydrates, fats and proteins.
Some of this potential food may be transferred to decomposers.
This can happen when leaves are shed, fruits and seeds are dispersed
and when the plant itself dies.
Decomposers benefit by obtaining energy from the dead plant tissues.

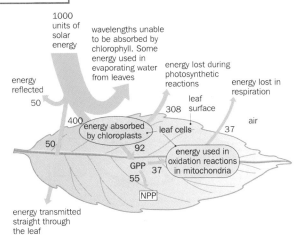

The amount of solar energy intercepted by green plants depends a great
deal on geographical location. In Britain this is estimated as approximately
1×10^6 kJ m^{-2} year^{-1}, but at least 95% of this is unavailable to plants
for photosynthesis

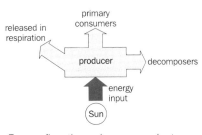

Energy flow through a green plant

▷ Energy flow through consumers

Transfer of energy from producers to primary consumers, or from plants to herbivores, also involves energy 'wastage'. It is estimated that for every 100 g of plant material available, only about 10 g ends up as new herbivore biomass. This represents a conversion efficiency of 10%.

So what are the reasons for the 90% energy wastage between trophic levels?

- Some plant material may not be consumed in the first place, for example the bark of a tree or a plant's roots. The energy will eventually go to decomposers in dead remains.
- Some plant material is not digested and passes out of the herbivore's body in the faeces.
- Much of the energy in the food will be used by the herbivore for respiration.

Similar losses of energy occur between subsequent trophic levels.
Carnivores are more efficient at energy conversion.
Some are able to achieve as much as 20%.
That is, 20% of the herbivore biomass eaten ends up as carnivore biomass.
This is because they are able to digest their high protein diets more efficiently.
It is this loss of energy at each trophic level that gives ecological pyramids their characteristic shape.

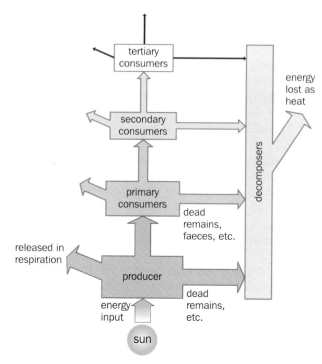

Energy flow through a community

▷ Energy budgets

If the amounts of energy entering, being used up and leaving an animal can be measured, then we can work out an **energy budget**.

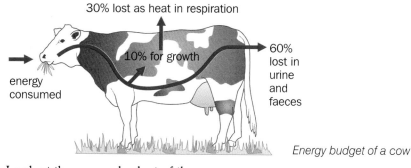

Energy budget of a cow

Look at the energy budget of the cow.
You can see that, of the energy in the grass that the cow consumes, over half of it is passed out of the body in the faeces.
A lot of energy is used up in respiration to fuel the chemical reactions in the body and for movement.
A proportion goes to produce new biomass in growth.
The remainder is excreted as metabolic waste in urine.
The energy budget of a cow can be summarised as:

energy intake	=	energy transfer in respiration	+	energy transfer into biomass	+	energy in faeces	+	energy in urine

▷ Nutrient cycling

As you know, all living organisms need energy.
Energy enters ecosystems as sunlight trapped by producers.
It is then transferred up various trophic levels, eventually being released as heat.

But living organisms also need organic and inorganic nutrients.
Plants obtain inorganic nutrients from the soil and water.
As with energy, these nutrients are transferred to consumers along the food chain.
But unlike energy, these nutrients are later released back into the environment so that they can be reused.
There is a fixed amount of nutrients on Earth and they constantly move from air, water and soil into living organisms and back again.
We say that nutrients are **cycled** between the biotic and abiotic environments.

Most living matter (95%) is composed of just six elements:
carbon, hydrogen, nitrogen, oxygen, phosphorus and sulphur.
A good way to remember this is the mnemonic 'CHNOPS'.
These are **macronutrients** needed in large amounts by green plants (as we saw in Chapter 17).
Other nutrients, called **trace elements**, are only needed in minute amounts, for example iron, manganese, copper, zinc and boron.
However, if these are lacking, plants will develop deficiency symptoms.

▷ Decomposition

Fragments of dead and decaying matter are called **detritus**.
Can you remember what we call the small animals that feed on detritus?
Detritivores include animals like worms, woodlice and maggots.
They shred up detritus into minute particles that decomposers are able to act upon.
Without detritivores, the process of decomposition would take much longer.

Decomposers (bacteria and fungi) release enzymes which break down their food by **extracellular digestion**.
They then absorb the digested products in much the same way as we absorb digested food from our gut.
The decomposers use this food for growth and energy.
The decomposers may be eaten by other organisms, passing on nutrients in this way, or the nutrients may be released into the soil or water.

Decomposer food chain:

dead leaves → fungus → beetle → frog

Detritvore food chain:

dead animal → blowfly maggots → blackbird → sparrowhawk

As you will see in the carbon cycle and the nitrogen cycle, decomposers play a key role in the cycling of nutrients.

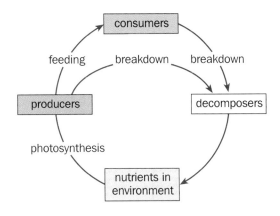
Cycling of nutrients in an ecosystem

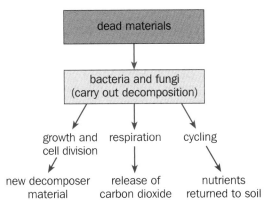
The roles of bacteria and fungi in decomposition

▷ The carbon cycle

All living organisms need carbon.
Organic molecules such as carbohydrates, proteins, fats, nucleic acids and other important compounds all contain carbon.

Two processes dominate the carbon cycle: photosynthesis and respiration.

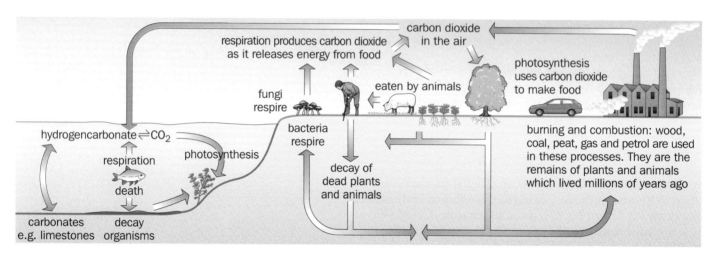

Carbon dioxide is readily available in the air and, because it is highly soluble in water, it is freely available to freshwater and marine plants.
As you can see from the diagram, carbon dioxide from the air and water is fixed into organic compounds during photosynthesis.

$$6CO_2 + 6H_2O \xrightarrow[\text{chlorophyll}]{\text{sunlight}} C_6H_{12}O_6 + 6O_2$$

carbon dioxide · water · glucose · oxygen

Photosynthesis provides the input for carbon into food chains.
Primary consumers eat the producers and may, in turn, be eaten by secondary consumers, and so on.
All animals rely upon plants, directly or indirectly, for their source of carbon.

How is carbon released back into the environment?

● Plants and animals use a lot of their organic food in respiration.
The carbon is released back into the environment as carbon dioxide.
This carbon dioxide can be used for photosynthesis again.

$$C_6H_{12}O_6 + 6O_2 \longrightarrow 6CO_2 + 6H_2O + \text{energy}$$

glucose · oxygen · carbon dioxide · water

● Decomposers use dead plants and animals for food.
They use some of their food in respiration, releasing carbon dioxide.
● Fossil fuels such as oil, coal, peat and gas contain carbon.
When they are burned, carbon dioxide is released back into air and water.

The burning of fossil fuels releases carbon dioxide back into the environment

These processes put back carbon dioxide into the air and water at about the same rate as plants remove it for photosynthesis.
So the amount of carbon dioxide in the atmosphere and water should stay the same.
As you will know, the level of carbon dioxide in the air is increasing.
The possible consequences of this in terms of the 'greenhouse effect' and possible global warming are dealt with in Chapter 24.

▷ The nitrogen cycle

Despite making up nearly 80% of the air, nitrogen (N_2) is an unreactive gas.
Living organisms need nitrogen for amino acids, proteins, nucleic acids
and other important organic molecules.
But plants and animals are unable to use nitrogen gas.
It has to be converted to **nitrates** before it can be absorbed and used by plants.
It can then be transferred to consumers along the food chains.
So how does nitrogen gas get changed into nitrates?

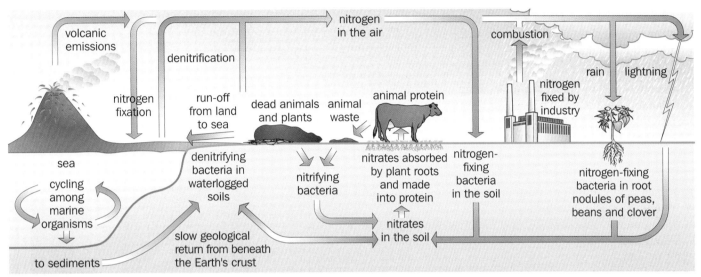

If you look carefully at the diagram you will see that the key organisms
in the nitrogen cycle are *bacteria*.

- **Decomposing bacteria**, along with fungi, decompose dead plants
  and animals, faeces and urine into simpler molecules.
  The complex molecules such as proteins, amino acids and urea are
  broken down and nitrogen is released to the environment in the form
  of ammonium ions (NH_4^+). This is called **ammonification**.

- **Nitrifying bacteria** are able to convert the ammonium ions into
  nitrates, under aerobic conditions.
  Nitrosomonas oxidises ammonium ions to nitrite.
  The nitrite is then oxidised to nitrate by *Nitrobacter*.
  This process is called **nitrification**.
  The nitrates formed can be absorbed by plants and so make proteins
  and nucleic acids and enter the food chains.

- **Nitrogen-fixing bacteria** take nitrogen gas out of the air
  and convert it into organic form. Free-living microorganisms such as
  Azotobacter in the soil and *Nostoc*, a cyanobacterium found in
  freshwater, account for 90% of nitrogen fixation.
  The bacterium *Rhizobium* is found in the roots of legume plants such
  as peas, beans, clover and gorse. The roots swell to form **root
  nodules**.
  The bacterium forms a relationship with the legume plant
  which is beneficial to both partners.
  The bacterium fixes nitrogen and gives the plant a source of nitrogen;
  in return, the bacterium obtains carbohydrate from the host plant.
  This type of relationship where both partners win is called **mutualism**.

- **Denitrifying bacteria** get their energy source by converting nitrates
  and ammonium ions back into nitrogen gas.
  Denitrification occurs in the absence of oxygen, for example in water-logged soils.
  Pseudomonas and *Thiobacillus* gain their energy from denitrification.

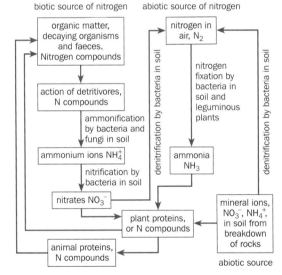

The role of bacteria in the nitrogen cycle

Root nodules of a legume plant

401

▷ Biology at work: Sustainable timber production

World War I alerted the Government to the dangers of running out of timber, so it set up the Forestry Commission in 1919.
Its brief was to establish a national forestry reserve.
Since then, vast areas of non-native conifers have been planted, particularly in Scotland.
Currently, woodland covers 10% of the UK, but 9% is made up of these plantations and only 1% by native woodlands.
Conifers have been planted rather than native hardwoods because they produce more timber in a shorter time and can grow on infertile soils.

Coniferous plantation in Perthshire, Scotland

The two main aims of Government forestry policy are

● the sustained management of existing woods and forests,
● a steady expansion of tree cover to increase the many diverse benefits that forests provide.

Can a landscape rich in wildlife also produce a **sustainable** supply of timber? The following actions will help:

● better management of existing woodlands,
● planting more native trees,
● using natural regeneration and more sensitive planting methods,
● siting well-managed commercial forests on surplus agricultural land.

The UK is a major importer and user of timber.
Most of this comes from the temperate forests of Scandinavia and North America, often involving clear-felling of old growth.
We could reduce the need to import so much timber by reducing consumption of wood products, recycling paper and only using wood which has come from sustainably managed forests.

Cutting down coniferous timber in USA

Native woodlands

The native woodlands that are left should be preserved.
They should be allowed to grow and expand to form a network of woodland reserves across the country.

There should be a clear commitment towards sustainable forestry in order to

● maintain and enhance biodiversity by providing woodland habitats for the great variety of species that live there,
● produce timber at a rate the forest can sustain,
● use non-renewable resources sparingly to avoid needless consumption and pollution.

To achieve this there should be

● major research and survey work carried out to classify woodlands according to their environmental quality,
● restoration of woodlands by allowing them to grow naturally or, where this is difficult, by planting native species,
● sensitive management of woodlands to mimic natural ecological processes.

Native woodland in Cornwall

▷ Biology at work: Intensive farming

Intensive farming involves attempts to maximise food production through the careful control of growing conditions.

It can be seen in a number of examples, such as the use of chemicals and glasshouses in crop production, careful monitoring of food and environmental conditions in poultry farming, and also in fish farming.

In the UK, the main farmed fish are salmon and trout.
True marine fish farming (for example with plaice) has proved less commercially successful.

Fish farms are usually based on a series of ponds, or cages suspended in freshwater or the sea.
Where ponds are used it is obviously easier to control growing conditions.
The depth, for example, is kept to about 1.5 m to avoid the development of a **thermocline**.
This is where a cooler layer of water (unsuitable for growth) develops below the warmer suface layers.

The quality and reliability of the water is crucial to successful growth.
It should be clear, with a neutral to slightly alkaline pH.
The flow rate must provide both adequate oxygenation and also adequate dispersal of metabolic wastes such as ammonia and carbon dioxide.
A high flow rate will cause the fish to expend energy simply to maintain their position.
This energy is therefore not available for growth.

A high protein diet is given, usually in the form of fish meal together with a mix of appropriate minerals and vitamins.
Anti-louse compounds are also added in order to control the spread of disease in overcrowded conditions.

In the UK, fish-farmed trout reach a marketable size of between 180 and 280 g in around 11 months, depending on temperature.

The reality with fish farming is that it is more likely (at least in the foreseeable future) to provide a source of variety to the human diet rather than being a major additional source of protein.

A sea loch salmon farm using cages

A trout hatchery

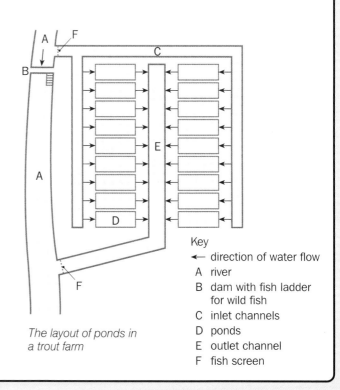
The layout of ponds in a trout farm

Key
← direction of water flow
A river
B dam with fish ladder for wild fish
C inlet channels
D ponds
E outlet channel
F fish screen

403

Summary

- Ecology is the study of how living organisms interact with each other and with their environment.
- A habitat is the place where an organism lives. A niche is the role that an organism plays in its environment.
- A population is a group of individuals of the same species. A community consists of all the species in a particular habitat. An ecosystem is made up of the community and the habitat.
- Feeding relationships can involve producers, consumers, detritivores and decomposers.
- Food chains and food webs chart the feeding relationships in a community.
- Pyramids of number give information about the quantities of organisms involved.
- Biomass pyramids reflect the mass of organisms involved but do not show their productivity.
- Energy pyramids are the most accurate method of representing feeding relationships.
- The overall efficiency of energy conversion in photosynthesis is low.
- Net primary production = gross primary production − respiration.
- Transfer of energy from producers to consumers involves energy 'wastage'.
- The longer the food chain, the more energy will be lost.
- Decomposers are the key organisms involved in the cycling of nutrients in ecosystems.
- Bacteria play a number of vital roles in the cycling of nitrogen.

▷ Questions

1 What is meant by each of the following ecological terms:
   a) a community,
   b) a population,
   c) a niche?

2 Look at the diagram showing the food web. Each letter in the diagram represents a different species of organism.
   a) Suggest one letter that represents
      i)   a decomposer,
      ii) a herbivore,
      iii) a secondary consumer,
      iv) trophic level 1.
   b) Identify, by letter, one organism in the food web that is found in the trophic level which contains most energy.

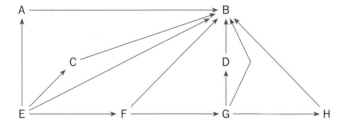

3 The diagram shows part of a food web in a freshwater pond.
   a) Name examples of the following from this food web.
      i)   an omnivore,
      ii) a producer,
      iii) a secondary consumer,
      iv) a tertiary consumer.

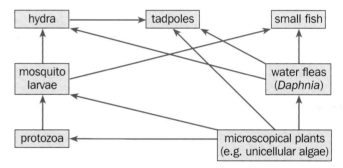

   b) Can you find a food chain in this web that consists of five trophic levels?
      Draw a pyramid of energy to represent this chain. Label your diagram to show the organisms at each energy level.

4 The table shows the numbers of organisms obtained at each trophic level in a sampling study of an oak tree.

Trophic level	Number of organisms
producer	1
primary consumer	260 000
secondary consumer	40
tertiary consumer	3

   a) Draw a pyramid of biomass to represent this food chain.
   b) Suggest two reasons why there is such a large difference between the numbers of primary and secondary consumers.

5 Here are three pyramids of number from different food chains.

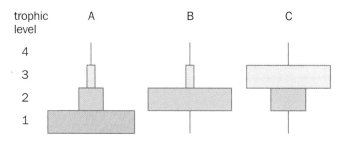

a) Name the four trophic levels in pyramid A and give a typical example of an organism found at each trophic level. (The organisms you choose should all come from the same food chain.)

b) Account for the shapes of pyramids B and C.

6 The table shows the net primary productivities in some aquatic communities.

Community type	Mean net primary productivity
swamp and marsh	2000
continental shelf	360
lake and stream	250
open ocean	125

a) i) What is meant by net primary productivity?
   ii) What units could net primary productivity be measured in?

b) Why do you think that the net primary productivity is much higher for the continental shelf community than for the open sea community?

c) The diagram shows a biomass pyramid for a lake in June.
   i) Why is the biomass of the producers smaller than that of the primary consumers?
   ii) Draw an energy pyramid for this community.

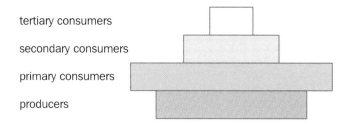

7 Detritivores and decomposers are both important in the processes of decomposition. The graph shows the activities of microorganisms involved in the breakdown of leaf litter and the effects of the number of woodlice (detritivores).

a) Why is rate of respiration a good way of measuring the activity of microorganisms?

b) What is meant by a **detritivore**?

c) i) Describe the effects of introducing woodlice on the activity of the microorganisms.

ii) Try to suggest a reason for these effects.

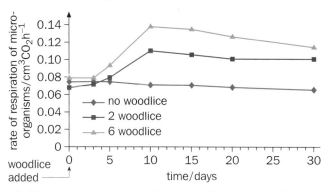

8 a) Name one compound produced by plants which needs a source of nitrogen.

b) The diagram shows some stages of the nitrogen cycle.
   i) Why are animals not essential to the nitrogen cycle?
   ii) Name the processes carried out by bacteria at points A, B and C in this cycle.

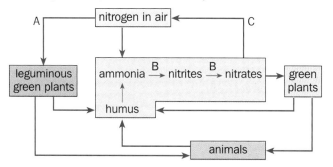

9 An experiment was carried out to investigate the disappearance of leaf litter. Discs cut out of oak leaves were put into nylon mesh bags and buried in the soil. The table shows the disappearance of the oak discs from bags of 7 mm and 0.5 mm mesh over a period of months.

a) Plot the results of the experiment as line graphs.

b) i) Describe the effect of mesh size on the rate of disappearance of leaf litter between the months of June and October.
   ii) Explain the variation in the rate of disappearance of leaf litter from the 0.5 mm mesh bags during the experiment.
   iii) The nitrogen released as a result of this decomposition acts as a fertiliser, but only some of it is available to plants. Suggest one way in which nitrogen is lost from the soil.

Month	Percentage oak leaf area remaining in bags of mesh size	
	7 mm	0.5 mm
June	100	100
August	81	94
October	30	91
December	13	66
February	9	62
April	6	60

Isle Royale is an island on Lake Superior in North America. It is thought to be the only site where the moose, a large herbivore, and its predator, the wolf, co-exist unhunted by humans.

The moose reached the island in about 1908, probably by swimming from the mainland. Their numbers increased as they browsed on the leaves of trees and aquatic plants. Visitors to the island in 1934 found many dead and emaciated moose carcasses. The population had crashed due to overgrazing. In 1948, wolves reached the island across the ice. They established a pack and started to kill the moose for food. At present there are about 1000 moose on Isle Royale, producing about 440 calves a year and supporting about 24 wolves. The populations appear to be in balance with each other and with the vegetation on which the moose browses.

moose

wolf

▷ Populations

A population is a group of individuals of the same species living in the same place at the same time and interbreeding. These are all populations:

- aphids on a sycamore tree,
- a shoal of herring in the sea,
- bluebells in a wood.

Why do you think that individuals live in populations?

- Individuals may be more successful in breeding and rearing their young.
- Many animals gain protection from predators in a group.
- Some animals can locate new food resources as a group.

But as a population grows, individuals **compete** for scarce resources such as food and space. Some individuals will be better adapted to compete than others. They are more likely to survive and pass on their genes to their offspring.

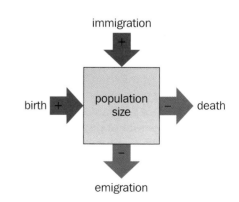

A population of sardine in Oman

▷ What determines population growth?

The growth of a particular population at a particular time is determined by
birth rate – the reproductive capacity of the population,
mortality – the death rate of organisms in the population.

Individuals can also enter or leave a population. It is easy to imagine animals being able to do this, but plants too can use seed dispersal to enter or leave a population.

Immigration is the movement of individuals into a population.
Emigration is the movement of individuals out of a population.

immigration
+
birth + | population size | – death
–
emigration

▷ How populations grow

What happens when a species colonises a new area?
If conditions are favourable, the birth rate will *exceed* the
death rate and lead to **exponential growth**.
With this type of growth the population ***doubles*** per unit time.
15 individuals become 30, then over the same period of time,
30 individuals double to 60, 60 to 120, and so on.
As you can see, exponential growth can lead to a massive
explosion in numbers.

Some species of algae can achieve this sort of growth if
conditions of light, temperature and nutrients are favourable.
This can result in algal blooms but if nutrients are used up
and become a ***limiting factor,*** then the population can fall as
quickly as it rose.

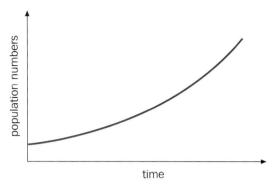
Exponential population growth

The characteristic **J-shaped** growth curve is often called
a 'boom and bust' curve. Insect pests that produce many
generations in a single year often have this sort of growth curve.

Population growth involves three main factors:

- the **biotic potential** of the population,
- **environmental resistance** of the habitat,
- the **carrying capacity (k)** of the environment.

The **biotic potential** of a particular population is the maximum
rate at which it can reproduce, given all the resources it needs.
Environmental resistance means that populations seldom ever
achieve their biotic potential.

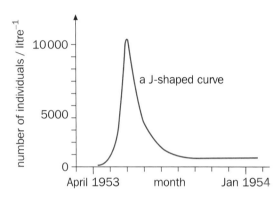
Changes in the population size of a brown alga

Environmental resistance includes all the factors that may limit
the growth of a population, such as accumulation of waste
products, scarcity of resources such as food and space, or adverse
climatic conditions.

Environmental resistance also takes in biotic factors such as the
effects of predators, parasites and competitors.

When the rate of increase stops and the birth rate balances
the death rate, the population has reached the **carrying capacity**
of the environment.

This is the maximum population size that can be
supported by a particular environment.

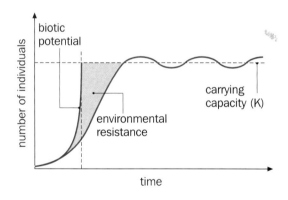

The S-shaped curve

As a population encounters environmental resistance, such as
food shortage, its rate of growth slows and it approaches
the carrying capacity.
The **S-shaped** curve is typical of species colonising new habitats.
There is a period of slow growth as the species adapts to the
habitat, followed by a period of rapid growth with little
environmental resistance.
The graph then levels off as the population reaches its carrying
capacity. If a particular factor becomes scarce, it can limit the
growth of the population, which can then go into decline.
Look at the different phases demonstrated in an S-shaped curve.

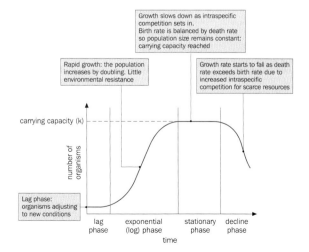

▷ Checks on population increase

Population growth slows down due to environmental resistance. This may be due to abiotic or biotic factors.

Abiotic factors

Abiotic factors include climatic factors, such as extremes of temperature, drought, floods or storms.
Lack of shelter exposes individuals to a harsh climate.
Plants need light of the correct intensity, wavelength and duration if they are to achieve optimum growth.
Shortage of oxygen can limit the numbers of aquatic species.
Water quality is affected by pollution and intolerant species may die.
Pollution from the local accumulation of toxic materials can affect populations on land, sea and air.

Migrating wildebeest

Biotic factors

Individual plants and animals may have to compete for scarce resources such as food, light, water and space.
Predators can reduce the numbers of a prey species.
The higher the density of a population, the more rapidly a disease could spread through it. Similarly, parasites reduce the ability of the host species to survive and reproduce.

Density-independent factors affect **all** the plants or animals in a population irrespective of the population size.
For example, a severe winter will affect **all** the birds in a population of robins. Density-independent factors may be abiotic, for example chemical pollution affecting water fleas in a pond, or biotic, for example the effects of disease on a vole population.

Density-dependent factors vary in the effect that they have on a population, depending on the size of the population.
So the size (or density) of a population affects its growth rate.
For a fixed food supply, the larger the population gets, the less food there will be for each individual and the slower the growth rate.
Other density-dependent factors include space, competition, predation and parasites.
Density-dependent factors are **always** biotic.

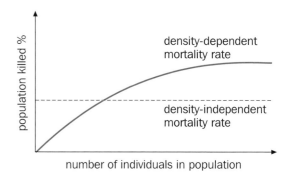

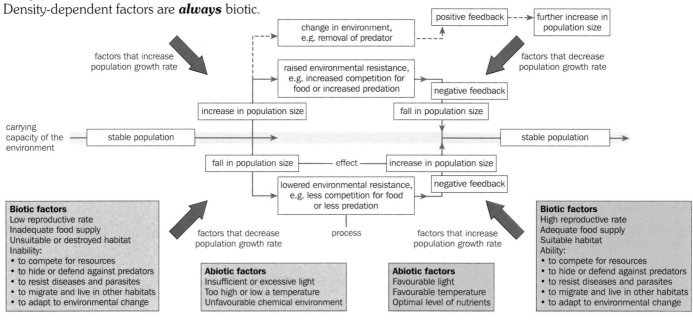

▷ Competition

The word 'competition' suggests a race in which all the competitors
try their hardest to win.
In nature, plants and animals struggle for survival.
They compete with each other for scarce resources.
As you have seen, plants compete for light, space, water and nutrients.
Animals compete for things like food, space and mates.
Many animals have to establish a **territory** if they are to attract a mate
and breed.
There are two types of competition: **intraspecific** and **interspecific**
competition.

Intraspecific competition between lesser black-backed gulls

Intraspecific competition

Intraspecific competition is competition between individuals of
the *same* species. Seedlings of the same species of plant compete
for light, water, space and nutrients.
Gulls of the same species compete for nesting sites.

Intraspecific competition is *density-dependent*.
As the population density increases, a greater proportion of the
population fails to survive.
Growth rate, reproduction and length of life are also affected.
For instance, in crop plants, intraspecific competition can result
in smaller plants with a decrease in biomass, or in fewer seeds
being produced per plant.

Living organisms tend to produce far more offspring than
the habitat can support.
It is this overproduction that results in intraspecific competition.
Those individuals that are best adapted to take advantage
of scarce resources have a better chance of survival.
This ensures that their alleles are passed on to their offspring.
It also ensures that environmental resources are not over-exploited,
as in the case of too many herbivores over-grazing vegetation.

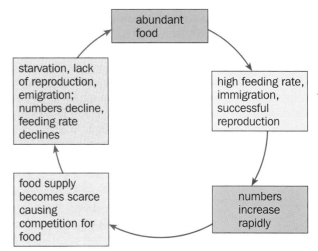

Changing population numbers caused by intraspecific competition

Interspecific competition

This is competition between individuals of *different* species.
In winter, different species of garden bird visit a bird table.
They all compete for the food that is put out.

Weeds are excellent competitors.
A weed is a plant growing where it is not wanted, for instance the
field poppy (*Papaver rhoeas*) growing in a barley crop.
Poppies compete with barley for light, water, nutrients and space.
They grow and complete their life cycle before the crop plant
has reached its full height and shaded them out.
But how are they able to do this?
The diagram will give you some clues.

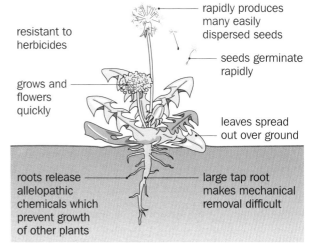

Weeds are successful interspecific competitors

- Weeds are able to reproduce quickly and produce huge numbers of seeds.
- Their seeds germinate quickly in poor soil.
- Weeds grow very quickly, and flower and set seed before other plants can.
- They can grow in poor soil, often become resistant to herbicides, and have
  adaptations such as spiny leaves and poisonous chemicals which make them
  unpalatable to grazers such as cattle.

409

▷ Competitive exclusion

Interspecific competition is most intense when two different species attempt to occupy the same niche.

A Russian biologist, G.F. Gause, cultured two different species of the unicellular organism *Paramecium* in laboratory conditions.
When grown separately with controlled amounts of food, *P. caudatum* and *P. aurelia* both showed typical S-shaped growth curves.
When they were grown together, the two species were able to co-exist for a limited period of time.
But eventually, *P. aurelia*, the smaller, faster-growing species, tended to out-compete the larger, slower-growing *P. caudatum*.
P. caudatum eventually died since it could not occupy the same niche as *P. aurelia*.
This work demonstrates the **competitive exclusion principle** under controlled laboratory conditions.

There are two native barnacles that are common on UK shores, *Semibalanus balanoides* and *Chthamalus montagui*.
Chthamalus is able to live higher up on the shore than *Semibalanus*, because it is more resistant to desiccation (water loss).
Lower down the shore, *Semibalanus* is able to feed for longer periods and grows more quickly.
So on the lower shore *Semibalanus* out-competes *Chthamalus* for space.

During the Second World War, an Australian barnacle, *Elminius modestus*, invaded British shores.
It arrived in this country on the hulls of ships and quickly spread around the south coast.
In many situations, *Elminius* has been able to out-compete both *Semibalanus* and *Chthamalus*, because

- *Elminius* can withstand lower temperatures than *Chthamalus*,
- *Elminius* can withstand higher temperatures than *Semibalanus*,
- *Elminius* can tolerate lower salinities so can colonise estuaries,
- *Elminius* has a faster feeding rate and rate of growth.

The ability of *Elminius* to occupy a niche at the expense of the native barnacles demonstrates competitive exclusion.

In the 1870s, the grey squirrel was introduced into this country from North America. Our native red squirrel was found in both deciduous and coniferous woodland throughout the British Isles.
By the beginning of the 20th century, the grey squirrel had spread at the expense of the native red squirrel.
Today, red squirrels are only found in coniferous woods and isolated areas which grey squirrels have not colonised.
Grey squirrels do not physically drive out reds squirrels.
So the question is *how* does the grey out-compete the red?
The answer may well be in their food source.
Grey squirrels can digest acorns and hazel nuts more efficiently than red squirrels can.
Grey squirrels also seem to be broad-leaved woodland specialists, whereas the smaller, nimbler reds do better in conifers where they feed on pine cones high in the canopy.
It seems that competitive exclusion is at work and that the niches of the two squirrels are so similar that only one can survive in a particular habitat.

Competition between two species of Paramecium

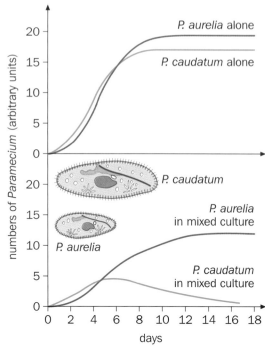
Elminius modestus

Native red squirrel

Grey squirrel

▷ Predation

Predators kill other animals (their **prey**) for food.
Predators are usually larger and fewer in number than their prey.
If they are to survive, then they must be well adapted for killing.

What do you think makes a good predator?

- It needs the weapons to kill: claws or talons to grasp the prey and sharp teeth or beak to kill and tear it up.

- It needs speed to pursue the prey and camouflage to escape detection when stalking.

There are other less obvious strategies that help predators:

- Group hunting enables predators to surround the prey and also means that together they can kill larger prey.

- Catching prey that is young, old, sick or injured means that the prey is easier to overpower and kill.
  This also 'weeds out' some of the weaker individuals in the prey population, leaving better-adapted individuals to pass on their genes.

- Catching large prey provides the predator with more food per kill.

- Having a variety of prey species reduces the chances of starvation in the event that any one prey species declines in number.

- Migrating to areas where the prey is more plentiful.

A prey's guide to survival

However well adapted the predator, some of the prey escape.
Prey species are adapted to avoid capture, although they are never completely successful.

- Many try to out-run, out-swim or out-fly their predators.

- Staying in large groups, like herds of antelope and shoals of fish, distracts a predator from aiming at one particular individual.

- Some potential prey, for example bees and wasps, can sting a predator. Others simply taste horrible, like some types of ladybird. Either way, predators learn to take them off the menu.
  These species often have **warning coloration** to act as a reminder to the predator.

- Some prey species 'mimic' these warning colorations.
  A hoverfly has yellow and black stripes like those of a wasp, although it has no sting.

- Camouflage is often used by prey species to avoid capture. Many animals blend in with their surroundings, whilst others look like something else, twigs or leaves for instance.

- **Startle mechanisms** involve a sudden and conspicuous change in appearance of the prey, designed to confuse or alarm the predator.
  Can you see how the eyed hawkmoth might startle off a hungry bird?

Brown bear catching salmon

Spotted hyenas and jackels with prey

A six-spot Burnet moth showing warning colours

Katydid insect

Eyed Hawmoth

▷ Predator–prey cycles

It's pretty obvious that predators affect the size of prey populations. But have you ever considered the effect that the prey can have upon the predator population?

What would happen to the predator population if its prey were affected by disease?
Such drastic events are not common place, but if its prey becomes scarce then the predator suffers too.

The diagram shows a model for a predator–prey cycle that has been worked out mathematically.

1. The prey have plenty of food.
   They survive to breed and their numbers increase.
2. The increase in prey numbers means that there is more food for the predator. So more predators survive to breed and their numbers increase.
3. As there are now more predators, the rate of predation rises and the number of prey goes down.
4. There is now less prey for the predator to feed upon.
   Fewer predators survive to breed and their numbers decline.
5. With fewer predators, more prey will survive to breed.
   Prey numbers will increase and so the cycle continues.

Predator–prey cycles are naturally self-regulating.
Notice that there are fewer predators than prey and also that predators tend to reproduce more slowly than their prey.

- So the fluctuations in predator numbers are smaller than those in numbers of prey,
- and the fluctuations in predator numbers lag behind the fluctuations in numbers of prey.

The lynx and the snowshoe hare

One of the most widely documented examples of a predator–prey cycle is that of the snowshoe hare and its main predator, the lynx.
Records of their numbers were kept by the Hudson Bay Fur Trading Company in Canada, between 1845 and 1935.
The numbers of hare and lynx pelts brought in by trappers were accurately recorded over this period.
The relationship between predator and prey can be clearly seen in the graphs.

Predator–prey relationships are also affected by interactions at other levels, for instance plant–herbivore relations.
The snowshoe hare feeds on conifer buds and twigs of aspen, alder and willow, so-called browsing vegetation.
If the amount of browse vegetation falls below that needed to support the hare population over winter, malnutrition occurs.
Weakened hares are much more vulnerable to predation.
Intense predation lowers the number of hares and means that inevitably the lynx will suffer its own food shortage.
Meanwhile, since the vegetation is not being browsed by so many hares, growth increases.
With the decrease in predation and the growing abundance of winter food, the hare population rises, starting another cycle.

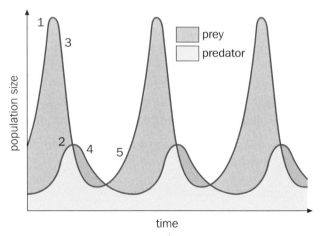

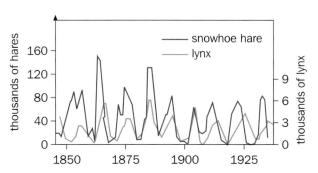

The relationship between the numbers of lynx (predator) and snowshoe hare (prey)

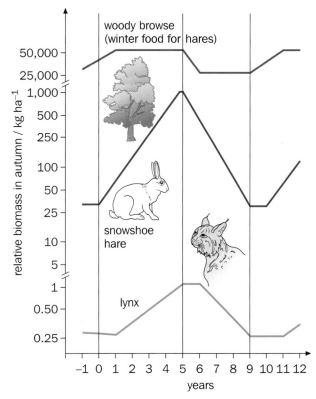

Three-way interaction between woody vegetation, snowshoe hare and lynx

▷ Biological control

A pest is any organism that competes with or adversely affects a population of plants or animals that are of economic importance to humans. As with many living things, the population of a pest is normally regulated by its natural predators and parasites. Many alien species, introduced into a country by accident, can become pests since they are no longer controlled by a natural predator. Biological control is the use of predators, parasites and pathogens to keep the numbers of pests below the **economic damage threshold**.

The economic damage threshold is reached when the pest numbers are causing so much damage (say to a crop) that it is worth spending money on controlling the pest. The predator, parasite or pathogen used is called the **biological control agent**.

Biological control agents

- Biological control agents must be *specific* to the pest. They must target the pest and no other species.
- If the biological control agent becomes established and is successful in controlling the pest for long periods of time, then the high initial expense is justified, and over the long term this form of control is relatively inexpensive.
- Biological control has none of the detrimental effects upon the environment associated with persistent chemical pesticides.

There are, however, drawbacks associated with biological control.

- If a farmer has a sudden invasion by a pest, rapid control is required in order to minimise damage to the crop. Biological control agents are fairly slow to react to a surge in pest numbers.
- Most crops suffer from several pests during their growth. This would require several biological control agents for one crop.
- Crops may have only occasional pest attacks. In the years that the pest was absent, the biological control agent would die out and so would have to be continually reintroduced.

A classic case

In 1868, the cottony-cushion scale insect (*Icerya purchasi*) was accidentally introduced to California from Australia.
Away from its natural enemies, the scale insect decimated the citrus groves, threatening the future of the industry.
American scientists went to Australia to search for a predator of the scale insect.
They found a ladybird predator (*Rodolia cardinalis*).
The ladybird was imported into California in1888 and quickly succeeded in controlling the scale insect threat.
Rodolia has proved to be a successful biocontrol agent in 35 countries.

Try drawing a graph to show the relationship between the numbers of a pest and the numbers of its biocontrol agent over time.
Will the graph look similar to a predator–prey cycle?

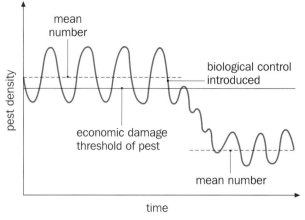

Graph showing the principle of biological control

Graph showing resurgence of a pest after the application of a broad-spectrum insecticide

Comparison	Control method	
	Biological	Chemical
time to take effect	slow	fast
pollution, danger to humans and domestic animals	none	considerable
ecological dangers	few	considerable
permanence of control	permanent	usually temporary, repeated treatment needed
development of pest resistance	very rare if ever	common

Cottony-cushion scale insects on citrus trees

▷ Succession

An area of bare ground left to nature does not remain devoid
of vegetation for long.
Weeds are usually the first plants to invade the site, followed
by grasses and tall herbs.
After a long period of time, the area would turn to woodland.
This one-directional process of community change with time
is called **succession**.

> **Succession is the change in structure and species
> composition of a community over time.**

The different stages in a succession when particular communities
dominate are known as **seres.**
Succession continues until the community reaches an equilibrium
with its environment and no further change occurs.
This is then known as the **climax community**.

Primary succession occurs on newly formed habitats
that have not previously supported a community.
Examples can be found on rocks exposed by landslides,
volcanic larva flows and sand dunes.
The first organisms to colonise the bare rock are lichens and algae,
so-called **pioneer species**.
These slowly erode the rock as their hyphae penetrate tiny cracks
and absorb minerals.
Debris and other organic material become trapped in these cracks,
providing the basis of a soil.
Mosses are next to colonise the area, arriving by means
of wind-blown spores.
They trap water, and their own dead remains build up
the organic content of the soil.
Shallow-rooted grasses and herbs are able to establish themselves
as a result of the improved soil conditions.
As the soil builds up, deep-rooted shrubs appear.
Over a much longer time scale, these eventually give way
to trees such as beech or oak, so reaching the climax community.

Although we have looked at succession in terms of vegetation in
this example, it is important to remember that the whole community,
including animal species, is involved in succession.

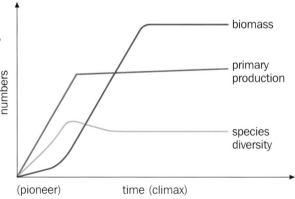

*Succession from cleared ground to oak
hornbeam forest over 150 years, in
south Poland*

A number of ***trends*** develop as succession proceeds.

- The soil develops – it increases in depth, has greater organic content,
  and different layers can be identified as it becomes a mature soil.
- The height and biomass of the vegetation increases.
- The primary production increases with soil development.
- Species diversity increases, from simple communities of
  early succession to richer communities of late succession.
- The number of food chains increases.
- Changes in height and density of vegetation provide
  a greater variety of microhabitats.
- The community becomes more stable.
  In the early stages of a succession, populations rapidly replace
  one another. The climax community is stable and dominated
  by long-lived plants.

Changes in vegetation during succession

Secondary succession

Secondary succession occurs at sites that have previously supported a community.
It occurs after a major environmental disturbance disrupts a previous succession.
Forest fires, the ploughing of grassland and road building are examples.

Following such major disruption, the process of succession will begin again in the new environmental conditions.
After a fire, many species of plant will disappear.
But some seeds will remain viable in the soil and will germinate.
Pioneer species from adjacent sites will be quick to colonise by means of their seeds.
Without periodic fires, the prairies of North America and the African grasslands would become dominated by woody vegetation.

The building of motorways is clearly disruptive to communities.
However, motorway verges soon start to undergo secondary succession.
Soon colonised by herbaceous vegetation, with time young shrubs such as hawthorn and trees like sycamore and beech establish themselves.
Relatively undisturbed by humans, motorway verges have become important reservoirs for our native wildlife.

Secondary succession following a forest fire

Motorway verges are important havens for wildlife

Deflected succession

Succession does not always proceed through to the climax community.
The process is halted, often by the management practices of humans.
This is known as **deflected succession**.

Grazing by sheep prevents grassland such as the South Downs from being colonised by scrub and developing into woodland.

Heather moorland is managed by controlled burning.
This maintains the heather and stops the succession to woodland.

Even mowing and weeding the lawn preserves grass as a result of deflected succession.
If you were to study an unmown lawn over a period of 10 years, you would notice changes in species composition as herbs and shrubs invade it.

Explain what is meant by a climax community.

Explain how each of the following changes occur during succession:
    i) species diversity increases,
    ii) gross production increases,
    iii) stability of the ecosystem increases.

Give two reasons why farmland in the UK does not reach a climax community.

Deflected succession: sheep grazing

▷ Sampling

Ecologists often need to estimate the abundance and distribution
of animals and plants.
They may need to know if a population is changing, perhaps in order
to conserve the species or monitor the level of a pest species.
It is not usually possible to count all the individuals in a particular population.
Instead, samples are taken which will hopefully be representative of the
population as a whole.

There are two main types of sampling strategy: **random** and **systematic**.
To take a random sample, a grid is used to divide up the area.
Then, a random numbers table or a calculator with a random
number key is used to give coordinates.
The sample is taken where the coordinates intersect.
In practice, it is easier to draw a grid on paper and then
pace out the coordinates.
Systematic sampling is better if you are looking for a pattern,
for instance the effects on the vegetation of a change in soil type.
A grid is again used to divide the area up into sampling units.
But this time the sampling points are taken at regular intervals.

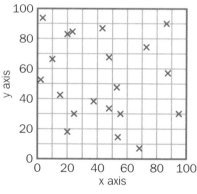

random sampling

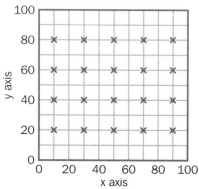

systematic sampling

Transects

Transects are commonly used for systematic sampling.
The samples are taken along a line laid out across the sample area.
Transects are useful for recording changes in the abundance and
distribution of species where some sort of transition occurs.
For instance, in the zonation of species along a rocky shore, or
in the succession that can be highlighted along sand dunes.
There are two common types of transects.
The **line transect** involves laying a tape across the sample area
and any species that touch the tape are recorded.
This is a quick technique but is useful for distances over say 20 m.
The **belt transect** involves laying down a **quadrat** at intervals
along the tape and estimating the species found within it.

Quadrats

Quadrats are often used in sampling plant communities and are
traditionally used in rocky shore studies, since many of the animals
are slow-moving and stay within the quadrat.

A **frame quadrat** is a square, the most common size being 0.25 m².
It can be made out of wood or bought commercially.
The quadrat is laid down at sampling points within the sample area,
or at points along a transect, and the organisms within it estimated,
often as **percentage cover** (the percentage of the area within
the quadrat that the species covers).

A **point quadrat** was devised to give a more objective
assessment of cover.
Ten pins are dropped through a low-standing frame onto the vegetation.
As each pin touches a plant of a particular species a **hit** is recorded.

$$\text{percentage cover} = \frac{\text{hits}}{\text{hits} + \text{misses}} \times 100$$

So if the point quadrat is used 15 times and the number of hits for one

particular species is 20, the percentage cover $= \dfrac{20 \times 100}{150} = 13.3\%$

A frame quadrat in use

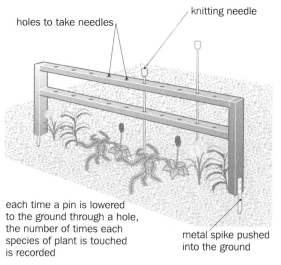

knitting needle

holes to take needles

each time a pin is lowered
to the ground through a hole,
the number of times each
species of plant is touched
is recorded

metal spike pushed
into the ground

A point quadrant

◁ Measures of abundance

Four measures of abundance are commonly used.

- **Density**: the mean number of individuals per unit area.
- **Frequency**: the number or percentage of sampling units in which a particular species occurs.
- **Biomass**: the dry weight of plants or animals in a certain area at a certain time, often referred to as **standing crop**.
- **Percentage cover**: the percentage of the ground covered by a species within the sampling unit.
  This is commonly used for estimating plants and does away with the need to count all the individuals.

this plant covers 4 whole + 5 half
squares = 26%

each square
= 4% area

to measure percentage cover:
  lay a frame quadrat over the selected area;
  count the number of squares occupied by the plant species in question;
  count those squares that are partially occupied;
  estimate how many full squares this would represent and add it to the total.

◁ Sampling animal populations

Animals are more difficult to sample than plants.
For one thing, many won't stay inside a quadrat to be counted!
Many hide during the day and only come out at night.
So some form of net or trap must be used to sample them.

A technique called **mark, release, recapture** (**MRR**) can be used to work out estimates of animal populations.
The population size is then estimated using the **Lincoln Index**:

$$P = \frac{M \times S}{R}$$

P = the estimate of the population size,
M = the number of animals captured, marked and released in the first sample,
S = the number of animals captured in the second sample,
R = the number of marked animals recaptured in the second sample.

> **Worked example:** 20 ground beetles were caught in a pitfall trap.
> Each was marked with a small dot of paint and when it was dry they were released. After 2 days, a second sample of 18 beetles was taken.
> Of these, 6 were marked individuals from the first catch.
> Estimate the total population of beetles.
>
> Number in first catch = 20
> Number in second catch = 18
> Number of marked individuals in second catch = 6
>
> Total population = $\dfrac{20 \times 18}{6}$ = 60

When using the Lincoln Index, we make a number of assumptions.

- The marked individuals must redistribute themselves randomly amongst the unmarked individuals.
- The marks must not come off between marking and recapture.
- The marks must not affect the behaviour of the animals nor make them more noticeable to predators.
- Being caught in the first sample must not increase or decrease the chances of capture in the second sample.
- Ideally, there should be no movement of individuals into or out of the population during the exercise. Neither should any births or deaths occur in the population.

How would the disappearance of a mark or the death of some individuals affect the population estimate?

Mark, release and capture

catch a sample of the animals you want to study and count them

↓

mark each one in a way that will not harm them or make them more noticeable to predators

↓

release your sample back into their habitat and allow one or two days for them to mix back into their own population

↓

take a second sample and count the total numbers along with the number marked from the first sample

Marking a wood cricket Nemobius sylvestris *as part of a mark–release–recapture exercise to estimate the number of wood crickets in an area of woodland*

▷ Collecting invertebrates

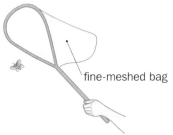

Butterfly net: used to catch flying insects. Short handle for ease of use. Large mesh bag can be folded over frame to prevent catch escaping.

Sweep net: used to catch invertebrates in low-growing vegetation. Long handle, robust frame with a small mesh bag. The net is brushed through vegetation, dislodging animals that fall into the bag.

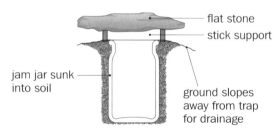

Pitfall trap: collects invertebrates that are active on the soil surface or in leaf litter. Basically a yoghurt carton sunk into the soil to ground level. A piece of wood or stone keeps the rain out. Pitfalls are cheap and easy to use but the catch often reflects the activity of a particular species as well as its abundance.

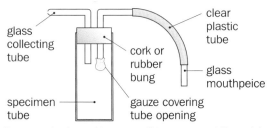

Pooter: tube for sucking up small insects, especially useful for insects in cracks and crevices. Small invertebrates are drawn into the collecting tube by sucking through the mouthpiece. A piece of gauze prevents the insect from ending up in your mouth!

Dredge net: can be used to sample invertebrates on a pond bed or in grassland. D-shaped frame mounted on steel runners supports a coarse meshed bag. Towed over the bed of a pond or lake to sample bottom-living invertebrates, or hauled over the surface of grassland to dislodge insects.

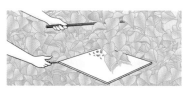

Beating tray: used to sample invertebrates in bushes and trees. This can be as simple as a white plastic sheet spread out under a bush. A branch is then shaken, dislodging the invertebrates which fall onto the sheet. They can be collected from the sheet by means of a pooter.

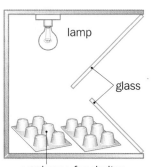

Light traps: collect night-flying insects such as moths. The insects attracted to the light hit the baffles and fall into the base of the trap. Pieces of egg carton are put in the base for shelter and subsequent ease of handling.

Pond net: collects freshwater invertebrates by 'kick sample' or sweeping. Long handle, strong supported frame, rot-proof bag with 1 mm mesh. Kick sampling dislodges invertebrates on stream bed, current sweeps them into the net bag.

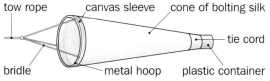

Plankton net: used for sampling phytoplankton and zooplankton in marine and freshwater habitats. Robust frame supports long conical net when full of water. Collecting jar holds filtered plankton. Net is towed by a boat at 1 to 1.5 knots or anchored against the current in a stream.

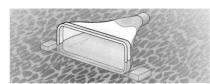

Drift net: samples invertebrates drifting downstream. Rectangular frame is secured to the river bed by metal stakes. The invertebrates float into the bag on the current and are collected in a sample bottle at the end of the tapering bag.

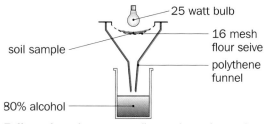

Tullgren funnel: extracts small invertebrates from soil and leaf litter. Easily made from a plastic funnel and a flour sieve. The soil sample is placed on the gauze under a 25 watt light bulb. The invertebrates move down, away from the light and the heat, and slide down the funnel into a collecting jar.

▷ Monitoring the physical environment

As part of an ecological study, you may need to measure
physical and chemical factors in the environment, since these will
influence the abundance and distribution of the organisms.

There are now a wide variety of battery operated meters available
for use in field conditions.
Electronic probes can be attached to data logging equipment so that
readings can be recorded at regular intervals over a period of time.
For instance, measurements of temperature, oxygen concentration
and pH in an upper shore rock pool over 24 hours in summer.

Temperature

Temperature directly affects an organism's metabolic processes.
Most living organisms have an optimum temperature range below
which these processes tend to slow down.
This is particularly true of ectotherms. During the severe winter of 1962–63,
when the sea actually froze, over 80% mortality was recorded in limpets.

Migrating snow geese

Endotherms take steps to avoid extremes of temperature.
Swallows are summer migrants to our country from South Africa, and
Bewick swans are winter migrants to the UK from the Arctic Circle.
Some small mammals, like the dormouse, avoid severe winters by hibernating.

When recording temperature with an electronic field thermometer, it is
important to note the time of day and location (aspect, altitude or depth).

Light

Light is of great importance to photosynthesising plants, both the light intensity
and the wavelength.
Light meters are available that measure light intensity, but the problem is
that the level of illumination can fluctuate greatly, for example with cloud cover.
In ecological investigations it is probably more relevant to estimate the
total amount of light falling on the vegetation during the course of the study.
For instance, if you were studying the conditions inside a wood, you may take
a series of measurements at regular intervals and record them with a datalogger.

Light penetration in a wood will change during the year

pH (acidity and alkalinity)

Aquatic plants and animals have differing pH requirements.
Some are tolerant to low pH, others are pH sensitive.
Hill streams with acid water (pH below 5.7) are often completely lifeless.
The pH can be affected by a number of factors, including precipitation,
type of bedrock and soil type.
But only extremes of soil pH will directly affect plant growth.
Usually pH has an indirect effect in that it affects the release of soil nutrients.
Many of these are soluble in acid conditions, so aluminium and manganese
ions are mobilised in acid soils.
Calcifuges are plants such as heathers, which thrive in acid, calcium-deficient
conditions.
Calcicoles, on the other hand, are plants such as dog's mercury,
which prefer alkaline soils with plenty of calcium.
We shall look at the effects of extremes of pH on ecosystems in the next chapter.
Universal indicator can be used to test soil pH over a range of 4.0 to 11.0.
However, pH meters are usually more convenient and reliable for estimating
the pH of the soil, seawater or freshwater.

Using a pH meter

419

Oxygen

Oxygen concentrations vary very little in the atmosphere.
However, oxygen levels in aquatic ecosystems can vary considerably.

Oxygen concentration is probably the most important element
in overall water quality.
Most organisms are **aerobic** – they require oxygen.
But if organic waste, such as sewage, gets into a freshwater system,
oxygen depletion can occur.
Bacteria break down the organic waste. As they do so, the increased
bacterial respiration imposes a high oxygen demand on the waters.
The consequent low level of dissolved oxygen can have a detrimental
effect upon the plant and animal life.
We will look at organic pollution in more detail in the next chapter.
Electronic oxygen meters have tended to be the least reliable of
the environmental meters in the past.
They are much improved nowadays but still require careful calibration.

A rapid flowing upper hill stream

Conductivity

The conductivity of a water sample refers to its ability to carry an
electrical current. Since electricity is carried in solutions by migrating ions,
the conductivity of a solution indicates the level of dissolved salts.
The conductivity of pure water is zero, so adding any ions will
increase the conductivity.

Conductivity measurements do not differentiate between salts.
So if you need to estimate chloride, for instance, you need to carry
out a separate test (a silver nitrate titration).
For most ecologists, conductivity measurements are good enough.
The increase in salinity in an upper shore rock pool, which has been
isolated for a number of days as a result of neap tides, can be shown
using conductivity data.
Conductivity meters are accurate and very reliable.
They are also easy to use in the field.

Testing a water sample

Soil type

Soil can be sampled simply by digging to show a **soil profile** or
by using a **soil auger** to take a core sample.
Sieves with different mesh sizes can be used to categorise the
various soil components, as shown in the diagram.
Depending upon your particular investigation, you may need to
estimate the water content, organic content, temperature or pH
of the soil.
For instance, samples taken along a line transect across sand dunes
will show changes in organic content, chloride and pH with succession.
To measure soil water content, you need to dry your sample in an
oven at 110 °C overnight. Then work out this equation:

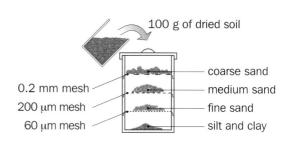

Separating soil compounds by sieving

$$\% \text{ soil water} = \frac{\text{weight loss on drying}}{\text{weight of fresh soil}} \times 100$$

To measure organic content, you take the dry soil sample and heat it in a
crucible to red heat for 15 minutes to incinerate all the organic matter.
Then work out this equation:

$$\% \text{ organic matter in dry soil} = \frac{\text{weight loss on burning}}{\text{weight of dry soil}} \times 100$$

▷ Biology at work: Bolivian savanna interactions

The Beni Biological Station (BBS) in Northern Bolivia is an area comprising of representative samples of tropical forest, savanna and swamp, and is noted for its high **biodiversity**. In 1986, the Station became the world's first Man and Biosphere Reserve as part of a 'Debt for Nature' swap.

A view of typical savannah vegetation in Northern Bolivia

The BBS has 14 characteristic vegetation types and over 2,000 species of vascular plants within the reserve. The fauna is made up of at least 100 species of mammal, about 500 species of bird, 45 species of amphibian and 200 species of fish. Many of these are endangered and the subject of research.

Neotropical savannas are under as much threat as tropical rainforests due to the increase in heavy cattle grazing and the associated annual burning of the scrub during the dry season. The irregular occurrence of fire is a natural, and quite beneficial, phenomenon of the savanna ecosystem.

With such high biodiversity, it is not surprising that species interact with each other.

- **Mutualism** – both species benefit from the association. Symbiosis is a specialised form, which involves some form of physiological interdependence between two species.
- **Commensalism** – one species benefits whilst the other is unaffected. Phoresy is a specialised form, which involves one species benefiting from being transported by another that is unaffected.
- **Predation** – one species eats another species, so one species benefits whilst the other loses. Parasitism is a specialised form of predation where the host is harmed but is not normally killed.
- **Competition** – both species suffer from this interaction.

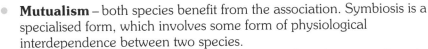

Species 1 Species 2	positive (+)	negative (−)	no interaction
positive (+)	mutualism symbiosis	predation parasitism	commensalis phoresy
negative (−)	predation parasitism	competition	
No Interaction	commensalism phoresy		ammensalism

Classification of species interactions

Umbrella tree and ants – the hollow stems and branches of the tree are inhabited by a fierce species of ant (*Azteca* spp.). These provide protection for the plant by killing or driving away predators. In return, the ants gain access to edible bodies on the plant and leaf nectaries. This is an example of mutualism.

Termites and bacteria – termites are primitive social insects, which feed mainly on the cellulose component of plant material. They do not contain the enzymes necessary to do this but rely on bacteria found in their gut. In return, the bacteria gain shelter and access to a supply of sugar. This is an example of symbiosis similar to that found in ruminants.

Most bromiliads are epiphytic and grow on the branches of other trees

Bromiliads and their fauna – some bromiliad varieties collect water in their tight, over-lapping leaf axils. These trap leaves and other detritus, forming food-rich, temporary aquatic ecosystems. These are inhabited by a diverse range of competing invertebrate species, which may be eaten by frogs and reptiles.

Leafcutting ants and fungus – the most conspicuous ant species in the savanna forms large columns of individual ants, each carrying a leaf fragment several times its own size. These are chewed into a paste, which forms the substrate to grow fungus, on which the ants live, another example of mutualism.

Bats and flowers – there are 106 bat species in Bolivia with 46 being found in the BBS. These include frog and fish eating bats, vampire bats and those like the short-tailed leaf nosed bats (*Carollia* sp.) which pollinate the savanna tree (*Pseudobombax* sp.). This is another example of mutualism.

The future of the savanna depends upon a deep understanding and knowledge of species interactions and the role they play in complex and intricate ecosystems. Without this it would be very difficult to assess the impact of human activity and hence propose appropriate management and conservation strategies.

Pseudobombax sp.

Summary

- A population is a group of individuals of the same species living in the same habitat.
- The numbers of individuals in a population are increased by births and immigration and decreased by deaths and emigration.
- The size of a population at a particular time is determined by biotic potential, environmental resistance and the carrying capacity.
- Population changes may be density-dependent due to biotic factors such as competition for food, or density-independent due to biotic or abiotic factors such as adverse weather.
- Many populations show a pattern of growth that follows an S-shaped growth curve.

- Competition may be intraspecific between individuals of the same species, or interspecific between individuals of different species.
- If species compete for the same niche, it can lead to the exclusion of a species.
- Both predator and prey species have evolved adaptations to enable them to survive.
- Predator–prey cycles show the relationships between the two populations.
- Biological control is the use of predators, parasites or pathogens to control the numbers of a pest.
- Succession is the change in the structure and species composition of a community over time.
- Sampling can be random or systematic. Quadrats and transects are common sampling strategies.

▷ Questions

1 Explain what is meant by the following terms and give an example in each case:
a) a density-dependent factor,
b) a density-independent factor,
c) intraspecific competition,
d) interspecific competition.

2 a) What is the name for this type of growth curve?
b) What does the dotted line represent?

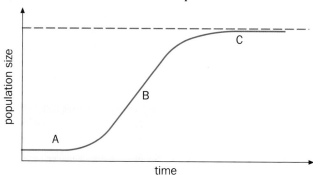

This growth curve can be used to show the growth of a bacterial population and a rabbit population.
c) i) Describe and explain the growth of the bacteria at points A, B and C.
ii) Describe and explain the growth of the rabbit population at points A, B and C.

3 A light trap was used to sample a particular species of moth. In the first sample, 30 moths were caught and each one was marked and released. The next night another sample produced 24 moths, of which 6 were marked from the previous catch.
a) Estimate the total population of moths.
b) Why is it important that
i) a suitable period of time passes before the second catch is taken,
ii) the mark is not toxic nor does it make the moth conspicuous,
iii) the mark does not rub off too soon?

4 Ten identical plots of land were cleared of weeds and then sown with pea seeds. After sowing, nine of the plots were kept free of weeds for different lengths of time. After 9 weeks, all the plants were harvested from each plot and weighed. The results are shown in the table.

Period plot kept weed-free (weeks)	Yield at harvest (arbitrary units)	
	Pea plants	Weeds
0	4	80
2	37	44
4	58	24
6	72	12
8	79	4

a) Plot the data in a suitable form on graph paper.
b) What conclusion can you draw about the competition between pea plants and weeds?
c) How could you estimate the total mass of weeds growing in a large field?
d) Design an experiment to test the prediction that pea plants grown at a high density produce fewer peas per plant than those grown at a low density.

5 a) What is mean by the term 'succession'?
b) How is succession different from zonation?
c) What happens to the following during a succession sequence:
i) plant height and biomass,
ii) species diversity,
ii) primary productivity,
iv) community stability?
d) Explain what is meant by deflected succession and give examples based on agricultural practices.

6 The table shows the populations of lynx and snowshoe hares in Canada between 1885 and 1895.
   a) Explain the low figure for hares in 1886.
   b) How long did it take the hares to regain their original density?
   c) When the hares reached this peak, what happened to the lynx population? Explain your answer.
   d) Explain the high figure for the lynx population in 1886.
   e) Explain the high figure for the hare population in 1890.

Year	Lynx population	Hare population
1885	70 000	135 000
1886	80 000	14 000
1887	35 000	90 000
1888	10 000	35 000
1889	7500	20 000
1890	7500	50 000
1891	10 000	55 000
1892	15 000	65 000
1893	25 000	60 000
1894	40 000	80 000
1895	55 000	135 000

7 a) Explain what is meant by 'biological control'.
   b) The graph shows how biological control can reduce the numbers of a pest species.
   Explain why the pest numbers fluctuated before the biological control agent was introduced.

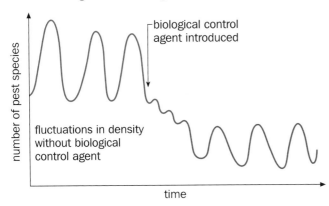

   c) Suggest two features that a successful biological control agent should have.
   d) Explain the advantages and disadvantages of using biological control, rather than chemical, to control pests.

8 A group of students investigated the distribution of plants across a salt marsh. The diagram shows the results.
   a) Describe the techniques that the students could use to obtain the data in the diagram.
   b) The distribution of plants in the saltmarsh is governed mainly by abiotic factors.
   Suggest two abiotic factors that could restrict the distribution of sea rush and cord grass in this habitat and explain how each factor would have its effect.

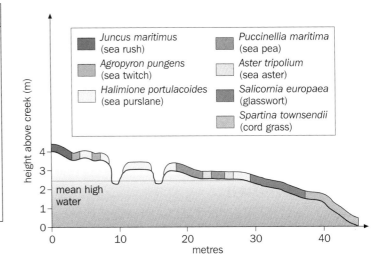

9 The table shows the results of investigations of several ponds in mid-Wales.
   a) Describe the relationship between the pH of these ponds and the numbers of invertebrate animal species.
   b) Mere Pool has the greatest species diversity. Why do you think this is?
   c) Which pond would you expect to be least stable? Explain your answer.

Pond	pH of pond water	Number of plant species	Number of invertebrate species
Mawn Pool	4.4	8	4
Rhulen Hill	4.8	11	5
Llanbadan	5.7	16	9
Mere Pool	6.6	23	19
Beilibedw	8.1	21	14

Humans have many influences upon the environment, one of the most obvious being pollution.
Pollution is defined as
'the release of substances or energy into the environment by man, in quantities harmful to plant or animal life, and which causes damage to structure or amenity'.

But a simpler and perhaps more appropriate definition could be 'the wrong amount of the wrong substance in the wrong place at the wrong time'!
As you will see, some pollutants are biodegradable, for example sewage, whilst others persist in the environment, such as broad-spectrum pesticides, and tend to accumulate along food chains.

Sewage effluent being discharged

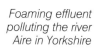

Foaming effluent polluting the river Aire in Yorkshire

▷ Deforestation

Forests help to maintain the balance of carbon dioxide and oxygen in the atmosphere.
This is important, because carbon dioxide is a 'greenhouse gas'.
It absorbs outgoing radiation and accumulation leads to global warming.

Forests also act as 'stores of water', with their canopies slowing down both the rate of evaporation and the rate at which water reaches the soil.
So deforestation means more water reaches the soil and more quickly.
With no roots to bind the soil together, soil erosion occurs.
This decreases the overall productivity of an area because essential nutrients are washed out of the soil (**leaching**).

Forests conserve soil because the decomposition of their leaves adds to the organic content (**humus**) of the soil, although in the case of tropical rainforests this is less true.

Factory chimneys discharging

High temperatures and high rainfall lead to high productivity, so the forest grows quickly.
As a result, most of the nutrients are located in the biomass, so chopping down trees essentially removes the nutrients from the forest.

Landfill site

So what are the reasons for the large scale clearance of forests?

- The world demand for tropical hardwoods as building materials.

- The demand for paper for newsprint, photocopiers, printers and office consumption.

- The clearing of land for farms, cattle ranches and plantations.

- The building of new road networks through the region.

- To provide firewood and charcoal as fuels.

Felling of rainforest trees

▷ The greenhouse effect

There are a number of 'greenhouse gases' in the atmosphere. Some of these gases such as carbon dioxide, water vapour and methane are naturally occurring, whereas others are man-made, for example chlorofluorocarbons (CFCs) and nitrogen oxides (NOx).

Greenhouse gases allow solar energy to pass through the atmosphere to warm the Earth's surface up. But when the Earth radiates the heat energy back into space, some of it is absorbed and trapped by the greenhouse gases, causing the air to warm up.

It is important to understand that the **greenhouse effect** is a *natural* process, and that without it the average temperature on Earth would be about $-17\,^{\circ}C$.
However, over the last hundred years there has been a build-up of these gases, which has increased the greenhouse effect.

- There has been an increase in the amount of fossil fuels being burnt by power stations and for domestic heating and transport. About 50% of the greenhouse effect is thought to be caused by carbon dioxide derived from these sources.
- As you have seen, deforestation has resulted in large areas of land being cleared and the trees being burnt. So there are fewer trees to take up carbon dioxide for photosynthesis.
- Methane has increased from a number of sources. There has been an expansion in rice growing and cattle rearing. Methane is belched out from the stomachs of cattle and it is also released from rice crops, as a result of the anaerobic conditions in paddy fields.
  Another source of methane is rotting material in landfill sites.
- CFCs have been used as aerosol propellants and as coolants in refrigerators and freezers. Although only present in small amounts, CFCs are many times more active than carbon dioxide as a greenhouse gas.
- Nitrogen dioxide, nitric oxide and nitrous oxide, together termed NOx, are emitted from vehicle exhausts.

Of all the greenhouse gases, the most significant increase has been in carbon dioxide levels, which have risen by 10% over the last 30 years.

Burning rain forest

Industrial pollution

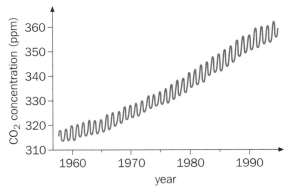

Atmospheric CO_2 concentrations recorded at the Mauna Loa monitoring station, Hawaii

▷ Global warming

A possible consequence of global warming is a rise in sea levels as a result of melting glaciers and the thermal expansion of water.
This would cause flooding of low-lying areas, and coastal erosion.
There could also be a change in wind patterns and distribution of rainfall, leading to more extremes in the weather.
If the Earth was to slowly warm up, there would be a shift in climate belts, so the production of grain could be affected.
It could cause massive reductions in the grain crops of North America and Central Asia.
This could affect the pattern of world food production, with obvious economic and political consequences.

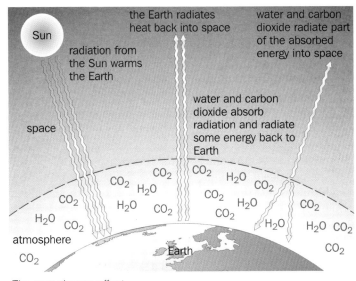

The greenhouse effect

▷ Acid rain

Rain water is naturally slightly acidic, because it reacts with carbon dioxide in the air producing carbonic acid with a pH of about 5.6. **Acid rain** is classed as rain with a pH below 5.6. Europe and North America have rain that is ten times more acidic than this with a pH value of 4.0.

The main pollutant responsible for acidification is sulphur dioxide (SO_2). Although there are natural sources of sulphur dioxide such as volcanoes, most of it comes from the burning of fossil fuels, mainly as emissions from power stations. Various oxides of nitrogen (NOx) are given off from vehicle exhausts. These gases combine with water vapour in the atmosphere to form sulphuric acid and nitric acid.

Acid rain is no respecter of boundaries. The polluting gases can ride the clouds for days and be carried long distances before coming down as acid rain. Britain is by far the greatest contributor to acid rain in Norway. Similarly the USA is responsible for much of Canada's acid rain problem.

Effects of acid rain

Research has shown that the acidity of forest soils has increased 5–10 fold over the last 20–50 years across vast areas of Europe and North America.
The effects may be reduced if the soil is alkaline with a high calcium and magnesium content, as it will neutralise the effect of the acid to some extent.
Many of the soils of northern Europe are thin and cover granite. The low calcium content means the buffer capacity of these soils is low.

- The acid leaches out important minerals from the soil, such as calcium, magnesium and potassium, which are needed for plant growth.
- Toxic minerals like aluminium are mobilised, finding their way into freshwater systems. Here they become deposited on the gills of fish. The fish then produce mucus, which clogs the gills, and they die. Many Scottish lochs are now completely fishless.
- Acid rain causes extensive damage to conifers. Thinning of the crown, shedding of leaves, damage to root hairs and decreased resistance to drought and frost are all symptoms of acid rain.
- Decomposition in the soil is inhibited by the acid.
- Acidified lakes look crystal clear, devoid of life except for a luxuriant growth of moss and algae.

The clean up

The technology exists to combat acid rain.
- Chemical plants can be installed to remove the sulphur from emissions before they reach the atmosphere.
- Low-sulphur fuels could be used. Crushing coal and washing it with a solvent can reduce the sulphur content.
- Flue gas desulphurisation removes the sulphur from power station chimneys by bombarding the waste gases with jets of wet powdered limestone. The acid gases are neutralised to form a sludge.
- Catalytic converters can be fitted to reduce nitrogen oxides in the exhaust fumes of cars.

These solutions are expensive but they are gradually being introduced as the cost of the effects of acid rain start to outweigh the cost of the solutions.

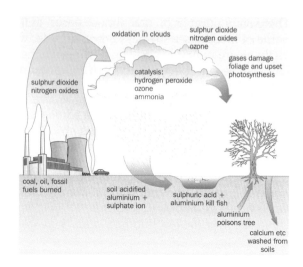

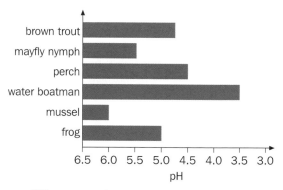

Different aquatic organisms have varying sensitivities to higher acidity (low pH)

▷ Ozone depletion

The **ozone layer** is present some 10-45 km up in the stratosphere.
It is formed by the effects of ultraviolet radiation on oxygen.
The ozone layer acts as a screen, preventing much of the damaging UV light from reaching the Earth's surface.

In 1985, a large 'hole' was discovered in the ozone layer over the Antarctic.
It was found that the ozone layer had thinned to as much as 67% in places.
The size of the hole seems to be increasing each year, and a similar hole has now developed over the Arctic too.

The cause of this ozone depletion is a group of chemicals called **CFCs**.
Chlorofluorocarbons also act as greenhouse gases.
CFCs are remarkably inert gases that rise unchanged into the stratosphere where they are converted by UV light into free chlorine atoms.
The chlorine reacts with the ozone breaking it down into oxygen.

The use of CFCs is now restricted, but in the past they have been used as propellants in aerosol cans and coolants in refrigerators and air-conditioners.
Less ozone in the stratosphere allows more UV light through.
UV radiation is known to be associated with an increased incidence of skin cancer.
The use of blocking creams and wearing a hat reduces the risk of skin cancer.

▷ Lead

Lead has been known to be toxic for many years.
In the past, it was used in domestic water pipes, although this is not thought to have been a major hazard, since lead is not easily absorbed from the gut.

Of far more concern is the lead that is emitted from vehicle exhausts.
Tetraethyl lead has been added to petrol as an anti-knock agent.
This makes the burning of petrol more efficient and raises its octane rating.
But the lead emitted in the exhaust fumes can be absorbed by the lungs.

The toxic effects of lead in the body include

- brain damage and mental retardation in children,
- other problems associated with the nervous system, such as convulsions,
- abnormalities in the digestive system such as intestinal colic,
- kidney malfunction.

In the UK, the use of unleaded petrol, leadless paints and the switch to copper or plastic pipes has helped to reduce the input of lead into the environment.
However, emissions of lead from vehicles are increasing on a global basis as economies in Asia develop and become more affluent.

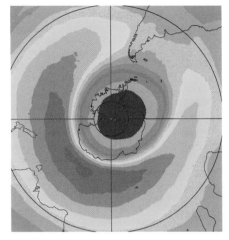

Measurements of column ozone in the Southern Hemisphere showing ozone hole in the centre

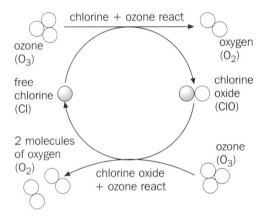

ozone (O_3)
chlorine + ozone react
oxygen (O_2)
free chlorine (Cl)
chlorine oxide (ClO)
2 molecules of oxygen (O_2)
chlorine oxide + ozone react
ozone (O_3)

▷ Thermal pollution

Water is often taken from rivers and used as a coolant by industries.
The water that is returned to the river has a higher temperature
than when it was taken out.
This discharge of warm water into rivers is called **thermal pollution**.
The warmer temperature decreases the solubility of oxygen, so lowering
the amount of dissolved oxygen in the water.
Higher temperatures also increase the rate of metabolism of fish.
Valuable game fish, such as trout, cannot survive in water above 25 °C
and will not reproduce in water warmer than 14 °C.
Coarser fish such as pike and carp, can tolerate temperatures as warm as 35 °C.
In fact, the warmer water enhances their growth rate.
The problems of thermal pollution include

- thermal shock, which can cause death to organisms in extreme cases,
- a decrease in oxygen levels, which affects organisms that live
  in well-aerated waters and alters the food chains and food webs of a river,
- an increased susceptibility of aquatic organisms to disease,
  parasites and toxins.

This is an example of **synergism**, where two pollutants act together
producing an effect that is greater than the sum total of their
separate effects. For example, increased water temperature makes:

- fish more susceptible to the effects of heavy metals,
- an acceleration in the rate of eutrophication by encouraging
  the growth of bacteria,
- a change in species composition, as we have mentioned,
  where trout may be replaced by coarse fish.

▷ Radiation

About 87% of the radiation that we are exposed to every day is
natural radiation.
This comes from space as cosmic rays, or from rocks in
the Earth's crust which contain radioactive materials.
About 12% comes from medical sources, such as the use of X-rays
for diagnosis and from **radiotherapy** used in the treatment of cancers.
Only 1% of the radiation that we are exposed to comes from nuclear
power stations or nuclear weapons.

As with most types of pollution, problems arise when too much
of the pollutant is emitted in one place over a short period of time.
In 1986 there was an accident at the Chernobyl nuclear power station
in south-west Russia.
A huge cloud of radioactive material was released into the atmosphere.
The winds blew the cloud across Europe, and areas like Poland and
Scandinavia were showered with radioactive chemicals.
Upland areas of North Wales, Scotland and Cumbria were also affected
as the rain washed the radionuclides out of the sky.
Often the effects of radiation are more long-term in nature.
Some forms of radiation are known to act as mutagens, which induce
genetic mutations.
The bombs dropped on Hiroshima and Nagasaki during the Second World
War, resulted in a high incidence of birth defects and cancers.

Fish killed by thermal pollution

Rugeley power station in Staffordshire

Nuclear power station

428

▷ Organic pollution

Organic pollution includes sewage, slurry from intensive livestock units, silage effluent (silage is stored grass to feed cattle in winter), washings from dairies and paper mill wastes.

Organic wastes are '*oxygen-requiring*' because they are decomposed by microorganisms, which use up oxygen and reduce the oxygen level of the water.
The wastes act as food for large numbers of bacteria and these need oxygen to carry out respiration.

We say that the bacteria place a high **oxygen demand** upon the water.
The quality of a body of water can be measured by taking a sample and finding its **biochemical oxygen demand** (**BOD**).
BOD is measured by taking a water sample of known volume and recording its dissolved oxygen content in mg litre $^{-1}$.
The sample is then incubated in the dark at 20 °C for 5 days.
The dissolved oxygen is then remeasured so that the amount used up by the effluent can be calculated as mg O_2 used per litre over 5 days.
The **lower** the BOD, the fewer bacteria present, indicating **less** organic material in the water.

Whenever organic waste such as sewage gets into a river, there are changes in the river's chemical and biological components downstream from the point of discharge.

- Initially, the increased loading of organic matter provides food for bacteria and their numbers increase dramatically. Bacterial respiration means that a lot of dissolved oxygen is used up, creating a high BOD.

- Clean water invertebrates, such as stonefly and mayfly larvae, and fish, such as trout, swim away or are killed by the low level of oxygen.

- Pollution-tolerant species such as sludge worms (*Tubifex*) and midge larvae (*Chironomus*) increase in numbers by feeding on the organic matter and through reduced competition and predation.

- Eventually the bacterial population starts to decline as the organic matter becomes used up and protozoa begin to feed on them.

- Sewage fungus increases and then declines as the organic matter becomes used up.

- Further downstream, photosynthetic algae increase as light penetration increases and nitrifying bacteria convert ammonium ions in the effluent into nitrates.

- Eventually, pollution-intolerant species are found as the dissolved oxygen increases as a result of photosynthesis and the reduction in the volume of organic material.

- Pollution-tolerant species decline due to increased predation and competition.

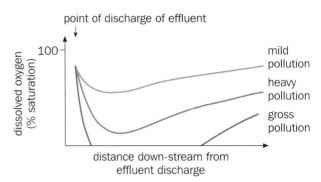

Stonefly larvae: pollution intolerant species

Sludge worms: pollution tolerant species

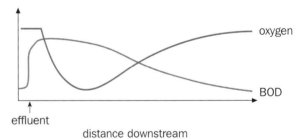

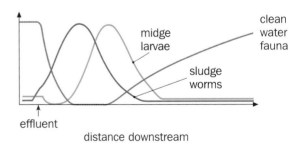

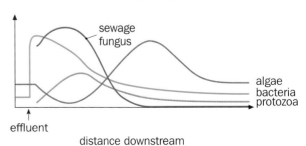

▷ Eutrophication

Eutrophication is the naturally occurring process of **nutrient enrichment** of freshwater and coastal waters. However, artificial enrichment of water bodies is occurring as a result of human activities, changing the biological communities found in our lakes, pond, canals and some rivers.

Causes of nutrient enrichment

Eutrophication can be accelerated by the following:

- increased leaching and run-off of nitrate-rich and phosphate-rich fertilisers from agricultural land,
- release of phosphate-containing detergents,
- run-off from slurry spread on agricultural land,
- drainage of washings from intensive livestock units,
- untreated sewage discharges,
- increased soil erosion as a result of deforestation.

Eutrophication results in marked changes in plant and animal life.
The Norfolk Broads is a series of small, shallow lakes in East Anglia, which used to support a community with a rich flora and diverse fauna.
But over a period of 60 years, the waters have become heavily contaminated with phosphate (a common limiting factor in plant growth). This appears to be due mainly to sewage effluence as a result of the large tourist industry in the area.

The effects of eutrophication on aquatic ecosystems can be summarised as follows.

- Increased nitrate and phosphate loading causes massive increases in algae (microscopic plants). These form so-called **algal blooms**.
- Although the algae do release some oxygen from photosynthesis, their dense surface growth cuts down light penetration to the lower depths, reducing the numbers of large rooted plants (macrophytes).
- There is a general decrease in the diversity of species not only the plant community but also the animals that rely on them for food and shelter.
- Dead algae sink to the bottom and are decomposed by aerobic bacteria. This uses up a lot of dissolved oxygen (producing a high BOD).
- Oxygen depletion means that many species of invertebrates and fish die. Many food chains will collapse.
- Turbidity increases. That is, the water becomes more cloudy and the rate of sedimentation increases. Less light penetrates for photosynthesis.

These effects may create a number of problems to humans:

- water removed for drinking may have an unacceptable taste or odour,
- the water may be harmful to health,
- its appeal to tourists and its value as a conservation area may decrease,
- increased vegetation may slow water flow and navigation by boats,
- important fisheries may be lost.

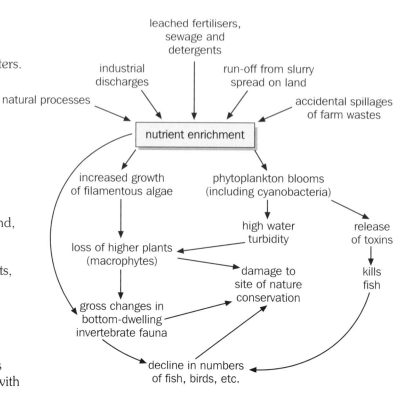

Algal bloom in Basingstoke canal following warm weather

Cutting water weeds in Basingstoke canal

▷ Fertilisers

There has been a massive increase in the use of inorganic fertilisers over the past 50 years.

Prompted by the need for Britain to be self-sufficient in food during the Second World War, 1939–45, the application of fertilisers proved to be a cornerstone of the post-war boom in British agriculture.

The major plant nutrients that have contributed to this increase in crop yield are nitrogen and phosphorus, as nitrates and phosphates.

Not all of the fertiliser applied is taken up by crop plants.
A large proportion either washes off the soil surface (as run-off) or else trickles through the soil (a process called **leaching**) to eventually find its way into our waterways.
This can damage the environment by encouraging the growth of algae and so contribute to the process of eutrophication.

Fertilisers need to be added to the soil when the plant's demand for nutrients is greatest, that is when growth is rapid.
Fertilisers applied in the autumn may well be leached away because of slow plant growth and the likelihood of heavy rainfall.
Inorganic fertilisers such as ammonium nitrate are particularly soluble and prone to leaching if applied at the wrong time of year.
Over-application of fertilisers also leads to nutrient drainage.
This is detrimental to the environment, and the farmer also loses money if expensive fertilisers are washed out of the soil.

Once in the watercourses, the fertilisers do what they are supposed to do on the land, they stimulate plant growth.
They trigger the cycle of events that we have outlined in eutrophication.
There is also particular concern about nitrates building up in the ground water.
The European Union (EU) limit on nitrate in water is 50 mg dm^{-3}.
Medical opinion is that 80 mg dm^{-3} poses no threat to human health but water from lowland rivers in England often has in excess of 100 mg dm^{-3} and has to be diluted with low nitrate water before it is drinkable.

High levels of nitrates in drinking water are known to be the cause of 'blue-baby syndrome'.
Bacteria in the baby's gut reduce the nitrate to nitrite.
The baby's haemoglobin picks up the nitrite in preference to oxygen, resulting in respiratory failure.
Only a handful of cases have occurred in Britain but even so, nursing mothers in agricultural areas of south-east England have been given bottled water because their drinking water exceeds the EU nitrate maximum.

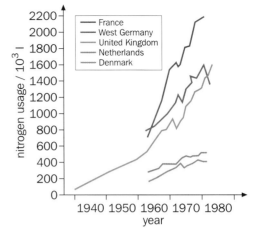

Fertilizer usage in western Europe

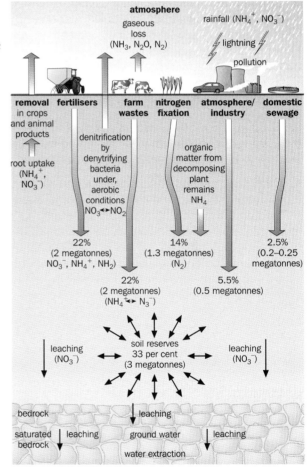

The leaching of nitrogen into ground water

A number of changes in farming strategy could reduce the current loss of nitrates to rivers and streams.

● Avoid over-use of nitrate fertiliser by matching application to crop needs.
● Avoid winter application when soils are wet and prone to leaching.
● Do not apply fertilisers too early in the spring or just before heavy rain is forecast.
● Split fertiliser applications: do not apply it all in one go.
● Use slow-release fertilisers, which give up their nitrogen gradually.
● Avoid ploughing up grassland, which releases large amounts of nitrogen.

▷ Oil pollution

We tend to associate oil pollution with oil tanker disasters
but intentional discharge can occur if a tanker takes on seawater
to wash out its tanks, or for ballast after the cargo has been delivered.
The blow-out of the IXTOC 1 oil platform in the Gulf of Mexico
in 1979 produced the largest spillage, until the Iraq occupation of
Kuwait in 1991.
Iraqi forces deliberately damaged nearly 900 Kuwaiti oil wells and
hundreds of thousands of tonnes of oil spilled into the Arabian Gulf.

The Amoco Cadiz sinks off the coast of Brittany

Effects on wildlife

We have become familiar with press photographs of oil-covered
seabirds.

Oil pollution causes harm in the following ways.

- Oil coats the feathers of seabirds, reducing their buoyancy and insulation.
- If swallowed, oil causes intestinal irritation and can cause pneumonia.
- Mussels are unable to feed if coated with oil and it also affects their
  reproductive capacity.
- Oil destroys certain algae, which are important primary producers
  in marine food webs.
- Little effect is experienced by fish because they just swim away.

Quite often, the most damaging effects of an oil spillage are a result of
the actions of government who, prompted by press coverage, need to
be seen to be doing something about the disaster.

An oiled razorbill at Great Yarmouth

- Detergents and dispersants are often used, which are 10–100 times
  more toxic than the oil itself. Even worse, these kill the bacteria that
  feed on the oil and break it down naturally.
- Expensive inflatable booms have been used to limit the spread of
  oil slicks but these are useless in bad weather.
- Mechanical methods such as bulldozers can do great damage to
  intertidal organisms if used in an attempt to clear a beach.
- Attempts have been made to set the oil alight. In 1967, 22 000 tonnes
  of bombs were used in an attempt to break up the wreck of the
  Torrey Canyon on the Seven Stones reef, but it was only hit once!

Let nature take its course

Current scientific opinion favours the decomposition of oil by natural
bacterial populations.
The recovery time in temperate waters is 2–3 years (slower in polar
regions and faster in the tropics, because degradation is
temperature-dependent).
Growth of the oil-degrading bacteria may be limited by availability of
nutrients (particularly nitrates and phosphates).
Bags of fertiliser can speed up bacterial growth and aid recovery.
Phosphorus and nitrogen can be sprayed onto oil-covered rocks to
encourage bacterial growth.
In the wake of the Kuwaiti disaster, extensive growths of blue-green
microbial mats were found over oil-covered areas of the coast.
The major constituent was a cyanobacterium, *Microcoleus*.
Although the cyanobacteria are photosynthetic, they produce sticky
mucilage, which traps the oil-degrading bacteria, preventing them from
being washed out to sea.
Their photosynthetic partner also provides them with oxygen.

A burning oil well in Kuwait

432

▷ Bioaccumulation

Bioaccumulation is the build-up in body tissues of substances that are neither used (metabolised) nor excreted by cells. Many chemicals cannot be broken down and so they accumulate in the soil or in the aquatic environment.

Many of these chemicals are released into the environment as a result of human activities.
They include

- a number of pesticides, such as Dieldrin, DDT and DDE,
- heavy metals, such as cadmium, mercury, tin and lead,
- industrial chemicals, such as polychlorinated biphenyls (PCBs).

Pesticides such as DDT have been used to combat malaria by controlling the mosquito **vector**.
They have also been used to control crop pests, and as a result have saved millions of people from starvation.
But because these sorts of chemicals do not readily break down, they persist in the environment and tend to accumulate in the body tissues of organisms.

Rodents such as rats and mice are becoming resistant to many anticoagulant poisons that have been used to control their numbers.
As a result, these chemicals are building up in their body tissues. This makes it more likely that predators such as the barn owl will become poisoned.

Bioaccumulation is considered to be most significant in marine and freshwater environments.
Many aquatic animals are filter feeders, passing vast quantities of water over their gills in order to extract food particles.
As a result, even if a pollutant is present in minute concentrations, over a period of time it can accumulate in large quantities.
The oyster, for example, has been shown to accumulate DDT to a level at least 70 000 times greater than that present in seawater.

Bioaccumulation need not simply refer to individual organisms. It also refers to the increasing concentrations of chemicals at successively higher trophic levels in food chains.
So each time an organism containing a pollutant is eaten by a predator, the pollutant is passed on and builds up in its tissues. By consuming many prey, an animal can accumulate high concentrations of the pollutant, which can eventually prove toxic.
The diagram shows how a very low level of DDE pesticide at the producer level can become at least a thousand times more concentrated in the top carnivores.

Legislation and stricter testing of pesticides has resulted in greater control of these toxic chemicals.
The use of alternative methods such as biological control has also reduced the hazard of persistent broad-spectrum pesticides.

Pesticide spraying in S.E. Asia

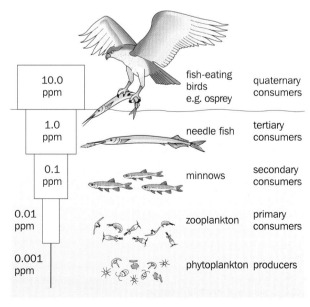

DDE concentrations in a food chain

▷ Biology at work: Bioaccumulation of mercury

In the lakes of north-eastern USA in the state of Maine, a water bird called the loon has become a symbol of conservation because of efforts to preserve its breeding grounds.

These efforts may be in vain because mercury poisoning is threatening the loon's survival, and the survival of other organisms, including humans which depend upon the same freshwater ecosystem.

A female loon on a nesting platform, Aziscohos Lake, Maine, USA

Loons are bioaccumulators of mercury. **Bioaccumulation** is the build-up in body tissues of substances that are not used by or excreted from cells. Increasing concentrations of chemicals occur at successively higher trophic levels in the food chain.

At the higher trophic levels, concentrations may reach fatal levels. Fish-eating birds like the loon appear at the top of the food chain.

Human activities such as waste incineration, coal burning and chlorine production have doubled or tripled natural mercury levels in the atmosphere. Each year, the level increases by 1–2%.

In lakes and ponds, bacteria convert inorganic mercury to methyl-mercury. This organic form is much more toxic to living organisms.

Invertebrates eat the bacteria and the methyl-mercury becomes more concentrated. In turn, fish eat the invertebrates.

Mercury then concentrates in muscle tissue as the fish get older and larger. When humans eat contaminated fish, the methyl-mercury is readily absorbed through cell membranes into the bloodstream.

From here, it easily crosses into the brain, where it attacks the central nervous system, destroying brain and nerve cells.

Mercury also crosses the placenta and enters the fetus in pregnant women. The human health effects of exposure to methyl-mercury from eating contaminated fish may include irritability, tremors, tunnel vision, reduced hearing, poor memory and difficulty chewing and swallowing.

1. Rain or snow washes mercury out of the atmosphere and deposits it on the land or in lakes and rivers.
2. Some of this mercury cycles back into the atmosphere from evaporation or forest fires and other disturbances.
3. In lakes and ponds, bacteria convert mercury into methyl-mercury. Highly acidic lakes which are warmer and higher in dissolved carbon produce more methyl-mercury.
4. Methyl-mercury enters the food chain and bioaccumulates from bacteria to invertebrates to fish to loons and humans

Loons are the best model for demonstrating how mercury flows through the ecosystem because
- they catch fish on the lakes where they also breed,
- they live for 20 years or more,
- they are large in size,
- they can swallow large fish in their expandable throats,
- they eat a large quantity of fish,
- they are tolerant to high levels of mercury whilst displaying a range of effects.

Monitoring involves taking regular blood and feather samples from caught loons. These reveal an increase in methyl-mercury levels from 1 ppm in Alaska in the west to 5.3 ppm in Maine in the east.

These high levels of mercury don't kill loons outright. Sub-lethal effects, however, have a broader impact.

Reproductive effects cause loons to lay fewer eggs or no eggs at all. Alterations to behaviour include failure to incubate eggs and the abnormal care of chicks. Only one-fifth the level of methyl-mercury needed to cause observable effects in adult loons is needed to cause lethal effects in chick embryos.

The implication of this research for human health has led to a move to reduce the level of industrial mercury emissions in the north-eastern states of the USA by 50% by 2003.

▷ Biology at work: Natural treatment of man-made waste

In several European countries, the common reed *Phragmites* is used in the treatment of domestic and industrial waste.

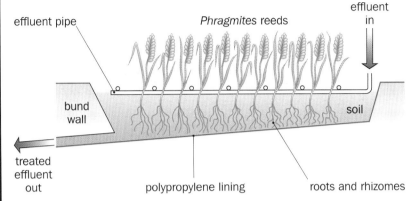

A reed bed system

The roots and rhizomes (underground stems) of the reeds grow both vertically and horizontally through the soil, aiding the passage of the effluent.
Oxygen enters through the stomata of the leaves, passes down the hollow stems and out through the roots into the soil.
Reed beds are shallow and allow the effluent to keep moving, so maintaining oxygen levels.

Aerobic bacteria collect and degrade organic material, releasing harmless substances such as carbon dioxide, nitrogen and water.
The bacteria break down organic material in the effluent that would otherwise starve aquatic life of oxygen.
They also break down nitrogenous waste, and phosphates that can be absorbed onto the materials that the reeds grow in.

Some anaerobic decay also occurs in the less-well-oxygenated areas of the reed bed and this contributes to the removal of the pollution.

Some of the waste from chemical plants, such as this one, can be treated in reed bed systems

Where these beds have been used to treat domestic sewage, there has been an 80–90% reduction in the biochemical oxygen demand (BOD).
BOD is the amount of oxygen used up by microorganisms in a water sample kept in the dark at 20 °C for 5 days.
It reflects the amount of organic material in the water that is broken down by the microorganisms.

Reed beds containing a variety of microbes have also been used to treat industrial effluents from the chemical industry, such as phenol, methanol and acetone, and to remove heavy metals.

Reed beds have low running costs and, unlike other treatment plants, are not unsightly.
However, they do require large areas of land if they are to be effective.

The traditional approach to treating effluent

Summary

- Human activity can have great influence on the environment at global and local levels.
- Deforestation means the loss of important habitats, soil erosion and a change in the balance of atmospheric gases.
- Increasing levels of carbon dioxide are causing the greenhouse effect and global warming.
- Emissions from power stations and vehicle exhausts result in acid rain.
- CFCs are causing ozone depletion and exposing us to harmful UV radiation.
- Organic material, fertilisers, detergents, toxic chemicals and heat all contribute to water pollution.
- Eutrophication is the enrichment of nutrients that upsets the ecological balance of ponds and lakes.
- Oil pollution has dramatic effects on the wildlife of marine ecosystems.
- Some pesticides and toxic heavy metals accumulate along food chains.

▷ Questions

1 a) Describe and explain the long-term effects of large scale deforestation on the Earth's atmosphere.
   b) The world-wide use of fossil fuels has increased rapidly during this century.
      i) Give two reasons for the increase in the amount of fossil fuels used.
      ii) Give two effects on the environment of this increase.
   c) Power stations often use water in cooling processes and then discharge warm water into rivers. Describe how this warm water might affect organisms that live in the river.

2 Lichens have been found to be reliable indicator species for sulphur dioxide in the air. The table shows the percentage cover of a species of lichen at different distances from the centre of a large city.

Distance from city centre in kilometres	Percentage lichen cover
5	3
8	22
11	45
16	75
19	75

   a) Draw a graph to show the relationship between lichen cover and distance from the city centre.
   b) What percentage cover of lichen would you expect at 10 km from the city centre?
   c) i) Explain the trend in percentage lichen cover between 5 and 16 km from the city centre.
      ii) Suggest why this trend is not continued between 16 and 19 km from the city centre.

3 The table shows the soil characteristics of a deciduous woodland in 1994 and 1997. In the winter of 1995, 90% of the woodland was cleared.
   a) Suggest what effect these changes will have had on the rate of decomposition. Explain your answer.
   b) Suggest an explanation for the changes in the soil nutrient levels.

Soil characteristic	1994	1997
mean soil temperature (°C)–day	9.1	11.5
mean soil temperature (°C)–night	5.2	3.0
soil moisture content (%)	32	21
soil nitrogen (mg kg^{-1})	13.6	2.3
soil potassium (mg kg^{-1})	11.0	1.9
soil calcium (mg kg^{-1})	15.3	4.8
pH	7.4	6.9

4 The graph shows some changes that occurred in a river following pollution by organic waste.

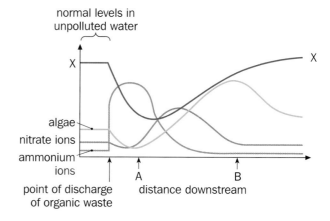

   a) i) Suggest an abiotic factor represented by curve X.
      ii) Name one organic pollutant which would result in these changes.
      iii) State one difference in appearance between fresh samples of water taken from the river at points A and B.
   b) i) Give two physiological characteristics you might expect organisms in the polluted water community to possess.
      ii) Name a group of organisms you would probably find near the point of discharge of the pollutant.
   c) Explain each of the following changes:
      i) the increase in concentration of ammonium ions after the point of discharge,

ii) the subsequent increase in the concentration of nitrate ions.
d) Give two possible reasons for the initial fall in the algal population after the discharge of organic waste.
e) Briefly explain the subsequent rise and fall in the algal population further downstream.

5 The graphs show the effect of untreated sewage on a stream.
a) Graph A shows physical and chemical effects (ammonia, nitrate, dissolved oxygen, suspended solids). Identify each of the lines 1–4, giving the reasons for your choice.
b) Graph B shows changes in the plants and animals (algae, midge larvae, stonefly larvae, sludge worms and 'water-lice'). Identify each of the lines 5–9, giving reasons for your choice.

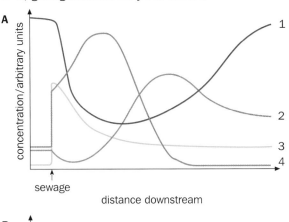

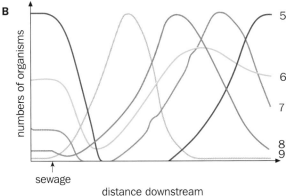

6 The map shows a small area in the Midlands. The sites indicated by letters **A**, **B** and **C** are sources of pollution. For each of the sites suggest

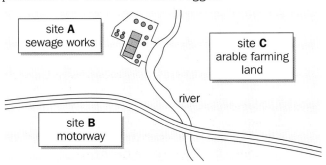

a) the main pollutants associated with each,
b) explain how these pollutants affect the living organisms inhabiting the site.

7 The Norfolk Broads (large areas of freshwater) have become heavily contaminated with phosphate over the last 100 years. The drawings show the effect this has had on the community of plants and animals in the Broads.
a) Suggest one reason for the large increase in the phosphate concentration in the Broads over the last 100 years.
b) Explain the reasons for the changes to the community that occurred
i) by the middle of the 20th century,
ii) between the middle and late 20th century.

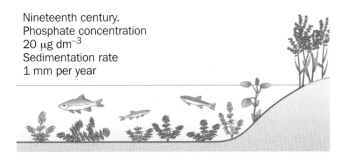

Nineteenth century.
Phosphate concentration
20 μg dm^{-3}
Sedimentation rate
1 mm per year

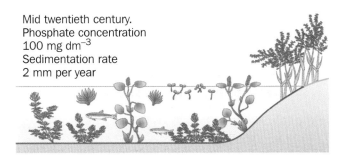

Mid twentieth century.
Phosphate concentration
100 mg dm^{-3}
Sedimentation rate
2 mm per year

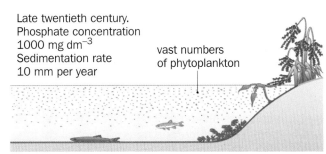

Late twentieth century.
Phosphate concentration
1000 mg dm^{-3}
Sedimentation rate
10 mm per year

vast numbers of phytoplankton

437

Further questions on continuity and environment

▷ Inheritance

1 Some cats have white patches on their coats. This effect is produced by action of the spotting gene, **S**. This gene has two codominant alleles, S^1 and S^2. The coats can have large patches of white, small white patches or no white patches at all.
   a) Explain the meaning of the term *codominance*. [2]
   b) A cat with no white patches, homozygous for S^1, had small white patches. Some of the offspring produced had coats with small white patches and the rest had no white patches.
      In the space below, draw out the genetic diagram to show this cross and include the expected ratio of phenotypes on your diagram. [4]
      (London) **[6]**

2 In mice, the dominant allele (**B**) of a gene for coat colour gives a black coat, the recessive allele (**b**) of this gene gives a brown coat. A second gene determines the density of the coat colour. The dominant allele (**D**) of this gene allows expression of coat colour, its recessive allele (**d**) dilutes the colour converting black to grey and brown to cream.
   a) A breeder crossed a male black mouse with a female brown one. The offspring produced showed four different coat colours: black, grey, brown and cream.
      i) State the genotypes for the black parent and the brown parent giving an explanation for your answer. [5]
      ii) Copy and complete the Punnett square to show the genotypes of the gametes and the offspring. [2]

      iii) State the expected phenotypic ratio. [1]
   b) With the aid of a genetic diagram, explain how the breeder could determine which of the black offspring were homozygous for the full colour allele (**D**). [4]
      (Edexcel) **[12]**

3 In the fruit fly, *Drosophila melanogaster*, the allele for grey body colour (**G**) is dominant to that for ebony body colour (**g**). The allele for normal wings (**N**) is dominant to that for curled wings (**n**).
   A student crossed a grey-bodied, normal-winged fly with an ebony-bodied, curled-winged fly. The offspring were as follows.

Phenotype	Numbers
grey body and normal wings	33
grey body and curled wings	23
ebony body and curled wings	28
ebony body and normal wings	16

   a) Show how this cross should have produced offspring in the ratio 1 : 1 : 1 : 1. [2]
   b) i) The Chi squared test (χ^2) can be used to test whether the observed results fit the expectation. Complete the table below in which E represents the expected number of each type of fly in the above cross, and O represents the number actually observed.

Phenotype	Number observed (O)	Number expected (E)	Difference (O–E)	Difference squared $(O-E)^2$
Grey body, normal wings				
Grey body, curled wings				
Ebony body, curled wings				
Ebony body, normal wings				

[2]

      ii) Calculate the value of χ^2 using the following formula.

$$\chi^2 = \sum \frac{(O - E)^2}{E}$$

[1]

      iii) Use the following extract from the χ^2 table to decide whether the observed numbers of offspring are significantly different from those expected. Explain how you reached your answer.

Degrees of freedom	Probability (p)						
	0.90	0.50	0.20	0.10	0.05	0.02	0.01
1	0.02	0.46	1.64	2.71	3.84	5.41	6.64
2	0.21	1.39	3.22	4.61	5.99	7.82	9.21
3	0.58	2.37	4.64	6.25	7.82	9.84	11.34
4	1.06	3.36	5.99	7.78	9.49	11.67	13.28

[3]
(AEB) **[8]**

4 a) Distinguish between the terms *gene* and *allele*. [3]
   b) The diagram at the top of the next page shows a family tree in which the blood group phenotypes are shown for some individuals.

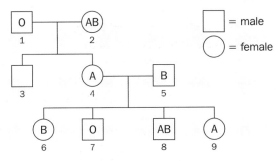

i) Using the symbols I^A, I^B and I^o to represent the alleles, indicate the genotypes of the following people: 1, 2, 4, 5, 6. [5]

ii) State the possible blood groups of person 3. Explain your answer. [3]

(Edexel) [11]

5 a) Doctors in some clinics claim that they can separate individual sperm cells so that the sex of a human child can be pre-determined.
Explain the genetic principles which enable the sex of a child to be pre-determined. [2]

b) The diagram below shows the inheritance of a rare hereditary form of rickets in a human family.

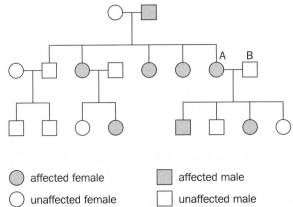

● affected female   ■ affected male

○ unaffected female   □ unaffected male

The condition is caused by a dominant allele (**R**). This allele may be present on the X chromosome (**X^R**), but not on the Y chromosome.
Copy and complete the genetic diagram to explain how this type of rickets was inherited by the children of parents **A** and **B**.

	A	**B**
Parental phenotypes	affected female	affected male
Parental genotypes		
Genotypes of gametes		

Genotypes of children				
Phenotypes of children	affected male	unaffected male	affected female	unaffected female

[3]
(NEAB) [5]

▷ **Selection, evolution and classification**

6 Commercial crop varieties have a relatively uniform genotype. Interbreeding two such varieties makes only small differences to quantitative characteristics, such as fruit size, yield and growth rate, which all show continuous variation.

a) Distinguish between *continuous variation* and *discontinuous variation*. [2]

b) Explain each of the following.
  i) The genetic basis of continuous variation [2]
  ii) Why commercial crop varieties have a 'relatively uniform genotype'. [2]
  iii) The *disadvantages* of growing a crop with a relatively uniform genotype. [2]

(Camb) [8]

7 The diagram below shows the relationship between six different species (A, B, C, D, E and F), which have evolved from a common ancestor.

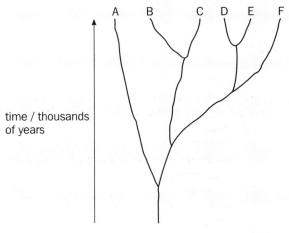

a) i) State which *two* species are most closely related. [1]
  ii) Use the information in the diagram to explain why species A and species B are *less* closely related to each other than B and C. [1]

b) If you had been provided with specimens of species A, B and C, instead of the diagram, how could you tell which *two* were the most closely related? [1]

(WJEC) [3]

8 Beetles belonging to the genus *Colophon* are unable to fly and are found on hilltops in South Africa. The dotted lines on the map on the following page show the distribution of three species of this beetle. Suggest an evolutionary explanation for each of the following statements.

a) All of these beetles are of very similar general appearance. [1]

439

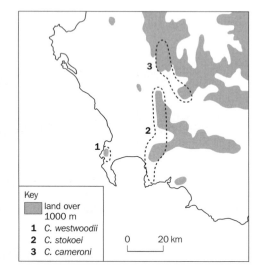

Key
land over 1000 m
1 *C. westwoodii*
2 *C. stokoei*
3 *C. cameroni*
0   20 km

b) There are slight differences between the species of *Colophon* found in the three areas. [2]
c) The fact that beetles of the genus *Colophon* are unable to fly has been important in the evolution of twelve different species of the genus in a small area of South Africa. [2]

(*AEB*) **[5]**

9 The diagram below shows one way of representing the classification of living organisms into five kingdoms. Box A has been drawn overlapping the other boxes, since its members share characteristics with the other kingdoms.

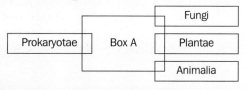

a) Which kingdom is represented by Box A? [1]
b) Give *one* structural characteristic that members of the kingdom represented by box A may share with (i) Fungi and (ii) Prokaryotae. [2]
c) Give *two* reasons why the Fungi are placed in a separate kingdom from the Plantae. [2]

(*AEB*) **[5]**

10 *Testudo ephippium* is one of the species of giant tortoise found on the Galapagos Islands. Complete the table below to show its classification.

Kingdom	Animalia
	Chordata
	Reptilia
	Chelonia
Family	Testudinidae
Genus	

(*NEAB*) **[3]**

▷ Energy and ecosystems

11 The diagram below represents a food web in a heathland ecosystem.

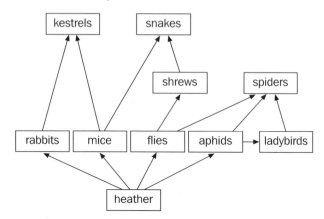

a) In this foodweb, name the following.
   i) The tertiary consumers [1]
   ii) The organism which has the largest population biomass [1]
b) Give *two* reasons why all the light reaching the heather cannot be used in photosynthesis. [2]
c) The acidic conditions present in the soil of heathlands inhibit the growth of bacteria. Suggest *two* ways in which this ecosystem may be affected by having few bacteria in the soil. [2]

(*NEAB*) **[6]**

12 a) What is meant by each of the following ecological terms?
   pyramid of energy; productivity; trophic levels; [6]
b) The biomass of organisms in an aquatic system was determined. The results are given in the table below.

Type of organism	Dry mass / g m^{-2}
Phytoplankton	7
Herbivorous plankton	30
Carnivorous fish	4

Account for the differences in the amounts of dry mass in this ecosystem. [4]
c) Suggest a method for measuring the dry mass of the phytoplankton in the ecosystem. [4]

(*O&C*) **[14]**

13 a) Define the following terms:
   habitat; niche; community; population; [4]
b) In the United Kingdom, deciduous trees lose their leaves in October or November and new leaf growth takes place during April to May of the following year.
   Diagram P below shows a pyramid of biomass for a deciduous woodland (in the UK) in July.

i) Explain how the biomass of the second trophic level would be determined. [4]

ii) Explain why the biomass decreases at each trophic level. [2]

iii) Diagram Q below represents a pyramid of biomass for the same woodland in January. This pyramid is drawn to the same scale as diagram P.

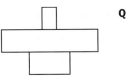

With reference to diagrams P and Q, explain the changes in biomass of each of the trophic levels in the woodland between July and January. [4]

(Camb) [14]

14 The diagram below represents the energy flow (kJ m^{-2} year^{-1}) through the community in an area of the sea.

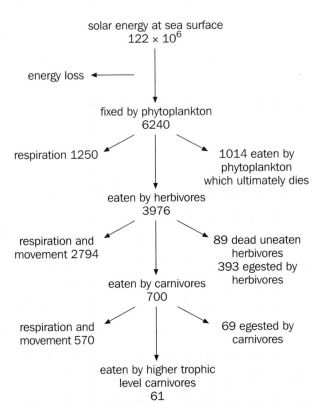

a) i) Calculate the percentage of solar energy which did *not* enter the food chain. Show your working. [2]

ii) State *three* reasons why this figure is so high. [3]

Further questions on continuity and environment

b) i) What percentage of the energy which enters 1. the herbivores and 2. the carnivores is used in respiration and movement? [2]

ii) Account for the difference in the results you have obtained in 1. and 2. above. [2]

c) Why are there so few top carnivores in a food chain? [2]

(O&C) [11]

15 The diagram below shows part of the nitrogen cycle.

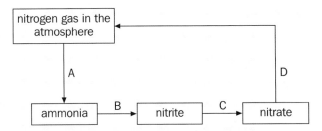

a) Name a genus of bacteria which is responsible for each of the reactions A, B, C and D. [4]

b) Describe the conditions in which the bacteria responsible for reaction D will thrive. [2]

(London) [6]

▷ **Interactions between organisms**

16 The roach is a freshwater fish. The water flea is a small crustacean, about 3 mm in length, which swims in the surface waters. The graph shows data concerning the populations of roach and water fleas in a small lake.

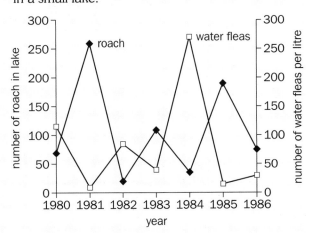

a) Explain how the data support the hypothesis that roach eat water fleas. [1]

b) In 1981, there was a very small number of water fleas. Suggest why the population of roach did not die out. [1]

c) Suggest a method for obtaining a reliable estimate of the number of water fleas per litre in the lake. [3]

(NEAB) [5]

Further questions on continuity and environment

17 a) Describe how biological control of *one named* pest is achieved. [3]
   b) Give *two* advantages of using biological control rather than pesticides to control insect pests. [2]
   (NEAB) **[5]**

18 A survey was carried out on a rocky shore to determine the distribution of two species of marine mollusc, *Littorina saxatilis* (the rough periwinkle), and *L. littorea* (the common periwinkle). Both species are primary consumers. A profile of the rocky shore is shown on the diagram below. At low water mark, the shore is covered by sea water most of the time. The sea reaches high water mark twice each day.

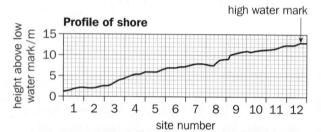

The sites of sampling were 10 metres apart, starting at the low water mark. The distributions were assessed by means of an abundance scale with 5 representing the greatest abundance. The results are shown as bar charts in the diagrams below.

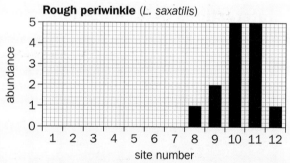

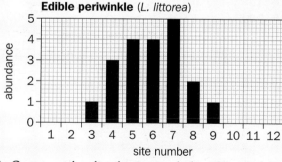

a) Compare the distribution and abundance of these two species on this rocky shore. [3]
b) Suggest which of the two species is likely to be more tolerant of desiccation. Explain your answer. [2]
c) Suggest *two* factors, other than desiccation, which might account for the difference in distribution of the two species. [2]
   (London) **[7]**

19 If you went to a rocky seashore at low tide and walked up from the water's edge towards the high water level, you would see changes in the species present and their abundance as you moved higher. The most obvious changes would be in the seaweeds present.
   a) How would you collect data and construct a kite diagram showing the distribution and abundance of seaweeds? [4]
   b) Near the top of the shore, you might find large numbers of sea slaters. These are mobile animals about one centimetre in length. Describe how you could use the mark, release and recapture method to estimate the size of the sea slater population. [4]
   c) An exposed rocky shore is one which receives the full force of the wind and waves. A sheltered rocky shore is protected from the wind and waves. On which shore would you expect species diversity to be greater? Explain your answer. [4]
   (NEAB) **[12]**

▷ Human influences on ecosystems

20 Acid rain is a matter of serious environmental concern. Sulphuric acid is present in acid rain and has adverse effects on both plants and animals.
   a) (i) Name *two* acidic components of acid rain other than sulphuric acid. [2]
      ii) Describe how acid rain is formed. [3]
   b) An experiment was carried out to investigate the effect of dilute sulphuric acid on the growth of cress seedlings. Batches of seeds were sown in glass dishes on filter paper to which dilute sulphuric acid was added. The dishes were then incubated. The root and shoot lengths were measured after 65 hours. The results are shown in the table below.

Sulphuric acid concentration / mol dm^{-3}	Mean root length / mm	Mean shoot length / mm
0	55.5	25.2
1×10^{-3}	63.4	18.4
3×10^{-3}	6.5	9.5
4×10^{-3}	2.0	4.6
6×10^{-3}	2.8	0.8
7×10^{-3}	1.5	0.5
8×10^{-3}	1.3	0.3
9×10^{-3}	1.3	0.0
1×10^{-2}	1.0	0.0

   i) Describe the relationship between the concentration of sulphuric acid and the growth as shown by the results in the table. [2]
   ii) Compare the effects of sulphuric acid on the growth of roots and shoots. [3]
   iii) Suggest *two* reasons why cress seedlings are suitable for investigating the effect of acid rain on plants. [2]
   (London) **[12]**

Synoptic questions

1 The diagram below shows the structure of a mitochondrion.

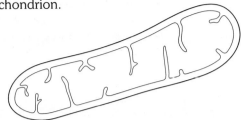

a) Describe where, in the mitochondrion, (i) the electron carrier system is found, and (ii) the reactions of the Krebs cycle take place. [2]
b) Give *two* similarities in structure between chloroplasts and mitochondria. [2]
c) Give *two* products of the light-dependent reaction which occurs in chloroplasts. [2]
(NEAB) **[6]**

2 Cystic fibrosis is a genetic disorder caused by a mutation in the gene which codes for a protein known as the CFTR protein. This protein is involved in the transport of chloride ions through the cell surface membrane.
The diagram below shows how the normal CFTR protein is believed to function in the cell surface membrane.

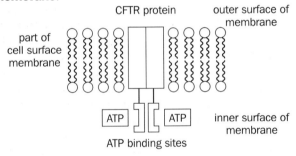

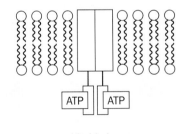

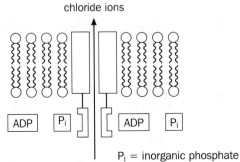

P_i = inorganic phosphate

a) (i) Describe the sequence of events that takes place when ATP is present. [3]
(ii) What is the function of ATP in this sequence of events? [1]
b) One symptom of cystic fibrosis is the production of very sticky, thick mucus which cannot easily be moved. This occurs particularly in the lungs, pancreas and testes.
Suggest an explanation for each of the following.
(i) Many people affected by cystic fibrosis suffer from repeated lung infections. [1]
(ii) Reduced ability to digest starch in the small intestine is common among people affected by cystic fibrosis. [1]
(iii) 95% of males affected by cystic fibrosis are infertile. [1]
(London) **[7]**

3 a) Graph 1 below shows the dissociation curves for human oxyhaemoglobin in the absence of carbon dioxide and in the presence of 5% carbon dioxide. Graph 2 shows similar curves for crocodile oxyhaemoglobin.

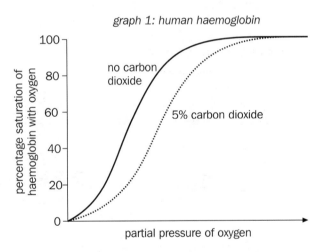

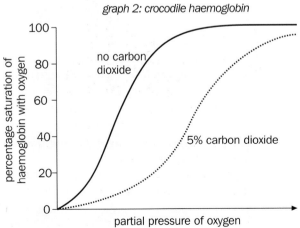

(i) Use graph 1 to describe the effect of carbon dioxide on human haemoglobin. [1]

443

(ii) Explain how this *effect* enables respiring tissues to obtain oxygen. [1]

(iii) Crocodiles are able to stay under water longer than humans. Explain how the different effect of carbon dioxide on the dissociation of their oxyhaemoglobin helps them to do this. [2]

b) The diagram below shows the structure of a molecule of crocodile haemoglobin.

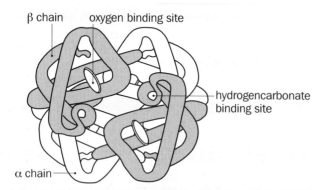

What is the evidence that this protein has (i) a tertiary structure, and (ii) a quaternary structure? [2]

c) In terms of molecular shape, suggest how the presence of hydrogencarbonate binding sites might account for the amount of oxygen released by the crocodile haemoglobin. [2]

(AEB) **[8]**

4 The Colorado beetle is a pest of potato crops. A soil bacterium, *Bacillus thuringiensis,* produces a substance called Bt which kills Colorado beetles but is harmless to humans. Scientists have isolated the gene for Bt production from bacteria and inserted it into potato plants so that the plant produces Bt in its leaf tissues.

a) (i) What is a gene? [2]

(ii) Suggest how the gene for Bt production could be isolated from the bacteria and inserted into cells of the potato plant. [4]

b) Bt can also be used as a spray. Colorado beetles may be killed if they ingest potato leaves which have been sprayed with Bt.
Suggest and explain *one* reason why using Bt-producing potato plants might increase the rate of evolution of Bt-resistance in the beetles compared with using Bt as a spray. [2]

(NEAB) **[8]**

5 The toxicity of certain substances can be determined by the use of an LD_{50} test. LD_{50} is defined as the concentration of a substance which results in the death of 50% of a population of test organisms in a given time period.
An investigation was carried out to test the effectiveness of a new insecticide on the larvae of the mosquito, *Anopheles* sp. Groups of larvae were

treated with the insecticide at concentrations ranging from 0.1 to 5.0 parts per million and the percentage mortality was calculated after 2 days. The results are shown in the graph below.

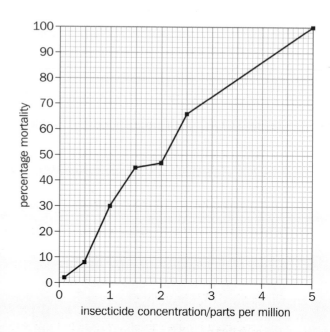

a) i) From the graph, find the LD_{50} for this insecticide. [1]

ii) Suggest and explain *one* long-term effect on mosquito populations of repeated use of this insecticide at concentrations lower than the LD_{50}.

b) Suggest a suitable control for this investigation and explain why it is necessary. [2]

c) The larvae of mosquitoes live in freshwater pools. Further tests on the insecticide showed that it was soluble in water and chemically stable. Suggest *three* reasons why the insecticide might be unsuitable for general use. [3]

d) (i) Some insecticides function as non-competitive inhibitors of enzyme activity. Explain how a non-competitive inhibitor works. [2]

(ii) Suppose that an insecticide acted as an inhibitor of the enzymes acetylcholinesterase, which breaks down acetylcholine. Suggest what effects this may have on the body of an insect. [3]

e) Predators of mosquito larvae, such as the water boatman, *Notonecta* sp., are important natural control agents in areas such as rice fields in the southern United States.

ii) State *two* advantages of the use of natural predators, rather than chemical insecticides, for the control of insect pests. [2]

iii) State *one* disadvantage of the use of natural predators, rather than chemical insecticides, for the control of insect pests. [1]

(London) **[16]**

6 a) Microorganisms present in a rabbit's gut are able to digest carbohydrates in the plant material that they eat. The diagram below shows the biochemical pathways by which cellulose and starch are digested in the gut of a rabbit.

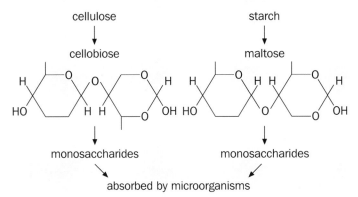

i) Describe how a molecule of cellulose differs from a molecule of starch. [1]
ii) Draw a diagram to show the molecules produced by digestion of cellobiose. [2]
iii) Cellobiose and maltose are both disaccharides. Explain why amylase enzymes produced by the rabbit are unable to digest cellobiose. [3]

b) One way in which rabbits cause considerable damage to agricultural land is by competing for plant material that would normally be eaten by domestic animals.

Table 1 below shows some features of the energy budgets of rabbits and cattle living under the same environmental conditions. All figures are kilojoules per day per kilogram of body mass.

Feature	Rabbits	Cattle
Energy consumed in food	1272	424
Energy lost as heat	567	311
Energy gained in body mass	68	17

(i) What is the purpose of giving these figures per kilogram of body mass? [1]
(ii) Explain the difference in the figures for the amount of energy lost as heat. [2]
(iii) Use information given in the diagram for (a) to explain why all the energy consumed in food cannot be converted to body mass or is lost as heat. [2]

c) Rabbits were introduced to Australia in the middle of the last century. Their population grew rapidly and they are now major agricultural pests.

Table 2 below compares some features concerned with heat loss in cattle and rabbits at a temperature of 30 °C.

Feature	Cattle	Rabbits
Percentage of body heat lost by evaporation	81.0	17.0
Core temperature of the body	38.2	39.3

Use information given in parts b) and c) of this question to explain each of the following.
(ii) How evaporation helps cattle to maintain a constant body temperature [2]
(iii) The main way in which a rabbit would lose heat at an environmental temperature of 30 °C. [2]
(iv) Why rabbits are major agricultural pests in Australia [2]
(v) Why rabbits are better able to survive than cattle in the hot, dry conditions found in many parts of Australia [3]

(AQA) **[20]**

7 ATP can be considered as a temporary energy store. It supplies energy to cells for a range of processes. During aerobic respiration ATP is mainly produced in mitochondria by oxidative phosphorylation. In photosynthesis it is produced in chloroplasts during the light-dependent reaction.
a) Describe the similarities and differences in the ways in which ATP is produced in respiration and photosynthesis.
(i) similarities
(ii) differences [6]
b) Describe how ATP is used in processes within cells. [6]

(NEAB) **[12]**

8 a) Active transport and osmosis are two of the ways by which substances move in and out of cells. Give *two* differences between these processes. [2]
b) Explain the part played by active transport and osmosis in each of the following.
(i) The uptake of substances from the soil by a root [5]
(ii) Selective reabsorption in the proximal convoluted tubule of a nephron [5]

(NEAB) **[12]**

Study skills

▷ Revision skills

When you revise, you need to
balance your time between:
- learning your notes
- practising past paper questions

The next four pages concentrate mainly on how you can learn your notes
effectively so that you have a good knowledge and understanding of biology
when you go into the exam room.

Before you start:

- Get a copy of the syllabus (specification) from your teacher
  or the Awarding Body.

- Be clear about which topics you need to revise for the exam you are about
  to take. If you check the website at www.nelsonthornes.com you will find a
  section which will help with this. There is a Specification Guide on page 459.

- Work out which are your strong topics and which you will need to spend
  more time on. One way of doing this is to look at tests or exams that you
  have done in the past to identify any weaknesses.

Some helpful ideas

1. Work out your best way of learning. Some people learn best from
diagrams/videos whilst some prefer listening (perhaps to taped notes) and
making up rhymes and phrases. Others prefer doing something active with
the information like answering questions or making a poster on a topic.

If you know which way you prefer, then this will help you to get the most
out of your revision. Also a *variety* of learning techniques can help.

2. Test yourself! Just reading through notes will not make them stick.
Get someone to test you on a section of work or write down some questions
testing your knowledge of the topic. A quick way of doing this is to tape the
questions and then play them back to yourself.
Check your notes if you can't answer any of the questions.

3. Teach others. If you can find someone to teach a topic to (friends or
family?) then this is sometimes the best way to learn. You and some friends
might take in turns to present a topic to each other.

4. Make sure that you understand the work! It is unlikely that you will
remember much biology if you do not understand it!

Having said that, there are still things that you need to learn by heart.
For example, if you don't know that a triglyceride is made up of 3 fatty acid
molecules and a molecule of glycerol, there is no way to work that out from
first principles. So know your basic facts!
But don't waste your time learning data that will be given in the exam.
If you aren't sure, ask your teacher for guidance.

Some revision techniques

1. Get an overall view of a topic first.
Before you start revising a topic, quickly read through the whole topic so that you have a general understanding of it and of how the different bits of it connect with each other. A good place to start is with the summary shown at the end of each chapter.

2. Highlight key words and phrases in your notes using hi-lighter pens in different colours.

3. Make notes.
Rewriting and condensing notes is a good and active way of reading and then understanding what you need to learn.

4. Make yourself cards with notes on one side and a diagram on the other.
Test yourself by looking at the diagram and seeing if you can recite the notes.

5. Visualisation.
When you are memorising material, always try to get a bold and bright picture in your mind that will help you to remember.
It helps if the picture is something which is very important to you because it is easily remembered (girl/boyfriend? football team? rock group?). Sometimes imagining something outrageous that can be connected to the fact may help.

Use visualisation

6. A poster.
You can summarise a topic with a poster which you can put on the wall of your bedroom. Include important words and phrases in large, bold letters. If you are a *visual* person then include bright, colourful diagrams which illustrate the ideas.

7. A mind map.
This is a poster which summarises a topic by showing the links between the different concepts that make it up. Making a mind map forces you to think about a topic and will help your understanding of it.

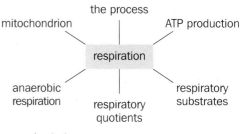

A mind map

8. Use rhymes and phrases.
Some people are good at rhymes or raps and this can be a way of memorising work. Phrases such as **R**ichard **o**f **Y**ork **g**ave **b**attle **i**n **v**ain, which is used to remember the colours of the spectrum (red, orange, yellow, green … etc.), can be useful.

9. Revision CD ROMs.
These can be bought in many shops and often have questions for you to test yourself. They are an active way of revising which may suit you.

10. Practice calculations.
In biology these often appear in questions on energy flow and genetic crosses in tests of significance (see p. 360). You can learn the techniques involved in these calculations as follows:

Find a worked example to look through in your notes or book.
Make sure you understand the logical steps between lines in the calculation.
Then cover the answer and try to solve the problem yourself.
If you get the answer wrong, this method can show you straight away where you went wrong. Or if you get stuck, you can reveal the next line, and then carry on.

You should then try some other problems from scratch.

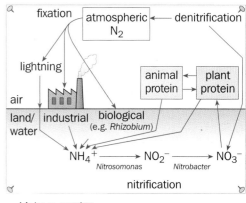

Make a poster

▷ Organising revision

Do you have difficulty starting revision and feel that there is so much to do that you will never complete it?

Do you constantly put off revising and find other things to do?

There are ways in which you can help yourself:

1. Think about the positive effects of starting.
When you have finished a session you will feel good that you have made progress and will feel less anxious about not getting enough work done.

2. Think about the negative effects of delaying.
What will happen and who will be affected if you put off starting?

3. Give yourself rewards.
Think of things with which you can reward yourself at the end of a session, e.g. a cup of coffee or listening to some favourite music.

4. Get help!
Think of ways to involve friends and family which will make revision easier and more enjoyable.

Reward yourself AT THE END of a planned revision session!

Making a revision timetable

Some recent research suggests that some students do better in exams than others because they;

- start their revision earlier

- use better techniques for learning work such as testing themselves, rather than just reading their notes

- get help from others rather than working alone

- have a planned revision timetable which includes working on their weaknesses.

Start your revision early

You can use these ideas to help you plan a **revision timetable**.

1. Start your revision a long time before your exams (at least eight weeks). Plan to spend quite a lot of the last two weeks before your exam on revising your weaker topics again.

2. Note down when you will cover each topic and stick to this!

3. Spend more time on your weaker areas.
   Try to get extra help on them from your teacher.
   (Don't just do the things you are good at already!)

4. Give yourself enough time to do past questions.

5. Arrange in some revision periods to work with someone who can help.

6. Do some social activities in between revision sessions, so that you don't go completely crazy!

Do some social activities between revision sessions

What will you revise?

You will need to divide your time between:

1. Learning the work which you have covered so that you have a good knowledge and understanding of it, including knowing genetic crosses and definitions of terms such as a community, habitat and niche.
2. Practising past questions so that you know what to do when you get a similar question in the exam. This can be useful in learning work, because you will often need to read your notes to help you answer a question. You can also judge where your weaknesses are.

You need to work out what is best for you – how much time should you spend on each and which should you start first?

How long should you revise for?

Research suggests that if you start revision with no thought of when you will stop, then your learning efficiency just gets less and less.

However, if you do decide on a fixed time, say 30 minutes, then you learn the most at the beginning of a session and just before you have decided to stop. This is when the brain realises that it is coming to the end of a session. (See the first two graphs.)

Which would be better, one two-hour session or four 25 minute sessions with a break of 10 minutes in between them?

The four sessions would be much better, as shown by the second graph. It is important, though, to stick to the 25 minutes and have a break, rather than just carrying on!

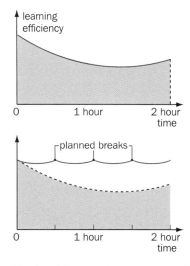

Short revision sessions are more effective

How often should you revise?

The third graph shows what percentage of revised material is remembered after you have stopped.
As it shows, you very quickly forget material that you have revised.

The first graph below shows that, if you revise work again after 10 minutes, then the amount you remember increases.

So what should you do after you have had your 10 minute break after working for 25 minutes?

You should briefly read again what you have been studying.

If you then revise this material again after a day and then after a week then you remember even more of the work, as shown by the last graph.

The trick is to briefly revise a topic again at regular intervals!

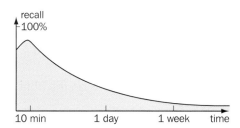

Recall falls rapidly after one revision session

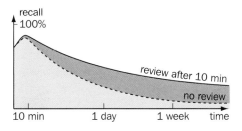

(Horizontal axes not drawn to scale!)

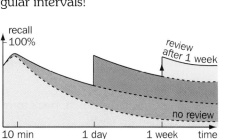

Recall improves by reviewing revised material regularly

▷ Exam technique

Before the exam

1. Make sure that you carefully check the times and dates of all your exams, so that you are not late!

2. Make sure that you know which type of paper (e.g. multiple-choice, short answer) is on which day, and which topics are being examined on which paper.

3. Make sure that you know how many questions you have to do on each paper, how long it is and whether you will get a choice of question. Plan how long you will spend on each question on a paper.

4. Make sure that you are familiar with the chemical formulae of the compounds named in your syllabus (specification).

5. On the night before the exam, it may help you to steady your nerves by briefly looking through your notes. But don't do too much!

6. Make sure that you get a good night's rest before your exam.

On the day of the exam

1. Aim to arrive early at the exam and try to get into the room as early as possible. This will help you to settle your nerves and give you time to prepare.

2. Don't drink alcohol before an exam, or eat too much or too little food.

3. Make sure that you are properly equipped with pens and pencils (and spares in case they break), a rubber, ruler, calculator (check the batteries) and a watch.

During the exam

1. Don't waste time when you get the paper! Write your name and exam number onto the front of any sheets of paper or answer booklets that you are going to use.
   Read the instructions on the front page of the exam.

2. Read each question very carefully and underline important parts. If you have a choice on which questions to attempt, then read **all** of the questions on the paper. Remember that some of the later parts of some questions can be easier than the first parts.

3. Don't dive into a question without reading all of it first.

4. Do not spend too long on any question! If you are stuck just leave some space so that you can go back to it later. *It is easier to get 50% on all the questions than 100% on half of them.*

5. Sometimes you may be stuck on one part of the question. Check to make sure that there are no later parts which you can do easily.

6. Write neatly and in short sentences that will be easier for the marker to understand. Try to be precise and detailed without writing too much, so that you don't waste time.

7. Make your diagrams clear and neat but do not spend a long time on them to make them perfect.

8. Check that you have done all the required questions – for example, sometimes people don't see that there is a question on the last page of the paper!

9. Check your answers! The first thing that you could check is whether an answer is much too big or too small.
   You must also check units and significant figures.

Don't spend too long on any one question

Some hints on answering questions

1. If an exam paper shows that a question is worth 4 marks then put down 4 separate points in your answer.

2. Use correct scientific words as much as possible.

3. When you do calculation questions you must show your working – for example, there is often a mark for writing down the right equation which you will get even if you don't finally get the right answer.

4. Don't forget units and to give the answer to the same number of significant figures as the numbers in the question.

5. In a multiple choice question narrow down your options by crossing out those answers which can't possibly be right. If you are then not sure … guess!

6. When you are asked to draw a graph, label the axes (including units) and plan a sensible scale to fill most of the grid.

7. Words that are used in exam questions are chosen very carefully. Each word has a precise meaning which you will need to understand if you are to respond to the question with a relevant answer. Here are a few words that often occur in questions together with their meanings:

Use the correct scientific words

Briefly or Concisely:	give short statements of the main points
Compare:	point out similarities
Contrast:	point out the differences
Define:	state the exact meaning of a word or phrase
Describe:	give a detailed, factual account
Discuss:	explain, then give two sides of the issue
Explain or Account for:	give reasons for how and why it is
Evaluate:	assess the effectiveness/validity of something
Illustrate:	use clear drawings and diagrams
List:	give a sequence of words
Outline:	give the main points
State:	present in brief, clear form
Suggest:	put forward ideas
Summarise:	give a concise, clear explanation of the main points, leaving out details and examples

Practical skills

Your practical skills can be assessed by a practical examination
or by your teacher as you work through the course.
In either case you need to develop your skills in 4 areas:

1. Planning

2. Implementing

3. Analysing and drawing conclusions

4. Evaluating

These skills are grouped differently by different awarding bodies.
So you must make sure that you know how yours will judge
your level in the areas it defines. However the following advice
will be useful whichever exam you are taking.

▷ Planning

Your planning skills will be assessed in the context of work
you do in your AS and A2 modules. You will be expected
to use the knowledge gained in lessons and from secondary
sources like textbooks and CD ROMs.

One idea would be to study the effect of pH on the activity of
the enzyme catalase. This enzyme catalyses the breakdown
of hydrogen peroxide into water and oxygen gas.
You need to plan your method *in detail*.

What must you think about to get good marks in this investigation?

- what will you use as your source of the enzyme (potato works well)?
- what range of pHs will you investigate (this requires prior research)?
- which product of the reaction will you measure?
- what apparatus will you need?
- how many measurements will you take (think about replicates!)?
- over what time period will you record (here you need to think not only
  biologically but also about the time available to you)?
- how will you control other variables such as temperature,
  and the concentration of the enzyme?

Investigating the action of catalase

All of these points are crucial to the ***reliability*** of your evidence.
But you also need to show an understanding of the biology behind
the practical, showing in your planning that you understand the theory
behind factors that affect enzyme activity. This should be evident in
areas like your choice of pHs.
It is also important that you show some evidence of ***risk assessment***,
in this example the safety issue surrounds the corrosive nature
of hydrogen peroxide.

▷ Implementing

This skill looks at the way that you carry out investigations and you will need to be familiar with a variety of practical techniques.
As well as the technique for measuring oxygen release due to the action of catalase, the techniques below might be useful, depending on the nature of your activity.

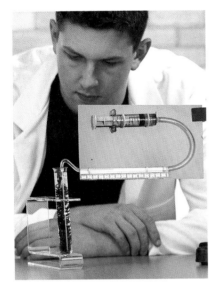

The photosynthometer is used to measure oxygen production from photosynthesising pond weed

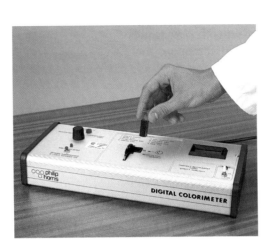

The colorimeter could be used to measure the release of pigment from beetroot tissue exposed to different temperatures

Data logging can be a useful way to gather data, particularly over long periods of time or in very fast reactions

The key areas in this skill are:

- competence in assembling and operating the apparatus
- taking detailed and accurate measurements
  e.g. reading accurately from the meniscus in the burette
- taking care to obtain reliable results (this is where replicates are vital)
- having assessed risks in the planning, do you take adequate precautions to minimise them i.e. by wearing safety specs?

This skill also focuses on the clear and logical recording of your measurements.
As in any branch of science this will invariably involve a table.
The usual format involves putting the variable you have changed in the first column.
This is the **independent variable** and in the example would be the range of pHs.
The second column will contain your measurements of the **dependent variable**, in this case volume of oxygen produced.

Remember that one of the ways that you can show precision and reliability in your results is through this table, therefore make sure that all columns are clearly labelled, and that you have used appropriate units.

pH	Time (mins)	1	2	3	4	5
				Total oxygen produced (cm³)		
6	Attempt 1	2.5	4.8	7.1	9.4	11.6
	Attempt 2	2.3	5.2	8.2	9	12.6
	Attempt 3	2.6	5.3	9	12	15
	Average	2.47	5.1	8.1	10.13	13.07
7.2	Attempt 1	3.3	7	11.1	14.9	18.5
	Attempt 2	3.1	8	12.7	16	19.7
	Attempt 3	5.1	11	16.2	20.7	24.6
	Average	3.83	8.67	13.33	17.2	20.93
9	Attempt 1	3.2	7	10	13.4	16.2
	Attempt 2	0.9	3.4	6.4	9.4	12.4
	Attempt 3	3.4	7	11	15	18.4
	Average	2.5	5.8	9.13	12.6	15.67

▷ Analysing

Once you have a set of data, then your analysis begins.
The skills you use will depend upon the data gathered
or given to you. They could include:

- calculations (to the appropriate number of significant figures)
- use of simple statistical techniques like chi-squared
- drawing graphs (using lines of best fit or curves, and recognising anomalous results)
- using these graphs to spot trends and patterns
- drawing conclusions that are **consistent** with your results
- explaining these conclusions with detailed and appropriate biological knowledge.

Here are some examples to put these points into context.

1. The effect of pH on the activity of catalase.
This graph shows data from the investigation that you have already
considered in the planning and implementing sections.
From this data you can see that:

- the rate of reaction of catalase is fastest at pH 7.2
- the rate of reaction of catalase is slower at pHs more acidic **and** more alkaline than pH 7.2

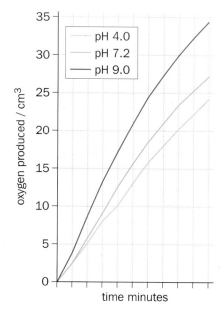

These are trends and patterns and from them you can conclude that :

- pH does affect the activity of catalase and that it is less active at extremes of pH.

What you **cannot** conclude (for reasons that will become clear
when you consider the skill of evaluation) is that :

- catalase has an optimum of pH 7.2

In trying to explain your conclusion you would need to refer to the fact
that enzymes are stable over a limited range of pH and that at extremes
outside this range they can be denatured. In your write-up you would
of course discuss this in more detail.

2. The effect of light intensity on photosynthesis.
This graph shows the results of varying light intensity on photosynthesis
in Canadian pondweed (*Elodea*). Here the student measured oxygen
production over five minute periods.
From this data you can see that:

- oxygen production increases with light intensity
- this increase is most pronounced at lower light intensities.

From these patterns you can conclude that:

- the rate of photosynthesis increases with light intensity
- but at high intensities light begins to have less effect.

For relevant biological knowledge you would need to consider the effect of
'limiting factors' upon the rate of photosynthesis.

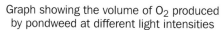

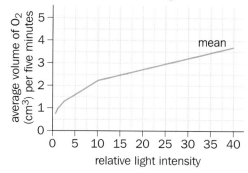

Graph showing the volume of O_2 produced
by pondweed at different light intensities

▷ Evaluating

The final skill area involves reflecting on your working methods, the quality of evidence produced and therefore the strength of any conclusions drawn.
In order to gain high marks you should think about:

- the suitability and limitations of your method
- any errors in your procedures, including measuring equipment used
- suggestions for reducing the main sources of error
- the reliability of the data (i.e. are your results repeatable?)
- suggesting how to gather more reliable data, if appropriate
- any anomalous results and explaining why they are out of line with the rest of the data
- the strength of the conclusions you can draw from a set of data
- what you could do to gather further evidence to support your conclusions.

(You might consider the number of measurements made, or the range over which they were taken. Will any generalisations made be true for readings taken outside the range within which your data lies?)

If you consider the examples of biological investigations already discussed, what limitations can you identify?

- the source of enzyme is diced potato, so there is no guarantee that the enzyme concentration is constant between different pHs
- even if each potato sample is accurately measured there is no guarantee that each sample has the same surface area exposed to the substrate
- each sample may not have come from the same potato (particularly likely if the investigation was carried out over more than one lesson)
- have you read the meniscus on the burette accurately?
- have you accounted for air expelled from the flask when the substrate is added?
- are the pHs chosen adequate in terms of number and range?

This latter point explains why a conclusion that states 'the optimum pH for catalase activity is 7.2', would not be valid.

A better statement would be
'within the range chosen the optimum pH for catalase activity is 7.2, but further tests using a narrower range of values around this figure would be necessary to confirm the actual optimum'.

There is no set list or number of limitations. What the awarding bodies are looking for is an awareness of the tentative nature of results and the need for subsequent further investigation .

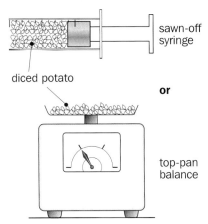

Which apparatus would give the consistency when preparing different potato samples?

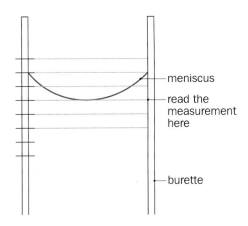

A common source of error – misreading a burette

Key Skills in Advanced Biology

When you study biology you learn about living things, the ways in which their bodies work and the ways in which they interact.
You also learn about a variety of ways in which biologists solve problems.
But one of the best things about studying A levels (any A levels) is that you learn how to do lots of other things which you will find useful at work or at university even if you do not become a professional biologist.
Three important areas are using the skills of communication, number and IT.

To recognise this, the Government has introduced a new qualification called the Key Skills Qualification.
To get this qualification, you have to achieve three units:
- one in Communication,
- one in Application of Number, and
- one in IT.

For each unit, you have to produce a portfolio of evidence (better known as coursework) and pass a test (like a short exam).
You can pass a unit at any Level from 1 to 4 and you should aim as high as you can.
Level 3 is probably the right level for an A level student to aim for.

The other key skills – working with others, problem solving and improving your own learning – are just as important as those listed above but are not examined.

The Qualification is separate from your A level course;
in fact, it is also available to people taking GNVQs, degrees, Modern Apprenticeships, or any other kind of education or training.
However, the idea is that you should develop these Key Skills and get your portfolio of evidence (as much as possible anyway) within your A level course.
But you don't have to get all the evidence from your A levels, and certainly not all from A level Biology.
Your tutor will advise you about this.

The main thing is that you should aim to develop the skills where they are needed naturally, not force them in where they don't fit.
Biology is a good subject for some of the Key Skills, for instance, you are communicating all the time, and IT is becoming an ever more essential tool for research and analysis.
But, perhaps using numbers is a skill that occurs more frequently in say, Chemistry or Physics.

The next few pages give you some ideas to help you make the most of the opportunities in A level Biology to become good at the Key Skills and to get the portfolio of evidence you need.

But remember, an important part of Key Skills is that you take the initiative yourself. So, whenever you produce a piece of work, you should ask yourself: 'Have I used any of the Key Skills, and are there any more Key Skills I could have used?'

Communication

Communicating our ideas to other people is one of the most important things we ever do, both in discussions and in writing. Scientists sometimes have a poor reputation when it comes to communication. But we know that some scientists communicate very well. How do they do that?

Throughout this book you will find opportunities to develop your communication skills. There are open-ended questions that require you to research a topic and discuss issues.

For example on pages 156–157 you are asked for your views on GM foods. On page 155 you are asked to evaluate the advantages and disadvantages of genetic engineering.

Many of the 'Biology at work' pages introduce you to the latest developments and would also be suitable for further research. This could be followed by a presentation to the rest of your group. Examples might include collagen replacement therapy (page 25), training at altitude (page 178), the effects of drugs on synaptic transmission (page 342), sustainable timber production (page 402), intensive farming (page 403) or the natural treatment of man-made waste (page 435).

The Level 3 Communication unit (you should ask your tutor for your own copy of the Key Skills units) says that you should be able to:

- contribute to discussions, in twos and threes and in larger groups

- make a presentation to an audience (a small one will do!)

- select, read and understand quite long articles and sections from books, and take out the bits you need at the time

- write essays, reports, etc. in a way that suits what you are trying to communicate. This includes using diagrams, graphs, tables, etc. if they help you say what you want to say. In biology, they usually do make your work more clear.

You will do most of this in a biology course anyway. If you can learn how to do it at Level 3, you will be well on the way to being a good communicator, in biology or anywhere else.

Application of Number

When you start to learn biology you don't get very involved with numbers. But you will find that use of numbers comes in more as your course progresses, especially when you carry out investigations. For instance, when investigating the effects of light intensity, temperature and carbon dioxide on the rate of photosynthesis you need to take measurements, carry out calculations and draw and interpret graphs. When investigating the results of genetic crosses you may need to use a statistical test such as the **chi-squared test (χ^2)** to test the validity of your results (see page 360). Statistics are often used in ecological studies, for instance you can use **standard deviation** to test whether your sample of dog-whelks from a sheltered rocky shore is representative. The higher the standard deviation, the greater will be the spread of data around the mean. Many ecological projects involve collecting two or more sets of data from different locations and comparing them. For instance the numbers of earthworms in soils on chalk and on limestone. Tests of significance like the chi-squared test will enable you to find out whether the differences between two sets of data are truly significant or are purely due to chance. Remember though that you do not have to produce **all** this evidence in biology. You should practise the skills in biology, but you may find that in the case of application of number, you can get the evidence more easily in another subject such as physics. This is for you to decide, after talking it over with your teacher.

For your Application of Number portfolio, you will need to have evidence to show that you can:

- work out what numerical data you need for what you want to do

- get it from somewhere, maybe including your own measurements

- carry out the right calculations, and get the right results

- check your work and correct any mistakes

- decide what the results are telling you

- present the results in a way that suits the situation, using graphs etc. where they help make your point.

Information Technology

Information technology is about using computers to help you to do your work more quickly, to present your work more professionally, to make measurements and process the results, or to give you access to information that would be difficult to find in books. We will look at each of these in turn.

In experimental work you often find that you have a large number of measurements and have to work on them in order to find the quantity you want. The usual way to deal with these is to draw a table with suitable headings. But using a spreadsheet can often do the job more effectively.

You will probably not want to word-process all your work because you will have to write with a pen in your biology module tests and examinations. But it is a good idea to set yourself a goal to produce a piece of word-processed work at least once per month, say. Discuss this with your teacher and take his or her advice.

Computers are ideal for collecting data over a very short or very long period. Computers can be used to collect data on reactions that are complete in a one hundred millionth of a second! You will not be doing any reactions that are quite as fast as that, but computers can record changes in mass, temperature, colour, etc. much better than human beings because they do not forget to take readings, misread the thermometer, or get called away to another lesson. And they can often produce a graph or other chart as they log the data, giving you an instant picture of what is going on during the reaction. You should find some opportunities for data logging during your course.

Finally, you should not ignore opportunities for finding things out on the Internet or CD ROMs. These have a wealth of information and give you access to information which you would find difficult to assemble in any other way. In other words, do what you have to do in biology anyway, but use IT so that you can do it more effectively.

Remember, though, that you also have to pass a test in each of the three Key Skills, so you have to be sure you understand all the techniques that underlie the skills and can answer questions about them under exam conditions.

Your school or college will have arrangements to help you develop your Key Skills, assemble your portfolio, and prepare for the test. Find out what these are and always ask your tutor if you are not sure what you should be doing.

Key Skills are not a soft option. They earn you UCAS points, and employers are very keen on them. Over the next few years, more and more employers are going to be expecting people to have Key Skills qualifications. Anyway, life is much easier if you are good at communicating, using numbers and using IT.

For your IT Key Skills portfolio at Level 3, you will have to have evidence that shows you can:

- decide what information you want and where you are going to get it (CD ROM? Internet? Your own experiments?)

- select the right information for what you want to do

- use spreadsheets, databases, etc. to input this data and do calculations, test hypotheses, find the answers to questions, and so on

- check that your results are accurate and make sense

- present your results effectively

▷ Grid matching specifications with Advanced Biology for You chapters

Chapter	Examination Boards' Specifications (syllabuses for biology)							
	AQA (AEB) A	AQA (AEB) Human A	AQA (NEAB) B	Edexcel	Edexcel Human	OCR	WJEC	NICCEA
1 Biological molecules	P6–27	P6–27	P6–27	P6–27	P6–27	P6–27	P6–27	P6–27
2 Cells	P28–47	P28–47	P28–47	P28–47	P28–47	P28–47	P28–47	P28–47
3 Cell surface membrane and transport	P48–62	P48–62	P48–62	P48–62	P48–62	P48–62	P48–62	P48–62
4 Enzymes	P63–79	P63–79	P63–79	P63–79	P63–79	P63–79	P63–79	P63–79
5 Digestion	P80–92 (A2)	P80–92 (A2)	P80–92	P80–92	P80–92	P80–92 (A2) part module 2805 component 05	P80–92 (A2)	P80–92 (details of digestive enzymes not required)
6 Nucleic acids and protein synthesis	P99–112	P99–112	P99–112	P99–112	P99–112	P99–112	P99–112	P99–112
7 Cell division	P113–127 (not stages of meiosis)	P113–127 (not stages of meiosis)	P113–127 (not stages of meiosis)	P113–127 (not stages of meiosis)	P113–127 (not stages of meiosis)	P113–127 (not stages of meiosis)	P113–127	P113–127 (not stages in meiosis)
8 Reproduction	P140	P132–142		P128–142	P132–142	P128–142 (A2) component 01	P128–142	
9 Gene technology	P143–159	P143–159	P143–159	P143–159 (A2)	P143–159 (A2)	P143–159 (A2) components 02 + 04	P143–159	P143–159
10 Gas exchange	P170–180 (AS) P164–169 (A2)	P170–180	P164–180	P164–180	P170–180	P164–169	P164–180	P164–180
11 Transport in animals	P181–192	P181–198	P181–198	P181–198	P181–198	P181–198	P181–198	P181–198
12 Transport in plants	P199–214 (A2)		P199–214	P199–214		P199–214	P199–214	P199–214
13 Diet and health		P220–238(A2)		A2 option B P220–238	A2 option B P220–238	P220–238 (AS)		
14 Exercise and health		P239–254 (AS)	P243–245	A2 option C P239–254	A2 option C P239–254	P239–254 (AS)		
15 Infectious disease and immunity	P258–279	P255–279 (AS)	A2 option module 6Q P255–279	A2 option A P255–279	A2 option A P255–279	P255–279 (AS)	P255–279 (A2)	P255–279 (A2)
16 Respiration	P284–297	P284–297	P284–297	P284–297	P284–297	P284–297	P284–297	P284–297
17 Photosynthesis	P298–309	P298–309	P298–309	P298–309		P298–309	P298–309	P298–309
18 Homeostasis	P310–325	P310–325	P310–325	P310–325	P310–325	P310–325	P310–325	P310–325
19 Control and coordination	P326–341	P326–341	P326–341	P326–341	P326–341	P326–341	P326–341	P326–341
20 Inheritance	P354–369 (plus stages in meiosis)	P354–369 (plus stages in meiosis)	P354–369 (plus stages in meiosis)	P354–369	P354–369	P354–369 (plus stages in meiosis)	P354–369	P354–369 (plus stages in meiosis)
21 Selection, evolution and classification	P370–389	P370–389	P370–389	P370–389	P370–389	P370–389	P370–389	P370–389
22 Energy and ecosystems	P390–405	P390–405	P390–405	P390–405 (AS)	P390–405 (AS)	P390–405 (AS)	P390–405 (AS)	P390–405 (AS)
23 Interaction between organisms	P406–423	P406–423	P406–423	P406–423	P406–423	P406–423 (A2) component 03	P406–423 (AS)	P406–423 (AS)
24 Human influences on ecosystems	P424–425	P424–425	P424–439	P424–439 (AS)	P424–439 (AS)	P424–439 (A2) component 03	P424–439 (AS)	P424–439

Index

Acknowledgements

I would like to thank Mark Wasserberg and the Governors of Poynton High School for arranging my secondment in order to write the bulk of this book.

My thanks also go to Bob Wakefield, Dr Graham Reid, Sally Morgan, Erica Clark and Nick Paul for reviewing and improving the manuscript. In addition, I should like to acknowledge the work of Erica Clark and Sally Morgan on the Further Questions, Nick Paul on Practical Skills, Andy Raw on Study Skills and David McGivern's contribution to the Biology at Work spread 'African Cassava Mosaic Virus'.

Throughout the writing of this book I have had a great deal of encouragement and support from both my family and colleagues, particularly Damian Allen, Nick Paul and Sue Adamson.

Particular thanks are due to Keith Johnson for his advice and insight into the ways in which we learn and what makes a good textbook. His influence on my writing of both this book and GCSE Biology for You, has been huge.

Thanks also to Adrian Wheaton, Rosie Heywood, John Bailey and Sheila Tarrant of Nelson Thornes for their invaluable advice and support.

Acknowledgement is made to the following Awarding Bodies for permission to reprint questions from their examination papers:

AQA	Assessment and Qualifications Alliance
EDEXCEL	
NICCEA	Northern Ireland Council for Curriculum Examinations and Assessment
OCR	Oxford, Cambridge and RSA Examinations
WJEC	Welsh Joint Education Committee

Other books by Gareth Williams

Biology for You
Spotlight Science 7, 8, 9 with Keith Johnson and Sue Adamson
Science: On Target with Keith Johnson and Sue Adamson

Ace Photolibrary 220B (Custom Medical), 229 (Benelux Press), 252B (Mugshots), 261M (Andrew Conway), 346B (Karka); Adams Photolibrary 415M; Allsport 11M (Al Bello), 181 (John Gichigi), 223T (Mike Powell), 236L (Stu Forster), 245T (Gary M Prior), 253T (Shaun Botterill), 285T (Richard Baker); Alpine Club 284T,M; Aquarius Picture Library 273T; Ardea 355 (AP Paterson), 366T (Don Hadden), 402T, 428M (James Marchington); Barnaby's Picture Library 334; bbsrc 77 (IACR), 157B (JIC), 366M, B (thanks to David McGivern); Biophoto Associates 28M, 31, 32T, B, 33, 34T, B, 35T, 40M, B, 41a ,c, e, f, 44, 48, 49T, 58, 85, 86, 113B, 114, 118a–f, 119T, 166ML, MR, 200a–e, 201B, 205B, 208T, 235T, 247T, 255b, c, 314, 331B, 332T, 338, 339, 379T, 385b, 411e; biota@ccon.org 370T; Bridgeman Art Library 374T; British Diabetic Association 76B; Britstock-IFA 306 (H Schmidbauer); Bruce Coleman 131T, 381MR (Hans Reinhard), 129, 199B, 211M, 377 (Kim Taylor), 164 (Pacific Stock), 165T (Jane Burton), 165B (Dr Frieder Sauer), 312 (John Cancalosi), 320 (Bob and Clara Calhoun), 381T (Paul Van Gaalen), 382BL (Adriano Bacchella), 387ML (Erwin and Peggy Bauer), 406 (Charles and Sandra Hood), 411b (Leonard Lee Rue); Camera Press 264T (Stills); Capital Pictures 221B (Hugo Dixon); Colorsport 230T; Damian Allen 421a, b, d; David Pegg 59B (University of York), 60T (Tissue Bank, Cambridge), B (Alabama Tissue Bank); Dr Angela Robinson 125; Ecoscene 166BL (Mark Carey), 212B (Chinch Gryniewicz), 295T (Joel Creed), 337 (Sally Morgan), 346T (Peter Currell), 379B (Martin Jones), 402B (Andrew Brown), 403T (Stephen Coyne), 41b, 430T, B (Sally Morgan), 435B (J Wilkinson); Empics 244 (Neil Simpson); Frank Lane Picture Agency 11BR (Panda, G Cappelli), 391B (Martin B Withers), 403B (Walther Rohdich), 415T (David Hosking); Gareth Williams 394; Gene Cox 41h, 172, 175B, 193, 207B, 267T, 326T, 331T; Health Development Agency 226T; Holt Studios International 22T, 166BR, 167, 211T, 237B, 344 (Nigel Cattlin), 413; ICI 22B, 298; Image Bank 220T (Paolo Curto), 233T (Mike Brinson), 245B (Simon Wilkinson); Image Select 374B (Ann Ronan); John Walmesley Photolibrary 225T; Kings College London 45 (Laser confocal images by kind permission of Dr Andrew Sincock); Martyn Chillmaid 8, 13, 14B, 15T, 18B, 51, 63, 76, 151, 188M, 202, 205T, 211B, 223T, B, 227, 235B, 246M, 260B, 276T, B, 310, 346M, 358T, 419M, 427; Maximuscle 236R; National Health Service 323B; Natural Visions 11T, 284B (Peter Herring), 301, 384, 387MR, 395, 410TR, 411d (Brian Rogers), 429T, 432M; News International 259; Nick Cobbing 154, 156; Nordic Track 370B; Novosti (London) 155B; Ohio University 59T Professor John Eastman; Ornis Scand 6/33 1975 414 (Glowacinski and Jarvinen); Oxford Scientific Films 15B (Satoshi Kuribayashi), 28T (Godfrey Merlen), 29 (Scott Camazine), 42L (Science Pictures Ltd), 38 (CG Gardener), 41d, 56T, 166TR (London Scientific Films), 150B (Ian West), 165M (G I Bernard), 266T (G I Bernard), 381B (Bob Gibbons), 401 (Breck P Kent Earth Sciences), 409 (Mark Hamblin), 424b (Ronald Toms), 429B (JAL Clarke), 434T (Daniel J Cox); Panos Pictures 307T (Jeremy Hartley); Photri Inc 225T, 402M; Popperfoto 266B (Eric de Castro, Reuters), 292 (Corinne Dufka, Reuters); Rex Features 232T, 256, 275M, 294T (J Sutton-Hibbert), B (Nils Jorgensen), 39b; Robert Harding Picture Library 107 (Tom Pantages), 221M, 248B (Liason Int.), 226B (Charlie Westerman, Int'l Stock), 242, 255d, 261T (Dr Dennis Kunkel), 269, 323T (Phototake), 275B (Barts Medical Library), 420B (Carolina Biological Supplies), 424c; Ronald Grant Archive 233B, 332B; Royal Botanic Gardens, Kew 387CL, CR (by kind permission of the Directors and Trustees); Sally and Richard Greenhill 232M; Science Photolibrary 6 (Frank Zullo), 7 (Dept. of Nuclear Medicine, Charing Cross Hospital), 11BL, 411C (Claude Nuridsany and Marie Perrennou), 18T, 65, 66, 208B (JC Revy), 25B (J Gross, Biozentrum), 30 (Moredon Animal Health Ltd), 42R, 89B, 131B, 152, 175T (Dr Jeremy Burgess), 36L (KR Porter), R (Quest), 41b (John Walsh), 43T (Maximilian Stock Ltd), 49B (Don Fawcett), 56B (Astrid and Hanns-Frieder Michler), 74 (Ken Eward), 80M (Dr Tony Brain), 82, 268, 373T (BSIP, VEM), 87 (CNRI), 89T, 175M, 212T (Andrew Syred), 107 (John Wilson), 102T (Ken Eward), M (Science Source), B, 103T (A Barrington Brown), B (Div. of Computer Research and Technology, National Institute of Health), 110 (Secchi-Lecaque-Roussel–UCLAF, CNRI), 119B (Weiss/Jerrican), 124b (Michael Abbey), 128 (Neil Bronshall), 138L, R (Petit Format, Nestlé), 139 (Hank Morgan), 146T (Dr Gopal Murti), 144T (Mark Clark), B (James Holmes, Cell Tech Ltd), 145 (Andrew McClenaghan), 148T (Maximilian Stock Ltd), B 222T (Sinclair Stammers), 150T (PH Plailly, Eurelios), 149 (Simon Fraser, RVI, Newcastle Upon Tyne), 170, 387T (Alfred Pasieka), 184, 285B (Manfred Kage), 188T (Dr Gopal Murti), 190 (Ken Eward), 225M (Princess Margaret Rose Orthopaedic Hospital), 231M, B (Peter Menzel), 234 (Biophoto Associates), 237T, 239T, 271T, 315T (Saturn Stills), 246T (Dr Tony Brain), 248T (John Greim), 250 (Jerry Wachter), 251B, T, 252T (Simon Fraser), B (CNRI), 255a (Dr Kari Lounatmaa), 260T (USDA), 262 (Dr Linda Stannard, UCT), 263 (NIBSC), 264M (David Parker), 267B (David Scharf), 275M, 277, 385a (AB Dowsett), 286 (Oxford Molecular Biophysics Laboratory), 291 (Institut Pasteur, CNRI), 304 (Geoff Tompkinson), 315B (Garry Watson), 327 (Volker Steger IFN), 358B (Rosenfeld Images), 371 (Cecil H Fox), 378 (Omikron); Stockmarket 224T (L Long), 246B (John Henley), 373M; Stone 28B (Robert Brons, BPS), 37 (Newcomb and Wergin, BRS), 41g (Spike Walker), 43B (Tim Flach), 80T (Michele Westmorland), 80B (David E Myers), 89M (James Solliday, BPS), 105 (Peter Poulides), 113T (Peter Dazeley), M (Spike Walker), 115 (Philip Matson), 116 (Spike Walker), 119M (Spike Walker), 124a (Barts Hospital), 124c (Ben Edwards), 136T, B (Yorgos Nikas), 143 (Barry Bomzer), 147 (Charles Thatcher), 150M (Fern and Ivaldi), 173 (Claudia Kurun), 176 (John Millar), 182 (Warren Rosenberg, BPS), 186 (Peter Cade), 188B (Yorgos Nikas), 189T, B (Andrew Syred), 199T (Ken Biggs), 201T (Andrew Syred), 247B (Stewart Cohen), 264B (Andrew Errington), 273B (Bruce Ayres), 373B (Rich Frishman), 386B (LSHTM), 391M (S Purdy Matthews), 421c (Tim Flach), 432T (Martin Rogers); Telegraph Colour Library 221T (Klaus Reisinger, Black Star), 231T (Andrew Holbrooke), 258 (Barry Willis), 261B (Malcolm Linton), 386T (VCL), 424a (Planet Earth, Chris Howes), 432B (Jim Lukowski, Blackstar); Topham Picturepoint 400 (Vladimir Akimov); TRIP 275T (B Seed), 379M (Anon); UKAEA 428B; Universal Pictorial Press and Agency 232B, 343B; University of Manchester 417 (Dr SER Bailey); Wilderness Photolibrary 177 (John Noble); www.johnbirdsall.co.uk 224M, 273M

Acknowledgements for diagrams and tables

AAAS 60; Allen D 397, 408; Applin D 222, 233; BBC News 277; Biozone International 145, 251, 345M, B, 380; BMJ Publishing 177; Cambridge University Press 77T, M, 139T, 149, 271; Collins Educational 140, 187, 257, 294; Francis Chichester Ltd 196TR; Guardian Newspapers 265; Heinemann 295; John Murray 90 (C Clegg); John Wiley and Sons 435; Longman 412B; NIH 196TL; Noble P 125T; Northeast Dermatology Associates 25; Nottingham Trent University 156; Office for National Statistics 234; Open University 212; Rowland M 276, 344; Royal College of Physicians 249B; Sander DM 366; Saull 431B; TMIP 236BL, BR; Veuger J 426B (Acid News); Zeneca Pharmaceuticals 196B

The publishers have made every effort to contact copyright holders, but apologise if any have been overlooked.